Clinical Handbook of Pastoral Counseling, Volume 2

Studies In Pastoral Psychology,
Theology, and Spirituality
Robert J. Wicks, General Editor

also in this series

Clinical Handbook of Pastoral Counseling (volume 1)
edited by R. Wicks, R. Parsons, and D.Capps
Adolescents in Turmoil, Parents Under Stress
by Richard D. Parsons
The Art of Clinical Supervision
edited by B. Estadt, J. Compton and M. Blanchette
The Art of Passingover
by Francis Dorff, O. Praem
Losses in Later Life
by R. Scott Sullender
Pastoral Care Emergencies
by David K. Switzer
Choosing Your Career, Finding Your Vocation
by Roy Lewis
Spirituality and Personal Maturity
by Joann Wolski Conn
Christointegration
by Bernard J. Tyrrell
Adult Children of Alcoholics
by Rachel Callahan, C.S.C. and Rea McDonnell, S.S.N.D.
Health Care Ministry
edited by Helen Hayes, O.S.F. and Cornelius J. van der Poel, C.S.Sp.
Surviving in Ministry
edited by Robert R. Lutz and Bruce T. Taylor
The Healing Imagination
by Ann and Barry Ulanov
Renewal in Late Life through Pastoral Counseling
by James N. Lapsley

Clinical Handbook of Pastoral Counseling, Volume 2

Robert J. Wicks
and
Richard D. Parsons,
editors

Integration Books

paulist press/new york and mahwah

Acknowledgments
The article entitled "Pastoral Care and Counseling and Issues of Self-Esteem" is adapted and condensed from material published in *God Images and Self-Esteem: Empowering Women in a Patriarchal Society* by Carroll Saussy, copyright 1991. Reprinted by permission of Westminster/John Knox.

Library of Congress Cataloging in Publication Data

(Revised for vol. 2)

Clinical handbook of pastoral counseling.

(Integration books)
Includes bibliographies and indexes.
1. Pastoral counseling. I. Wicks, Robert J. II. Parsons, Richard D. III. Capps, Donald. IV. Title. V. Series.
BV4012.2.C54 1985 253.5 84-62559
ISBN 0-8091-2687-7 (v. 1 : pbk.)
ISBN 0-8091-3325-3 (pbk.)

Published by Paulist Press
997 Macarthur Boulevard
Mahwah, New Jersey 07430

Printed and bound in the
United States of America

Contents

Robert J. Wicks
Introduction 1

I. THE EXPANDED CHALLENGES AND OPPORTUNITIES OF PASTORAL COUNSELING

Ann Belford Ulanov
Barry Ulanov
1. Reaching to the Unknown: Religion and the Psyche .. 7

Siang-Yang Tan
2. Lay Christian Counseling 27

Chris R. Schlauch
3. Re-Visioning Pastoral Diagnosis 51

Edward P. Shafranske
4. The Contributions of Short-Term Dynamic Psychotherapy to Pastoral Psychotherapy 102

II. THE CHALLENGES AND OPPORTUNITIES OF SPECIAL POPULATIONS

David W. Augsburger
5. Cross-Cultural Pastoral Psychotherapy 129

Richard W. Voss
6. Pastoral Counseling with Families-at-Risk 144

Christie Cozad Neuger
7. A Feminist Perspective on Pastoral Counseling with Women 185

Robert J. McAllister
8. Mental Health Treatment of Religion Professionals ... 208

Gail Lynn Unterberger
9. Counseling Lesbians: A Feminist Perspective 228

Richard Byrne, O.C.S.O.
10. Pastoral Counseling of the Gay Male 267

III. THE CHALLENGES AND OPPORTUNITIES OF LIFE STAGES

Margaret Gorman, R.S.C.J.
11. Midlife Transitions in Men and Women 297

Paul R. Giblin
12. Marital Conflict and Marital Spirituality 313

David Blackwelder
13. Single Parents: In Need of Pastoral Support 329

IV. THE CHALLENGES AND OPPORTUNITIES OF THE DE-VALUED AND ABUSED

Carroll Saussy
14. Pastoral Care and Counseling and Issues of Self-Esteem 363

William J. Sneck, S.J.
15. Guilt 390

Howard W. Stone
16. Depression 415

Sharon E. Cheston
17. Counseling Adult Survivors of Childhood Sexual Abuse 447

Marie M. Fortune
James Poling
18. Calling to Accountability: The Church's Response to Abusers 489

Eileen A. Gavin
19. Words Can Never Hurt Me? The Psychological/ Emotional Abuse of Children 506

V. PROBLEMS, CHALLENGES, AND OPPORTUNITIES OF THE ADDICTED

Paul A. Mickey
20. Bulimia and Anorexia: Signs of the Times 521

Paul D. Lininger
21. Pastoral Counseling and Psychoactive Substance Use Disorders 543

Rachel Callahan, C.S.C.
Rea McDonnell, S.S.N.D.
22. Adult Children of Alcoholics 577

Joseph Ciarrocchi
23. Pathological Gambling and Pastoral Counseling 593

VI. SPECIAL CHALLENGES AND OPPORTUNITIES FOR THE 1990S

David W. Foy
and Kent D. Drescher, Allan G. Fitz, Kevin R. Kennedy
24. Posttraumatic Stress Disorder 621

Richard D. Parsons
25. Suicide Survivors: Intervention—Prevention—Postvention 638

Roy Lewis
26. Pastoral Care to the Unemployed 664

Walter J. Smith, S.J.
27. Embracing Pastoral Ministry in the Age of AIDS 679

Notes on the Contributors 711

Indexes 718

Robert J. Wicks

Introduction

In 1985 the *Clinical Handbook of Pastoral Counseling* was published. It was designed to bring the "clinical handbook" model, which is commonplace in psychiatry and psychology, into the arena of pastoral counseling. In this ecumenical work leading Christian professionals incorporated basic theory and practice with the use of illustrated examples. It integrated theory and basic skills in pastoral counseling and ministry and addressed the unique challenges of how one works with different populations.

In this new work, *Clinical Handbook of Pastoral Counseling, Volume 2,* the goal is to build on the original work and to supplement the new expanded edition of the original *Clinical Handbook of Pastoral Counseling.* As in its predecessor, Volume 2 has been prepared by leading pastoral care professionals from different Christian denominations. It too is designed to be practical, thought-provoking, balanced, clinically sound, and theologically oriented.

Every effort was made to secure the best possible person with relevant experience in each area being addressed. In preparing for the activities of pastoral care and the specialized form of ministry we call pastoral counseling one must assimilate a good deal of information so as not to be guilty of "Christian romanticism." When persons wish to be medical missionaries—and be capable of providing something more than first-aid—they must obviously first study medicine and/or nursing. Similarly, if someone wishes to do more than basic pastoral care as a minister in the counseling arena, he or she must become skilled in the behavioral sciences. This is the reason for the publication of both the *Clinical Handbook of Pastoral Counseling, Volume 1—Expanded Edition* and the *Clinical Handbook of Pastoral Counseling: Volume 2,* as well as other fine sourcebooks now available in this area. (Two other examples are the rich, encyclopedic work, *Dictionary of Pastoral Care and Counseling* (general editor: Rodney J. Hunter; associate editors: H. Newton Malony, Liston O. Mills, and John Patton), and the extremely helpful *The Clinical Handbook to*

[Howard Clinebell's] *Basic Types of Pastoral Counseling* (edited by Clements and Stone).

Being *technically* proficient in the practice of counseling though is not enough. *Pastoral* counseling is more than a religious person helping others in distress. It is a response by a baptized person to the call to help others in a quite defined way. It is also an activity that involves the integration of psychology and theology in which (as Charles Gerkin described in his creative work *The Living Human Document*) the theological hermeneutic must take its place alongside the psychological one and at times even take precedence over it.

In pastoral counseling then, understanding of the client's problems and growing edges is essential. However, this understanding must always also set the stage for *metanoia* (conversion). Persons being treated are not only being helped to restore a greater level of emotional health in their lives and to set the foundation for further psychological growth, but also to open themselves up to God's free initiative of grace so they can take a more psychologically healthy and spiritually sound role in their respective Christian communities.

Since pastoral counseling involves both the action of God's grace and conscious attention given to the human effort of the minister and client involved, a discussion of the theory and practice of this process (as is reflected in the following contributions) will probably raise as many questions as it answers. Part of this is based on different theological as well as therapeutic stances. For instance, from certain theological vantage points there will be a concern that in trying to gain an understanding of the process of pastoral counseling and the role of grace, one of the prominent dangers will be a diminishment of the divine role or sovereignty of God in life. For others the concern comes from the other end of the spectrum: that in emphasizing the important place of grace and God's free initiative in our lives, a diminishment of the human role might occur. That these age-old questions and differences exist is natural—and good! Debate around the topic of "grace and the theology of ministry" have long been present. They are helpful because they remind us that experiencing the relationship between God and the human person is above all a *mystery*—and we must never forget this existential reality.

Volume 2 is divided into six sections, each with its own introduction. Articles are clustered around the challenges and opportunities of pastoral counseling in general, special populations, certain life stages, the devalued and abused, the addicted, and special issues of the 1990s. As in any edited work, the contributions vary with the intent, the unique clinical experience, and the background and orientation of individual authors as well as the level of sophistication of the available literature.

As in any handbook of this type, this book is not meant to be read through from cover to cover. Instead, each piece is designed to stand by itself and be a good beginning reference for the topic in question. As is the case in the expanded edition of the original *Clinical Handbook of Pastoral Counseling*, every effort was made to provide enough information in each chapter to offer a solid introduction to the area in question, thereby surfacing the issues and problems surrounding the topic and directing the reader to additional sources if further study is desired.

The editors did not try to meld the individual "voices" of the contributors into a seamless garment so as to approximate a textbook on pastoral counseling. (There are enough of those now available in their own right.) Rather, the diversity and sometimes passionate stands on certain positions where psychology/anthropology and theology intersect are prized and presented to you with editing only designed to encourage readability while not interfering with the content or unique process of argumentation presented by individual authors.

Finally, although both volumes of the *Handbook* deal with a great array of important material and the editors feel that together they provide a respectable contribution in the area of pastoral counseling, their combined articles are by no means to be considered as comprehensive coverage of all the major concerns in the field. Just as the editors and publisher felt that the first volume needed to be expanded and a second volume prepared to deal with the many other important areas in the field of pastoral counseling not covered in the original volume, more can still be written and said. In deciding to offer each contributor enough space to deal in a more than cursory way with his or her topic, some areas had to be deleted so the volume could be kept manageable and affordable for individuals looking for resources for their own professional development or for course texts. Also, we recognize that in publication of this volume we are hopefully furthering discussion and study in certain areas of the pastoral counseling field rather than offering the final word on any particular section of it.

In conclusion, it is our hope that you will find the individual contributions as helpful and thought-provoking as the editors have. The dedication, professionalism, knowledge, creativity, and compassion of the authors involved certainly made working with them a real joy.

SECTION I
THE EXPANDED CHALLENGES AND OPPORTUNITIES OF PASTORAL COUNSELING

Although the primary focus of this, the second volume of the *Clinical Handbook of Pastoral Counseling,* is on challenges and opportunities of those whom we serve, there are a number of challenges and opportunities that sit at the core of the role and function of the pastoral counselor in the '90s. The presentations in Section I make it clear that the need to be consistently and constantly aware of the "calling of the spirit"; to be trained and competent; and to integrate our pastoral, theological, and human science resources in an authentic, consistent, and coherent manner remain of prime importance.

Ann and Barry Ulanov provide a unique look at pastoral counseling as the process by which two individuals come to identify and embrace the spirit of God (Chapter 1). The Ulanovs suggest that pastoral counselors integrate their theology with depth psychology in order to see the many ways, oftentimes symbolic, that the unknown touches their lives and the lives of their clients. Further, the authors' suggest that it is the special "calling" of the pastoral counselor to assist his or her clients to see that their desire to be known and to know that they matter are evidence of the reality of the transcendent —a reality that they are sought by the spirit of God.

Attention to the movement of God in our lives and the lives of those whom we serve is not restricted to those who are ordained. The growing interest and involvement of lay people in pastoral counseling may signal the increased potential for helping those who struggle. However, the benefits to be gained are clearly tempered by the degree to which such counseling is done competently. Siang-Yang Tan provides a biblically based model for effective lay Christian pastoral counseling (Chapter 2). Further, Tan provides an insightful review of the evaluative research on the effectiveness of lay counseling and suggests models for selection, training, and supervision.

Chris Schlauch challenges us to "re-vision" our models and definitions of pastoral diagnosis (Chapter 3). Schlauch argues that contrary to most commonly held views, "pastoral" is not incompatible with "diagnosis." Chapter 3 also offers a very creative and challenging look at the concept of diagnosis and reframes diagnosis to mean an ongoing activity of "knowing apart certain qualities and features of the current state of another's self and suffering." Schlauch argues that since what and how we know about the person's current state is inherently related to the goals toward which we will work, as well as the means by which we envision getting there; "diagnosis is at the heart of our overall clinical perspective."

The challenge to our professional orientation and practice, started by Schlauch's invitation to revisit and re-vision our use and definition of pastoral diagnosis, is continued in Edward Shafranske's call to a model of short-term dynamic pastoral psychotherapy (Chapter 4). With the current trends in mental health pointing to the increased need for cost-containment, time-limited therapy, and increased accountability, Shafranske's essay is timely and quite useful. It provides the reader with one model of time-limited and short-term intervention that, while acknowledging its theoretical underpinnings to psychoanalytic thought, is unique in that it offers clients the opportunity to work intensively toward the resolution of one focal conflict. While providing an introduction to the essential features common to short-term treatment approaches, he is quick to emphasize that short-term psychotherapy requires not only careful selection of clients, but also specialized training and skills of the pastoral counselor.

Thus, Section I provides the reader with many challenges, opportunities, and clarifications for pastoral counseling in the '90s and beyond.

Ann Belford Ulanov
Barry Ulanov

1. Reaching to the Unknown: Religion and the Psyche

Every algebra problem makes students conscious of the fact that they are seeking an unknown X. We all do the same thing, however little we may be conscious of it. We seek to connect our side of the equation with the unknown on the other side. We seek the experience of knowing that we are known, that we matter, that our living and loving make a difference, not because we are particularly gifted or good or true, but because we are sought, each in our turn, by the heart of life on the other side, the spirit, God. The possibility of connecting makes all the difference, makes us hope to live imaginatively in a world of shared existence with others. The idea that connection is sought from both sides not only makes the algebra easier, but anchors our faith in the midst of the suffering we all experience.

It is an ancient truth that we do not remember pain. But we do remember only too well that we have suffered pain. It may have been physical pain of an all but unendurable intensity that turned out oddly enough to be endurable. We are here, after all, remembering how unendurable it all was. It may have been—may still be—those small tortures of head or stomach or tooth or limb or back that seem to be built into the human condition. It may, most seriously of all, have been or still be that dysfunction of the psyche or spirit that makes us wonder whether we are in anything like full possession of an ego or a self and sends us looking for professional help. It is so much a part of our life, trivial or profound in its visitations, and has been with us so long that we can accept Wittgenstein's oracular pronouncement, "You learned the *concept* 'pain' when you learned language" (Wittgenstein 1958, p. 118).

We long ago learned the concept; we did not understand why it was as fundamental to our lives as language itself. We spent agonizing days when we were young trying to learn to deal with pain. We have spent years, as we have grown older, trying to deal with the scandal of suffering, its undemocratic excesses in the lives of some people, its appalling inroads on whole families, tribes, neighborhoods, cities, even nations. How do we connect with it? Where do we find understanding? How do we account for the misery, abstract in a sense when it is out there and belongs to other people, fearfully concrete when it is our own, and especially if its terms are psychological or spiritual. The unknown X quantity in pain and suffering, our own or others', is bedeviling. How do we even describe it? More often than not, we choose not to talk about it—too general, too woolly, hopelessly philosophical, or worse, theological. But it is there, as difficult and elusive to deal with as the most obscure unknown figure in mathematics or the physical sciences and a good deal more important, for it is in one respect not at all unknown to us, this unknown X. It is present, here, very much with us, and one way or another, in our own suffering or that of others, almost all the time.

Behind every presenting symptom brought to those who work professionally with the psyche lurks this seeking, this reaching to the unknown X. But people rarely say this straight out; the identifying symbols of the transcendent are difficult to discern. The religious vocabulary has lost a lot of its punch. Religious symbols have faded for many people; they no longer carry the power of the Divine. Many people discard the vocabulary altogether or use it only defensively to mask or avoid what does not fit easily into their lives—the pulls and pushes of sexual needs and the pressures of unlived aggression. For many, the religious vocabulary simply fails to express a world-view. Instead, the words hang emptily in the air, neither grounded in the depths nor reaching to the heights. There the words hang, flapping in the winds of the late twentieth century, failing to touch us just when we need them most, to express the unspeakable experiences of the psyche.

Pastoral counselors, those in any of the mental-health professions who count themselves believers, stand out from their colleagues in their explicit articulate recognition of the unknown X in the consulting room where, for believers and unbelievers alike, religious issues always turn up. But we need seeing eyes to see them and hearing ears to hear them. We need training to spot the unknown X as it moves toward us, seeking its persons from the other side of the equations they bring into therapy. The religious dimension in work with the psyche is obscure to the sight; we can easily overlook it, discount its importance in terms of our own equations, or just deny its presence altogether. We need to learn to respond, and we need to learn when to keep quiet. For always, we run the risk of indulging in empty chatter about "spiritual" things, things which will waft us up out of the grit and safely distance us from the anguish of suffering of daily life.

There is an unmistakable difference between spiritual chatter and an understanding that goes to the heart of things and finds words to describe the experience. The gift of the spirit that reaches so far beyond the banal and the aimless is almost always characterized by a psychological habit of mind, if not precise training in the psychological disciplines. Thus it is that the psychiatrist Maurice Drury, in his brilliant little study in philosophical psychology, *The Danger of Words,* says he "would describe St. Augustine's *Confessions* as perhaps the most profound psychological analysis ever carried out." It is not just a general encomium. Drury has a very specific element of the great book in mind: "If it be true, as indeed it is, that '*Fecisti nos ad Te, et inquietum est cor nostrum donec requiescat in Te*' (You made us for yourself, and our hearts are restless until they rest in you), then any psychology which ignores the persistent inquietude of the human soul is a shallow and superficial affair" (Drury 1973, pp. 31–32).

The issue for Augustine, as for Drury and all who work in psychology with any pastoral concern, is the failure to recognize this central truth—"the persistent inquietude of the human soul"—and to speak openly out of it. In a sermon notable for its calm good sense and precision about prayer, Augustine says, "Imagine yourself under a physician, and in weak health, as is true of all of us, for all of this life of ours is a weakness, and a long life but a prolonged weakness." He is not being pessimistic but practical. We are troubled, insistently uneasy; why then do we not ask about our condition, pray about it, look for help? His physician, his invariable refuge, is the Lord, but his procedure is the procedure of the clinic and the consulting room freed of ambiguity and diffidence. "Imagine yourself, then, sick, under a physician's hand. You want to ask your physician to allow you to drink some fresh wine. You are not forbidden to ask, for it may not do you any harm; it may even be good for you. Do not hesitate to ask, then. Ask, do not hesitate" (B. Ulanov 1983, p. 16).

The religious phenomena that turn up in the clinic and the consulting room show the same ambiguity they do in all the other areas of life. It takes a responsive and practiced eye to perceive them. By their nature religious phenomena as we experience them are ambiguous because the transcendent, the unknown X, is too big to fit precisely into our finite capacities. We sense that the transcendent lies far outside and beyond our categories. It stirs our emotions and introduces a problem of identification for us of what or who mediates between it and us. We feel tiny, contingent, fragmentary before the Vast, the All, the Whole. We respond with deep feeling to the unknown X as absolute and unconditioned. Our religious symbols create themselves out of this fundamental form of response through which, with whatever indirectness or uncertainty, we glimpse the transcendent. We feel a sense of respect and obligation to it, and with it an inevitable breaking of the rules in our relation to it. But even transgressions are gathered up in the operation of these new creative forces that bring with them symbols of forgiveness of sin, of repentance, of reparation.

We come again and again to the question of mediation. Are our religious symbols more than projections of our inner conflicts, of our psyche's archetypal images for the unknown X, of collective representations that function to order our society? Do these symbols spring from our side of the equation only? The breaking in of grace with the figure of Jesus Christ answers these questions, not with a new philosophical formulation or a political cause or mental-health plan, but through a person. This radically narrows the gap between us and the unknown, and in the intensity of the religious experience bridges it. But that is the rare event. For most people the gap between the two sides of the equation and the urgent need to reach to the unknown X remain. They must ask how they can receive what Jesus brings, how they can relate to him.

A further complication arises from the fact that in our earliest life as little children, and even in our deepest psychic life as adults, religious experiences come to us in pre-verbal or non-verbal modes of apprehension. We know no words to express what we see or hear or smell or taste or touch. The boundaries are fluid. We live on the borders of the unfathomable. We depend upon religious gestures and rituals and symbolizations to communicate experience at these depths. Psyche and soul not only overlap here; they interweave and mix with each other (A. and B. Ulanov 1975, chap. 5). This compounds their ambiguity and ambivalence, leaving us open to the charge that we are merely dressing up our psychic needs in religious clothing. But their closeness also allows us to see, if we have the eyes to see, that the increasing thrust in recent years of depth psychologies of all schools farther and farther back into the origins of human life to birth and the first months of life represents efforts to investigate the origins of being itself, of what it means to be human and to be held in being.

The ambiguity and ambivalence of religious symbols are by their very nature, as Dorothy Emmet says "not the result of pious vagueness or confusion of thought. . . . It is a precise way of conveying the fundamental dilemma of religious symbolism, which presents an analogue of the transcendent in the forms of the phenomenal, of the infinite in the finite" (Emmet 1957, p. 105). This means we simultaneously accept two apparently contradictory facts, that what comes to us from the unknown is a sign of divine presence, and that our sign is not in itself the divine. Its independent life exceeds our grasp. It is infinitely more important than our symbols for it. We do glimpse, grasp, and receive the unknown X, but in indirect, non-literal ways, in and through our embodied life, in the here and now.

This is the sort of knowing that the counselor trained in religion as well as depth psychology brings to the consulting room—an ability to see and deal with and even talk about clients' symbols for the unknown that touch their lives, that must be understood as both true and yet incomplete, as promoting wholeness and yet always only a part of a much greater whole. These symbols operate in and through psychological compulsion, depression, anxiety attacks, fragmentation, and perversion as well as every other part of a client's life. In some instances the compulsion may even result from an inability to get on with creating religious symbols, the way the neurosis itself, as Jung said long ago, results from a refusal to suffer legitimately, that is, religiously (Jung 1958, p. 75, par. 129).

How do we suffer legitimately? We suffer legitimately when we acknowledge our pain. We do so best, it may be, when we are informed by the majestic symbols of the Judeo-Christian inheritance and the tutelage in understanding and living through them of those most practiced in their graces because most open to them. We need not look for honeyed words. There is no need to follow the lines of scripture or the language of set prayer, however rich and instructive these may be. It may be that the best instruction for us, those who seek to heal or to be healed, is in the example of others like us, victims of the tortures of modernity, but perhaps unlike us in their resourcefulness in dealing with those tortures.

The French poet Max Jacob has much to tell us here. His psyche and spirit were tutored by the Surrealist movement, by close association with Picasso and Guillaume Apollinaire, by religious vision, and by the terror of the Nazis when they occupied France in World War II. He was arrested by the Gestapo as he was leaving morning Mass and sent to a concentration camp, where he died. But he had known another terror, far worse: "Absence of God—that's the real hell! In memory I compare my life without God to my life today!" The most terrible suffering was to believe there was no way out of it, no one to help, to offer support. "Sick as a dog" is the best way, he says, to describe that dreadful experience (Jacob 1972, p. 71).

Jacob's nostrums are simple. "God is all around us if we want him to be, and we do want him." All around us? Yes, he says, "in the host and in our stomachs. He is in our ears and in our eyes inside us. He speaks to us and we try to speak back in spite of our stupidity" (Jacob 1972, p. 95). In his meditative life the poet saw and heard with the ears and eyes of interiority the possibility of being constantly aware of God, in every moment, in every place, in everything around him. To allow God to be distant, to be absent, was to assure that constant deafening emptiness, that maddening life which was a life without God, which is to say, without reality.

Nothing is lost in such a construction of reality. The Christian poet remains as much a Surrealist as ever, but with larger resources, with a deeper palette, a thicker one. In the sharp, blunt images of his prose poems he offers a mythology in brief of psyche and soul. He calls the collection *Le Cornet à des (The Dice Cup)* and like Mallarmé not so long before him offers testimony that there is much more than meaningless chance in the throw of the dice. In his cosmology "God (there is a God) looks at the earth. . . ." What the Creator sees in his creation "is a few teeth with cavities." Something to lament over, to repudiate? No. "My eye is God! my eye is God! The teeth with cavities show a kind of infinitely tiny drop which classifies them. . . . To me, the universe is as it is to God" (Jacob 1979, p. 75).

In such a reading of the universe one discovers a new geography, a burgeoning spirituality, a confident inner life. Jacob responds to the most promising command of scripture, "Knock and it shall be opened," with characteristic imagination and religious subtlety. "If you moved back . . . and moved back still, saying every ten thousand yards: 'This is unimportant!' you would eventually meet God," he tells us. "After travelling through indifference, you could remain motionless and God would abandon the pleader no longer." If in your travels over the huge terrain of indifference you kept on moving backward, Jacob promises, you would finally come to God's dwelling-place "and the point from which He created the skies and the earth" (Jacob 1979, p. 119).

Jacob's pastoral counseling is strong, clear, unhesitant. See the religious dimension in everything. Claim it. Do not hesitate, claim it all, and claim it quickly, and claim it in any way that you can. In a world which Jacob characterizes as "a few teeth with cavities," we are not to scruple over inadequacies, clumsinesses, past failures, the nagging uncertainty of what it is that gives our life meaning, of who it is that stands behind us. Move backward over the endless miles of what is far worse than uncertainty, that is, *indifference*. For indifference, after all, is another way of saying absence, and absence, we know from Jacob, is hell. A subtle religiosity? Yes, but we must remember that another meaning of *subtle* is "pervasive," which is the opposite of *absent*.

Clinical examples of subtle religious happenings in the consulting room abound.[1] A woman in her mid-forties rushes into her session scattering words, jacket, purse, even shoes, as she drops into a chair. Her work requires numerous phone calls, meetings, appointments, last-minute changes of plans, constant arrangements for future business deals. She is harassed to the point of madness. Tensely erect, on the edge of her chair, her words burst forth: "Five times yesterday, I felt suicidal. I was falling into pieces." And she means it. Her body crumples. She falls back against the chair. Her life, her sense of person, her soul-hold on its vision of the center threaten to break up into fragments. "Like Humpty Dumpty," was the response of the analyst, who did not know really what brought that rhyme to her mind with such force. The patient paled. This particular nursery rhyme had never been mentioned before, nor was it one often in the mind of the analyst. The patient confided that the nursery rhyme had haunted her childhood—negatively. She had loved all nursery rhymes except Humpty Dumpty. It brought fear and foreboding to her. She knew something irretrievably awful was going to happen. And it did: "Humpty Dumpty had a great fall. And all the king's horses and all the king's men couldn't put Humpty Dumpty together again." The rhyme conveyed her greatest fear to her, the one that prompted her to seek help in the first place: she feared she would herself break up into tiny fragments that could not be pasted together again.[2] She feared simply dropping out of existence. The rhyme spoke to her of annihilation of her self. It was not just pain she suffered at those moments, but agony. Suicide would be a relief.

But here, in the session, a connection rose through the unexpected enunciation of Humpty Dumpty. At some pre-verbal, unspoken level, the unknown came through this surprising appearance, across the gap over to her side of the equation. She felt literally held in being. Instead of plunging headlong into the gap to relieve her agony over disintegrating, she knew she was known. Right there in the place of breakdown, something had broken through, a human connection that made her unspeakable anxiety bearable.

The connection that held her in being and the accompanying sense of something breaking through to her were so great that they moved her to give something right back. She left beautiful bunches of tulips right outside the analyst's office door, to surprise, to greet, to connect.

The religious factor in this example is in the sense that both persons felt of being held by something greater, that generated the Humpty-Dumpty association which so firmly hit the mark, and then arose again in the generous giving of flowers. Something had broken through in the very place the patient felt herself breaking up. It was a connection that lasted. It sustained her when suicidal thoughts threatened again. A string of connections supported her now. When she felt suicidal, she remembered Humpty Dumpty and her fear of breaking up. She linked all to that sense of being cared for, held, that arose right in the midst of fear, that she celebrated by the tulips. The unknown X that had reached out to her stayed with her; it was portable or, as we might say in religious language, it was incarnated.

Is the religious aspect of this episode merely in the eye of the beholder? Is it reducible to the terms of countertransference projection on the part of the counselor? Yes and no. Part of what the religiously trained mental-health professional brings to clients is precisely a countertransference sensitivity to the religious dimension of the work. As with all other countertransference phenomena, the professional must analyze it and know when its content applies to a personal complex that needs more work (the "abnormal" or "subjective" countertransference), when it arises in response to the client (the "normal" or "ordinary" countertransference), and when it is induced by the client's complexes (the "objective" countertransference that gives information about the client's unconscious struggles).[3] In addition, however, any mental-health professional must have analyzed the range and function of his or her own God-images (Rizzuto 1979, p. 4). The religiously trained counselor knows this and acts accordingly. Very few training institutes include this dimension, and thus counselors are often left as blind and as unhearing in the religious area as they would be in the sexual, aggressive, or object-relations areas if those psychic experiences were omitted from training.

Religiously trained counselors must know what their conscious God-images are and what their unconscious God-images are and what the gap is between them (A. B. Ulanov 1986, chap. 12; A. B. Ulanov 1988, chap. 1). They may consciously worship the Johannine God of love, for example, and unconsciously dream of worshipping a giant pig, of all mad things. How do these compete? What effect does that conflict have on clients? They must know what touches off their own dread of the infinite and what range of defenses automatically marches in to protect them. The reductionist argument that such dread is nothing but fear of the judgmental father or the devouring mother may, in fact, be only a rationalized version of the defense of denial.

The need to be trained to see how religious phenomena mix with dynamic interchanges between client and counselor springs from two sets of facts. First, such phenomena truly exist; they exhibit truth; they point to the reality of the transcendent. Second, seeing this, the counselor can respond in gesture, expression, breathing rhythm, tone of voice, as well as words, in ways that convey to the client a larger picture, a glimpse of endlessly complex patterns that surround and undergird and hold in being all that happens. This enlarging of awareness will be picked up by the client as a sorely needed added perspective, radically changing the view of what he or she is suffering (A. and B. Ulanov 1987, pp. 14–20). Religious knowledge, it becomes clear, is endlessly useful in defining and diagnosing not just problems, but reality itself. In the threat of breaking-up, for example, that the woman's suicidal fantasy defended against, and in the joy of two persons connecting in the midst of that agony, the woman saw a larger pattern of connection and interconnection in reality, one that supported her and indeed all of us. It was as if she had found herself floundering in a river when suddenly her foot touched a rock far beneath the surface and she knew she could stand on it. It was really there. This changed her whole understanding of suffering. When the fear of breaking-up occurred again it took on a large signifying function. She knew what it meant and remembered the experience of connection. The heightened consciousness afforded her relief because she understood what was happening. In addition, she remembered that tantalizing glimpse, her experience of the human link and discovery of a rock to stand on. She saw, however briefly, that even in her worst fragmentation, something larger and stronger was there supporting her, that unknown X showing itself through the connection that can be made between persons. This is more than conscious insight, more than corrective emotional experience with a "good" object. This is a small theophany in the midst of the ordinary work and suffering of the consulting room.

The counselor in such an instance may think of honored scriptural attestation to such manifestations of the transcendent, that, for example, even in hell God is with us (Ps 139). The counselor does not necessarily need to articulate this association; often it would be intrusive to do so. In this instance the woman was not formally religious and, in fact, had violent negative feelings about the Judeo-Christian tradition as a system of male oppression of women. The purpose of psychological work is clearly not to proselytize or engage in religious debate. The point is that when the counselor knows his or her own religious stance and problems and is working deliberately with them, a connection to this dimension of reality opens for the client to find his or her way in relation to it.

As is so often true, suffering provides the best of terrains for understanding here. A man worked a number of years in therapy and came through to some surcease of intense suffering. A drinking problem rose to the surface and he dealt with it. His feeling of being compulsively identified with his persona, the public face that his job demanded of him, he now recognized for what it was. The compulsion yielded. What he discovered in the process, however, was his almost total ignorance of what else he wanted to be and to do in his life. The work could go no further. It just went round and round in circles, with nothing new presenting itself. Little hints from dreams did not flower. Fantasy images for new attitudes or actions in his life bubbled for a moment on the surface of consciousness and then disappeared right back into the unconscious. It was as if there were not enough psychic energy to forge a new attitude or even hope for a new direction. And so the work stopped.

Several years later this man called in great distress. He felt he was having a "breakdown." Weeping, shaking, terror, an anxiety of uncontrollable proportions threatened to undermine him completely. Their target was precise: his public figure, functioning on the job. That was the place he felt himself breaking apart. Again, the religious perspective of the counselor could effect a radical revaluation of psychological distress. The man was suffering gravely. Immediate and numerous, even daily sessions were called for. Yet in the midst of the emergency the counselor felt a great opportunity. The energies accumulating in the unconscious had finally gathered enough intensity to break through to consciousness. The man was being served notice that no longer could he confine his life to definition by his work. The unlived parts of his psyche now insisted on being admitted. They wanted to live too. If he could receive them they would be added to his life. If he could not, they would push his life out of the way, like so much waste. What excited the counselor to the point of hope was the notion of this man being given a chance to live life "abundantly," much the way Jesus announced he was bringing into the world.

The abundant life reaches down into us as much as up. Our most neglected parts, most enslaved, nearest to dead, are to be gathered into plenitude just as much as our most differentiated sensibilities. Isn't this the meaning of the fact that Jesus Christ, the divine one, is crucified like a slave? In one nature he combines the highest of the high—he is the Son of God—and the lowest of the low—he is the most abased and enslaved of us, the Son of humankind, all of it, the most absurd and abused very much included. What matters crucially for the person suffering, indeed what determines whether the outcome will be breakdown or breakthrough, is whether the new that is coming comes in a form that can be assimilated. Sometimes therapy needs to concentrate on just that—a widening of consciousness, a strengthening of flexibility and resiliency, an enlarging of its potency to see in symbolic terms—in order to accommodate what the unknown X is making known. In religious terms such ego-enlarging can be seen as getting big and flexible enough to correspond with grace —the breaking in of more life to be lived (A. and B. Ulanov 1983, chap. 13). This man felt calmed by the steady presence of the counselor, but also amazed at their different perspectives on what was happening. He felt that he was falling apart; she felt that at last something could break through to be lived that would inhabit that emptiness he had so long complained of in the first phase of work, years before.

If we cannot assimilate the unknown we must experience its presence as breaking us, as God's curse. We experience what Jung called the dark side of the God, (Jung 1958, pp. 366, 455, 461; pars. 561, 739, 747). Though Jung thought that was an evil contained in God, we find it more useful to see it as that aspect of the Holy that exceeds our grasp. We might even hazard that the mythological depictions of punishment in hell are the result of our inability to receive the Holy, so we experience them negatively. The envious, in Dante's *Purgatorio,* endlessly circle the mountain, the hand of one on the shoulder of another, blind from having their eyes sutured shut with threads of iron. Looked at one way, that is punishment for the evil eye of envious looking to spoil or steal the good of our neighbor. Looked at another way, the shuttered eye is forced to look within to receive the crumb of good that is our own (A. and B. Ulanov 1983, chap. 6). Similarly, a man breaking down needs to see what is coming through from the side of the unknown X and to pay close attention to the images in which it presents itself.

Psychoanalysis has taught us to look for an endless complexity in the life of images. Displacement, substitution, the negation of negation—these disguises and recastings of images in the unconscious have become almost commonplace to us in our examination of dreams and fantasies. They have made many of us, votaries of Freudian or Neo-Freudian or Kleinian or a dozen other schools, believe that the unknown is simply a generic term for what we have not yet identified. As with so many scientistic zealots, who take for granted that all that is now hidden from us will one day be revealed with the tools of the sciences, so the over-determined dream-and-fantasy pursuers run down their signs, their symbols, their tales, their dramas. They promise to resolve all, if not immediately, then with just the shortest of delays.

They are selfless, we are assured, dedicated to scientific truth-seeking, as Freud was when he determined to publish his *Interpretation of Dreams* "at all costs, even if it meant sacrificing his personality." So we are told by the analyst-scholar who produced what is surely the most voluminous account that will ever be made of *Freud's Self-Analysis.* "From Saint Augustine on, many men had written their confessions with the aim of edifying their fellow human beings or achieving literary fame." Not Freud. He "was the first person to do so for strictly scientific reasons" (Anzieu 1986, p. 426). And so, not looking to edify or to become famous as a writer, free of everything but scientific concern and bitter antireligious bias, he could pursue the unknown.

The irony is Dostoevskian. As the Russian novelist's proclaimers and organizers of utopian society became masters of deceit and tyranny, so the unshackling of the unconscious by Freud and his followers became for some an opportunity to manufacture new impediments and restraints. Let us by all means look for the unknown, isolate it, identify it, explain its life in the psyche—and explain away whatever presents itself in spiritual clothing.

It may seem late in the day to be concerned by the antireligious attitudes, arguments, distortions, and defamations of Freud and those who follow him in these matters or adopt his often questionable anthropology to dispose of the unwelcome entry of the numinous. It is certainly no longer necessary to take on the arguments, to answer the attacks, to recover from the Freudian wasteland what is useful even in these combats. What is urgent is some serious recognition of just how powerful the presence of the spirit really is in our lives, to discover, for scientific reasons among others, how much human interiority wears the colors, speaks in the accents, moves in the gestures and postures of the numinous. The unshackling to which Freud contributed so much needs now to proceed in terms of this recognition, in this presence, freely, thoughtfully, watchfully acknowledged.

Watching for the way the unknown presents itself means that the counselor must constantly turn and return to the experience of touching and being touched by the numinous, but as a servant, not as a master. We experience the numinous in our lives gripping us, in ecstatic moments where we are all but identified with its energy, or in an agony of feeling know ourselves shut out from such intensity of presence.

One woman in her forties said she ached to give herself to something large outside herself. She wanted to be caught up in its life and give herself to making it intelligible to others. The divine spirit, as the Freudian text tells us, comes and goes, blowing where it will. It never consents to be our possession even though it is our constant temptation to reify it, catch it, label it, even bottle it and sell it.[4] That is the wrong ego-attitude. The better approach is the servant-attitude taught us by the Suffering Servant of the gospels, being on the watch for its arrival, ready to admit it and pay close attention to what it wants. Usually it arrives just where we do not expect it. The Christ still gets born in a stable—though now it looks like a consulting room —in the muck of an obsessive complex, a dogging anxiety, the pain of realizing how much our hate and passivity have detoured us.

Hate is the concentration camp of the soul. Passivity is the psyche's straitjacket. Caught in the prison of our contempts and aversions, we utterly lose our freedom of person. There is no room for the self in the concentration on other people's iniquities. Fixed on their failure to deal with us properly, to really see us, we do not recognize the anterior fact—that we do not deal with ourselves as we should, that we do not really see ourselves. Looking for the unknown, we put ourselves in the position, when hate is at the center of our being, where nothing is knowable. All we have is nothing—no thing, no being, Augustine's definition of evil, the privation of being, the ultimate absence.

In passivity, that fall from grace that apes the appearance of civility and rectitude, we descend again into nothingness. Our good manners are in fact an absence of manners. Our rectitude is hollow—we have at best a thin coating of the words or postures of good faith. What really possesses us is a fear of being possessed. We live a life of detour. We do not dare to face being. We haven't the courage or the determination to take on the spiritual combat; its risks are too great. All we ask, we tell ourselves, is a moment's peace every now and then.

And we tell this to ourselves as analysts or patients, as counselors or counseled. We want to be out of things, free from events, as little touched as possible by the embroilments of personhood.

In part because of a belief in scientific impartiality, in part because of a true wisdom borrowed from scripture, psychology in all its disciplines eschews judgment. "Judge not that ye be not judged" could well be stitched in samplers for the consulting rooms and clinics of psychoanalysts, psychiatrists, psychologists, pastoral counselors. Their patients come to be probed, to be taken apart, to have their psyches hacked and sawed and left in little pieces—impartially. No judgment. No right or wrong. Hate? Let us find the trauma. A shell-like existence, disconnected, untouched by feeling, unrelated to anyone? We will seek the punishing father, the envious mother, the wretched mate responsible for that terrible emptiness of being.

We say "no judgment," but even as we say it we make a judgment.[5] We point a righteous finger, over many sessions, at "the other," the demon responsible for our patients of violent affect, of inner void. That is, we do so unless we are willing, as by our very adoption of the role of pastoral counselors we must be, to allow some room for the spirit. We do not make the judgment of no judgment now, but allow ourselves to mix our scientific impartiality with some religious partiality. We retain some sense of the value of seeking first an understanding of the psyche's stance, some penetration of the unconscious, without any trace of moralizing interference. But we hold too to the wisdom of the spirit, which counsels not moral judgment but correspondence with grace. We seek light where light has been so liberally bestowed, in text and example, by the great practitioners of the life of the spirit.

If we combine our experience and training as analysts of the psyche with what we have learned as votaries of the spirit, we are bound to recognize, perhaps with glee, how wonderfully intertwined are psyche and soul. Almost mischievously, passivity recommends itself now as a positive way of life for the psyche when it is openly tended by the soul. We can say, out of an abundance of examples, that there is a waiting quietly, a standing aside, that is a splendid exercise of the spirit. It is a kind of passivity, but not one we simply fall into out of a dereliction either of psyche or soul. We prepare for it; we set ourselves up to it. We say with Hamlet prepared at last for death, "the readiness is all," as we prepare for life. We echo Emily Dickinson, that readiest of souls waiting to be received,

You taught me Waiting with Myself—
Appointment strictly kept—

If we follow her talking "in slant," as she called it, we know what she means in this context when she says

Yet—there is a Science more—

The Heaven you know—to understand
That you be not ashamed
Of Me—in Christ's Bright Audience
Upon the further Hand—(Dickinson 1960, p. 363).

We pay attention to such learned counsel because it comes from long engagement in the turbulent encounters of psyche and soul. Out of a life of quiet struggle, lived far from the turmoil of her mid-nineteenth century world, Dickinson crafted a doctrine of elegant imbalance. Her passivity never countenances nothingness. But neither does it stand unequal to pain and suffering, her own or others. Addressing a friend wounded in the Civil War from a sick bed of her own, in an illness of some nine months, and mindful of the recent death of the writer Nathaniel Hawthorne, she confides

The only News I know
Is Bulletins all day
From Immortality (Dickinson 1971, pp. 184–85).

Emily Dickinson's is a sprightly passivity. Its informing principle is clear. Two quatrains sum it up. We should read them as verse, but live them as prose.

The Soul should always stand ajar
That if the Heaven inquire
He will not be obliged to wait
Or shy of troubling Her

Depart, before the Host have slid
The Bolt unto the Door—
To search for the accomplished Guest,
Her Visitor, no more—(Dickinson 1960, p. 481).

Again, the readiness is all. If we do not prepare ourselves, if our waiting is simply inattention, we can expect what we have earned—nothing, absence. And this absence, we have been taught, is separation from being, is hell. A learned passivity, we are being taught, is the passivity of grace, in which the soul always stands ajar.

It is a road of carefully nurtured imbalance we are being led along. Here the passivity, which earlier acted to detour us, has been turned around and has brought us back to the center of things. In the playful, but oh, so serious paradoxes of the spirit, we will learn, too, that the violence of our contempts and aversions can also be steered back to the center. We need that force of which Jesus speaks in the words that leap from his discourse on John the Baptist: "the violent bear it away" (Mt 11:12). *It* is heaven. We must seize it with force, he is saying. Heaven does not come quietly. It is a risky undertaking. It demands all. But how could it ask less since it offers all? Flannery O'Connor makes her most bold foray into the thorny fields of grace in the novel she constructed around these words, *The Violent Bear It Away.* Her central character, appropriately named for the American south and the charged world of the spirit, Tarwater, is a man maddened into prophecy, truly mad, and in time a true prophet of the spirit.

These are the lights of the spirit, revealed in literature and scripture and the example of those who have lived in their illumination. They speak to us again and again in the language of paradox and coincidence. They turn the displacements and substitutions of the unconscious into affirmative inaction. They make the negation of negation into a counsel of grace. They warn us, like Simone Weil, that "the search for equilibrium is bad because it is imaginary." In a time, an event, a personhood wracked with pain, we must hold, as Weil does, with that "something" in ourselves that "does not suffer and remains in contact with a universe which is not impaired" (Weil 1952, p. 6). We must make our sufferings "come down like a deposit, collect them into a point and become detached from them. . . . Prevent them from having access to *things.*" Paradox and coincidence. The appropriate use of violence takes nothing less than heaven. The passivity in which the soul stands ajar is noisy with being. Prophecy coincides with madness.

Sometimes the spirit breaks through the most startling coincidences, in synchronistic moments, when two events without causal connection occur simultaneously and strike us with their deep intertwined meaning. We glimpse again an order larger than anything we had imagined. Outer and inner seem linked in one continuum. Our little psychic universe and the huge universe around us bespeak one whole.

We find this sort of experience in the example of a struggling, committed Christian man. As a young boy, he had missed out on the royal authority of all children—to be welcomed and recognized as a unique and valuable person, feeling his own loving received as precious by others. He was shunted off. An experience of the kind that symbolizes in its traumatic impact all the little cumulative traumas (Kahn 1974) of feeling negligible occurred one night at bedtime. Like many children, and indeed as with many of us adults who suffer from not feeling received, he had trouble passing from waking into sleep. The loss of control in the darkness quickened his latent anxiety over not really existing as a person in his own right. So, as a child will, he wheedled and nagged. He needed extra water and bathroom time, another bedtime story, and repeated callings of "good night." (The similarity of children's demands all over the world, across cultures and historical periods, is the best proof of Jung's notion of archetypes. Clearly, there is a bedtime archetype.) In this instance his parents lost patience. In an explosion of anger his father grabbed him out of his bed and hurled him into a dark attic, shut the door, and locked him in.

He knew real terror. He screamed to get out, and the screaming carried through his life. Only through exploration of the interweaving of this trauma with a compelling fetish did it come to light that more had happened than just the bedtime drama. For a few seconds, he said, he had known annihilation; he had gone out of existence. The fetish activity that plagued him as he grew up, with its sexual accompaniment of masturbation, served in effect to bridge the gap of those seconds when he was not out of existence. Because of his terror, he had split off both his rage at being so mistreated and the ruthless level of his own aggressive self-assertion. The dissociation hampered him in his work. When he had to fight, he did not know how because he feared killing his opponent. He felt he had to protect the other from his own brutal aggressiveness. In one session all these connections were made, an interpretation finally reached that had been accumulating over many previous sessions.

All this made a deep impression on him. The next session he reported something that had come in the mail right after the pivotal session. It had bowled him over, seemed like a sign from heaven. An old neighbor of his parents, from whom he had not heard in years, sent him a newspaper clipping, complete with picture, reporting that the attic room in which he had been locked up in his childhood house had burned. Only the attic room, nothing else. This happened two days before the pivotal session. It was reported in the paper published two days after the session, and the patient received it before the next session, a miraculously quick arrival in the mail.

So it is that being breaks through, one room at a time, one person at a time. It may be destructive in the service of the good. It may serve its purposes—our purposes—in the most openly constructive manner. But always some shred of mystery remains. Now perhaps we must look for the mystery, learn from the mystery, live from the mystery in a white laboratory coat, persuading ourselves that it is all part of the great scientific enterprise. With some weariness Jung sums up our flight from the gods to Reason, the great goddess of the French Revolution, in the last pages of his last work, *Symbols and the Interpretation of Dreams:*

> The great religions of the world suffer from increasing anemia, because the helpful numina have fled from the woods, rivers, mountains, and animals, and the God-men have disappeared underground into the unconscious. There we suppose they lead an ignominious existence among the relics of our past, while we remain dominated by the great *Déesse Raison,* who is our overwhelming illusion (Jung 1976, p. 261).

Still, whatever we name our ruling deity, however we explain our procedure, we pursue the unknown. What gives heart to those of us for whom the deity comes in the old familiar ways, wearing the beautiful old vestments, answering to the old faith-enfolded names, is that the pursuit goes on under all the new rubrics. Countless expeditions set off to find what may have disappeared underground into the unconscious and, what is more, return safely, with astonishing finds. The unknown still calls to us. Connection is made as it always has been. There may be no end to pain and suffering, but there is, we discover once again, purpose.

Notes

1. All clinical examples are from the practice of Ann Belford Ulanov, presented with gratitude to the persons who gave permission to use their material.
2. This dread of fragmentation characterizes the suffering in a borderline condition (see Kernberg 1975, chap. 1; Winnicott 1965).

3. For discussion of types of transference, see Winnicott 1975; A. B. Ulanov 1974 and 1982.

4. Paul Ricoeur says, "The reason man projects himself into the Wholly Other is to grasp hold of it and thus fill the emptiness of his unawareness.

"This objectifying process is the origin both of metaphysics and of religion: metaphysics makes God into a supreme being; and religion treats the sacred as a new sphere of objects, institutions, and powers within the world of immanence. . . .

"This diabolic transformation makes religion the reification and alienation of faith: by thus entering the sphere of illusion, religion becomes vulnerable to the blows of a reductive hermeneutic" (Ricoeur 1970, p. 530).

5. For a discussion of how analysts use the psychoanalytic vocabulary as a weapon of contempt against their patients, see Miller 1981, chap. 3.

References

Anzieu, D. 1986. *Freud's Self-Analysis.* Trans. Peter Graham. London: Hogarth Press and Institute of Psycho-Analysis.

Dickinson, E. 1960. *The Complete Poems.* Boston: Little, Brown.

——. 1971. *Selected Letters.* Cambridge: Belknap/Harvard University Press.

Drury, M. O'C. 1973. *The Danger of Words.* New York: Humanities Press.

Emmet, D. M. 1957. *The Nature of Metaphysical Thinking.* London: Macmillan.

Jacob, M. 1972. *Meditations.* Paris: Gallimard.

——. 1979. *The Dice Cup.* New York: SUN.

Jung, C. G. 1958. *Psychology and Religion.* Trans. R. F. C. Hull. *Collected Works,* vol. 2. New York: Pantheon.

——. 1976. *The Symbolic Life.* Trans. R. F. C. Hull. *Collected Works,* vol. 18. Princeton: Princeton University Press.

Kahn, M. 1974. "The Concept of Cumulative Trauma." In *The Privacy of the Self.* New York: International Universities Press.

Kernberg, O. 1975. *Borderline Conditions and Pathological Narcissism.* New York: Aronson.

Miller, A. 1981. "The Vicious Circle of Contempt." In *Prisoners of Childhood.* Trans. Ruth Ward. New York: Basic Books.

Ricoeur, P. 1970. *Freud and Philosophy.* Trans. Denis Savage. New Haven: Yale University Press.

Rizzuto, A. M. 1979. *The Hands of the Living God.* Chicago: University of Chicago Press.

Ulanov, A. B. 1974. "Follow-up Treatment in Cases of Patient-Therapist Sex," *Journal of the American Academy of Psychoanalysis* 7, no. 1.

——. 1982. "Transference/Countertransference." In *Jungian Analysis,* ed. M. Stein. La Salle: Open Court.

——. 1986. *Picturing God.* Cambridge: Cowley.

——. 1988. *The Wisdom of the Psyche.* Cambridge: Cowley.

Ulanov, A. and B. 1975. *Religion and the Unconscious.* Philadelphia: Westminster.

——. 1983. *Cinderella and Her Sisters.* Philadelphia: Westminster.

——. 1987. *The Witch and the Clown.* Wilmette: Chiron.

Ulanov, B. 1983. *The Prayers of Saint Augustine.* New York: Seabury.

Weil, S. 1952. *Gravity and Grace.* Trans. Emma Craufurd. London: Routledge.

Winnicott, D. W. 1965. "Ego Integration in Child Development." In *The Maturational Process and the Facilitating Environment.* New York: International Universities Press.

——. 1975. "Hate in the Counter Transference." In *From Paediatrics to Psychoanalysis.* New York: Basic Books.

Wittgenstein, L. 1958. *Philosophical Investigations.* Trans. G. E. M. Anscombe. Oxford: Blackwell.

Siang-Yang Tan

2. Lay Christian Counseling

Lay counseling as a field has grown tremendously in recent years. It has not only become an important part of the contemporary mental health scene (see Alley, Blanton, and Feldman 1978; Gershon and Biller, 1977; Guerney, 1969; Robin and Wagenfeld, 1981; Sobey, 1970), but it also occupies a significant place in current Christian ministry and local church contexts (see Becker 1981; Collins 1980, 1986; Tan 1981, 1987b, 1990, 1991a, 1991b). Lay counselors have been called nonprofessional or paraprofessional counselors who lack the training, education, experience, or credentials to be professional therapists, but who, nevertheless, are involved in helping people cope with personal problems (Collins 1986).

The literature on lay counseling, both secular and Christian, has also proliferated in recent years, reflecting the rapid growth in the field. The purpose of the present chapter is to review the current or present status of lay *Christian* counseling, including lay pastoral counseling in the context of lay pastoral care in the local church (Clinebell 1984; cf. Sunderland 1990), focusing on biblical models and programs of lay counseling, selection, training, and supervision of lay counselors, evaluation research on the effectiveness of lay counselor training and lay counseling, and legal and ethical issues. Future directions in these areas of lay Christian counseling will also be briefly discussed. The Christian literature available on these topics will therefore be the primary literature covered, but relevant secular literature on lay counseling will be referred to where helpful or necessary.

Biblical Models and Programs

A number of biblical models of lay Christian counseling have been proposed and programs of training and ministry based on several of these models have been described in the literature. Among the better known and more widely used are Jay Adams' nouthetic counseling (Adams 1970, 1973, 1981), Larry Crabb's biblical counseling

(Crabb 1977; Crabb and Allender 1984), Gary Collins's people-helping (Collins 1976a, 1976b), William Backus's misbelief therapy (Backus 1985, 1987; Backus and Chapian 1980), Charles Solomon's spirituotherapy (Solomon 1975, 1977), and Kenneth Haugk's Stephen Series (Haugk 1984), which is actually both a biblical model and a systematic program of training lay people in pastoral care[1] but does include basic lay counseling skills training. Many other biblical approaches to lay Christian counseling have been proposed or described (see Carol Baldwin 1988; Martin and Deidre Bobgan 1985; Duncan Buchanan 1985; John Drakeford 1978; John Drakeford and Claude King 1988; Timothy Foster 1986; Stephen Grunlan and Daniel Lambrides 1984; Selwyn Hughes 1982; Isaac and Shirley Lim 1988; Stanley Lindquist 1976; Horace Lukens 1983a; Paul Miller 1978; Paul Morris 1974; Evelyn Peterson 1980; Harold Sala 1989; Abraham and Dorothy Schmitt 1984; Melvin Steinbron 1987; Joan Sturkie and Gordon Bear 1989; Gary Sweeten 1987; Siang-Yang Tan 1981, 1986a, 1987b, 1991a; Barbara Varenhorst with Lee Sparks 1988; Richard Walters 1983; Waylon Ward 1977; Paul Welter 1978, 1987; Everett Worthington 1982, 1985; and Norman Wright 1977).

Most of the biblical models and programs cited have been developed for use in local churches, but several parachurch organizations also have biblical models and programs for training lay counselors in the context of their particular ministries, for example, James Oraker's Counselor Training for Young Life staff and George Sanchez's seminar on interpersonal relationships through the ministry of the Navigators (Collins 1980, p. 82).

Some exciting recent developments, which hopefully will receive greater attention in the near future, include the use of lay Christian counselors in community settings other than churches, such as retirement centers and nursing homes (Welter 1987), and the training of missionaries in peer helping skills (Schaefer, Dodds, and Tan 1988). Missionaries actually need training not only in peer helping but also in lay Christian counseling skills, especially in a cross-cultural context (see Augsburger 1986; Hesselgrave 1984), in order to minister more effectively to the people they have been sent to, many of whom have only limited or no access to professional counseling services. Peer counseling (peers in age, status, and knowledge helping each other) as a significant part of lay Christian counseling, especially in the context of the local church, has received much attention (see Miller 1978; Sturkie and Bear 1989; Varenhorst with Sparks 1988). There is even a secular organization called the National Peer

Helpers Association based in San Francisco, which has begun holding annual national conferences on peer counseling. It has committees and interest groups on research and evaluation, ethics and standards, publications, minority involvement, and programs that are church/religious based, high school or middle school or elementary school based, community/social agencies/business based, higher education/university based, or district wide. Lay Christian counseling leaders should perhaps become more significantly involved in such an organization.

A comprehensive textbook or handbook on lay Christian counseling has recently been published (Tan 1991a). It covers the need for and biblical basis of lay counseling ministries; the literature of lay counseling; a biblical model for effective lay counseling; how to set up or build a lay counseling ministry; the selection, training, supervision and evaluation of lay counselors; examples of lay counseling ministries in local churches; and potential ethical and legal pitfalls in lay counseling.

Tan's biblically-based model for effective lay Christian or pastoral counseling includes the following key points with regard to a *basic view of humanity:* (1) Basic psychological and spiritual needs include needs for security (love), significance (meaning/impact), and hope (forgiveness); (2) the basic problem of human beings is sin—but *not* all emotional suffering is due to personal sin; (3) the ultimate goal of human beings is to know and enjoy God and spiritual health; (4) problem feelings are usually due to problem behavior and more fundamentally, problem thinking—however, biological and demonic factors should also be considered; (5) a holistic view of persons includes the physical, mental/emotional, social, and spiritual dimensions.

The following *basic principles of effective lay counseling from a biblical perspective* are also provided in Tan's model: (1) The Holy Spirit's ministry as counselor is crucial; (2) the Bible is a basic and comprehensive (*not* exhaustive) guide for counseling; (3) prayer is an integral part of biblically based counseling; (4) the ultimate goal of counseling is maturity in Christ and fulfilling the Great Commission; (5) the personal qualities of the counselor are important, especially spiritual ones; (6) the client's attitudes, motivations, and desire for help are important; (7) the relationship between counselor and client is significant; (8) effective counseling is a process involving exploration, understanding, and action phases, with a focus on changing problem thinking; (9) style or approach in counseling should be flexible; (10) specific techniques or methods of counseling should be consistent with scripture—cognitive-behavioral ones may be especially helpful, with qualifications; (11) cultural sensitivity and cross-cultural counseling skills are required; (12) outreach and prevention skills in the context of a caring community are important; and (13) awareness of limitations and referral skills are also critical.

Comprehensive handbooks on lay Christian counseling that cover more than just training of lay counselors or basic counseling skills will, therefore, be forthcoming in the near future, and they will serve a great need for more practical information on the "nuts and bolts" of how to establish and run a lay counseling ministry, particularly in a local church context with more specific groups of counselees like youth or seniors. Several churches have already developed policy and procedure manuals for lay counseling ministries (e.g., Creative Counseling Center of Hollywood Presbyterian Church, Hollywood, California, and Counseling Resource Center of First Presbyterian Church, Boulder, Colorado).

The need to survey existing church-based lay counseling ministries so that such practical information can be collected and shared among interested churches should receive more systematic attention in the future. Some efforts in this direction have already been made recently. For example, in 1986 the Center for Church Renewal in Plano, Texas, surveyed fifteen lay counseling ministries based in evangelical churches ranging in size from 450 to 9,000 members, with a variety of denominational affiliations, geographic locations, and counseling models. The resulting report is helpful and interesting (see Tan 1991a).[2]

A similar survey was more informally conducted by Richard Walters and volunteers from The Counseling Resource Center of First Presbyterian Church in Boulder, Colorado, in 1985. Walters presented a brief summary of his survey findings at a National Convention of the Christian Association for Psychological Studies. An earlier survey focusing more specifically on the training of Christian paraprofessional counselors has been published (Lukens 1983b).

There are now available a number of well-known biblical models of and programs for lay Christian counseling, so that anyone interested in establishing a lay counseling ministry has many resources to draw from. In fact, another recent development in the field has been the publication of comprehensive curricula and materials for training including books, manuals, audiotapes, and videotapes (for reviews, see Tan 1991a, 1991b).

More refined, biblically based models of lay caring and counseling ministries will be developed in the near future, with a focus on the significance of the ministry of the Holy Spirit, including appropriate spiritual gifts (e.g., exhortation, healing, wisdom, knowledge, discerning of spirits, and mercy) and spiritual power in effective lay *Christian* or pastoral care and counseling (Tan 1990; also see Gilbert and Brock 1985, 1988).

With the plethora of materials available comes the need for more critical evaluation, both biblically and psychologically, of the models or programs described in them. It is also important to differentiate the different levels of lay counseling ministry possible, ranging from basic caring or encouragement skills for all Christians to learn and use in general interpersonal relationships, to sophisticated and specialized helping or counseling skills for some gifted Christians to learn and use in a more specific, focused ministry of lay counseling to people facing problems in living. I have suggested that another potentially helpful way of conceptualizing the different levels of lay counseling ministry is to divide them into three major models or categories (Tan 1991a): 1) the *informal, spontaneous* model, which assumes that lay Christian counseling should occur spontaneously and informally in interactions and relationships already present in the existing structures of the church, and hence only some basic caring skills training should be made available to as many leaders and interested members in the church as possible; 2) the *informal, organized* model, which assumes that lay Christian counseling should be an organized and well-supervised ministry that should, however, still occur in informal settings as far as possible (e.g., in homes, hospitals, restaurants, etc.), with the Stephen Series being a good example; and 3) the *formal, organized* model, which assumes that lay Christian counseling should be an organized and well-supervised ministry conducted in a formal way in the context of a lay counseling center or service established in a local church. Lukens has suggested that all lay counseling services should be overseen by a licensed or certified mental health professional, but such a suggestion may be most applicable to the formal, organized model just described (Lukens 1987). Consultation with mental health professionals should, however, be done whenever necessary in all models of lay counseling ministries.

Those interested in establishing a lay Christian counseling ministry should first decide which model or models may be best suited to their local church or parachurch context and needs. The choice of specific programs and training materials from the great variety now available will be a little easier once the decision is made about which to use. It is my contention that the informal, organized model is a particularly helpful and appropriate one for many local churches, especially in some ethnic churches where there may be a stigma against both formal counseling and lay or nonprofessional counseling.

Finally, as Bufford and Buckler have pointed out, a biblical model of lay Christian counseling must place such counseling in the context of the multifaceted mission of the church, centering on loving submission to God and loving ministry to people, and therefore not elevate lay counseling above other ministries of the church (Bufford and Buckler 1987).

Selection, Training, and Supervision of Lay Counselors

Selection

G. R. Collins has proposed several helpful requirements for the screening of potential lay counselors: First, a brief, written statement from the potential lay counselor affirming his or her adherence to the doctrinal positions or statement of faith of a particular local church, as well as reasons for wanting to be involved in a lay counseling ministry. Second, letters of recommendation from two or three people who know the potential lay counselor well. Third, an interview of the potential lay counselor by the director of the lay counseling ministry and another church leader in order to assess his or her spiritual maturity, stability, and motivation. Finally, psychological testing of the person if possible. Collins mentions the 16PF or the Taylor-Johnson Temperament Analysis, but other tests which have been used include the Minnesota Multiphasic Personality Inventory or MMPI, the Personal Orientation Inventory or POI, and the Myers-Briggs Temperament Type Indicator (Collins 1980). Although Collins does not mention the use of measures other than personality tests, there are a number of other helpful instruments designed to assess a person's spiritual qualities and spiritual gifts, such as the Shepherd Scale, which is a measure of orthodox Christian belief and adherence to a Christian lifestyle (Bassett, et al. 1981), the Spiritual Well-Being Scale (Ellison 1983), the Character Assessment Scale, which is a measure of Christian character or maturity (Schmidt 1983), the Wagner-Modified Houts Questionnaire, which is a spiritual gifts inventory (Wagner 1985), and the Spiritual Leadership Qualities Inventory (Wichern 1980a, 1980b; Townsend and Wichern 1984). Another somewhat promising measure of optimal religious functioning and Christian religious maturity is the Religious Status Interview (Malony 1988), which is now available in a self-report version.

Regarding specific criteria for the selection of lay counselors, different churches use somewhat different but generally overlapping criteria (cf. Cerling 1983). I have proposed the following nine categories as important criteria to use (Tan 1986a): spiritual maturity; psychological stability; love for and interest in people; appropriate spiritual gifts (like exhortation); some life experience; previous training or experience in people-helping (preferable but not essential); age, sex, education, socioeconomic status and ethnic/cultural background (appropriate to the needs of the lay counseling ministry); availability and teachability; and ability to maintain confidentiality.

Future work in this area of selection of lay counselors should include establishing more common criteria for selection and determining which methods and tests are particularly useful for predicting which lay counselors will eventually do well in a lay counseling ministry.

Training

As already mentioned, there are many programs, books, or manuals currently available for the training of lay Christian counselors. I will not review them in detail but instead will draw out some commonalities and important guidelines to use in the training of selected or specially chosen lay counselors, following the informal, organized or formal, organized models.

Many training programs include a minimum of forty to fifty hours of training over a period of several months. The number of lay counselors selected for such basic but intensive training is usually limited to between eight and fifteen. They meet on a regular basis, usually weekly or biweekly for two to three hours. During the training sessions they are given opportunities to learn counseling skills and knowledge by listening to lectures, reading, observing, and experience (e.g., through role-plays or use of an "experimental client" or friend, or the use of real-life cases). Sometimes a special weekend seminar or retreat is organized as part of the training program. Leaders in a lay counseling ministry may also attend special intensive training seminars for a weekend, several days to a week, or longer, conducted by well-known figures in the field, for example, Larry Crabb's Biblical Counseling Seminars, Kenneth Haugk's Stephen Series Leader's Training Course, or Gary Sweeten's Counseling with Power Seminars.

Collins has suggested that the training curriculum should include: (a) basic biblical knowledge, especially that relevant to people-helping, personal problems, and the ministry of the Holy Spirit; (b) knowledge of counseling skills, with opportunity to practice them; (c) understanding of common problems like discouragement, anxiety, excessive stress, or spiritual dryness; (d) awareness of ethical and legal issues, and dangers in counseling; and (e) knowledge of the importance and techniques of referral (Collins 1980).

Many training programs focus on the development of basic counseling skills such as listening and relationship-building skills, but others have included training in basic problem-solving and cognitive-behavioral interventions (Backus 1985, 1987; Worthington 1982), as well as inner healing or healing of memories (e.g., Lukens 1983a; Sweeten 1987; Tan 1987b). Some have also included training in marriage and family counseling (e.g., Lukens 1983a; Osborn 1983). Training materials that are particularly helpful for lay counselors include books by Adams (1973, 1981), Backus (1985; also see Backus and Chapian 1980), Baldwin (1988), Collins (1976a, 1976b, 1988), Crabb (1977, 1987, 1988), Crabb and Allender (1984), Foster (1986), Grunlan and Lambrides (1984), Haugk (1984), Miller (1978), Peterson (1980), Seamands (1985), Solomon (1975, 1977), Sturkie and Bear (1989), Tan (1991a), Walters (1983), Ward (1977), Welter (1978), Worthington (1982, 1985), and Wright (1977). G. R. Sweeten has also developed training materials, including books, audiotapes and videotapes, covering his discipleship counseling approach to lay counseling, which integrates psychology, theology, and the power of the Holy Spirit (Sweeten 1987).[3]

If a variety of training resources are used, it is important for the trainer or instructor to provide an integrative framework that is biblically based (cf. Hurding 1985; Tan 1981), with qualifying comments that help clarify areas where some of the cited authors may disagree.

A recent trend in training has been to extend the minimum number of hours required for basic lay counselor training beyond forty or fifty hours, sometimes up to 100 or more hours (Tan 1986b). Further research is necessary to help determine the optimal length of basic training for lay counselors. Whatever it is, further training and supervision should be provided for lay counselors after they have completed their basic training and begun to see clients in their lay counseling ministry.

In the field of professional training, there has been a recent call to train professional counselors or psychotherapists using a competency model. In other words, more specific criteria for assessing the competency or skills of the trainee are needed, and recommendations have been made to use more specific treatment manuals for particular types of therapy (e.g., cognitive therapy, interpersonal therapy, psychodynamic therapy, experiential therapy, and behavior therapy) in the training of professional therapists.[4] Such recommendations are also relevant to the training of lay counselors. Training programs for lay counselors should be as specific as possible regarding the counseling competency or skills expected of the lay counselors, and such skills should be clearly taught. Comparative studies evaluating the relative effectiveness of different types of lay Christian counselor training programs can then be more easily conducted to determine if one approach to lay counseling is superior to others (see Collins 1987).

Finally, the need for lay counselors in the church trained in prevention and outreach services, including cross-cultural counseling skills, has been emphasized by J. S. Prater since many traditional lay Christian counselor training models have largely ignored such services and skills. Lay Christian counselors should also receive training as far as possible in the following areas: assessment of the role of environmental stressors (e.g., poverty, unemployment, racism, sexism, and lack of social support) in the development and maintenance of emotional problems; techniques of community outreach and empowerment; cultural awareness and sensitivity (including cross-cultural counseling); awareness and utilization of existing support systems and services within churches; development of new support systems within the church where needed; and active communication on a regular basis with leaders of other outreach ministries in the church resulting in a more integrated and coordinated package of church ministries (Prater 1987).

Supervision

After completing a basic training program and beginning their lay counseling ministry lay counselors require ongoing supervision as well as further training. The literature on supervision of lay Christian counseling is sparse compared to that on training. However, E. L. Worthington, Jr., has written a helpful article on issues in supervision of lay Christian counseling. He points out that supervision issues can be divided into two main categories: issues during the *training* of lay counselors, and issues during *ongoing lay counseling* provided by lay counselors who have completed their basic training program. Issues during the training of lay counselors include determination of an appropriate model of supervision (hopefully one which includes observation of the lay counselor in action through role-plays, and audiotapes or videotapes of role-play or actual counseling situations, or through co-counseling); decision between theoretical or developmental models of supervision; choice of who will serve as supervisors (e.g., pastors, elders, experienced lay counselors, or professional counselors); balance between emphasizing the lay counselor's strengths or weaknesses (with the recommendation that supervisors should stress what friends do and don't do well, and the need to make good referrals to professional counselors where appropriate and necessary); and correction of poor counseling styles (e.g., "formula driven counseling" that is insensitive and rigid). He raises the following supervision issues during ongoing lay counseling: economic and legal issues including lawsuits; continuing education of lay counselors; confidentiality of client information; evaluation of lay counseling; and utilization of prayer during supervision, which should also be viewed as an opportunity for discipleship of the lay counselor. Worthington urges lay Christian counseling programs to ensure that responsible supervision takes place, pointing out that supervision of lay counseling is crucial for producing lay counselors who improve (Worthington 1987). He cites a national survey (Wiley 1982) that found mere counseling experience did not help counselors improve their ability. Counselors improved most when they received regular face-to-face supervision. Further research is needed to show whether regular supervision of *lay Christian counselors* also results in significant improvement in the competency as well as effectiveness of such counselors.

Supervisors of lay counselors also need training in supervision skills and knowledge. A number of helpful books on supervision are now available in the secular literature (e.g., Hart 1982; Hess 1980; Hoffman 1990; Kaslow 1977; Mead 1990; Robbins 1988; Stoltenberg and Delworth 1987), as well as a few helpful journals on supervision (e.g., *Counselor Education and Supervision*, and *The Clinical Supervisor*). In 1987 a special series of articles on advances in psychotherapy supervision appeared in *Professional Psychology: Research and Practice*, (vol. 18, no. 3, pp. 187–259). A recent book on clinical supervision from the perspective of pastoral counseling is also available (Estadt, Compton, and Blanchette 1987). There is also the *Journal of Supervision and Training in Ministry*.

There is a need, nevertheless, for more materials and books on supervision of lay Christian counselors written from a biblical, Christian perspective. Integration issues in supervision, parallel to integration issues in therapy or counseling, should receive more attention. L. E. Lipsker has pointed out that the use of spiritual resources like prayer and the scriptures, and discussion of spiritual values (cf. Tan 1991b) can play a significant role in the training of student therapists (or lay counselors) in the context of the supervisor-trainee relationship. He discusses the enhancement of the supervision relationship as well as modeling of overt integration practices as crucial components of integration in graduate student-therapist supervision, but much of what he has written also applies to the supervision of lay Christian counselors (Lipsker 1988). A particular focus in integration issues should be the dimension of intrapersonal integration, especially the spirituality of the therapist or supervisor, and its development (cf. Tan 1987a).

Evaluation Research on the Effectiveness of Lay Counselor Training and Lay Counseling

There has been relatively little evaluation research to date on the effectiveness of training programs for lay Christian counselors, as well as the counseling provided by such counselors. However, some encouraging attempts have begun.

A small number of studies have now been published evaluating the effectiveness of lay Christian counselor training. Boan and Owens found peer ratings of lay counselor skill to be useful measures, which are related to client satisfaction, but they did not include a more direct evaluation of their training program with measures given before and after training, and no control or comparison group was used (Boan and Owens 1985). Tan has reported preliminary results using the Counselor Training Program Questionnaire (Tan and Sarff 1988), a self-report measure of knowledge of counseling and Christian counseling, competence in counseling and Christian counseling, and confidence in one's competence levels, which showed that lay counseling trainees improved significantly more than a control or comparison group of students who took a Bible course at Ontario Bible College in Toronto, Canada. The need to use more comprehensive and sophisticated evaluation measures in addition to such a self-report instrument is obvious.

Welter used a variety of evaluation measures, which were administered at the end of training, including an external evaluation of concepts learned, evaluation by the leader, evaluation by the participants, and evaluation of the trainers, in his study on the effectiveness of a lay counselor training program for retirement center and nursing home staff and residents, with basically positive findings (Welter

1987). Schaefer, Dodds, and Tan also reported positive changes in attitudes toward peer counseling and several scales on the POI in a small number of subjects who received growth facilitator training for cross-cultural ministry (Schaeffer, Dodds, and Tan 1988).

Two other evaluation studies on the effectiveness of a lay counselor training program in two different local churches have been completed with generally encouraging and positive results. Tan and Sarff found that lay counseling trainees in a Chinese evangelical local church context rated themselves as more knowledgeable and competent in both counseling and Christian counseling after the training program. They also chose more understanding and less evaluative or supportive response styles, and were rated as being more empathic, respectful, and genuine in an audiotaped role-play counseling situation by two independent raters. They scored higher on existentiality and self-acceptance on the POI after the training program, but did not show changes in spiritual well-being or spiritual growth, presumably because they already scored high on these two measures of spirituality at the beginning of the training program (Tan and Sarff 1988). Another study, using similar evaluation measures but including a comparison group of subjects who participated in weekly Bible study classes unrelated to counseling at the same church as the lay counseling trainees, also found some positive results. The lay counseling trainees improved significantly more than the comparison group on self-ratings of knowledge about counseling and Christian counseling, competence in counseling and Christian counseling, and confidence in such competence, as well as ratings of genuineness in a videotaped role-play counseling situation, by two independent raters, when post-training scores were compared to pre-training scores on such measures (Jernigan, Tan, and Gorsuch 1988).

The results from these two studies, using more comprehensive evaluation measures, as well as a comparison or control group in one of them, are therefore significant and represent relatively more sophisticated research. There is, nevertheless, still a need for more evaluation research on the effectiveness of lay Christian counselor training programs for improving counseling skillfulness or competency as well as facilitating personal and spiritual growth in lay counselors or trainees. In particular, more specific competency-based measures of lay counselor skillfulness that are related directly to the counseling skills or intervention methods taught in the training program are needed and should be used in future studies. Similar recommendations have been made in the professional training literature (see Shaw and Dobson 1988). The relationship between lay counselor skillfulness or competency and the effectiveness of lay counseling in terms of therapeutic outcome also requires further investigation, since such outcome can be influenced by factors other than lay counselor competency (e.g., client motivation, nature of clinical problem presented, client-counselor match, etc.).

Nevertheless, a critical test of the effectiveness of any lay Christian counselor training program must eventually involve the evaluation of the effectiveness of the lay counseling provided by the trained lay counselors in terms of therapeutic outcome. Evaluation research on the effectiveness of lay Christian counseling is still relatively scarce. J. Harris found that the use of non-paid, nonprofessional lay helpers in combination with professional pastoral counseling resulted in a more favorable increase in self-esteem for clients, compared to private professional pastoral counseling only (Harris 1985). In 1987 R. P. Walters reported that the lay counselors in his church compared favorably with Family Service Association (FSA) professionals on measures of client change and client satisfaction. Walters used mail survey evaluations sent out to clients six months after termination of counseling. This report has provided encouraging but tentative outcome findings because of methodological problems obvious in such a retrospective evaluation study, with no control groups used (Walters 1987).

The secular research literature has shown that lay counselors generally are as effective as professionals in producing therapeutic outcome (see Durlak 1979; Hattie, Sharpley, and Rogers 1984; Berman and Norton 1985). There are, however, some methodological shortcomings in several of the comparative outcome studies which only further research can address or overcome, and there are no well-controlled comparative studies involving individual or group therapy for middle- or upper-class clients (see Durlak 1981; Nietzel and Fisher 1981). It is still unclear whether training (including supervision or assistance given by a professional) and experience of lay counselors are significant factors affecting the therapeutic outcomes of counseling provided by them. Hattie, Sharpley, and Rogers, in their meta-analysis of the data available from most of the studies reviewed by Durlak (1979), concluded that paraprofessionals or lay counselors show greater therapeutic effectiveness the longer their training or the more experienced they are (Hattie, et al. 1984). However, Berman and Norton in a more careful meta-analysis of only the better comparative outcome studies found that variables like extensive preparation (training) or prior experience with the therapy task, or frequent supervision by a professional, could not account for the lack of difference between professionals and paraprofessionals or lay counselors in terms of their therapeutic effectiveness (Berman and Norton 1985). Further clarification of the role of training and supervision, as well as experience on the therapeutic effectiveness of lay counselors is therefore needed.

Durlak has noted that "as future investigators achieve stricter control of therapist, treatment, and client characteristics, paraprofessionals' functioning under different circumstances can be assessed more accurately and reliably in order to challenge or qualify the general conclusions offered here" (Durlak 1979, p. 90). The results of two new studies do in fact indicate the need for some qualification of the effectiveness of lay counselors. One was a study conducted by Brigham Young University psychologists Gary Burlingame and Sally Barlow, which showed that group therapy clients led by both professionals and nonprofessionals improved significantly more than subjects assigned to a waiting-list control group. At the mid-point of the fifteen-week group therapy series, clients seen by nonprofessionals had improved significantly whereas those seen by professionals had actually deteriorated. At the end of therapy, however, clients seen by professionals had caught up, and there were no significant differences between them and those seen by nonprofessionals. However, at a six-month follow-up, clients seen by nonprofessionals had gotten worse while those seen by professionals maintained their gains and even built on them (Burlingame and Barlow 1988). More comparative studies of lay counselors versus professionals with follow-up assessments are needed to more clearly delineate long-term therapeutic effects.

A second study (Carey and Burish 1987) involved a specific behaviorally based technique of relaxation training provided to cancer chemotherapy patients using three delivery techniques: professionally administered, paraprofessionally administered (i.e., by a trained volunteer), and audiotaped administered. Professionally administered relaxation training was found to be superior to both paraprofessionally administered and audiotaped administered relaxation training in reducing particular symptoms like emotional distress and physiological arousal. However, as Carey and Burish pointed out, the medical setting of a hospital in which the study was conducted may have been more difficult or troublesome for the volunteer therapists than the professionals, who were also more technically skilled in relaxation training and more clinically experienced in general. Nevertheless, this recent study did find professionals to be more effective than paraprofessionals in providing relaxation training to cancer chemotherapy patients seen in a hospital setting.

Durlak's concluding statements made a decade ago are still pertinent:

> Data indicate that paraprofessionals can make an important contribution as helping agents, but the factors accounting for this phenomenon are not understood. . . . It would be a mistake to continue using paraprofessionals without more closely examining their skills, deficiencies, and limitations (Durlak 1979, p. 90).

Further evaluation research investigating more specifically such skills, deficiencies, and limitations of *lay Christian counselors* is definitely needed.

Legal and Ethical Issues

Space does not permit a lengthy discussion of legal and ethical issues involved in lay Christian counseling, especially in the local church context. However, some brief comments are necessary.

W. W. Becker has written a helpful article covering legal and ethical considerations pertinent to the paraprofessional or lay counselor in the church. He emphasizes that trust is the essence of the counseling or therapeutic relationship, and it should be developed in three main areas: the confidentiality of the counseling relationship, the competence of the counselor, and the client's freedom of choice. He also delineates seven high-risk situations that lay counselors should avoid in order to minimize possible litigation or malpractice lawsuits and makes several helpful suggestions for practice. Examples of high-risk situations include charging fees or asking for "donations"; using psychological tests without proper training or supervision; having simplistic beliefs that can lead to superficial treatment, misdiagnosis, and harm; counseling those with severe problems requiring professional intervention; giving advice against medical or psychological treatment; ignoring statements of intent to harm or signs of violent behavior; counseling with a relative or employee; and developing a romantic or sexual relationship with the client. Becker recommends that lay counselors follow the ethical standards and guidelines of professional counseling organizations like the American

Association of Counseling and Development, American Psychological Association, and the American Association for Marriage and Family Therapy (Becker 1987).

It should also be noted that a code of ethics for Christian counselors has been published (Beck and Mathews 1986). The application of ethical standards and guidelines of professional counseling to lay counselors, however, does require some further reflection and possible modification since lay counseling often involves peer or friendship counseling, and there are some significant differences between some types of lay counseling, especially those following a more informal model, and professional counseling. Legal and ethical aspects of *supervision* of lay Christian counselors also require further attention (cf. Harrar, VandeCreek, and Knapp 1990).

The issue of malpractice insurance for lay Christian counselors has received significant attention and discussion in recent years in local church lay counseling centers. Since such malpractice insurance can be very expensive or not easily available, some centers have chosen to have an emergency fund instead. This is used to obtain legal advice or services in case a malpractice suit is filed against them and/or their lay counselors. Others have decided to function without any malpractice insurance or emergency fund, but follow ethical guidelines or community standards for the practice of professional counseling in order to minimize the risk of litigation.

A somewhat related issue has to do with the limits to confidentiality in the lay counseling situation. Many lay counseling centers in California, for example, have decided to follow the state law, which mandates professional counselors to report incidences of reasonably suspected child or elder abuse (physical or sexual), and to warn appropriate individuals if the client intends to take harmful, dangerous, or criminal action against another human being or against himself or herself. In such centers clients are therefore informed of the limits to confidentiality and informed consent forms are signed before beginning counseling. Directors of lay Christian counseling centers or even more informal lay counseling ministries should, therefore, familiarize themselves with the specific laws of the state in which they are working concerning mandatory reporting and limits to confidentiality in the professional counseling relationship, and decide whether to follow them for lay counselors.

It should be noted that in some states the title *counselor* may need to be used with caution or qualification or even eliminated, depending on the licensing laws of a particular state governing the use of such a title. Some lay Christian counseling ministries have used other titles like *lay helper, lay caregiver,* or *lay minister* in place of *lay counselor,* and terms like *lay helping, lay caregiving, lay pastoring,* or *lay shepherding* in place of *lay counseling.*[5]

Conclusion

The vast literature now available on lay Christian counseling, including lay pastoral counseling in the context of lay pastoral care in the local church, has been reviewed, documenting both the present status and future directions of lay Christian counseling in the following areas: biblical models and programs; selection, training, and supervision of lay counselors; evaluation research on the effectiveness of lay counselor training and lay counseling; and legal and ethical issues. The tremendous development of the field of lay Christian counseling in recent years is encouraging and can result in help and blessing in ministry to many troubled people to the glory of God, provided such counseling is done in a biblical, Christ-centered way, within appropriate ethical and legal limits, and with the best of selection, training, supervision, and evaluation possible.

Notes

1. For more information, contact Stephen Ministries, 1325 Boland, St. Louis, MO 63117. Telephone 314-645-5511.
2. The Lay Counseling Survey results can be obtained by writing to Floyd Elliott, Director of Counseling and Family Renewal, Center for Church Renewal, 200 Chisholm Place, Suite 228, Plano, TX 75075.
3. Sweeten's materials are available from Equipping Ministries International, 4015 Executive Part Drive, Suite 309, Cincinnati, Ohio 45241 (513-769-5353).
4. For more information, see "Training to Competency in Psychotherapy," *Journal of Consulting and Clinical Psychology* 56, no. 5 (1988):651–709.
5. For further discussion of legal and ethical issues relevant to lay Christian counseling and clergy ministry, see Malony, Needham, and Southard 1986. Hart's *Counseling the Depressed* also contains a good chapter on avoiding legal problems (Hart 1987, chap. 17).

References

Adams, J. E. 1970. *Competent to Counsel.* Grand Rapids: Baker Book House.

——. 1973. *The Christian Counselor's Manual.* Grand Rapids: Baker Book House.

——. 1981. *Ready to Restore: The Layman's Guide to Christian Counseling.* Grand Rapids: Baker Book House.

Alley, S., Blanton, J., and Feldman, R. 1978. *Paraprofessionals in Mental Health: Theory and Practice.* New York: Human Sciences Press.

Augsburger, D. 1986. *Pastoral Counseling across Cultures.* Philadelphia: Westminster.

Backus, W. 1985. *Telling the Truth to Troubled People.* Minneapolis: Bethany.

Backus, W. 1987. A Counseling Center Staffed by Trained Christian Lay Persons. *Journal of Psychology and Christianity* 6(2): 39–44.

Backus, W., and Chapian, M. 1980. *Telling Yourself the Truth.* Minneapolis: Bethany.

Baldwin, C. L. 1988. *Friendship Counseling: Biblical Foundations for Helping Others.* Grand Rapids: Zondervan.

Bassett, R. L., Sadler, R. D., Kobishen, E. E., Skiff, D. M., Merrill, I. J., Atwater, B. J., and Livermore, P. W. 1981. The Shepherd Scale: Separating the Sheep from the Goats. *Journal of Psychology and Theology* 9: 335–51.

Beck, J. R., and Mathews, R. K. 1986. A Code of Ethics for Christian Counselors. *Journal of Psychology and Christianity* 5(3): 78–84.

Becker, W. W. 1981. A Delivery System within the Church: The Professional Consultant and the Laity. *C.A.P.S. Bulletin* 7(4): 15–18.

Becker, W. W. 1987. The Paraprofessional Counselor in the Church: Legal and Ethical Considerations. *Journal of Psychology and Christianity* 6(2): 78–82.

Berman, J. S., and Norton, N. C. 1985. Does Professional Training Make a Therapist More Effective? *Psychological Bulletin* 98: 401–7.

Boan, D. M., and Owens, T. 1985. Peer Ratings of Lay Counselor Skill as Related to Client Satisfaction. *Journal of Psychology and Christianity* 4(1): 79–81.

Bobgan, M., and Bobgan, D. 1985. *How to Counsel from Scripture.* Chicago: Moody Press.

Buchanan, D. 1985. *The Counseling of Jesus.* Downers Grove, Ill.: InterVarsity Press.

Bufford, R. K., and Buckler, R. E. 1987. Counseling in the Church: A Proposed Strategy for Ministering to Mental Health Needs in the Church. *Journal of Psychology and Christianity* 6(2): 21–29.

Burlingame, Gary, and Barlow, Sally. 1988. *Psychology Today* (April): 14.

Carey, M. P., and Burish, T. G. 1987. Providing Relaxation Training to Cancer Chemotherapy Patients: A Comparison of Three Delivery Techniques. *Journal of Consulting and Clinical Psychology* 55: 732–37.

Cerling, G. L. 1983. Selection of Lay Counselors for a Church Counseling Center. *Journal of Psychology and Christianity* 2(3): 67–72.

Clinebell, H. 1984. *Basic Types of Pastoral Care and Counseling.* Nashville: Abingdon.

Collins, G. R. 1976a. *How to Be a People Helper.* Santa Ana: Vision House.

Collins, G. R. 1976b. *People Helper Growthbook.* Santa Ana: Vision House.

Collins, G. R. 1980. Lay Counseling within the Local Church. *Leadership* 7(4): 78–86.

Collins, G. R. 1986. *Innovative Approaches to Counseling.* Waco, Tex.: Word Books.

Collins, G. R. 1987. Lay Counseling: Some Lingering Questions for Professionals. *Journal of Psychology and Christianity* 6(2): 7–9.

Collins, G. R. 1988. *Christian counseling: A comprehensive guide.* (rev. ed.) Waco: Word Books.

Crabb, L. J., Jr. 1977. *Effective Biblical Counseling.* Grand Rapids: Zondervan.

Crabb, L. J., Jr. 1987. *Understanding People: Deep Longings for Relationship.* Grand Rapids: Zondervan.

Crabb, L. J., Jr. 1988. *Inside Out.* Colorado Springs: Now Press.

Crabb, L. J., Jr., and Allender, D. 1984. *Encouragement: The key to Caring.* Grand Rapids: Zondervan.

Drakeford, J. W. 1978. *People to People Therapy.* New York: Harper & Row.

——, and King, C. V. 1988. *WiseCounsel: Skills for Lay Counseling.* Nashville: The Sunday School Board of the Southern Baptist Convention.

Durlak, J. A. 1979. Comparative Effectiveness of Paraprofessional and Professional helpers. *Psychological Bulletin* 86: 80–92.

Durlak, J. A. 1981. Evaluating Comparative Studies of Paraprofessional and Professional Helpers: A Reply to Nietzel and Fisher. *Psychological Bulletin* 89: 566–69.

Ellison, C. W. 1983. Spiritual Well-Being: Conceptualization and Measurement. *Journal of Psychology and Theology* 11: 330–40.

Estadt, B. K., Compton, J. R., and Blanchette, M. C. 1987. *The Art of Clinical Supervision: A Pastoral Counseling Perspective.* New York: Paulist Press.

Foster, T. 1986. *Called to Counsel.* Nashville: Oliver Nelson.

Gershon, M., and Biller, H. B. 1977. *The Other Helpers: Paraprofessionals and Nonprofessionals in Mental Health.* Lexington, Mass.: Lexington Books.

Gilbert, M. G., and Brock, R. T., eds. 1985. *The Holy Spirit and Counseling: Theology and Theory.* Peabody, Mass.: Hendrickson Publishers.

Gilbert, M. G., and Brock, R. T., eds. 1988. *The Holy Spirit and Counseling: Principles and Practice.* Peabody, Mass.: Hendrickson Publishers.

Grunlan, S., and Lambrides, D. 1984. *Healing Relationships: A Christian's Manual for Lay Counseling.* Camp Hill, Penn.: Christian Publications, Inc.

Guerney, B. G., Jr., ed. 1969. *Psychotherapeutic Agents: New Roles for Non-professionals, Parents, and Teachers.* New York: Holt, Rinehart and Winston.

Harrar, W. R., VandeCreek, L., and Knapp, S. 1990. Ethical and Legal Aspects of Clinical Supervision. *Professional Psychology: Research and Practice* 21: 37–41.

Harris, J. 1985. Non-Professionals as Effective Helpers for Pastoral Counselors. *The Journal of Pastoral Care* 39(2): 165–72.

Hart, G. M. 1982. *The Process of Clinical Supervision.* Baltimore: University Park Press.

Hart, A. D. 1987. *Counseling the Depressed.* Waco, Tex.: Word Books.

Hattie, J. A., Sharpley, C. F., and Rogers, H. J. 1984. Comparative Effectiveness of Professional and Paraprofessional Helpers. *Psychological Bulletin* 95: 534–41.

Haugk, K. C. 1984. *Christian Caregiving—A Way of Life.* Minneapolis: Augsburg.

Hess, A. K., ed. 1980. *Psychotherapy Supervision: Theory, Research, and Practice.* New York: John Wiley and Sons.

Hesselgrave, D. 1984. *Counseling Cross-culturally.* Grand Rapids: Baker Book House.

Hoffman, L. W. 1990. *Old Scapes, New Maps: A Training Program for Psychotherapy Supervisors.* Cambridge, Mass.: Milusik Press.

Hughes, S. 1982. *A Friend in Need.* Eastbourne, E. Sussex: Kingsway.

Hurding, R. F. 1985. *The Tree of Healing.* Grand Rapids: Zondervan.

Jernigan, R., Tan, S. Y., and Gorsuch, R. L. 1988. *The Effectiveness of a Local Church Lay Christian Counselor Training Program: A Controlled Study.* Paper presented at the International Congress on Christian Counseling, Lay Counseling Track, Atlanta, Georgia (November).

Kaslow, F. W., ed. 1977. *Supervision, Consultation, and Staff Training in the Helping Professions.* San Francisco: Jossey-Bass.

Lim, I., and Lim, S. 1988. *Comfort My People: Christian Counseling—A Lay Challenge.* Singapore: Methodist Book Room.

Lindquist, S. E. 1976. *Action Helping Skills.* Fresno: Link-Care Foundation Press.

Lipsker, L. E. 1988. *Integration in Graduate Student-Therapist Supervision.* Paper presented at the International Congress on Christian Counseling, Clinical Supervision Track, Atlanta, Georgia (November).

Lukens, H. C., Jr. 1983a. Training of Paraprofessional Christian Counselors: A Model Proposed. *Journal of Psychology and Christianity* 2(3): 61–66.

Lukens, H. C., Jr. 1983b. Training paraprofessional Christian counselors: A survey conducted. *Journal of Psychology and Christianity,* 2(1), 51–61.

Lukens, H. C., Jr. 1987. Lay Counselor Training Revisited: Reflections of a Trainer. *Journal of Psychology and Christianity* 6(2): 10–13.

Malony, H. N. 1988. The Clinical Assessment of Optimal Religious Functioning. *Review of Religious Research* 30(1): 3–17.

Malony, H. N., Needham, T. L., and Southard, S. 1986: *Clergy Malpractice.* Philadelphia: Westminster.

Mead, D. E. 1990. *Effective Supervision: A Task-Oriented Model for the Mental Health Professions.* New York: Brunner/Mazel.

Miller, P. M. 1978. *Peer Counseling in the Church.* Scottsdale, Penn.: Herald Press.

Morris, P. D. 1974. *Love Therapy.* Wheaton, Ill.: Tyndale House.

Nietzel, N. T., and Fisher, S. G. 1981. Effectiveness of Professional and Paraprofessional Helpers: A Comment on Durlak. *Psychological Bulletin* 89, 555–65.

Osborn, E. B. 1983. Training Paraprofessional Family Therapists in a Christian Setting. *Journal of Psychology and Christianity* 2(2): 55–61.

Peterson, E. 1980. *Who Cares? A Handbook of Christian Counseling.* Wilton, Conn.: Morehouse-Barlow Co.

Prater, J. S. 1987. Training Christian Lay Counselors in Techniques of Prevention and Outreach. *Journal of Psychology and Christianity* 6(2): 30–34.

Robbins, A. 1988. *Between Therapists: The Processing of Transference/Countertransference Material.* New York: Human Sciences Press.

Robin, S. S., and Wagenfeld, M. O., eds. 1981. *Paraprofessionals in the Human Services.* New York: Human Sciences Press.

Sala, H. 1989. *Coffee Cup Counseling: How to Be Ready When Friends Ask for Help.* Nashville: Thomas Nelson.

Schaefer, C. A., Dodds, L., and Tan, S. Y. 1988. *Changes in Attitudes Toward Peer Counseling and Personal Orientation Measured During Growth Facilitator Training for Cross-Cultural Ministry.* Manuscript submitted for publication.

Schmidt, P. F. 1983. *Manual for Use of the Character Assessment Scale,* 2d ed. Shelbyville, KY: Institute for Character Development.

Schmitt, A., and Schmitt, D. 1984. *When a Congregation Cares.* Scottsdale, Penn.: Herald Press.

Seamands, D. 1985. *Healing of Memories.* Wheaton, Ill.: Victor Press.

Shaw, B. F., and Dobson, K. S. 1988. Competency Judgments in the Training and Evaluation of Psychotherapists. *Journal of Consulting and Clinical Psychology* 56: 666–72.

Sobey, F. 1970. *The Nonprofessional Revolution in Mental Health.* New York: Columbia University Press.

Solomon, C. R. 1975. *Handbook to Happiness.* Wheaton, Ill.: Tyndale House.

Solomon, C. R. 1977. *Counseling with the Mind of Christ.* Old Tappan, N.J.: Revell.

Steinbron, M. J. 1987. *Can the Pastor Do It Alone? A Model for Preparing Lay People for Lay Pastoring.* Ventura, Cal.: Regal.

Stoltenberg, C. D., and Delworth, U. 1987. *Supervising Counselors and Therapists: A Developmental Approach.* San Francisco: Jossey-Bass.

Sturkie, J., and Bear, G. 1989. *Christian Peer Counselors: Love in Action.* Waco, Tex.: Word Books.

Sunderland, R. 1990. Lay Pastoral Care and Counseling. In *Dictionary of Pastoral Care and Counseling* edited by R. Hunter, H. N. Malony, L. Mills, and J. Patton pp. 632–34. Nashville: Abingdon.

Sweeten, G. R. 1987. Lay Helpers and the Caring Community. *Journal of Psychology and Christianity* 6(2): 14–20.

Tan, S. Y. 1981. Lay Counseling: The Local Church. *CAPS Bulletin* 7(1): 15–20.

Tan, S. Y. 1986a. Care and Counseling in the New Church Movement. *Theology News and Notes* 33(December): 9–11, 21.

Tan, S. Y. 1986b. Training Paraprofessional Christian Counselors. *The Journal of Pastoral Care* 40(4): 296–304.

Tan, S. Y. 1987a. Intrapersonal Integration: The Servant's Spirituality. *Journal of Psychology and Christianity* 6(1): 34–39.

Tan, S. Y. 1987b. Training Lay Christian Counselors: A Basic Program and Some Preliminary Data. *Journal of Psychology and Christianity* 6(2): 57–61.

Tan, S. Y. 1990. Lay Counseling: The Next Decade. *Journal of Psychology and Christianity* 9(3): 59–65.

Tan, S. Y. 1991a. *Lay Counseling: Equipping Christians for a Helping Ministry*. Grand Rapids: Zondervan.

Tan, S. Y. 1991b. Religious Values and Interventions in Lay Christian Counseling. *Journal of Psychology and Christianity* 10(2).

Tan, S. Y., and Sarff, P. 1988. *Comprehensive Evaluation of a Lay Counselor Training Program in a Local Church*. Invited paper presented at the International Congress on Christian Counseling, Lay Counseling Track, Atlanta, Georgia (November).

Townsend, J. S., II, and Wichern, F. B. 1984. The Development of the Spiritual Leadership Qualities Inventory. *Journal of Psychology and Theology* 12: 305–13.

Varenhorst, B. B., with Sparks, L. 1988. *Training Teenagers for Peer Ministry*. Loveland, Col.: Group.

Wagner, C. P. 1985. *Wagner Modified Houts Questionnaire for Discovering Your Spiritual Gifts*. Pasadena: Fuller Evangelistic Association.

Walters, R. P. 1983. *The Amity Book: Exercises in Friendship Skills*. Grand Rapids: Christian Helpers.

Walters, R. P. 1987. A Survey of Client Satisfaction in a Lay Counseling Program. *Journal of Psychology and Christianity* 6(2): 62–69.

Ward, W. O. 1977. *The Bible in Counseling*. Chicago: Moody Press.

Welter, P. R. 1978. *How to Help a Friend*. Wheaton, Ill.: Tyndale House.

Welter, P. R. 1987. Training Retirement Center and Nursing Home Staff and Residents in Helping and Counseling Skills. *Journal of Psychology and Christianity* 6(2): 45–56.

Wichern, F. B. 1980a. *Spiritual Leadership Qualities Inventory*. Richardson, Tex.: Believer Renewal Resources.

Wichern, F. B. 1980b. *The Spiritual Leadership Qualities Inventory Instruction Manual.* Richardson, Tex.: Believer Renewal Ministries.

Wiley, M. O'L. 1982. *Developmental Counseling Supervision: Person-Environment Congruency, Satisfaction, and Learning.* Paper presented at the Annual Convention of the American Psychological Association, Washington, DC (August).

Worthington, E. L., Jr. 1982. *When Someone Asks for Help: A Practical Guide for Counseling.* Downers Grove, Ill.: InterVarsity Press.

Worthington, E. L., Jr. 1985. *How to Help the Hurting: When Friends Face Problems with Self-esteem, Self-control, Fear, Depression, Loneliness.* Downers Grove, Ill.: InterVarsity Press.

Worthington, E. L., Jr. 1987. Issues in Supervision of Lay Christian Counseling. *Journal of Psychology and Christianity* 6(2): 70–77.

Wright, H. N. 1977. *Training Christians to Counsel: A Resource Curriculum Manual.* Santa Ana: Christian Marriage Enrichment.

Chris R. Schlauch

3. Re-Visioning Pastoral Diagnosis

Many pastoral clinicians regard "pastoral diagnosis" as an oxymoron. "Pastoral" and "diagnosis" are less like apples and oranges than oil and water. Pastoral implies care of the person; diagnosis, in contrast, implies treatment of the disease. Clinicians intent on preserving an uncontaminated vision of pastoral *care* pride themselves in avoiding diagnosis, maintaining the illusion that if they don't use the term, they're not engaged in the procedures. As a consequence, they don't critically reflect upon and evaluate their actual diagnostic commitments and judgments.

Other pastoral clinicians, on the other end of the spectrum, understand that a sound theory and practice of diagnosis is central to clinical care. In conjunction with this they may have embraced the American Psychiatric Association's *Diagnostic and Statistical Manual* (*DSM III-R*) as a kind of clinical scripture. Usually, these diagnostically sensitive clinicians pursue one of two directions. On the one hand, they diagnose according to this medical perspective and provide ongoing care from a practical theological perspective, remaining unaware of their fundamentally inconsistent commitments (Mitchell 1987). They become a "doppelganger, a person who inhabits two parallel universes" (Muehl 1990, p. 27). On the other hand, they may disregard entirely the authentically pastoral contributions of their confessional theological traditions; their practice and theory of care in general, as well as of diagnosis in particular, are secular. In either case pastoral diagnosis is a misnomer.

Another group of pastoral clinicians understands pastoral diagnosis as theological diagnosis. These practitioners regard religious and theological language not as professional jargon but as a "grammar" appropriate to the everyday life of every person (Holmer 1978). They make faith, theology, and spirituality operational, interpreting clinical data through and in relation to theological symbols and scriptural stories (Asquith 1980; Boisen 1936; Browning 1983; Capps 1980, 1981, 1984; Draper 1965; Draper, Myer, Parzen, and

Samuelson 1965; Draper and Steadman 1984; Ellens 1984; Fairbanks 1952; Gaskill 1984; Gerkin 1984, 1986a; Hiltner 1943, 1949, 1972, 1976; Hobson and Jacob 1985; Ivy 1987, 1988; Jordan 1986; Nouwen [unpublished]; Patton 1983, 1985; Pruyser 1976a, 1976b, 1979, 1984; Schlauch 1985, 1987, 1990a, 1990b; Schneider 1986; Underwood 1982; Wahking 1987; Yeomans 1986). Earlier (Draper 1965; Fairbanks 1952; Hiltner 1943, 1949) as well as more recent contributions (Hiltner 1972, 1976; Pruyser 1976a, 1976b, 1984; Underwood 1982; Gaskill 1984; Hobson and Jacob 1985) restrict attention, for the most part, to the use of scriptural metaphors and theological constructs, as if including any connections to or conversation with secular concepts and approaches would jeopardize the validity or diminish the significance of their efforts. At the same time, however, using only theological resources is not without its hazards. First and foremost, a pastoral clinician cannot capture all of human experience through only one universe of discourse. Second, a pastoral clinician cannot identify precisely the varieties of suffering through language that tends to characterize human experience in broad strokes, in rather abstract terms. Third, a pastoral clinician cannot afford to be isolated from colleagues in the helping professions and from their respective resources and contributions. Pastoral diagnosis is in this approach singularly, yet narrowly theological.

While there are merits as well as liabilities to these respective approaches, none reflects a vision which *integrates pastoral-theological and social and human science resources in an authentic, consistent, and coherent manner,* and which recognizes that *the practice and theory of diagnosis is integral to and must be consistent with one's overall perspective of pastoral clinical care.* With these concerns in mind, I suggest that a newly emerging approach is the most promising for our field.

Several contemporary authors characterize pastoral clinical care as an expressly *interdisciplinary* enterprise that is interpreted through concepts and resources of confessional *and* secular traditions (Browning 1983; Estadt, et al. 1983; Patton 1983; Gerkin 1984, 1986; Jordan 1986; Schlauch 1985, 1987, 1990a, 1990b). In this approach every aspect of the theory and practice of pastoral clinical care, including pastoral diagnosis, is interpreted in an interdisciplinary manner. Interestingly, however, except for a comparatively few perspectives (Browning 1983; Capps 1980, 1981, 1984; Schneider 1986), the vast majority of discussions of pastoral diagnosis typically exclude any reference to non-confessional contributions. The majority of existing literature on pastoral diagnosis, then, is inconsistent with contemporary approaches to pastoral care, counseling, and psychotherapy. This inconsistency not only reflects but also contributes to pastoral clinicians continuing to isolate pastoral diagnosis from pastoral clinical care.

We need a vision of pastoral diagnosis that is consistent with and integral to our interdisciplinary understanding of pastoral clinical care; that encourages and requires us to incorporate the full range of resources at our disposal in authentic, consistent, and coherent ways; and that is increasingly more valid and reliable (Feighner and Herbstein 1987; Grove 1987; Cloninger 1989; Dohrenwend 1989; Robins and Guze 1989).

I suspect that one of the primary reasons we have had such difficulty developing an integrated vision is because of the peculiar but standard way we have all been trained to characterize diagnosis. Diagnosis is regarded as a separate procedure initiated and completed at the outset of care, interpreted through a "theory" of diagnosis independent of one's theory of care. In other words, clinicians in general have been accustomed to regarding the practice and theory of diagnosis as separable from the practice and theory of care.

In response to this, I will present my ideas in two related parts. In the first part, a prolegomenon, I outline a re-visioning of diagnosis. Considering the etymology of the term leads me to refer to diagnosis as *an ongoing activity* of "knowing apart" certain qualities and features of the current state of another's self and suffering. What and how we know apart about the person's current state is inherently related to the goals toward which we will work, as well as the means by which we envision getting there. In other words, diagnosis is part of a triad of related clinical activities—diagnosing, goal-setting, and treatment-planning—and is thus at the heart of our overall clinical perspective. As a consequence, we have to approach the system of concepts and categories through which we interpret and classify—the so-called "diagnostic variables"—in a broader context.

It is precisely because diagnosis is integral to and must be consistent with one's overall clinical perspective that my discussion of pastoral diagnosis can not be limited to a presentation of diagnostic variables. Such a presentation would mistakenly separate diagnosis from its context and contribute to the continuing tendency and dilemma of isolating the practice and theory of diagnosis from the practice and theory of care. It is only by re-visioning the structure that we are led to appreciate most deeply how the criteria according to which we know apart any features of another are part and parcel of a broader context.

In elaborating upon that broader context I characterize an overall clinical perspective as an expression of underlying root-metaphors we have of the person (of "human nature") and of care, and I suggest that we incarnate and enact these root-metaphors in a basic "clinical attitude." Thus, our "diagnostic variables" are the structure through which we make our clinical attitude operational. In this re-visioning *pastoral diagnosis is an ongoing activity within a clinical perspective that is the expression of root-metaphors, which are enacted in a clinical attitude and made operational in diagnostic variables.*

In the second part of this essay, I outline a particular approach to pastoral diagnosis. I propose the root-metaphor of "faithful companioning," drawn from New Testament passages, and relate that to the root-metaphor of "collaborative translating," taken from studies of clinical care as a hermeneutic activity. I suggest that these root-metaphors are incarnated and enacted in an understanding of clinical attitude that draws from but expands upon Heinz Kohut's psychoanalytic psychology of the self, the "introspection and empathy of the psychologist-theologian-ethicist." Finally, I suggest that this attitude operates in certain diagnostic variables—a basic dual focus on self and suffering, and the domains of content, affect, and action.

My purpose in this second part is twofold. In a more limited sense readers might make use of the substance of my particular metaphors, attitude, and diagnostic variables. In a more important sense, however, I hope that my text effectively illustrates a *method* of configuring pastoral diagnosis that encourages readers to re-vision their own practice and theory of pastoral clinical care reflective of their own respective metaphors, attitude, and variables.

The Prolegomenon

What Is Diagnosis?

The word *diagnosis* derives from the Latin, and prior to that, from the Greek, *diagnosis.* The oldest form of this Greek word was *diagignoskein,* comprised of *dia* (meaning "two," or "apart") and *gignoskein* (meaning "to know or perceive"). It has been translated "to distinguish," "to differentiate" (Nathan 1967, p. 16), "to discern," "grasping things as they really are, so as to do the right thing" (Pruyser 1976b, p. 30), "to know apart." When we "know something apart," we "lift it out of context," we "highlight" it. We engage in a comparative process; that is, something is now figure as compared to ground, or foreground as compared to background. When, for example, we meet with a person who reports feeling "sad and overwhelmed," we try to identify what the experience of being "sad and overwhelmed" is like. We try to understand the experience apart from yet in the context of the person's overall presentation.

Our attempt to understand by knowing apart is a natural human procedure. We want to know how "sad" contrasts with "dejected," "sorrowful," "unhappy." We compare "overwhelmed" with "helpless," "powerless," "overpowered." Knowing is *comparative:* "Judgment is always binary; we can grasp nothing in itself but only as related to and set apart from something else" (McFague 1982, p. 39). In addition, we understand "sad and overwhelmed" in the context of the other's presentation as a whole, and in the context of our overall clinical perspective. Knowing is innately contextualizing and organizing. As we contrast and compare, we are fitting the data into a context which pre-exists that data's appearance.

As a natural and inevitable comparative procedure, diagnosis is an ongoing activity. We are seeking to know apart at any and every moment. Rather than regarding diagnosis as a specific act or series of procedures restricted to the outset of clinical care, it is more appropriate to understand diagnosis as taking place all the time. It is with this in mind that I propose that *diagnosis is the identification of the current state* of the self and the suffering of the client.

As a natural and inevitable contextualizing and organizing procedure, identifying the current state is inextricably bound with other judgments. We don't seek to know anything in abstraction, or in a vacuum; we seek to know in order to act. Our diagnosing is intentional: we know in a certain way so as to be equipped to intervene in light of that understanding. Implicit, then, in the judgments of knowing apart are related clinical judgments: Where are we going, in what general direction or toward what general objective(s)? How might we move in that direction, toward that objective? We cannot engage in diagnosis, that is, identifying the current state of the client's self and of her or his suffering, independently of identifying the endpoint of care and the path through which we will move to and toward that endpoint. Thus, diagnosis is an ongoing, integral dimension of the clinical process and relationship.

Re-visioning diagnosis as an ongoing procedure integrally related to other clinical activities has several significant implications. First, we cannot simply use a diagnostic orientation, such as *DSM III-R* or Paul Pruyser's "diagnostic variables for pastoral assessment" (1976b, p. 61) as if it were an independent clinical procedure. It is not simply that our diagnostic orientation must be consistent with our overall clinical perspective. Rather, our diagnostic orientation lies at the heart of our clinical perspective. Second, we have to discern and evaluate critically the diagnostic commitments and criteria according to which we have been *implicitly* operating?

Diagnostic Variables

Most discussions of diagnosis focus expressly on diagnostic variables, on systems of classification. We tend to assume that a commonly employed system is normative. At times we act as if the concepts and categories of a diagnostic system ontologically correspond to the entities they label. For example, we might falsely presume that an "entity" termed "affective disorder" exists in time and space (Menninger, Mayman, and Pruyser, 1963; Holland, 1985). It is more accurate, however, to think of diagnostic concepts and categories as terms we use to name or refer, "conventions" which have the status of "hypotheses." As Theodore Millon (1987) notes, "no classification in psychopathology today 'carves nature at its joints,' that is, is an inevitable representation of the 'real world.' Rather, our classifications are, at best, interim tools for advancing knowledge and facilitating clinical goals" (p. 4). Our "interim tools" are subject to confirmation, disconfirmation, modification. Aaron Lazare (1979) notes that every clinician approaches every interview in light of "partial formulations based on his [or her] previous experience," which become "hypotheses to be tested." "Each new observation can now be considered in terms of its relevance to a limited number of hypotheses under consideration, instead of being one of thousands of possible facts" (p. 132). Millon's (1987) comments are again helpful, and deserve to be quoted at length:

> Because the number of ways we can observe, describe, and organize the natural world is infinite, the terms and concepts we create to represent those activities are often confusing and obscure. For example, different words are used to describe the same behavior, and the same word is used for different behaviors. Some terms are narrow in focus, others are broad, and some are difficult to define. Because of the diversity of events to which we can attend, or the lack of precision in the language we employ, different processes are confused and similar events get scattered hodgepodge across a scientific landscape; as a consequence, communication

> gets bogged down in terminological obscurities and semantic controversies.
>
> One of the goals of formalizing the phenomena comprising a scientific subject is to avoid this morass of confusion. Not all phenomena related to the subject need be attended to at once. *Certain elements may be selected from the vast range of possibilities because they seem relevant to the solution of a specific question.* And to create a degree of reliability or consistency among those interested in a subject, its elements are defined as precisely as possible and classified according to their core similarities and differences (p. 6, emphasis added).

When we diagnose, we are acting according to particular procedures, which are selected precisely because they are relevant to the solution of a particular question. The procedure of knowing apart therefore varies depending upon the question we are seeking to solve. We select certain data for certain purposes, to solve a certain question. We construct specific diagnostic variables because they enhance the likelihood of gathering data by which we might answer our question.

The diagnostic variables we employ, like the overall clinical activities in which we engage, reflect an underlying clinical attitude. As we operationalize a clinical attitude we approach another through variables, we seek to know apart, in a manner which answers a particular question. In the following, I will discuss the idea of clinical attitude, and subsequently consider how attitude is an expression or incarnation, so to speak, of underlying root-metaphors.

Clinical Attitude

Several writers have drawn attention to the formative and pivotal role of the clinician's attitude (Ewing 1976b; Kohut 1987; Schafer 1983; Schlauch 1990a; Shapiro 1989). David Shapiro (1989) opens the Preface to his delightful and enlightening text, *Psychotherapy of Neurotic Character*, with these words:

> My teacher, Hellmuth Kaiser, once expressed a dilemma to me about the teaching of psychotherapy. He said it was no use teaching what to do or what to say because *the significance and effect of what the therapist did or said depended on the attitude with which it was expressed.* With the right attitude on the part of the therapist, he thought, all else would follow easily (p. ix, emphasis added).

The attitude with which anything is expressed, or more precisely, *from or out of which* it is expressed, is deeply influential. Roy Schafer (1983) concludes that the core of psychoanalytic practice is the attitude of the clinician. In *The Analytic Attitude* he observes that behind key concepts, metapsychology, and clinical technique, is the attitude of the practitioner.

It is clear from these remarks that Schafer and Shapiro recognize how central the clinician's attitude is to the therapeutic relationship and process. *Everything the clinician says or does, observes, analyzes, and interprets, is a function of, is informed and guided by, her or his clinical attitude.* It lies in the background, behind the scenes, shaping all of what unfolds. Though typically outside of awareness, and thus not a matter of discussion, the clinical attitude directly bears on all of the therapy relationship and process. What and how we know apart is a function of that attitude.

Kohut (1987) writes in a similar vein:

> I teach the patient an attitude toward himself. I create an atmosphere—not artificially, however, because it truly is mine—in which a broadened understanding for oneself is encouraged. My own interest is in what is going on in the patient—not only in what he experiences, but also in how he experiences and relates to his difficulties. This is in essence an attitude of an expanded self-empathy—an expanded capacity to be empathic with one's own past, and with aspects of oneself that one really does not own, or does not own fully, including even aspects of oneself that have not yet expanded—in other words, one's future possibilities (p. 188).

Kohut extends Shapiro's and Schafer's assertions and deepens our appreciation of the influence and function of a clinical attitude. He brings it into the foreground by recognizing that a client may be influenced not only by what is conveyed "through" that attitude, but by the conveying and learning "of" the attitude itself. He describes how clients "learn" by identifying with the clinician, internalizing the attitude through which the clinician engages them. Clients comes to relate to themselves in a manner similar to that in which they have experienced the clinician to have related to them. The clinician's attitude toward each client—a feature of an interpersonal relationship—has become a part of the client's attitude toward himself or herself—a feature of an intrapsychic relationship. In a sense, the client may become adept at self-diagnosis, having learned what and how to know apart.

The clinician's attitude is thus pivotal to the therapeutic relationship and process in two dramatically different but equally profound ways. As a tacit map it guides every feature of the clinician's activities. As a map that the client may (will) internalize, at least in part, it will come to influence many features of the client's activities.

Thus, as I suggested above, our diagnostic variables are not a set of isolated ideas, but concepts and categories through which we operationalize our clinical attitude. It is at this point that I would like to take the discussion a step further and consider how our clinical attitude is itself an expression and incarnation, if you will, of underlying root-metaphors.

Root-metaphors

Imagine sitting in the room with a person who is there because he is suffering. In the infinite data that are presented, you are aware of his clothing, posture, tone of voice, facial expressions, pace of speech, eye contact, mannerisms. As you listen to and talk with him, you make a series of choices and decisions, some of which are conscious, most of which happen outside of your awareness. You experience something *as* something else; you re-cognize it because you are prepared to see and hear something *as* something (Hanson 1969; Carnes 1982). You attend to certain features and select out as less than salient a multitude of data which do not fit into your approach. In fact, the data excluded are far more numerous than those included. You want to know what his suffering has been like, how long he has experienced being sad and overwhelmed, what kind of support he has, if he is any danger to himself. Your procedures differ, depending on whether you understand your role as to attend to him in his "crisis"; to enable him to find appropriate support and help from other professionals or family and friends; or to help him make some major changes in himself and his life. You have, in the background, a theoretical map in which you locate where a person is, where he might be, and how to intervene so as to enhance change. You have a vision or perspective according to which you are judging how "normal" his suffering is, what he might expect to do, how long any process of care and healing might take. In other words, you are attending in a certain way as part of an overall picture: while explicitly making diagnostic judgments about him and his suffering, you are implicitly making judgments and decisions about "goals of treatment" and a "treatment plan." For example, are you seeking to change his patterns of behavior, identify unconscious motives, modify an erroneous belief system? Operationalized in your diagnostic variables, and underlying your attitude, are formative root-metaphors which capture your vision of the person and of care (Mehrabian 1968; Lakoff and Johnson 1980; McFague 1982; Browning 1983, 1987b; Tilley 1985).

Let me illustrate this further. Imagine, again, sitting in the room with this suffering man. How do you envision who he is? How do you conceive of your joint enterprise? Speaking metaphorically, do you think of this person as a seed which will grow, so that care is a process of organic unfolding in which the caretaker is a cultivator-farmer? Might you consider him as a pilgrim, wherein care is a kind of journey to some destination with the therapist as guide? Do you find it more appropriate to regard him as a person in the throes of labor, with the therapist as midwife in a process of birthing? Or, can you capture an essential feature by way of the idea that he is or has a story, with the caregiver as an editor or a co-author who provides care by assisting in the identifying, telling, and transforming of the story? Is he the host of some disease, and the therapist a skillful surgeon whose task it is to excise the pathology? Is he a helpless child who needs a parent-manager to teach him more mature ways of thinking and behaving?

Each of these metaphors both represents and guides your overall theory and practice of clinical care, and your diagnostic acts and procedures in particular. The cultivator-farmer, the guide, the midwife, the editor, the surgeon, the parent-manager each wants to know different phenomena for different motives and purposes. Each wants to understand and know in order to act in a particular way. What we know apart is chosen in conjunction with what we intend to do (Pruyser 1979; Rice and Greenberg 1984).

I am, through these comments, re-visioning diagnosis. In contrast to traditional views, I suggest that diagnosis is not a procedure which is initiated and completed at the outset of care, according to an isolated set of criteria and commitments. Rather, one must regard diagnosis in an expanded context, as an ongoing procedure of knowing apart—identifying the current state of the client's self and of her or his suffering. It is integrally related to the clinical procedures of identifying goals of care and a plan of care. In addition, diagnosis involves a set of diagnostic variables which answer a certain question, operationalize a clinical attitude, and express root-metaphors.

It is in this context that I will illustrate a particular vision of pastoral diagnosis in conjunction with this pastoral question: How can we effectively discern features of another's self and suffering in order to be able to intervene collaboratively in a manner which enhances the person's well-being and authentically represents our pastoral identity and context as we employ the resources of our confessional tradition and those of the human and behavioral sciences in a consistent and coherent manner?

By casting the basic question in this manner, I am contrasting my understanding of pastoral diagnosis with other (pastoral as well as non-pastoral) approaches to diagnosis (cf. Draper 1965; Draper, Myer, Parzen, and Samuelson 1965; Draper and Steadman 1984; Fowler 1981; Ivy 1987, 1988; Hiltner 1943, 1949, 1972, 1976; Muslin and Val 1987; Othmer and Othmer 1989; Pruyser 1976a, 1976b, 1984; Roth 1987; Seligman 1986; Wolman 1978). Pastoral diagnosis is *not* a procedure done by and for the clinician; independently of the client; solely at the beginning of care; focusing on a particular dimension (such as "mental disorder," "religious phenomena," "faith development," an "implicit creed," or "lived theology"); in terms of the resources of a particular disciplinary framework (such as *DSM III-R*, psychoanalytic concepts, Piagetian theory, or theological symbols and concepts). Rather, *pastoral diagnosis is an ongoing collaborative process of clinician and client companioning the self of the client as she or he emerges in and through unfolding experience, through an interdisciplinary theological approach* (inclusive of confessional and human and behavioral science resources).

I will propose that both the clinician and the client have multiple identities, so to speak, as psychologists-theologians-ethicists. The pastoral clinician engages the other in and through these identities, taking into account how each will interpret the variety of clinical data from psychological, theological, and ethical frames of reference. I will suggest that pastoral diagnosis can be viewed as answering the question, *How do the client and I know apart certain data in order to intervene therapeutically in a collaborative way?* We know apart in a manner expressing an attitude of introspection and empathy, which I interpret as expressing the root-metaphors of faithful companioning and collaborative translators. Finally, we attend to the mutually informing domains of content, affect, and action.

This represents an authentically pastoral perspective on pastoral diagnosis in two distinguishable ways. First, clinical care and diagnosis are "pastoral" in part because the clinician engages the client through concepts and categories which are religious and theological in nature. Whether or not a clinical conversation involves the explicit use of religious language, that language will contribute to shaping how the clinician and the client engage one another.

This is the approach implicit in most of the literature on pastoral diagnosis. Whether focusing on a psychological analysis of religious phenomena (Draper 1965; Draper, Myer, Parzen, and Samuelson 1965; Draper and Steadman 1984), a diagnosis of faith development (Fowler 1981; Ivy 1987, 1988; Schneider 1986), using expressly theological constructs to interpret (all) clinical material (Browning 1983; Capps 1980, 1981, 1984; Ellens 1984; Gerkin 1984, 1986a; Hiltner 1943, 1949, 1972, 1976; Patton 1983, 1985; Pruyser 1976a, 1976b, 1984; Wahking 1987; Yeomans 1986), discerning an implicit creed (Nouwen [unpublished]), or an implicit "lived theology" (Jordan 1986), most theorists of pastoral diagnosis have proposed that what makes pastoral diagnosis pastoral is the focus on religious phenomena in conjunction with theological concepts.

The approach I am presenting is authentically pastoral in a second, equally important sense. The care in which the pastoral clinician engages is ministry. That ministry follows from, is an expression of, the clinician's pastoral-faith identity. Both care-as-ministry and identity are formed and interpreted through theological reflection. I presume that theological reflection is an interdisciplinary, "transmethodological" enterprise (Tillich 1939), correlating confessional theological and non-confessional resources. In this regard the participants, their relationship, the various clinical procedures, and the ways of making sense, are *all* interpreted through theological reflection. The approach is properly pastoral in a foundational, horizonal way, precisely because every dimension of the identity, practice, and theory is inherently pastoral-theological.

Illustrating an Approach to Pastoral Diagnosis

In this second section of this essay I will present the outlines of a particular approach to diagnosis to illustrate as well as substantiate the prolegomenon.

Underlying Metaphors in One Pastoral Approach

Each of us has favorite scriptural passages, stories, and statements which articulate something particularly meaningful and helpful. It may be the Twenty-Third Psalm, a song of comfort and inspiration; the Sermon on the Mount, a vision of the kingdom; John 3:16, a testimony of God's love; accounts of Jesus' birth; accounts of the Exodus; the Road to Emmaus story. These passages have a special power to speak something pivotal, something particularly meaningful as we carry on day-to-day.

The following scriptural passages have "chosen me." They are texts which represent something fundamental about my understanding of myself and my ministry. They are probably familiar to most Christians, beginning with a statement of the kerygma, and moving through some of Paul's reflections. Of course, I am not nominating them for special theological status, only focusing upon them because they express crucial aspects of my own personal vision of Christian life and ministry. As I proceed to consider these passages, and implicit metaphors, I think it would be helpful for the reader to identify passages and implicit metaphors that are pivotal for her or him.

Mediating a Gift

In I Corinthians 15: 3–4, Paul writes, "For I delivered to you as of first importance what I also received, that Christ died for our sins in accordance with the scriptures, that he was buried, that he was raised on the third day in accordance with the scriptures." This, the kerygma of the gospel message, captures several significant points. Paul conveys that something of first importance has been delivered to him, which he has been called upon to receive and to deliver to others. This is a gift regarding Jesus Christ having died for our sins and being raised again. It is in the receiving and delivering of this gift that Paul bears witness to the fact that something of first importance, forgiveness of sins, has been given. Paul thus understands himself to be *mediating a gift*.

Elsewhere, Paul exhorts us to "be imitators of me, as I am of Christ." (1 Cor 11:1), to follow his model, as he imitates Christ. As imitators of Paul, we are called to receive and deliver the gift of forgiveness. In other words, *we* are called to mediate a gift. Paul notes, however, that both his mediating and ours are modeled on Christ; it is Christ who mediated the gift of God's love and forgiveness. As John records Jesus' words, "I have come down from heaven, not to do my own will, but the will of him who sent me" (Jn 6:38). Somehow our mediating a gift is captured in not doing our own will but the will of God who created us.

Through Holy Regard

Paul describes how we are to witness, to mediate:

> So if there is any encouragement in Christ, any incentive of love, any participation of the Spirit, any affection and sympathy, complete my joy by being of the same mind, having the

> same love, being in full accord and of one mind. Do nothing from selfishness and conceit, but in humility count others better than yourselves. Let each of you look not only to his own interests, but also the interests of others. Have this mind among yourselves, which you have in Christ Jesus, who, though he was in the form of God, did not count equality with God a thing to be grasped, but emptied himself, taking the form of a servant (Phil 2:1–7a).

We witness and mediate God's gift in and through Jesus Christ by "being of the same mind," "having the same love," doing "nothing from selfishness and conceit but in humility [counting] others better than [ourselves]." We mediate the gift given to us through our witnessing *by who and how we are.* We deliver something that comes *through* us by our participation in the Spirit. We mediate the gift by following the model of Christ, by emptying ourselves, taking the form of a servant, looking to others' interests as well as our own. Indeed, it is precisely in emptying himself—in becoming transparent to God and thereby mediating between God and persons—that Jesus the Christ was the Christ. It is therefore in following this model of mediation by emptying ourselves that we express God's incarnation fully in Christ and God's presence in us. As Paul expresses it, "I have been crucified with Christ; it is no longer I who live, but Christ who lives in me; and the life I now live in the flesh I live by faith in the Son of God, who loved me and gave himself for me" (Gal 2:20).

We receive and deliver—we mediate—the gift by having the same love, by following Christ's example: in emptying ourselves, it is Christ who lives in and through us; it is God and God's love that lives in and through us. "From now on, therefore, we regard no one from a human point of view" (2 Cor 5:16a). We no longer regard ourselves and others as "merely human," but rather as being mediators and bearers of the gift: the Christ in each of us. In other words, we relate to ourselves and others—we mediate the gift—through a holy regard of all persons, others and ourselves. Ours is a holy regard precisely because it is the Christ in us (and through us) that regards and relates to the Christ in (and through) the other.[1]

These passages express how we are given the gift of life that we receive, confirm, and give by emptying ourselves, by taking the form of a servant, by looking to others' interests as well as our own. As "imitators of Christ" (1 Cor 11:1), we are willing to be "the good shepherd" through whom others are known by God, and know God, through whom they are loved by God, and love God.

When we mediate this gift through holy regard, we convey or carry over something given to us, that can be given *through* us. We participate in the Spirit who works through us. We become transparent to Christ in us, present through us with and to another. What comes through us to another may be carried in and through our words, our actions, our person. It is not in being "full" of ourselves that we know and convey what is to be given, but in "emptying" ourselves that we become instruments of God's grace and will. To appreciate that we give something through us is to recognize that it is not given directly but indirectly.[2] Others do not experience God's love and forgiveness simply by being told that God loves them; words are empty unless made manifest in deed. These words have to be incarnated in us so that God's love and forgiveness are shown through us.

If we mediate through holy regard, by incarnating the gift given to us, we do so by our way of being with people. Most profoundly, it is in being with them genuinely and consistently. That means our holy regard is constant, ever-present. Even as they go through the valley of the shadow of death, even as they descend into hell, they can know that nothing can separate them from the love of God in Christ Jesus. They know that, as Ruth said to Naomi, "where you go I will go." "God is faithful" (1 Cor 1:9a).

In Faithful Companioning

These sacred stories arise from as well as generate various symbols and metaphors. I have chosen to represent features of these stories in the following way: We *mediate a gift through holy regard in incarnating* that gift in the quality and nature of our presence. We mediate God's presence to the other through the holy regard of the other as Christ. I have come to capture these various aspects of Christian identity and ministry in the metaphor of faithful companioning.

The other who is with me suffers in part because she or he is alone in that suffering. The person may have lost, or never had, the experience of being loved and accepted and therefore knowing that he or she is love-able, and accept-able. The person may have lost, or never had, the experience that suffering may be sustained in a different way when one is accompanied. He or she may have lost, or never had, the sense that God is present and faithful in that suffering, whether or not a person experiences it, trusts it, accepts it. In this sense, in being faithfully companioned such people have the opportunity to experience being love-able, accept-able, mediated through our being faithfully present to them, regardless of how deep their pain, how alienating their brokenness.

The other who is with me suffers in part because she or he may have lost, or never had, faith in the other. The person's past and present may be peopled with individuals who have done harm by neglect, disregard, selfishness, abuse. He or she may have learned that others hold the power and opportunity to hurt, and that he or she requires vigilant protection from that likely prospect. In being faithfully companioned, such people have the opportunity to experience faith in others, in the goodness and love-ableness of others.

The other who is with me suffers in part because she or he may have lost, or never had, membership in a sustaining community that holds and supports its members. Such a person may have not felt a part of anything, but remained isolated and apart from others. In being faithfully companioned, such people have the opportunity to experience the faithfulness of a community, the sustaining presence of a shared vision which helps make sense of the past and provides a context for making sense of the future.

The other who is with me suffers in part because she or he may have lost, or never had, hope in the future. Such persons may prepare for what is to come not as being full of sustenance, redemption, or healing, but as holding future primitive agonies from which they have to protect themselves. They may have lost, or never had, the sense that they have authorship in their lives and future, that they can contribute constructively to what will unfold. They may have lost faith in their future. In being faithfully companioned, they have the opportunity to experience that faith and hope in their future.

The other who is with me suffers in part because she or he may have lost, or never had, faith. In being faithfully companioned, such persons have the lived sense that the other who is present with and to them shares their brokenness, doubts, agonies, struggles about lovableness, acceptableness, hopefulness. They have a sense that despite, and because of, that authentic known appreciation of such unfaith, the other brings a sense of courage and hope. In other words, in being faithfully companioned, they have the opportunity to experience faith that embraces unfaith. They are lent an appreciation that suffering can be taken up into care, despair into hope, doubt into faith, brokenness into redemption, loneliness into community, alienation into acceptableness. They live in the presence of, and are lent, faith that can become appropriated.

Having proposed that the metaphors of my pastoral identity and context are those of faithful companioning, mediating God's gift of love and forgiveness through holy regard that is incarnated, it is important to recognize that one embodies these metaphors in ways that vary depending on context and relationships. Faithful companioning takes on a particular sensibility given the unique context of the ministry of pastoral psychotherapy. Faithful companioning is a theme on which there are variations. I would like to elaborate further on the metaphor of faithful companioning by way of the metaphor of collaborative translating.

Collaborative Translating

Many theorists in various circles have come to regard psychotherapy as an interpretive hermeneutic process. Roy Schafer (1981, 1983) and Donald Spence (1982) in psychoanalysis, Arthur Kleinman (1988) in psychiatric care, and Charles Gerkin (1984, 1986a, 1986b), John Patton (1983, 1985), Don Browning (1983), and Donald Capps (1980, 1984) in pastoral care and counseling have considered how hermeneutics is central to their respective activities.

These theorists appreciate that the person seeking help and the professional providing care approach their joint enterprise from diverse contexts, by way of dissimilar universes of discourse. The prospective client has a unique way of capturing and representing who she is and what her suffering and pain is, and the clinician has a different way of identifying and making sense of what is presented. In a sense, the clinician naturally sees and hears something as something else.

Arthur Kleinman (1988) expresses this particularly well in his differentiating between illness and disease. "Illness refers to how the sick person and the members of his [or her] family or wider social network perceive, live with, and respond to symptoms of disability" (p. 3). Sick persons present their suffering through "explanatory models" which enable them to order, communicate, and thereby symbolically control symptoms. The illness narrative is the sufferer's unique, more or less coherent but disguised biological, psychological, cultural, ethnic, religious account of what hurts.

Practitioners listen to and attempt to understand the patient by way of their own technical concepts and explanatory models. "Disease is what practitioners have been trained to see through the theoretical lenses of their particular forms of practice" (Kleinman 1988, p. 5). Diagnosis is a *semiotic* act transforming lay speech into professional categories. The practitioner creates another entity when transforming illness into disease.

When we regard care in general, and diagnosis in particular, as hermeneutic activities, we realize how both parties in the collaborative enterprise are constantly translating what they see and hear. Participants presume that their conversation is meaningful and constructive and disavow that misinterpretation is the order of the day. They deny the confusion, and the accompanying anxiety, trying to act "sooner rather than later." They typically collude to endow the professional with special powers and responsibilities for taking the pain away.

These root-metaphors of faithful companioning and collaborative translating are incarnated in a particular clinical attitude. In the following, I elaborate on an attitude, drawing upon yet revising some of the central ideas of Kohut's psychoanalytic psychology of the self. I examine the psychologist-theologian-ethicist employing the introspective-empathic approach.

Features of a Particular Pastoral Clinical Attitude

The Engagement of Psychologist-Theologian-Ethicist

At the heart of my pastoral clinical attitude is the deep appreciation of how each person and each relationship may be experienced, observed, understood, and interpreted from a variety of angles of vision. The pastoral clinician has a manifold professional identity, having been trained to function as psychologist, theologian, and ethicist. Below I will argue that we consider the client as a lay psychologist, lay theologian, lay ethicist. This will lead to the suggestion that we regard pastoral clinical care as the engagement of persons of manifold identities, wherein they come to know and relate to one another, as well as attempt to understand and explain what unfolds between them, as psychologists-theologians-ethicists.

All human beings, by virtue of being human, constructively formulate ways of making sense of their interior life, the interiority of others, their behavior, motives, habits, and tendencies. *Every human being is, in a functional sense, psychological.* Furthermore, *every human being is a lay psychologist.*

All human beings, by virtue of being human, constructively formulate ways of making sense of their life in certain ways and organize their life according to fundamental values, myths, purposes, and have a sense of who God is, what is sacred, holy, meaningful. *Every human being is, in a functional sense, religious.* Furthermore, *every human being is a lay theologian.*

All human beings, by virtue of being human, constructively formulate ways of making sense of their responsibilities, and the responsibilities of their communities, in certain ways. They have some at least implicit sense of what they are supposed to do, of who they are supposed to be or become. *Every human being is, in a functional sense, moral.* Furthermore, *every human being is a lay ethicist.*

Thus each relationship between the client and the pastoral clinician may be recast as the engagement between psychologist-theologian-ethicist and psychologist-theologian-ethicist.[3] Together they may examine and evaluate what is happening and decide what to do from several vantage points. More accurately, together they may engage one another about their various ways of making sense of what unfolds in their collaborative enterprise. The focus in this perspective is less on the various *interpretations* of the data that each person may construe than on the engagement of persons-as-psychologists, persons-as-theologians, persons-as-ethicists.

The Introspective-Empathic Attitude

The attitude through which the clinician engages the client may be characterized as attending to the ongoing experience of two different persons through dual concurrent processes: introspection and empathy. On the one hand, the clinician introspects, that is, pays careful attention to her or his own ongoing inner experience. The clinician monitors what she or he is becoming aware of—thoughts, feelings, sensations. In conjunction with this introspection the clinician at the same time pays attention to the experience of the other. Through empathy, what Kohut (1959/1978) terms "vicarious introspection," the clinician introspects as if she or he were the other. Thus, at the heart of the clinician's attitude is a fundamental duality: the clinician attends to her or his own experience via the procedure of introspection, while concurrently (alternatingly) attending to the experience of the other via the procedure of vicarious introspection, that is, empathy. As the terms suggest, the clinician is tracking the internal experience of self and other through two related procedures.

The introspective-empathic attitude is particularly complex and difficult to characterize. I have found that one effective means of describing some of its many features is by way of a series of dualities (Schlauch 1990a). I will examine the basic duality of attending to one's self and the self of the other through these polarities: *self-experience, internal-external, surface-depth, doubting-believing.* These pairs of terms originate from various contexts and help to articulate central features of ways in which the clinician knows and relates to himself or herself and to the self of the other. The terms are, for the most part, heuristic devices which I use to discriminate features of a process that is ongoing and dynamic, more circular than linear. In other words, while I am capturing dimensions of the attitude and process by way of dualities, I am acknowledging how these mutually informing, interpenetrating qualities are features of a cyclical, dialectical, hermeneutic process.

SELF-EXPERIENCE

The clinician's focus on both self and other is dual. The clinician wants to identify *the subject who is experiencing* and *the nature of the experience.* The clinician wonders *who is the self* who is having and reporting the experience and *what is the experience* that the self is having and reporting. Thus the clinician tracks the self and experience of herself or himself (via introspection), in conjunction with tracking the self and experience of the other (via vicarious introspection).

There are several ways in which the clinician can develop a fuller sense of who the client is and what the client experiences. I, as clinician, might wonder, from what I provoke or evoke in the client, how I can infer—from the client's sensations, feelings, associations, fantasies—what she might be experiencing at this moment. By imagining myself saying what she is saying—by cautiously but intentionally projecting myself imaginatively into her situation—how might I infer what she might be experiencing at this moment? From what I know from my real-life contact with others in somewhat similar situations, how might I generalize from that understanding to attempt to infer what she might be experiencing at this moment? From my readings, studies, and training, how might I infer what might she be experiencing at this moment?

The clinician is, at the same time, wondering, who am *I* as I am experiencing, and, what am *I* experiencing as I listen to her, as I am with her? How do I feel? What am I thinking about? What sensations emerge as we meet? What is my baseline or norm in this kind of moment? In what ways am I departing from that baseline? What are my own tendencies, strengths, weaknesses in this kind of situation?

INTERNAL-EXTERNAL

Philosophers, and following them psychologists, have for a long time characterized aspects of human nature and experience by way of the metaphors internal and external. This way of thinking about ourselves has become normative in Western culture; most of us have learned to distinguish between events which take place inside a person, in the mind, from events occurring outside a person, in the external world. Internal refers to something private, known only to a subject herself or himself; external refers to something public, available to the observation of several persons.

The clinician working from an introspective-empathic stance is presented with considerable data about the client—physical appearance, clothing, body posture, gestures, facial expression, mannerisms. These are data which are presented externally, publicly, available through "extrospection." At the same time the clinician also observes and attempts to make sense of the client and the client's experience through "vicarious introspection." The clinician can imagine, "If I were this person, speaking and acting in this way, what might I be sensing, feeling, thinking as this unfolds?" In other words, what would it be like to be on the inside looking out as I am presenting publicly in this manner?

As a clinician working from an introspective-empathic attitude, I make ongoing judgments about who the person is, and is experiencing by paying attention to what she or he is expressing "on the outside" in conjunction with what she or he is expressing "on the inside." I develop hypotheses from what these sources of information provide, how they do and don't fit together, shaping and reshaping my impressions and hypotheses in deciding how and when to intervene.

For example, I try to appreciate the sadness, despair, and longing that a man is experiencing and expressing as he meets with me, drawing from the content of his words, the pace and tone of his comments, his drooping posture, his infrequent eye contact. While I gather and make use of data from outside and inside, the primary vantage point from which I want to track, monitor, attend to a self and that self's unfolding experience is "from the inside," or "from within." And, the self to whom I address my comments, the self with whom I relate, is that self I have sought to grasp and picture "from the inside," "from within." I am in an ongoing way seeking to grasp, imaginatively, what it is like to be the self who is reporting his experience, while speaking to and engaging that self.

While I am involved in the process of attending to and relating with the self of the client, I am also involved in making ongoing judgments about *my* self and *my* experience by attending to internal and external data. While I am tracking my own feelings, words, posture, and mannerisms through introspection, I am aware of the client's responses to me. While, for example, I had imagined that I was acting sensitively, he gives me the impression that he experiences me to be rather disinterested and aloof. I have to consider in what ways that feedback not only reveals something about him, but also discloses something about me of which I am not yet aware. In other words, I am open to feedback about me and my experience that is "external" to me.

In this way the duality of internal-external captures the various mutually informing, fluidly interrelated sources of data—inside and outside both participants—which are available to the clinician. In addition, the duality provides a context in which to capture the internal vantage point from which the clinician in the introspective-empathic attitude proceeds: *attending to and relating with the imaginatively constructed self as subject of the client's ongoing experience.*

SURFACE-DEPTH

It's not uncommon when discussing everyday conversation to draw a contrast between what is communicated directly, that is, "denoted," and what is implied by the speaker and inferred by the listener, that is, "connoted." A statement conveys apparent meaning and betrays hidden or disguised meaning. We can recast this contrast in terms of the spatial metaphors surface and depth: something is at the surface, illumined, available to be seen and heard, and something more or other is in the depths, beyond the light. Not infrequently, surface brings with it connotations of superficial, and depth, of foundational, elemental, profound. When we bear in mind how conversation always involves surface and depth, we become suspicious of what is obvious, and search for what is disguised and hidden.

I am proposing that our knowing and relating to ourselves and another reflect the tension and paradox of attending to both surface and depth, recognizing that what is "manifest" will be in competition and potential conflict with what is "latent." Consider, for example, the situation where a client wants the length of therapy sessions to remain flexible, depending upon his moods. He might feel "really understood" were I to extend the hour when he felt depressed and shorten the hour when he felt okay. He becomes anxious and troubled when I do not accede to his wishes. While he might have experienced me to be more attuned to him by agreeing to his request, I am suggesting that knowing and relating "paradoxically" at both surface and depth means appreciating what is experienced and reported consciously while at the same time appreciating what is dimly sensed and implied preconsciously (unconsciously). Thus, it does *not* mean being attuned to a person in her or his conscious awareness and experience. Nor does it mean being simply attuned to the person "in the moment," as if the moment were "out of time." On the contrary, the introspective-empathic attitude inclusive of surface and depth extends across the boundaries of consciousness. It thus means being *with and for the other* in a context wider than the other's consciousness, broader than the moment.

Being with another in surface *and* depth is therefore being with that person across time. We understand the conscious experience of the moment in conjunction with, in the context of, the other's unfolding life history. It is the knowing of and relating to a person in his or her developmental context. To return to the clinical illustration, I am relating via an introspective-empathic attitude with this man when I appreciate his experience inclusive of depth, across the boundaries of conscious, preconscious, unconscious, when I appreciate his experience in time (in history), across the boundaries of past, present, and future.

Because a pastoral psychotherapist functions as theologian as well as psychologist (and ethicist), she or he is attentive to the ways in which depth may be approached. Gabriel Marcel (1950) has written about the difference between a "problem" and a "mystery" (pp. 211ff.) In the former we approach something as potentially available to be solved, something which can be rendered intelligible. In the latter we approach something as fundamentally beyond our comprehension. While we may respect problems, we approach them as opportunities for knowledge and mastery. In contrast, we approach mysteries with awe and fascination.

When we function as if depth were problem, we are enlisted to work unflaggingly, to the limits of our capacities, to understand and know what is presently unknown. When we function as if depth were mystery, we are encouraged to respect the limits of our capacities to know and to appreciate that at most we can be in the presence of something beyond us. In some sense it is helpful to approach depth as problem *and* as mystery. Most important, "Our first task in approaching another . . . is to take off our shoes for the place we are approaching is holy. Else we may find ourself treading on another's dream. More serious still, we may forget . . . that God was there before our arrival" (Augsberger 1986).

DOUBTING-BELIEVING

I have found Peter Elbow's (1973) comments in *Writing Without Teachers* to be very helpful in articulating how we may approach persons we want to know and understand—others as well as ourselves. In his essay "The Doubting Game and the Believing Game—Analysis of the Intellectual Enterprise" Elbow characterizes two "basic games" to play in trying to find the truth. "The doubting game seeks the truth by seeking error. Doubting an assertion is the best way to find an error in it. . . . The truer it seems, the harder you have to doubt it. . . . To doubt well, it helps if you make a special effort to extricate yourself from the assertions in question" (p. 148). "In the believing game the first rule is to refrain from doubting the assertions. . . . We are trying to find not errors but truths, and for this it helps to believe. . . . To do this you must make, not an act of self-extrication, but an act of self-insertion, self-involvement" (p. 149).

In the introspective-empathic stance I "believe" what the client says *and* "doubt" what the client says. I accept what the other says as "plausible," "real," "true," and at the same time remain curious and "suspicious." I apply what Paul Ricoeur (1970) referred to as a hermeneutics of suspicion and a hermeneutics of restoration. When this man tells me about his sadness, for example, I am aware of the fact that by the end of an hour I feel exhausted, wishing I had had a cup of coffee before meeting with him. I am wondering about the fact that while he says he wants to tell me everything so that I can do something, I am also aware that I have struggled to put words to his experience and that he has disclosed very little. While I must in part believe what he says, in order to understand, I must doubt, in part, the accuracy of what he says, in order to understand.

Doubting-believing characterizes an important feature of the introspective-empathic attitude that we enact in knowing and relating to ourselves as well as to the other. We proceed, most naturally, to believe and trust the accuracy of our own experience: what, how, and why we understand and know we almost take for granted. By the same token, however, it is important that we bring the same doubting attitude to ourselves as we do to and with the other. If we take the notion of surface-depth seriously, particularly as it is expressed in the contrast of conscious-unconscious, we appreciate that *what* we see and hear may be surface more than depth, subjective more than objective. Furthermore, *how* and *why* we see and hear may be more surface than depth, subjective than objective—may need to be doubted as well as believed.

Having discussed features of the pastoral clinical attitude in light of the polarities of self-experience, internal-external, surface-depth, and doubting-believing, I will now examine the diagnostic variables through which this attitude is operationalized.

Diagnostic Variables: The Dual Focus and the Three Domains of Pastoral Clinical Care

In this section, I will examine the client's presentation in terms of the *dual focus* of "self" and "suffering," and the *three domains* of "content," "affect," and "action." I have chosen to structure and characterize this material in this way because I believe that the language of pastoral care, counseling, and psychotherapy—and thus pastoral diagnosis—must be "close-to-experience" (Patton 1985, p. 74), or "experience-near" (Kohut 1971, 1984), for a number of reasons. Each of us experiences a slippage between our ongoing felt-experience and the words we use to try to capture that experience, to ourselves as well as to another. Because any enterprise which so intimately involves the careful use of language is fraught with such innate difficulties, it is important that our own professional language remain as close as possible to colloquial expression rather than technical jargon. Second, because each of us experiences and names experience in a somewhat unique manner that requires that we collaboratively translate, it is additionally necessary that we not confound the territory by introducing abstract, experience-distant concepts. Third, given that empathy, "tracking," or "faithful companioning" may be integral to the process of successful care, avoiding jargon enhances the likelihood that we remain close to experience. Finally, I expect that this language will not necessarily compete or conflict with the constructs and categories of the wide variety of pastoral clinical approaches which integrate diverse psychological and confessional resources in differing ways. Clinicians from a diversity of pastoral perspectives might be able to use the following concepts and categories.

A BASIC DUAL FOCUS: SELF AND SUFFERING

Every clinician approaches the clinical situation in light of and in conjunction with a theory or theories which inform what and how they observe, how they organize their data, and how they intervene. Regardless of orientation, most clinicians typically focus their attention on a particular constellation or cluster of data—the area of pain, and dysfunction. Whether that area is interpreted in terms of psychic processes, behavioral patterns, cognitive beliefs, or family myths, most clinicians attend to what is "wrong" or "broken," variously labeled "chief complaint," "presenting problem," or "psychopathology." Under the influence of medical practice, we are geared toward identifying a single specific cluster of data. Following the image of a circle, it's as if we develop a picture with the pathology at the center.

When we proceed in this manner, we attain a grasp of the other's pain and dysfunction, in breadth and depth. We do that in part by differentiating what we understand to be its "essence" from a range of alternative interpretations. However, our commitment to identify and focus on the nature of the pathology has its own problems. Often our concerted attention to the "pathology" is achieved at the expense of attention to the person who seeks our help. Investing so much energy in identifying the *problem* leaves us comparatively little energy to invest in understanding the *person*. Our investment of energy betrays that we are not there to care for the person; we are there to treat the illness, for which the client just happens to be the carrier or host. Clients may experience a sense of being "missed," as if they are only an appendage to their pain. The most attention they might receive is when we ask them to describe their experience of their suffering. Then again, they experience being regarded only through the lens of their illness.

In contrast to this I propose that the picture we want to construct—and continually modify through the ongoing process of care—is less like a circle than an ellipse, with *two* focal points. Amid the infinity of data that are presented in clinical hours, I have found it helpful to focus on two interrelated, mutually informing features of the client's presentation: Who is this person, or more technically, who is the "self" of the person? What is the suffering of this person? The mutually informing features of self and suffering are related in a complementary manner, as context and foreground. In order to understand who a person is, it is invaluable to identify particular expressions and qualities of that person, such as in and through her or his suffering. By the same token, in order to understand a person's suffering, we need to identify the person who suffers in that particular way.

It is important to note that our dual attention to the self and the suffering of the person can be enhanced by, but does not focus expressly on her or his mental status. A person's mental status is assessed in terms of **J**udgment, **I**nsight, **M**ood, **M**emory, **O**rientation, **T**hought processes and content, **S**peech, **I**ntelligence, **G**eneral appearance and behavior, and **A**ffect (JIM MOTSIGA) (Draper and Steadman 1985, p. 127). Data from these various domains contribute to a picture of a person's current state and provide some indications of long-term functioning and capacities.

One of the best ways to convey what I mean by the dual features of self and suffering is through illustration. A man who has recently lost a friend describes his suffering as sadness, hopelessness, despair.

Our first concern, however, is not to focus on "the" sadness, recast as "a mood disorder," but to ask this person to help us understand as fully as possible how he is experiencing what hurts. Embedded in this approach is our dual focus: How are *you* experiencing *what hurts?* We listen to how he elaborates both on who he is, how he experiences, how he thinks, communicates, relates, as well as on a particular dimension of his experience that leads him to seek help—the particular suffering. Because I will be providing care for a person, and prospectively developing a relationship with him, I do not want to restrict my attention to his complaint, nor do I want to restrict my attention to him through his suffering, as if he were merely a person with the complaint. I want to identify and relate to the person, and work *with* him to identify and work toward helping him with his suffering. Thus, as I explore features of how he hurts, I keep in mind, "Who is this *person* who is reporting his particular experience in this way?"

Given the fact that I am functioning as a psychologist-theologian-ethicist in conversation with a psychologist-theologian-ethicist, I am always listening-interpreting-recasting-translating the client's report of his experience into a variety of language games and engaging the client in light of my various understandings. I am hearing and responding to self and suffering as a psychologist intent on identifying character structure, strengths, recurrent conflicts, deficits, and symptomatology. I am engaging as a theologian who is trying to identify how the other may be denying God's presence, action, and participation in unfolding events, and replacing God in mistakenly presuming the wisdom, authority, and responsibility to act independently of God, while also seeking to mediate God's presence in faithful companioning through holy regard. Finally, I am engaging as an ethicist who is trying to discern the client's and our sense of responsibility. In and through each of these respective "identities," I am attempting faithfully to companion, in mutually translating our respective interpretations of our different experiences. In doing so, I am expressing certain metaphors through my pastoral clinical attitude.

THREE CENTRAL DOMAINS: CONTENT, AFFECT, ACTION

The pastoral clinician who focuses on the dual features of self and suffering may differentiate among three related domains: content, affect, and action. *Content* refers to the cognitive, ideational dimension of a person's experience, captured and articulated in the form of words. *Affect,* in contrast, is an area of emotions and feelings, usually experienced in bodily sensations, captured only gradually and usually only approximately in words. I am using *action* to refer to what is enacted and expressed in particular behaviors and patterns of behavior.

CONTENT

The most obvious manner of gathering data and formulating a picture or "working model" (Greenson 1960) of the self and suffering of the other is by way of the content of the person's report. We can listen to the other's thoughts, ideas, memories, not only to enable us to understand more fully what is currently wrong, but also to construct a picture or model of who that other is who is realizing something is wrong. Many of us begin the process of information-gathering by focusing on the other's suffering. We might ask simply, "What hurts?" or more elaborately, "Can you tell me a little about what is happening that brings you to meet with me?"

It is important to be equally intentional about gathering data about the other's "self." One way of initiating that process is to bear in mind a rather simple question. Imagine that after your initial meeting with this person, you are going to consult with a colleague. You will want to orient your colleague's attention to a particular quality or feature of the person's presentation that you somehow have come to regard as quintessential or prototypical of that person. What feature of the person's presentation seems to capture and represent symbolically something fundamental or pivotal about the other's self? For example, you might recall that the client's shoulders were remarkably rounded, her posture sagging, as if to convey that she is carrying too heavy a burden. Or, you might think about the fact that she wears her hair in such a way that you can never really see her face, as if to suggest her not wanting to be seen. Or, you could flash back to an image of her sitting on the edge of her chair, and infer that she is desperate to hear a word of comfort and wisdom that could help her. You would have come to any of these images subsequent to your meeting, choosing one or another precisely because in light of everything that was presented, you concluded that this or that captured a pivotal quality.

Alongside our formulating a picture of the self, we are trying to construct a picture of the other's suffering. We ask questions about sadness: What does he mean by sadness? What does he experience that he chooses to label it in that way? This tactic serves several purposes and conveys several messages. First and most obviously, it enlists the other to try to specify as carefully as possible what it is that she or he is experiencing. Second, and not less significantly, it contributes to the client's coming to appreciate that words may not correspond to particular states, which human beings universally share, but are more terms each of us has chosen in her or his personal lexicon to name some hidden, interior experience. Furthermore, the client might recognize how the terms may conceal and obfuscate as much as they disclose. Although every person uses the word *sadness* and experiences feelings she or he names sadness, it is productive to specify and clarify one's own felt-experience and the linkages between that felt-experience and one's language world.

Appreciating some of the quality of that sadness requires understanding its history and course. When we inquire, "How long have you been feeling this sadness?" we enlist the client to put suffering in historical context. Is it something that just began? Is it lifelong? How would the client contrast sadness with some un-sad (premorbid) state? What was taking place when the suffering began? To appreciate what *sad,* and *empty,* and *depressed* have come to mean, it is important to identify three features of the origins of these feelings: the context, the precipitants of the suffering, and the precipitants of the request for help. "What was happening at the time when you first experienced feeling sad?" "What in particular precipitated, provoked, caused your sadness?" "What in particular precipitated, provoked, caused you to seek help?"

Most of us take for granted, regardless of how we account for it theoretically, that present experience—patterns of perception and behavior, for example—are in part expressive of past experience. As a psychoanalytically informed clinician, I presume that much of what a person experiences reflects "continuing the past in the present—(unconsciously) repeating particular patterns of expectation (unconsciously) reenacting patterns of relationship. With this in mind, I presume that the present experience is, in part, a repetition of the past, and that the precipitants both of the experience of suffering as well as of the request for help are themselves repetitions. On the one hand, I examine what, in particular, contributed to what had been a more-or-less balanced self becoming more injured, more out of balance. The nature of that event again informs us about how the self is made and what its past history has been like. On the other hand, I examine what, in particular, contributed to the development in this injured self of the need, and the hope, of restored balance. The nature of this moment, of this event, gives us clues about past experiences of seeking care, and thus about the way in which the self is built.

As we listen for what precipitated a person's seeking help, we identify what made that help not only necessary, but possible. The other is informing us about how he or she has experienced help in the past. It is a safe assumption, then, that the person will approach us with the expectation that we might respond in a manner similar to others in their past. I explore precisely that area when I ask, "How can I help you?" More specifically, "What did you hope, expect, anticipate, that I might do, or how I might be, that would make a difference?" Through that, I am in a position to formulate hypotheses not only about how he or she has gotten "help" in the past—personally as well as professionally—but about the nature and makeup of the self who engages others in particular ways. For example, the client might respond, "I thought by just getting these things out with a sounding board that I'd feel some relief." Talking or catharsis helps. The client also reveals, however, that care is a rather impersonal or depersonalized process between someone who gets "relief" from "getting things out" with a "sounding board." How different my impression of the client were she or he to respond, "I know there are ways in which I've gotten depressed and felt lost when I've lost someone who feels like a part of me, and I've found it helpful for someone to help me identify why I am stuck in this pattern." This reveals someone who is able to connect this experience with similar experiences, to experience a pattern, wherein another will help discern something she or he is unable to know alone.

If I take for granted that the past continues into the present, that a person's seeking help in particular reveals how they have received, or at least longed for, care in the past, I can also presume that a person's decision to meet with me in particular is a repetition of some kind. My exploring with the client, "How did you come to the decision to see me in particular?" "What do you know of me, of what I do, that contributed to your seeking me out?" will not only tell me something about her or his present expectations, but about past experiences. For instance, the person might respond, "I've heard that you are a warm and sensitive person, someone 'pastoral,' and I felt safer with that than with someone who might challenge me or hurt me." I know through these words that this individual has learned that she or he needs to be protected from the prospect of being confronted, and injured, by someone. Were the client to have said, "I'd rather come to a pastoral counselor than a secular therapist, because I trust that God will be present in our work," I would learn that God is a part of the other's experience. The client also implies that God is not present in work with non-pastoral caregivers, and possibly that there is a special, even magical, way in which my being "pastoral" invokes God's presence.

Because I regard diagnosis—judgments regarding the present state—to be intimately connected to formulating goals of care—judgments regarding the end state—and because I regard pastoral clinical care in general and pastoral diagnosis in particular as collaborative enterprises, it is to be expected that I would explore with a person what she or he hopes and intends to accomplish through prospective work with me. At times, I will ask, "What objectives do you have for our work?" "What do you hope to achieve, or attain?" Over the years, I have tended to ask that in a different way, from the "inside" more than from the "outside": "What do you anticipate you will experience that will serve as a clue or signal that you have attained what we have worked for, and are ready to begin preparation to end our work together?" For example, a client might say, "I just want to feel better about myself." When he is unable to specify what that might mean, he reveals that his interior life may be rather colorless, and we would want to assess to what degree that is "state" or "trait"—characterological or situational, chronic or acute. If he were to say, "I want to be in a new relationship, to get married," we would have to explore in what ways that was meant as a replacement for the present loss and/or as the building of a different kind of relationship.

As I enlist the person to collaborate in diagnosing and in formulating goals, I naturally explore how the other envisions moving from where she or he is to some desired place. "How might we work together in a way that you anticipate will help?" The response about "getting things out with a sounding board" indicates an implicit plan. I might then pursue this further, "How have you found that to be helpful in the past?" We are then in a position to specify that "getting things out" means "exposing secrets," or "confessing sins," and that a "sounding board" is a person who is "objective," "not encumbered by his or her own values and needs." I could reinterpret these comments and observe, "You suggest that some of what is causing you to suffer has to do with some experiences of 'sinning,' and you want me to be present in such a way that I don't interfere with your getting those painful things out."

Each of the above series of questions will inevitably lead clinician and client to move readily across time and space, to look at what is happening in the here and now in conjunction with past experience. While it is extremely helpful and important to formulate a history of the suffering (a history of the chief complaint), it is even more important to formulate a history of the person—of the self. One way of proceeding would be to ask him to provide an overview of his life, beginning with earliest memories and moving through time to include memories that are important to him and his story. The client should be asked to include some understanding of his family, the relationships among family members, as well as how we can understand who he is by how he fits (and doesn't fit) within that family context. Throughout, it is valuable to attend to themes and variations which emerge in listening to the client's own "working model" of his "self." It is from and in conjunction with that working model that we develop our own.

Each of the responses to these questions raises another important issue. While I am working to help the client to help us both understand more fully her or his self, suffering, goals, and plan of care, I am conveying some of how I work and will work. In other words, implicit in all my questionings are "hidden" communications about me, my attitude, my method of care. I am not saying in words, but I am revealing in actions, some of the following messages: "We need to take care in identifying as fully as possible who you are and what you are experiencing." "While I might know about persons, and about clinical care, I am ignorant of who you are and need you to help me. Together we will judge what is wrong, consider the goals of care, and plan a course of care." "It is important for us to identify how what I understand you to imply—what I infer—plays an important part in our making sense of what is happening and what to do: what is beyond the obvious, what might be hidden, is very relevant." "I respect your way of experiencing and naming things and will honor what you want to do and how you envision doing that, but I want to proceed carefully and sensitively, so that we work collaboratively enough, even though you might experience me not only as an ally but also as an adversary."

It is important to convey genuine respect for the integrity of the other's experience and judgment; we must also convey an authentic respect for the integrity of our own experience and judgment. If we are genuinely collaborating, we must come to some shared sense of who the client is, what the client's suffering is, what are reasonable goals of work, what are reasonable means of attaining those goals. For example, I could not agree that the client's getting married is a reasonable goal, but I might suggest developing more life-giving relationships as an alternative objective. I would not agree that we will stop the client's painful thoughts, only that together we might come to understand more about those thoughts, where they come from, why they are so painful.

What this points to is the fact that in a collaborative process the clinician is not an objective data-gatherer who in her or his wisdom and expertise magically arrives at a masterful private assessment which empowers her or him to act in some way with or on the client. Rather, the clinician should be presenting to the client what she or he is identifying and how that is being put together. For example, I would, in an ongoing way, tell this man who recently lost his friend that as he talks about being depressed, he sounds more and more frightened about the possibility of becoming as depressed and powerless as he had been years ago. I would want him to hear how I have heard him, so that he could correct my "hypothesizing" and the direction in which I was moving. He could then help me, as a collaborative translator, to reshape my picture of his anxiously anticipating the primitive agony of being helpless and alone. As he contributes to reshaping my picture, he is also implicitly, if not explicitly, challenging and enhancing his own picture of himself and his suffering.

The questions why, why now, where from, why me, where to, and how, are questions relevant to every moment of every session. They contribute to what and how we know apart. The data we gather will be expressed and disclosed in ways that will require a continual process of translating, in two different ways. In one sense, I take for granted that the particular words and the overall language world of each person is somewhat unique, capturing and expressing somewhat unique experiences. Thus I have to translate what another is conveying in terms of my own lexicon of interior experience, which will of course overlap but will be in part exclusive. Translation takes place "between" the participants. In a second sense, I also take for granted that the person is fundamentally unaware of much of who she or he is, and what her or his suffering is about. Taking the unconscious seriously, I listen for "content" being presented at several levels: the "manifest content," material which is for the most part acceptable and intelligible to the person (what I am told directly); the preconscious content, what is dimly sensed by the client, implied in their words and actions, can be reasonably inferred, is implicit, present, but in part hidden; the unconscious content, what is implied (which I infer), presented, but not available to the awareness of the client. Thus the client, with the clinician's help, has to translate what she is conveying to her self, carrying from one area of experience (unconscious) into another area (conscious). Translation takes place "within" the participants.

In the context of such translation within and between the participants, it is difficult to recognize to what degree the evolving meanings of unfolding experience have more to do with what is implied by the client or what is inferred by the therapist. It is only through collaborative conversation that the participants come to discriminate what was hidden from and by the client that enhances their joint deeper and more accurate grasp of the client's self and her or his suffering.

AFFECT

Another central domain of every person's self and suffering is the affect she or he experiences. By affect I'm referring to the feeling-tone, the emotional flavor of a person's self-presentation and report. A client might remark quite directly, "I feel sad and overwhelmed." She might convey "sadness" in her posture, her facial expression, her tone of voice, her movements. She might betray sadness by provoking in the therapist a sense of sadness, while simultaneously conveying little directly about how she feels in her words and actions. As we can see, affect is conveyed or communicated in a variety of ways, some directly, others indirectly.

Regardless of how it is communicated, it is important to realize that attending to and understanding affect is a central project of effective clinical care. That is because every thought and every action of every person is not only influenced but motivated by affect (Basch 1988b, p. 69). We engage in behaviors, establish relationships, and pursue activities which are likely to enhance our experiencing positive feelings and minimizing negative feelings. Most important, we experience, perceive, apprehend in a manner which enables us to enhance positive feelings and minimize negative feelings. We deny, repress, select out of awareness, painful memories or the pain of some memories. We select out of awareness features of current experience which might evoke pain. We select out of awareness features of the future which might precipitate pain, frequently by protecting ourselves from anticipated dangers by limiting our actions and relationships.

A person with whom we are meeting confirms that affect motivates all thinking and action. She is seeking our help because she is suffering, because she is experiencing pain, and the help she seeks is to alleviate the suffering, mitigate the pain. Sheldon Roth (1987) says it well: "Sometimes thoughtful therapists are dismayed when patients candidly acknowledge that insight is not their primary goal in psychotherapy; they just want to feel better. Actually, such comments are closer to the affectual wishes that bring people to seek the help of a therapist" (pp. 274–75). Our concern, then, is to be able to appreciate and grasp her affect, with the awareness that it is precisely this dimension of her self and suffering she seeks to change. One of the ways of accomplishing that task of appreciating and grasping is by encouraging and enabling her to name her feelings more and more accurately.

The effort of naming feelings accurately is an inherently difficult project for a variety of reasons. Affect is a dimension of human experience that is present from birth and becomes patterned in quality, shape, and meaning from a very early age. Our affective experience is, as research reveals, initially a genetically encoded reflex phenomenon (Basch 1988b p. 72). In a manner similar to other reflex actions, such as the knee jerk or blinking, this response does not involve any reflective evaluation of what precipitated its occurrence: it "just happens" (p. 77). Often it seems that, even as adults, we feel something —which we only subsequently identify—that stimulated our response and why we responded that way. Our earliest and most enduring experiences of affective states, then, are of patterned, reflexive, preverbal moods which happen to us.

Affects confront us in patterned, reflexive ways and are embedded in our experience and memory in a preverbal way. Gradually, of course, we acquire the capacity to communicate in words, to become verbal, having by this time a preverbal history and storehouse of affective experience and patterns. But language is a double-edged sword: "It drives a wedge between two simultaneous forms of interpersonal experience: as it is lived and as it is verbally represented" (Stern 1985, p. 162) Interpersonal experience has been lived, has a history, before it becomes verbally represented. "There is a stretch of time in which rich experiential knowledge 'in there' is accumulated, which somehow will later get assembled (although not totally) with a verbal code, language" (p. 168). As these comments indicate, we lead two lives—"original life as nonverbal experience and a life that is a verbalized version of that experience" (p. 174).

As Stern explains, there are many ways in which language is not adequate to the task of communicating about lived-experience. There will be "points of slippage" (p. 178). One of these points of slippage is in the realm of internal states, because "affect as a form of personal knowledge is very hard to put into words and communicate" (p. 178). What is true of "original global experience" is thus true of affective states:

> Several different relationships can exist between nonverbal global experience and that part of it that has been transformed into words. At times, the piece that language separates out is quintessential and captures the whole experience beautifully. Language is generally thought to function in this

> "ideal" way, but in fact it rarely does, and we will have the least to say about this. At other times the language version and the globally experienced version do not coexist well. The global experience may be fractured or simply poorly represented, in which case it wanders off to lead a misnamed and poorly understood existence. And finally, some global experiences . . . do not permit language sufficient entry to separate out a piece for linguistic transformation. Such experiences then simply continue underground, nonverbalized, to lead an unnamed (and, to that extent only, unknown) but nonetheless very real existence (p. 175).

Language, then, affords the opportunity to contribute to naming accurately certain qualities of internal states, while misnaming, and leaving unnamed, other qualities of internal states. As we acquire the capacity to be verbal and to name internal states, our experience of affect undergoes developmental, maturational shifts to what Basch (1988b) calls "feeling" and subsequently, "emotion." Affect becomes feeling "when the involuntary basic affective reaction begins to be related to a concept of the self" (p. 78). "Emotion, a further step in affective maturation, results when feeling states are joined with experience to give personal meaning to complex concepts such as love, hate, and happiness" (p. 78).

One way of understanding this evolution of affect-feeling-emotion is in the gradual acquisition of a way of identifying and making certain states of experience meaningful, through which they are owned as part of, expressions of, a self. By doing so the self attains a sense of connection and possibly of mastery. Typically the process of identifying and making meaningful involves, or essentially amounts to, the process of putting experience into words. But this procedure of putting experience into words is, as we have seen, a hazardous one.

> Prior to language, all of one's behaviors have equal status as far as "ownership" is concerned. With the advent of language, some behaviors now have a privileged status with regard to one having to own them. The many messages in many channels are being fragmented by language into a hierarchy of accountability/deniability (Stern 1985, p. 180).

Some affect-feeling-emotion is known and owned, other unknown and disowned. Thus our effort to discern and identify the affect-feeling-emotion of any other person, of any client, is as central to our healing enterprise as it is magnificently difficult. Affects are at the heart of motivation for all thinking and acting. Affects are, at the same time, extraordinarily difficult to capture, express, and modify, though that is at the center of our work.

When meeting with a client who describes suffering as feeling "sad" and "overwhelmed," we need to explore, "What is it like when you are sad?" "How do you experience that?" We presume that there is considerable "slippage" between vocabulary and felt-experience, and that in the area of affect and feelings, such slippage is most acute. Thus at all times we should try to be present to and with another in their unnameable affect, appreciating how feeling-states can be understood and shared apart from words. At other times we might modify this slippage—by helping the person to develop a more extensive "personal vocabulary of affect." Roth (1987) notes,

> It has been my observation that for most people, the most significant change in psychotherapy—the product of insight as contrasted with the process of insight—is the suppression and repression of the moment-to-moment insights of treatment and their replacement by an altered, condensed, sustained affective state. This affective state is the crystallization of the personality changes achieved through the therapeutic process. It is reflected in an altered, basic characterological mood, dispositions to mood and affect, and new capacities to acknowledge, bear, and experience affective states (p. 275).

A person would be helped to achieve "an altered, basic characterological mood, dispositions to mood and affect, and new capacities to acknowledge, bear, and experience affective states" by experiencing the collaborative presence of the clinician, at times in the experience of unnamed sharing and intuitive understanding, at other times in identifying and naming painful emotional states which led the person to seek and continue to need help.

ACTION

Action refers to the ways in which persons disclose features of self and suffering by the behavior they engage in. In this "existential" dimension, the clinician attends to how significant features of the client's self are enacted in behavior. The clinician can be alert to and anticipate how the suffering that has been expressed in content, and conveyed in affect, will be enacted. I find it helpful to differentiate between two different areas, that of the *process* of the engagement, and that of the helping (therapy) *relationship*.

THE PROCESS OF THE ENGAGEMENT

Compare the following scenarios with the question, "What does this reveal about self and suffering?" in mind. A woman contacts us through our emergency service, late at night, and asks us to call "as soon as possible." She tells us that she got our name from an acquaintance several weeks ago and had not wanted to call until she "absolutely had to." She says she feels "desperate and alone" and wants to see us "as soon as possible." When we meet with her at our next available time, the following evening, she comes in agitated, launching into what is happening. She speaks at a frantic pace, with little eye contact, as if gathering steam. She leaves little entrance for questions, comments, or observations. She appears exhausted by the end of our initial meeting, uncertain what to do. After meeting with her for several sessions for purposes of evaluation, we agree to meet regularly, on a weekly basis. As our work proceeds she reveals a ritualized style that can be expressed in this way: each hour is filled with words, ideas that seem to have some apparent connection to her but feel to us at times tangential. There is a frantic pace, as if "filling up the time," "making sure everything that needs to be said is said," "getting everything out."

Here is another story. A man calls us during working hours, asking if it would be possible for us to meet. He tells us he is sad and overwhelmed, and wonders if it would be possible for us to see him in his home rather than in our office. He says he feels uncomfortable being "seen" going to a therapist. With some firm encouragement he reluctantly agrees to meet in a few days in our office. Although he appears forthright at the outset, he rarely responds directly to any of our initial questions, instead choosing to tell us things that he hopes will help us understand. A couple of times he remarks, "I think you'd really get to know and understand me if you would see me in my home." We agree to try to work together, in the office, and become aware that the sessions have a kind of pattern. He begins each hour remarking about the weather and describes what he is wearing that "keeps him protected from the elements." He then asks us how we are, whether we feel any of the effects of the fluctuations in weather. He goes on, slowly, almost painstakingly, to tell us about what we would see were we to visit him in his home. He deflects any observations about how his tone of voice sounds so sad, about how important it is for him to be understood through his home.

The process of the time together reveals a lot about the self and the suffering of each client. The woman can only come when things are beyond her ability to manage, and then she "uses the time" frantically and desperately "to get things out." It makes us wonder about why she withheld care for herself for so long, as if she didn't deserve it. Can she only ask for help in emergencies? Is she afraid that she will not be responded to unless she presents in an emergency? Is she aware that her presumptuousness in calling so late, and in dumping so much on the therapist, alienates the caretaker from being as present as he or she might be?

The man needs protection. He senses an inability to communicate who he is and what he needs, as if he will be unable to help the clinician to understand him. While he wants us to see him for who he really is, that can only happen by our seeing his home; otherwise, he has to protect himself and hide from inquiries and observations about how he is experiencing his loss.

As these scenarios demonstrate, clients reveal a lot about who they are and how they hurt by the very process of contact and ongoing work. The data discerned from the *process* should be used to amplify and enhance the pictures we are generating, the hypotheses we are formulating, as we take into account the content and affect presented to us. Most important, we are concerned with content, affect, and process not as ends in themselves, and not as categories which exist independently of one another. Rather, we appreciate that each of these dimensions or areas are "entrances" into the self and the suffering of the self, which together contribute to our constructing an accurate and useful understanding with and for the client.

RELATIONSHIP

A person conveys essential aspects about her or his self and suffering through a second area of action, that is, in the relationship that is formed between that person and the clinician. The various literatures on care, counseling, and psychotherapy abound with discussions of the helping *relationship*. In the following, I will not attempt to be comprehensive or exhaustive, but will focus on one aspect of the clinical relationship as it is characterized in psychoanalytic theorizing, particularly in the psychoanalytic psychology of the self.

Psychoanalytically oriented theorists differentiate among various dimensions of a clinical relationship that co-exist: the real relationship, the classical transference, the narcissistic transference, and the working alliance. Thus, for example, I can interpret the relationship forming between a sad, depressed person and me in terms of these different sub-relationships.

Psychoanalytically informed care centers around the identification and working through of the transference. Like all psychoanalytic concepts, however, transference has been described and defined in innumerable ways. My own description draws from several sources.

> Transference refers to the clinician's interpretation of certain features of the client's perception, understanding, and experience of the clinician, which the clinician regards to be distorted, biased, inappropriate, having to do more with the client than with the clinician and having to do more with the reexperience/reenactment of patterns of perception, experience, and relationship with past significant figures of which the client is not fully aware.

In formulating this description of transference I have taken into account a number of important issues. First, because a clinician is a participant-observer—is part of the field of observation—she or he never attains an ultimately objective understanding of anything that occurs. All of the clinician's interpretations, including interpreting certain phenomena as transference, have the status of *hypotheses.* As such, they require verification, are subject to disconfirmation or falsification, and require ongoing collaborative exploration. Second, the hypotheses about transference do not capture the totality of the clinical relationship or the totality of the client's experience of the clinician and of the relationship; transference refers to certain limited dimensions or qualities. Third, by virtue of having become more or less familiar with her or his own personality in her or his own therapy experience(s), and by virtue of having become more or less familiar with how she or he is experienced as a clinician, the clinician develops a sense of a "baseline"—what is more or less typical of her or him. In conjunction with this sense of a standard or norm, somewhat generalizable from clinical relationship to clinical relationship, the clinician will at times hypothesize that certain features of the client's experience are "distorted." Fourth, the judgment that certain perceptions or experiences have more to do with the client than with the clinician is always an assessment of relative proportions. Fifth, the hypothesis about a reexperience of, reenactment of . . . with past figures refers to the "genetic orientation"—one makes sense of the present in terms of the past. To put it differently, one assumes that the client has learned to experience people in a certain way, and that it is appropriate and beneficial to explore and understand the nature, problems, and limitations of that learning. Finally, the claim "of which the client is less than fully aware" refers to the "topographic assumption" that the client is not conscious that certain features of what she or he is experiencing says as much if not more about her or his self than about what is "out there." By definition, it also assumes that the client is unaware precisely because to be aware causes pain. In other words, the client doesn't entirely want to become aware of what she or he has kept from consciousness. This, then, assumes both the "dynamic" and "economic" points of view—the client wishes to reveal and to conceal.

Kohut's writings have added considerably to our capacity to "recognize" certain phenomena as expressions of transference. He proposes that we approach the client as a self which seeks restoration of equilibrium, cohesiveness, and self-esteem through including another in her or his self as "selfobject," as a part of or extension of the self of the client. To be experienced as a selfobject means to be experienced not as an object, or self, but as a function in the service of the client's self's equilibrium, cohesiveness, and self-esteem. By observing the nature of the relationship, then, the clinician is able to recognize what function or functions she or he is providing for the client that the client is unable to provide on her or his own behalf. In other words, the therapist is able to recognize the "structural deficits" in the self of the client.

By attending to the functions I serve on behalf of the self of the client, I locate the deficits in that self: what was not made a part of her or his self through past relationships, what was not internalized. From that I can infer something about the nature and quality of the selves with whom the client had relationships that failed to afford the opportunity to build a self which included those psychic functions. By understanding the deficits, I am attentive to the "fixation" of the self: this client cannot but engage me in a relationship which conveys her or his level of psychic development—what she or he has been able to internalize, and what she or he has not yet been able to internalize. Thus I understand the repetition in life experience to be a function not only of repetition compulsion, or repetition of patterns of experience and expectation, but as an expression of engaging others from a certain place wherein the self has certain functions and requires certain functions from selfobjects. When the clinician is alert to patterns of engagement and relationship in selfobject transferences that express deficits, the fixation of the self, that clinician is implicitly locating the self of the client in a developmental context. That clinician is judging what was and was not available to be internalized, what level of development the self has attained. In other words, the clinician is formulating a developmental diagnosis or diagnosing developmentally.

For example, a woman who has recently lost an important person is sad, hopeless, despairing. I feel drained through the process of the interview, exhausted by the time it's over. I feel as if my vitality, my lifeblood, has been drawn from my body, as if the energy I had has been taken from me. In some ways I have become aware, usually after the fact, of having to provide something—energy, vitality—which she has in too short supply. As I continue to meet with her, she expresses concerns that this is not the first time she has lost someone dear to her. In remembering past losses she reveals that somehow these were brought about because something was wrong with her. She didn't deserve to be happy. She didn't deserve to enjoy life. She was supposed to suffer. I become aware of the feeling that I "should" contradict her self-accusations; at moments I feel compelled to try to make her feel better. I catch myself extending the time of the initial consultation, as if to provide some attention, even affection. Again, but in a slightly different dimension, I become alert to being required/enlisted to provide something for her that she has in too short supply and cannot provide for herself.

I want to identify how the self's structure includes the clinician, how the intrapsychic processes are interpersonalized, are enacted between client and me. I regard the client's experiences of others, including me, to be an expression of an internal, intrapsychic structure. I go through a process of recasting: when the client says she or he experiences me in such and such a way, I recast this not as a transference or displacement of a figure from the past, although that might be an intermediate step. Rather, I recast this as an experience the client has of her or his self, which the client becomes aware of by experiencing it in and/or with me. In other words, when I take for granted that at some level I am a part of the client's self, I am now acknowledging how the client becomes aware of features of her or his self by first experiencing it in or with an extension of that self.

A central feature of my understanding of the relationship, of the way in which I am a part of the client's self, of the transference, is to attend to my own inner experience. We are now in the realm of *countertransference*, a term that has innumerable meanings and uses. I am restricting its use to what the clinician experiences as being summoned to do or be that departs from her or his baseline; it somehow betrays less about her or his own history, issues, biases, unconscious, than about the history, issues, biases, and unconscious of the client. In other words, by attending to her or his inner experience, her or his countertransference, the clinician is in a position to identify, now indirectly, another dimension of the self of the client, expressed through the transference and identified via the countertransference. Often we can infer the nature of the transference by becoming aware, usually after the fact, of elements of countertransference.

In attending to the transference, to the unique qualities of the relationship which convey unique qualities of the self of the client, I am listening to ways in which the self engages and experiences self and others. In addition, and most significantly, I also presume that there is a fundamental connection among different expressions of self and suffering—across content, affect, process, and relationship. Most especially, I listen to ways in which statements about suffering will be "enacted" in the relationship with me. To use the example, in what ways will the client enact the fear of losing me, and of losing me because she doesn't deserve me or deserve to be happy? In other words, how can we attend to how the client will enact with me some of the central features of her or his self and pain?

It is in this dimension that diagnosis and care is most profound. And, it is this dimension that distinguishes this kind of diagnosing from other more "objective" forms. (In fact, Kohut argues that "*the crucial diagnostic criterion* is to be based not on the evaluation of the presenting symptomatology or even of the life history, but on the nature of the spontaneously developing transference" (Kohut 1971, p. 23, emphasis added).) My concern is to bring into felt-experience and dramatic focus how both of us can understand most fully and deeply who the client is and what she or he is suffering when we can observe its appearance firsthand, in the room, in the relationship. Rather than focusing on some isolated objective entity, or some idea, or something "out there," we are collaborating on identifying what is confirmed and amplified "in here."

Summary Reflections on Pastoral Diagnosis

Some among us function without a critical practice and theory of diagnostic procedures; others live and practice in two parallel universes; others neglect pastoral identity, resources, and traditions; still others practice in a restricted, isolated manner. While there are merits as well as liabilities in several contemporary approaches to pastoral diagnosis, few reflect a vision which integrates pastoral-theological and social and human science resources in an authentic, consistent, and coherent manner, and which recognizes that the practice and theory of diagnosis is integral to and must be consistent with one's overall pastoral clinical care perspective.

I have argued that each of us engages in procedures of pastoral diagnosis, whether or not we do so intentionally, consciously, and critically. As a consequence, it is important to identify and evaluate the procedures we follow. I have proposed that we regard diagnosis as *an ongoing activity of "knowing apart" certain qualities and features of the current state of another's self and suffering.* Because what and how we know apart about the person's current state is inherently related to the goals toward which we will work, as well as the means by which we envision getting there, *diagnosis is at the heart of our overall clinical perspective.*

Because that is the case, I could not limit my discussion of pastoral diagnosis to an analysis of diagnostic variables per se. Such a restricted approach would implicitly, if not explicitly, perpetuate the tendency and dilemma of isolating the practice and theory of diagnosis from the practice and theory of care. In other words, diagnosis must be understood within the context of our overall perspective—as integral to and consistent with that perspective.

In elaborating upon that, I proposed that we regard an overall clinical perspective as an expression of underlying root-metaphors we have of the person and of care and suggested that we incarnate and enact these root-metaphors in a basic "clinical attitude" and operationalize that attitude through our "diagnostic variables." In sum, pastoral diagnosis is an ongoing activity within a clinical perspective that is the expression of "root-metaphors" which are enacted in a "clinical attitude" and operationalized in "diagnostic variables."

I hope that this re-visioning will be helpful in two ways. First, some might make use of the substance of my particular metaphors, attitude, and diagnostic variables. For example, some might reconsider how integral "companioning" and "translating" are to care. Or how a dual focus on self and suffering enhances how the clinician engages those with whom they minister. Or how the questions we ask at the outset of care are relevant to every moment of every meeting with a client. Second, and in a more important sense, I hope that this essay enables readers to reconsider what pastoral diagnosis is about: that it is integral to and must be consistent with one's overall perspective; that behind the diagnostic variables are a clinical attitude and underlying metaphors which inform and guide the relationship and process. Within this structure of re-visioning pastoral diagnosis, some might be encouraged and enabled to identify their own commitments and criteria, particularly underlying metaphors and basic clinical attitude, as well as how and what they know apart.

Notes

1. Many authors, in various contexts, have considered the importance of how we regard and are regarded. Our understandings of ourselves are very much a function of how we have been understood, and related to. Sartre has a well-known discussion of the regard of the other, in which in the experience of being object/objectified we lose our self. By comparison, Kohut has an interesting comment about how the mother (or primary caretaker) relates to the infant as if it were a self, and in and through that imputing and regarding the other as a self the infant experienced-as-a-self experiences itself as a self. Dewey's analysis of the self as in part made up of the other's regard of us is also relevant.

Probably the most well-known analogue to my proposal of holy regard is Rogers' "unconditional positive regard." Both Thomas Oden, in *Kerygma and Counseling*, and Don Browning, in *Atonement and Psychotherapy*, understand unconditional positive regard to be possible, and constructive, because it is an expression of God's love for us. I consider holy regard to be of a different order. I am not referring to love, *per se*, or to a love that is impossible. I am referring to a way of experiencing and relating to another as the Christ in her or him, as if that other were Christ. That means an infinite respect and reverence, a devotion to the well-being of the other, a sense of deep humility of how to care for the other—and most important, a way of experiencing and relating to another that is made possible precisely because of God's holy regard of us, through others. To speak about holy regard, then, keeps in the forefront our appreciation that I and another are mediating a presence greater and other than both of us, that is present in and through both of us.

2. I'm reminded of Soren Kierkegaard's helpful distinction between direct and indirect communication.

3. Please note that functioning as psychologist implicitly involves functioning as psychologist of religion and religious phenomena. As a consequence, the pastoral clinician-as-psychologist may utilize a variety of "psychological" perspectives, including *DSM III-R*, psychoanalytic concepts, structural psychology, or systems theory. The pastoral clinician-as-psychologist-of-religion may make use of Draper 1965; Draper, Myer, Parzen, and Samuelsen 1965; Draper and

Steadman 1984; Fowler 1981; Ivy 1987, 1988; Schneider 1986. Among the many resources the pastoral clinician-as-theologian may use, I suggest Browning 1983; Capps 1980, 1981, 1984; Ellens 1984; Gerkin 1984, 1986a; Hiltner 1943, 1949, 1972, 1976; Patton 1983, 1985; Pruyser 1976a, 1976b, 1984; Wahking 1987; Yeomans 1986.

References

American Psychiatric Association. 1987. *Diagnostic and Statistical Manual of Mental Disorders.* 3d ed. rev. Washington, D.C. Referred to in text as *DSM III-R.*

Asquith, G. H., Jr. 1980. "The Case Study Method of Anton T. Boisen." *The Journal of Pastoral Care* 34: 84–94.

Augsberger, D. W. 1986. *Pastoral Counseling Across Cultures.* Philadelphia: Westminster.

Basch, M. F. 1988a. "How Does Treatment Help? A Developmental Perspective." In *How Does Treatment Help? On the Modes of Therapeutic Action of Psycholanalytic Psychotherapy,* edited by A. Rothstein, pp. 127–33. Madison, Conn.: International Universities Press.

———. 1988b. *Understanding Psychotherapy: The Science Behind the Art.* New York: Basic Books.

Boisen, A. 1936. *Exploration of the Inner World: A Study of Mental Disorders and Religious Experience.* Philadelphia: University of Pennsylvania Press.

Browning, D. 1983. *Religious Ethics and Pastoral Care.* Philadelphia: Fortress Press.

———. 1987a. "Mapping the Terrain of Pastoral Theology." In *Pastoral Psychology* 36: 10–25.

———. 1987b. *Religious Thought and the Modern Psychologies: A Critical Conversation in the Theology of Culture.* Philadelphia: Fortress Press.

Capps, D. 1980. *Pastoral Counseling and Preaching.* Philadelphia: Westminster.

———. 1981. *Biblical Approaches to Pastoral Counseling.* Philadelphia: Westminster.

———. 1984. *Pastoral Care and Hermeneutics.* Philadelphia: Fortress Press.

Carnes, J. 1982. *Axiomatics and Dogmatics.* New York: Oxford University Press.

Cloninger, C. R. 1989. "Establishment of Diagnostic Validity in Psychiatric Illness: Robins and Guze's Method Revisited." In *The*

Validity of Psychiatric Diagnosis, edited by L. N. Robins and J. E. Barrett, pp. 9–18. New York: Raven Press.

Dohrenwend, B. P. 1989. "The Problem of Validity in Field Studies of Psychological Disorders' Revisited." In *The Validity of Psychiatric Diagnosis,* edited by L. N. Robins and J. E. Barrett, pp. 35–55. New York: Raven Press.

Draper, E. 1965. *Psychiatry and Pastoral Care.* Englewood Cliffs, N.J.: Prentice-Hall.

———, Myer, G., Parzen, Z., and Samuelson, G. 1965. "On the Diagnostic Value of Religious Ideation." *Archives of General Psychiatry* 13: 202–7.

———, and Steadman, B. 1984. "Assessment in Pastoral Care." In *Clinical Handbook of Pastoral Counseling,* edited by R. J. Wicks, R. D. Parsons, and D. Capps, pp. 118–31. New York: Paulist Press.

Ellens, J. H. 1987. "Biblical Themes in Psychological Theory and Practice." In *Christian Counseling and Psychotherapy,* edited by David G. Benner, pp. 22–33. Grand Rapids: Baker Book House.

Estadt, B. K., Blanchette, M., and Compton, J. R., eds. 1983. *Pastoral Counseling.* Englewood Cliffs, N.J.: Prentice-Hall.

Fairbanks, R. J. 1952. "Diagnosis in Pastoral Care." *The Journal of Pastoral Care* 6.

Feighner, J. P., and Herbstein, J. 1987. "Diagnostic Validity." In *Issues in Diagnostic Research,* edited by C. G. Last and M. Hersen, pp. 121–40. New York: Plenum Press.

Fowler, J. 1981. *Stages of Faith.* San Francisco: Harper & Row.

Gaskill, H. S. 1984. "The Diagnostic Interview." In *Psychiatry, Ministry, and Pastoral Counseling,* edited by A. W. R. Sipe and C. J. Rowe, pp. 78–102. Collegeville, Minn.: Liturgical Press.

Gerkin, C. 1984. *The Living Human Document: Re-Visioning Pastoral Counseling in a Hermeneutical Mode.* Nashville: Abingdon.

———. 1986a. "Faith and Praxis: Pastoral Counseling's Hermeneutical Problem." *Pastoral Psychology* 35: 3–15.

———. 1986b. *Widening the Horizons: Pastoral Responses to a Fragmented Society.* Philadelphia: Westminster.

Greenson, R. 1960. "Empathy and Its Vicissitudes." *International Journal of Psychoanalysis* 41: 418–24.

Grove, W. M. 1987. "The Reliability of Psychiatric Diagnosis." In *Issues in Diagnostic Research,* edited by C. G. Last and M. Hersen, pp. 99–119. New York: Plenum Press.

Hanson, N. R. 1969. *Perception and Discovery.* San Francisco: Freeman, Cooper and Co.

Hiltner, S. 1943. *Religion and Health.* New York: Macmillan.
———. 1949. *Pastoral Counseling.* Nashville: Abingdon.
———. 1972. *Theological Dynamics.* Nashville: Abingdon.
———. 1976. "Toward Autonomous Diagnosis." In *Diagnosis and the Difference It Makes,* edited by P. Pruyser, pp. 175–94. New York: Jason Aronson, Inc.
Hobson, D. P., and Jacob, M. 1985. "Possibilities and Pitfalls of Pastoral Diagnosis." *Pastoral Psychology* 34: 30–41.
Holland, N. 1975. *Five Readers Reading.* New Haven: Yale University Press.
———. 1985. *The i.* New Haven: Yale University Press.
Holmer, P. 1978. *The Grammar of Faith.* New York: Harper & Row.
Ivy, S. S. 1987. "A Model for Pastoral Assessment." *The Journal of Pastoral Care* 41: 329–40.
———. 1988. "Pastoral Diagnosis as Pastoral Caring." *The Journal of Pastoral Care* 42: 81–89.
Jordan, M. R. 1986. *Taking on the Gods: The Task of the Pastoral Counselor.* Nashville: Abingdon.
Kleinman, A. 1988. *The Illness Narratives.* New York: Basic Books.
Kohut, H. 1959/1978. "Introspection, Empathy, and Psychoanalysis: An Exploration of the Relationship Between Mode of Observation and Theory." In *The Search for the Self,* edited by P. Ornstein, vol. 1, chap. 12. New York: International Universities Press.
———. 1971. *The Analysis of the Self.* New York: International Universities Press.
———. 1984. *How Does Analysis Cure?* Chicago: University of Chicago Press.
———. 1987. "Extending Empathic Understanding, Sharing an Attitude." In *The Kohut Seminars on Self Psychology and Psychotherapy with Adolescents and Young Adults,* edited by M. Elson. New York: W. W. Norton.
Lakoff, G., and Johnson, M. 1980. *Metaphors We Live By.* Chicago: University of Chicago Press.
Lazare, A. 1979. "Hypothesis Testing in the Clinical Interview." In *Outpatient Psychiatry: Diagnosis and Treatment,* edited by A. Lazare, pp. 131–40. Baltimore: Williams and Wilkins.
McFague, S. 1982. *Metaphorical Theology: Models of God in Religious Language.* Philadelphia: Fortress Press.
Marcel, G. 1950. *The Mystery of Being: I. Reflection and Mystery.* Trans. G. S. Fraser. London. Harvill Press, Ltd.

Mehrabian, A. 1968. *An Analysis of Personality Theories*, Englewood Cliffs, N.J.: Prentice-Hall.

Menninger, K., Mayman, M., and Pruyser, P. 1963. *The Vital Balance: The Life Process in Mental Health and Illness.* New York: Penguin Books.

Millon, T. 1987. "On The Nature of Taxonomy in Psychopathology." In *Issues in Diagnostic Research*, edited by C. G. Last and M. Hersen, pp. 3–86. New York: Plenum Press.

Mitchell, K. 1987. "The Book That Has Most Influenced My Practice of Pastoral Psychotherapy." *The Journal of Pastoral Psychotherapy* 1: 77–82.

Muehl, W. 1990. "Opinion: A Statement of Communication." *Reflections* (Yale Divinity School), pp. 26–27.

Muslin, H., and Val, E. 1987. *The Psychotherapy of the Self.* New York: Brunner/Mazel.

Nathan, P. 1967. *Cues, Decisions, and Diagnoses: A Systems-Analytic Approach to the Diagnosis of Psychopathology.* New York: Academic Press.

Nouwen, H. J. M. Unpublished manuscript. *Ronald: A Study in Pastoral Diagnosis.*

Oden, T. 1966. *Kerygma and Counseling.* Philadelphia: Fortress Press.

Othmer, E., and Othmer, S. C. 1989. *The Clinical Interview Using DSM-IIIR.* Washington, D.C.: American Psychiatric Press, Inc.

Patton, J. 1983. *Pastoral Counseling: A Ministry of the Church.* Nashville: Abingdon.

———. 1985. "The New Language of Pastoral Counseling." In *Spiritual Dimensions of Pastoral Care: Witness to the Ministry of Wayne E. Oates*, edited by G. L. Borchert and A. D. Lester, pp. 72–89. Philadelphia: Westminster.

Pruyser, P. W., ed. 1976a. *Diagnosis and the Difference It Makes.* New York: Jason Aronson, Inc.

———. 1976b. *The Minister as Diagnostician.* Philadelphia: Westminster.

———. 1979. *The Psychological Examination: A Guide for Clinicians.* New York: International Universities Press.

———. 1984. "The Diagnostic Process in Pastoral Care." In *Psychiatry, Ministry, and Pastoral Counseling*, edited by A. W. R. Sipe and C. J. Rowe, pp. 103–16. Collegeville, Minn.: Liturgical Press.

Rice, L. N., and Greenberg, L. S., eds. 1984. *Patterns of Change:*

Intensive Analysis of Psychotherapy Process. New York: Guilford Press.

Ricoeur, P. 1970. *Freud and Philosophy.* New Haven: Yale University Press.

Robins, E., and Guze, S. B. 1989. "Establishment of Diagnostic Validity in Psychiatric Illness: Its Application to Schizophrenia." In *The Validity of Psychiatric Diagnosis,* edited by L. N. Robins and J. E. Barrett, pp. 1–7. New York: Raven Press.

Roth, S. 1987. *Psychotherapy: The Art of Wooing Nature.* Northvale, N.J.: Jason Aronson, Inc.

Schafer, R. 1981. "Narration in the Psychoanalytic Dialogue." In *On Narrative,* edited by W. J. T. Mitchell. Chicago: University of Chicago Press.

———. 1983. *The Analytic Attitude.* New York: Basic Books.

Schlauch, C. R. 1985. "Defining Pastoral Psychotherapy." *The Journal of Pastoral Care* 39: 219–28.

———. 1987. "Defining Pastoral Psychotherapy II." *The Journal of Pastoral Care* 41: 319–27.

———. 1990a. "Empathy as the Essence of Pastoral Psychotherapy." *The Journal of Pastoral Care* 44: 3–17.

———. 1990b. "Expanding the Contexts of Pastoral Care." *The Journal of Pastoral Care* 44: 359–71.

Schneider, C. D. 1986. "Faith Development and Pastoral Diagnosis." *Faith Development and Fowler,* edited by C. Dykstra and S. Parks, pp. 221–50. Birmingham: Religious Education Press.

Seligman, L. 1986. *Diagnosis and Treatment Planning in Counseling.* New York: Human Sciences Press.

Shapiro, D. 1989. *Psychotherapy of Neurotic Character.* New York: Basic Books.

Spence, D. 1982. *Narrative Truth and Historical Truth: Meaning and Interpretation in Psychoanalysis.* New York: W. W. Norton.

Stern, D. 1985. *The Interpersonal World of the Human Infant.* New York: Basic Books.

Tilley, T. 1985. *Story Theology.* Wilmington, Del.: Michael Glazier.

Tillich, P. 1939. "The Conception of Man in Existential Philosophy." *Journal of Religion* 19: 201–15.

Underwood, R. L. 1982. "Personal and Professional Integrity in Relation to Pastoral Assessment." *Pastoral Psychology* 31: 109–17.

Wahking, H. 1987. "Therapy with Theological Constructs and Tactics." In *Christian Counseling and Psychotherapy,* edited by D. G. Benner, pp. 15–22. Grand Rapids: Baker Book House.

Wolman, B. 1978. "Classification and Diagnosis of Mental Dis-

orders." In *Clinical Diagnosis of Mental Disorders: A Handbook,* edited by B. Wolman, pp. 15–46. New York: Plenum Press.
Yeomans, M., ed. 1986. *Clinical Theology.* London: Darton, Longman, and Todd.

For Further Reading

Basch, M. F. 1980. *Doing Psychotherapy.* New York: Basic Books.
———. 1983. "Empathic Understanding: A Review of the Concepts and Some Theoretical Considerations." *Journal of American Psychoanalytic Association* 31: 101–26.
Belenky, M., Clinchy, B., Goldberger, N., and Tarule, J. 1986. *Women's Ways of Knowing.* New York: Basic Books.
Bollinger, R. A. 1985. "Differences Between Pastoral Counseling and Psychotherapy." *Bulletin of the Menninger Clinic* 49: 371–86.
Browning, D. S. 1966. *Atonement and Psychotherapy.* Philadelphia: Fortress Press.
Cone, K. 1984. "Sociology of Knowledge and Pastoral Psychotherapy." In *Religion and the Sociology of Knowledge: Modernization and Pluralism in Christian Thought and Structure,* edited by B. Hargrove, pp. 301–31. New York: The Edwin Mellen Press.
Elbow, P. 1973. *Writing Without Teachers.* London: Oxford University Press.
Schafer, R. 1976. *A New Language for Psychoanalysis.* New Haven: Yale University Press.
Spence, D. 1976. "Clinical Interpretation: Some Comments on the Nature of the Evidence." *Psychoanalysis and Contemporary Science* 5: 367–88.
Wolf, E. S. 1988. *Treating the Self: Elements of Clinical Self Psychology.* New York: Guilford Press.

Edward P. Shafranske

4. The Contributions of Short-Term Dynamic Psychotherapy to Pastoral Psychotherapy

Pastoral counseling draws upon its roots in pastoral care, practical theology, and the behavioral sciences in its daily practice. Developments in each of these disciplines inform, shape, and define its unique provision of pastoral care. Advances within the behavioral sciences are particularly relevant for contemporary pastoral counseling as the profession endeavors to respond to increasing numbers of individuals for whom psychological and emotional difficulties play a constituent role in their appeal for guidance.

Within the behavioral sciences considerable attention has been paid to understanding and evaluating the process and effectiveness of psychotherapy (Garfield and Bergin 1986; Luborsky, et al. 1988; Strupp 1980; Weiss and Sampson 1984). Within the context of such investigation, models of psychotherapy have been recently developed which emphasize focal, short-term, and time-limited approaches to the treatment of psychiatric disorders (Davanloo 1978, 1979, 1980, 1986a, 1986b; Horowitz 1984; Luborsky 1984; Malan 1976, 1979; Mann 1973; Sifneos 1972, 1987; Strupp and Binder 1985; Winston 1985; Wolberg 1965). An emerging research literature suggests that significant resolution of psychological conflict can be attained through such approaches (Davanloo 1986–1991; Mandel 1981). This chapter presents an introduction to the processes and procedures which constitute a focal, short-term, psychodynamically oriented approach to psychotherapy. This exposition will not present a particular system of short-term or time-limited treatment. Neither is it presumed that through such an introduction one would be enabled to practice such an approach. Rather, it aims at discussing certain clinical issues which have particular relevance for pastoral psychotherapy. Further, it is suggested that the insights derived from the short-term treatment approaches may contribute to the practice of pastoral psychotherapy, which amplifies its distinctive identity as pastoral.

An Introduction

Short-term and time-limited[1] approaches to treatment have their origins in the clinical observation that many clients derive significant benefits from brief experiences of psychotherapy. Alexander and French (1946), building on the insights of Ferenczi and Rank, were the first to systematically examine the assumptions inherent in long-term, open-ended psychoanalytic treatment and to offer an alternative psychodynamic model. Emphasizing the role of the "corrective emotional experience," they advocated an active role for the therapist in conducting brief, focal psychotherapy. Although criticized during its day, this seminal work set the stage for not only an appreciation for shorter forms of treatment but, more important, for the investigation of specific aspects of the clinical process which promote personality and behavioral change.

The works of Balint (1957; Balint et al. 1972) and Malan (1963, 1979) marked the commencement of the contemporary study of focal psychotherapy. Balint demonstrated the efficacy of establishing a therapeutic focus and elucidated the role of the activity of the therapist in providing counteroffers to the client's projections. In his treatment approach Balint stressed the dynamic interaction of the client and the therapist and the function of the therapist's activity in the reactivation and resolution of psychological conflicts. Further, through his workshops Balint encouraged the systematic investigation of the clinical case process which has become the hallmark for research in short-term and time-limited psychotherapies. Malan further established the utility of applying the psychoanalytic paradigm within short-term treatment. Through the active interventions of the therapist the patient is put "in touch with as much of his true feelings as he can bear," which brings out the core psychological conflicts (Malan 1979, p. 74). Through the emergence of genetic and transference material the client accomplishes insight into his or her current difficulties and works through the neurotic compromise. In keeping with psychoanalytic principles, Malan stresses the analysis of defenses and the transference in leading to a successful treatment outcome. His innovation is found in his emphasis on activity rather than passivity as a counteroffer to the patient's resistance.

In keeping with the contributions of Balint and Malan, a number of prominent analysts, for example, Davanloo, Horowitz, Mann, Sifneos, and Strupp, have developed systems of short-term or time-limited psychotherapy. Each uniquely emphasizes the importance of establishing a focus for the psychotherapeutic inquiry and proposes techniques which the therapist enlists in confronting and interpreting the client's conflictual compromises. An explication of each model is beyond the scope of this chapter. Our discussion will address the heart of these approaches, which involve the establishment and working through of a focal theme, the dynamic use of the structure of treatment and the therapeutic relationship, and those specific interventions which have been demonstrated to contribute to therapeutic efficacy.

As an introduction to our discussion of specific techniques it is timely to note that short-term approaches to psychotherapy are not merely truncated or briefer forms of psychoanalysis or psychoanalytic psychotherapy. These approaches are unique in their specificity of technique and process. Freud (1913, p. 123) used the metaphor of chess in describing the procedures guiding the practice of psychoanalysis. He suggested that there are rules for defining the opening and closing phases of this interaction, but few rules and myriad possibilities in between. The contributions of the short-term psychotherapies are particularly relevant as they provide important direction to all phases of the treatment process. It is to these approaches, techniques, and therapeutic rules or recommendations that we now turn.

Establishing the Therapeutic Focus

The establishment of the therapeutic focus is of paramount importance in short-term psychotherapy. The selection of a central theme or focus is crucial in that all interventions are aimed at the elucidation and working through of this identified focal conflict. This is particularly the case in certain short-term psychotherapy orientations in which deviations from the identified focus are systematically confronted as resistance or in time-limited treatments in which the termination date rapidly approaches.

An appropriate therapeutic focus is one which embodies the patient's privately felt, rarely verbalized, present and chronically endured pain and psychodynamic conflict (cf. Mann and Goldman 1982, p. 21). Mann and Goldman's (1982, p. 23) definition articulates the understanding of the therapeutic focus common to psychodynamic practitioners working within short-term models:

> The statement of the central issue in terms of the present and chronically endured pain reverberates from the deepest levels of the unconscious, through the layers of ego defenses, and in the patient's conscious experience of himself in the present. It spans the patient's experience of time from remote past to the immediate present to the expectable future. It speaks with exquisite poignancy with which each person privately experiences his being.

The focal conflict is the present expression or derivative of an inveterate experience of the self or in Davanloo's (1986b, p. 239) words, "the core neurotic structure." The problem that will be addressed in treatment is not necessarily the presenting problem. Rather, it is the life problem of which the client has a degree of conscious or seemingly preconscious awareness or which is clearly manifested in the client's futile attempts at resolution. The focus that is selected is also one in which the client can be reasonably expected to achieve a degree of mastery within the parameters of short-term psychotherapy. Through a detailed history-taking and through a careful reading of the content and process data exhibited within the initial clinical interactions a therapeutic focus is established.

Attention should be paid to the relationships between the client's affective tone, symptoms, presenting problem, and life history. The contiguity between the expression of content and affect together with any physical signs of tension may provide important indices of the client's present and enduring psychical pain and neurotic structure. Redundancy of particular themes or recurring configurations of particular object relations and need states offer significant input toward the identification of the focal conflict. Davanloo (1978, 1979, 1980, 1986a, 1986b) pays particular attention to consistent themes across past self-parent, self-other, and self-therapist relations. Horowitz (1984) points to shifts in "states of mind" as clinically relevant. For example, that a patient's affective tone demonstrates a shift from confident to anxious while mentioning a past relationship suggests the presence of psychological conflict. Themes embedded with the aforementioned clinical observations are culled together within the organizing context of psychoanalytic theory. These themes typically express the universal conflicts surrounding Oedipal attachment and competition, object loss and narcissistic injury, separation and individuation anxieties, and identity conflicts.

Within the context of pastoral psychotherapy the hermeneutical context expands beyond psychoanalytic conceptions to include consideration of ontological, teleological, and religious-spiritual meanings of the client's present and chronically enduring pain. It is the pastoral psychotherapist's charge to identify the religious complement as to the psychodynamic underpinning of the client's malaise. It is through such an undertaking that pastoral psychotherapy affirms its distinctive identity. Power (1990), in a recent article, provides a framework through which ontological themes might be discerned in identifying "limit questions" within the client's presenting problem and clinical material. Drawing on Toulmin's work on ethics, Power's essay suggests that limit questions embody the concerns addressed within pastoral counseling. In this view, limit questions exist at the limit of moral reasoning and the apprehension of the nature of the vicissitudes and finitudes that are expressed throughout human experience. Power (1990, p. 85) concludes that:

> Because pastoral counseling focuses on limit questions and experiences, its proper domain will overlap with nonpastoral counseling. Limit questions and experiences both begin and end in the finite, everyday world. They arise when the ground of everyday confidence, meaning and worth is called into question or revealed; and they are resolved with a reassurance of that everyday confidence, meaning, and worth. Like any kind of counseling, pastoral counseling is meant to help individuals to work through crises. Yet pastoral counseling, must focus on the ultimate questions that life crises raise. Pastoral counseling, in the strict sense, goes beyond concern for mental health to a concern for the Kingdom of God.

The challenge of short-term pastoral psychotherapy includes, therefore, the identification of a therapeutic focus which, although wedded to psychodynamics, constitutes a limit experience. It is suggested that the aforementioned themes involving eros, competition, loss, autonomy, and identity are significant human dilemmas, which at their ontological heart pose limit experiences. The distinctive potential of pastoral psychotherapy is revealed in the apprehension of human suffering within the contexts of a science of psychodynamics, the disciplines of theology and biblical studies, and the traditions and revelatory experiences of the client's faith community.

The identification of the therapeutic focus constitutes the close of the evaluative phase in short-term psychotherapy and marks the commencement of the explorative process, which fosters insight and contributes to the working through of the conflict. Davanloo (1979, 1986a, 1986b) and Malan (1976) among others utilize the therapeutic focus implicitly, drawing upon confrontations, clarifications, and interpretations in assisting clients to become more fully aware of their personal psychodynamics and intrapsychic conflict. Sifneos (1987) and Mann (1973, 1981), on the other hand, explicitly offer the therapeutic focus to the client for consideration and elicit agreement that this will constitute the central theme for the therapeutic work. Sifneos (1987, p. 65) suggests that "the therapeutic contract serves the purpose of making the patient take an active responsibility in the development of his psychotherapeutic work and sharing the difficulty encountered as an *equal* partner, not as one dependent on the evaluator." The establishment of a focus, whether expressed explicitly in a therapeutic contract or implicitly through the therapist's selection of interventions, is essential to the practice of short-term psychotherapy.

Determining the Appropriateness of the Client for Short-Term Psychotherapy

In consort with the identification of a therapeutic focus, the initial contact with the client concerns the evaluation of the appropriateness of the client for short-term psychotherapy. To a significant extent the ability of the client to work collaboratively with the therapist to arrive at a therapeutic focus will provide important information upon which to select the most efficacious treatment approach. The process and the extent to which a nascent therapeutic relationship is established, as well as the content of the therapeutic focus and diagnostic impression, contribute to the assessment of the client's abilities to benefit from short-term psychotherapy.

There is general consensus regarding the characteristics of clients who are most appropriate for briefer and more confrontive forms of psychotherapy. They consist of the qualities which correlate with successful outcome for all forms of treatment and might be characterized as indicating ego strength, psychological mindedness, and a high level of adaptational functioning and personal motivation (Koss and Butcher 1986). There is less agreement regarding the extent to which a client must possess these psychological assets to benefit from short-term psychotherapy. Davanloo (1979, p. 15), drawing on twenty years of systematic research, concluded "that those criteria which are based on severity and duration are basically of no value. . . . Many patients suffering from long-standing psychoneurotic disorders with severe psychopathology . . . have obtained deep-seated dynamic changes." Others, including Sifneos (1987, p. 51), suggest that clients possessing relatively high ego strength and presenting difficulties involving primarily "unresolved Oedipal conflicts, grief reactions, and certain problems relating to loss and separation issues are the foci which, when they are resolved, give rise to the best therapeutic results." Clients present on a continuum of strengths, adaptational resources, and limitations in ego functioning. There are few contraindications that are absolute, and those are clearly suggestive of significant ego deficits and underlying psychotic processes or vulnerabilities.

The assessment of clients for short-term psychotherapy consists, therefore, of a multidimensional understanding of the client which includes diagnostic, psychodynamic, and therapeutic process features. A consideration of the following variables has been found to be relevant in assessing the suitability of the client for short-term dynamic psychotherapy.

Establishment of a Therapeutic Focus

The extent to which a client is able to work with the therapist to establish a therapeutic focus is indicative of certain psychological attributes which are essential for effective short-term psychotherapy. In selecting a circumscribed conflict, the client demonstrates the ability to manage anxiety and to tolerate with limited regression the demands psychotherapy will exact. The selection of a focus suggests the properties of an observing ego function through which the client can utilize interpretations and develop insight. Clients who cannot arrive at such a focus often experience their world and their suffering in a diffuse manner, cannot contain anxiety, and are susceptable to debilitating regressions. In some clients this is suggestive of severe impairments in object relations and a precarious psychological structure. Therefore, the ability to limit the therapeutic work to a single focus demonstrates ego strength and is suggestive that the client possesses the psychological resources required to benefit from a short-term psychotherapy approach. Further, the accomplishment of a therapeutic focus indicates the ability to work collaboratively with the therapist and bodes well for the creation of a therapeutic alliance (Greenson 1965) upon which treatment is based.

Psychological Mindedness

Psychological mindedness refers to the ability to examine the intrapsychic conflict underlying the symptom or the discordant interpersonal situation the client brings to treatment. Such an ability is not simply based on intelligence but also involves some measure of flexibility in the use of defenses. This involves suspending the operation of defenses; for example, allowing affect to emerge rather than employing intellectualization, or sitting with a painful insight rather than using a display of emotionality to cloud awareness. In keeping with the concept of an observing ego function, clients must be able to develop insight into their personal, psychological contributions to their presenting problems. This involves being able to tolerate conflicting states of mind, the emergence of repressed mental contents, awareness of their contributions to their difficulties, and the range of meanings associated to the focal problem. Psychological mindedness refers, therefore, to both intellectual and personality factors that set parameters on the client's ability to explore the psychodynamics which underlie his or her difficulties. Cognitive and affective inflexibility and reliance upon denial and projection as primary defenses pose significant challenges to the psychotherapeutic process. Clients who are unable or unwilling to look at all into possible psychological constituents of their difficulties are not well suited for short-term psychotherapy.

Motivation for Change

Not surprisingly, clients who are highly motivated for change are the most suitable for short-term psychotherapy; in fact, it may be the treatment of choice. It may be said that all clients who present for psychotherapy evidence motivation. We know as clinicians, however, that there is a wide range of motivation despite each client's verbalized desire for change in his or her life situation. The point might be best made in terms of *where* clients expect the change to take place.

Highly motivated, psychologically sophisticated clients anticipate that the change in their lives will predominantly come from a change in themselves. They have a knowing awareness of the nature of resistance and possess the psychological resources to embark on a path to inner and external change. Poorly motivated clients, on the other hand, possess many of the limitations described in the discussion on psychological mindedness. They expect benefits to come solely from changes outside of themselves; they expect and demand that their therapists provide the changes for them or in their world. They abdicate responsibility for the situation they are in, have low tolerance for conflicted states of mind, and possess limited self-awareness. These clients may, however, experience progress in short-term psychotherapy. Davanloo (1986a, 1986b), for one, suggests that a confrontational, short-term psychotherapy approach may be the most likely to achieve therapeutic results in such highly resistant persons. To commence such treatment, a therapist must be well trained and personally prepared to confront actively the client's stronghold of defenses through which resistance is maintained. Most clients fall somewhere between the highly motivated and the poorly motivated. They struggle with the paradox that, although they are dissatisfied with the ways in which they are living, these ways are in fact functional. Their compromise formations serve to some extent both the expression of needs and their desires for safety. They simultaneously desire change and want things to remain the same; such is the nature of the resistance which psychotherapy is aimed to challenge.

Sifneos (1978, 1987) reported that variables related to motivation to change correlated significantly with successful treatment outcome. The following factors were found to be clinically useful in assessing the client's motivation: (1) willingness to participate in the psychiatric evaluation; (2) honesty in reporting about himself or herself; (3) ability to recognize that the symptoms are psychological in origin; (4) introspection and curiosity; (5) openness to new ideas; (6) realistic expectations of the results of treatment; and (7) willingness to make a reasonable sacrifice. A reading of these variables contributes to the determination of the appropriate treatment approach.

History of Meaningful, Reciprocal Relationships

Short-term psychotherapy requires that a therapeutic alliance be formed at the outset of the treatment process. The work is collaborative as the client and therapist determine the therapeutic focus, actively confront resistances, and uncover and work through the psychodynamics underlying the person's difficulties. Although the focus of treatment may concern the client's conflicts in relationships, short-term psychotherapy is not well suited to treat individuals for whom deficits in their ability to relate to others constitute their life circumstance. Persons suffering from such ego and object relations deficits, particularly those diagnostically within the borderline spectrum, are generally not suited for a short-term psychotherapy approach, which assumes the ability to develop a reciprocal interpersonal relationship.

The level of object relatedness can usually be gleaned through a careful taking of history, by the nature and presentation of interpersonal relations and difficulties, and by paying attention to the dynamics within the therapeutic relationship. Clients who present histories of unstable and intense interpersonal relationships, marked shifts in affective response to the therapist and to others, confusion in self-identity and object representations are generally considered to be inappropriate candidates for this approach to treatment. The treatment that they require is of longer duration and will focus on the vicissitudes of forming a stable interpersonal relationship with the therapist. Short-term treatment assumes that such an ability exists; it is the prerequisite upon which a stable therapeutic alliance will be formed. Persons presenting a history of current and past meaningful, reciprocal relationships are best suited for short-term psychotherapy.

Ability to Utilize a Confrontational-Interpretive Process

Short-term psychotherapy involves the capacity of the client to "allow for rapid affective involvement" in the therapeutic process (Mann and Goldman 1982, p. 56). The ability to utilize this treatment process is based on the client's capacity to respond affectively to the confrontations and interpretations of the therapist. The client must be able, as well, to contain the impulses and affective reactions to the therapist and to tolerate the de-repression of conflictual material. Patients who present histories of psychotic episodes, poor impulse control, tendencies for marked regression and decompensation, paranoia, and significant suicidal and homocidal potential are poor candidates for a time-limited, confrontational-interpretive process.

The assessment involves, in addition to the aspects previously discussed, a reading of the client's responsiveness to confrontations of resistance and interpretations during the initial interview. Advocating the use of a trial therapy as one component in evaluation, Davanloo (1980, p. 99) concluded that "no one can really tell anything about the patient's likely response without exposing him to some of the important ingredients of the therapy that he [or she] will receive. Therefore a specific kind of psychotherapeutic session—amounting in fact to trial therapy—is an essential part of the evaluation process." Although each system of short-term psychotherapy initiates the treatment process differently, each considers the client's responses to the therapist's early interventions to be salient in evaluating the appropriateness of the treatment for the client. Important information can be garnered through testing the limits of the individual's capacity for confronting resistance and gaining insight through interpretations. A measure of the flexibility of cognition and defenses may be obtained through the offering of confrontations and interpretations within the evaluation interview.

These assessment procedures are performed to ensure that clients will be presented with a treatment regimen aimed not only at the resolution of the presenting problem but, more important, tailored to the psychological resources they have at their disposal. Through a consideration of the client's history and a reading of the dynamics within the initial session the therapist determines the appropriateness of short-term psychotherapy for the client. Such an evaluation takes into account, as well, a consideration of the therapist's clinical acumen and personal qualities, which will necessarily contribute to the treatment outcome.

In the event that such an approach is assessed not to be suited to the client, care should be given to the manner in which open-ended psychotherapy or a referral is offered. Malan (in Davanloo 1980, p. 187) reminds practitioners "to take care of the consequences of the interview for the patient, and especially to avoid leaving him or her with a mass of unresolved feelings." We will now turn to a discussion of the techniques of short-term dynamic psychotherapy.

The Process of Short-Term Psychotherapy

The essential feature of short-term psychotherapy is the application of techniques to focus unrelenting attention on the therapeutic issue. Through the strategic use of time and through the interventions of confrontation, clarification, and interpretation, pressure is placed upon the client in such a way as to mobilize and to overcome resistance. Following the de-repression of hidden affects, impulses, and cognitions, clients develop insight into the underlying psychodynamics of their present and chronically endured pain. The origin of the focal theme in childhood is explored with an eye toward its appearance with present relationships and within the interactions with the therapist. Through such a process clients come to understand their core neurotic structure, the inadequacy of previous compromise formations, and the repetitions of unresolved conflict in present life. Through treatment an individual has the opportunity to modify his or her defensive structure and is encouraged to seek more appropriate and effective expressions of thought, impulse, and affect. These aspects are recognized as cardinal features of psychoanalytic treatment with one exception: the activity of the therapist to focus unrelenting attention to the therapeutic issue.

The crucial distinction is found in the high degree of activity employed by the therapist when faced with the client's resistance. Malan (in Davanloo 1980, p. 13) "stated categorically that in the early part of this century Freud unwittingly took a wrong turning which led to disastrous consequences for the future of psychotherapy. This was to react to increasing resistance with increased passivity." Short-term psychotherapy is designed to respond to resistance with *increased* activity. We will now examine the structure and techniques which constitute its response to the client's difficulties and encumbering resistances.

The Function of Time

The first challenge to the client's resistance is found in the function of time within the structure of the treatment. This function is dramatically applied in time-limited approaches, in which the client is presented at the beginning of treatment with a termination date. This setting of a precise, predetermined ending stimulates the working alliance and assists the therapist in maintaining attention on the therapeutic focus. It forestalls the regressive pull of open-ended psychoanalytic treatment and short-circuits infantile expectations and dependence on the therapist (cf. Mann and Goldman 1982, pp. 43–44). The time limit contributes pressure throughout the exploration of the focal theme.

Mann (1973, 1981, Mann and Goldman 1982) suggests that time itself becomes the focal issue as the termination date approaches. By the reality of impending termination the client is faced, again, with the crucible of separation and loss. Whatever the content of the unexpressed dependency needs or latent desires to find a way to recreate the past, the termination date will not allow enough time for this wished-for aim. "In this highly affective setting, it becomes the therapist's task to help the patient to see clearly the transference nature of these inappropriate responses: *that which once was no longer is*" (Mann 1981, p. 41). Through this work the client may find resolution to the images of the self which have their origin in the past and which serve, in part, to preserve the wish for a change of the past. The confrontation of present and future time experienced within the therapeutic relationship offers the client an opportunity to ascribe new meanings and possibilities to the self.

In other short-term treatments a specific termination date may not be explicitly set; however, the function of time is expressed in the implicit knowledge that therapy is intended to be brief. The therapist, being aware of the function of time, may be more apt to apply pressure and to resist the regressive demands of the client. Further, the pressure of time may prompt the therapist to be more mindful of the mutual collusion that staying within the safe harbor of resistance offers to both. The function of time, seen psychodynamically, illustrates the contention that short-term treatment is not merely an abbreviated form of long-term psychotherapy. It is a unique form of intervention in which time plays a crucial clinical role.

Maintaining the Focus

In this work an emphasis is placed on maintaining attention on the focal issue. Whatever the client discloses is understood within the context of the client's present and enduring pain. The goal is to foster insight and work through past and present conflict through the derepression of memories and through the expression of associated affects and impulses. The full explication of the conflict is achieved through the linking of past, present, and transferential expressions of the theme as presented in Figure 1. Difficulties which arise in the client's relationship—for example, with her husband—are related to conflicted relations with her mother. Dynamics within the therapeutic relationship are linked, as well, to past conflicts and to difficulties in relationships outside of treatment. The continual shifting of emphasis from one relational context to another demonstrates to the client the pervasive influence of the focal conflict or, as Luborsky (1984) puts it, the "core conflictual relationship theme." This leads to increased insight and to a further experiencing of the hidden affective response to the psychological pain embedded in the focal conflict.

This enterprise is not aimed at obtaining an intellectual grasp of the pervasive influence of the past on the present. Rather, its aim is the full expression of the hidden feelings and impulses which maintain the neurotic compromise. Through maintaining attention on the therapeutic focus the client is encouraged to disclose fully the history and meaning of his or her present and enduring conflict and pain toward the aim of abreaction and mastery.

Within the unique setting of pastoral psychotherapy, the expression of the focal conflict is explored as well within the client's relationship with God. It is particularly relevant to address the client's total response, including the intellectual, emotional, impulse, and faith aspects, to the limit experiences within the focal conflict. In

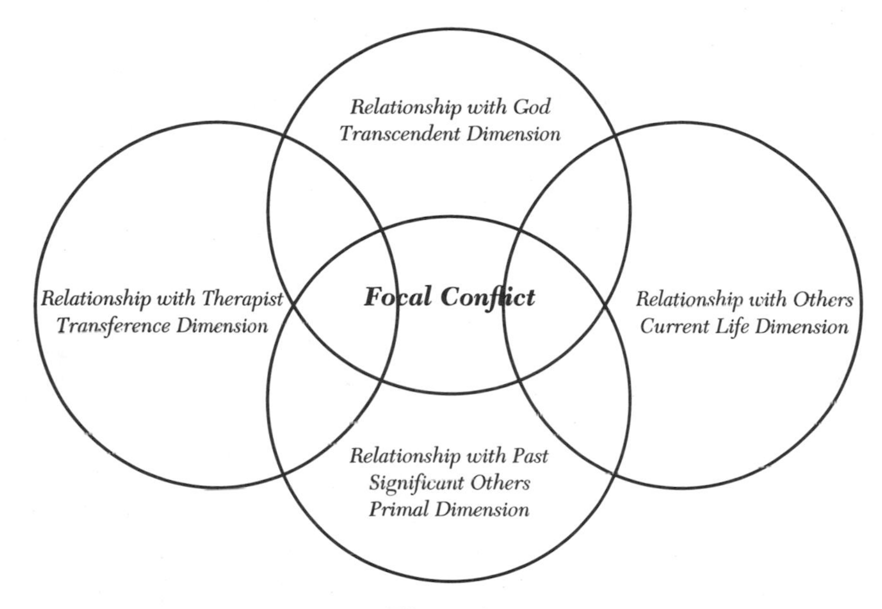

Figure 1.
Spheres of Relationship

addition, an analysis of the client's image of God respective of past significant others and present life difficulties is useful. Within this context, incongruencies between the client's experience of God and his or her theology or beliefs about God may be explored. Spero (1990) and others (Jones 1991; Shafranske 1987, 1988, 1991 in press) have suggested that within psychotherapy believing and non-believing clients may have the opportunity to locate their belief orientation within the context of their life experience and may come to a deeper and, at times, modified integration of their personal theology in their daily lives. This may be particularly the case in pastoral psychotherapy, which explicitly draws attention to the limit experiences which convey the religious and ontological dimensions of human existence. As is often noted in grave circumstances of loss, for example, the death of a child, an individual may experience a profound shattering in other relationships and a questioning of religious beliefs and his or her relationship with God. Through pastoral psychotherapy all aspects within the spheres of relationship may be addressed in treatment.

The use of detail has been found to be effective in the uncovering of memories and in encouraging the expression of associated emotions. The client is prompted to describe past and present events in as much detail as possible. The therapist may repeat the client's recollections in "experience-near" detail and set the tone for an active, lucid recovery of the past event. Through this process of repetition and challenge for detail, the client's resistance may dissolve and the hidden feelings and impulses may be enjoined to the memories promoting abreaction and leading to the working through of the conflict and the negative experience of self.

Dealing with Resistance

Inevitably resistance is encountered as the therapist maintains attention on the exploration of the focal conflict. Defenses come into play as the client attempts to forestall the uncovering of the conflicted, affectively charged, impulse-laden memories in which the negative self-image was established. Each treatment approach differs in the priority it assigns to the analysis of defenses and the strategic use of this analysis in the abreaction of the core neurotic conflict. Sifneos (1987) and Luborsky (1984), for example, recommend sidestepping defenses at times and advocate continuing to focus on the affects and impulses within the focal conflict. To illustrate, if a client were speaking about his anger toward his boss and then shifted to a new subject, the client would be directed back to his discussion about his supervisor. The defensive operation would have been observed by the therapist but not necessarily interpreted.

An alternative approach is offered by Davanloo (1986a, 1986b; see also, Davis 1987a, 1987b; Malan 1986). Resistance is viewed as the opportunity through which access into the core neurotic structure will be accomplished. In the first interview the therapist pressures the client toward the experience of the feelings associated with the focal conflict. As the client resists feeling the affective concomitants of his or her problem, the therapist challenges the resistance. Through a systematic and relentless challenge of the defenses, an intensification of transference ensues and a "head-on collision" between the client and therapist occurs. The forces of repression and expression come into immediate conflict within the actual and transferential relationship of the client and therapist. Through the exhaustion of the defenses the resistance is broken and the client and therapist have unmediated access to the complex transferential feelings and the conflicted material underlying the therapeutic focus. Through this de-repression the client is enabled to experience the affect and impulse components, as well as to gain insight into the historical and psychodynamic rudiments of his or her problem (cf. Davanloo 1985).

In conjunction with an understanding of the relational contexts in which the focal conflict appears, a simultaneous analysis of the defenses is undertaken. The client is shown through confrontations and interpretations the means by which defenses are engaged to contain anxiety and to maintain a repression of the hidden affects and impulses. The therapeutic work is accomplished through an analysis of two interrelated aspects of the focal conflict: the repetition of the conflict in multiple settings, and the defensive structure which preserves repression. A comprehensive presentation of Davanloo's approach is beyond the scope of this chapter. Suffice it to summarize that there are two general approaches that can be taken to resistance within short-term psychotherapy. One involves a relative de-emphasis on the analysis of defenses and recommends maintaining focus on the central issue. The second approach considers the analysis of defense to be essential to the therapeutic enterprise and advocates a relentless challenge of resistance.

Transference

A central feature of psychodynamic treatment is the analysis of transference (Gill 1979). Transference may be referred to as the universal tendency to experience present relationships under the sway of past relational experience and conflict. Modes of perceiving, conceiving, and relating with a person are influenced by the effects of other, past, significant relationships, particularly those in which unresolved conflict exists. In psychoanalysis the treatment situation is structured to facilitate the development of a transference neurosis through which the therapeutic work will be conducted. In psychoanalytic psychotherapy, and to some extent in psychotherapy in general, transference is viewed as the vehicle by which early pathogenic ideas are apprehended and worked through. Therapy models which rely upon free association and are open-ended in respect to time and focus encourage the activation of transference repetitions.

In short-term psychotherapy, owing to the activity of the therapist, regression is curtailed; this restricts the development of a transference neurosis. That is not to say, however, that transferential (and countertransferential) elements are not experienced within the course of treatment. As pressure is brought to the focalization and interpretations of the conflict, the client's response may be influenced decisively by transference phenomena. In particular, transference constellations involving helplessness, dependency, and passivity are immediately confronted in short-term treatment (Been and Sklar 1985, p. 6). Strupp (1981, pp. 229–30) comments, "It seems clear than any interpretive activity can become effective only to the extent that a conflict becomes 'alive' in the transference, that is, sufficient affect has been mobilized, and the patient is actively struggling with a painful content in the here and now." Transference is actively confronted and is immediately brought within the context of the therapeutic focus. This forthright confrontation of transference accomplishes both the containing of therapeutic focus and an intensification of the pressure through which a ventilation of associated affects will be achieved. Transference interpretations are strategically aimed at furthering the focalization of the treatment process and the expression of the present and enduring conflict and pain. These activities enable clients to develop insight into their maladaptive resolutions of conflict and prepare them to work through their present and longstanding difficulties.

Working Through and Termination Processes

The working through process consists of ongoing exploration of the therapeutic focus with particular attention paid to interactions in which the client "holds on" to the conflictual mode of being in the world. Such an instance may occur within the therapeutic setting when clients resort to an affectless recounting of their concerns or in their personal or professional life when they adopt a powerless position in addressing their needs. Such occurrences are understood within the context of the therapeutic focus and the resistance to change is confronted. Through the use of the spheres of relationship, shown in Figure 1, an understanding of the psychodynamics that influence all modes of relating is facilitated. Clients see the relationships between the ways in which they related to important figures in the past and in their current relationships, the relationship with the therapist and, in pastoral psychotherapy, within their faith orientation and relationship with God. This phase of treatment can be most rewarding for both the client and the therapist as the insights of treatment are applied to the resolution of current conflicts. Additionally, the client may experience an increase in self-esteem and confidence as he or she works through the neurotic aspects of a negatively tinged self-image and forges a more realistic sense of self and self-efficacy in the world.

As termination approaches the client may experience a regressive pull (this is particularly the case in time-limited treatment) as he or she faces the inevitability of separation and loss. In short-term psychotherapy this issue is placed within the context once again of the therapeutic focus. The acceptance of the ending of treatment parallels the client's growing acceptance of other limitations which are faced throughout life. As clients accept that the past cannot be changed, despite the wishes and compromises that they proffer, a more realistic and mature appraisal of the opportunities life affords can be appreciated.

In pastoral psychotherapy the client becomes better able to address the limit questions within the context of articulated faith and belief. The disappointments and injustices within the human condition are appreciated not only within the context of psychodynamics but are also addressed through an examination of faith. The exploration of the psychological contributions to the client's religious experience allows for a maturing of faith in the same manner as an understanding of psychodynamics fosters a greater facility in participating in healthy interpersonal relations.

Short-term psychotherapy concludes successfully with the client having gained insight and having worked through to a significant extent the psychodynamics of the chronically endured and present conflict and pain that prompted the person to seek treatment. Although the treatment has centered on one specific focal conflict, the experience of resolution and mastery of this psychological difficulty, in consort with the internalization of the therapist's observing ego, fosters the client's ability to resolve other psychological difficulties.

Conclusion

Short-term psychotherapy, while acknowledging its theoretical underpinnings to psychoanalytic thought, is a unique form of treatment which offers to appropriate clients the opportunity to work intensively toward the resolution of one focal conflict. Through the structure of time-limited and short-term approaches, and through the application of specific techniques, clients are encouraged to confront the nature, genesis, and consequences of their present and chronically endured neurotic conflict and pain. Short-term approaches are particularly relevant to the provision of mental health services in light of their therapeutic and cost effectiveness. Such treatments are potentially availability to many individuals who otherwise would not be provided with psychological treatment. Further, the focalization of the treatment within these approaches may be structured to pay particular attention to those issues in which the faith dimension plays a significant role.

This chapter has presented an introduction to the essential features common to short-term treatment approaches. By intent, the specificity of particular treatment approaches has not been discussed in any detail. Rather, a general overview has been provided that, hopefully, has stimulated interest in the clinical merits of short-term, psychodynamically oriented psychotherapy. It is noted, as well, that there are many forms of short-term treatment, drawing from the cognitive-behavioral, family systems, and existential-humanistic schools of practice, that have shown clinical merit (Budman 1981; Hawton, Salkovskis, Kirk, and Clark 1989). These approaches offer, as well, important contributions to the field of mental health. In closing, it is prudent to share the caveat of many of the theorists from whose work we have drawn: short-term psychotherapy is a unique form of treatment that requires not only careful selection of clients but also requires specialized training and skills of the practitioner.

Note

1. The term *short-term psychotherapy* will be used to indicate those approaches which have the intention of producing specific outcomes within a brief course of psychotherapy; *time-limited psychotherapy* will indicate those particular short-term psychotherapies in which a strategic use of the dimension of time through the setting of a termination date at the outset of treatment is utilized.

References

Alexander, F., and French, T. 1946. *Psychoanalytic Therapy.* New York: Ronald Press.

Balint, M. 1957. *The Doctor, His Patient and the Illness.* New York: International Universities Press.

Balint, M., Ornstein, P. H., and Balint, E. 1972. *Focal Psychotherapy.* London: Tavistock Publications.

Been, H., and Sklar, I. 1985. "Transference in Short-Term Dynamic Psychotherapy." In *Clinical Issues in Short-Term Dynamic Psychotherapy,* edited by A. Winston, pp. 2–18. Washington, D.C.: American Psychiatric Press.

Budman, S. H., ed. 1981. *Forms of Brief Therapy.* New York: Guilford Press.

Davanloo, H. 1978. *Basic Principles and Techniques in a Short-Term Dynamic Psychotherapy.* New York: Spectrum Publications.

———. 1979. "Techniques of short-term dynamic psychotherapy." *Psychiatric Clinics of North America* 2(1): 14–24.

———, ed. 1980. *Short-Term Dynamic Psychotherapy.* Northvale, N.J.: Jason Aronson, Inc.

———. 1985. "Training in Short-Term Dynamic Psychotherapy." Cape Cod, Mass. (July)

———. 1986a. "Intensive Short-Term Dynamic Psychotherapy with Highly Resistant Patients I." *International Journal of Short-Term Psychotherapy* 1: 107–33.

———. 1986b. Intensive Short-Term Dynamic Psychotherapy with Highly Resistant Patients II. *International Journal of Short-Term Psychotherapy* 1: 239–55.

———, ed. 1986–91. *International Journal of Short-Term Psychotherapy* 1–4.

Davis, D. 1987a. "The Process of De-repression in Intensive Short-Term Dynamic Psychotherapy: Part I." *International Journal of Short-Term Psychotherapy* 2: 59–78.

———. 1987b. "The Process of De-repression in Intensive Short-Term Dynamic Psychotherapy: Part II." *International Journal of Short-Term Psychotherapy* 2: 187–203.

Freud, S. 1913. "On Beginning the Treatment." *Standard Edition of the Complete Works of Sigmund Freud.* vol. 12. London: Hogarth Press.

Garfield, S. L., and Bergin, A. E., eds. 1986. *Handbook of Psychotherapy and Behavior Change.* New York: John Wiley and Sons.

Gill, M. 1979. "The Analysis of the Transference." *Journal of the American Psychoanalytic Association* 27: 263–88.

Greenson, R. 1965. "The Working Alliance and the Transference Neurosis." *Psychoanalytic Quarterly* 34: 155–81.

Hawton, K., Salkovskis, P. M., Kirk, J., and Clark, D. M., eds. 1989. *Cognitive Behaviour Therapy for Psychiatric Problems.* Oxford: Oxford University Press.

Horowitz, M. 1984. *Personality Styles and Brief Psychotherapy.* New York: Basic Books.

Jones, J. 1991. *Transference and Transformation.* New Haven: Yale University Press.

Koss, M. P., and Butcher, J. N. 1986. "Research on Brief Psychotherapy." In *Handbook of Psychotherapy and Behavior Change,* edited by S. L. Garfield and A. E. Bergin, pp. 627–70. New York: John Wiley and Sons.

Luborsky, L. 1984. *Principles of Psychoanalytic Psychotherapy.* New York: Basic Books.

Luborsky, L., Crits-Christoph, P., Mintz, J., and Auerbach, A. 1988. *Who Will Benefit from Psychotherapy?* New York: Basic Books.

Malan, D. H. 1963. *A Study of Brief Psychotherapy.* Springfield, Ill: C. C. Thomas.

———. 1976. *The Frontier of Brief Psychotherapy.* New York: Plenum Medical Book Company.

———. 1979. *Individual Psychotherapy and the Science of Psychodynamics.* London: Butterworths.

———. 1986. "Beyond Interpretation: Initial Evaluation and Technique in Short-Term Dynamic Psychotherapy." *International Journal of Short-Term Psychotherapy* 1: 55–82.

Mandel, H. 1981. *Short-Term Psychotherapy and Brief Treatment Techniques. An Annotated Bibliography: 1920–1980.* New York: Plenum Press.

Mann, D. 1973. *Time Limited Psychotherapy.* Cambridge, Mass.: Harvard University Press.

———. 1981. "The Core of Time-Limited Psychotherapy: Time and the Central Issue." In *Forms of Brief Therapy,* edited by S. Budman, pp. 25–44. New York: Guilford Press.

Mann, D., and Goldman, R. 1982. *A Casebook in Time-Limited Psychotherapy.* Washington, D.C.: American Psychiatric Press.

Power, F. C. 1990. "The Distinctiveness of Pastoral Counseling." *Counseling and Values* 34: 75–88.

Shafranske, E. P. 1987. "Transference and Transformation of God Representations in the Course of Psychotherapy." Paper presented at the meeting of the California State Psychological Association, San Francisco, Cal. (February).

———. 1988. "The Contributions of Object Relations Theory to Christian Counseling." Paper presented at the International Congress of Christian Counseling, Atlanta, Ga. (November).

———. 1991, in press. "God Representation as the Transformational Object." In *Object Relations Theory and Religion,* edited by M. Finn and J. Gartner. New York: Praeger.

Sifneos, P. E. 1972. *Short-term Psychotherapy and Emotional Crisis.* Cambridge, Mass.: Harvard University Press.

———. 1978. "Motivation for Change: A Prognostic Guide for Successful Psychotherapy." *Psychotherapy and Psychosomatics* 29: 293–98.

———. 1987. *Short-Term Dynamic Psychotherapy.* New York: Plenum Medical Book Company.

Spero, M. H. 1985. "The Reality and Image of God in Psychotherapy." *American Journal of Psychotherapy* 39: 75–85.

———. 1990. "Parallel Dimensions of Experience in Psychoanalytic Psychotherapy of the Religious Patient." *Psychotherapy* 27(1): 53–71.

Strupp, H. 1980. "Success and Failure in Time-Limited Psychotherapy: A Systematic Comparison of Two Cases." *Archives of General Psychiatry* 37: 595–603.

———. 1981. "Toward the Refinement of Time-Limited Dynamic Psychotherapy." In *Forms of Brief Therapy*, edited by S. Budman, pp. 219–42. New York: Guilford Press.

Strupp, H., and Binder, J. 1985. *Psychotherapy in a New Key: A Guide to Time-Limited Psychotherapy.* New York: Basic Books.

Weiss, J., and Sampson, H. 1984. *The Psychotherapeutic Process.* New York: Guilford Press.

Winston, A. 1985. *Clinical Issues in Short-Term Dynamic Psychotherapy.* Washington, D.C.: American Psychiatric Press.

Wolberg, L. R., ed. 1965. *Short-Term Psychotherapy.* New York: Grune and Stratton.

SECTION II
THE CHALLENGES AND OPPORTUNITIES OF SPECIAL POPULATIONS

Section II easily might have been called pastoral counseling to the oppressed. Each of the chapters within this section explicitly or implicitly points to the devastation of oppression and the need for a liberation model of pastoral counseling.

David Augsburger starts Section II with a very poignant and prophetic call for pastoral counseling to "dare under no circumstances remain local and mono-cultural" (Chapter 5). Augsburger suggests that pastoral counseling must broaden its horizons to become not only intercultural but also transcultural. The model presented calls for pastoral counselors to expand their hermeneutic to include intracultural empathy (i.e., experience another's phenomenal world), intercultural interpathy (i.e., a cognitive and effective entry into a foreign world of experience), and transcultural pathos (i.e., profound feeling of humanness). Further, the reader is provided a heuristic model and an articulation of specific characteristics as guides to becoming an intercultural pastoral counselor.

The value and role of cultural is further articulated in Richard Voss's "Pastoral Counseling with Families-at-Risk" (Chapter 6). Voss provides the reader with an ecosystemic, liberation theology approach to treating the oppressed. He also reviews the existing professional literature regarding counseling with the poor and multiproblem family and poignantly challenges the field of pastoral counseling, and each of us as pastoral counselors, to examine our own actions on behalf of the poor and oppressed. Voss then invites us to consider a broader, community-based approach rooted in the ongoing call to personal conversion, shared confidentiality, and community teamwork.

In Chapter 7, Christie Cozad Neuger reminds us that despite considerable evidence that the cultural context is significantly responsible for women's psycho-spiritual distress, pastoral counseling all too often fails to take the cultural system into account when assessing and treating women. While committed to advocacy of the oppressed and empowerment of those who are striving toward wholeness, our theological traditions arise out of a deeply patriarchal point of view and thus, according to Neuger, block our understanding of the cultural and systemic needs of women. Neuger offers a feminist perspective on pastoral counseling with women and suggests specific guidelines for the feminist pastoral counselor of women. For Neuger, the use of a feminist liberation approach is the "only way in which a counselor may bring real and lasting healing to women in distress."

The theme of psycho-spiritual distress is further explored in Robert McAllister's essay, "Mental Health Treatment of Religion Professionals" (Chapter 8). Noting that religion professionals are notorious for taking poor care of their own psychological needs, and considering the reality of the current stress, low morale, and tarnished image experienced by most religion professionals, McAllister argues that religion professionals are prime candidates for pastoral support. The author notes that while religion professionals bring the same kinds of pathology, the same dynamic complexities, the same psychological defense to the therapeutic encounter that others bring, there are obvious and yet unusual characteristics and demands to which the counselor needs to be sensitive. Through his discourse McAllister emphasizes the need to understand the source of resistance exhibited by religion professionals, their tendency toward moralizing and intellectualizing as defense, and the unique levels of dependency typically fostered through their religious and ecclesiastical experiences.

Oppression and the need for empowerment are themes which carry through "Counseling Lesbians: A Feminist Perspective" (Chapter 9). In this chapter Unterberger provides a feminist liberation theology as integrated into psychological theory, research, and practice, as a model for working with lesbian clients. In fulfilling the mandate to put experience of the oppressed first, she notes that understanding the experience of lesbian women is the foremost criteria for the formulation of theological and ethical viewpoints, which feminist pastoral counseling affirms concerning same-sex orientation. Unterberger urges the consideration of a gay-affirming, feminist pastoral counseling stance which determines that lesbianism per se is not a disease; rather it is a minority sexual orientation. Further, she suggests that competent pastoral counseling requires that we be aware of the systemic effects of discrimination and oppression upon the overall health and well being of the lesbian parishioner or client.

Chapter 10, "Pastoral Counseling of the Gay Male," further explores this call for the church—and pastoral counseling in particular—to serve as agents of liberation for those who have been oppressed due to sexual orientation. Richard Byrne argues that the full acceptance of homosexuality within the framework of the gospel imperative to love serves as the basic presupposition to working with gay males. He suggests that pastoral counselors take the stance of "full acceptance" of homosexual love as a way of imaging God. He further suggests that such full acceptance is needed to further the gay male's movement toward wholeness and health. Employing Adrian van Kaam's model of "intraspheric formation powers" (i.e., apprehension, appraisal, affirmation, and application), Byrne depicts the twofold purpose of pastoral counseling with gay men to be the following: to assist the client in the movement toward a radical self-affirmation as a gay man; and to foster an integration of the affirmed identity in the total context of the client's life field, including his relationship with the mystery that permeates this field.

David W. Augsburger

5. Cross-Cultural Pastoral Psychotherapy

Pastoral psychotherapy at the beginning of the twenty-first century dare under no circumstances remain local and mono-cultural. Every pastoral encounter occurs in a complex of dilemmas which threaten all human life—the tragedy of world hunger, the exploitation of the poor, the crisis in ecology, the expanding population, the inequities of resource distribution, the problem of debtor nations, the destructiveness of the arms race, and the threat of a nuclear holocaust. For practical theologians the oppression of sexism, ageism, racism, and the fragmentation of family and community, the alienation of accelerated individualism, and the erosion of traditional values only begins the listing of changes in human community and in human personalities which result from and create that community.

Not only are we inextricably connected to all other humans by the worldwide dilemmas of our age, but each human group is necessary to the others for understanding culture (who knows but one culture knows no culture) and for understanding humanness (who knows but one developmental pattern knows none). No longer can we be defined by sexual (males are the norm), racial (whites are superior), religious (Brahman castes are definitive), hemispherical (Western autonomous, linear, teleological experience is paradigmatic of authentic humanness), or sectarian (my faith is the true faith) values. A pastoral psychotherapy must offer breadth capable of addressing both universal humanness and the particular human. Theological ethics must address issues from international to individual concerns. Biblical hermeneutics must be universally responsible while locally relevant. Pastoral theologians who are open to multiple world perspectives observe how familiar concepts become disturbing and unsettling when read through third-world eyes.

> We must be in dialogue not only with the Bible but also with Christians in other parts of the world who read the Bible in a very different way. . . . When third world Christians listen to

> the Bible, *they hear different things than we hear.* It often seems as though they and we are reading different books (Brown 1984, pp. 11–12).

These different worlds actually bring us closer to the strange world of the Bible and the multiple strange worlds of the Judeo-Christian heritage. The differing world-views offer an equal challenge to our psychological and personality theories and stimulate a discovery of a human identity with both a more accurate individual and more authentically corporate existence in the eve of the twenty-first century.

The pastoral psychotherapist can no longer define a self within an isolated context; we live in a global neighborhood. We are in the midst of social and historical change of huge proportions.

In any analysis of the relationship between a renewed sense of human identity and theological-therapeutic practice, we need the correction and confrontation of other cultures to enable us to see our own context clearly. To view individual problems as separate from their context is to misunderstand them. They need to be seen in the system, network, society, and culture if they are to be realistically understood.

When we see individual problems in only an individual context, we fail in two serious ways. First, the individual problems are manifestations of systems which extend far beyond the personality, family, and locality. Second, to treat individual problems in the immediate context is to fail to approach persons as theologically informed therapists, since our concern is with the indivisible salvation of the world. Our caring must be for the person, family, community, and society, since assistance given those near at hand without regard for the larger context all too often means helping some at the expense of others.

Intracultural, Intercultural, and Transcultural Counseling

Pastoral psychotherapy on a cultural boundary requires the resolution of conflicts within, between, and beyond the cultures involved: *within,* since all counseling is cultural adjustment; *between,* since all cross-cultural transactions are cultural adaptation; *beyond,* since all effective pastoral psychotherapy transcends particular cultural values and views. Pastoral counseling is an intracultural consultation, an intercultural intervention, and a transcultural translation of human values.

Intraculturally, therapeutic effectiveness is dependent on its contextual congruence. The person's charge, growth, and psychic integration must result in interpersonal reconciliation within that person's cultural-contextual experience. We may visualize ourselves as individuals, but we live our lives in relationships, in groups and networks. Therapy which is contextually incongruent substitutes one dysfunction for another in the hope that novelty heals.

Interculturally therapeutic effectiveness is determined by its multicontextual clarity; therapists must be congruent with their own cultural self-definitions, the clients progressively congruent with theirs, and the process contextually congruent with the community in which it occurs. Standing on the boundary, pastoral counselors maintain their own rootedness in their culture and context, which grants the grounding of personhood necessary to clear identity and personal integrity while intentionally entering another world of experience.

Transculturally, therapeutic effectiveness is destined by its supracultural relevant point, but what is truly universal, what is cultural, what is individual? Can any therapist be pretentious, arrogant, triumphalist enough to claim knowledge of those transcultural criteria or constructs that offer a base for therapeutic being beyond doing? Is it possible that the pastoral psychotherapist finds in the servant of the Lord—the suffering servant—or in the Christ of the road, the mountain, the garden, the cross, and the transforming tomb a model of human encounter with pain, death, and rebirth that is beyond cultural limitations?

Thus, we might say at a deeper level that all pastoral counseling is an intracultural empathy, an intercultural interpathy, a transcultural pathos.

Intraculturally its authenticity is grounded in its capacity to be empathic. Empathy, the ability to enter cognitively, emotively, experientially into another's phenomenal world, is requisite to all effective therapy. It is facilitated by, dependent upon, showing a common frame of reference which allows the protective identification of therapist with client. The other's experience becomes the picture; one's own experience the frame (Augsburger 1986, p. 31).

Interculturally, the pastoral counselor must experience interpathy. Interpathy is a cognitive and effective entry into a "foreign" world of experience, which allows the therapist to envision and to experience a different epistemology and to feel its commensurate effective impact. To see as another sees with culturally different eyes and to allow oneself to feel what that person feels in consequence of those perceptions, contradictory as they may be to one's own cultural congruence, is the interpathic adventure. In interpathy the other's experience becomes both picture and frame.

Transculturally, the pastoral counselor touches pathos. Pathos is that profound feeling of humanness which plumbs the universal, intuits the essential, and tentatively, humbly, heuristically ventures to identify the absolutes in human experience. We are united, as human beings, by more than our biology, by more than our interracial, intercultural capacity to offer egg or sperm in procreation. We are the same in deep essential thrusts—thrusts toward relatedness, toward individuation, toward growth, toward meaning that transcends the cultural pathways and patterns which provide their content (Kimper 1972).[1]

The pastoral counselor is a boundary creature, living on personal, familial, cultural, national, transnational boundaries, crossing over, coming home, and returning to the boundary as his or her natural habitat. It is on the boundary that one becomes fully aware, truly alive, wholly available. The therapist "who knows but one culture knows no culture," and the therapist who becomes a member of a third culture, a bridging culture, begins to understand, respect, and utilize culture fully and freely in the healing of human pain. As a third-culture citizen, a universal human, the effective intercultural agent prizes both cultures as aesthetically valuable (beauty is in the eye of the beholder), as relationally capable (all persons experience solidarity and solitude), as linguistically equivalent (there are no primitive languages), and as theologically viable (all cultures are equidistant from God). As a therapeutic presence, available, authentic, agapeic, the pastoral counselor sees the second culture with the equal regard of authentic love.

To prize the client is to prize the client's culture as a matrix of maturing which possesses its own homeostatic integrity, creativity, and authenticity. The cultural encapsulated counselor finds the preceding tedious, the boundary nonexistent, the task of treatment as essentially similar regardless of tradition or heritage. The outcome is tragic, the impact a renewal of colonialism and psychological imperialism, paternalism, or maternalism. But for the therapist who has come to love the boundary as the proper domain of all pastoral psychotherapy, the sensitivity to contrasting values, world-views, internal controls, identity formation, familial solidarity, gender definition, ethical direction, and meaningful life direction alters the entire process of consulting as counseling.

Pastoral counseling, on the boundary between cultures, requires construction of models of the person which return to traditional understandings of the individual-in-community yet retain the understandings of the individual-in-depth. Although the interiorization of communal process is increasingly present in urbanized cultures, each individual becomes an internal community of all the significant people of his or her life and creates a homeostatic balance of these characters so that the personality becomes a full congress of such representatives and differentiates legislative and judicial powers to complete the inner quorum.

Figure 1 offers a model which unites person and context, not as a universally applicable construct but as a heuristic sketch which is corrected when reconstructed in each culture. It posts at the core the development process of the person (1) which emerges from, is directed by, unfolds within culturally prescribed pathways, and fulfills the (2) basic assumptions of family, group, and wider culture, which empowers this particular sub-unit of the society. As identity forms in either fidelity to or flight from the cultural expectations (3) the particular personality emerges from the developmental process of childhood. Now the person is able to enter into authentic encounter (4) as expressed in that cultural context in intimacy with other persons. The (5) cultural, relational rooms define and delimit the patterns and pathways of human community. Out of this emerges (6) the sense of life project in expression of and under the influence of larger community, vocation, and vision, which command the person's life and work.

The degree of influence from the cultural context varies sharply from those inner directed cultures which value "inner control and inner responsibility" to the more collective cultural values which affirm more "external control and external responsibility" as necessary for life in solidarity with family and community.

The Western ethos in which our training for pastoral care and counseling occurs is a context marked by the following five significant and interrelated elements.

Pluralism of values, of languages for interpretation of what the world is about. Most persons in any given day move through three or four contexts, each governed by different primary languages of interpretation.

Relativism. Each of the many worlds through which a person moves has its own moral values. This leaves the person chameleonlike in a fragmented world with no cohesive moral context.

Tribalism. Persons retreat into one meaning affirming group and so insulate themselves from differing perspectives, from alternate worlds; the rigidity of these boundaries creates a cultural return to tribalism.

Privatism. Life and meaning worlds are divided neatly into public and private realms, often with contradictory values.

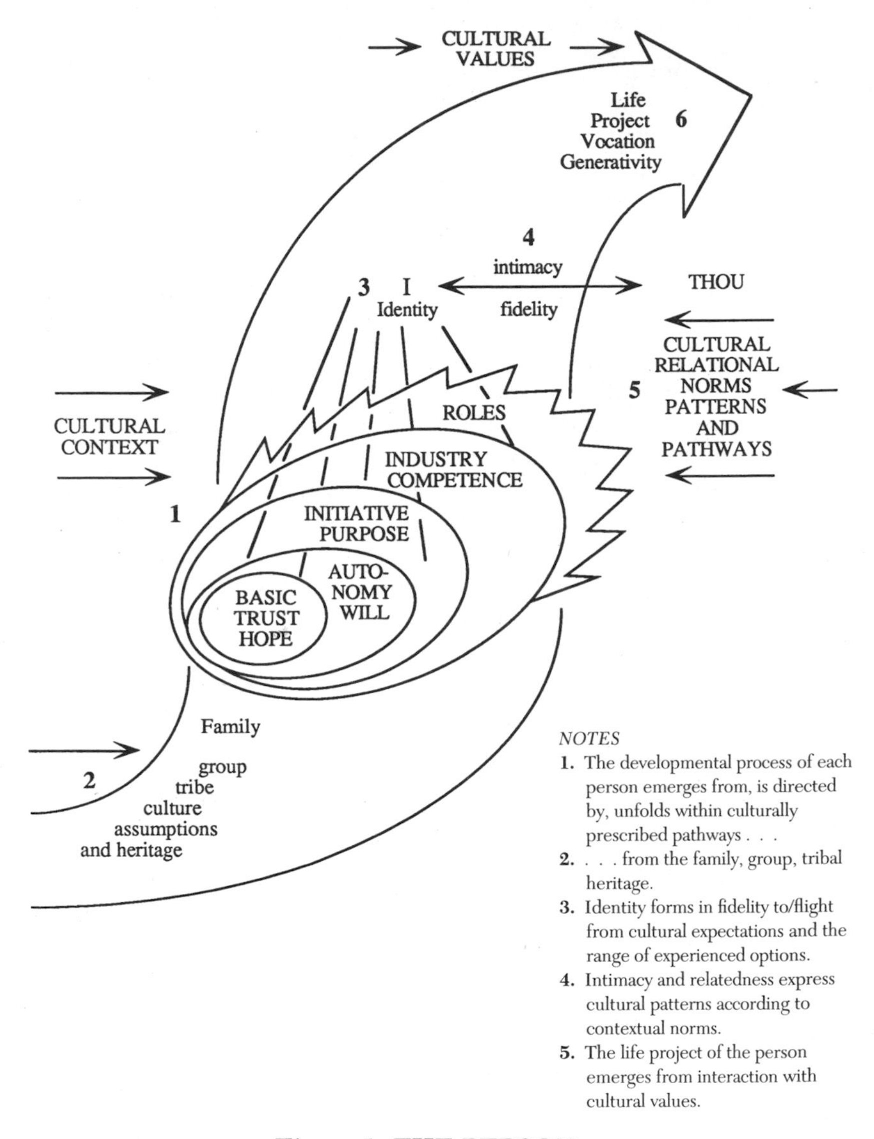

Figure 1. THE PERSON IN CONTEXT IN CULTURE IN COMMUNITY

Narcissism. The current focus of the psychotherapeutic community is on the borderline character disorders where persons are fragmented in deep levels of personhood. What hysteria was to the twenties, and obsessive compulsive disorders to the mid-century West, narcissism is in the last half of the century (Gerkin 1986, pp. 16–17).

Identity, for the modern Westerner, is "peculiarly differentiated." Traditional personhood was experienced with an internal and external coherence which required little differentiation—differentiation here is defined as the discrimination of distinctions, differences, boundaries, and part processes with explanatory power to resolve tensions. This differentiation process has the following social antecedents as developed by Peter Berger (Berger, Berger, and Kellner 1973, pp. 77–78).

1. A pluralism of social worlds in modern society has replaced the single coherent world which seemed firm and inevitable in traditional society.

2. The structures of each particular world in the pluralistic situation are experienced as relatively unstable and unreliable, thus the experience of their vulnerability and their overlapping boundaries makes every one of them relative.

3. The institutional order of marriage, family, community, and society undergoes a certain loss of reality. The "accent of reality" consequently shifts from the objective order of institutions to the realm of subjectivity and personal interiority.

4. The individual's experience of the self becomes more real than the experience of the objective social world. So the person seeks to find a foothold in reality within the self rather than outside in the human context.

5. The individual's subjective reality (what is commonly regarded as the person's psychology or the study of the psyche) becomes increasingly differentiated, complex, and interesting to the self.

6. Subjectivity, interiority, and exploration of a differentiated elaborated psyche acquire previously unconceived depths.

This focus on individual interiority permeates the Western educational process. Personality theory, faith formation, spirituality, human growth, and development all possess richly diversified depths and elaborate inner structures. Contemporary use of the concept of *self*, for example, is a study in constructs and contrasts with the simplicity of the biblical meanings of the word. With an expanded lexicon of metaphors for individual, internal psychic explanations, the Western pastoral counselor constantly returns to the personal unconscious rather than the group mythology and tradition to understand the dynamics of human behavior. The balance between individual and collective, personal and social must be restored in the pastoral caregiver's understanding of healing, health, and growth.

The Intercultural Pastoral Counselor

In *Pastoral Counseling Across Cultures* I have argued the following eleven characteristics as necessary for the pastoral counselor who works on cultural boundaries and becomes culturally aware when working in the culture of origin. The intercultural pastoral counselor is:

1. Culturally aware, interpathically skilled, and authentically present in dialogue with persons of other cultures, values, and faiths, unafraid to cross over and return from alternate world and religious views.

2. Culturally sensitive to what is universal, cultural, or individual; and values humans as essentially of ultimate worth, culturally of comparable worth, individually of equal worth.

3. Conscious of both individuality and solidarity with others in his or her self-identity, in its infinite variety in other cultural, familial, and personal identities; and sees the individual-in-community as the basic unit of humanness.

4. Sensitive to the wide variation of human controls—anxiety, shame, guilt—in the different human contexts, respectful of the positive as well as negative functions of each emotion and its moral as well as functional content.

5. Aware of values—their nature, universality, uniqueness, variety, and power in directing life—and sensitive to the core values of each culture, group, or person.

6. Concerned with essential human groups—family, marriage, and kinship groups—as well as individuals; and sees relationships of integrity as essential to personal integration and health.

7. Aware of the inequities of gender roles, sensitive to the exploitation and abuse of women, and committed to work for justice and the liberation of all who suffer oppression.

8. Aware of the moral character of human choice, reasoning, and behavior, of the constancy of form and contrasts in content in ethical stories and storytellers.

9. Sensitive to world views which accept middle zone experience; which utilize metaphorical, mythical, and supernatural explana-

tions for human pain, tragedy, and disorder; and which demand power confrontations with evil and the demonic.

10. Aware of the cultural shaping and labeling of mental illness, respectful of the wide variation in what is normative and normal in each culture; and responsive to human frailty and suffering with insight and compassion.

11. Open to the many metaphors for psychotherapy which exist in various cultures, recognizing in each the possibilities of an experience of grace and truth inviting integrity and wholeness.

These elements are integral to effective intercultural pastoral caregiving, which will take many forms with richly varied content. The goal is not the construction of a single integrative model, but the recognition of the need for as many models as there are cultural contexts, and the call for pastoral counselors to work creatively, flexibly, humbly, and redemptively on the boundaries where crossing over and returning enrich and transform our vision of human life and destiny (Augsburger, 1986, pp. 272–73).

Pastoral Care/Counseling in Multi-Cultural Perspective

Although its grounding in theology should have protected it, pastoral counseling has been a discipline held hostage by a mono-cultural psychological imperialism producing a pastoral parochialism. Although the data for a broadened world-view have been in reach, we in Western pastoral psychotherapy training have continued persistently or persisted continuously as though Western models, values, and views of human nature and community were normative for all humankind. Our Western psychotherapy, viewed through Eastern eyes, is immediately recognizable as an institution of Western society. Rooted deeply in the Western cultural heritage, it affects and transforms the soil and the era in which it thrives. The Western mental health movement may be viewed as both a symbolic and substantive cultural undertaking to meet the deficits in the Western way of life and to attempt to cope with the negative implications of its premises (Pande 1968, p. 425).

In the period following World War II the Western pastoral counseling movement was shaped by two central assumptions. These, as defined by historian E. Brooks Holifield are, first, that self-realization has priority among all human strivings. Self-actualization, self-fulfillment, self-determination, self-motivation were goals all focused on self-realization and the discovery of the potentials of the individual.

Second, most corporate institutions and social structures interfere with rather than support the fulfillment of the self. Thus helping persons free themselves from family constraints, moral constraints of social respectability, and corporate restraints which block persons from realizing their individual freedom became a central assumption and unquestioned function of pastoral care (Holifield 1983, p. 260).

The pastoral care movement is recognizing its need for "widening the horizons," although often it is doing well to broaden the focus to the family unit, and on occasion it addresses the larger community and social context. Most recently a major theorist, Charles Gerkin, has taken the leap of addressing the American culture.

> If pastoral care must at all times be sensitive to the particularity of human needs, then the situation of radical pluralism in which we now find ourselves has great significance for what pastors should be keeping at the center of their attention. To take the pluralistic situation seriously, pastors will need to widen the horizon of their pastoral interests from the concern with psychological and relational well-being that has been the focus of the recent past . . . to the pain and confusion produced by living at this particular time in our culture (Gerkin 1986, pp. 19–20).

These signs of movement from individual to familial to communal to social to cultural frames of reference are promising, but they tend to be a widening of present horizons. The temptation is to extend present assumptions, to project our agenda onto others in unwitting psychological imperialism. We may claim to be universal in theory and practice while grounding our hypotheses in an inadequate sample.

Any psychology or theology which pretends to be a-cultural or a-historical in its conception of the individual is reductionistic regardless of its breadth or depth. Tragically, the a-cultural, a-historical, apolitical conception of individuals remains the paradigmatic favorite in counseling theories and in much theology. Training and practice models must be grounded in sociocultural systems thinking. All human psychology is embedded in its cultural context, and all counseling must take the personal and the contextual with equal seriousness.

Two central issues in training intercultural pastoral counselors are, one, the belief in the paradigmatic primacy of seeing individual development as embedded in and inseparable from its social and cultural context; and two, the development of ministry models and training programs which appreciate the validity of "the second culture" equally with that of the dominant culture of the training or the care delivery context. Individual and group differences must be seen not just as the products of different environments, but as existing now in the context of a particular setting of cultural traditions, perspectives, and norms. Any therapeutic intervention must be congruent with the context in which it occurs.

Every theory or therapy of psychology, psychiatry, or psychotherapy emerges from some kind of philosophical, theological, political, and ethical presuppositions. There is no apolitical, a-economic, amoral, a-cultural system of counseling theory. Each has its own philosophical, theological, economic, and ethical bases, which must be owned, integrated, corrected, utilized.

One culture values harmony with nature, another domination of and exploitation of nature and its reserves; one assumes an economy of geometric possibilities and exponential growth, another sees limits to growth as necessary; one perceives humans as destined by fate, Karma, providence, or fortune, another insists that all are self-defined, self-determined, and therefore responsible and capable of change. For almost any cultural assumption held by a counselor there are other equally skilled therapists who question its validity. Thus we may take as rules of therapeutic judgment the following propositions.

One, cultural assumptions shape all clinical applications.

There are human universals, but these are experienced within cultural contexts, expressed through cultural world-views, and acted upon in culturally defined pathways and patterns. Within any given culture there is a broad range of individual variation and for many cultures the differences within a culture may be greater than those between paired cultures. Yet in their variety and in their commonality, the cultural assumptions still shape the clinical directions required to facilitate reconciliation and healing.

Two, clinical practice is grounded in cultural depths.

There are superficial similarities across many cultures created by northern hemisphere dominance, economic interdependence, communications homogenization, educational and informational interchanges in the urbanization, technological revolution, and militarization of our world. Beneath these common elements of world culture, or of those shared patterns we frequently call Westernization, are the cultural patterns rooted in the personal development journey, the familial history and heritage, the group ethos and values, the collective assumptions and belief systems of the culture of origin. It is from these depths that the sustaining and transforming metaphors for stability and change arise in clinical dialogue. Although clients may report a greater freedom in owning and expressing feelings in a second language (such as Japanese counselees utilizing English with its more value-free connotations learned in later life-stages and thus less freighted with primal trust, anxiety, shame, or guilt issues), nevertheless their growth lies in integrating learning from other contexts with their cultural depths as it colors or discolors, forms or deforms the psyche.

Three, all claims "to know" must be justified.

Culturally capable counselors are engaged in a continuous self-critique which examines what they think they know, what they can know with certainty, and how they know what they know in humility. Truth is both culturally defined and at the same time transcultural. It is never the unique property of any culture, subculture, or a school of psychotherapy derived from any of these (i.e., analytic development of classic rabbinic wisdom, Jungian elaboration of reformed theology blended with mystic anthropology, or behavioral systemization of American empiricism and pragmatism).

Four, all therapy must be contextually congruent.

The counselor's presuppositions about the nature of human beings, concerning the human mind and psyche, pertaining to human difficulties, conflicts and distortions, and leading to resolution, reconstruction, and reconciliation must have the requisite "fit." Congruence between person and process, psyche and ethos, inner depths and their cultural roots must be established and maintained throughout the course of therapy. The clinical application of any cultural healing system involves the counselor's capacity to evoke an integrative resolution of conflicts by making changes in the counselee's basic assumptions, whether directly or indirectly. To accomplish this change, we challenge the counselee's basic structures, examine the unexamined assumptions, make explicit the implicit beliefs, and contradict the repetitive conclusions about human difficulties and their resolution. To attempt such challenge or change from an alternate context is both vanity and insanity.

Five, we must hold our assumptions tentatively, provisionally, heuristically open to challenge and change.

Psychology, psychiatry, and the practice of psychotherapy are healing arts grounded on at least four bases. Only one of these is scientific, and it is subject to ongoing review and revision. The other three legs of collective cultural mythology; theoretical constructs on human development, personality, and relationships; and philosophical, theological, or metaphysical speculations are all constantly debated and frequently employed even after they have been disproven or discarded by most practitioners. For almost every psychological assumption held by one therapist, there is another psychologist who considers it unimportant or invalid. The work of William James from a hundred years ago has nearly the same claim to accuracy at crucial points as the most recent formulations. We have many different school of therapy created from utilitarian models and claiming some degree of authority and finality but without an objective demonstration of validity beyond select cases, clinical circularity, and self-validating longitudinal studies which are shaped by the presuppositions peculiar to the theorist and the theory.

Six, we must learn to move rhythmically between universal facts, their applications and implications AND cultural facts with their translations and interpretations. Culturally valid meanings are negotiable within the culture as well as between cultures. As we seek to discern and define the cultural values and vision of both client and counselor in any therapeutic interaction we alternate between contextual meanings and universal significance. Both are important. The universal keeps us from sacralizing what is transitory; the cultural stops us from imposing what is foreign to the particular instance.

Seven, we could well concede that our Western theories of counseling are arbitrary, contestable, and frequently contested by our own colleagues. For every perspective on doing therapy there is a colleague who holds an equally supported and opposite position. We do not have empirical grounding and verification of more than the most parsimonious behavioral hypotheses. One theory is as effective as another, one approach is as healing as its opposite, leaving us to conclude that it is presence not proposition, process not theoretical formulation, which unite our richly varied approaches.

Eight, we need a theological ground, a transcultural relevant point which provides a center for our thinking, acting, and being. Discovering such a theological center is painful, slow, demanding work. It is best done in community with other counselors, not alone. A primary step toward such theological formation is a concerted effort of all pastoral theologians to work at theology from the other side, from alternate visions, from multiple cultures. *Theology is faith seeking understanding from within a cultural context.* The three elements of this definition of theology offer three propositions.

1. Theology relates human values to God, who transcends all cultures while being absolutely related to each. Every culture is equi-

distant from God, none has primary access, familiarity, divine superiority.

2. Theology is done within a cultural context, and Christian theology, if incarnational, is local and cultural in its particular situation and application.

3. Theology seeks understanding, a coherent relationship between divine and human values that allows one to speak of both universals and particulars, of the translocal and the local, of cross-cultural and of cultural perspectives.

Universal values can be sought in many contexts, but they are "values" as they are prized in a particular context. A theology which takes incarnation seriously, Barbara Zikmund notes, "is hard put to find universal values. The scandal of particularity reminds us that God does not engage the human condition 'in general,' but always in particular acts and events, through a chosen people or through the Christ event we encounter the Divine. So . . . instead of saying that cultures need to be permeated through and through by the gospel and its values, perhaps we need to say that the gospel needs to be sought more and more diligently in the many cultures of the world" (Zikmund, 1986, 41).

The cross-cultural pastoral counselor is a seeker of this God who loves the world, is at work and at love through out all the cultures of the world, and who prizes all of creation, creatures, and their re-creation.

Summary

Pastoral theology, pastoral counseling, and psychotherapy must broaden their horizons to become not only intercultural but also, at some moments, transcultural. This requires moving beyond intracultural empathy to intercultural interpathy.

The entrapment in Western individualism, the seduction of psychological reductionism must be transcended as the pastoral theologian expands the vision of what humanness, the human psyche, and the human being are and can become.

Sensitivity to God, who calls us to love the world; to the world, which calls us to embrace diversity; and to the uniqueness of persons, which calls us to discover the particularities of God at work in each human experience can free us to discard old models and join in the creation of new—as many new models as there are cultures, groups, and visions of life's meaning.

Note

1. Frank Kimper, perhaps the most radical, insightful, creative pastoral counselor of our generation, who is recognized by only his students (since he chose to counsel, mentor, encounter, rather than publish), has offered these essential human dynamics as transcultural constants in human experience, which can be directed creatively in transforming ways.

References

Augsburger, David. 1986. *Pastoral Counseling Across Cultures.* Philadelphia: Westminster.

Berger, Peter with Brigitte Berger and Hansfield Kellner. 1973. *The Homeless Mind.* New York: Random House.

Brown, Robert M. 1984. *Unexpected News: Reading the Bible with Third World Eyes.* Philadelphia: Westminster.

Gerkin, Charles. *Widening the Horizons.* 1986. Richmond: Knox.

Holifield, E. Brooks. 1983. *A History of Pastoral Care in America.* Nashville: Abingdon.

Hough, Joseph and John Cobb. 1985. *Christianity Identity and Theological Education.* Chico, CA: Scholars Press.

Kimper, Frank. 1972. Unpublished clinical notes. School of Theology at Claremont.

Pande, S. 1968. "The Mystique of Western Psychotherapy: An Eastern Interpretation." *Journal of Nervous and Mental Disorders* 146: 425–32.

Zikmund, Barbara. 1986. "Response." *Theological Education.* Vandalia: ATS (Autumn).

Richard W. Voss

6. Pastoral Counseling with Families-at-Risk

Leonardo Boff, a Franciscan theologian, notes that "Today's dominant classes . . . have inherited a profound scorn for the poor. They consider them to be socially disqualified; they avoid contact with them, going around them, insensitive to their misery" (Boff 1984, 51).

The Signs of the Times: "The Situation is Grim and Getting Worse!"

> The joys and the hopes, the griefs and the anxieties of the men of this age, especially those who are poor or in any way afflicted, those too are the joys and hopes, the griefs and anxieties of the followers of Christ. (*Pastoral Constitution on the Church in the Modern World,* Abbott 1966).

A recently published government report, *No Place to Call Home: Discarded Children in America* (Miller 1990) provides evidence that the situation of certain American families is grim and getting worse. Rather than decreasing, the reports of child abuse and neglect have risen 82 percent between 1981 and 1988, representing 2.2 million children (Miller 1990, p. 8). In 1988 the number of children who died from abuse exceeded twelve hundred, representing more than a 36 percent increase in just three years (p. 8). These findings are disturbing in light of data supporting the lack of appropriate follow-up treatment for these children.

Another survey, *Abused Children in America: Victims of Official Neglect* (Miller 1987) showed that mental health services for abused children barely exist in many places. These findings are consistent with an earlier study, *Safety Net Programs: Are They Reaching Poor*

Children?, which showed that between 1979 and 1984 approximately three million more children fell below the poverty line (based upon a four-person family income of $10,609), representing a 31 percent increase (Miller 1986, p. 2). This increase raised the total number of American children living in poverty conditions to thirteen million (p. 2). While the number of children living in poverty conditions increased, the survey also showed that they participated less in government-sponsored children's programs (p. 13).

Between the years 1987 and 1988 the U. S. Conference of Mayors reported an 18 percent increase in requests for shelter by homeless families. Homelessness was cited as a factor in over 40 percent of the foster care placements of children in New Jersey in 1986 (p. 8). It was estimated that between 70 and 80 percent of emotionally disturbed children did not receive appropriate mental health services, or they received no services at all (p. 8).

Excessive client caseloads have overburdened the system's ability to provide even minimal care and appropriate services to children and families (p. 9). One report on child welfare services in the District of Columbia showed that as of September 1989, approximately seven hundred reported cases of child abuse and neglect had not been completed (p. 9). One survey of seventy-eight drug treatment programs in New York City found that 54 percent of them refused to treat pregnant women, 67 percent refused to treat pregnant women on Medicaid, and 87 percent had no services available to pregnant women on Medicaid addicted to crack (Chavkin 1989).

These statistics reflect a kind of "social recession" in America that is affecting the quality of caring for the most vulnerable citizens in our nation. It affects those families and children least likely to cope with the problems of living. This social recession also affects those professionals involved with these families. Fiscal restraints frequently require hiring young, inexperienced, entry-level professionals to provide services to some of the most complex and troubled families one is likely to encounter.

Historically, social workers were among a minority of professionals that ventured into the world of the poor in America (Richmond 1908, 1917, 1920; Rich 1956; Hartman 1970; Holbrook 1983; Moffic, et al. 1983; Parsons 1986; Auslander and Litwin 1988; Breton 1989). This professional topography and commitment to providing services to the poor is changing and now includes the fields of community psychiatry (Clausen and Kohn 1954; Robinson et al. 1954; Redlich 1960; Auerswald 1968, 1972, 1985, 1987; Minuchin 1968, 1970(a), 1970(b)) and community psychology (Sarason, et al. 1966;

Rappaport 1977; Susskind and Klein 1985). But where is pastoral counseling in the world of the multi-risk poor?

Literature Review

A review of the pastoral counseling literature on the poor reveals that there is limited literature on this topic. In fact, there is no coverage on the specific topic of pastoral counseling with poor families. There are, however, a few articles about issues often associated with the poor.

There is literature about a pastoral response to violent and abusive families (Bentley 1984; Garanzini 1988), and specifically about child abuse reporting responsibilities (Denham 1986; Bullis 1990) enumerating liability and immunity issues for clergy. Related literature also looks at the heightened emotional stress encountered by the pastoral counselor in working with abusive families (Henning 1987), and another article discusses the need to coordinate counseling when working with congregants who have abused or neglected their child (Bentley 1984).

One article discusses the reluctance of clergy to become involved with the problems of domestic violence among members of their congregation (Thompson 1989), and another evaluates the overall effectiveness of the helping efforts of clergy with battered women indicating that they tended to be more successful with middle-class clients than with working-class clients (Bowker 1982). The only other article related to the topic was "Social Pastoral Care in the Urban Setting" (Johnson 1978), which examines the role of community organization in the congregation and identifies models of group intervention in urban settings. Interestingly, this author notes the following:

> Unfortunately, the pastor often seems more interested in being the star player than in being the coach. While this may be fine for *his* or *her* ego-involvement and feeling of positive contribution to the community, it does not go very far in providing the congregation with the resources for self-help —a need which is crucial for congregation in urban communities (Johnson 1978, p. 253).

Even considering the related literature to the topic of pastoral counseling with the poor, one senses a perception of *risk* involved in providing counseling services to this population. Pastoral counseling with families at risk is not "counseling as usual"! This arena is uncharted terrain, and the path has many unknown perils and dangers that confront the pastoral counselor—emotionally, ethically, and spiritually.

This is not to insinuate that the church has not cared for the poor. As Harry J. Aponte notes:

> The notion of love of the poor, identification with the poor and total self-dedication to serving the poor is a peculiarly Christian concept which by now has been incorporated into cultures that are traditionally Christian. The church has not only revolutionized attitudes toward the poor, but has institutionalized them through its various religious orders and charities that care for the poor (personal communication, 1990).

Traditionally, church services to the poor have been organized and provided through social work service agencies. But is there an appropriate role for pastoral counseling?

Interrogating the Silence in the Literature

In light of Matthew 25:31–46, the criterion by which Jesus' followers will be judged include ministering to the basic needs of one's fellows, especially to the poor and the powerless. Thus the question emerges why the pastoral counseling literature is so silent in grappling with relevant issues associated in working with impoverished, multi-risk families. This Matthean passage is weighty theologically. Recall Jesus' words: "As long as you neglected to do it to one of these least ones, you neglected to do it to me" (v. 45). This passage could be paraphrased to say that the pastoral counselor's ministry is judged entirely on service to the poor, the least among Jesus' brethren (McKenzie 1968, p. 107).

The silence may reflect the basic ambiguity of the term *poor.* Who are the poor, really? The term is equivocal, and may include the "poor at heart," "poor in spirit," and "the morally bankrupt" as well as those "lacking in basic material means." The lack of discussion of the topic may be a matter of semantics, related to how pastoral counselors articulate their counseling ministry. It could be that pastoral counselors do not differentiate socioeconomic variables in their ministry or in their writing: "In Christ 'There is no Greek or Jew . . . slave or freeman' " (Col 3:11).

On another level the silence may also reflect an alignment of the profession with traditional psychotherapeutic approaches to treatment. Such an alignment may unwittingly sustain the belief that pastoral counseling can only be beneficial to those clients who are able to be involved and motivated to engage in traditional, nondirective psychotherapy (Abramczyk 1981; Arnold and Schick 1979; Crews 1966; Hudson 1955), that is, clients who are psycho-socially able to attend to, and thereby able to discuss their spiritual strivings. The poor, it has been argued, are too focused on survival issues, and are more in need of social work service.

On yet another level of consciousness, the silence may reflect a lack of awareness of the dynamics of social oppression by therapists (pastoral counselors) from the middle-class majority, who may not understand how their role fits within the bigger picture of services to the poor. This lack of consciousness may reflect a privatized notion of pastoral counseling more aligned with traditional psychotherapies that precludes involvement in the public sectors (the marketplace) where the poor are likely to be.

Have we taken John's passage—"The poor you always have with you" (Jn 12:8, *NAB*)—as the basis for complacency or for a self-critical hermeneutic? The poor are the chronic, unrequiting, prophetic, living testimony of the risen Lord, confronting, interrogating, and disrupting our comfort and sensibilities. Their plight is the basis for a moral indictment and becomes an embodiment of the "divine pathos" heard in the voice of Hosea:

> Hear the word of the LORD, O people of Israel,
> for the LORD has a grievance
> against the inhabitants of the land:
> There is no fidelity, no mercy,
> no knowledge of God in the land (Hos 4:1, *NAB*).

This article will look at the pastoral imperative in ministering faithfulness, mercy, and knowledge of God to the poor. It will also offer a paradigm for pastoral counseling with multi-risk poor families. It is hoped that this endeavor will shed light onto an appropriately troubling but not totally hopeless subject.

Clarifying Terms: Who are the Poor?

In this essay the terms *poor* and *impoverished* will follow the definition developed by Michel Mollat, who defined the poor in this way:

> He is the one who temporarily or permanently finds himself in a situation of weakness, dependence, humiliation, characterized by the lack of means, variables according to the age and society, means of power and social consideration: money, relationships, influence, power, science, technical qualifications, honorable birth, physical strength, intellectual ability, personal freedom, and dignity. Living day to day, the poor man has no possibility of changing his state without the help of another. A definition like this one could include all those who are frustrated through their own fault, the asocial, the marginated; this definition is not specific to an age, to a region, or to an environment. Nor does it exclude those who, because of an ascetic or mystic ideal, reject the world, or those who, through devotion, choose to live poverty among the poor (Mollat 1978, p. 14).

Throughout this chapter references to "impoverished" and "poor" families refer to the condition of material and social dependence and not the spiritual or moral condition alone. While the discussion may have some relevance to middle- or upper class families, who have attained some level of socioeconomic success but may also experience multiple and complex problems, the focus will be on those multi-risk families who experience multiple problems *and lack the material and social (family and community) resources* to resolve them.

Clinically—Who are the Multi-Risk Families?

These multi-risk families, as I will describe them, are not typically seen in private community agencies or hospitals on any regular basis. If they do come to voluntary agencies or private counseling centers for help, it usually is to request financial or material assistance (food, shelter, clothing, fuel) for problems that have reached crisis proportions.

Clinically these families are typically viewed as "not amenable to treatment," which means that they are not "highly motivated to change" and they "lack insight into their problems," two basic assumptions or prerequisites for engagement in traditional therapies. Frequently these behaviors make them "inappropriate candidates" for traditional insight-oriented therapy, making them prone to experience a kind of "treatment discrimination" by professional helpers (see Robinson, et al. 1954; Adams and McDonald 1968; Billingsley 1969; Pierson 1970; Rubenstein and Bloch 1978).

I argue that the pastoral counselor, trained in traditional methods of treatment, may also be prone to subtle forms of treatment discrimination. If one of the client's symptomatic behavior is "under-organization," which includes lack of motivation, lack of initiative, lack of insight, and so on, and one's therapeutic approach requires these characteristics as prerequisites for treatment, clients whose "clinical problem" includes familial under-organization are effectively excluded from traditional psychotherapeutic treatment.

Do these impoverished, multi-risk families only need a social worker to help them with their material needs or is this a professional maneuver to avoid changing one's pastoral counseling approach to meet the client "where they are"? Do we pastoral counselors give witness to the inherent worthiness of the poor? By our practice do we recognize and affirm in word and action the spiritual foundation to self-worth, or do we overly emphasis self-worth from the psychological perspective? Beyond the comfort-oriented materialism of our dominant culture, do we see the spiritual glue binding us all together as co-pilgrims? Aponte has noted that, unfortunately, "professionalism has injected a whole new set of values as well as methods of helping, which have not been based on any special love of or commitment to the poor" (personal communication, 1990).

Frequently the multi-risk poor families do not perceive their behavior as problematic. They may be involved in antisocial or asocial behaviors (as viewed from the value perspective of the majority community standard); they may not view themselves (behaviorally) as much different from their neighbors. When they do perceive a problem, they often lack the material resources to pay for treatment and lack the organizational skills to obtain and/or follow through with appropriate treatment in an effective way. Their lives reflect and simultaneously reinforce environments of chaos, despair, hopelessness, and powerlessness.

These are the families historically described as "multiproblem families" in the literature (Booth 1892; Buell 1948; Buell et al. 1952, 1958; Dick and Strnad 1953; Page and Axelrod 1955; Birt 1956; Geismar and Ayres 1958, 1959; Voiland 1961; Geismar 1961; Voiland and Buell 1961; Geismar, La Sorte, and Ayres 1962; Geismar and La Sorte 1963, 1964; Spencer 1963; Geismar and Krisberg 1967; Geismar et al. 1972; Geismar 1973; Rutter and Madge 1976; Geismar and Geismar 1979, Geismar 1980; Colon 1980; Geismar and Wood 1989). Classically such families have been distinguished by their conflict with the prevailing community's standards of living. Their attitudes and practices of personal interaction, hygiene, sanitation, medical care, and child rearing often place them at odds with the larger community (Geismar et al. 1972; Brown 1968; Spencer 1963; Warren 1960; Hallinan 1959; Regensburg 1954; and Overton 1953). They have been the subject of massive social research for over forty years, and they have provided an important hermeneutic about what constitutes therapy. As social researchers faced persistent failure in identifying successful methods of treating these "problem families," therapists began to look more carefully at themselves in relation to working with these families.

Families of the Slums: An Exploration of Their Structure and Treatment (Minuchin et al. 1967) documented the need for therapists to be flexible enough to change and adapt their approach to treating the "disorganized family" (Minuchin and Montalvo 1966b, pp. 880–997) based upon the unique needs, values, and experiences of each family. This work was further supported and expanded by others (Aponte 1974a, 1974b, 1976a, 1976b; Fleischer 1975; Foley 1975; McAdoo 1977; Hardy-Fanta and MacMahon-Herrera 1981; Edwards 1982), who identified the difficulties facing the middle-class therapist trying to adapt to the reality of impoverished or otherwise oppressed people.

The magnitude of the problem was graphically illustrated by Harry J. Aponte in the following observation:

> Poverty associated with a cultural minority can present an impenetrable barrier to a middle-class therapist who is not a member of that minority. It must be made clear that the problems for the therapy created by these differences are not the result of any pathology in the minority patient—a rationalization that can protect the therapist from a sense of failure in therapy. The distance between the walls of the canyon is no greater if measured from one side than if measured from the other (Aponte 1976b, p. 432).

The poverty of these at-risk families is not the destitution of widespread famine and starvation of the Third World. Their poverty is a living mirror of our decaying social and moral infrastructure in our high-tech world and the human byproduct of who we are and what we value as a society. While many of these families live in the decaying cities, they are not exclusively situated in urban settings. Many rural and suburban communities also include multi-risk families, but they tend to be less visible.

These families lack access to the human and material resources to "get by" in a materialistically competitive society; they are consequently dependent upon numerous community agencies for their material and moral survival. Contrary to the popular myth, this dependence on community agencies is frequently involuntary. Multi-risk families do not *choose* to experience the humiliation of being welfare recipients; there are no viable alternatives for them under our present political, economic, and social welfare structures. Human reality for these families is shaped by their intergenerational impoverishment, which alienates them from the larger technologically competent community. They lead a kind of "fourth-world" existence in the land of plenty. Both psycho-socially and environmentally exposed and vulnerable to the worst our society has to offer, these families reflect *our* convoluted and muddled values, indicative of a larger social moral malaise.

My use of the term *multi-risk families* does not refer to the well-functioning poor who have been able to maintain strong family ties and muster sufficient resources to meet the demands of everyday living. My usage of the term is not intended to equate people who live in impoverishment with abusive lifestyles. It is intended to convey the recognition, however, that impoverished families are more visibly dependent upon the public systems for support, and are, therefore, much more vulnerable to the lack of ample social supports, which further contributes to the magnitude of risk experienced by these families. The term refers to those impoverished families who cannot manage their family relationships and life tasks and are dependent upon others for their material and moral well-being and survival. Without such intervention these families would face death and destruction.

Multi-risk families have adapted their lifestyles and living strategies in such a way as to survive in their environment. They cope with their unpredictable, seemingly capricious, and dangerous world by developing patterns of under-organization (Aponte 1976b). Instead of dissolving as a family unit, these families tend to become under-organized, creating more fluidity in some ways and more rigidity in others. Against dangerous odds these families *do* survive.

These families have learned not to trust anyone, not even themselves. They live in tremendous isolation, even amid crowded living conditions. They have learned to be self-reliant—from childhood members have learned to be unrealistically self-sufficient. They have learned not to rely on others to meet their needs. They have learned to solve *their* problems, *their* way, even if this way is harmful and damaging to them or to their children. The intergenerational and intrafamilial cycle of this behavior is clinically documented in any public agency that tracks case flow, as well in the literature (Oliver and Taylor 1971; Harrell 1980).

In summary, multi-risk families are identified by three historic characteristics that place them at risk: 1) they experience severe and multiple problems of living[1]; 2) they are involved on an involuntary basis with at least one community agency of social control, such as Child Protection Service agencies or law enforcement agencies, and 3) they are members of a cultural and/or racial minority group whose values and family practices conflict with those recognized as socially acceptable in mainstream American society, many of which are codified into family law.

Theological Methodology: Christian Pastoral Counseling

The theological methodology used in this reflection about pastoral counseling is drawn from liberation theology (as articulated by Gutiérrez and Boff), which reestablishes the emphasis in Christian analysis on *action* (praxis) in light of the gospel. This theological methodology emphasizes the role and importance of authentic Christian behavior (orthopraxy) in relation to authentic Christian truths (orthodoxy). It is a theological method that emphasizes personal actions and social activities in the life of being a Christian. This theological method is "new" in the wake of a historical tradition that has emphasized the reflective and meditative aspect of theological activity. Schillebeeckx reflects the fundamental impulse for the renewed emphasis on action in the following:

> It is evident that thought is also necessary for action. But the Church has for centuries devoted her attention to formulating truths and meanwhile did almost nothing to better the world. In other words, the Church focused on orthodoxy and left orthopraxis in the hands of nonmembers and nonbelievers (Schillebeeckx 1970).

It is simply not sufficient to articulate what makes pastoral counseling "pastoral." A more foundational question emerges, What makes pastoral counseling *Christian*? Jon Sobrino argues that two principles make a university Christian: 1) the university's awareness of the presence of the anti-kingdom in the present reality; and 2) the university's willingness to align itself with the poor (Sobrino 1987).

Pastoral counselors need to take stock of their real involvement with poor, multi-risk families. We cannot just leave that up to the specialists who work with the poor. Are we open to learn ways of becoming involved in the treatment of these at risk families? Are we willing to work with under-organized families? To make home visits when office appointments are missed? To attend court hearings and agency staff meetings? To reschedule missed appointments as often as necessary until we have engaged the family? To attend to creatively and respond to the pace and lifestyle of multi-risk families? Are we willing to provide a proportion of our services based upon a client's ability to pay? Have we looked at ways of developing pastoral counseling cooperatives among colleagues to promote and sustain counseling services to this population, pooling transportation resources, financial assistance, and mutual support?

Sobrino notes that the university can be guided by a Christian inspiration, but that this can also be distorted and actually promote sin (the values of the world) more than gospel values. Sobrino is clear about this alignment. He writes unequivocally:

> For a university to be truly of Christian inspiration, it must place its whole social weight at the service of the poor, through its roles of teaching, research and social involvement, building the kingdom of God from its option for the poor (Sobrino 1987, p. 1).

This praxis-oriented (action-based) insight prompts the liberation theologian to attend to, and critically to reflect upon the suffering and social ills (evil) in the present moment, *denounce this evil*, and then seek a gospel application in concrete action to the present reality, thereby *announcing the moment of liberation*, the "inbreaking of the kingdom." This theological methodology invites and initiates the liberation theologian into an interactive (ecological) dialogue with his or her community (national) reality.

Sobrino's principles express the twofold dynamic of denouncement-announcement offered by liberation theologians to make the gospel message a living testimony of Jesus standing for the poor (Gutiérrez 1973). This method prompts the theologian to reflect upon, identify, and denounce the presence of sin, oppression, and darkness in the present moment, and to reflect upon, identify, and announce the saving activities (orthopraxis) of the gospel made incarnate in the life of the Christian.

It implies a familiarity with the concrete experience of the people, sustained with the belief that this is the locus of revelation in the light of the gospel. "It implies openness to the world, gathering questions it poses, being attentive to its historical transformations" (Gutiérrez 1973, p. 12). This methodology is also reflected in Congar's words:

> If the Church wishes to deal with the real questions of the modern world and attempt to respond to them . . . it must open . . . a new chapter of theologico-pastoral epistemology. Instead of using only revelation and tradition as starting points as classical theology has generally done, it must start with facts and questions derived from the world and from history (Congar 1967, p. 11).

In a reappropriation of Sobrino's insights into what makes a university Christian (Sobrino 1987) this article asserts that it is the degree to which the pastoral counselor is aligned and *doing work with impoverished multi-risk families in their local communities* that makes pastoral counseling *Christian*, not solely the pastoral counselor's explicit religious affiliation.

The Structural Basis of the Crisis of Gentleness and Care in Our Communities

Anyone who has worked in the public sector of mental health, community medicine, social services, law enforcement, or inner-city pastoral work knows that there is a terribly harsh and complex reality that devastates certain families in all of our communities. This devastation is seen in those families whose lifestyles, historical patterns of interpersonal relationships, and life experiences are characterized by violence in the family and random neighborhood violence, drug abuse, child abuse, death, destruction, and all kinds of human exploitation.

The firsthand witnesses to this devastation include those professionals who become involved in trying to help these families. Shortly after becoming involved with multi-risk, impoverished families (this can occur after the first contact) professionals will frequently identify with a sense of "being in the trenches." This poignant analogy, often heard by staff who "work on the front line" with these families, touches upon the heart of the difficulty in working with this impoverished clientele—they bring *us* into contact with their unbearable pain, fear, and vulnerability. Professionals engaged in providing mental health care services to the poor cannot escape sharing in their vulnerability. They are touched by a global sense of hopelessness, helplessness, and apathy that are part and parcel of the larger socioeconomic fabric, which views the poor as an unwelcome social burden. As a result, staff feel as though they are in darkness, in combat, and living off limited supplies in a danger zone.

To a certain degree these professionals share in this devastation experienced by their clients/patients through the chronic lack of sufficient resources and program cutbacks that occur unpredictably and without warning, due to ever-tightening budgets, both on local and federal levels.

There is a chronic fiscal crisis which parallels the human service crisis; this results in inadequate services to meet the catastrophic, intergenerational, and multi-disciplinary needs of these families. This fiscal crisis is a direct result of the Nixon era's "New Federalism," which sought to cut back drastically the social programs initiated in the so-called War on Poverty (Lyndon B. Johnson, March 1964). In response to an attempt to eliminate social services entirely from federal auspices, Walter Mondale and Jacob Javits introduced legislation aimed at preserving key elements of existing social welfare programs under the Nixon administration (Mott 1976, p. 28).

Mondale and Javits succeeded in passing the Social Security Act (Title XX).[2] This law set forth a model by which the federal government would encourage the provision of social services for individuals and families by the states. While Title XX affirmed the obligation of the government "to assist society's most vulnerable people to attain the highest possible level of independent living of which they are capable," it also asserted that these services "can best be provided by a combination of public and private agencies, all determined at the state and local levels, and not prescribed federally." (Mott 1976, p. 49).

Neither local governments nor private sector agencies, however, were prepared to pick up this complex task. So, on a state-by-state level the crisis in effective programming for the poor has varied greatly. By and large they are under-served, and those involved with them know this firsthand and cope with the service shortfall on a day-to-day basis.

Anyone working with the poor needs to develop bifocal vision to "see" the effects of the social-moral recession that is affecting our social infrastructures of family support and creating numerous problems in working with the poor. Both the multi-risk families and the people in the multi-risk treatment systems face harsh and unsympathetic realties. There is too little care and not enough gentleness to go around—no one wants to pay for these "social commodities." The prospects for change are not good for many self-serving political and economic reasons; there are few signs for an optimistic assessment of where this crisis will lead.

The only hope I see is if we begin to change our minds (in the sense of a society-wide *metanoia*) about what is *most* important to us as a nation. Maybe if we begin to take our future seriously, we will begin to take our present more responsibly. So far we have not been willing to pay the price for humane, gentle, and effective care of the poor. We seem committed to other national priorities, and we pay other costs. We continue to see the "enemy out there" and do not see the "enemy within"—our own insensitivity to our most vulnerable citizens. The deteriorating plight of the poor, our spiraling social-moral recession, has not yet been perceived as a national problem or a real security risk.

Ecosystemic Pastoral Counseling with the Poor

In providing ecosystemic pastoral counseling to the poor, multi-risk family, one must consider a number of specific factors. By definition these families are unmotivated and under-organized. They are not appealing or attractive clients. They often follow a violence-prone lifestyle, reinforced by violence-ridden communities. They have problems with honesty; their self-report often leaves major gaps or distortions in information. Multi-risk families are troublesome and disturbing on many levels.

The core element for involvement in ecosystemic pastoral counseling with poor, multi-risk families centers on the ongoing need for personal conversion on the part of the pastoral counselor. Without a change of heart, of mind, and of what constitutes "therapy," it is unlikely that pastoral counselors will be involved with these multi-risk families on any significant basis. In hope of building upon such a personal conversion, some of the clinical principles and practice implications will be discussed below. These will utilize various case illustrations composed of factual elements drawn from numerous families and case situations. Portions of verbatim interview materials have been included using fictitious names and altering some of the specific circumstances of the actual cases. Finally, a model of pastoral counseling with poor, multi-risk families will be explored.

"But All the Members, Many Though They Are, Are One Body" (1 Cor 12:12, *RSV*)

When we speak about an ecosystemic approach to pastoral counseling of the poor, we mean an approach that sees the interconnectedness and the interdependency of client, family, community, therapist, and body politic. An ecosystemic approach recognizes these "players" in the treatment system are not disconnected, but are intimately related and even interdependent in the provision or the failure to provide effective treatment of the multi-risk, impoverished family.

An ecosystemic approach to pastoral counseling with poor, multi-risk families means that pastoral counselors recognize that once they become involved with the multi-risk family, they also become profoundly influenced by powerful system dynamics. Pastoral counselors know that this system (in which they are an integral part) may organize in many expected and unexpected ways around the presenting problem identified by each member of the system concerning the multi-risk family. Pastoral counselors engaged with these multi-risk families quickly learns that if community funding for social services is inadequate, certain "needed" services will not be forthcoming. Pastoral counselors will also be aware that there may be a move to provide inappropriate services that may be available, just because something needs to be done! The sad social-political fact remains: we live in an affluent society that does not give priority to those families in our communities who are most in need, who are fragmented and literally falling apart. Multi-risk families who cannot function independently in our society are directly affected by any fiscal downturn. This becomes a very powerful system dynamic.

In working with this vulnerable population, pastoral counselors open themselves up to a side of life most Americans do not see or prefer not to see.

To use an analogy, pastoral counselors become aware of the ebb and flow of the ripples in the ecosystemic realities that affect the multi-risk family. Just as pond life is dependent upon and vulnerable to the presence of toxins or other dramatic changes in the ecosystem of the woodland pond on the fringe of an industrial center, so too is the multi-risk family dependent upon the multiple influences in the treatment system. Pastoral counselors need to become attuned to the movement and activities of the numerous persons involved in the treatment of the at-risk family, each making some change that affects the ecosystem of the client as well as each member of the treatment system.

Recalling the pond analogy, everyone involved with the multi-risk family has an impact that affects not only the client or family, but all others involved with the family as well, very much like the multiple, expanding, interlocking ripples that reverberate out to the pond edge and then return to the center when the water is disturbed. These ecosystemic effects (ripples) are not only one-way. They reverberate back and forth among the interacting members of the whole.

Therapists and counselors trained in clinical processes and strategies for helping middle-class Americans may not see what they can do for families overwhelmed with basic human needs and problems of concrete living. Their training, which primarily focuses upon intrapsychic or interpersonal problems, may obscure the impact poverty makes both on the multi-risk family *and* on the therapist's attitudes about the multi-risk family (Aponte 1974, 1982, 1986) in a society that overly values material success and competence.

When working with multi-risk families, the pastoral counselor becomes a member of a larger treatment team, frequently composed of numerous professionals. These professionals usually include social workers, probation officers, lawyers, psychotherapists, drug and alcohol counselors, psychologists, teachers, nurses, clergy, detectives, police, and judges. Together, whether they are consciously aware of their ecosystemic interrelatedness or not, these professionals form the treatment team of the multi-risk family.

Pastoral counselors engaged with multi-risk families need to be flexible and be able to develop realistic expectations and goals both for themselves and with the multi-risk family. Just because a family lacks insight into its problem does not mean it cannot benefit from pastoral counseling intervention. It may mean that the pastoral counselor has to include more behaviorally oriented goals and objectives. It may also mean that the pastoral counselor will take an active role in coordinating services with other community agencies and organizations to ensure that the treatment objectives developed by the numerous professionals involved with the multi-risk family are appropriate and coordinated in an effective and compassionate way. When needed services are not available in the local community, the pastoral counselor will be a mobilizing voice to denounce the inequity and to seek out appropriate remedies with other community professionals.

Ecosystemic Organization

Professionals who work with this multi-risk population must realize that the complex systems they will encounter *and become a part of* have their own organic movements, responses, and resistances—like individuals. The complex treatment systems that develop in the treatment process with the multi-risk family can, themselves, be functional or dysfunctional, or they may also include elements of both, depending on how each member organizes himself or herself around the "problem issue."

A general tenet in working with the poor is to be informed about the nature of the problem issue and then observe how the various members of the treatment eco-system (which includes family, mental health, social service, medical, and law enforcement professionals) organize around that issue. The ecosystemically sensitive pastoral counselor notices the predominant configuration of the systemic organization. The organization may emerge as one of two possible descriptive trends. These trends, which follow along a continuum, are identified as "systemic convergence" (Aponte, personal communication, 1990) and "systemic fission."

Systemic convergence is a type of ecosystemic organization around the multi-risk "problem issue." It may be understood as that point at which the larger treatment ecosystem comes together. This means that the goals, objectives, expectations, values, and purposes implicitly and explicitly held by the members of the system are reasonably coherent, consistent, and aligned. An example is when professionals engaged in the treatment process have a good understanding of the legal processes, and the law-enforcement professionals, in turn, understand and appreciate the sensitivities and parameters of the therapeutic process. Of course, since this is a theoretical concept, its precise occurrence has not been empirically tested. Nonetheless, it can be a crucial reality in the effective and appropriate treatment of the multi-risk family.

Conversely, the ecosystemic organization may also take the form of *systemic fission*. This is another type of ecosystemic organization around the "problem issue," but may be understood as that point where the larger treatment ecosystem breaks apart. Through this organizational trend, the goals, objectives, expectations, and purposes among the various players in the larger ecosystem are conflicted, inconsistent, and counter-aligned.

Systemic fission occurs when there are conflicting goals and objectives among the various professionals engaged in the therapeutic work with the multi-risk family. It is a kind of splintering among the family, social agency, court, pastoral counselor, and other professionals involved with the client that creates chaos, confusion, and may well be counterproductive. Unfortunately, there are numerous elements which reinforce systemic fission, not the least of which is inadequate funding for appropriate services for these families as well as interprofessional competition and "professional" squabbling.

Neither of these concepts is totally new; they are adaptations and further developments of Harry J. Aponte's ecostructural approach to treatment (Aponte 1974, 1976, 1990) and Tilman Furniss's work on conflict-by-proxy and resolution-by proxy dynamics in the systemic treatment of incest and child sexual abuse (Furniss 1983, 1984, 1987).

A Case Illustration: Magdalina's Baby

A case illustration may help flesh out some of these preliminary concepts in working with multi-risk families. This case illustration is a composite, recreated from actual case material from numerous cases. It involves a woman whom I will name Magdalina.

Magdalina was diagnosed with an organic brain syndrome, which contributed to her impaired ability to supervise her child effectively. She became involved with the child welfare agency after her three year old was found wandering outside their trailer home and onto the main road. Magdalina lacked the ability to provide appropriate supervision for her child due to her extremely high levels of distractibility, which left her virtually unable to concentrate on any two things at once. Hence, if she became engaged in some household chore, she become totally unaware of her need to monitor or supervise her child. Her mental handicap also left her with very poor impulse control; she tended to express herself in highly volitile outbursts. Her personal style tended to provoke anyone who attempted to help her.

An important ecosystemic reality for Magdalina was her limited (subsistent) income from public assistance. This qualified her to receive subsidized child care, but there were no providers available in the rural community where she lived. Her mental condition, exacerbated by her income deficiencies, social alienation, and lack of neighborhood resources, coupled with the unavailability of subsidized day care in her community, created a complex risk situation which eventually culminated in the allegation of neglect.

When the social worker from the child protection service agency informed her of the allegation of child neglect, Magdalina launched into a tirade of obscenities and counter-accusations. She repeated this behavior at the court hearing set to decide whether custody of the child should be awarded to the agency. Magdalina argued with the judge, but the "facts" were persuasive. She lost custody of her child. She also established a "bad reputation" in the system. Magdalina's handicapping condition and difficult personal style, the lack of available day care or in-home assistance, limited family support, and the community's desire to "protect its children" all contributed to a type of systemic fission.

In this instance the pastoral counselor easily could have been put off by the systemic fission and apparent chaos of the situation, frequently part and parcel in working with the multi-risk family. Magdalina's loud and offensive personal style, perhaps, made her more at risk for systemic fission. However, she called the pastoral counselor who had attended the court hearing and had provided some consolation for her. Magdalina continued her tirade against the social worker, the judge, and the whole "damn system" in speaking to the pastoral counselor on the telephone.

However, familiar with the report of neglect and the client's court performance, the pastoral counselor agreed to meet Magdalina that same day. Magdalina was able to find transportation and agreed to meet in his office. During the counseling session the pastoral counselor picked up on the broader systemic problem issue of the allegation of child neglect and confronted the client directly, in the immediacy of the counseling relationship:

> *Counselor:* I'd be happy to talk to you about your interest in getting custody of Jimmy back, but not if you are going to scream at me like you screamed at the judge.
>
> *Client:* I want to talk, and get my point across—she really got me mad. She's lucky I didn't pop her one!
>
> *Counselor:* You really got upset, Maddy, and you screamed and cussed—you know, that can frighten people. It's hard for people to talk to you when you are screaming at them. If you are willing to talk rationally with me I'll do everything I can to help you.

Client: (calmly, tearfully) I'm so scared that I won't see Jimmy again. . . . They said I neglected him, but I love him. I wouldn't do anything to hurt him . . .

Counselor: I know that you love Jimmy. I wonder if you let the social worker and judge know that?

Client: I really messed up. I just want to see Jimmy again . . . that's what made me so crazy . . . I'm not always that way.

Counselor: I know that, Maddy. Have you talked to the social worker about these worries like this?

Client: No.

Counselor: Maybe if you explained to her the way you explained to me, it would be a start to get your point across—that you really love Jimmy, and would like to see him.

Client: (crying) I really didn't mean to insult anybody . . . I just want to see my baby.

Counselor: If you like, you can call Ms. Jones from my telephone right now. Talk to her just like you've talked to me about it.

Allowing and inviting the client to call the social worker from the counselor's office is a concrete step in providing a "therapeutic" opportunity for the multi-risk client. Failing to provide such concrete assistance could necessitate the client calling the social agency from a public telephone booth, which is frequently the poor's only access to agencies. They cannot conveniently receive return messages when requested by agency secretaries to do so. If they are placed on hold for an extended period on a public phone, which frequently is the case at overloaded agency switchboards, they may be inadvertently disconnected, all of which sets up a situation of frustration and discouragement that easily evokes the client's customary dysfunctional response and reinforces failure in working with the very system she is required to negotiate with. Calling from the counselor's office also gave the client confidence and helped her maintain her perspective on the larger "problem issue."

In this illustration the pastoral counselor did not become part of the *systemic fission,* which may happen when a professional allies with the client *against* the apparent infringement made by the system, the social agency, and the court. The alternative is to ally *with* systemic intervention *and* with the client. This may be achieved by helping the client consider the reasonableness of the court action *and* by empathizing with the client's feelings about the situation. Within this therapeutic activity the pastoral counselor and client are in a better position to develop systemic convergence, whereby the goals and objectives of all parties—the social agency, court, and family—could be achieved.

By confronting the client about her behavior at court the pastoral counselor helped the client consider the unreasonableness of her style of communication and the possibility for a more reasonable alternative. In this situation the pastoral counselor was instrumental in helping the client develop the level of self-control needed to give rational testimony about her love and care for her child as well as her need for a child-care resource in her community. As a result, the court ordered the social agency (county government) to provide an appropriate day-care provider in the client's local community.

As we attempt to understand and help the families who live on the socioeconomic fringe, we are met with a sobering glimpse of our own inadequacies, sense of hopelessness, and limitations reflected and reinforced by the social reality. The problems facing these families tend to be extremely complex, with no simple solutions. There are pressures to maintain the status quo of noninvolvement. These problems involve both the intrapsychic confusion and extra-social malaise of the impoverished, multi-risk family, which reflects the failure of the larger body politic to provide adequate care and sustenance to meet the needs of its most dependent citizens. Pastoral counselors can make a difference!

The Person of the Pastoral Counselor: Personal Conversions

Pastoral counselors who seek greater involvement with the poor will invariably make three professional shifts or conversions in their thinking and in their therapeutic activity.

The first conversion will involve a shift away from a self-definition or perception of power and expertise to a position of shared powerlessness and helplessness. This preliminary conversion will entail a personal change from a position of clinical objectivity/indifference (repulsion) to the plight of the poor, to a position of an empathic embrace (inclusion) with the plight of the poor. This personal conversion will enable the pastoral counselor to greet the impoverished client as an equal, a co-journeyer, rather than an inferior or "someone who cannot benefit from counseling and really needs a social worker."

The second conversion will involve a professional shift from an autonomous, privatized model of therapy to a more inclusive, collective, and collegial model of therapy. This shift will enable the pastoral counselor to become a partner in a larger community-based treatment team. In making this shift the pastoral counselor will come to realize that sometimes "therapy is not therapeutic" and sometimes non-therapy is (Furniss 1987). A "therapy" that does not confront and contain violent, exploitative, or otherwise abusive behavior may tacitly reinforce it and actually be counter-therapeutic.

Conversely, sometimes non-therapy activities can be therapeutic. A policeman, caseworker, probation or parole officer, or judge, confronting a client with evidence presented in court, is not therapy as such, but can have a powerful therapeutic effect in containing dangerous, violent, or otherwise destructive behavior. Here the pastoral counselor sees the importance and role of non-therapist allies involved with the multi-risk family. These allies include law enforcement agencies, social agencies, and the courts—sometimes perceived as antagonistic to traditional, privatized models of therapy.

The third conversion will involve a political shift from being a passive community observer to becoming an active community participant in the political and fiscal processes, especially those that allocate funds and set priorities for services in the local community.

Involvement with the poor will take the pastoral counselor outside his or her office to the broader therapeutic environment of the larger community-based treatment system for the poor. The change prompted by the ecosystemic exposure will also prompt a spiritual expansion within the pastoral counselor from a spirituality of introspective contemplation (attuned to interior ripples) to a spirituality of ecospective liberation (attuned to both the interior and exterior ripples)—whereby the pastoral counselor sees the client/patient in living and interacting relationship with a community that can further assist or further threaten the well-being of the multi-risk family.

In making the shift away from a perception of power and clinical expertise to a position of shared powerlessness and an empathic embrace (inclusion) with the plight of the poor suggested above, the pastoral counselor will discover that the formal clinical boundaries of traditional psychotherapy become more fluid and flexible. By pacing his or her intervention to the lifestyle, level of socioeconomic subsistence, cultural (meaning) context, and needs of the family, the pastoral counselor becomes deeply aware of the limitations and possibilities experienced by the clients, as well as the deep interconnectedness between economic assistance and clinical intervention.

Aware of the reality of these economic limitations, the pastoral counselor can then be responsive to helping the family overcome economic barriers in a creative way as well as overcoming psychodynamic resistances. They are no longer viewed in an either-or construct.

Professional Boundaries or Barriers?

In another case a pastoral counselor, in conjunction with a local children's theater group, obtained a number of free tickets to distribute to economically disadvantaged children for a lively, interactive children's play. As part of this arrangement, the pastoral counselor also helped to fund transportation to and from the theater. For the middle class, transportation is usually a "given." For the multi-risk poor it is not a "given"; the lack of transportation frequently prevents the poor from attending not only cultural events, but therapeutic opportunities as well! So in providing the tickets as well as a rented van and a counselor-aide to transport the children, the pastoral counselor reached out to an otherwise anonymous group of children from multi-risk families.

In route to a performance one of the children told the driver (who was also a co-therapist) that she was afraid of her father, and that he had beaten her mother. The family had formerly been seen in family counseling, but due to the father's frequent crack addiction relapses, withdrew from counseling on numerous occasions. With this child's contact through the children's theater event, the counselor was able to reestablish contact with the mother to offer services—to which she readily agreed. Shortly afterward, the father requested counseling after learning that he was HIV positive. The children's play (a non-therapy activity) served as the opportunity for re-engagement of the family into therapy. While the theater intervention was separate and distinct from the therapy intervention, the two formed an ecosystemic intervention through the common link of the family counselor-aide who provided transportation and supervision services for the children. Children will frequently disclose their concerns to trusted adults at their own pace and in their own time.

Invariably the question of professional boundaries arises. In providing pastoral counseling to poor, multi-risk families, the pastoral counselor will discover that professional boundaries have less to do with social convention—control of time, place, and duration of therapy, and so on—and more to do with his or her own professional integrity. Rather than ascribe to any set social conventions to define the therapeutic parameters of helping, the pastoral counselor engaged with the poor must creatively develop therapeutic responses in pace with the family's actual needs. These responses will not be one-dimensional, as *psycho*logical, but multidimensional, and will include *socioeconomical* assistance as an integral component of the pastoral therapeutic intervention (Fleischer 1975).

Pastoral counselors need to challenge the assumption that because a multi-risk family cannot or does not follow the same social conventions for therapy as a middle-class client (e.g., arrive on time, have its own source of transportation, be capable of arranging child care, etc.) that it is "not appropriate for treatment." Poor people do not have the socioeconomic luxury to compartmentalize their therapy needs. As a consequence, pastoral counseling with the poor must be integral. It must address the whole person—psychological, social, spiritual, and economic (see *Populorum Progressio,* 1967; *Toward a Renewed Catholic Charities Movement,* 1976).

When engaged with poor people pastoral counselors will not be able to limit themselves to a 50-minute hour or to a formal appointment in an office or to an inflexible schedule. Following such middle-class conventions only serves to alienate the multi-risk family even more and sustains the unavailability of *any* pastoral therapeutic treatment. Pastoral counselors will need to adjust and pace their interventions to the realities of their clients and will need to schedule meetings with families or clients in their home, at the social agency, at the welfare office, at the school, or at the courtroom, depending upon the situation and need (Aponte 1976a).

For the pastoral counselor engaged with the multi-risk, impoverished family professional boundaries are not maintained by a rigid, prescribed, and preconceived notion of "what therapy is." Involvement with the multi-risk family, where there is chronic and pervasive deficiencies and limitations in human and social services, demands creativity and imagination on the part of the pastoral counselor and therapist. In this context professional boundaries are maintained by the *person* of the pastoral counselor—by his or her attitude, therapeutic orientation, and personal style (Aponte 1982). Such professional boundaries are based upon recognized ethical and practice standards that are not solely drawn from the values and prerogatives of the white, male, middle-class majority, which are often based upon power, control, dominance, and economic competition.

Serendipitously, the pastoral counselor can act both as *counselor* and *advocate* for the multi-risk family and can become an agent of compassion and *caritas,* not only sitting with the impoverished client in the counseling session, but standing by the client as well, being wherever systemic intervention requires the counselor to be.

Another Case Illustration: Evie's Ribs

How does the principle of shared powerlessness and empathic embrace (inclusion) with the plight of the poor look in clinical practice? One poignant example may be seen in the case of a family involved in a child abuse investigation. To illustrate this discussion another factual case situation has been reconstructed using non-identifying and disguised data that maintains the integrity of the actual case. This case is not atypical.

The case situation involves parents who brought their infant to a hospital emergency room because she was having trouble breathing. Medical examination revealed that the infant had serious fractures to her legs, allegedly due to becoming tangled in the vertical bars of her crib. While the parents asserted the injuries occurred by accident, the father was suspected as the "perpetrator" (abuser) since the child was under his care at the time of the alleged accident. The father vehemently denied any wrongdoing, and his wife vouched for his explanation of the injuries.

The child welfare agency, unconvinced, requested a long-bone study, in which a total X-ray scan of the skeleton is done to detect older injuries. The family protested, and it was not until a court order was obtained by the child welfare agency that the complete skeleton study was done. The findings were startling. The study showed previous fractures to the child's ribs. The parents attributed these injuries to a time when they had the baby sleeping with them. The father, who was a stocky man, said he "rolled over on her in his sleep."

The depth of denial and ambiguity in working with multi-risk families is deep and troubling. It was not until the child welfare agency called in a recognized child abuse expert examiner (after three local community physicians had equivocated about the implications of the X-rays) that the specific type of the fractures was identified as being caused by deliberate lateral motion, breaking the infant's legs as one would break a pencil.

In this case the pastoral counselor had been involved with the family around parent-support issues, the mother's depression and her feelings of being overwhelmed, as well as the economic problems associated with the father's lack of employment, which left the family on the verge of eviction from their apartment. Once the allegations of serious physical abuse were made by a hospital social worker, the pastoral counselor became a confidante to the parents and was an important source of support through the systematic child abuse investigation and subsequent court processes. The pastoral counselor was extremely helpful, not in isolation, but in concert with the larger agency-court intervention with this family and infant.

Throughout these processes the father consistently denied any wrongdoing and blamed the social workers for "trying to destroy my family." The equivocation by medical personnel only served to reinforce the client's denial of abuse and exacerbated the systemic fission. Empathizing with the parents, but appreciating the investigative work of the child welfare agency and the court, the pastoral counselor maintained a viable, ongoing relationship with the family, avoiding being pitted against the social agency. The pastoral counselor kept a delicate balance and worked toward systemic convergence. For example:

> *Client:* I don't like talking to her (the social worker). I can't trust her. She writes down everything I say, and then goes and tells the judge. . . . They're all against me.
>
> *Counselor:* It isn't easy going through a child abuse investigation, Mr. Jones. The social workers are required to ask a lot of tough questions, and they are legally required to report back to the court on their findings. It may seem that "they're all against you," but they have reason to do the investigation. . . . Those injuries were serious enough to require the agency to be involved with you. As difficult as it is, you have to work with them. They are trying to understand what happened to Evie—how she got hurt—so it won't happen again.

While the pastoral counselor maintained an empathetic posture toward the client, he did not collude with or affirm the client's mistrust of the investigation process. Instead, the pastoral counselor helped the client see the reasonableness of the investigation and helped focus the client on the goal of the investigation—the protection and safety of the child. In this way the pastoral counselor avoided systemic fission and contributed to the possibility for systemic convergence.

In addition to meeting with the young couple (the infant was placed in foster care during the investigation process), the pastoral counselor also provided transportation services for the family to and from court, the agency, and to supervised visits with their infant. The pastoral counselor was not only available formally during the "therapeutic hour" of counseling, but was available informally, as a friend, companion, and provider of practical help and assistance to the family (e.g., periodic rent assistance, child care, and transportation).

It was during the ride home after a particularly distressing cross-examination process that the father disclosed to the pastoral counselor that he "could have killed Evie . . . her crying was so bad . . . he could have just killed her." The father stated, without any remorse evident in his voice or manner, that she was lucky he didn't kill her. Upon reflection he admitted, "If I had (killed her), we'd all be a lot better off!"

Half believing what he had heard the father say, the pastoral counselor asked for clarification. The father explained how he had held the baby (causing the specific injuries to the child) and demonstrated how he had attempted physically to silence the baby's crying. Finally he resorted to punishing her by clutching her limbs in a grotesque fashion. The pastoral counselor confronted the father about this disclosure, reminded him that by law he was required to give the child welfare agency this information, and urged the father to be honest with the investigation process. The pastoral counselor clarified the seriousness and life-threatening nature of what the father said. At this confrontation the father broke down into tears, recalling his own abusive childhood, his lack of readiness for parenthood, and his frustration in not being able to keep a steady job.

In this therapeutic moment the entire heretofore undisclosed drama unfolded before the pastoral counselor while driving home from the court hearing. The pastoral counselor was available to hear an honest disclosure which the father of the infant had been hiding from the court, from his wife, from the abuse investigation, and from his own conscious awareness. Within the pastoral counseling relationship, prompted by the agency and court action, this man was able to disclose his own violent behavior toward his child with disarming honesty.

This father's disclosure was not the result of any one intervention, but rather the result of an effective ecosystemic convergence. The success of this therapeutic organization was made possible through the ongoing cooperation and collaboration among the mental health, social welfare, and law enforcement professionals (including the pastoral counselor) throughout the process of investigation, confrontation, cross-examination, and therapy. In this case the goals, objectives, and purposes of the social agency and court were not seen as aversive to the therapeutic goals, objectives, and purpose.

In a very real way the pastoral counselor was part of a team intervention which gradually resulted in the father's disclosure of his intention of infanticide. Without rejecting the client, in fact in an ongoing process of unconditional acceptance, the pastoral counselor was able to confront this parent with the seriousness of his actions and the importance of being honest in the investigation process. The counselor was instrumental in coming to a clearer understanding of the domestic violence problems faced by the family and the mortal vulnerability of the infant.

The pastoral counseling efforts, child welfare agency, and court intervention were mutually instrumental in effectively organizing (i.e., achieving ecosystemic convergence) around the real treatment issues. These included the father's own unresolved abusive childhood, his deep unresolved feelings about his own infant, the mother's unspoken fear of her husband's violent temper (which she covered up), and the need for alternate family care to safeguard this infant from more serious harm, very possibly death.

By providing concrete assistance (i.e., transportation services together with supportive counseling services), this pastoral counselor provided pastoral therapeutic services to this family *based upon its unique needs and problems*. By embracing the family's limitations and powerlessness, economically as well as psycho-socially, the clinician became a credible helper to this multi-risk family.

The other foundational principle of our model of pastoral counseling with multi-risk families illustrated in the above case summary is the shift from an autonomous, privatized model of therapy to a more inclusive, collective model of therapy.

While the pastoral counselor was engaged with the couple in pastoral counseling, by accompanying them to the court hearings he was also very much aware of the family's involvement with the child welfare agency and the court. Rather than assume a detached role from the child abuse investigation process, this pastoral counselor assumed an active role with this family. While the pastoral counselor was not required to provide testimony at court—since the father did admit his abusive behavior to the court—the therapeutic involvement of this pastoral counselor was not antagonistic toward the broader community concerns identified about this family by the child welfare agency and court.

Core Clinical Principles

While clinical intervention with multi-risk families requires the same level of clinical expertise, accountability, and care as traditional person-centered clinical intervention, the unique systemic complex affecting the multi-risk family, that is, the involvement of the community agencies of social control (the police, child welfare agencies, domestic relations, etc.) requires a number of additional clinical guidelines.

Clinical intervention with multi-risk families requires that the pastoral counselor develops interprofessional coordination and leadership skills as well as the ability to become an interacting member of a larger treatment team composed of clinicians as well as non-clinical professionals (e.g., law enforcement personnel). Such work requires the ability to see the larger clinical perspective of the family, not only the individual clients' self-reports but also the data received by and from the involved social and law enforcement agencies as well.

Being a member of a team need not be a physical activity such as meeting on a regular weekly or monthly basis, although in some cases it may. Team intervention does require a conceptual awareness of larger, interrelated components of the clinical and law enforcement foci of the case in the pastoral treatment. While there are numerous unique elements to clinical work with these families, there are two distinctive elements the pastoral counselor should consider when he or she becomes clinically involved in these complex cases.

Shared Confidentiality

In the illustrations the pastoral counselor respected client confidentiality *within legal parameters* but was also aware of the limitations of professional confidentiality. Professional confidentiality is not an absolute value. It does not, for example, exempt pastoral counselors from reporting instances of "suspected child abuse" or "neglect" (*The Juvenile Act*, 42 Pa. C.S.A. Sec. 6301, 1981). The laws in most states which protect children from abuse and neglect also include penalties for professionals mandated to report who fail to do so, making it a second-degree misdemeanor [e.g., New Jersey Stat. Ann. (9:6–8. 14 1976); North Dakota (Century Code 50-25. 1–13 (1989

Interim Supp.)] and immunities, that is, protection from civil or criminal liabilities that might arise when a mandated reporter makes a report of child abuse to the respective authority [e.g., New Jersey statute 9. 6–8. 13 (1989 Cum Supp.)].

The pastoral counselor, in the above illustration involving the infant who experienced severe physical abuse was not a neutral party. He was involved in a much larger therapeutic effort that included the social (child welfare) agency and the court. This involvement carried certain ethical and legal responsibilities, not only to insure the confidentiality of the client contacts, but also to insure the safety of the child, the alleged victim of serious physical abuse.

In this case, if the father had not disclosed his experience with his infant to the court, the pastoral counselor would be required to do so both ethically and legally. To fail to report disclosures of abuse when mandated to do so tacitly reinforces the violent behavior and is counter-therapeutic, in addition to being illegal and unethical.

While this principle may be widely acknowledged, there is considerable social pressure to minimize the seriousness of child abuse and a tendency among (adult) therapists to ally with the parent (adult) perpetrator of the abuse. In a society that tolerates tremendous levels of violence, confronting abuse in the clinical situation becomes almost counter-cultural. I know of one incident where a pastoral counselor was relieved of counseling duties in a congregation for making a report of child abuse involving a parishioner. The mandated report by the pastoral counselor was perceived by the pastor as "unprofessional" and "unpastoral." The irony, conflict, and paradox here is self-evident, but real.

Intersystem Consultation/Clinical Teamwork

Whenever there is an allegation of child abuse, an elaborate system of community intervention is brought into play. The primary concern of the community agencies is the protection of the child and the safeguarding of family life. Since this "line" is often narrow and controversial, the family court system is often involved in ascertaining facts about the case as well as ensuring compliance of family members in the investigation process while protecting the civil liberties of all the parties involved.

Once the "abuse" has been established by the child protective service agency or "founded" in court (which bears greater legal weight), based upon court testimony, the multi-risk family is assigned a case manager who is responsible for developing and monitoring an appropriate treatment plan, called a *Family Service Plan (FSP)*. The *FSP* is a legal document that binds the child protective service agency, family, and involved professionals to a coordinated treatment plan, which is reviewed on a six-month basis by the team. Such legal intervention frequently provides the "therapeutic leverage" that might motivate an otherwise unmotivated family and can be a valuable therapeutic force in the treatment process. The *FSP* also helps to establish, clarify, and coordinate appropriate treatment goals to resolve the abusive situation.

The outcome of court involvement is usually a court order or a consent decree, legal documents of varying enforceable weight. These usually include stipulations—specific and legally binding actions to which the parties agree. Frequently the elements of the court order are included in the *Family Service Plan*. Since there is historically great resistance to treatment by multi-risk families, the stipulations included in court documents and the *Family Service Plan* can provide powerful incentives for the multi-risk family to enter treatment or face legal consequences.

In the above illustration the parents were required to enter counseling or risk losing custody of their infant. Since they had been involved with a pastoral counselor in the past, they were encouraged to return to this counselor. At this point the pastoral counselor became a member of the treatment team.

When involved with multi-risk families on an involuntary basis (court referral), the pastoral counselor should request to see any court order or consent decrees that may be in effect as well as the name of the family's case manager. The case manager may be a social worker or an other professional mandated by the primary public social agency to oversee the case. Case managers are usually key players in the development of the treatment plans for multi-risk families and should be contacted by the pastoral counselor, with the client's informed permission.

Whenever it is known that a client is involved with agencies of social control or law enforcement (e.g., child welfare, domestic relations, parole, the court, etc.), permission to contact the respective agency should be obtained by the pastoral counselor to learn about any treatment expectations that may already exist. Frequently multi-risk families have long and difficult "histories" with the court and social systems, and these data are critical materials for effective clinical intervention.

Pastoral counselors need to reach out to community agencies and establish a face-to-face contact with at least the intake worker. Social agencies, while frequently overwhelmed, are usually amenable to providing case consultation prior to a counselor's making a report. Such advance consultation enables the counselor to determine whether a situation warrants reporting and also helps facilitate a referral if one is to be made. Thus it can help humanize what can very easily become just a routine bureaucratic process, "just another abuse case."

The pastoral counselor need not be the outsider looking in. He or she can play an important role in the development and implementation of a treatment plan that really addresses the complex needs of the multi-risk family. By entering this process the pastoral counselor may also be an advocate for obtaining additional social or family services needed by the clients.

In light of the overwhelming needs of abused children and their families and the limitations of the social systems to adequately meet the needs of these clients (as cited in the above literature review), there is an emerging and critical role for the pastoral counselor engaged with multi-risk families.

Conclusion

The third conversion discussed above touched upon the pastoral counselor's need to develop sensitivity and awareness of the direct impact the political reality of the local community has on the allocation of funding services for the poor. Pastoral counseling with the poor, multi-risk family is complex. It expands the role of the pastoral counselor to include involvement with community planning activities. The pastoral counselor should know how, what, and why community funds are allocated, and subsequently, advocate that services needed by the poor be included in the local budgets.

Most public community agencies have citizen advisory boards and conduct annual meetings or hearing to review their proposed budgets. My experience with these processes is that they are seldom attended by the public at large. Pastoral counselors can attend these public meetings, ask basic questions pertaining about housing, emergency services, day care, and look at the proportion of funding allocated to social and family services. These activities are inherently pastoral. They give public testimony that the church is standing with the poor and recognizes the relationship between good mental health treatment and decent living conditions.

Administrators of child welfare and mental health service agencies need all the public support they can muster—rallying support for much needed social services in the local communities is a practical application of making an option for the poor. Pastoral counselors must not wait for an invitation to community involvement. The gospel mandate is crystal clear about the acceptable response in ministering to the least among us.

By reaching out to community agencies, by meeting administrators, establishing rapport with supervisors and frontline workers in child welfare agencies and family court judges, important bridges are built and the foundation reinforced for renewed hope in serving poor, multi-risk families in our communities.

Postscript

Some might argue that such a community-oriented approach to pastoral counseling dilutes the unique role of the pastoral counselor, and that, functionally, he or she may be no different from a social worker. I think such an argument begs the question. In developing community-oriented approaches to pastoral counseling in the service of the poor, the pastoral counselor is not functioning as a social worker, nor is the role pastoral counselor role "diluted." What happens is that the pastoral counselor stretches some of the therapeutic limits imposed by the traditional medical models of treatment that have influenced the field to include more fluid and flexible limits for therapy, limits that are integral for more community-oriented therapeutic models. This professional process is one of liberation, not dilution.

What we are proposing here is that the pastoral counselor co-opt treatment methods that social workers, as well as community-oriented psychiatrists and psychologists, have found necessary and essential to treat the multi-risk families.

Pastoral counselors need to learn ways to define their roles based upon their own personal integrity and their willingness to stand with the poor. It is our willingness to seek out the needs of poor, multi-risk families and meet them to whatever extent is necessary that defines whether or not what pastoral counseling we do is "Christian." This will not be an easy task.

Notes

1. By this I mean that these families face catastrophic problems on three levels: (1) they face severe socioeconomic stress that places them in material danger (they lack adequate food, shelter, and security); (2) they experience severe psycho-social stress (they lack emotional and psychological resources to cope with the demands of living); and (3) they are exposed to severe environmental stress (they subsist in substandard living conditions).

2. "Social Services Program for Individuals and Families: Title XX of the Social Security Act." *Federal Register,* vol. 40, no. 125 (June 27, 1975).

References

Abbott, Walter, M., ed. 1966. *Documents of Vatican II.* New York: Guild Press.

Abramczyk, L. W. 1981. "The Counseling Function of Pastors: A Study in Practice and Preparation." *Journal of Psychology and Theology* 9, 3: 257–65.

Adams, Paul, and McDonald, Nancy. 1968. "Clinical Cooling Out of Poor People." *American Journal of Orthopsychiatry* 38, 4: 457–63.

Aponte, Harry J. 1974a. "Psychotherapy for the Poor: An Eco-Structural Approach to Treatment." *Delaware Medical Journal* (March): 1–7.

———. 1974b. "Organizing Treatment Around the Family's Problems and Their Structural Bases." *Psychiatric Quarterly* 48: 209–22.

———. 1976a. "The Family-School Interview: An Eco-Structural Approach." *Family Process* 15: 303–11.

———. 1976b. "Underorganization in the Poor Family." In *Family Therapy: Theory and Practice,* edited by J. Guerin. New York: Gardner Press.

———. 1979. "Diagnosis in Family Therapy." In *Social Work Practice: People and Environments,* edited by C. Germain. New York: Columbia University Press.

———. 1982. "The Person of the Therapist: The Cornerstone of Therapy." *Family Therapy NetWorker* (March–April): 19–21, 46.

———. 1986. "If I Don't Get Simple, I Cry." *Family Process* 25: 531–48.

Arnold, J. David, and Schick, Connie. 1979. "Counseling by Clergy: A Review of Empirical Research." *Journal of Pastoral Counseling* 14, 2: 76–101.

Auerswald, Edgar H. 1968. "Interdisciplinary Versus Ecological Approach." *Family Process* 15: 202–15.

______. 1972. "Families, Change, and the Ecological Perspective." *Family Process* 18: 263–80.

______. 1985. "Thinking About Thinking in Family Therapy." *Family Process* 24: 1–12.

______. 1987. "Epistemological Confusion in Family Therapy and Research." *Family Process* 26(3): 317–30.

Auslander, Gail, and Litwin, Howard. 1988. "Social Networks and the Poor: Toward Effective Policy and Practice." *Social Work* 33, 3: 234–38.

Bentley, Steven. 1984. "The Pastoral Challenge of an Abusive Situation." *Journal of Religion and Health* 23(4): 283–89.

Billingsley, Andrew. 1969. "Family Functioning in the Low-Income Black Community." *Social Casework* (December): 563–71.

Birt, Charles J. 1956. "Family-centered Project of St. Paul." *Social Casework* (October): 41–47.

Boff, Leonardo. 1984. *St. Francis: A Model for Human Liberation*, trans. John W. Diercksmeier. New York: Crossroad Publishing Co.

Booth, Charles, ed. 1892. *Life and Labour of the People in London*, vol. 1. London: Macmillan.

Bowker, Lee H. 1982. "Battered Women and the Clergy: An Evaluation." *Journal of Pastoral Care* 36(4) (December): 226–34.

Breton, Margot. 1989. "Liberation Theology, Group Work, and the Right of the Poor and Oppressed to Participate in the Life of the Community." Ninth Annual Symposium for the Advancement of Social Work with Groups. *Social Work with Groups* 12: 3, 5–18.

Brown, G. 1968. *The Multi-Problem Dilemma*. Metuchen, N.J.: Scarecrow Press.

Buell, Bradley. 1948. "Know What the What Is." *Survey Midmonthly* (October).

______ and Associates. 1952. *Community Planning for Human Services*. New York: Columbia University Press.

Bullis, Ronald K. 1990. "Child Abuse Reporting Requirements: Liabilities and Immunities for Clergy." *The Journal of Pastoral Care* 44(3) (Fall): 244–48.

Chavkin, Wendy. Testimony at Hearing. "Born Hooked: Confronting the Impact of Perinatal Substance Abuse." Select Committee on

Children, Youth, and Families. U.S. House of Representatives. Washington, D.C.: April 27, 1989.

Clausen, J., and Kohn, M. 1954. "The Ecological Approach in Social Psychiatry." *American Journal of Sociology* 60: 140–51.

Colon, F. 1980. "The Family Life Cycle of the Multiproblem Poor Family." In *The Family Life Cycle: A Framework for Family Therapy,* edited by E. A. Carter and M. McGoldrick, pp. 343–81. New York: Gardner Press.

Congar, Yves M. J. 1967. *Situations et tâches presentes de la théologie.* Paris: Les Editions du Cerf.

Crews, D. W. 1966. "Counseling Behavior and Religious Beliefs of Methodist Ministers." Doctoral Dissertation, University of Florida. *Dissertation Abstracts International* 27: 3329A–3330A, University Microfilms No. 67-034, 84.

Denham, Thomas E. 1986. "Avoiding Malpractice Suits in Pastoral Counseling." *Pastoral Psychology* 35, 2: 83–93.

Dick, Kenneth, and Strnad, Lydia J. 1953. "The Multi-problem Family and Problems of Service." *Social Casework* 34, 7: 349–55.

Edwards, Andrew W. 1982. "The Consequences of Error in Selecting Treatment for Blacks." *Social Casework* 63, 7 (September): 429–36.

Fleischer, Gerald. 1975. "Producing Effective Change in Impoverished, Disorganized Families: Is Family Therapy Enough?" *Family Therapy* 2, 3: 277–89.

Foley, V. 1975. "Family Therapy with Black Disadvantaged Families: Some Observations on Roles, Communications, and Techniques." *Journal of Marriage and Family Counseling* 1: 29–38.

Furniss, Tilman. 1983. "Mutual Influence and Interlocking Professional-Family Process in the Treatment of Child Sexual Abuse and Incest." *Child Abuse and Neglect* 7: 207–23.

———. 1984. "Conflict Avoiding and Conflict Regulating Pattern in Incest and Child Sexual Abuse." *Acta Paedo-psych.* 50: 299–313.

———. 1987. "A Meta-Systemic Approach to Child Sexual Abuse: The Inter-Locking Process Between Family Dynamics and Professional Systems." Workshop presented at the International Structural Family Therapy Conference, Philadelphia Child Guidance Clinic.

Garanzini, Michael J. 1988. "Troubled Homes: Pastoral Responses to Violent and Abusive Families." *Pastoral Psychology* 36(4) (Summer), 218–29.

Geismar, Ludwig. 1961. "Three Levels of Treatment for the Multi-Problem Family." *Social Casework* 42, 3: 124–27.

______. 1973. *555 Families: A Social-Psychological Study of Young Families in Transition.* New Brunswick, N.J.: Transaction Books.

______. 1980. *Family and Community Functioning,* 2d ed., Metuchen, N.J.: Scarecrow Press.

______, and Ayres, Beverly. 1958. *Families in Trouble.* St. Paul, Minn.: Family Centered Project.

______, and Ayres, Beverly. 1959. *Patterns of Change in Problem Families.* St. Paul, Minn.: Family Centered Project.

______, and La Sorte, M. A. 1963. "Research Interviewing with Low-Income Families." *Social Work* 8, 2: 10–14.

______, and La Sorte, M. A. 1964. *Understanding the Multi-Problem Family: A Conceptual Analysis and Exploration in Early Identification.* New York: Associated Press.

______, La Sorte, M. A., and Ayres, B. 1962. "Measuring Family Disorganization." *Marriage and Family Living* 24, 1: 52–60.

______, and Krisberg, J. 1967. *The Forgotten Neighborhood: Site of an Early Skirmish in the War on Poverty.* Metuchen, N.J.: Scarecrow Press.

______; Lagay, G.; Wolock, I.; Gerhart, U. C.; and Fink, H. 1972. *Early Supports for Family Life.* Metuchen, N.J.: Scarecrow Press.

______, and Geismar, S. 1979. *Families in an Urban Mold.* New York: Pergamon Press.

______, and Wood, K. 1989. *Families at Risk: Treating the Multiproblem Family.* New York: Human Sciences Press.

Gutiérrez, Gustavo. 1973. *A Theology of Liberation.* Translated and edited by Sister Caridad Inda and John Eagleson. Maryknoll, N.Y.: Orbis Books.

Hallinan, Helen W. 1959. "Co-ordinating Agency Efforts in Behalf of the Hard-to-Reach Family." *Social Casework* 40, 1: 9–17.

Hardy-Fanta, Carol, and MacMahon-Herrera, E. 1981. "Adapting Family Therapy to the Hispanic Family." *Social Casework* (March): 138–47.

Harrell, F. 1980. "Family Dependency as a Transgenerational Process: An Ecological Analysis of Families in Crisis." Ph.D. diss. University of Massachusetts, Amherst.

Hartman, Ann. 1970. "To Think About the Unthinkable." *Social Casework* 51 (October): 459–68.

Henning, Lawrence H. 1987. "The Emotional Impact of Treating Child Abuse." *Journal of Religion and Health* 26(1) (Spring): 37–42.

Holbrook, Terry L. 1983. "Going Among Them: The Evolution of the Home Visit." *Journal of Sociology and Social Welfare* 10, 1: 112–35.

Hudson, R. V. 1955. "A Survey of Counseling Techniques as Used by the Clergy." Ph.D. diss., Purdue University, 1950. *Dissertation Abstracts* 15: 2294 (University Microfilms No. 00-138, 13).

Johnson, Eric D. 1978. "Social Pastoral Care in the Urban Setting." *The Journal of Pastoral Care* 32(4) (December): 251–55.

McAdoo, Harriet. 1977. "Family Therapy in the Black Community." *American Journal of Orthopsychiatry* 47 (1) (January).

McKenzie, John L. 1968. "The Gospel According to Matthew." In *The Jerome Biblical Commentary*, vol. 2. Englewood Cliffs, N.J.: Prentice-Hall.

Miller, George. 1986. *Safety Net Programs: Are They Reaching Poor Children?* (Report No. 99-1023). Select Committee on Children, Youth, and Families, U. S. House of Representatives. Washington, D.C.: U. S. Government Printing Office.

———. 1987. *Abused Children in America: Victims of Official Neglect.* Select Committee on Children, Youth, and Families, U. S. House of Representatives. Washington, D.C.: U. S. Government Printing Office.

———. 1990. *No Place to Call Home: Discarded Children in America* (Report No. 101-395). Select Committee on Children, Youth, and Families, U. S. House of Representatives. Washington, D.C.: U. S. Government Printing Office.

Minuchin, Salvador. 1968. "Psychoanalytic Therapies and the Low Socio-economic Population." In *Modern Psychoanalysts*, edited by J. Marmor. New York: Basic Books.

———. 1970a. "The Use of an Ecological Framework in the Treatment of a Child." In *The Child in His Family: Vol. I*, edited by E. J. Anthony and C. Koupernick. New York: John Wiley, pp. 41–57.

———. 1970b. "The Plight of the Poverty-Stricken Family in the United States." *Child Welfare* 49 (March): 124–30.

———, and Montalvo, B. 1966b. "Techniques for Working with Disorganized Low Socioeconomic Families." *American Journal of Orthopsychiatry:* 880–87.

———; Montalvo, B.; Buerney, B. G.; Rosman, B. L.; and Schumer, F. 1967. *Families of the Slums: An Exploration of Their Structure and Treatment.* New York: Basic Books.

Moffic, Steven H.; Brochstein, Joan; Blattstein, Abraham; Adams,

George L. 1983. "Attitudes in the Provision of Public Sector Health and Mental Health Care." *Social Work in Health Care* 8, 4: 17–28.

Mollat, M. 1978. *Les pauvres au moyen-age.* Paris.

Mott, Paul E. 1976. *Meeting Human Needs: The Social and Political History of Title XX.* Columbus, Oh.: National Conference on Social Welfare.

Oliver, J. E., and Taylor, Audrey. 1971. "Five Generations of Ill-treated Children in One Family." *British Journal of Psychiatry* 119: 473–80.

Overton, Alice. 1953. "Serving Families Who 'Don't Want Help.' " *Social Casework* 34, 7: 304–7.

Page, Harry O., and Axelrod, S. J. 1955. "Community Teamwork by Public Health and Welfare." *Public Welfare* 12, 2: 53–57.

Parsons, Robert. 1986. "Practice and Patch: Passivity Versus Participation." *British Journal of Social Work* 16: 125–48.

Pierson, Arthur. 1970. "Social Work Techniques with the Poor." *Social Casework* (October): 481–85.

Rappaport, J. 1977. *Community Psychology: Values, Research and Action.* New York: Holt, Rinehart and Winston.

Redlich, F. C. 1960. "The Influence of Environment on Mental Health." *Bulletin of the New York Academy of Medicine* 30: 608–21.

Regensburg, Jeanette. 1954. "Reaching Children Before the Crisis Comes." *Social Casework* 35, 3: 104–11.

Rich, M. D. 1956. *A Belief in People: A History of Family Social Work.* New York: Family Service Association of America.

Richmond, Mary E. 1908. *A Real Story of a Real Family.* In *A Belief in People: A History of Family Social Work*, edited by M. E. Rich New York: Family Service Association of America (1956).

———. 1917. *Social Diagnosis.* New York: Russell Sage.

———. 1920. "Some Next Steps in Social Treatment." *Proceedings of the National Conference of Social Work*, Chicago: University of Chicago Press.

Robinson, H. A., Redlich, F. C., and Myers, J. K. 1954. "Social Structure and Psychiatric Treatment." *American Journal of Orthopsychiatry* 24: 307–16.

Rubenstein, H., and Bloch, M. H. 1978. "Helping Clients Who are Poor: Worker and Client Perceptions of Problems, Activities, and Outcomes." *Social Service Review* 52 (March): 69–84.

Rutter, M., and Madge, N. 1976. "Multiple Problem Families." In

Cycles of Disadvantage: A Review of Research, pp. 246–56. London: Heinemann.

Sarason, S.; Levine, M.; Goldenbery, I.; Cherlin, D.; Bennett, E. 1966. *Psychology in Community Settings.* New York: John Wiley and Sons.

Schillebeeckx, Edward. 1970. "La teologia," In *Los catolicos holandeses.* Bilbao: Desclee deBrouwer.

Sobrino, Jon. 1987. "The University's Christian Inspiration." *ECA,* No. 468.

Spencer, John C. 1963. "The Multi-Problem Family." In *The Multi-Problem Family: A Review and Annotated Bibliography,* edited by Benjamin Schlessinger, pp. 3–54. Toronto: University of Toronto Press.

Susskind, E., and Klein, D., eds. 1985. *Community Research: Methods, Paradigms, and Applications.* New York: Praeger.

Thompson, Carolyn. 1989. "Breaking Through Walls of Isolation: A Model for Churches in Helping Victims of Violence." *Pastoral Psychology* 38, 1: 35–38.

Voiland, Alice L. 1961. *Family Casework Diagnosis.* C. R. A., New York City.

Voiland, Alice, and Buell, Bradley. 1961. "A Classification of Disordered Family Types." *Social Work* (October): 3–11.

Warren, Ronald L. 1960. *"Multi-Problem Families"—A New Name or a New Problem?* New York: State Charities Aid Association.

For Further Reading

Aponte, Harry J. 1979. "Family Therapy and the Community." In *Community Psychology: Theoretical and Empirical Approaches,* edited by M. S. Gibbs, J. R. Lachenmeyer, and J. Sigal. New York: Gardner Press.

Auerswald, Edgar H. 1974. "Thinking About Thinking in Health and Mental Health." In *American Handbook of Psychiatry* 2, edited by G. Caplan. New York: Basic Books.

Buell, Bradley, Beisser, Paul T., and Wedemeyer, John M. 1958. "Reorganizing to Prevent and Control Disordered Behavior." *Mental Hygiene* 42 (April).

Creden, J. R., and Casarego, J. I. 1975. "Controversies in Psychiatric Education: A Survey of Residents' Attitudes." *American Journal of Psychiatry* 32: 270–74.

de Lora, Cecilio, Marins, Jose, and Galilea, Segundo. 1970. *Communidades cristianas de base.* Bogotá: Indo-American Press Service.

Enzer, Norbert B., and Stackhouse, Jacqueline. 1968. "A Child Clinic Approach to the Multiproblem Family." *American Journal of Orthopsychiatry* 38, 3: 527–38.

Martin, Susan E. 1989. "Research Note: The Response of the Clergy to Spouse Abuse in a Suburban County." *Violence and Victims* 4(3) (Fall): 217–25.

Minuchin, Salvador; Auerswald, E.; Kind, C. H.; and Rabinowitz, C. 1964. "The Study and Treatment of Families Who Produce Multiple Acting-out Boys." *American Journal of Orthopsychiatry* 34: 125–33.

______, and Montalvo, B. 1966a. "An Approach for Diagnosis of the Low Socio-economic Family." *Psychiatric Research Report* 20, American Psychiatric Association.

Populorum Progressio ("On the Development of Peoples"). Pope Paul VI, March 26, 1967. Washington, D.C.: United States Catholic Conference.

Proceedings. 1910. First Annual Meeting of the National Conference of Catholic Charities. Washington, D.C.: National Conference of Catholic Charities, p. 10.

Rappaport, Mazie F. 1960. "Clarifying the Service to Families with Many Problems." *Journal of Social Work Process* 11: 77–87.

Reissman, Frank. 1973. "New Approaches to Mental Health Treatment for Low-Income People." In *Interpersonal Helping: Emerging Approaches for Social Work Practice,* edited by Joel Fischer, pp. 529–44. Springfield, Ill.: Charles C. Thomas.

Richards, H., and Daniels, M. 1969. "Sociopsychiatric Rehabilitation in a Black Urban Ghetto: Innovative Treatment Roles and Approaches." *American Journal of Orthopsychiatry* 39: 662–76.

Toward a Renewed Catholic Charities Movement: A Study of the National Conference of Catholic Charities. 1976. Final Report. Washington, D.C.: National Conference of Catholic Charities.

Voiland, Alice L., and Buell, Bradley. 1961. "A Classification of Disordered Family Types." *Social Work:* 3–11.

Warren, Ronald L. 1968. "A Multi-Problem Confrontation." In *The Multi-Problem Dilemma,* edited by Gordon E. Brown. Metuchen, N.J.: Scarecrow Press.

Weitzman, Jack. 1985. "Engaging the Severely Dysfunctional Family in Treatment: Basic Consideration." *Family Process* 24: 473–85.

Christie Cozad Neuger

7. A Feminist Perspective on Pastoral Counseling with Women

A Case Study

Joan walked into the office of a pastoral counselor. She was anxious, depressed, and hopeless. She felt that her world was overwhelming her and no matter how hard she worked to make things better, she constantly failed. Her marriage was a disaster. Her husband had married her because she was pregnant and felt that, by that act, he had done all that was necessary on behalf of the marriage. She constantly tried to get him to care more for her but without success. Her job was frightening to her. She had moved into a management position and felt that all the women hated her and all the men scorned her. She wondered whether she was competent enough to handle her new work responsibilities. Her life was busy but empty. She felt guilty about her erratic mothering of two small children whom she both loved and resented. She felt spiritually dead. She experienced no connection to a God who, in her eyes, had abandoned her. She had no image of a meaningful future. She felt powerless to make things different for her and her family. And, she felt to blame for all the chaos and despair of her life.

This is the story of one woman and yet nearly every woman who reads this will feel some cords of identification and response. Much of what this woman experienced was intimately linked to living in a world in which she is devalued and limited because she is a woman. A feminist approach to pastoral counseling takes the reality of systematic sexism or patriarchy as central in the formulation of theory, theology, and clinical practice. The purpose of this chapter is to explore some of the dimensions of one feminist approach to pastoral counseling. We will return to this case later in the chapter.

A Framework for Pastoral Counseling

It is important to note from the beginning that there is a careful balance to draw in developing a theory/theology of a feminist pastoral counseling. On the one hand, women share a world in which they are threatened by normative violence against them, in which they are devalued by the limited roles approved for them, and in which they are deprived of the social, economic, and psycho-spiritual resources necessary to a full life. On the other hand, each woman's experience in this world is different, deeply influenced by race, class, sexual preference, family of origin background, age, and life experiences. The particularities of women must be kept in mind as the broad strokes of "women's world" are painted. My own social location as a white, middle-class, well-educated, married, mother of two profoundly influences my insights and priorities in writing a feminist approach to pastoral work. For most of us, the areas of the culture from which we benefit (in my instance, class, race, sexual preference, and so on) are the areas in which we are most blind. Consequently, this chapter represents *one* perspective on a feminist approach; it needs to be complemented and challenged by other feminist/womanist perspectives.

Pastoral counseling is both deeply suited for and antithetical to a feminist perspective. Counseling of any sort is always deeply informed by a philosophical perspective. The practice of caregiving is an activity grounded in questions about human nature, the role of community, the values that guide human behavior, and the meanings of living. These philosophical/theological questions are central to our counseling work. Pastoral counseling has always overtly claimed these questions as it has developed approaches to people in need. The questions of value and meaning have been at the center of the discipline, and there has never been a claim to value neutrality.

Of these value and meaning concerns, the tendency to take up the part of the oppressed and to offer advocacy to those systematically deprived of power has been present. In addition, there has been a strong link or correlation between people's ongoing lives and the fabric of the community or culture. The phrase "the personal is political," which has been a watchword for the feminist movement, could equally apply to the dominant themes of our theological heritage. Throughout our faith histories the needs of the self could not be separated from the needs of the community. One's own sense of salvation was made manifest in a commitment to God's creation. In addition, the form of the culture affected the shape that faith positions took. Prophetic voices responded out of their own faith to the injustices of the time, which touched both the spiritual health of the prophets and that of their community. These values central to our religious traditions are congruent with a feminist liberation approach to pastoral counseling.

On the other hand, our religious traditions have consistently contributed to the oppression of women on a variety of fronts. For the most part women's stories have not been recorded in the scriptural history of the people of faith. Where women are remembered in the Bible, they have often served either as symbols of evil and seduction or as impossible ideals of self-sacrifice and perfect love. Theologians in the early church and in more recent times have used those limited symbols as ways to characterize women. Women have traditionally not been seen as worthy of public church leadership but have been expected to work behind the scenes, instrumental in the more "earthy" functions of the congregation. Many women have found considerable benefit in having a place in the church even if it was in the domestic sphere. However, there was still a message communicated to the women that they were not valuable enough to take their place in the meaning-making sphere of the church.

It becomes clear, then, that the context of pastoral counseling has natural proclivities and natural antipathies to a feminist perspective on its work. It is the responsibility of every pastoral counselor and of the discipline as a whole to take seriously this ambivalence in the ongoing theory building of its healing ministry.

It is not just the theological issues that need to be evaluated and reformulated in a feminist approach to pastoral counseling. Over the past twenty-five years pastoral counseling has borrowed from and relied heavily upon the social science disciplines of psychology, sociology, and psychotherapy. These disciplines also have been formed in the context of patriarchy and rely heavily on normative male assumptions, experience, and research. As is evident in much of the literature reporting on research done on women's lives, theory built around women's experience is very different and leads to very different therapeutic implications than that done on men's lives. Every traditional theory of psychology and psychotherapy must be held suspect of sexism and be subject to extensive critique. Some theories may not be reclaimable in any form. Others must be enlarged and reconstructed around women's experience. New theories must be born directly out of an understanding of women's lives in patriarchy. This work is underway, and the material in this chapter reflects the important work being done by feminist theorists, psychotherapists, and theologians as they seek to offer healing and empowerment to women in distress.

General Principles of Feminist Counseling

Although one must be careful not to paint in too broad a stroke, it is possible to identify some principles which are central to a feminist perspective on pastoral counseling. Some of these reflect broad agreement in various dimensions of feminist research and others are more personally compelling to my perspective. However, they reflect a general consensus in feminist work.

1. An Awareness of Patriarchy and Depression

The first and most primary principle of feminist counseling is an awareness of patriarchy as a fundamental dynamic in the formation of women's distress. As Mary Ellen Donovan and Linda Sanford conclude in their extensive study on women and self-esteem: 1) Low self-esteem is primarily the result of being female in a male-dominated culture; and 2) low self-esteem is at the root of many of the psychological problems that women experience, and attempts to cure these problems without addressing the causes of low self-esteem lead to other problems (Donovan and Sanford, 1984, p. xiv). In addition, a recent panel of the American Psychological Association, formed to study the epidemic of women's depression, decided that neither biology nor psychology could adequately explain the epidemic. The panel members stated that the depression that women of all ages, races, and classes experience is clearly linked to societal attitudes and behaviors that are detrimental to women ("Women and Depression" 1990). The reality that the "personal is political" is fundamental to looking at women's "pathology" and in developing an approach to the counseling.

The phrase "the personal is political" means that one does not treat women's emotional and psycho-spiritual distress as primarily internal and idiosyncratic in nature. Women's *dis*-ease is understood as fundamentally related to various dimensions of oppression in a world which operates to "keep women in their place." Sexism is still a real and dominant experience for women in the society. As Nicole Benokraitis and Joe Feagin state in their work on modern sexism:

> Sex discrimination is not an illusion. It is at least as robust as it was in the 1950's, 1960's, and 1970's. Why, then, are many men and women today so accepting of sex inequality and so complacent about the future? A majority of people are convinced that sex inequality is no longer a high priority problem. This conviction is based, first and foremost, on a

> lack of information. Most Americans rarely see or pay attention to statistics that show that sex discrimination abounds. Even when such statistics are provided, the initial reaction is denial (Benokraitis and Feagin 1986, p. 2).

The fact that all women experience sex discrimination and damage due to that discrimination is complicated by its renewed hiddenness. Women are taken by surprise when they are hurt. I have received letters from women graduates asking why we didn't tell them that sexism was alive and well out in the world. They were seduced by the greater visibility of women in positions of authority into believing that sexism was no longer a problem. It is true that women have made some visible gains, particularly in terms of economic and employment opportunities. These gains, as we shall see, are not all we would hope them to be but, nonetheless, they confuse us in our analysis of ongoing sexism. The reality is that the more subtle dimensions of patriarchy still operate powerfully upon the women in this culture. Women still live in a world which does them considerable harm because of their sex, and the hiddenness of this world makes it doubly destructive.

Women's World

I hold the basic assumption that men and women are embedded in very different worlds even as they share the same institutions and families. Women and men both have been denied systematic access to this knowledge, although women know about both worlds, at least at some level. It is crucial for women and men to be exposed to the statistics which outline these two different worlds so that the source of much of women's distress can be clearly identified. It is in knowing the world of patriarchy and its effects on the lives and faiths of women and men that we will be able to engage in effective pastoral counseling and even have a chance at working toward a more just and healthy environment for all. This is at the heart of the first principle of a feminist approach.

The purpose of the following statistics is to paint a beginning portrait of the women's world. The knowing and naming of this world is a central part of pastoral counseling with women and is the starting place for knowing women's lives and pain. The statistics about seemingly disparate dimensions of life, when seen together, begin to show the systemic oppression that women experience. These statistics become like snapshots of a system of oppression which has become a morally normative justification for the dominance of one group over another. It is again important to note here that, despite the commonality women have of experiencing a world of patriarchal oppression, each woman's class, race, family history, and life experience deeply affect the way that this oppression is experienced and understood. The particularities belong to each counseling client, and it is the larger context within which those particularities are found that these statistics reveal.

ECONOMICS

In 1987 over 26 percent of families who were singly headed by white women were below the poverty line in comparison to 8 percent of families singly headed by white males. Over 50 percent of all black families singly headed by women were below the poverty line compared to 29 percent of those singly headed by black men (Hoffman 1990, p. 561). Approximately 43 percent of all black families are singly headed by women (Rix 1990, p. 71). In addition, by the time women are sixty-five years or older, 15 percent of white women, 50 percent of black women, and 25 percent of Hispanic women are below the poverty line (Swenson, Siegal, and Doress 1985, p. 23).

The average white woman college graduate earns less as a full-time worker than the average white male with only a high school diploma. The average black woman college graduate working full time earns less than 90 percent of her white counterpart's salary—or the equivalent to the earnings of a white male high school drop out (Rix 1990, p. 176). Hispanic women who work full-time earn only about 82 percent of what comparably employed white women earn.

In 1955 full-time women workers earned about 64 percent of the full-time wages of men. In 1990 they earn about 69 percent of men's wages. The biggest change is that there are many more women in the work force, but the reality of work segregation by sex has not changed much. In the mid 1980s 60 percent of all women were in either clerical, retail sales, or service jobs (Benokraitis and Feagin 1986, p. 52). Currently most women work in jobs that are at least 75 percent female. Eighty percent of women workers earn *less* than $20,000 annually, while 80 percent of men workers earn *more* than $20,000 annually (Benokraitis and Feagin 1986, p. 52). Different people interpret these numbers differently, but Sara Rix writes: "Research has concluded that characteristics such as education and experience cannot account for more than one-half of the current gender gap in earnings. Moreover, on the whole, women who make comparable investments in time, preparation, and experience still advance less far and less quickly than men" (Rix 1990, p. 171). According to the 1983

World Health Organization Report, two-thirds of the world's work is done by women, but they receive only one-tenth of the world's income (Ballou and Gabalac 1985, p. 69).

The work hours of women are significant, too. One author suggests that what has changed in the past twenty years is that more women work at what she calls "double days" (one shift at home and one at work) (Benokraitis and Feagin 1986, p. 7). In 1988 a University of Florida study found that wives average about thirty hours per week on household tasks and husbands average about six hours. Full-time employed wives do about 70 percent of the housework compared to full-time housewives, who do about 83 percent (Rix 1990, p. 33). The issue of double days is a significant factor in the lives of women who are depressed and/or discouraged about their lives.

ABUSE

Almost six million women are beaten by male friends or spouses each year. This translates into somewhere between 50 percent and 75 percent of all women being beaten sometime in their lives by a boyfriend or husband. Attacks by husbands on wives result in more injuries requiring medical treatment than rapes, muggings, and automobile accidents combined. A recent Bureau of Justice report suggests that, "based on evidence collected in the National Crime Survey, as many as half of the domestic 'simple assaults' actually involved bodily injury as serious as or more serious than 90% of all rapes, robberies, and aggravated assaults" (Langan and Innes 1986, p. 1). One-third of all women homicide victims are killed by their husbands. (Benokraitis and Feagin 1987, p. 49). And 48 percent of all domestic violence against women discovered in the National Crime Survey had not been reported to the police for reasons of fear of reprisal, desire for privacy, or fear that it wasn't important enough to be taken seriously (Langan and Innes 1986, p. 1).

Rape is another common form of abuse against women. The Statistical Abstract of the United States for 1987 reported that there were 87.5 forcible rapes per 100,000 women (Statistical Abstract of the U.S., 1989). However, there is considerable consensus that only 20 to 50 percent of rapes are ever reported. It is estimated by many that between 20 and 30 percent of women over twelve years old will be victims of attempted or completed rape sometime in their lifetime (Bourque 1989, p. 12). It is no wonder that women, though often deeply traumatized by the experience of rape, are rarely surprised by it. Several studies indicate that nearly all women live in pervasive fear of violence against them.

In addition, approximately 40 percent of all girls are sexually molested or abused by the age of eighteen—either inside of or outside of their families (MacKinnon 1987). Estimates about the occurrence of incest vary from 5 percent to 20 percent of all girl children. Women learn very early that the world is not a safe place for them.

MEDIA

It is also important to note that the media carry many of these messages of the threat of violence and the lack of worth to women. For example, a majority of children's stories still show men who achieve and women who get rescued. Male biographies outnumber female biographies by as much as six to one, and the stories and accomplishments of women, especially women of color, are still in large part left out of our history books. These realities are changing, but very slowly. In addition, the quantity of pornography is on the rise, and it is becoming increasingly violent. There are close to two hundred pornographic magazines in the United States with about fourteen million readers. In comparison there are fewer than one million readers of feminist magazines.

There have been a variety of studies that report on the consequences of violence against women in the media, even when it is not sexual violence. A recent study by Linz, Donnerstein, and Penrod concluded: "When subjects are continually exposed to graphically depicted film violence against women, individual feelings of anxiety and depression begin to dissipate. Material that was anxiety provoking became less so with prolonged exposure. . . . Material once found somewhat degrading to women was judged to be less so after prolonged exposure" (Linz, Donnerstein, and Penrod 1987, p. 114). In this same study the subjects also became less sympathetic to a rape trial victim and in fact judged her more harshly after watching films depicting violence against women. In other studies it was demonstrated that even after watching R-rated levels of *non-sexual* violence against women, subjects were more judgmental against rape victims then they had been before watching the movies (Linz, Donnerstein, and Penrod 1987, p. 114). Subjects also became less supportive of sexual equality, espoused more traditional views about the roles of women, and became more lenient in assessing punishment to a convicted rapist (Zillman and Bryant 1982, p. 10–21). This kind of aggression and violence against women is pervasive in media, not only in movies and television but even in the music industry. According to some studies, more than one-half of the music videos on MTV present hostile sexual situations or show males abusing women for fun (Benokraitis and Feagin 1986, p. 10). These media presentations, in books, television, movies, music videos, newspapers, and so on seem not only to communicate the threat of violence to women, encouraging them to live in fear, but in fact increase the likelihood of violence and ongoing sexism.

IMPLICATIONS

The overall picture of these statistics portrays a part of the world in which women live. For the most part this world is minimized, trivialized, and hidden. When women are abused or devalued or made to feel crazy, they tend to believe that they are alone and to blame for this experience. It is important to communicate the world which makes these experiences normative for women so that they can begin to trust themselves and their experiences and come out from hiding to take their appropriate place in society. The pastoral counselor must first look through the lens of patriarchy rather than through the lens of personal pathology when attempting to assess the distress that a woman client is experiencing.

This lens is at the core of the principle incorporated in the phrase "the personal is political." It also reorients the goal of counseling from one of adjustment to one of empowerment. It would be destructive to help a woman adjust to a culture which is destructive to her even if it appears that it would be more comfortable. We can assume that it was adjustment to that culture that probably gave birth, at least in part, to her symptoms of distress. The counselor's goal is to empower a woman through an increased awareness of her environment and through an ability to connect with other women so that she can more readily withstand and even attempt to change the patriarchy which has been so damaging. The personal and political link means that part of women's empowerment in counseling is to begin to join other women in some form of transformation of this destructive patriarchy. Unless she does, she will continue to be vulnerable to patriarchy's power. If she joins other women in working to change the society, to work against the oppressions of sexism, racism, classism and other isms, then she will be able to move in an active way toward her own and others' empowerment. This will become more clear as we move on.

2. *The Counselor/Client Relationship*

A second fundamental principle of feminist thought is the nontraditional relationship between counselor and counselee. Traditionally counselors have been seen as experts who have the answers and who will tell the counselee what she needs to do in order to get "well." Usually this prescription was adjustment oriented. A feminist approach to pastoral counseling suggests that the role between counselor and counselee be egalitarian. This does not imply that there is a complete mutuality between counselor and counselee. The relationship is still a contract in which the counselor is to provide informed care and guidance for the counselee and not vice versa. However, the difference that exists is one of function not of essence, and the counselor's role is to help the counselee learn to know her own story, to believe in herself, and to claim herself in the company of other women and in the face of patriarchy. It is a role of empowerment, not one of repair or cure.

Involved in this relationship are a number of characteristics that do not fit with traditional counseling work. For example, it is often the case in a feminist perspective that the counselor is an advocate for the counselee. In other words, the counselor assumes on behalf of the counselee. Instead of looking for the "illness" she or he looks for and facilitates the client's strengths. The counselor believes in the counselee's story and her interpretation of that story, and by trusting the counselee the counselor conveys permission for the counselee to trust herself. The counselor, in this advocacy role, may also join the client in her anger or blame rather than encouraging the counselee to look rationally at all sides. This relational advocacy cheerfully breaks the myth of therapeutic neutrality and operates on behalf of the woman counselee.

Another trait of the egalitarian relationship may be that of mentor. The counselor, having gone through her own awareness and consequent struggles regarding her life in patriarchy, uses appropriate self-disclosure over the process of counseling and thereby gives hope and a sense of possibility to the counselee. It is important, of course, not to assume that the counselee's journey should or will replicate that of the counselor, but appropriate self-disclosure on the part of the counselor can be an important dimension of the counseling process. Counselor distance and withholding are not the norm in this approach.

The egalitarian nature of the therapeutic relationship should not get in the way of the counselor recognizing how much influence she or he has in the counseling process. It is not wise to ignore one's own therapeutic power or pretend that the relationship is mutual. The counselor is highly influential, and it is important to remember that the goal is that of empowerment of the counselee rather than of "fixing" her. The counselee's story and her particularities and needs and goals are the primary values in the counseling process.

3. The Group Component

A third principle in this feminist approach to pastoral counseling is the need for a group component to the counseling work. Helping a woman to experience a community of women who will hear her story and validate it through the sharing of their own stories is a fundamental dimension of this healing work. Women live in a world where they experience constant, pervasive messages about who they are and who they are not; about what is possible for them and what is denied to them; and about what they are valued for and in what ways they lack value. Women's experience, for the most part, is defined for them by the dominant culture. Most women doubt their own realities. It is a common experience for a battered woman or a rape victim to agonize over how she brought this abuse on herself. Most women who are depressed define their experience as due to their own failure. Many women who are overwhelmed by their double days of work and the unending nature of their responsibilities are puzzled and self-blaming about why they can't do what every other woman is able to do.

A counselor can only introduce the possibility that there are other ways to understand the experiences that the woman counselee has had. The counselor cannot convince or validate the systemic and widespread nature of the counselee's context. Most women do not feel entitled to see injustice toward themselves (Major 1987, pp. 124–48). They are much more able to identify abuse against other women. It is only when they join with others and hear their own stories from other women and have their own realities affirmed over and over that a new way of viewing their lives becomes possible. Reality testing, believing in one's self, building a base of trust in self and in other women, learning options for surviving and thriving—these are the activities of the counseling group for women that operates in conjunction with the individual counseling. It is in the community that one finds one's self. This is not unfamiliar to the history of the Christian church. When one lives in a world that denies that which is life giving, it is crucial to find a community in which life can be found. Women's support/counseling groups can provide the healing context in which hope and life can be found. And, almost any group in the church where women gather regularly can become this kind of support community if women are encouraged to be honest and authentic and if they are able, through their dialogue, to open their eyes to the cultural sexism and patriarchy around them.

If a profeminist man is doing this counseling work, it becomes even more crucial for a women's group to be included in the counseling plan. Churches should have ongoing women's support groups available to women at any point needed. Men cannot provide the reality testing and story sharing that a woman counselor can (and even her input alone isn't enough). Consequently, the group becomes the major part of the counseling work when a profeminist male is doing the counseling.

It is in a group that damaging behavior, ingrained in many women from an early age, gets challenged. For example, it is a lot more natural and acceptable to "good Christian women" to experience guilt and self-deprecation rather than anger in response to situations which don't live up to their own or others' expectations. It is much easier for a woman to be a giver (she is protected from accusations of selfishness and she is in control) than to be a receiver (vulnerable and able to be rejected). Women tend to give up themselves and their own "gifts and graces" for others out of a deep fear of being left alone. These attitudes and behaviors run deep in women's fragile self-esteem and are hard to challenge and even harder to give up. A women's group where these behaviors are shared and seen more clearly in one another gives both the motivation and the support to move toward more authentic and healthy ways of being.

4. A Woman-Centered Approach

The fourth general principle of this feminist approach is two pronged. It has to do with the need to take women's particularities as central in formulating a counseling approach with each woman. The first dimension to this suggests that it is important to apply consistently the counselee's values and experience, along with knowledge about women's world, as critical in exploring any issue brought into the counseling office. For example, a counselor who wishes to be an advocate for a battered woman who has come for help might feel inclined to encourage her to stand up to her spouse or to leave the home without considering the specifics of her experience and the realities for women in general. Frequently we hear counselors express frustration and confusion about why battered women don't just leave their batterers. Yet, such a woman probably has a deep fear of reprisal if she should stand up to her spouse. Since one-third of all homicides of women come from battering, it is natural for her to have fear. In addition, she might have limited financial resources or economic opportunities so that if she leaves the home, she may find herself to be part of the fastest growing homeless population—women and their young children. She may also worry about reprisals to her children or to other people dependent upon her if she looks after herself. She may very well worry about what people will think of her if she leaves her husband—she may be blamed for breaking up a perfectly viable family. She may have been told to try to be more understanding of her husband as he goes through this stressful time, a very common pastoral response to battered women. And, very likely, she has a self-esteem which is congruent with being battered and which saps her motivation and her hope of having a different, abuse-free life. If these factors aren't explored and taken seriously, if women's criteria aren't used in evaluating the circumstances a woman finds herself in, more damage may be done right in the counseling office.

The second aspect of this principle has to do with the need to consider the particularities of race, class, sexual preference, age, and so on. If the counselor belongs to a culturally dominant race or class, for example, she or he will not fully understand the race or class world of the counselee who is of color or from the working class. These particularities are not peripheral to the counseling work. They are central and the counselor must be willing to be taught the implications of these particularities. Values, responsibilities, goals—all these are profoundly affected by the particularities of race, class, sexual preference, and other dimensions of the society. The counselor must also take responsibility to learn as much as possible about the worlds to which she or he does not belong. For a white, middle-class, feminist counselor it is very important to read widely in womanist and working-class literature as well as that written by women of color.

5. *The Patriarchal Context*

The fifth principle of this feminist approach to pastoral counseling is hopefully self-evident. This principle has to do with the reality that both psychological and theological formulation has been done in the context of patriarchy, without much or any awareness of that context. Consequently, these sex-biased formulations have served to reinforce and reify a status quo which is destructive to women.

PSYCHOLOGY

As stated above, the psychological theories in all of the major schools of thought (psychodynamic, behavioral, humanistic, and family systems) are products of a world which has, at best, ignored women's experience and has, at worst, sought to damage women. These theories require considerable critique and cannot be utilized in working with women counselees without that critique. There has been considerable work in feminist psychotherapeutic theory and some in womanist theory, which is available to the pastoral counselor. Much of it is eclectic and most does not address the spiritual needs of women. Nonetheless, it does give guidance to the pastoral counselor in terms of critique and construction within the context of traditional psychotherapeutic theory.

One place where the feminist/profeminist counselor of women must pay particular attention is in the dominant diagnostic categories used in the mental health system. When one explores the diagnostic categories most commonly applied to women, it is easy to see that many of the criteria for diagnosis are merely extensions of expected but exaggerated stereotypical feminine behavior. For example, borderline personality has many descriptive criteria which mirror expected feminine behavior—dependency, indecisiveness, emotionality, and so on. Depression, as we have suggested earlier, is a more acceptable affect for women (passivity, sadness, withdrawn behavior, etc.) than anger or other less passive responses. Co-dependency, as it has been extended in recent years, is an "illness" much more common in women than men and focuses on the need to take care of others and hold oneself responsible for the needs and behaviors of others. These are expected feminine behaviors. As Carol Plummer writes:

> Co-dependency is, in fact, a smorgasbord of behaviors used by all types of oppressed people when with their oppressors. It is a set of survival skills when one is in a subservient position economically, emotionally, politically, or spiritually. The list of co-dependent characteristics is true not only of women, but of workers with their bosses, or the poor with those in power. Telling women to "heal themselves" in a culture which trains them in co-dependency cannot work without transforming the context of their behaviors" (Plummer 1990, p. 10).

Plummer concludes:

> If women don't have the "disease" [of co-dependency], it is only because they have worked very hard against their gender socialization (Plummer 1990, p. 11).

As pastoral counselors we must be careful in our assessment work in general as we often operate with different diagnostic criteria than the field of psychiatry, which doesn't take the spiritual dimension of people seriously. In working with women we must be especially careful with these categories at the risk of perpetuating injustice and oppression.

THEOLOGY

In a like manner we must be very careful with our traditional theological categories as we work with the faith lives and concerns of our women counselees. Again, there is considerable work by feminist theologians working with deconstruction and reconstruction of theological positions available to pastoral counselors. However, the pastoral counselor must do some integrative work to make these revisions and constructions applicable to the counseling situation.

Let's look at two areas of theological concern to pastoral counselors for illustrative purposes. The first has to do with traditional theological categories, which are proclaimed from the pulpit, consistently presented in the liturgies, and reinforced by pastoral care. For example, we persistently confess in our liturgies on Sunday morning the sin of pride and for our putting ourselves first. For most women this is not a central element to her alienation from God, self, and neighbor. It is more likely that she does not think highly enough of herself or regard herself as worthy of God's care. She probably does not think of herself as able to engage publicly in the work of God's realm. She probably tends to put herself last. For her to confess consistently to pride misses the opportunity for authentic self-searching and transformation.

The same may be true when we primarily identify Christian mission with that of the suffering servant. It is not greater willingness to suffer that women usually need but a willingness to not suffer. Many pastors have told battered women who have come for advice that this is their cross to bear and that their suffering has earned them a place in heaven without ever considering that their suffering is not chosen—not redemptive—but meaningless suffering for the most part. This requires a reevaluation of some central theological tenets. Atonement and its primary metaphors need rethinking in order for them to be meaningful to women. Sin, especially sin as pride, needs deconstructive work in order to be applicable to women. In addition, women have been traditionally held to be more responsible for bringing sin into the world than men. The story of Eve's presentation of the apple to Adam is certainly better known then the stories of the women who were the last at the cross and the first at the tomb. Negative images of women in our faith traditions are intimately linked to the negative spiritual health and spiritual depression of women and to the integrative potential of the women who come to us for pastoral help. These are not dry, abstract theological luxuries for our eventual perusal. They are, rather, at the core of our pastoral counseling formulations. If, as we said at the beginning of this chapter, pastoral counseling, indeed all counseling, is at its heart a philosophical/theological enterprise, then these instances of theological destructiveness to women deeply affect our potential helpfulness in our healing ministries. We need to be about the work for which we have been particularly trained—the work of reflective theology for the sake of ministering to the spiritual needs of those in our care.

A second illustration of needed theological work has to do with imagery for God. It is clear that the predominant image for God has been, and is, that of God as father. According to a number of feminist theologians this image is not only destructive for many women, but the image itself has become an idol. We do not think of God as a father; rather God *is* a father. We have limited God in such a way that the image of father is no longer as useful in connecting with the richness of God's presence and power.

Again, this is not just an abstract concept. In research that I conducted with women in spiritual growth groups, it became clear that expanding imagery for God—especially when images included the potential for the reflection of self in the divine image—allowed women to be more active in their faith search and in their integration of their faith into the rest of their lives. A side advantage, which was not predicted, was the improvement in women's self-esteem as they found God through this new set of metaphors and images. When they were able to expand their images beyond that of a father who takes care of his daughter (replicating much of the hierarchical, paternalistic world of patriarchy) they presumably found more value in themselves. If, as we discussed earlier, much of women's problems are a result of a culture which pervasively squelches women's self-esteem, then working with imagery for God and for themselves which expands possibilities for life and faith becomes an important dimension of pastoral counseling. (For more on the use of imagination in pastoral counseling, see Neuger 1991).

These, then, are the general principles within the feminist approach to pastoral counseling described here. They do not encompass all the dimensions to a pastoral counseling approach to women, nor do they address the specifics of counseling work with a variety of problems. They are, however, the primary elements of the lens through which a pastoral counselor should look as she or he works to formulate a counseling plan with each particular counselee. They are fundamental and foundational in approaching the psycho-spiritual distresses that women bring to pastoral counseling.

Applications

Let's take these principles and see how they apply in two commonly experienced problems women bring to pastoral counseling—situational depression, and marriage and family distress.

DEPRESSION

Depression is at an epidemic level among women. There are a variety of studies and estimates about women's depression, but at the very minimum twice as many women are depressed as men. Some studies estimate that as many as six times more women than men are depressed. There are several theories suggested for this difference in numbers of depressed men and women, but feminist research agrees that the major reason for it is "an abiding, unconscious rage at our own oppression which has found no legitimate outlet" (Greenspan 1983, p. 300). A feminist approach to counselees with depression focuses on the need for women to understand their own lives in the context of cultural sexism. Power dynamics in relationships, in families, and in institutions are taken as seriously as the psycho-spiritual symptoms that are the result of the depression. Consequently it is essential for the pastoral counselor to understand the psychological, social, and theological dynamics of patriarchy in working with women who are depressed.

There are a number of types of depressions. The type addressed here is the most common form, what would be called in diagnostic manuals "depressive neurosis." I am not talking about either major depression or bipolar depression, which seem to have biochemical roots and respond best to medication. However, depressive neurosis responds best to a counseling approach that takes seriously the sociocultural reality of the woman's depression. These sociocultural factors express themselves in various dimensions of the counselee's life—her family, her work, her faith, her social life.

This kind of depression can cause tremendous pain in a woman's life. She generally feels hopeless and powerless; she sees no possibility of change. She has generally spent a lot of her energy caring for other people and still feels unnecessary and impotent. She is frequently resentful but afraid to admit or acknowledge her anger, even to herself. She doesn't know much about self-care and even if she does, she is afraid of her own potential selfishness. She has been accused of and seen as over-involved in the family. Because she is depressed and because she has become desperate in her attempt to maintain relationships, she now seems to be the problem in the family. She is the "sick" one, and she has begun to believe this myth. Sometimes she turns to religion as a justification for her suffering and her hope is in God to help her see life as hopeful again.

By the time this woman comes to counseling her agenda is for the counselor to help her be "normal" again and stop being a drain on the family. Too many counselors buy into this agenda and work to help her adjust better to an oppressive environment. However, the role of the pastor is to empower this woman to hear and believe her own experience, to understand her life in a world that frequently is not interested in her wholeness, and to help her network with other women for the sake of ongoing support and reality testing. Finally, the hope is that she will continue to work toward her own wholeness by ongoing recognition of her role in working to change patriarchy.

This means that the counselor begins by offering hope to the woman by normalizing her depression and by listening deeply to her story. Nelle Morton, a feminist theologian, has offered us the phrase of "hearing a woman into speech," which means that we listen deeply to the pain, the hopes, the anger, the doubt, and the various life experiences of a woman until she comes to trust and know her own story. In the midst of this process she is encouraged to begin to use some of her energy to care for herself so that she loses some of her fear of helplessness in the face of abandonment. She is supported in her rage and in her ambivalence about change. After all, depression is the most familiar and acceptable way for her to be. And she is helped to develop a support community of women where she will begin to trust that her experience of hurt and deprivation is, in some form, the experience of all women. In that solidarity there is great hope and possibility.

A pastoral counselor can draw from various techniques, especially from the cognitive approaches which seem so effective in working with depression, as long as they are always used in the context of the world in which women live. All theories have been limited, even family systems theory, in that they have ignored the cultural system which is primary in the development of women's distress. As long as they are appropriately critiqued and used in the cultural context, a variety of theoretical approaches may be useful.

MARITAL DISTRESS

In many cases of women's depression, marital and/or family issues also emerge. It is very common for the dynamics of the culture to be mirrored within the family. Generally there is a considerable power difference between the spouses even though it looks as though the wife has more family power. She generally focuses her power toward the family because she does not have the broader power base that her spouse does. Further, women tend to feel powerless in the family because the major decisions are still made by the husband.

Family systems theory has not taken seriously the differences in cultural power brought into the family. The theory has tended to say that men and women have equal access to power and, in fact, choose each other in order to live out their preferred roles and rules. However, feminist family therapy suggests that the rigid rules and roles in a family are greatly influenced by the rules of the culture and both systems (the family and the culture) must be considered as changes are attempted in the counseling setting.

Case Study

When a woman comes in to counseling and talks about marital problems such as we saw in the case study that introduced this chapter, it is important to assess a number of factors. First, what are the power dynamics in the family? It is easiest to assess this if both members of the couple come to the session. Joan did not feel that her husband would come, but she did invite him. He came for the first session but was clear that he felt that the problems in the family belonged to Joan both in terms of perception and in terms of cause. He said that he was basically happy in the marriage as long as Joan did not expect anything from him. He liked his children and occasionally spent time with them on Saturdays, but for the most part he felt that his job, his social life, and his relaxation time in front of the TV comprised a fully satisfying life. When Joan shared her discontent, he said that he didn't know what he could do to change and she would just have to deal with it. He was also not willing to continue with the counseling. This meant that Joan would have to make the choice to continue alone or terminate the counseling work. She decided to continue.

Sometimes, when the family power dynamics are such that the woman feels powerless, it can be important to do some work to build self-esteem, develop self-care, and encourage an awareness of various realities of the counselee's world. Joan began to explore the world in which she lived, which included her family, her work, and her lack of a social life. She was feeling overwhelmed at work, without a support network. By advancing in her career she became afraid that she would lose any possibility of community. We worked to test this by having her take some initiative with other women in the department. She was able to develop a reasonably satisfying support community. However, this led to another problem. The group of women with whom she began to associate decided that it would be fun to go out to supper together one night a week. Unfortunately, Jim was not willing to help out at home by picking up the children from day care and making them dinner. Joan decided that it was important enough to her to hire a babysitter to pick up the children and make them dinner. After a while Jim decided that he would rather not have someone in the house, and he began to pick up the kids and make them dinner this one time a week. His willingness to do this helped Joan feel closer to him, and she did not behave with such hostility at home.

Joan also began to develop a list of self-care behaviors that she would act on during the week. They were as simple as taking a walk, reading a novel, taking a bubble bath, and so on. This self-care made her feel less needy in her marriage, and she worried less about Jim's unavailability. She became less depressed and enjoyed her life more. We worked on these issues and on her learning to trust herself and her needs more fully. We explored the images she had of herself and she did some re-imaging of her own potential. We also paid attention to the areas in which Joan was most likely to compromise herself out of her cultural and family learning. She got involved in a noontime support group of women and heard much of her story in the stories of the other women. This program of counseling helped her a great deal. However, it also made her more aware that her needs were not being met in her marriage relationship.

About this time Jim came with Joan to a counseling session. He said that he saw that Joan had made a lot of changes, and he wasn't sure that he liked them. He acknowledged that she seemed happier, but he felt that she had withdrawn from the family. The three of us agreed to work together for several sessions. During that time Joan told Jim what she had learned about herself, about the ways she had not claimed herself, and the ways in which she felt the marriage was unsatisfactory. Jim found that he did want the marriage to continue and was willing to negotiate more so that the needs of both of them could be met. This included attending church together, as they felt they had completely ignored that aspect of their lives. They felt this would be one area where they would enter at the same place and grow together. It also included going out together periodically (they had never really dated), doing without television for the hour after supper so that they could talk with each other, sharing child-care responsibilities, and developing more intimacy in various dimensions of their life together. The power had been balanced in the relationship to a certain extent by helping Joan to know the ways in which power had been denied to her and by helping her to learn how to claim the power that was available to her. Her empowerment through counseling allowed her to have a position from which to negotiate within the marriage.

This is a very superficial description of a complex process. However, it does illustrate, at least in part, the need for the counselor to be aware of women's experience and tuned into the needs of the counselee in the face of a normatively unjust environment. Without an awareness of the systematic sexism that is mirrored in all aspects of women's lives, the counselor cannot effectively work with women individually or in families.

Conclusion

The use of a feminist liberation approach to pastoral counseling is not one option of many. It is the *only* way in which a counselor may bring real and lasting healing to women in distress. The cultural factors are central to the lives of women and cannot be seen as a side issue in pastoral counseling. They form the lens through which a counselor must look at the woman counselee, and they form the material which, when made appropriately available to the counselee, can make seemingly disparate and crazy pieces of her reality fall into place. This does not mean that the counselor lectures about patriarchy, but rather that she or he works out of the knowledge of patriarchy and shares elements of that knowledge as it becomes appropriate.

It is in keeping with the traditions of our faith to serve as advocates for people who have experienced systematic oppression. It is important to integrate that perspective into our counseling work in order to help women find the strength and empowerment authentically to know themselves, their community, and their God. In that, they will be better able to understand and respond to God's call to be full and dynamic participants in the ongoing activity of creation.

References

Ballou, M., and Gabalac, N. 1985. *A Feminist Position on Mental Health.* Springfield, Ill.: Charles C. Thomas.

Benokraitis, N., and Feagin, J. 1986. *Modern Sexism: Blatant, Subtle, and Covert Discrimination.* Englewood Cliffs, N.J.: Prentice-Hall.

Bourque, L. B. 1989. *Defining Rape.* Durham, N.C.: Duke University Press.

Donovan, Mary Ellen, and Sanford, Linda. 1984. *Women and Self-Esteem: Understanding and Improving the Way We Think and Feel About Ourselves.* New York: Penguin Books.

Greenspan, M. 1983. *A New Approach to Women And Therapy.* New York: McGraw Hill.

Hoffman, M., ed. 1990. *World Almanac and Book of Facts 1990.* New York: Pharos Books.

Langan, P., and Innes, C. 1986. "Preventing Domestic Violence Against Women." *Bureau of Justice Statistics Special Report.* Washington, D.C.: Bureau of Justice (August) pp. 1–5.

Linz, D., Donnerstein, E., and Penrod, S. 1987. "Sexual Violence in the Mass Media: Social Psychological Implications." In *Sex and Gender,* edited by P. Shaver and C. Hendrick, pp. 95–123. Newbury Park, Cal.: Sage Publications.

MacKinnon, C. 1987. *Feminism Unmodified: Discourses on Life and Law.* Cambridge, Mass.: Harvard University Press.

Major, B. "Gender Justice and the Psychology of Entitlement." In P. Shaver and C. Hendrick (ed.), *Sex and Gender,* edited by P. Shaver and C. Hendrick, pp. 124–148. Newbury Park, Cal.: Sage Publications.

Neuger, C. 1991a. "Imagination and Pastoral Care." In *Clinical Handbook to Basic Types of Pastoral Care and Counseling,* edited by Clements and Stone. Nashville: Abingdon.

——. 1991b. "Women and Depression: Lives at Risk." in *Women in Travail and Transition.* edited by Moessner and Glaz. Minneapolis: Fortress Press.

Plummer, C. 1990. "Refusing Co-dependency." *MCC Women's Concerns Report* (July–August): 9–11.

Rix, S., ed. 1990. *The American Woman 1990–91: A Status Report.* New York: W. W. Norton.

Statistical Abstract of the United States, 1987, 109th ed. 1989. Washington, D.C.: U.S. Bureau of the Census.

Swenson, N., Siegal, D., and Doress, P. 1985. "Health: Women and Aging." In Drake McFeely (ed.), *The Women's Annual Number Five*, 1984–85, edited by Mary Drake McFeely, pp. 22–42. Boston: G. K. Hall and Company.

Timrots, A., and Rand, M. 1987. "Violent Crime by Strangers and Non-strangers." In *Bureau of Justice Statistics Special Report*, pp. 1–7. Washington, D.C.: U.S. Department of Justice.

Wilkinson, C. 1985. "Work: Challengers to Occupational Segregation." In *The Woman's Annual Number Five*, 1984–85, edited by Mary Drake McFeely, pp. 149–65. Boston: G. K. Hall and Company.

"Women and Depression." 1990. *Chronicle of Higher Education*. 19 December 1990, p. A7.

Zillman, D., and Bryant, J. 1982. "Pornography, Sexual Callousness, and the Trivialization of Rape." *Journal of Communication*. 32:10–21.

Robert J. McAllister

8. Mental Health Treatment of Religion Professionals

Therapists for Mental Health Professionals

Mental health professionals espouse a broad range of theoretical positions in their approach to serving the emotional needs of religion professionals. At one end of the spectrum there are therapists who insist that matters of religion, of belief, of spirituality are not germane to the therapeutic setting. These therapists argue that the belief system of the therapist is as alien to the therapeutic setting as the religious practices of the clients. Mental health professionals of this persuasion approach the treatment of religion professionals[1] in the same way they approach the treatment of any other client. These therapists are not hostile toward religion; in fact, they may be quite religious themselves. They view matters of faith and of spirituality as belonging to another sphere and not being pertinent, except perhaps incidentally, to emotional life.

At the other end of the spectrum, there are mental health professionals who support the stand that religion professionals should be taken care of only by therapists who are also believers. The extreme of this position shows up in those mental health professionals who present their professional credentials to the public based more on their religious orthodoxy than on their educational background and professional experience.

Variations occur between these two extreme positions, but highlighting their divergence provides a distinct base from which to delineate a philosophical approach to the treatment of religion professionals. The pivotal issue can be stated in a more direct manner. Can religion professionals be appropriately treated by the same professionals who treat the general population, including persons of various beliefs and practices, including agnostics, apostates, and atheists? Can religion professionals with emotional problems be ably treated by therapists using the same techniques they use to treat other emotionally ill persons? Or do religion professionals require special techniques of therapy which only certain kinds of therapists possess? Are the unique qualifications of these therapists dependent on some special training, some particular belief system, some composite of religious practices, or some high standard of virtue? These questions are not just theoretical speculation. They represent positions which have a marked impact on the therapist's approach to religion professionals and which interrelate with characteristics of religion professionals in their approach to therapy.

Because of the critical significance of the theoretical stance adopted by the mental health professional, this requires further exploration. If mental health professionals assume that the beneficial treatment of religion professionals requires special techniques, they must be able to state what those techniques are. In addition, they need to produce reliable evidence that these special techniques produce more beneficial results than those techniques which belong to the armamentarium of all well-trained mental health professionals. Are these special techniques only used in working with religion professionals or other highly religious persons, or are they used in working with nonreligious clients? Are they suitable techniques for the treatment of nonbelievers?

Some mental health professionals apparently attempt to establish their competence based on their belief system or on their particular religious affiliation. If belief system is important, if religious affiliation is a credential, one must ask what belief system and what religious affiliation is required? What standards of orthodoxy arise? Is it sufficient for the therapist to be Catholic, or must he or she also oppose birth control? Increasing numbers of mental health professionals promote their competence based on the fact that they are "Christian." The suggestion is, of course, that they are better suited for the treatment of other Christians and naturally for the treatment of Christian religion professionals. Does this mean they are better equipped to treat *all* Christians, including fundamentalist Baptists, conservative Catholics, charismatic Lutherans, and traditional Methodists? Does the common belief in Jesus as the Son of God open the door to a new standard of treatment offered by Christian therapists? Economic realities and marketing needs may contribute as much to this presentation of therapeutic excellence as spiritual realities and special techniques do.

A treatment approach based on belief system has been most prominently supported in the Catholic church, where church administrators have established and financially supported a hybrid system of mental health care which is financially inefficient and which frequently fosters institutional dependence. This system depends on the premise that priests and vowed religious of the Roman Catholic Church require special treatment settings and therapists who are church affiliated and responsive to church attitudes. This system of care serves to highlight some of the treatment issues which occur in church-affiliated approaches and which will be discussed later in this chapter.

A very basic decision must be made in approaching the treatment of religion professionals. They either possess the same emotional components that other people have, or they do not. They either experience the same gamut of emotional responses that other people do, or they do not. They either develop the same kinds of pathology that other people develop, or they do not. They can either be treated by the same therapeutic techniques used for other people, or they cannot. If the therapist answers these statements affirmatively, then the therapist approaches the treatment of religion professionals with the same style, the same comfort, the same techniques, and the same self-reflection as he or she approaches other clients. If the therapist answers these statements in the negative, then the therapist must possess a whole system of techniques and theoretical premises especially designed to work with this group of clients who do not fit in with the rest of humanity.

Origin of Treatment Philosophies

One might ask why this dichotomy of treatment philosophies has occurred in the first place. Early antagonism between Mother Church and Father Freud was ignited by Freud, who, calling himself "the infidel Jew," described religion as a "universal obsessional neurosis" and who relegated the figure of God to a mere psychic projection. Religious defenders rose to the occasion and soon labeled psychiatry as atheistic, materialistic, and hedonistic. In the 1930s and 1940s the war was waged in the radio oratory of Catholic Bishop Fulton J. Sheen and in the nebulous territory which university programs designated as philosophical psychology. The 1950s and 1960s saw a lessening of tensions and sound attempts at rapprochement. Gregory Zilboorg, Karl Stern, Noel Mailloux, and Thomas Verner Moore were prominent Americans who endorsed the value of the behavioral sciences and attempted to bring their insights into the camp of religious believers. In Europe, Louis Beirnaert, Albert Ple, Maryse Choisy, Gerald Vann, and the great philosopher Jacques Maritain, together with several other writers, produced a landmark volume entitled *Cross Currents of Psychiatry and Catholic Morality* (Birmingham and Cuneen 1964), which recognized the value of the depth psychologies and integrated them into the richness of the Christian tradition. While some contributed to increased theoretical understanding, others attended to the more practical application of attempted resolution. In 1963 Braceland, an internationally prominent psychiatrist, and Stock, a Dominican psychologist, authored *Modern Psychiatry: A Handbook for Believers.* They wrote in their introduction, "The volume is especially directed toward allaying the fears of religious believers who still have doubts about this discipline or those who have been adversely influenced by the misinformation which is abroad concerning it" (Braceland and Stock 1963, pp. xi–xii). The efforts of these and many others have not completely allayed the early suspicions regarding the depth psychologies. There continues to be misinformation regarding the mental health professions and their response to the treatment needs of believers, especially religion professionals. Mental health care which perpetuates a kind of paranoia about mainstream mental health treatment does a disservice to the treatment of religion professionals and a disservice to the mental health professions. Encouraging religion professionals to believe that their "specialness" necessitates narrow specialization in a therapist limits their access to a broad range of competent professionals. Certifying mental health professionals because of some religious orthodoxy denigrates other members of the profession by implying that they are not competent in this area of work.

Braceland and Stock (1963) wrote, "Psychiatry, we have learned, is an empirical discipline, and as such it is neutral with respect to religious ideas, no matter how religious its practitioners" (p. 245). In 1990 the American Psychiatric Association published "Guidelines Regarding Possible Conflict between Psychiatrists' Religious Commitments and Psychiatric Practice." These guidelines, which were approved by the Assembly in November 1989 and by the Board of Trustees in December 1989, state:

I. Psychiatrists should maintain respect for their patients' beliefs.
   A. It is useful for clinicians to obtain information on the religious or ideologic orientation and beliefs of their patients so that they may properly attend to them in the course of treatment.

B. If an unexpected conflict arises in relation to such beliefs, it should be handled with a concern for the patient's vulnerability to the attitudes of the psychiatrist. Empathy for the patient's sensibilities and particular beliefs is essential.

C. Interpretations that concern a patient's beliefs should be made in a context of empathic respect for their value and meaning to the patient.

II. Psychiatrists should not impose their own religious, antireligious, or ideological systems of beliefs on their patients, nor substitute such beliefs or ritual for accepted diagnostic concepts or therapeutic practice.

A. No practitioner should force a specific religious, antireligious, or ideologic agenda on a patient, nor work to see that the patient adopts such an agenda.

B. Religious concepts or ritual should not be offered as a substitute for accepted diagnostic concepts or therapeutic practice ("Guidelines" 1990, p. 542).

Should other professional practitioners accept similar guidelines? Should psychologists accept them? Social workers? Pastoral counselors? The guidelines as stated seem generally suitable for adoption by other mental health professionals. Pastoral counselors may be better equipped "to obtain information on the religious or ideologic orientation and beliefs of their patients," and they may exhibit greater "empathy for the patient's sensibilities and particular beliefs" and greater "empathic respect for their value and meaning to the patient." However, it is essential to recognize that these treatment characteristics and ethical responsibilities are not the sole domain of the pastoral counselor or the Christian therapist. They should, in fact, be part of the professional standards of all mental health professionals.

The particular religious practices or faith system of any client need not be an obstacle to therapeutic engagement for the well-trained and reflective mental health professional. Countertransference issues often arise in the therapeutic relationship, and an awareness of countertransference issues in the field of religion has importance for all mental health professionals, whether they purport to be Christian, Jewish, or nonbelievers. An article by Cavanagh states this clearly:

> The only legitimate goal of a therapist is to help people make choices that are in the direction of personality growth. Two countertherapeutic situations can arise with regard to the therapist's religious attitudes. In the first case, the therapist believes that religion or religious life is inimical to personality growth . . . . In the second case, the therapist possesses religious values that he or she believes the person in therapy should also possess (Cavanaugh 1982).

Role of the Therapist

It is important for the mental health professional to be aware of countertransference issues. What is one's attitude about religion, what is one's attitude about this particular religion? Awareness of countertransference can permit a mental health professional to work with a broad range of religious clients. Being divorced does not keep a person from working effectively with people who are married or from working effectively with their marital problems. Having abandoned or never having had a personal religion or even a belief in God does not keep a therapist from working with individuals who are religious.

From time to time, all mental health professionals work with clients who have destructive influences in their lives, damaging relationships, hazardous health habits, unhealthy personal attitudes. It is appropriate to refrain from attacking these influences, and only the most highly directive therapist instructs clients to extirpate these influences from their lives. It is prudent to remember that these influences may not be as destructive as the mental health professional perceives them to be because he or she is viewing them through the translucency of the client's verbal reports. Therapeutic caution provides the wisdom to know that it is the client's task, not the therapist's, to study the many facets and influences of her or his emotional life and to integrate or to eliminate in a way that permits the client a degree of personal integrity in the face of life's realities—as known only to the client. At first appearance the over-protectiveness of a spouse, the intrusiveness of a parent, the degrading behavior of an associate may seem clearly destructive to the individual in therapy, but the therapist must be careful not to judge and not to act. The client can be encouraged to evaluate these relationships and assess their significance and their influences, both positive and negative.

The same approach can be used in working with religion professionals. If the mental health professional believes that a client has tyrannical parents, a tyrannical spouse, or a tyrannical employer, the task of the mental health professional is not to free the client of that tyranny, but to help the client look at it and evaluate its significance with the hope that the client may find a way to gain healthy self-determination. If the mental health professional believes that a religion professional has developed a tyrannical superego which is nourished by an autocratic church, the task of the mental health professional is somewhat the same. The role of therapist is not to rid the world of tyrannical parents or tyrannical churches. Clients can be encouraged to review these influences in their lives and sometimes can escape the tyranny but preserve the tie with parent or with church. There are ecclesiogenic neuroses just as there are iatrogenic neuroses, but the former are no more a basis for ridding ourselves of religion than the latter are reasons for ridding ourselves of doctors.

The development of the pastoral counseling profession is due at least in part to uncertainty about the value placed on religion by other mental health professions. Pastoral counselors have a serious responsibility to influence the future of other mental health professions based on the theoretical position they avow in relation to the treatment of religion professionals as well as other religious believers. Public relations, public opinion, and public acceptance have considerable significance for any profession, but they should not become the benchmark of professional practice. Neither should marketing needs shade the validity of professional claims. If certain mental health professionals demand territorial jurisdiction over certain classes of clients, they may at the same time abrogate the treatment of other classes of clients. If certain mental health professionals isolate themselves from the professional mainstream, they may discover that they have in fact become alienated and in their religiously influenced specialization developed a hybrid therapy which achieves limited acceptance and reduced effectiveness.

The "Uniqueness" of Religion Professionals

Whatever the philosophical framework the therapist adopts, the treatment of religion professionals does have certain peculiarities. The obvious unusual characteristic, which often appears when the first appointment is made, is the religion component. An appointment is made for "Reverend" or "Pastor" or "Rabbi" or "Sister" or "Brother" So-and-So. The religion professional often has expectations of others that he or she associates with this religious title. The position that the religion professional should be treated by a church affiliated or religiously endorsed therapist provides the linchpin for a number of expectations. Why should religion professionals be treated by mental health professionals who are "chosen" because of some special techniques, unique abilities, or graced presence? Why cannot mental health professionals who are reasonably skilled and professionally competent treat religion professionals as ably as they treat others? The unspoken implication is that religion professionals are special and require special care. Is the special care necessary because they are more delicate, more difficult to treat, or perhaps more dangerous? The religion professionals are, of course, left without an obvious answer. They sometimes assume that they are very special people who deserve special treatment, an attitude which contributes to their natural defensiveness and which helps them maintain a pedestal position from which they look down on the therapist with some disdain and say, "You really cannot understand me, can you?" They may also assume another answer for their specialness. They may interpret religiously affiliated therapy as a sign of their moral decay and an attempt to get them back on the path of righteousness. Morbid guilt may be stimulated, and they are twice stigmatized.

Religion professionals bring the same kinds of pathology, the same dynamic complexities, the same psychological defenses to the therapeutic encounter that others bring. Caretakers, whether they are religion professionals or mental health professionals, have difficulty accepting care from others, particularly emotional care. A surgeon with acute appendicitis is not likely to postpone recommended surgery. Emotions associated with his or her dependent role during recovery may be more difficult to accept. Professionals who work regularly with the emotional turmoil and needs of others typically find it difficult to face their own emotional vulnerability. This is particularly true with religion professionals because much of their training has taught them to discount their emotions, to devalue their emotions, and to disguise their emotions. Many times they do this so well that their emotional life becomes completely falsified. They recognize only their positive emotions. Negative emotions have been repressed so successfully and for such a long time that they are no longer available to them in early phases of therapy. Additional incentives for hiding their emotions come from those whom they serve in ministry. In spite of recent negative publicity and sensationalized accounts of behavioral deficiencies in religion professionals, lay persons continue to have high expectations of them. So religion professions, more cognizant of their representation of moral standards than of healthy emotional responses, conceal emotional reactions which may have moral sequelae, particularly erotic and hostile feelings. Most religion professionals have a sense of being "on duty" twenty-four hours each day, every day of the year. They have difficulty finding times when or persons to whom they can reveal these feelings. They often adopt a facade to conceal these emotions and to provide a consistent pattern of interacting with others.

A 54-year-old Catholic priest was admitted for inpatient treatment because he had become almost nonfunctional in his parish. He experienced severe insomnia, anhedonia, anergy, and irritability. He exhibited marked motor restlessness, indecisiveness, poor concentration, and decreased appetite. When approached by hospital staff or by peers, he was friendly, pleasant, and outgoing. Although he acknowledged all the signs and symptoms characteristic of a severe major depression, he could not recognize that he was depressed. Throughout his hospital stay he frequently commented on the fact that every day of his life had been a happy one and that he could not understand why he had lost that feeling. Antidepressant medication served as the primary factor in his recovery, along with a change of assignment away from the burdens of his former pastorate. Although it was clear to treatment personnel that his depression was the result of unusual burdens and continuing crises in his parish, he was never able to make the connection between his symptoms and these long-standing problems. He had coped with them in sound, rational, administrative fashion. He remained unaware that they had affected him emotionally and depleted that psychic component which moves people to interact dynamically with life events.

Religion professionals typically approach treatment reluctantly for a number of reasons. They are themselves in the role of caregivers. They are poorly acquainted with their own affective existence. They frequently have a sense of shame in having emotions which are not easily controlled. Religion professionals frequently lack clarity about the amoral nature of emotional life. They are prone to associate negative emotional reactions with sin. The therapist must move carefully and respectfully in this territory, which may appear solely affective to the therapist but seem totally moral ground to the client. Many religion professionals believe that anger is sinful, that sexual desires are sinful, that discouragement and despondency are sinful. Although religion professionals may profess an intellectual appreciation of the distinction between sinfulness and emotional upheaval, they may not be so convinced at an affective level. Sheehan and Kroll (1990) found that in a group of hospitalized lay patients, 23 percent believed that sin-related factors, such as sinful thoughts or sinful acts, were influential in their development of psychiatric illness (pp. 112–13). Mental illness continues to carry a stigma in our society, and it is safe to suggest that the stigma of emotional illness is directly proportional to the intensity of religious beliefs and practices in various segments of society. The therapist working with the religion professional must attempt cautiously to provide affective clarity to the borderland between emotion and sin. The reality that emotions are not immediately subject to intellect and will may need to be an area of focus. The fact that feelings of anger, of sexual desire, of despondency are automatic, stimulus-response kinds of reactions may need careful elucidation.

Moralizing, like intellectualizing, can be a defensive maneuver for religion professionals in therapy. They are often more comfortable in the arena of morality than in the mysterious land of emotions. Sinful transgressions can be immediately resolved by God's ever ready forgiveness. Emotional divergence requires time and effort to correct. Sinfulness raises one to an ethereal plane. Human pathology places one in direct contact with significant persons in one's life. Although a resolution to amend one's ways is part of the petition for divine forgiveness, peace comes to the individual before the corrections are made. In therapy peace comes only after some corrective measures are achieved. It is not surprising that the religion professional may chose to hide in the camp of sinners in order to avoid the painful struggle that probing psychotherapy can inflict. One of the most obvious examples of "escape into sin" occurs in the reactions of the pedophile. It is not unusual for a pedophile, under the duress of confrontation and exposure, to "confess" the behavior to a spiritual director, to church administrators, or even to legal authorities. Such pedophiles have no problem promising amendment, but they want that to be an end to it. To engage in therapy which brings them to scrutinize their behavior and review its significance in their lives and the lives of others is something of which they want no part. They confess to authorities who can do something about them, but they have difficulty being open with therapists who expect them to do something about themselves.

Religion professionals use intellectualization as a typical defense. Their native intelligence, their education, their respect for ideas rather than feelings, their facility with words, and their experience in dealing with a variety of persons, all of this provides a natural base in their approach to therapy and a host of response patterns which they have developed to hide their own emotions and to deal with others effectively but not affectively. These response patterns serve them well in their ministry, particularly when they are pressured by others. They provide armor against criticism and immunity from taxing and disquieting emotional reactions. The treatment setting brings these defenses to the fore, and the religion professional quickly engages the unsuspecting therapist in discussions about the traditionalism of the hierarchy, the failings of liberation theology, or the correlation between giving and the format of services. The closer therapists are identified with the field of religion, the more the defenses of moralization and intellectualization are likely to be successful, unless the therapists are alert to these maneuvers and particularly aware of their own vulnerability.

Dependency is always a hazard in the closeness of the therapeutic relationship. Many religion professionals have marked dependency needs, which have been fostered by their religious and ecclesiastical experiences. Religion professionals in certain denominations function quite independently of hierarchical structure or church administration. They act as independent agents who agree to provide services to congregations on a precise contractual basis. They are directly responsible to the congregation through some administrative body, and their continued employment depends on their productivity. Other groups of religion professionals, most noteworthy the Roman Catholics, have been trained and supported in a setting which assumes a great deal of administrative, financial, and psychological responsibility for them.

Those with strong dependency drives are often attracted to a system which appears to respond favorably to those drives. However, strong dependency needs in adults inevitably become frustrated by the limitations of reality. This frustration often leads to anxiety and depression or to obsessive compulsive symptoms. Overly dependent persons are rarely able to express their anger openly over frustrated dependency, although they sometimes manage to achieve rather immature outbursts. Their emotional responses to their frustrated dependency needs make them good candidates for administrators to refer for treatment. They are not always good candidates for therapeutic benefit. They bring their dependency needs to the therapeutic setting, and the frustration of those needs by an energetic therapist provokes responses similar to those for which they were referred to therapy. Active therapy to produce some change is an appropriate endeavor, but the limitations of intense therapy for many of these persons should be acknowledged by mental health professionals.

A 45-year-old female religion professional was referred for an independent evaluation because she was socially isolated, unable to maintain employment, apparently abusing prescribed medications, and generally uncooperative. History revealed that these behaviors and problems had recurred throughout her adult life. Early history showed significant emotional losses and unmet developmental needs. Clinical evaluation and psychological testing showed strong dependency needs. When these needs were not met, the result was social withdrawal, physical complaints (to which others typically responded), and lack of cooperation. She had engaged in outpatient therapy with the same therapist once or twice a week for the previous twelve years without noticeable improvement. Various psychotropic medications including antidepressants and anxiolytics had been tried. She had taken an anxiolytic for several years together with several other medicines including narcotic analgesics. Following the evaluation, the recommendation was made that any further treatment be confined to group therapy and twelve-step programs, specifically ACOA. All medications were discontinued except for non-narcotic analgesics. She was encouraged to consider less stressful employment, and not engage in professional responsibilities independent of close supervision. It was abundantly clear that this person attempted to meet her dependency needs through visits to physicians, ongoing psychotherapy, and the use of various medicines prescribed by different physicians.

A clergyman, age 52, was referred for inpatient treatment by a pastoral counselor because of concerns about vague suicidal ideation. He had been involved in outpatient psychotherapy for twenty-five years with a number of different therapists. There had been no improvement in functioning and no particular insights developed as a result of treatment. Various recommendations resulted from the evaluation, including one that individual therapy be terminated.

These two cases underscore the issue of dependency on the part of the religion professional. In addition, they shed light on countertransference issues which sometimes confuse church related therapists. The religiously dedicated counselor may find it difficult to cease rescue efforts for the religion professionals whom they treat. Good therapists recognize the limitations of treatment efforts with some clients and acknowledge that persons who remain unmotivated to change will not be changed by the most valiant treatment efforts. Rabbi Friedman in his delightful book *Friedman's Fables*, comments, "The colossal misunderstanding of our time is the assumption that insight will work with people who are unmotivated to change" (Friedman 1990, p. 5). Religiously oriented therapists are frequently trapped by their own beliefs that religion professionals are intrinsically motivated to improve their lives. Even if that may be true on a spiritual plane, it does not translate to the field of emotions. Church affiliated therapists and treatment facilities have a double investment in producing change in their patients. They want to bring about emotional health for the client's benefit, and they have their own need to bring about emotional health for the church's benefit. The latter involvement makes it difficult for the therapist to let go and often prolongs treatment that remains unfulfilling for the therapist, unproductive for the client, and extremely costly for the church administration.

A sense of entitlement may not be readily thought of as a defense mechanism, but the notion captures a special characteristic that many religion professionals bring to the treatment relationship. Religion professionals who have used the prestige of their position to dominate others, to elicit special treatment from others, or to keep others at an emotional distance present peculiar problems in the therapeutic encounter. They postpone therapy because they need to be certain they have the best therapist, the one most suited to their special situation. They engage in treatment cautiously, waiting to be certain that the therapist is clearly cognizant of their specialness. They either withdraw from treatment completely or decrease their involvement if they judge that some therapeutic exchange failed to recognize their uniqueness.

Religion professionals sometimes have another sense of entitlement regarding the very concept of therapy. They regard therapy as their right, as a sort of postgraduate course in psychological growth. Mental health professionals, characteristically those who are church affiliated, have contributed to this attitude of entitlement by supporting treatment for religion professionals when in reality it was far from necessary. Mental health care has become a major expense among some groups of religion professionals, especially some Catholic communities of men and of women. Individual religion professionals frequently approach treatment as a means to enhance their emotional well-being, to support their psychological development, or, on occasion, as a substitute for the lack of intimacy in their lives. These goals need to be achieved through personal reflection and experiences of living. Wealthy persons and famous persons can support having "a personal therapist" as a mark of their position. When religion professionals need therapy, it should be available to them. However, true entitlement comes from need and not from some assumed right.

A 24-year-old theology student was referred for a second opinion regarding his need for treatment. He had been seeing a pastoral counselor in weekly sessions for the previous two years. After giving a brief initial history, he discussed his reasons for engaging in therapy. He recognized some of his own immaturity and some of the conflicts he was experiencing in dealing with his desire to please others, especially authority figures. He knew that he needed to establish more mature patterns of interaction, and he assumed that therapy would bring this about. Mental health treatment is neither a conventional nor inexpensive method of attaining maturity.

Mental health professionals not only respond to the religion professional's sense of entitlement in providing unnecessarily prolonged treatment, but also in allowing the religion professional to set certain boundaries in the therapeutic encounter. Countertransference issues contribute to this arrangement. Religion professionals may signal the therapist that particular topics are tabu, topics which the therapist might normally want to discuss with clients. A number of commonly believed tenets about religion professionals can interfere with sound therapeutic exploration. "Clergy do not use illicit drugs." "Religion professionals do not tell lies." "Nuns do not abuse alcohol." "Married clergy are sexually faithful." "Religion professionals are law abiding." "Religion professionals do not resort to physical violence." Each of these positions exempts religion professionals from the failings that therapists confront regularly and easily in their work. If mental health professionals are not ready to hear about such behavior from religion professionals, their unpreparedness increases the religion professional's lack of readiness to speak of such things. The religion professional who speaks of behavioral problems manifested by a parishioner may be "testing the waters." The therapist who, for example, takes a judgmental stance or an ecclesiastically approved position regarding the religion professional's comment about a parishioner who is having an abortion may be closing the door on the need of the religion professional to discuss some personal experience with an abortion decision. The parent, the pastor, the teacher who says to another, "I know I don't have to worry about you doing this or that" is not likely to hear from that other person when in fact she or he has done this or that. Therapists need to be constantly on the alert neither to assume the goodness of clients before they have revealed themselves nor to assume their badness after they have revealed themselves. In work with religion professionals this non-judgmental stance is particularly difficult to maintain.

Low-Morale Among Religion Professionals

Perhaps one of the most common issues underlying therapy with religion professionals in contemporary society is their low morale and their tarnished public image. Public exposition of faults and failures, often sensationalized in the media, has cast a shadow over the ministry of all religion professionals. The power and prestige of religion professionals has, on occasion, permitted financial exploitation, psychological victimization, and sexual abuses, which have created an atmosphere of suspicion and at times contempt. It is difficult to maintain the ideals of one's profession when it is sullied by a few and maligned by many. This background may be an important issue for the religion professional approaching therapy. When the ministry of religion professionals is publicly questioned, self-doubts arise quickly, followed by struggles with spiritual practices and conflicts regarding faith itself. It is not unusual to find religion professionals, anxious and depressed, doubting the personal investment they have made in the field of religion, doubting their personal integration of meaningful values, and doubting the fundamental tenets of their belief system. Their ministry may have deteriorated to motions without meaning. They continue to serve others in their dedication to selflessness, but their service has lost its divine connectedness as well as any personal significance or reward. Therapists need an awareness of the rapid fall into this "dark night" religion professionals can experience. It is difficult for them to verbalize this experience because they do not want to believe their own loss of belief, and they do not want others to see what they perceive to be a fall from grace.

Another factor contributing to low morale is the training of religion professionals which frequently equates "good works" and "justification." The more one does for the kingdom, the more worthy one is. Natural inclinations, child-rearing practices, and formation training may all contribute to the compulsivity (sometime represented by scrupulosity) characteristic of many religion professionals. They easily become workaholics par excellence. Religion professionals frequently neglect their own emotional needs and even their own spiritual needs. As work expands with increasing responsibilities and increasing numbers to whom they minister, their natural response is to increase their working hours to meet these demands. They cannot create the additional hours they pray for, so they begin to allot the hours they have differently. Recreation falls by the wayside, and with recreation a number of supportive relationships are frequently lost or markedly curtailed. They reach a balance of prayer and work which some ancient spiritual writers acclaimed. Their inability to say no has not been modified, so additional demands from the bottomless well of human needs confront them and further encroach on their time. The next area to give way is prayer life, because it is a private matter unobserved by others, and because they often say "my work will become my prayer."

A 42-year-old Catholic sister brought in her daily schedule at the repeated request of her therapist. During the evening hours, when most people relax, she was busy correcting papers and preparing for the next day of classes. She always found additional work to do during the free periods of her teaching day. Her prayer life had not yet disintegrated because she arose at 4:30 a.m. to meet that demand. Weekends were taken up in various ministries to others. It was important in therapy to help this woman understand the connection between her poorly controlled anger, her deep-seated resentments, her chronic anhedonia, and the schedule which she had established in her own life. Her natural compulsivity and her religious formation made it very difficult for her to intervene in her own behalf.

Religion professionals notoriously take poor care of their own psychological needs. They often seem ignorant of sound mental health principles, although one may hear them weaving those principles into homilies or discussion with others. Although religion professionals are typically well acquainted with psychological principles, therapists should not assume that they apply them to themselves.

Wider Responsibilities for Therapists

An area that is receiving more attention in relation to the treatment of religion professionals is the relationship of the therapist to the administrative body of the religion professional's denomination. This is particularly true in those denominations which have a clearly designated church authority. The responsibility of the therapist remains primarily to the client, but the responsiveness of the therapist may extend to the religious administration. How can the therapist balance the privacy of contacts with the religion professional and the legitimate needs of church administrators to have certain information about those religion professionals for whom they may have moral and legal responsibility?

Professional confidentiality is a delicate area. A sacred trust is involved and must not be violated. However, a large percentage of religious who are in treatment have significant and emotionally debilitating conflicts with their community administrators, their peer professionals, or those to whom they minister. It is often essential that the therapist have access to information relating to these conflicts. Steps need to be taken by religious administrators and by treating professionals to open channels of communication that provide for the transfer of that information, thereby enhancing the treatment process and speeding treatment progress. Informed consent requirements often force a therapist to give the reasons for an opinion and to explain alternative treatment approaches. Society no longer tolerates the unchallenged position of care providers. The confidential nature of treatment is not violated by providing certain kinds of information to carefully selected others.

This is the era of managed care, which means very simply that those who pay the bills for health care demand an accounting of the reasons for the care. Utilization review agents of insurance companies demand to know what a patient is being treated for, what proof there is that the patient has that illness, what outcome is expected from treatment, and how long treatment will take. It is typically the insurance company that dictates to the treating professional how long treatment will take, stating that insurance will pay for only so many days in the hospital or only so many outpatient visits. Managed care, as represented by the insurance company, often recommends that a second opinion be obtained and sometimes insists on a second opinion before authorizing treatment. In keeping with all of this, relatives who pay the bills are more likely to demand an accounting, including a review of progress, anticipated length of treatment, prognosis, information regarding medicines being used with reasons for their use, side effects, and other pertinent questions. This is a time when the people who pay the bills have established their right to an accounting and their right to request a second opinion. In mental health there are legitimate questions to ask: What progress is being made? How much longer will treatment take? What is the likely outcome? Are there alternatives to this treatment, and what are they? What about a second opinion?

This dilemma may be in part resolved by distinguishing an evaluation requested by church authorities and treatment requested by the individual or perhaps recommended by church administration. The purpose of the evaluation is to acquire information regarding the emotional health and the stability as well as any current pathology of an individual. Some limited predictions may be made based on the evaluation, and recommendations relating to mental health needs, stress reduction tactics and functional limitations may be made. Full disclosure to the individual and the requesting religious authority is appropriate when the individual has given signed permission for such disclosure. The treatment contract differs in that it focuses on the psychological needs of the individual and is not established to respond to the needs of the church authority. If the administration has recommended that treatment occur, it can be beneficial at the outset for administrators to provide clear and relevant information to the individual and to the therapist regarding the reasons for recommending treatment. This is similar to the interventions addressed in twelve-step programs. In addition, the religious authority should have some access to the treatment relationship in keeping with managed care concepts. The legitimate questions that family members ask, that insurance companies ask, that employers ask, can be asked by religious administrators. What progress is being made? What is the estimated treatment duration? What is the likely prognosis? What are alternative treatments? What about a second opinion?

The Role of the Pastoral Counselor

Is there a special role for the pastoral counselor in the burgeoning field of mental health professionals? Two possibilities are on the horizon. Pastoral counselors can present themselves as peculiarly equipped to deal with issues relating to religion, faith, spirituality, prayer. They can claim that their profession gives them special insights into these areas and special techniques for dealing with conflicts or problems in these areas. They can assert that because of their training, their insights, their techniques, they are best suited to work with religious believers and especially with religion professionals, the leaders of religious believers. One must question whether or not such a direction on the part of pastoral counselors is substantiated by the facts or if such claims would not in reality lead to confusion and division within the profession and eventually be a disservice to the profession and to those whom they would profess to serve.

The other possible role that pastoral counselors might assume could provide an enrichment for all the mental health professions and establish pastoral counseling as a contributor to the betterment of those served by all mental health professionals. Each of the other principal mental health professions has provided a distinct contribution to mental health treatment and each has advanced the general care of the emotionally troubled by the contributions they have made. Social work has contributed remarkably to the practice of collateral involvement of significant others. Psychology has enhanced treatment by providing the benefit of testing to clarify diagnostic dilemmas and uncover dynamic issues as well as personality strengths and weaknesses. Psychiatry has provided a broad armamentarium of psychotropic medicines that not only have direct efficacy in certain conditions but which frequently make the client more amenable to verbal therapies. These three mental health professions generally employ the same standard techniques in working with patients, and in their psychotherapeutic approaches they probably vary as much within each profession as they do between any one profession and the other two.

The pastoral counseling profession can make a unique contribution to the mental health professions generally by encouraging an interest in and a respect for the religious beliefs, values, and practices of all clients. A review by Larson et al. (1986) indicated that only 43 percent of the members of the American Psychiatric Association were theists and possibly only 5 percent of the American Psychological Association members were theists. Although one can assume that all pastoral counselors are theists, the depth and vitality of their beliefs and practices must vary greatly.

In approaching the treatment of religion professionals, pastoral counselors have the most likely opportunity to join the family of mental health professionals by recognizing the particular contribution of each profession, including their own, in the understanding of emotional problems, their communality, and their resolution. Pastoral counselors can enrich the mental health field by encouraging information about, understanding of, and empathy for the faith systems and religious practices of all clients, including religion professionals. Pastoral counselors may become leaders in research, such as that conducted by Byrd (1988) at the San Francisco General Medical Center suggesting the power of intercessory prayer for patients in a coronary care unit. If religion professionals are recognized as sharing common emotional ground with the rest of humanity and needing the same basic treatment approaches as the rest of humanity, the standard of care for everyone can be raised. All clients deserve the same basic respect, the same professional dedication, the same clinical effort and expertise, and the same prayerful remembrance, if the latter is part of the professional approach of the clinician.

Note

1. The staff of the Isaac Taylor Institute of Psychiatry and Religion at Taylor Manor Hospital in Ellicott City, Maryland, has promoted the

use of the term *religion professionals* to designate the range of persons whom they serve. This terminology suitably encompasses Protestant ministers, Roman Catholic and Episcopal priests, rabbis, permanent deacons, and vowed brothers and sisters of various faith groups. It will be used as an inclusive term in the present context.

References

Birmingham, W., and Cunneen, J., eds. 1964. *Cross Currents of Psychiatry and Catholic Morality.* New York: Pantheon.

Braceland, F., and Stock, M. 1963. *Modern Psychiatry: A Handbook for Believers.* New York: Doubleday.

Byrd, R. 1988. "Positive Therapeutic Effects of Intercessory Prayer in a Coronary Care Unit Population." *Southern Medical Journal* 81: 826–29.

Cavanagh, M. 1982. "Psychotherapeutic Issues in Religious Life." *Human Development* 3: 24–30.

Friedman, E. 1990. *Friedman's Fables.* New York: Guilford Press.

"Guidelines Regarding Possible Conflict Between Psychiatrists' Religious Commitments and Psychiatric Practice." 1990. *American Journal of Psychiatry* 147: 542.

Larson, D., et al. "Systematic Analysis of Research on Religious Variables in Four Major Psychiatric Journals 1978–1982." 1986. *American Journal of Psychiatry* 143: 329–34.

Sheehan, W., and Kroll, J. 1990. "Psychiatric Patients' Belief in General Health Factors and Sin as Causes of Illness." *American Journal of Psychiatry* 147: 112–13.

For Further Reading

Lutz, R., and Taylor, B., eds. 1990. *Surviving in Ministry: Navigating the Pitfalls, Experiencing the Renewals.* Mahwah, N.J.: Paulist Press.

McAllister, R. 1986. *Living the Vows: Emotional Conflicts of Celibate Religious.* San Francisco: Harper & Row.

Wicks, R., et al., eds. 1985. *Clinical Handbook of Pastoral Counseling.* Mahwah, N.J.: Paulist Press.

Gail Lynn Unterberger

9. Counseling Lesbians: A Feminist Perspective

A call comes into the pastoral counseling center. The caller, who describes herself as a white woman in her 40s, asks for a woman counselor to help her make an important decision. The secretary triages the intake to me. At the time of our meeting the client appears, having just come from the office, dressed in a business suit with a lace ruffled blouse, clasped by a cameo at the neck. During the first half of the counseling session, Lisa [not her real name] tells me that she works as a top manager, a job not without its stresses, but one in which she is comfortable and challenged. The problem lies in her personal life. She has been dating a man for several months, and he has asked her to marry him. Her parents, with whom she has always lived, are encouraging her to accept the offer, as they don't want her to be "an old maid." Her three other siblings have long since moved out, gotten married, and had children. She has chosen to stay with her parents, she says, in order to take care of them as they age.

Upon further discussion she divulges the information that she is not attracted to her present "beau," indeed, though she likes him as a friend, she is "revolted" by his physical advances. In her Christian belief system she feels it would be sinful for her to have premarital sexual relations with him, or anyone else for that matter. Pressed for further details she admits that she has never had any romantic feelings for men, but she has felt strong longings for women. In fact, she feels she may be in love with a woman who works in a neighboring office. They are good friends, lunching together regularly. But Lisa does not want to let her friend know her heart beats so fast whenever she is in her presence. Lisa relates this last with great apprehension, apparently worried about my response.

It turns out that she has been aware of these "longing, loving feelings for women," in which she yearns to be "close to the woman in every way," since she can remember. Yet she has been taught that such "queer" feelings are not only sick but also sinful. So she has tried to ignore them and channel them into relationships with men. For two years she regularly attended a local Christian self-help group for lesbian and gay people who want to become heterosexual. She states that they and she have prayed "day and night" for Christ to change her feelings but, she says, apparently "Jesus has not seen fit to heal her of this disease, this evil part" of her. She wonders if she would get over this problem if she just married her current beau. She suggests she might be able to become cured if I, as an ordained minister, would continually pray for her and would remind her weekly that her homosexual longings are not only sick, but also sinful.

Introduction

Homosexuality has been compared to a fishbone caught in the throat of Protestant, Roman Catholic and Jewish congregations—an obstruction that can neither be swallowed whole nor ejected and forgotten (Rashke 1976, p. 28; Nugent and Gramick 1989). From time to time various denominations attempt to update their formal statements in response not only to calls for civil rights and inclusivity raised by the gay liberation movement itself, but also to requests by religious homosexuals for equal opportunity to serve the church and synagogue in both lay and ordained positions. In the meanwhile pastoral care givers have had to find ways to respond with love and integrity to the pastoral concerns and theological questions presented to them by lesbian and gay constituents. Such pastoral counselors have had to minister to the families and friends of gays and lesbians, as well as to address the issues of concern brought by the increasing number of heterosexual church members who are moving into solidarity with the goals of the gay and lesbian movement.

There can be no doubt that religious institutions have played a powerful role in the oppression of lesbians to a greater or lesser extent throughout history. The religious community's acceptance of male homosexuality has paralleled variance within Western culture from New Testament times to the present (Boswell 1980). Even so, religion has given theological, biblical, and doctrinal arguments to undergird homosexuals' status as social pariahs, sexual deviants, loathsome, and the worst of all sinners in the eyes of God. And religion has depicted lesbians as more degraded, depraved, promiscuous, and damnable than heterosexual women.

While most denominational policy statements stop short of endorsing the denial of civil rights of homosexuals, they often do not grant full acceptance to them either, specifying for example that homosexual activity, if not the orientation itself, is incompatible with Christian teachings. Progress is being made toward greater acceptance. Scholars of religion, sociology, anthropology, and psychology representing a wide range of denominations are challenging the traditional church stances based on new understandings from the fields of psychiatry, biology, biblical exegesis, theology, and ethics. Several mainline denominations are currently in the process of reevaluating their statements. Yet with the exception of the Moravian Church, the Friends, the Unitarian Universalists Association, and the Metropolitan Community Churches, presently most Christian denominations refuse to ordain self-affirming (self-avowed), practicing (as opposed to celibate) homosexuals. However, the American rabbinate for Reform Judaism has recently voted to admit acknowledged, sexually active homosexuals into its ranks. (Wall 1990, p. 1189). But the problem is not confined to the clerical side of the church. Many lesbian and gay church members report that they must hide their sexual orientation from fellow congregants for fear they would not be welcome in the congregations should the truth be known.

Defining Lesbian

While there is no single authoritative way of defining who is lesbian, care must be taken concerning the methodology of definition, since it is of utmost importance that lesbianism be a self-defined orientation. This is not because every lesbian knows and acknowledges, at once consciously and unconsciously, her sexual orientation. Indeed, many lesbians and bisexual women block out any same-sex romantic longings or sexual desires due to the terrible dread of acknowledging in themselves such feelings, which dominant society defines as loathsome. Lesbian history, like the history of many secondary-status groups, is not widely known (Vicinus 1989). Since self-identified lesbians often choose to "pass" for straight women, there are few well-known healthy role models for lesbians. Lesbians as portrayed by the dominant literature, media, culture, and narratives are usually not sympathetic personalities but are stereotypically depicted as unattractive, butch, bull-dykes, man-haters, "witches," and more.

In fact, lesbians are single, married, happy, sad, angry, complacent, well-adjusted, and maladjusted. They dress in stereotypically feminine as well as stereotypically masculine clothes along with any mix of the two, and they have an equally diverse sets of mannerisms.

They are in every walk of life, every culture, every society, and they pursue all careers open to women. As adults, lesbians look back and recognize they were "different" from other girls, at least insofar as they expressed their assumption that they would be economically self-sufficient as adults and to varying degrees rejected stereotypical female roles (Saghir and Robins 1973). Lesbians are teenagers, young adults, middle-aged women, and elderly. They comprise about 10 percent of all women, and they sit in the church pew, preach from the pulpit, say prayers on the Sabbath, and hold responsible offices in all levels of ecclesiastical hierarchy. Most of all they are in various stages of acknowledging their lesbianism, that is, of being "out of the closet" within ever-widening circles of their immediate relationships and the larger society.

Often lesbians distinguish themselves from bisexual women, who are able to entertain the possibility of having a sexual/romantic/emotional relationship with a male as well as a female. To be labeled bisexual is safer in heterosexual society, though in the lesbian community a bisexual woman is often either despised as one who implicitly denies her exclusive lesbianism or is tolerated as a lesbian who is simply on the journey to realizing exclusive lesbianism. She may be viewed as even more of a traitor to the lesbian community than straight women by certain lesbian communities. A bisexual woman, following the Kinsey continuum model, might see herself as positioned more or less in the middle of a continuum of human possibilities of attraction and sexual involvement. At one end of the continuum are persons who are attracted to and sexually involved with same-sex partners exclusively. The other end of the continuum includes those whose exclusive attraction and sexual involvement is with partners of the other sex (Scanzoni 1978, pp. 74).

There are numerous definitions of lesbianism, the least complex being a woman who "has taken a woman lover" (Grahan 1978, p. 67). This definition is based predominantly on sexual-genital contact, which does not address the situation of the pre–sexually active or celibate female, nor does it exclude bisexuals or the straight woman who has previously experimented with a lesbian relationship. Alternatively, problems arise if the definition of lesbianism is made on the basis of emotional, mental, or spiritual attraction, since that might then define as lesbians all women who have a fleeting sexual fantasy or an idle sexual thought about a possible sexual affair with another woman. All definitions are problematic in that even the act of labeling can bring up the very real fear of individual harassments or "witch hunts." However, for the purposes of discussion a five-part model, taken from a feminist theological perspective, may offer the most holistic understanding for pastoral counseling purposes. Certainly a definition of lesbianism must eschew traditional patriarchal constructs as well as simplistic, reductionistic approaches of the social sciences.

Mary Hunt (1989) considers these five elements essential:

1. *Context:* Paradoxically, labeling becomes important in a society which calls lesbians "outsiders, outlaws and even outcasts" (p. 106). In my experience self-avowed lesbians may be in a position to claim their orientation with pride or may need to conceal it for political and professional reasons even though they personally are comfortable and at-home with their own self-understanding. All of this depends on the dangers involved in the individualized coming-out process. In the counseling setting the counselor should establish a trusting, confidential relationship in which a woman will feel safe to explore and/or discuss her own process of self-identification without fear of judgment.

2. *Eros:* This is an essential dimension of being a lesbian. "Fantasy, touch, dreams and attractions all aimed at women are part of what it means to love women in a context which tells us not to" (p. 106).

3. *Community:* Especially since the beginning of the gay rights movement, the lesbian community is being established and defined. The particulars of overlapping communities may be defined by geographical proximity, professional group, local church, denomination or faith group, or the more widely dispersed group that acts as the community to whom lesbians "are held accountable for our behavior, including sexual conduct, fidelity to friends, use of resources, etc" (p. 107).

4. *Sexual experience:* Widely interpreted as ranging from casual sexual feelings to genital sexual activity these are "active, creative dimensions of sexual expression in the context of female-female relationships, as well as the healthy orientation or openness toward such experiences in a culture which considers them taboo" (p. 107).

5. *Spirituality:* Difficult to define, but essential to a holistic pastoral counseling definition, lesbian spiritualities are just now being articulated in the theological literature, though the sources have long been found in women's literature, music, poetry, and so on. While there is not one monolithic spirituality to be delineated, feminist lesbian spirituality includes a "celebration of relationships and the goodness of our woman love . . . which can involve commitment or covenant ceremonies for long term relationships and it certainly en-

compasses our efforts to honor and recall the lives of our foresisters" (p. 107).

Etiology of Lesbianism

During the last century theories about homosexuality have abounded though only recently have lesbians been addressed as a population apart from gay males. While the debate continues, the current consensus is that we do not understand definitively how it is that one person is homosexual and another heterosexual; there is no single correct explanation. Scientific researchers and political advocates have argued from both sides of a rather dualistic line with social constructionists on the one side and essentialists on the other. The former prefer to focus on lesbian *desires and acts*, since the expression of these change over time and across cultures. The latter discuss lesbianism in terms of *identity*, as a human sexual orientation, probably present at birth. The homosexual rights movement of the 1970s embraced essentialism.

Guy Menard notes how "scientific" approaches to homosexuality dating from the end of the nineteenth century "featured the development of a new frame of reference which first saw homosexuality transferred from the category of 'sin' to that of one type of 'sickness' or 'disorder' or another, until one other variant appeared among the rest, a possible and legitimate one: homosexuality as a 'sexual orientation' " (Menard 1989, p. 128). Laura Reiter (1989) differentiates between sexual orientation, which is determined in the childhood years, and sexual identity as it changes over time. She discusses how identity may or may not be congruent with orientation and how these affect self-labeling. Other researchers debate the functions of repression and denial and their role in subsequent self-labeling.

In any case homosexuality is actually a fairly new Western word connoting a new construct in terms of lifestyle, the discussions and studies of which have been dominated by male experience. Only very recently have lesbians become engaged in delineating the parameters of the discussion and naming the issues. Therefore it may be too early to determine whether arguments from social constructionist and essentialist theories elucidate or obscure lesbianism, or even whether they matter at all. But for many religious constituents, the matter of causality is paramount in terms of dictating the appropriate ethical response. For example, some well-meaning Christians breathlessly await definitive scientific evidence that would prove homosexuality to be a matter of genetics or prenatal hormones so they could then categorize the condition as a kind of chronic and immutable "disability" rather than a sinful predilection over which one has choice or a perverted illness that can be cured by psychotherapy or even (barring miracles) prayer. Alternatively, the Quakers have long since described homosexuality as no more inherently sinful or diseased than left-handedness, which occurs about as often in the population. Still, misinformation, myth, and a cloak of silence dominate in religious circles, with long-standing psychoanalytic viewpoints preferred over essentialist theories. In the meanwhile some Christians settle the issues with the well-known cliche, "love the sinner but not the sin," which sentences lesbians to lifelong celibacy in order for them to achieve acceptance. Otherwise intelligent and informed persons have been heard to espouse the idea that one can "catch" lesbianism from a teacher, parent, or mentor, though it is clear that most lesbians grew up in a heterosexual environment (Corley 1990, p. 4).

In summary, given the state of knowledge of psychology, therapists cannot look definitively to the woman's past or dwell on the intrapsychic structure to fix the "blame" for the woman's sexual orientation. Most lesbians are not interested in blaming anyone, and religious lesbians often are heard to proclaim, "If you have a problem with it, take it up with my Maker." However, it is crucial to note that in a hostile and predominantly heterosexual world, lesbians' feelings of anger, rejection, and hurt can exacerbate whatever situational, emotional, or developmental crises arise during the life cycle.

Pastoral Counselors: Caught in the Middle

Illness or Variation

Pastoral counselors, more than "secular" therapists, are often caught in the middle between the predominant assessments of the psychological sciences and the prevailing opinion of their religious group affiliations. For example, certain church groups, while they may not characterize homosexuals as sinful, resort to the label of "psychologically disturbed." This commonly occurs despite the fact that in 1974 the American Psychiatric Association removed homosexuality from the index of psychological pathology on the basis that most psychiatrists no longer considered homosexuality in and of itself a pathological adaptation. The American Psychological Association took similar action the following year. Or religious officials or concerned lay people may recommend that a lesbian seek counseling, though studies have shown that no psychotherapy has been successful across the board in transforming a person's exclusive sexual orientation to the opposite one on the continuum. While behavior change may result, usually only for a short period, a lesbian's deepest longings and passions remain with same-sex individuals. As Reiter notes in the post-1973, literature it has been shown how the so-called cures really were "instances of the suppression of homosexual behavior in bisexual people" whose behavioral changes "usually were not accompanied by a fundamental shift in underlying erotic preference" (Reiter 1989, p. 144).

The clinical pastoral education movement was influential in helping many clergy move from the earlier medical model to the essentialist model through exposure to increasing scientific evidence. Nugent and Gramick (1989) note:

> CPE was a more professional attempt to equip pastoral ministers with better skills to undertake direct helping relationships in a variety of human problems and situations. One of these areas was the reality of homosexual people encountered by clergy in every denomination and religious group. . . . Whether individual clergy personally undertook the counseling of homosexual clients or made referrals to other professionals, they soon acknowledged the apparent fixity of a genuine homosexual orientation and identity in certain individuals. Seeing that even intense and prolonged psychotherapy would not alter a true homosexual orientation, many were faced with the personal decision of having to adopt a kind of prophetic stance in their churches about homosexuality or else to remain silent (p. 13).

Sin or Part of Rich Diversity of Creation

Pastoral counselors are also caught in the middle of the theological debates between official church statements and contemporary scholarship. For example, faith groups may make certain declarations about the inherent sinfulness concerning either the nature (identity, orientation) or the sexual practice (acts) of lesbians, usually determining to what extent they can be barred from baptism, church membership, lay office, or ordination. Professional specialists in pastoral counseling have often taken extra courses or workshops on human sexuality, sexual ethics, and biblical exegesis, educating themselves concerning current scholarly debate and becoming informed as to the complex issues involved as opposed to making sweeping statements about sin or broad ethical judgments concerning homosexuality.

In particular, having undertaken studies in these areas of theology and sexuality, pastoral counselors often find themselves in diametric opposition with the prevailing denominational authorities, who have not become similarly informed. In other words, a counselor may be moving in the direction of greater acceptance of lesbians as persons with a minority sexual orientation. Indeed, one study (Hochstein 1986, p. 162) of a sample of pastoral counselors in the American Association of Pastoral Counselors showed that around 70 percent scored in the non-homophobic (high or low grade) range on the Hudson and Ricketts' *Index of Attitudes toward Homosexuals* (IAH). Such counselors may have integrated one of the liberation theologies, such as feminist, womanist Latin American, or Asian, as a basis for theological understanding of the praxis involved in the liberation of minorities. Or perhaps the counselor has utilized the specific literature on lesbian and gay spirituality emerging presently. In so doing the counselors find themselves faithful to their theology of liberation but at odds with the doctrinal or official faith statements of their governing religious authorities. Like the Roman Catholic priest who is asked by his parishioners in premarital counseling sessions about the ethical and practical issues of using birth control, pastoral counselors often answer with another question: "Do you want to know what the church thinks or do you want to know what I think?"

This latter possibility—categorizing oneself simplistically in opposition with the formal statements of one's own faith group—does not offer a quick and easy out for pastoral counselors. This is due to the fact that such a position lacks integrity unless it is also clear that the counselor is teaching, working, and/or writing to make changes in the religious institutional structures. An activist stance gives evidence that counselors are in solidarity with the aims of religious lesbians, because in so doing, pastoral counselors expose themselves, albeit only in small part, to the very dangers that the lesbian confronts every day of her life on a much grander scale. In turn, this deepens counselor empathy for lesbians.

In most ecclesiastical and theological communities it is ostensibly no longer tolerable to express racist views. It is also increasingly less fashionable to exhibit sexist beliefs and behaviors (despite political retrenchment on both fronts). Yet homophobia and heterosexism are rarely discussed, confronted, or confessed in the pulpit or Sunday

School. The liberal churches have failed utterly to take heterosexism seriously, and therefore have failed to do justice to women's lives "whether lesbian, heterosexual, bisexual, genitally active, genitally inactive, or celibate" (Heyward 1987, p. 37).

This makes counseling for liberation that goes on behind the closed doors of the pastor's office even more estranged from the life of the church when it comes to issues of homosexuality and heterosexism. The topic is silenced and lesbians remain invisible. Time and time again when I was serving as a parish minister, parishioners would tell me there were no gays in our congregation, that it was not an issue for our local church. Pastoral counselors are caught in the middle when we choose to counsel ethically and effectively while remaining silent on the subject in the pulpit; when we join in the quiet consensus on the part of many specialized ministers while not opposing those who proclaim that lesbianism is a threat to family values or against natural law.

Finally, there is a certain amount of fear within some denominational circles that if one's personal viewpoint as a clergyperson were known to be "gay affirming," ecclesiastical endorsement could be jeopardized. This leads to rampant paranoia on seminary campuses on the part of gay and lesbian ministerial candidates and prospective religious educators. But it is also a fear for straight people who are sympathetic to the cause of religious gay and lesbian movement.

"Neutral" Silence or Prophetic Endangerment

This dilemma is even more exacerbated for well-known pastoral counselors than for other scholars of religion. Certainly a number of systematic theologians, biblical scholars, and ethicists have been "silenced," threatened, or ostracized by religious constituents or authorities because they have made public through their writings, lectures, or preaching their call for greater acceptance of gays and lesbians by religious groups. But it is a very real danger for pastoral counselors to speak out on this as a justice issue since their tenure and ordinations are more firmly linked to their clinical practice and academic careers. For example, pastoral counselors certified by the American Association of Pastoral Counselors must be endorsed by their own faith groups. Their accreditation, hence their clinical pastoral ministry, is threatened should their ordination or endorsement status be revoked by their faith group, for whatever reason.[1]

Key to Effective Pastoral Counseling: Conscientization Through an Integration of Psychology and Religion

Given the previous understandings, certain assumptions follow concerning effective pastoral counseling of women minorities in general and lesbians in particular.

1. *Effective pastoral counseling of lesbians mandates counselor genuineness.*

Counseling is not a value-free enterprise. Every school of therapy prescribes empathy and genuineness as important counselor attributes. Competent counseling requires that one be able to relate empathically and exhibit genuineness since these, along with respect for the client, are at least the necessary if not sufficient conditions for establishing therapeutic alliance leading to client change (Rogers 1961). As Kohut wrote: "Empathy, the accepting, confirming, and understanding human echo evoked by the self, is a psychological nutrient without which human life, as we know and cherish it, could not be sustained" (Kohut 1978, p. 705). Basic helping manuals, such as Carkhuff (1987) and Egan (1990) stress the ability to respond empathically. But empathy, along with unconditional positive regard, must be genuine.

> Homophobic therapists can't help homosexuals. It's ridiculous to imagine entering into the spirit of a gay person and truly understanding their experience from the inside if you are uncomfortable with or revulsed by homosexuality. . . . If therapists do not, in fact, feel or think that homosexuality "just is," that it is neither bad nor good, healthy nor sick, but is simply a part of the cosmos, they will never be able to love gay patients (*all* of them) and help them grow (Fortunato 1982, p. 118).

It may be unreasonable to expect pastors and other pastoral counselors totally to have eradicated their personal homophobia before they can effectively counsel lesbians. However, it seems crucial that they be genuinely moving in the direction of more and more open-mindedness, confronting and transforming homophobic and heterosexist attitudes in themselves as a process of their personal spiritual and political journey.

Rigid, anti-gay viewpoints *will eventually* come through in the counseling process, just as misogynist or racist attitudes do. If one has not become sufficiently educated and conscientized to the psychological and religious implications in terms of justice for homosexual persons, then the viable ethical response is to refer lesbian parishioners or clients to a counselor who has. Comparisons can be made to the military chaplain who believes strongly that Jesus is the *only* way to salvation, not simply as a confessional statement for herself but as a universal truth applying to everyone. There are definite limits to how effective such a chaplain would be in counseling Jews or others in an interfaith context.

Self-knowledge is the starting point for the process of conscientization. As Egan writes, "Like everyone else, helpers are tempted to pigeonhole clients because of gender, race, sexual orientation, nationality, social status, religious persuasion, political preferences, lifestyle and the like. . . . The importance of self-knowledge . . . includes ferreting out the biases and prejudices that distort our listening" (Egan 1990, p. 118).

2. *Effective counseling with lesbians mandates adequate cross-cultural counseling skills.*

Counseling with minorities, including sexual minorities, is often a cross-cultural issue. Fortunately more and more pastoral care curricula are beginning to acquaint theological students with the basic skills of cross-cultural counseling in general and pastoral counseling across cultures specifically (Augsberger 1986). One need not be homosexual oneself to work successfully with lesbian parishioners or clients (Hall 1985). Rather, effective counseling not only involves capacity for empathic response but also involves affirming certain values important to cross-cultural counseling theory. It concerns cultural sensitivity, understanding, and skills competency. In this case understanding of gay and lesbian differences is important. For example, while gay males sometimes choose to work with lesbian therapists, the reverse is seldom the case. This may be because there are more cultural and psychological affinities among women, straight or gay, than there are between lesbians and gay men, though the latter certainly share the experience of heterosexist and homophobic discrimination.

3. *Effective pastoral counseling with lesbians requires utilizing the wider lenses of family systems and cultural analysis.*

Utilizing a family systems lens for understanding lesbians and their problems is critical, especially to determine to what extent problems and pain are exacerbated by societal stigma—the process by which certain groups, such as racial minorities, physically challenged people, and lesbians are considered unworthy or discredited. The problem worsens for lesbians to the extent that people view lesbianism as a moral failing. Still, to be "gay affirming" is similar to being feminist; that is, the women's liberation movement showed that the universal problem for women was not women but the problem of sexism and misogyny. Similarly, the civil rights movement brought to consciousness that the problem for African-Americans was not their blackness but the surrounding climate of racial prejudice and bigotry. So also the "problem" for lesbians is dominant culture's homophobia and heterosexism.

Homophobia can be described as the dislike, hatred or fear of gay men and lesbians, as well as discrimination against lesbians and gay men (*Bulletin* 1983, p. 1). Heterosexism is a predominant universal assumption that everyone's experience is heterosexuality. It also means a lack of support for any relationship that is not heterosexual. The practical problems include what Roth calls "direct invasion of the lesbian couple boundary by the heterosexual surround" which takes form in various ways:

> . . . as not including the partner as a relative at holidays and other major family-of-origin events, giving the partners separate rooms during visits to families of origin, depriving one partner of access to the other and/or of decision-making power in time of serious illness, and depriving the partners of legal protection in mutual ownership of property and in survivorship unless they take special action (Roth 1989, p. 290).

This climate makes it very difficult to affirm one's own experiences either as a single person or as a lesbian in a relationship, especially since whatever sensitization goes on around the subjects of homophobia or heterosexism are targeted at adult population and rarely involve children's literature and education. Few children learn about how prejudice functions with regard to homophobia and heterosexism. Some journals, such as *Open Hands,* help parents learn how to raise or educate children concerning homophobia, but it is difficult when the rest of the society, including the schools, do not participate in such liberating efforts. One has to constantly reteach emancipatory attitudes. Perhaps a personal story will illustrate:

> In raising my son, age 8, and daughter, age 6, to guard against prejudice in all of its forms, I endeavored to acquaint them early with the fact that some people happen to be able

> to fall in love with people of their own gender, while more people happen to be able to fall in love with people of the opposite gender. They seemed both clear and comfortable about this. One day we were invited to a Holy Union, a celebration of commitment between two lesbians at a local Metropolitan Community Church. Once again I reminded the children about sexual orientations and told them all I knew about the particulars of an MCC liturgy. My son, who gets very excited about going to any kind of celebration, was playing at a neighbor's house on the afternoon before the service. When his dad picked him up, he said enthusiastically, "I have to get going, we're going to a lesbian wedding tonight." "That ought to be interesting," said the friend's dad. My husband came home and remarked that he guessed he might not be asked to be den leader of the Cub Scouts any more.
>
> Later that evening at the service my daughter expressed dismay that the two participants weren't dressed in the traditional bridal regalia. I assured her that they could have worn such gowns, but perhaps they chose sparkling New Year's dresses because of the season. She seemed satisfied. My son, having been told about eucharist MCC style participated with an open attitude, receiving communion as a family at the altar and sharing embraces and kisses with the pastor. But after partaking of the wafer and cup, when we returned to our pew, he stated loudly, "Now *that* was weird." Alarmed, I shushed him up quickly, whispering, "What was so weird?" His reply was, "Why was it with those little crackers anyway? Don't they serve bread in this place?"

Sexism, which also is not sufficiently addressed in our educational systems, plays a major part in homophobia.

> Sexism lays the ground work for homophobia. As women we are assumed to be asexual if we are not involved with men. Women are not seen as having an independent, aggressive sexuality of their own" (Loulan 1984, p. 10).

Once certain women are viewed as lesbian by the larger culture, they are seen as purely sexual beings, defined only by their genital contact with other women. This makes it difficult for some women to identify themselves as lesbians if they are celibate, infrequently sexual, or "primarily companionate." Therefore internalized homophobia makes a lesbian doubt her own reality.

Homophobia and heterosexism, rampant in Western culture across racial, ethnic, and class boundaries, are perpetrated through socialization and cemented through institutionalization. This socialization is so powerful that it affects not only heterosexuals but lesbians as well. Just as women hold sexist and misogynist viewpoints "deep down" and racial minorities participate in their own oppression, so too lesbians internalize homophobia and heterosexism, effectively participating in their own self-hatred.

> Before any kind of feminist movement existed, or could exist, lesbians existed: women who loved women, who refused to comply with behavior demanded of women, who refused to define themselves in relation to men. Those women, our foresisters, millions whose names we do not know, were tortured and burned as witches, slandered in religious and later in "scientific" tracts, portrayed in art and literature as bizarre, amoral, destructive, decadent women. For a long time, the lesbian has been a personification of feminine evil. . . .
>
> . . . Lesbians have been forced to live between two cultures, both male-dominated, each of which has denied and endangered our existence. . . . Heterosexual, patriarchal culture has driven lesbians into secrecy and guilt, often to self-hatred and suicide (Rich 1979, p. 225).

Theorists, theologians, and spokespersons differ about whether heterosexism is a subset for sexism or whether it is a analytic construct in its own right. For lesbians and for pastoral counselors it hardly matters; the oppression is compounded in either case. Through a systems viewpoint the cultural problem of exclusivist, intolerant heterosexual attitudes becomes evident. Such attitudes have become institutionalized in societal and ecclesiastical tenets and structures. They also become internalized, through social learning, in both heterosexuals and homosexuals.

4. *Effective counseling of lesbians requires appreciation for the ways in which a variety of oppressions affect lesbians.*

Many lesbians experience further discrimination by virtue of their color, ethnic and religious background, physical disabilities, or primary language. Lesbians of color, for example, may experience sexism and racism in their work area, only to return home to their parents and experience their family's and culture's rejection of them for their sexual orientation. Barbara Cameron (1983), a Native American, notes:

> It is of particular importance to us as third world gay people to begin a serious interchange of sharing and educating ourselves about each other. We not only must struggle with the racism and homophobia of straight white america, but must often struggle with the homophobia that exists within our third world communities (p. 50).

Teenagers, in particular, may find there is no place that feels like "home" to them. These feelings, so acute during adolescence, never truly end, though they may lessen as adults come to self-identity and are able to claim it. As Latina Cherrie Moraga (1983) writes:

> When I finally lifted the lid to my lesbianism, a profound connection with my mother reawakened in me. It wasn't until I acknowledged and confronted my own lesbianism in the flesh, that my heartfelt identification with and empathy for my mother's oppression—due to being poor, uneducated, and Chicana—was realized. My lesbianism is the avenue through which I learned the most about silence and oppression, and it continues to be the most tactile reminder to me that we are not free human beings.
>
> You see, one follows the other. I had known for years that I was a lesbian, had felt it in my bones, had ached with the knowledge, gone crazed with the knowledge, wallowed in the silence of it. Silence *is* like starvation. Don't be fooled. It's nothing short of that, and felt most sharply when one has had a full belly most of her life (pp. 28–29).

Like a multi-stranded cable, structures of oppression—patriarchy, racism, sexism, classism, misogyny, and heterosexual imperialism—are intertwined and interconnected under conditions of patriarchy which the church sanctions through its patriarchal structures and tenets. Just as feminism could not sustain its movement for liberation of women without directly facing its heterosexism, the church cannot truly be a liberation force against sexism without also facing its homophobia and heterosexism.

5. *Effective pastoral counseling of lesbians must utilize a situation ethic of mutuality, reciprocity, and caring as moral evaluators for lesbian relationships.*

Utilizing the "full acceptance" theological position, being a lesbian and acting on one's lesbian identity is no more inherently sinful than being a heterosexual and acting out of one's heterosexual identity. The counselor cannot substitute moral absolutes for moral complexities. The standard for what is holy, wholesome, healthy, good, is not simply whether partners are same or differently gendered.

A more complex criterion on which to base ethical and moral discernment about sexual behavior is the extent to which any relational activity is life-enhancing. Sexual behavior should enhance and fulfill human beings rather than inhibit, damage, or destroy them. Any sexual activity that is selfish in expression, cruel, impersonal, or obsessive is unhealthy. Therefore effective ethical criteria may be concerned with the degrees by which any relationship is characterized by caring and concern, tenderness, mutuality, trust, and respect toward each other. Other values center around non-oppressive, non-coercive, non-hierarchical, consenting, loving adult acts expressed through shared commitment.

6. *Effective pastoral counseling is not the same as secular psychotherapy with lesbians.*

Pastoral counseling must not simply defer to secular psychotherapeutic and sociological research and formulations over against theological stance. The distinguishing marks of pastoral counseling are not limited to the fact that it is concerned with a holistic view of the person, although often lesbians come to pastoral counselors because they mistrust secular counselors.

> Jane, 43 years old, sought out a pastoral counselor because she had become terribly frustrated with her former therapist, who happened to be a psychologist. He did not take her seriously, she said, when she discussed the depth of her commitment to her personal spiritual journey. He seemed cavalier about her wish to integrate a "new" sense of morality into her relationships with women partners. She was searching for a way of living her life openly and with integrity. Her identity as a Christian woman was very important to her, and she wished her counselor would take it seriously as well.

In our culture, religion and spirituality have much to do with individual functioning, and the making of values of meaning throughout the lifespan. With confusing values all around, clients seek counselors who will take seriously their sense of spiritual depth, their hunger for meaning, and their sincere desires to make moral choices within the fullness of God's creation and blessings. In counseling lesbians, fortunately, we are not left only with the God of liberal theology, who is all too often imaged by lesbians as indifferent to them and their sexual orientation at best. That theology is not to be deemed completely negative; after all, it is based on the very same liberal theology, at least in part, on which pastoral counselors have centered their stance of quiet affirmation. Nevertheless, we may now move ahead because specific theologies, which are gay-affirming, articulated by gay and lesbian theologians, activists, clients, and other writers, are now becoming more available. Keeping theology and spirituality central to our perspective, we also have had for some time the resources emerging from the liberation theologies in general. These are widely accessible and are foundational to inform our work with parishioners and clients so they can make spirituality a central part of their healing journey as well, a journey which involves affirming rather than fighting their consonant experiences of identity.

Lesbian Psychology

With a few exceptions lesbians bring to counseling the same issues straight women bring. Such problems, however, may be more or less compounded by their sexual orientation, the social stigma of being lesbian, social ostracism, downright hatred and violence against them. As Gordon Allport (1954) noted, victims of prejudice may express certain symptoms related to their status as persecuted groups. Struzzo (1989) lists these briefly as

> . . . excessive concern and preoccupation with minority or deviant group membership; feelings of insecurity; withdrawal; passivity; neuroticism, strong in-group ties coupled with prejudice against out-groups; slyness and cunning; acting out self-fulfilling prophecies about one's inferiority; secrecy; and self-hatred (p. 198).

Anthony (1981–1982) mentioned among special areas of concern for lesbians the following: 1) establishing and maintaining lover relationships; 2) alcoholism; 3) certain life-cycle issues of lesbian adolescents and older lesbians; 4) bereavement; 5) unique issues related to parenting; and 6) problems of being a woman who is not associated with a male. This last should not be seen as simply an issue of living as a "single person." It has to do with major issues of what it means not to have access to males' money. Heterosexual privilege usually means greater status for women who "marry up." Often the poorest of the poor are lesbian couples who may bring in less total money because there is no male wage earner.

Several other factors interlaced with issues of oppression make it difficult for lesbians to form congruent and healthy self-identities.

Invisible History

As mentioned before, little has been written about lesbian history, and that which has is not widely disseminated as yet through the population. In part, the problem has been that early theorists disagreed about whether a biological background assumed its "naturalness" or whether homosexuality was an "acquired" condition. This confusion, according to Carole Vance (1989), meant that before 1960 medicine, biology, psychology, and sexology created "a new frame of reference, converting same-sex behaviours into biologically or psychologically based dispositions and subsuming all sexual arrangements between members of the same sex under them" (p. 7). In addition such writings focused solely on the studies about men. Further, as Vicinus (1989) points out, histories that have been recorded have not necessarily been done by trained and practicing historians. She traces a history of how sexual identity came to be the overarching issue for modern Euro-American lesbians over the past three hundred years. The historical suppression of female sexuality is at the heart of any process of tracing lesbian history.

For lesbians in counseling the lack of lesbian history and the invisibility of lesbians has meant not only a dearth of self-affirming role models, heroes, and mentors, but also the lack of knowledge that such a lifestyle even exists. A 56-year-old grandmother, when asked why she had just come out as a lesbian, responded, "I simply did not know there was any other way to live than heterosexual. I knew I was pretty miserable, but I just accepted that as part of the way things had to be (Lewis 1979, in Groves, p. 17).

Trouble with the Church of Their Childhood

Heyward notes that liberal churches have "always displayed some measure of tolerance toward those women and those homosexual people whose *public* presence has been strictly in conformity with patriarchal social relations" (Heyward 1987, p. 37). This is, in part, due to liberal religions making false dualisms of being and act, of person and eros, the body and soul. The problem comes about for the ecclesiastical organizations when lesbians no longer pass as straight women, when they begin to break the silence about their own orientation and the church's sexism and heterosexism.

We cannot minimize or discount the experiences of prejudice, oppression, and discrimination lesbians feel by categorizing sexual orientation as a compartment of human experiencing. Gay people often hear (especially from well-meaning, kind-hearted "liberal" religious people), "What you do in your own bedroom between mutually consenting adults is of no concern to me and no business to anyone else." Usually such a statement is followed by the admonition stated aloud or added implicitly, "Besides, we don't *want* to know." This reduces lesbians to sexual objects. Lesbianism is more than sexual activity, and as feminism has so long admonished, the personal is political. Sexual orientation is experienced as a lifestyle that is all-encompassing whether a person is gay, straight, or bisexual. Compartmentalizing is problematic with regard to sexuality. This is why it is so incomprehensible for lesbians to understand good-hearted church people who say, "I don't condemn you, I just condemn your sexual activity." This obvious variation of "love the sinner but hate the sin" becomes unbearable for most lesbians, who consider their sexual orientation to be as much a part of their constitution as their femaleness or the color of their skin.

The church has not been healthy place for lesbians. But many lesbians have been raised in the church, and while many have left the religion of their childhood and youth, it is hard to leave religion completely behind. This is especially true since biblical standards permeate Western society, and Jewish and Christian belief systems undergird much of our cultural symbols, rituals, and mindset. Most lesbians who have stayed in the congregation remain in the closet. Sometimes the very last place a woman will come out is to her church or synagogue.

When a lesbian comes to her pastor, it may be at the very beginning of a process of coming out to the church. Education in terms of the wide range of theological viewpoints on the subject of homosexuality may be an important aspect of her emancipation from parochial religious views. She can be alerted to the writings of biblical scholars, ethicists, and theologians whose works have helped lead individuals and church groups through the complex issues of Bible, traditions, human knowledge, and human experience to an affirmative stance on homosexuality from one of the traditional faith positions.[2]

Multiple Oppression

Excluding issues of heterosexual relationships, lesbians have all the same issues other women do, only more so, because their lifestyle is not appropriated by society. Lesbians have more in common with straight and bisexual women because of issues of common womanhood than they have with gay men (though there are some important affinities such as the fact that gay men and lesbians experience heterosexism and homophobia in all their contextualized and varied forms). But Gloria Anzaldua, one of the editors of *This Bridge Called My Back*, reports that while white lesbians are invisible, the lesbian of color is considered nonexistent. "Our speech, too, is inaudible. We speak in tongues like the outcast and the insane" (Moraga and Anzaldua, p. 165).[3]

Desire to Conform

Lesbians tell of desperately wanting to please their parents and to fit into "normal" society. Even though they may have been aware since early childhood of their sexual preference, they try to fit in with heterosexual teens, dating and having sex with young men. They may deliberately or inadvertently marry and bear children, sometimes in part to prove to themselves and others that they are no different from other women. It is only later that they come to the full realization of their primary orientation toward attraction to women.

Problems with Self-Esteem

Furthermore, as Miller (1986) has noted, self-esteem for women is largely defined by their relationships, particularly familial ones, whereas men tend to relate their self-esteem to their work (p. 103). If society defines a woman's primary emotional and romantic attachment with another woman as tabu it is hard for a lesbian to feel good about herself. If her true self is unacceptable to herself and others, and the false self is at odds with her authentic feelings and understanding of her own reality, self-hatred occurs. In addition, depending upon her family of origin's degree of homophobia, she may have a strained relationship with her primary affiliations from childhood and youth. Disownment and rejection may occur. If that is compounded with a work place where lesbians are ignored, feared, or have to live in the dread of being found out, healthy self-esteem may be a difficult, seemingly impossible, achievement. The path to self-esteem may be the arduous and costly process of living more and more openly as a lesbian.

Counseling Lesbians

Emerging Literature

Our work with lesbians in pastoral counseling has been hampered by the dearth of literature on the subject of pastoral counseling of homosexuals in general and of lesbians in particular. The Jewish and Christian religious communities (of which most pastoral counselors are a part) have been mistrustful of sexuality, and often homosexuality has not even been seen as a legitimate concern. The literature on pastoral care and counseling of lesbians is sparse; only a few articles are available. Struzzo's "Pastoral Counseling and Homosexuality" (1989) describes how he utilizes transpersonal psychology and creation spirituality to help gay men or lesbians "appreciate the basic goodness of all creation, including their sexuality, without becoming possessive and addictive" (p. 199). Topper (1986) shows how the gay or lesbian spirituality journey deepens through a complex search for meaning, which must be addressed in the pastoral counseling setting.

However, in the secular fields much more has been written, including the publication of journals (*Journal of Homosexuality, Women Changing Therapy, Women & Therapy,* for example) that regularly address issues of lesbian psychology, psychotherapy, mothering, and so forth. Due to the gay civil rights and feminist movements, increasing numbers of women are making their sexual orientation a matter of public knowledge, and a circle of professionals who take an interest in minority psychology is growing. Rather than review all the psychological literature, the reader is referred to such works as *Lesbian Psychologies* (Boston Lesbian Psychologies Collective 1987), which discusses issues of identity, diversity, bisexuality, intimacy, relationships, socialization, families, child-rearing, lesbian community, alcoholism, eating disorders, and a host of other clinical issues in doing therapy. Another important book is *Lesbian Studies* (Cruikshank 1982), which includes chapters on lesbians in academics and in the classroom, new research/new perspectives, and an excellent list of resources (books, journals, articles, and groups) for and about lesbians of color, lesbians with disabilities, elderly lesbians, lesbian mothers, and so on.

Similarly, there are many models for doing psychotherapy from the viewpoint of a variety of schools, such as family therapy (Roth and Murphy 1986), cognitive therapy (Padesky 1988), sex therapy (Nichols 1987), and treating alcoholism and eating disorders (Nicoloff and Stiglitz 1987; Brown 1987). Similarly much has been written about couples therapy for lesbians (Carl 1990; Berzon 1988; Roth 1989).

It is possible that one of the main reasons lesbians turn to their pastors or pastoral counselors is because they need help and wish for affirmation in the process of coming out Roth (1989) speaks of the need lesbian couples have for the therapists to "witness and validate" the coming together of their relationship, a "social role performed by ministers, rabbis and others in the heterosexual world" (p. 290). It seems to me that lesbians need support and pastoral care not only in their coming together as partners, but also at life's critical points. In general, each of these points is affected most by the degree to which the woman or couple is "out of the closet"; therefore, this section will focus on that issue.

In and Out of the Closet

Coming out in lesbian feminist terminology has come to mean the "process of self-labeling, self-acceptance, and sharing one's lesbian identity with others" (Groves 1985, p. 17). For most females, unlike males, the discovery of a love relationship often precedes awareness of sexual orientation. Although sexual orientation is usually fixed by the age of five, it is not uncommon for a woman to come out after she is in her middle years. Aside from totally closeted lesbians (who may not even be self-identified), lesbians are "more or less out," that is, a fewer or greater number of persons know about their lifestyle. The process of coming out goes on for a lifetime; indeed much time can elapse between personal awareness and open acknowledgment to family and friends.

The tradeoff for coming out is honesty in place of safety. Because lesbianism by nature implies sexual, emotional, and economic freedom from men (Abbott and Love 1972), patriarchal society is threatened by its very presence. In upsetting the "natural order" or structures of hierarchy, the status quo, lesbians pose a serious threat to the patriarchal notion that women exist for men. Therefore, a woman who comes out as a lesbian incurs the wrath of patriarchal society for upsetting the status quo, for reminding us of the hidden awareness that "the emperor has no clothes." Specifically, she may encounter a lack of support, loss of close friends, family rejections, loss of job, or loss of a possible romantic relationship. The therapist who works with lesbians must be knowledgeable about the issues involved in coming out and the contemporaneous issues of identity formation (Groves 1985, p. 18).

Paradoxically, some heterosexual women may envy lesbian women simply because of the greater connectedness lesbian women have with other women, in general. Straight women may envy that lesbians "get to sleep with their best friend." In heterosexual circles a high percentage of women widely acknowledge that their husband, partner, or lover is not, in fact, their best friend. Since collegiality is so difficult between men and women, a longing for a primary woman-woman relationship is often mentioned by straight women when open discussion is made possible.

While straight women may have a real or imagined romantic notion of what lesbian relationships are like, the fact is that lesbians have to give up their wish for real or imagined heterosexual privilege, which takes the form of access to male status, power, class, and economic privilege (earning power or accumulated wealth).

> Judy, a 32 year old mother of two, got married right after college. She put her husband through medical school and residency by working as a legal secretary. Her hours were long and hard, but so were his. Later, Judy quit her job to take care of two daughters. At one point it was necessary to take in a boarder to help pay the mortgage and to give Judy some time away from the house. Over several months, Judy found herself attracted to the boarder, Sandra, and began to have an affair with her. It reminded her of her last relationship before she married her husband, one in which she was with her best friend in college. At one point, her husband became a little suspicious about the growing closeness he noticed between his wife and Sandra. By now, he had a growing family practice, though he still continued to work long hours. He took Judy aside and said, if she wanted to "explore" her sexuality, if she wanted to find out whether or not she was gay, then he would allow her to do it. But she would have to leave the house and the children to do so. Judy came into counseling terrified that she would lose her chil-

> dren, and her very identity in life, were she to make a choice concerning leaving her husband to be with Sandra. Not only that, but she had grown accustomed to her lifestyle as a doctor's wife and with all the amenities just now coming into being after so many years of scrimping and getting by.

In general, greater health is established the more a woman is able to define her own identity and realize and embrace the fullness of her personality. For the lesbian, however, this may mean becoming more publicly self-affirming and self-declaring, which exposes her even more to the very oppression by which she is already victimized. Yet with support, as Gloria Anzaldua writes, "our vulnerability can be our power—if we use it" (Moraga 1983, p. 195). A supportive community is of utmost importance, as well as few negative beliefs about lesbian lifestyles.

The first coming out process is often to oneself. This involves an awareness of lesbian feelings that have, usually through some precipitating event, broken through the denial system concerning lesbian identity. Perhaps the woman has read some literature which has placed lesbianism in a better light, such as the current periodical *Outlook,* an upscale magazine for gay men and lesbians. Perhaps she has seen an educational movie which addressed her situation or has met an "out" lesbian who has broken all the stereotypes. As such, "the woman finds herself in the position of choosing between societal abuse if she lives openly as a lesbian and the self-alienating experience of living a lie if she continues the denial pattern" (Groves 1985, p. 18).

Groves (1985) notes that positive coming out experiences are related to the development of a self-esteem with regard to newfound identity and orientation, relinquishment of investment in the patriarchal system (which has been the source of her survival), the finding of positive lesbian role models, and the ability to overcome significant feelings of loss (p. 19). Feminist psychology notes that for women—straight or lesbian—to develop a positive sense of self, they need to define themselves outside patriarchal expectations. This situation is doubly precarious for lesbians, however, who must also define themselves beyond heterosexist expectations. Leaving the legitimacy of (even the possibility of) a heterosexual lifestyle is a major step.

As a client or parishioner works through her own self-definition, it is crucial that she experience her therapist as not interjecting heterosexual or homosexual bias into the counseling, for she may then feel pressure to adopt a lifestyle contrary to her own nature. While eschewing the use of labels themselves, counselors can encourage clients to explore their feelings, thoughts, and fantasies, and they may try out various labels in the process (Moses and Hawkins 1982). Groves writes, "The therapist must be careful not to determine the client's identity for her, but to validate lesbianism as an acceptable lifestyle" (Groves 1985, p. 21). For the pastoral counselor and the religious lesbian working through to self-definition, this often means integrating spiritual with psychological understandings. The pastoral counselor needs to make it clear to the parishioner or client that whatever identity she understands herself to be is the crucial issue.

Once a woman has begun to achieve a positive self-image as a lesbian, she may be ready to come out to her family. A pastor or pastoral counselor may be consulted with regard to this process. Often lesbians come out first to siblings. Then they may write a letter to both parents, or each parent individually, before discussing their sexual orientation with them in person. Many lesbians are particularly relieved to know that their mothers, at least, have guessed the situation for quite a while. Others are threatened with being cut off, emotionally and/or financially. If parents do not know better, they may "blame themselves" for their daughter's orientation. Groups such as Parents and Friends of Lesbians and Gays (PFLAG) can be very helpful for parents in coming to a deeper understanding of their children.

Another critical time for counseling is when a lesbian mother considers coming out to her children. Do the children have a right to know about their mother's sexuality? Some researchers say yes. Corley (1990) discusses all of the possible issues, explaining that children of all ages can be told in age-appropriate language. Children can understand, for example, that this "family secret" is not a secret because it is something shameful, but because some people will not understand, will not agree, or are not educated about lesbian lifestyles. The most important issue for children is the modeling of a positive lifestyle and relationship. Unless there are overarching reasons for nondisclosure (such as an ex-husband's using the information to prohibit the mother's visitation or custody rights), it may well be in the best interests of both mother and child to keep their relationship honest. "A child told nothing about her mother's homosexuality can only relate to a fantasized image based on deceit and misinformation, even though her mother's intentions may have been the best in the world" (Corley 1990, p. 10). The process of coming out to a child is greatly facilitated if the grandparents are supportive; then the child won't have to carry the information alone in the family system.

A pastoral counselor can be very helpful in this process by helping the mother, perhaps also in counseling with her partner or with her ex-husband, to discern the right timing for disclosure and the right phrasing. If the family undergoes especially disruptive experiences, the pastor can mediate through family counseling.

In terms of coming out in the work place, some careers are relatively safe, for example, certain types of self-employment, segments of the art world and literary world, performance arts, modeling, sports, areas of science, and others. But for some vocations it can mean virtually automatic firing, such as in most denominations of ministry, in the military, and in teaching children and youth. People in politics, along with many other highly visible public persons, live in great fear because their careers are in jeopardy if they are "found out." There are variations in terms of level of safety in work places in terms of the consciousness of the work place and overall community (for example, whether it is a rural or urban area), and the prevailing political climate.

Other Life Passages

Myriad other issues may arise as the pastoral counselor works with lesbians. These include determining commitment to a relationship, mothering, co-parenting, and so on. These issues can be addressed through individual, couples, or family counseling as needed. Religious lesbians may need help in deciding about making a commitment to a long-term relationship, with or without benefit of the holy union services available in some Jewish and Christian circles, and therefore may call upon the pastor for couples counseling when they are making a decision about the future of their relationship.

Being lesbian does not exclude women from the ability or the desire to mother. Therefore many lesbians, within or outside of a long-term relationship, may ask for help in deciding whether or not to have children (through adoption, artificial insemination, or self-insemination). As a single parent, an "out" lesbian can adopt children, from infants to teens, depending upon the part of the United States and the laws. A closeted lesbian may find it easier to adopt children. As same-sex partners, lesbians cannot legally adopt children together. Since laws differ from state to state, a pastoral counselor can often help most by referring parishioners or clients for legal advice or steer them toward educational material such as legal guides for lesbian and gay parents or to self-help groups such as a nearby chapter of Gay Parents. In the same vein it is important for lesbian couples to define their relationship through legal documents that allow the partners to make certain decisions concerning the other's health care if one were to become incapacitated as well as with regard to wills. In short, though parenting is never an easy task, there is abundant research that happy, healthy gay parents in happy, healthy relationships will not have bad effects on their children (Corley 1990, pp. 12–13).

Since it is often the case that women come to recognize a lesbian identity after they have experienced a heterosexual marriage and already borne children, co-parenting is an important issue that comes up in therapy. One or both of the partners may be birth parents from previous heterosexual relationships. In this case the new partner may take on the role of "helping" parent, although she does not take the place of the father. Legally, responsibilities go to the natural custodial parent, then to the noncustodial partner, and only then, by special arrangement, to the lesbian partner. In any case, the new partner along with the children should have a major voice in determining how they want to relate to one another within the blended family. Counselors can help by normalizing this procedure in the ways of new family structures.

Lesbian couples may request counseling not only at the beginning stages of the relationship with issues of coming out, but also as they learn more and more how to live in egalitarian relationship with the right mix of intimacy and separateness in a society where few role models are available. Couples may sometimes worry unnecessarily about frequency of sexual contact. Sexual desire, which is strong in gay male couples and less in heterosexual couples, may be even less in lesbian couples (Loulan 1984; Loulan and Nelson 1987). Similar to gay men, many lesbians remain friends with their ex-lovers much longer than heterosexual persons, sometimes for a lifetime. Pastors should be aware of this, especially in the contexts of hospital visitation, holy unions, funerals, or other developmental or situational events of the life-cycle where a host of ex-lovers may be present because they still hold deep friendships with the parishioner.

Other Pastoral Counseling Issues

Religious Lesbians

Lesbians have always been members of our congregations, tithing, ministering, providing outreach, holding church positions. Parishioners who come to their pastors for counseling often have an idea that the pastor will be open to their particular area of concern, so lesbians usually have sensed it is "safe" to approach the pastor or pastoral counselor. For example, if a United Methodist church is a part of the "Reconciling Congregation Program," lesbians will feel more free to join or to approach that pastor with issues of their deepest concern. The same is true for pastors of Presbyterian "More Light Churches."

Alternatively, many of the major denominations have organizations that exist for groups of self-affirming gay and lesbians, such as Dignity for Roman Catholics, Integrity for Episcopalians, Affirmation for United Methodists. Olson (1984) lists thirty-six Christian organizations that relate to homosexuals mostly in affirming ways, though a few of the groups noted are dedicated to "transforming" homosexuals to at least act as if they were heterosexual through prayer, peer support, and counseling. Pastors can become involved with their faith group's gay-affirming ministries, or they may refer their parishioners to such settings for support.

There are gay and lesbian clergy and rabbis in virtually every faith group. Unfortunately, the church often encourages dishonesty and secrecy about sexual orientation in order to become ordained. It is a terrible thing to be forced to lie about one's sexual orientation in order to be permitted to fulfill one's call to ministry. Pastoral counselors who are known to be gay-affirming are often called on by lesbian and gay clergy for pastoral care if not counseling, especially in the coming out process. An important support group for lesbian clergy and lay women is CLOUT (Christian Lesbians Out Together). Ecumenical, multiracial, and multi-cultural, CLOUT addresses church policies on ordination and networks with Jewish lesbians, postchristian, profeminist, and prowomanist gay men and other organizations of marginalized women and men.[4]

Once it becomes apparent within the lesbian community that a particular pastor is empathic and non-judgmental, lesbians who may not be affiliated with any congregation but are searching for a faith community may seek pastoral counseling. In the process they can be referred to a faith community which is most open and welcoming for them. Besides "reconciling" or "more light" churches, the MCC, and other denominations that take an welcoming stance, a local woman-church group is another place for ritual, community, and feminist liturgy. In any case, parishioners and other interested clients should be informed about the various gay and lesbian groups affiliated with many of the denominations.

Emerging Lesbian Theologies and Spiritualities

The goal of reformist feminist Christian and Jewish women scholars and activists is to seek ways to redeem the tradition, practices, and structures of the organization from patriarchy. For Christians, this involves a critical examination of the ways in which patriarchy, anti-Judaism, and exclusivism go to the core of the religion. A hermeneutic of suspicion is utilized to discover the images, traditions, and dogmatics which can be seen as messages for justice and wholeness. Recently attempts have been made to articulate a critique of heterosexist theology and to begin to articulate a theology, spirituality, and ethic from the perspective of the experience of religious lesbians. Carter Heyward, an Episcopal priest, has published numerous works (see Heyward 1982, 1984, 1987, 1989a, 1989b). Roman Catholic lesbian women have begun the effort (Zanotti 1986; Grammick and Furey 1988) as have Jewish lesbians (Balka and Rose 1989). Women in general, and lesbians in particular, may find their own experience articulated best in theologies that describe God as present in relationships characterized by mutuality and empowerment (Heyward 1982). As Virginia Mollencott (1987) has expressed it,

> God's presence is known in those relationships that are mutually sympathetic, helpful, and interdependent rather than in hierarchical one-up, one-down relationships. The goal here is . . . to grow intentionally toward the recognition of God's image in everyone and in everything, and toward the mutual respect that such responsibility entails (p. 4).

Just as any competent pastoral counselor should be familiar with the variety of faith symbols and religious resources involved in ecumenical and interfaith counseling, so also it is imperative that the pastoral counselor be knowledgeable about, or at the very least cognizant of, the resources of gay and lesbian theologies (Glaser 1990; Fortunato 1982; Heyward 1989a and b; Hunt 1991). Such theologies challenge the liberal traditions and call into question—as do Latin American, Asian, African-American, and feminist theologies—the supposition that there is any theology free of bias or ideology. In content, the God described in gay and lesbian theologies appears as one who is primarily relational, neither distant nor "above the fray . . . unaffected by the clamor and clutter of human struggle, including the passions, problems, and confusions of human sexuality" (Heyward 1987, p. 34).

By assisting a parishioner or clergywoman to find access to these emerging theologies and organizations, pastoral counselors help lesbians realize they are not alone in their search for identity and in their yearning for a respectful place within their own religious tradition. It may relieve them greatly to realize they have choices in the manner and ways of relating to their root faith or to discover new possibilities for faith and community beyond their heritage. Organizations and writings are available to let a lesbian know she need not necessarily make a choice between affirming her sexual orientation and growing self-esteem, on the one hand, and her religious tradition on the other. And it always helps to know she is not alone in the struggle.

Orthopraxis: Social Justice Issues

To do pastoral counseling with lesbians is to help individual clients and parishioners experience through the counselor's mediation the accepting, redeeming, and loving presence of God. While this is an important activity, it is not enough. Pastoral counselors who are involved in the life of the church can be involved in many areas of ministry to help bring about change, through preaching, lecturing, and workshops. Educational events must address issues of heterosexism and homophobia. We must work to confront the structures in church and society that perpetuate this violence against sexual minorities; we cannot be solely engaged in treating the victims, important as that is for the individuals. Prejudice is learned; it can be unlearned, especially as people come into dialogue with those they fear, those who are the "stranger." Anxiety subsides and stereotypes lessen as people become more and more acquainted with "real life" people who call themselves lesbians. Many lesbians report that people get to know them first as women who are assumed to be straight. As the bond of friendship grows, they feel safe to come out to such friends, causing them to confront their own stereotypes and prejudices. This is perhaps the best way for people to learn about others, though it puts an inordinate amount of pressure on the minority individuals to play such an immense role as central instigators for change. Now that so much literature is available, people can begin to educate themselves by reading about the lives and struggles of lesbians and their emerging theologies. Such theologies, incidentally, have a lot to teach the church in general about healthy sexuality, new images of God, and mutual friendship.

Pastoral counselors work for justice on all fronts; we must not step aside on this particular issue. It is critical to work within one's own denomination and faith stance as well as ecumenically to educate parishioners, local churches, and larger groups wherever possible to begin to eradicate the violence of gay-bashing, which takes form physically, emotionally, intellectually, and spiritually. We cannot be satisfied to work in a smaller scope to help people who come damaged by the church without also working to change the church's attitude and behavior toward the marginalized people. Religious institutions need to repent of sexism and heterosexism and move beyond their institutionalized homophobia. When they do, then the issues of counseling lesbians will change, because such women will finally feel at home in their congregations, free to live their lifestyle openly with integrity.

Consequently, counselors must denounce homophobia and heterosexism just as fervently as they condemn racism, sexism, classism, and other structures of societal injustice. In so doing they present the good news of love and justice. Women's well-being must be an important hermeneutic for judging all things pastoral and prophetic. This means not just heterosexual women but lesbian women as well. To work to free the "least of these," the disabled, working-class lesbians of color, is to work to free us all from all oppressions. Not only that, but we all gain from learning from lesbians how we can be a faithful community. As black lesbian Cheryl Clarke has written,

> If radical lesbian-feminism purports an anti-racist, anti-classist, anti-woman-hating vision of bonding as mutual, reciprocal, as infinitely negotiable, as freedom from antiquated gender prescriptions and proscriptions, *then all people struggling to transform the character of relationships in this culture have something to learn from lesbians* (Clark 1983, p. 134).

Summary

This chapter is written from the point of view of feminist liberation theology as integrated into sound psychological theory, research, and practice currently available. In so doing, it takes a gay-affirming stance, prevailing in the psychological and sociological literature, which determines that lesbianism per se is not a disease; rather it is a minority sexual orientation. As members of a minority group lesbians become the object of subjugation by the majority. All lesbians are subjected to the oppressive forces of sexism, heterosexism, and homophobia. Most lesbians also experience the debilitating effects of racism, classism, and/or ethnic and religious discrimination. Competent pastoral counseling requires that counselors be aware of the systemic effects of discrimination and oppression upon the overall health and well-being of the lesbian parishioner or client.

In terms of determining the morality of lesbianism—both orientation and acts—the chapter assumes the historic "full acceptance" position, considering that lesbian expressions may be ascertained to be moral or immoral by the extent to which they express authentic human loving. Feminist theory has discussed the values upheld and enacted by authentic loving. I do not assume human freedom to be value-free from a moral perspective, but consider the valuing of anyone's personal agency to be set first and foremost in the context of just social relations.

It is inconsistent within the feminist liberation theological stance to concern oneself only with furthering heterosexual women's physical, emotional, psychological, and spiritual health and flourishing. Therefore heterosexual pastoral counselors must recognize the epistemological privilege of the voices and writings of the experiences of lesbians within and outside the religious community. In fulfilling the mandate to put experience of the oppressed first, understanding the experience of lesbian women is the foremost criterion for the formulation of theological and ethical viewpoints which feminist pastoral counseling affirms concerning same-sex orientation. The authoritative nature of scripture, tradition, and reason are not discounted; rather their role in contributing to the historical stances of rejecting-punitive, rejecting-nonpunitive, and qualified acceptance can be critiqued and their content reevaluated and reinterpreted in light of further research, historical analysis, and biblical exegesis.

A feminist liberation theology affirms women's freedom in the context of just social relationship to express their natural right to sexuality. It therefore affirms lesbians' right to develop their sexuality within their understanding of their context of spirituality, mutuality, and reciprocity. It is the nature and quality of the relationship itself, rather than the gender of the persons involved, that is important. Therefore, a gay-affirming feminist pastoral counseling stance 1) denies the moral superiority of genital sexual activity for procreation; 2) rejects as unjust requirement of imposing upon all lesbians a lifetime of sexual abstinence; and hence 3) cannot use the criterion of marital bonding to apply to a group of women for whom this is not a legal or, in most cases, an ecclesiastical possibility. Any sexual activity is then judged by a complex set of criteria, ideally suggested first by the lesbian community itself, regarding such issues as mutuality, equality, level of commitment, and reciprocity.

It is not outside the pastoral counselor's role to be prophet of traditionally unpopular religious viewpoints, especially with regard to speaking out against injustice perpetrated by the majority upon minority groups. Pastoral counselors also have a mandate, insofar as they participate in the ecclesiastical circles, to call their religious groups to accountability for perpetuating such injustice. A systemic analysis shows the links among all the structures of oppression: sexism, racism, classism, and heterosexism. All oppressions are thus interconnected through patriarchy, which the church sanctions through being itself a patriarchal structure as well as through holding patriarchal tenets. Just as feminism could not sustain its movement for liberation of women without directly facing its heterosexism, the church cannot truly be a liberation force against sexism without also facing its homophobia and heterosexism. I acknowledge that such public proclamation and actions directed toward eradicating sexism and thus heterosexism within traditional religions comprise a dangerous and subversive activity, as lesbians well know. It is, although to a lesser extent than for their lesbian parishioners and clients, dangerous for pastoral counselors who nevertheless must choose between integrity and the personal duplicity of affirming privately while remaining silent in public.

In terms of diagnosis, it is crucial that a self-definition of *lesbian* be achieved by the client or parishioner who has sought pastoral counseling. This is best achieved when the pastoral counselor is gay-affirming and can help the person in the coming out process with neither naive and hollow reassurances about the response of society nor a blame-the-victim reaction. To come out as a lesbian in a homophobic and heterosexist society is to endanger oneself and one's loved ones in physical, emotional, and spiritual ways. At the same time, the counselor must eschew participation in dominant religious traditions' judgmentalism and blanket disavowal of either the orientation or the acts. Lesbians, no less than straight women, may need help with holistic self-definition in a patriarchal society and in finding ways to express themselves in mutual, responsible, and loving relationships with their partners, families, and friends. Only when pastoral counselors minister genuinely, respectfully, and with unconditional positive regard for lesbians as well as for heterosexuals can we effectively participate in God's healing and justice-making activity. As with other theologies of liberation, where minorities become agents for calling the faith communities to greater faithfulness, so lesbians have much to teach the church about how to *be* the church.

Notes

1. This situation is exemplified by the difficulty in finding a scholar and clinician with a Ph.D. in pastoral counseling who is "out" professionally and publicly to the extent that she would not feel her position compromised through being recognized as the author of such a chapter as this. Though I cannot write *as* a lesbian, my hope is to write *on behalf of* lesbians due to my personal and political stance, my experience in counseling lesbians, and my research methodology. The latter includes 1) interviewing members of lesbian communities on both coasts; 2) extensive review of the literature; and 3) remaining accountable to the communities through their kind and careful reviewing of the drafts. However, this should not in any way be seen as a simple substitute for having one or a group of lesbian pastoral counselors write on this subject for the pastoral counseling field, the religious groups, and the wider public. It is hoped that the urgency with which this chapter is written will make room for lesbians to do such writing more and more in the future.

2. See, for example, the writings of Lisa Cahill, Charles Curran, John McNeill, Norman Pittinger, Margaret Farley, James Nelson and Robin Scroggs, Beverly Harrison, James Spong, among a host of others. For a brief though certainly not exhaustive overview of the history of the progression toward acceptance which also references some of the major writers, see Nugent and Grammick 1989, pp. 7–46.

3. *This Bridge Called My Back* not only contains writings about the struggles of lesbians of color, but includes a bibliography of some writings of lesbians of color. Other articles, such as Greene (1986), address issues of interracial counseling in the lesbian community in comparison with the straight community.

4. For a description of CLOUT (P.O. Box 460808, San Francisco, CA 94146-0808), see *More Light Update* (February 1991).

References

Abbott, S., and Love, B. 1973. *Sappho Was a Right-on Woman: A Liberated View of Lesbianism.* Briarcliff Manor, N.Y.: Stein and Day.

Allport, G. 1954. *The Nature of Prejudice.* Reading, Mass.: Addison-Wesley.

Anthony, B. 1981–1982. "Lesbian Client-Lesbian Therapist: Opportunities and Challenges in Working Together." *Journal of Homosexuality* 7, 2/3: 45–57.

Augsberger, D. 1986. *Pastoral Counseling Across Cultures.* Philadelphia: Westminster.

Balka, C., and Rose, A. eds. 1989. *Twice Blessed: On Being Lesbian, Gay, and Jewish.* Beacon.

Berzon, B. 1988. *Permanent Partners: Building Gay and Lesbian Relationships that Last.* New York: Dutton.

Boston Lesbian Psychologies Collective. 1987. *Lesbian Psychologies: Explorations and Challenges.* Urbana: University of Illinois Press.

Boswell, J. 1980. *Christianity, Social Tolerance, and Homosexuality.* Chicago: University of Chicago.

Brown, L. 1987. "Lesbians, Weight, and Eating: New Analyses and Perspectives." In Boston Lesbian Psychologies Collective, *Lesbian Psychologies,* pp. 294–310.

Cameron, B. 1983. "Gee, You Don't Seem Like an Indian from the Reservation." In Moraga and Anzaldua, *This Bridge Called My Back,* pp. 46–52.

Carkhuff, R. 1987. *The Art of Helping VI.* Amherst, Mass.: Human Resource Development Press.

Carl, D. 1990. *Counseling Same-Sex Couples.* New York: W. W. Norton.

Clarke, C. 1983. "Lesbianism, an Act of Resistance." In Moraga and Anzaldua, *This Bridge Called My Back,* pp. 128–37.

Corley, R. 1990. *The Final Closet: The Gay Parents' Guide for Coming Out to Their Children.* Miami: Editech.

Cruikshank, M., ed. 1982. *Lesbian Studies: Present and Future.* Old Westbury, N.Y.: Feminist Press.

Egan, G. 1990. *The Skilled Helper: A Systematic Approach to Effective Counseling.* Pacific Grove, Cal.: Brooks/Cole.

Fortunato, J. 1982. *Embracing the Exile: Healing Journeys of Gay Christians.* San Francisco: Harper & Row.

Glaser, C. 1990. *Come Home! Reclaiming Spirituality and Community as Gay Men and Lesbians.* San Francisco: Harper & Row.

Grahan, J. 1978. "The Common Woman." In *The work of a Common Woman.* Oakland: Diana Press.

Gramick, J., and Furey, P. eds. 1988. *The Vatican and Homosexuality: Reactions to the "Letter to the Bishops of the Catholic Church*

on the Pastoral Care of Homosexual Persons." New York: Crossroad Publishing Company.
Greene, B. 1986. "When the Therapist Is White and the Patient Is Black: Considerations for Psychotherapy in the Feminist Heterosexual and Lesbian Communities." *Women and Therapy* 5, 2-3 (Sum/Fal).
Groves, P. 1985. "Coming Out: Issues for the Therapist Working with Women in the Process of Lesbian Identity Formation." *Women & Therapy* 4, 2 (Summer): 17–22.
Hall, M. 1985. *The Lavendar Couch: A Consumer's Guide to Psychotherapy for Lesbians and Gay Men.* Boston: Alyson.
Hasbany, Richard, ed. 1989. *Homosexuality and Religion.* New York: Harrington Park Press.
Heyward, C. 1982. *The Redemption of God: A Theology of Mutual Relation.* Lanham, Md.: University Press of America.
——. 1984. *Our Passion for Justice: Images of Power, Sexuality and Liberation.* New York: Pilgrim Press.
——. 1987. "Heterosexist Theology: Being Above It All." *Journal of Feminist Studies in Religion 3* (Spring): 29–38.
——. 1989a. *Speaking of Christ: A Lesbian Feminist Voice.* New York: Pilgrim Press.
——. 1989b. *Touching our Strength: The Erotic Power and the Love of God.* San Francisco: Harper & Row.
Hochstein, L. 1986. "Pastoral Counselors: Their Attitudes Toward Gay and Lesbian Clients." *Journal of Pastoral Care* 40, 2 (June): 158–63.
Hunt, M. 1989. "On Religious Lesbians: Contradictions and Challenges." in D. Altman, et al., *Homosexuality, Which Homosexuality?* 1989, pp. 97–113.
——. 1991. *Fierce Tenderness: A Feminist Theology of Friendship.* New York: Crossroad.
Kohut, H. 1978. "The Psychoanalyst in the Community of Scholars." In *The Search for Self: Selected Writings of H. Kohut,* edited by P. H. Ornstein. New York: International Universities Press.
Lewis, S. 1979. *Sunday's Women.* Boston: Beacon.
Loulan, J. 1984. *Lesbian Sex.* San Francisco: Spinsters Ink.
——, and Nelson, M. B. 1987. *Lesbian Passion: Loving Ourselves and Each Other.* San Francisco: Spinsters/aunt lute.
Menard, G. 1989. "Gay Theology, Which Gay Theology?" In Altman et al. *Homosexuality, Which Homosexuality,* pp. 127–38.
Miller, J. B. 1986. *Toward a New Psychology of Women,* 2d ed. Boston: Beacon.

Mollencott, V. 1987. *Godding: Human Responsibility and the Bible.* New York: Crossroad.

Moraga, C. 1983. "La Guera." In Moraga and Anzaldua, *This Bridge Called My Back,* pp. 27–34.

——, and G. Anzaldua, eds. 1983. *This Bridge Called My Back: Writing by Radical Women of Color.* New York: Kitchen Table.

More Light Update. Monthly journal by Presbyterians for Lesbian and Gay Concerns. Elder James Anderson, P.O. Box 38, New Brunswick, N.J. 08903.

Moses, A., Hawkins, Jr., E. Hawkins, Jr., R. 1982. *Counseling Lesbian Women and Gay Men.* New York: Mosbey.

Nichols, M. 1987. "Doing Sex Therapy with Lesbians: Bending a Heterosexual Paradigm to fit a Gay Life-Style." In Boston Lesbian Psychologies Collective, *Lesbian Psychologies,* pp. 242–60.

Nicoloff, L., and Stiglitz, E. 1987. "Lesbian Alcoholism: Etiology, Treatment and Recovery." In Boston Lesbian Psychologies Collective, *Lesbian Psychologies,* pp. 283–93.

Nugent, R., and Gramick, J. 1989. "Homosexuality: Protestant, Catholic and Jewish Issues; a Fishbone Tale." In Hasbany, *Homosexuality and Religion* pp. 7–46.

Olson, M. 1984. "Christians and Homosexuality," a booklet of reprints from the January, February, and April 1984 issues of *The Other Side.*

Open Hands. Quarterly Journal of the Reconciling Congregation Program in the United Methodist Church, P.O. Box 23636, Washington, D.C. 20026.

Padesky, C. 1988. "Attaining and Maintaining Positive Lesbian Self-Identity: A Cognitive Therapy Approach." *Women & Therapy* 8, *1-2*: 145–56.

Rashke, R. 1976. "Dignity like a Fishbone lodged in the Church's Throat." *National Catholic Reporter,* 6 April 1976, p. 28.

Reiter, Laura. 1989. "Sexual Orientation, Sexual Identity, and the Question of Choice." *Clinical Social Work Journal* 17, 2 (Summer): 138–50.

Rich, A. 1979. "The Meaning of Our Love for Women Is What We Have Constantly to Expand." In *On Lies, Secrets, and Silence: Selected Prose 1966–1978.* New York: W. W. Norton.

Rogers, C. 1961. *On Becoming a Person.* Boston: Houghton Mifflin.

Roth, S. 1989. "Psychotherapy with Lesbian Couples: Individual Issues, Female Socialization and the Social Context." In M. McGoldrick et al., *Women in Families,* New York: W. W. Norton.

——, and Murphy, B. 1986. "Therapeutic Work with Lesbian

Clients: A Systemic Therapy View." In *Women and Family Therapy,* edited by Marianne Ault-Riche, pp. 78–89. Rockville, Md.: Aspen Systems Corporation.

Saghir, M., and Robins, E. 1973. *Male and Female Sexuality.* Baltimore: Williams and Wilkins.

Scanzoni, L., and V. Mollenkott. 1978. *Is the Homosexual My Neighbor?: Another Christian View.* San Francisco: Harper & Row.

Struzzo, J. 1989. "Pastoral Counseling and Homosexuality." In Hasbany, *Homosexuality and Religion,* pp. 195–222.

Topper, C. 1986. "Spirituality as a Component in Counseling Lesbians-Gays." *The Journal of Pastoral Counseling* 21, *1* (Spring-Summer): 55–59.

Vance, C. 1989. "Social Construction Theory: Problems in the History of Sexuality." In D. Altman, et al., *Homosexuality, Which Homosexuality?,* pp. 13–34.

Vicinus, M. 1989. "They Wonder to Which Sex I Belong: The Historical Roots of the Modern Lesbian Identity." In D. Altman et al., *Homosexuality, Which Homosexuality?* pp. 171–98.

Wall, J. 1991. "Faith, Tribe, Nation: Top Story of 1990," *Christian Century 107,* 37: 1187–1190.

Zanotti, B., ed. 1986. *A Faith of One's Own: Explorations by Catholic Lesbians.* Trumansburg, N.Y.: Crossing Press.

For Further Reading

Altman, D. et al. 1989. *Homosexuality, Which Homosexuality?* London: GMP Publishers.

Council on Interracial Books for Children. 1983. "Homophobia and Education," *Bulletin* 14, nos. 3 and 4.

Edwards, G. 1984. *Gay/Lesbian Liberation: A Biblical Perspective.* New York: Pilgrim Press.

Grahan, J. 1984. *Another Mother Tongue: Gay Words, Gay Worlds.* Boston: Beacon.

Hoagland, Sara. 1988. *Lesbian Ethics: Toward New Value.* Palo Alto, Cal.: Institute of Lesbian Studies.

Scroggs, R. 1983. *The New Testament and Homosexuality.* Philadelphia: Fortress Press.

Richard Byrne, O.C.S.O.

10. Pastoral Counseling of the Gay Male

The Shaping Contexts of Culture and Church

The Culture in Transition

Any reflection upon a Judeo-Christian approach to pastoral counseling of the gay male must take into account the powerful shifts in attitudes toward homosexuality that have been taking place in the culture and churches during the past twenty-five years. The gay male comes to the pastoral counselor shaped by these often ambivalent and changing attitudes toward his situation. In turn, many pastoral counselors are undergoing change in their attitudes toward gay persons as a result of shifting cultural and ecclesial climates.

The Stonewall riots of 1969 in New York historically represent the emergence of gay culture from its closet of fear to an open posture of dialogue and debate with the normative heterosexual community. The dialogue insists upon recognition of the dignity of homosexual persons and the effective promotion of their political, legal, religious, and social rights by the culture as a whole and by its representative institutions in particular. While bigotry still exists in the majority of the population, great gains have been made in legislation protecting the rights of the homosexual population and in the promotion of more positive social attitudes toward gay people.

Like other movements of reform and revolution, gay liberation has employed many different strategies. Chief among them has been a consciousness-raising effort that makes people aware of the omnipresence of gays and lesbians in the culture. Gay people are everywhere, in all walks of life, in every profession, in each extended family structure. They embrace all temperaments and lifestyles, and hence can never be reduced to the traditional stereotypes of the effeminate, the queer, the faggot, the bull-dyke, or the sick invert. As part of the raising of consciousness, the media—film, television, literature, visual arts—have been much freer about treating gay themes and thereby helping the public become more aware of the prevalence of the gay population and the patterns of gay and lesbian life. Historians have uncovered the creative contributions of leaders of Western civilization whom gays today would number among their confreres—insofar as these leaders seem to have displayed an erotic and affectional preference for members of their own sex: Michelangelo, Leonardo da Vinci, Tchaikovsky, James Baldwin, W. H. Auden, Samuel Barber, Benjamin Britten, Willa Cather, Gertrude Stein, Michel Foucault, and an endless list of others (Duberman, Vicinus, and Chauncey 1989). Finally, the arrival of the AIDS virus has further revealed the face of the gay community to the wider population, which is witnessing the courage of those who live and suffer with the disease, as well as the overwhelming outreach of compassion and advocacy on their behalf.

There has indeed been a movement toward more humane and accepting attitudes toward gay persons in many segments of American culture. And yet, except on some streets in San Francisco and Manhattan, can two men walk down the street holding hands and express other ordinary signs of affection in public without ridicule? Most gays are still afraid to do so. This is because, despite gains of tolerance and acceptance within the culture as a whole, there still lurks a profound, instinctive fear of and distaste for homosexual persons in the hearts of a vast majority of the population. Despite the fact that the American Psychiatric Association removed homosexuality from its list of emotional disorders and sexual perversions in 1973, many persons think there is something wrong with the gay person, something wrongfully different. Whatever the cause of this deep-seated antipathy and fear, simple observation attests that it exists everywhere in our culture. The movement of gay liberation has helped modify prejudice; it has not eradicated it.

The Churches in Transition

The Judeo-Christian traditions in Western culture have a similar record of condemnation of homosexuality, although recent scholarship has documented that prior to the thirteenth century Christian churches often had a more tolerant and accepting approach (Boswell 1980). Christian prejudice against gay persons is partly rooted in a fundamentalist interpretation of certain biblical texts—and this on the part of scholars and readers who interpret the rest of scripture with well-informed hermeneutical understanding and flexibility. These texts are well-known: Genesis 19:1–29, the Sodom and Gomorrah story which in fact is an indictment of inhospitality and social injustice; and the Holiness Code in Leviticus 18:22 and 20:13, which was a condemnation of the sacral prostitution and sexual orgies in Canaanite fertility worship. The New Testament records no words of Jesus about homosexuality, either as act or orientation. The key references in the Christian scriptures are from St. Paul in Romans 1:18–32, 1 Corinthians 6:9–10, and 1 Timothy 1:8–11. Scholars have documented that none of these texts represents what we today would call a gay orientation or the responsible expression of intimacy between two persons of the same sex (Nelson 1978, pp. 181–88; McNeill 1976, pp. 37–66). In fact,

> The central biblical message regarding sexuality seems clear enough. Like every other good gift, it can be misused. The idolatrous dishonoring of God inevitably results in the dishonoring of persons, and faithfulness to God will result in sexual expression which honors the personhood of the other. Our sexuality is not a mysterious and alien force of nature but part of what it means to be human. It is a power to be integrated fully into one's selfhood and to be used in the service of love. That message, I am convinced, applies regardless of one's affectional orientation (Nelson 1978, p. 188).

A literalist reading of the scriptures and a convergence of socio-political, economic, and other factors resulted in the centuries' long story of Christian culture's persecution of gay persons. The story has been largely ignored because until recently there has been no gay history. Stoning, burning, exile, sexual mutilation, and the death penalty were common punishments for homosexuals (Crompton 1974).

The church approved of some of these brutalities, yet tended to be less physically violent. Nonetheless, the church was spiritually even more severe (Nelson 1978, p. 189). The homosexual was a sinner. The unrepentant gay person was ostracized by the community and refused participation in its sacramental life.

The situation in the churches today is in a state of transition, both on official and informal levels. The official teaching of most Christian churches still proclaims that homosexual activity represents objectively sinful behavior, while the homosexual orientation as such is not sinful. Churches tend to see the orientation as either morally neutral or a "disorder of nature."

For example, the Roman Catholic Congregation for the Doctrine of the Faith in its *Letter to the Bishops of the Catholic Church on the Pastoral Care of Homosexual Persons* (1986) states that a former Roman document, *Declaration on Certain Questions concerning Sexual Ethics* (1975) may have led to an "overly benign interpretation given to the homosexual condition itself, some going so far as to call it neutral or even good. Although the particular inclination of the homosexual person is not a sin, it is a more or less strong tendency ordered toward an intrinsic moral evil; and thus the inclination itself must be seen as an objective disorder" (par. 3). The text goes on to say that "special concern and pastoral attention should be directed toward those who have this condition, lest they be led to believe that the living out of this orientation in homosexual activity is a morally acceptable option. It is not" (par. 3).

This same document, as well as any number of pronouncements issued by church authorities since the early seventies, advocates compassion and pastoral outreach to gay persons as well as advocacy for social justice on behalf of the gay community (Nugent and Gramick 1982). A careful hermeneutic of these documents could demonstrate how positive they are and that, given the essentially conservative nature of church authority, not much more can be expected at this period of history. But the typical gay Christian does not concern himself with this level of hermeneutical sophistication. All he hears is that he is "disordered," that something is wrong with him, that he may not express his love in sexual intimacy. All he tends to see are some church leaders actively opposing city ordinances that protect the rights of the gay community against discrimination in housing and employment. Sitting in the midst of a family-centered, heterosexual congregation, he has never heard a sermon affirming the value of his way of loving. And hence he sits alone, alienated in the midst of the Christian assembly.

As in the culture, advocacy and support groups have been formed in recent years to offer a context of healing, reconciliation, and mission to gay and lesbian Christians. Dignity in Roman Catholicism, Integrity in the Episcopalian tradition, Affirmation in the Methodist church, Lutherans Concerned, and so forth, are barely tolerated by the governing bodies of these denominations, yet they exist and sometimes flourish as contexts where people can worship, support each other, and minister to the wider community as both gay and Christian persons.

As a summary of the experience of gays in our churches and culture, one can survey the range of contemporary moral and theological positions that prevail in Christian churches and by extrapolation in Western "Christian" culture. Nelson (1978, pp. 188–99) provides four helpful categories for this overview.

The first position is the *rejecting-punitive* motif, which has prevailed in Christian history. While few but the most fundamentalist leaders hold this position theologically today, it may still be the approach most favored by a large percentage of Christian people. At base, it is a vindictive prejudice, rooted in centuries of conditioning and fear of the "other," who is the gay person. The rejecting-punitive disposition may also be an expression of the classical defense mechanism of projection whereby sections of the population "scapegoat" a minority because they are unable to accept the hated quality—in this case, their own homosexual tendencies—in themselves.[1] Among more educated persons this prejudice rarely takes the form of physical violence. It is, however, expressed in modes of social exclusion, inequities in the work place, sarcastic humor about gay people, prejudicial attitudes handed on to children around the dinner table in the form of bigoted remarks, and so on. Why do most parents dread the prospect of having a gay son? Why do they look for signs that the child is a "regular guy" from earliest infancy onward? Somehow, being gay represents a tragedy and a stigma for most people. Some would even prefer a child who grows up a criminal to one who turns out to be gay.

The second position presented by Nelson is the *rejecting–non-punitive* motif. This is represented by one of the greatest theologians of our century, Karl Barth. Barth holds that humanity comes into its fullness only in relation to persons of the opposite sex. To seek one's fulfillment in a person of the same sex is "physical, psychological and social sickness, the phenomenon of perversion, decadence and decay" (Barth 1961, p. 166). Yet, convinced that the central theme of the gospel is grace and forgiveness, Barth advocates the condemnation of homosexuality but the acceptance of the gay person. This approach seems close to the official positions adopted by various Christian denominations that make a distinction between "orientation" and "activity" in the lives of homosexual persons. In other words, hate the sin but love the sinner.

A third approach is *qualified acceptance.* This option holds that while homosexuality is in some way against the order of creation, there are homosexually constituted persons who have no choice regarding this sexual orientation. The ideal for these is sublimated abstinence. If this proves impossible, then they should "structure their sexual relationships in an 'ethically responsible way' (in adult, fully-committed relationships). They should make the best of their painful situations without idealizing them or pretending that they are normal" (Nelson 1978, p. 196). This opinion has become fairly common among moral theologians and church leaders. A caricature of it would run: "If they have to be that way, then let them at least model their relationships on the Christian heterosexual norm and not flaunt their gayness as good."

The fourth possibility from the ethical point of view is that of *full acceptance*. Those who adopt this position accept fully the conclusions of medical and psychological research that the gay orientation is a simple *given*. Although no common agreement exists about the etiology of homosexuality, major theories cluster around either genetic or psychogenic explanations. All concur that subjects discover rather than invent their homosexuality. Christian theologians who advocate full acceptance interpret this "given" as "grace" (McNeill 1976; Pittenger 1977; Whitehead and Whitehead 1984). It is part of the mystery of divine creation according to which God created each person in God's image. Since God *is* love (1 Jn 4:8), then the human being in God's image *is* also love. Love is the deepest ontology of the human:

> To say that I am made in the image of God is to say that love is the reason for my existence, for God is love. Love is my true identity. Selflessness is my true self. Love is my true character. Love is my name (Merton 1961, p. 60).

In this view, sexual attraction and its loving expression are intrinsic to the mystery of personal identity—that is, to the "love" that each person *is* in the depths of his or her being where a person images God who is love. Homosexual love, then, becomes a way of imaging God, just as heterosexual love images God.

The slogan "gay is good" is thus more than just a cry for liberation or an expression of ego self-esteem. It articulates the deepest spiritual reality of gay persons. Far from having something wrong with them (their gayness), they in fact have something altogether right with them: the gift of a unique dignity, a unique way of loving, a unique mission to live their homosexual orientation as a way of imaging God. God's creative and redemptive love is less present in the world when individuals, aided and abetted by culture and church, deny their homosexual orientation or loathe themselves because of it.

Which of the four approaches—rejecting-punitive, rejecting–non-punitive, qualified acceptance, full acceptance—is morally "correct" is not the concern of this chapter. Theologians will continue to debate them. The focus of this chapter is the psychological maturity and spiritual growth of the gay male who approaches the pastoral counselor for help in facing the "problem" of his homosexuality.

As defined by the Association of Pastoral Counselors, pastoral counseling is "a process in which a pastoral counselor utilizes insights and principles derived from the disciplines of theology and the behavioral sciences in working with individuals, couples, families, groups, and social systems toward the achievement of wholeness and health" (Wicks, Parsons, and Capps 1985, p. 15). In light of the goal of pastoral counseling, the assumptive presupposition of this chapter is that the fourth theological option of full acceptance will best promote the gay male's movement toward wholeness and health.

Justification for the counselor's adoption of this most positive of the four approaches lies precisely in the adjective "pastoral" that describes his or her counseling ministry. Pastoral counselors are not moral theologians engaged in debate over ethical issues. Neither in their role as counselors are they official representatives of the current authoritative teachings of their denominations. They are always and above all *pastors,* that is, fellow Christian charged with the ministry of shepherding the depth dimension of human life, which is the "soul" or true self created in the image of God. Pastoral counselors draw upon whichever insights from the theological or human sciences seem best to foster the emergence of the unique person toward wholeness and health. They root their ministry in the long tradition of the "primacy of conscience," which is the freedom and duty of the individual to follow the voice of God speaking in the depths of his or her responsibly formed conscience, even if this may seem to go contrary to the current teachings or demands of religious institutions. Pastoral counselors try to help their clients listen to this "voice of God" as the primary directive for guidance in and through whatever problems are being faced in the counseling sessions.

In view of these considerations the full acceptance of homosexuality within the framework of the gospel imperative to love can thus form the basic assumption of our approach to pastoral counseling of the gay male.

For the effectiveness of this approach, however, counselors must recognize the extremely complex and ambiguous situation that obtains during a time when churches and cultures are in a crisis of transition in their valuation of homosexuality on all levels—moral, psychological, spiritual, and cultural. As this transition occurs, all the uncertainty and insecurity that accompany major attitudinal shifts are at least preconsciously present in the psyches of most people, including the client and the counselor. For instance, the death of their best friends' son from AIDS recently plunged a prejudiced couple into the throes of this transition. The couple love their friends, who had to struggle to accept and affirm their son's gay orientation upon learning about it through his illness. This caused the formerly prejudiced couple to question their negative attitudes, to read some enlightened literature on the subject, to respond to the special demands of AIDS bereavement within the wider context of supporting their friends, who had hitherto kept their son's gayness a secret, even from themselves. Stories like this—of passage from a rejecting-punitive stance to at least a posture of qualified acceptance—are occurring all the time as a part of the more positive cultural and ecclesial scene that has been described. Yet, the old stories of prejudice, fear, and rejection also remain in force as part of the shadow (in the Jungian sense) side of a culture and churches that cannot deal in distinctly human and Christian ways with the gay expression of God's creative love in this world.

The gay male who comes for pastoral counseling emerges from the lived context of secular and religious culture, not from a solipsistic record of individual experiences. Philosophers like Hans Georg Gadamer (1975) have protested the Enlightenment's rejection of tradition as profoundly explanatory of human behavior and understanding. Following them, psychologists have emphasized the necessity of understanding the contemporary climate and its lived traditions in the therapeutic encounter.

In this regard Adrian van Kaam, existential psychologist and spiritual author, postulates an aspect of the self called the "sociohistorical" dimension (van Kaam 1983, pp. 57–59), which is the matrix of all the other dimensions of the personality: the organismic-emotive, the egoic-functional, and the transcendent-spiritual. All of our organismic, egoic, and spiritual interactions with reality are at least partly shaped and colored by the sociohistorical dimension of the self. Van Kaam calls the dynamics of this dimension "pulsations" (pp. 260–61). Pulsations are often unconscious or preconscious. They represent values, attitudes, uncritical judgments, feelings that have been blindly introjected from family, culture, and church since earliest childhood.

Risking generalization, one could conjecture that in relation to homosexuality these pulsations are still most often negative among the majority of the population, including the gay client and his counselor. This negative sociohistorical conditioning has often been partly reformed by more humane, Christian approaches adopted later in life. Nonetheless, however enlightened one's attitudes may later become, residual deformative pulsations continue to affect the deepest self-estimation of gay clients as well as the attitudes of their pastoral counselors.

Counselors of gay males must, therefore, first of all have an educated awareness of the complexities and ambiguities of homosexuality in today's churches and culture. They will recognize that both they and their clients are in a period of transition in their perceptions and responses toward the facts of homosexuality. Counselors will examine their own consciousness, either in private reflection or with the aid of a supervisor, as to their own internalized pulsations on emotional, moral, and spiritual levels. They might recognize that in truth they retain a level of rejecting-punitive moral judgment; or that they are in fact afraid of gay men; or that they look prejudicially at homosexuals as "people with a problem" rather than as images of God endowed with a unique way of loving.

Whichever pulsations predominate in pastoral counselors' minds and hearts, it seems imperative that they acknowledge them so that these preconscious or unconscious reactions do not interfere with their mission to guide gay people toward wholeness and health, toward psychological maturity informed by a religious value horizon. If in this honest self-examination some counselors detect the presence of hidden or obvious prejudice and negative judgments about homosexuality that are difficult or impossible to reform before receiving the gay client, they are best advised to refer the client elsewhere. There are sufficient gay counseling centers and gay-related church organizations that can recommend or provide competent assistance.

Toward a Positive Gay Identity and Integration

Having surveyed the ecclesial and cultural climates from which the gay male comes for pastoral counseling, we are in a position to reflect more specifically upon the purpose, structures, and dynamics of a sequence of pastoral counseling sessions with a gay male. While it is impossible to characterize the gay male under general stereotypes, one may offer some informed general patterns of approach that may apply, at least in some instances, to the growth of gay males toward psychological and spiritual integration.

Two Working Hypotheses

Two convictions or working hypotheses undergird this approach to pastoral counseling of the gay male. The first is that the counselor's task is the evocation and support of the gay client's radical self-affirmation as one uniquely created in the image of God precisely as a gay person. Second, the counselor's work involves assisting the client's responsible choices in integrating his affirmed identity as a gay person in the context of his everyday life.

These statements of purpose correspond to the underlying dynamics in all human growth: disclosure and incarnation rooted respectively in consciousness and freedom, or intellect and will, or knowledge and love, cognition and behavior. There is always something and something more to be discovered about the mystery of the self within the horizon of divine mystery. Based on new disclosure, there is always something more that can be "done," incarnated, or integrated in order to approximate more deeply the true self or divine image that each of us already is and is on the way toward becoming.

In practice, this journey of disclosure and incarnation of the client's deepest identity is the core issue in all pastoral counseling, perhaps in a special way for homosexual persons who are necessarily preoccupied with issues of identity and integration because of constant challenges to them. To trace the inner dynamics of the journey, we shall examine what van Kaam calls the "intraspheric formation powers" of apprehension, appraisal, affirmation, and application (van Kaam 1985, pp. 66–78; 1987, pp. 140–43).

From the perspective of formative spirituality, whose conceptual paradigms have potential for use in pastoral counseling, the intraspheric formation powers are the primary tools of growth. They represent the counselor's and client's capacities of mind and will on both the transcendent/spiritual and functional/egoic levels. These primary interior capacities are aided by the auxiliary powers of imagination, memory, and anticipation that foster their insightful and free use at the service of human formation, reformation, and transformation (van Kaam 1985, pp. 108–64).

Overview of the Intraspheric Powers

From a Christian perspective, God speaks and communicates in and through life experience. History is the context of grace. The "life-field" of clients refers to the whole context of their life experience: their experience of self, others, situation, wider world, and, ultimately, their experience of the divine Mystery that both permeates and transcends these other dimensions of experience. Formative spirituality calls this context the "formation field" of the client (van Kaam 1983, pp. 286, 296). It is the integrating or disintegrating total context of one's life. The life-field is an interwoven network of directives or influences that shape and are shaped by the client. This approach is based on the assumption that all reality "speaks," that the matter of our life is not inert but is in fact brimming over with directives, meanings, messages, calls, promptings, inspirations, and clues. Some of these directives mediate God's call for the client; others do not.

The pastoral counselor's task is to help clients face and transcend, insofar as possible, those obstacles and problems that prevent the disclosure and incarnation of the true self of the client. In practice, this often means the counselor helps clients to discover and incarnate consonant directives in the context of their life-field. This assistance has traditionally been called the art of discernment, discretion, prudence, or appraisal. Although these terms derive from the tradition of Christian spirituality and the practice of spiritual direction, they are an integral part of the pastoral counselor's role insofar as the counselor is concerned ultimately to help clients discern and do the will of God in their lives.

Like spiritual directors, pastoral counselors must follow the scriptural admonition:

> My dear friends,
> not every spirit is to be trusted,
> but test the spirits to see whether they are from God
> (1 Jn 4:1, *NJB*).

Life experience is full of "spirits" or dynamics—both conscious and unconscious—that motivate our perceptions and behaviors. The pastoral counselor will help clients appraise whether these are consonant or dissonant in relation to human and Christian growth. Once a judgment is made as to the relative consonance or dissonance of a particular directive, the counselor encourages and supports the client's freedom in letting go of the negative options and embracing the positive directive.

This whole process at the core of the counseling situation involves four major steps that engage the transcendental operations of the human spirit, as indwelt, illumined, and empowered by the Holy Spirit: apprehension, appraisal, affirmation, and application of consonant directives for growth.[2]

APPREHENSION

In apprehension, counselor and client pay attention to the life-field of the client in as many of its dimensions and ranges as seem pertinent. This is the process of getting in touch with actual life experience and enabling the client to listen to it. The client is encouraged to narrate "what is going on" physically, emotionally, functionally, and spiritually in his self-experience and his relations to others, situation, wider world, and the mystery of God. The counselor evokes this narration, and receives it with empathic listening and helpful reiteration. It is a process of attention, contemplative seeing, making explicit the directives that are shaping or misshaping the client's growth. It can be called the process of conscientization, whereby relevant directives—conscious, preconscious, or unconscious—are raised to focal attention so that they can be evaluated (van Kaam 1983, p. 299). This is similar to the first step in social transformation advocated by pedagogues and theologians of liberation who encourage the raising to explicit consciousness of oppressive elements in the political and social situation, as well as awareness of the gifts that persons and communities bring to the task of social change (Freire 1982, pp. 27–56).

APPRAISAL

Following apprehension, the task of appraisal occurs. This parallels directly the central process of the traditional art of discernment, discretion, or prudence. Client and counselor together sift through the directives that have been uncovered. Their goal is to attain tentative but sound judgments about which are consonant and conducive to growth—in religious language, which directives might represent God's call to the client. Having received the client's narration of experience, the counselor now confronts with gentle and firm care the client's story. He or she engages the client in the appraisal process, which is an interpretive reading of the client's field of directives in order to seek the truth that will foster the client's growth in freedom (Jn 8:32). Questions of congeniality, compatibility, compassion, and competence form the heart of the interpretative dialogue (van Kaam 1985, p. 67 et passim).

Congeniality asks whether a particular directive, course of action, decision, feeling, or disposition (any aspect of experience) seems in harmony with my deeper self or my true nature as I glimpse it at this time of my life. For example, as an educator I have been invited to accept a promotion to an administrative position. Does this really fit? Would I find meaning behind a desk, doing paper work, confronting other personnel? Or am I a teacher who simply must teach to find some measure of contentment in life?

Compatibility addresses the life situation, our commitments, family life, and other responsibilities and asks whether the proposed directive at least does not offend the situation. Ideally it will foster greater harmony, peace, and justice within it. The administrative post will bring a salary increase, which will help my family. On the other hand, if I am miserable as an administrator, my family and others will suffer.

Compassion examines the limits and vulnerabilities in both self and significant others to see whether the proposed course of action takes these into account in compassionate ways. I will look to each member of my family and to possible future employees, trying to imagine how my decision will affect them. I will examine my energy level, my needs for privacy, and other areas of life to discover which is the more compassionate of the choices that face me.

Finally, there is the obvious question of *competence.* Do I have the training and expertise necessary for administration? Can I learn on the job? Or is my competence more confined to the space of the classroom where students have consistently rated me a good teacher?

The questions represent four criteria that may help one come to sound judgments in the appraisal process. They are ways into life experience and its meaning; they help us disclose the direction of our life. They are in no way exhaustive, but give some hints that enable us to listen with our clients to the fullest possible range of their life experience—and not, for example, just to their interior feelings or dysfunctional family history—in the adventure of disclosure of God's call and our true self. In the end, after all our questioning and careful appraising, the moment of insightful judgment usually comes as gift. It comes to me, for example, that I should take the risk of accepting the administrative position. This represents an "affinitive or affective" appraisal more than a strictly reasoned one. It is in the end more a judgment of the thinking heart than of the analytical mind (van Kaam 1987, pp. 195–96).

AFFIRMATION

The next step in the logic of the pastoral counseling process is affirmation. This act represents the client's decision to embrace directives that have been judged consonant and to let go of those discerned to be dissonant. The act of affirmation is an expression of the spiritual will. This is our deepest freedom to surrender to what we perceive to be the claim, will, or call of God upon our lives. Once the educator sees and judges that he should accept an administrative post, he integrates this judgment into the broader horizon of his life within the kingdom by the act of obedient surrender to God. This is the most authentic act of human and Christian existence. Through it we move toward health and wholeness, for we integrate our deepest freedom with God's purposes for the world insofar as we perceive these purposes, albeit through a glass darkly.

APPLICATION

Application represents the final structure of the counseling encounter. Under the influence of the spiritual will that has said yes to a perceived manifestation of God's direction, the more functional-egoic dimensions of the mind will begin to plan and execute the decision taken and to apply it within the daily reality of the life-field. In this attempt at incarnation clients may make many mistakes. They must realize that functional willing is secondary to growth and transformation in which spiritual willing, our deepest freedom, has primacy of place. The counselor's task is to encourage the trying and the testing of new behaviors. Even more it is the counselor's mission to support the very act of affirmation and surrender by various modes of encouragement and challenge.

Two things must be noted in conclusion about the structures of apprehension, appraisal, affirmation, and application. First, they are logical rather than chronological operations. That is, they do not pretend to be a four-step method for an effective series of counseling sessions. They are rather perspectives on the logic or meaning-structure of the counseling engagement. Although seldom a predictable situation, analysis of many forms of pastoral counseling and spiritual direction reveals that they have these four structures in common. They are balanced and ordered according to the demands of the problems presented and the individuality of the client.

Second, both counselor and client engage in these four operations together in a coformative dialogue. The steps form the process to which both parties are committed in appropriate ways. For example, the counselor hears the apprehensions of the client and challenges him to widen them. The counselor raises questions that move the client toward the act of tentative judgment, which the counselor may or may not explicitly support. The accent in affirmation is, of course, on the client and his or her freedom, which may have to be evoked and encouraged by the counselor; likewise for the task of application.

In terms of these structures, one could say that the entire aim of pastoral counseling is to evoke and sustain the art and discipline of apprehension, appraisal, affirmation, and application in the lives of the clients so that they become capable of living their own lives under the direction of the Spirit (see Gal 5:25).

Using the structure of the four "A's" as a point of departure, we will look more closely at the purpose, structures, and dynamics of pastoral counseling of gay males. We shall examine the progression of experience that might occur in a typical series of pastoral counseling encounters, recognizing all the while that the "typical" gay male does not exist except as a figment of a prejudicial culture's imagination. We shall first discuss disclosure of a positive gay identity as integral to the processes of apprehension and appraisal. Second, we shall address the authentic integration of gay identity through the structures of affirmation and application. To focus our discussion, we shall take a crucial period of every gay male's experience—the process of "coming out." It is at this developmental juncture that many gay persons seek pastoral counseling.

Apprehension and Appraisal: Toward Positive Gay Identity

As a guest in a parish house for dinner one evening ten years ago, I recall the pastor telling of his meeting that day with "a homosexual" who dropped into his office. The pastor went on, "It was very simple. I told him all he had to do to overcome his problem was to be silent and meditate for half an hour each day. Too much fuss is being made today over this 'gay thing.' " I asked timidly, "Did you invite this man to return for further pastoral conversations?" The pastor replied, "Of course not, there was nothing more to talk about."

While fairly typical ten years ago, such a conversation is less likely to happen today. What does occur in practice? Word gets around the gay community that Reverend Joan or Pastor James is a "good person to talk to." Or the prospective client will go to a pastoral counseling center, trusting that the professionalism encountered there will not be marked by discrimination. Or, attending church, the gay man will intuitively size up, correctly or incorrectly, the presider at worship and ask for an appointment. In each case the presenting problem has something to do with a suspected or clearly recognized homosexuality that the client perceives as problematic, as an impairment to his faith life, his family and social life, his professional occupation, his emotional health, and so forth. Clearly the client is in conflict, sometimes in desperation, over this problem and how to solve it.

Peter, age twenty-three, is the eldest of four siblings in a middle-class Methodist family. A college graduate, he lives on his own and works for an insurance company. He had a number of sexual encounters with men in college, but dismissed these as locker room antics. He has dated women since high school but has never fallen in love. A gnawing suspicion that "I might really be gay" has been eating at him for over a year. It throws him into fear and indeed panic.

Three months ago Peter and a buddy from the office went out drinking on Friday night. The evening ended in bed, which Peter ascribed to intoxication. The friend, however, pursued the relationship. He invited Peter for dinners and other social occasions. The attraction between them grew. Soon it dawned on Peter that for the first time in his life he was really in love and falling more deeply into it each day. He felt he couldn't handle the situation on his own. He sought the help of the pastor of a neighboring Methodist church, Howard. Peter had heard Howard was a good listener, a caring person, and "liberal" in orientation.

What was the focus of their first few sessions? In Rogerian terms, Howard gave Peter a quality of attention marked by "unconditional positive regard" (Hall and Lindzey 1978, p. 288–89). Howard evoked Peter's story in as many of its facets as possible. He encouraged him to explore as many aspects of his life-field as seemed relevant to the presenting problem of conflict due to perceived or suspected gay orientation. Through evocative questions and empathic listening, Howard gradually acquired some of Peter's "internal frame of reference" (Hall and Lindzey, pp. 303–4). At this point Howard's main intentionality was not explanation, advice-giving, or interpretation. He wanted to co-listen with Peter to all the interwoven directives in Peter's life-field that played a role in his present conflict—on the personal, interpersonal, situational, and religious levels.

For example, Howard evoked and heard the directives of attraction and excitement emerging from Peter's vital-sexual self in relation to his friend; spiritual longings for partnership with a beloved other; fears of what his family would think about the relationship; great anxiety about the work situation should the relationship become known; dread of divine judgment and the possible need of self-imposed exile from the church community; an uneasy sense of ostracization from normal and normative culture as he has always known it. Through these and many other directives woven into the conflict lurked Peter's ultimate question: "Is there something really wrong with me, and what can I do about it?"

This first stage of apprehension is crucial for growth. The counselor cannot pass lightly or quickly over Peter's life-field with its ranges of conflicted experience by suggesting or imposing his own positive interpretations of homosexuality. As Howard evokes and listens to Peter's story in all its relevant pathways and chapters, Peter is given to himself through his act of narration. He comes home to the truth of his own experience in all its ambiguity and conflict, but with some hope that, because the counselor seems to accept him, his story may also be one of hope and opportunity.

There are three levels going on all the time in the apprehension process: the co-listening and apprehension of Peter and Howard together of the dynamics and directives in Peter's life-field; the concomitant internal processing of Peter within his own psyche and spirit; the ongoing self-apprehensions of Howard, who must remain congruent with his evolving experience of the client. (In this regard, in relation to the gay male, pastoral counselors must be highly self-critical, as noted previously, about their actual feelings and dispositions toward the client. These may range from unconscious fear or repugnance for homosexuality that gradually surfaces to consciousness all the way to countertransferences such as falling in love with the client. The latter is more probable for counselors who have not dealt with the homosexual component of their own personalities.) Through the convergence of these three levels of apprehension Peter and Howard move together toward the best possible apprehension of Peter's situation, the best *understanding* that is available to them of Peter's experience. The client often experiences this phase of the process as a homecoming. This may be the first time in years that a client has been helped to "be himself," to come home to the truth, to allow the real self rather than the ideal self to prevail, at least in the counseling session (Horney 1950, pp. 17–86).

After evoking and hearing Peter's story in a process of co-apprehension of the conflicting phenomena in his life, the pastoral counselor directs Peter toward a more interpretative mode of exchange. Together he and Peter seek the deeper meanings of his situation so that Peter will come to mature insight and judgment about his life direction as a gay man. In the actual dynamics of the counseling session, this will involve a movement from a phenomenological (disclosing structures of experience) to a more hermeneutical stance (interpreting the underlying dynamics at work in the life-field). This hermeneutical process is the work of appraisal or discernment, using guidelines and norms for appraisal such as congeniality, compatibility, compassion, and competence.

The appraisal process is a conversation that aims to foster the client's mature assessment of his situation. Integral to the process is the counselor's ability to propose questions in a creative and non-controlling way. In *The Analogical Imagination* theologian David Tracy, following Gadamer, notes that hermeneutical understanding is best fostered by authentic conversation. About this type of conversation Tracy writes:

> Real conversation occurs only when the individual partners move past self-consciousness and self-aggrandizement into joint reflection upon the subject matter of the conversation. The back-and-forth movement of all genuine conversation (an ability to listen, to reflect, to correct, to speak to the point—the ability, in sum, to allow the question to take over) is an experience which all reflective persons have felt. . . . Real conversation occurs only when the participants allow the question, the subject matter, to assume primacy. It occurs only when our usual fears about our own self-image die: whether that fear is expressed in either arrogance or scrupulosity matters little. That fear dies only because we are carried along, and sometimes away, by the subject matter itself into the rare event or happening named "thinking" and "understanding." For understanding *happens*; it *occurs* not as the pure result of personal achievement but in the back-and-forth movement of the conversation itself (Tracy 1981, p. 101).

The conversation of appraisal or discernment will thus be a back-and-forth movement about the truth of the negative voices apprehended in the life-field that incline Peter toward self-loathing and rejection, as well as about the more positive directives that hold out hope and wider horizons for Peter's life. The criteria proposed for appraisal of congeniality, compatibility, compassion, and competence may be helpful in this conversation.

CONGENIALITY

The first and most significant matter for appraisal is a congeniality issue; namely, Peter asks, "Am I really gay?" Many gay men have no doubts about their predominately homosexual orientation. They have known it since childhood. Others are profoundly disturbed by the question and have great difficulty in accepting themselves as primarily gay. The pastoral counselor may have to offer pointed questions to help assess whether gayness is congenial for the client, in harmony with his true self. Usually some simple questions aimed at disclosing the spontaneous, pre-reflective orientation of the client's sexual and affective energies will promote the necessary self-knowledge. For example, "You see an attractive male/female couple walking down the street. Are you spontaneously drawn to the male or the female in your 'first look.' " "Is the primary content of your sexual fantasy life and your dreams more male or female-oriented?" These and similar questions can help the client appraise the actual direction of his sexual orientation.

The deeper congeniality question comes down to this: "If I am gay, is there something really wrong with me, and what can I do about it?" This is a pivotal question for the gay male at this stage of his development. The pastoral counselor cannot arbitrarily dismiss it or give a positive pat answer that does not take the anguish and depth of the question seriously. Instead, through the back-and-forth of the conversation (in which both parties open themselves to the subject-matter and let it hold sway) the counselor will help the client struggle his way toward the answer. There are many directives, for example, in Peter's life-field from church, family upbringing, and male culture that tell him: "Yes, there is something wrong with you. It is your sexual orientation. And all you can do is hide it, suffer it, and try not to make a fool of yourself. You can even try 'passing' as a heterosexual man. Maybe even get married; it might work. At least you'll have a respected position in society, and who knows, you may be capable of a loving and sexual relationship with just the right woman." These directives have long reinforced unconscious and conscious feelings of self-doubt and loathing in Peter's life.

Howard can offer other questions that may point Peter toward a more positive direction. He can appeal to their shared faith tradition, which appraises all that God has created as very good (Gn 1:31), especially humanity created in God's own image. Being gay, therefore, is not only a sexual attraction; it is a profound orientation of one's deepest embodied soul, created to image God by loving as a gay person. Howard can appeal to the vitality and lifting of low-grade depression that Peter is experiencing in his new relationship with the friend from work. He can stress that each of us has only one life to live, and that the greatest tragedy is never to be one's self. Holiness and wholeness consist in disclosure and incarnation of one's true self. Being gay is part of being one's true self. Howard can point to positive gay role models in the church, the wider culture, and in history. He can counsel that there is a world of relationships, an alternative religious and secular culture, for example, church groups for gays and lesbians, in which Peter could find spiritual and social support for his personal quest.

COMPATIBILITY

Another strand of the pastoral conversation will focus upon issues of compatibility for Peter. How will being gay relate him differently to others? Should he inform his family of his newfound identity? What about the work situation? Should he be open, discreet, or completely secretive about being gay? Especially in a pastoral counseling context, the issue of compatibility with the church may be a serious question. Can he remain a practicing Christian since he may be living in contradiction with his church's official teachings? Is it honest to do so? A significant number of gays have left their churches precisely because of this question and the refusal or inability to distinguish the institutional churches from the reality of God's kingdom of justice, peace, and mercy.

Other compatibility questions will focus upon more immediate and long-range bonding issues. What about the relationship with his new friend? Shall he pursue it? Should they live together? If they continue to grow in love, should they make a formal or informal commitment to one another—and what shape could the commitment take? Or, perhaps he is not the "marrying kind," either as a gay or straight person. Would he be better off living alone as a single person, even embracing a celibate life as an expression of gay loving?

COMPASSION

Taking into account one's own and others' limits and vulnerabilities is integral to the client's task of appraisal with the pastoral counselor. The questions of compassion help temper inappropriate expressions of the newly found gay identity and self-affirmation. Peter, for example, is temperamentally a private person with extreme sensitivities to the opinions of others. Compassion for his own vulnerability, therefore, might suggest he be most discreet about self-disclosure. He would not have the inner stamina to go public as a gay person, but could "come out" to a few trusted friends. Peter's family members have always been liberal in their views and committed to social justice issues. They have always insisted that their children live their own lives. Thus, Peter assesses that they will probably accept his gayness without too much conflict or suffering, and tentatively judges that he will come out to them in the near future.

COMPETENCE

In order to maintain and enhance their self-esteem, all humans seek to maintain the conviction that they are competent to give and receive shape, love, and direction in their everyday lives. Plagued by a history of self-doubt, many gay men suffer a lifelong history of diminished self-esteem, which sometimes leads to self-abusive activity in thoughtless promiscuity, alcohol and drug addiction, and self-defeating behaviors in other realms of life, such as the work place. All of this amounts to self-fulfilling prophecies based on a deep sense of incompetence.

In their shared assessment of Peter's situation, Howard and Peter may want to explore Peter's deeper feelings about his basic sense of potency in life. Does Peter generally feel that he "can do," so that he can identify with Paul's "There is nothing I cannot do in the One who strengthens me" (Phil 4:13, *NJB*)? Can he accept failure and defeat with the conviction that "It is, then, about my weaknesses that I am happiest of all to boast, so that the power of Christ may rest upon me. . . . For it is when I am weak that I am strong" (2 Cor 12:9–10, *NJB*). This sense of biblical competence is important for gay males, whose sense of self-esteem must be deeply internal in a culture and society that so often withhold their approval.

Affirmation and Application: Toward Wise Integration

Peter and Howard have had ten counseling sessions over a three-month period. Howard has helped Peter become present to the truth of his experience, to express himself freely as together they explore the many directives shaping Peter's life and make tentative but sound judgments about which directives are consonant with his life call—that is, congenial with his true self, compatible with his situation, compassionate toward self and others, and competent. Peter's overall judgment is that it is all right to be gay. In fact, it is a gift of God. From the judgment that "something is really wrong with me," he has moved toward the judgment that being gay means that "something is right with me." There has been a transformation of consciousness, an experiential shift in perspective. This new judgment articulates Peter's interior passage from the closet of fear to the open space of freedom. Peter has come out of hiding from himself, from the protected place of false security where the truth of his being never finds the light of expression (Whitehead and Whitehead 1984, pp. 134–35).

The next task for pastoral counselor and client is the engagement of the client's freedom through the spiritual capacity we call the "will." Peter has grown in awareness. For a mature integration of homosexuality into his human and Christian life, there must now occur the interior assent of his freedom to the truth he has disclosed.

Second, he must start incarnating his assent in daily life. These are the operations of affirmation and application.

As we have seen, affirmation is an expression of the spiritual will, which is that depth of our freedom where we are always able to say yes to the divine mystery, even when we cannot incarnate this assent immediately in our behaviors. Van Kaam (1979) calls it "intentional wholeness" and the "wholeness of good will" (p. 133). It is the foundation for further psychological and spiritual growth. Without this firm and free engagement of the spiritual will, the client runs the risk of mere behaviorism or voluntarism in his attempts to apply new directives in daily life.

In the context of Judeo-Christian pastoral counseling Peter has discerned that God seems to will his gayness, that God calls him to love as a gay person. While such a judgment is only probable, it is all we can achieve in our search for the unfathomable mystery of God's will, which always remains ultimately hidden in light inaccessible (1 Tm 6:16). Placing Peter's new judgments about his gay experience within a religious horizon and encouraging a response to the divine mystery in light of this horizon seem to be the characteristics that distinguish pastoral counseling from secular therapies.

Howard will encourage Peter to say yes to God by saying a profound and free yes to his graced sexual orientation. In that yes the dichotomy between sexuality and spirituality is overcome at its root. This yes is the only radical antidote to the internalized homophobia from which many gay men suffer. This assent is truly an exodus from the bondage of self-depreciation to the freedom of self-affirmation and celebration of Peter's essential goodness as a gay man.

Saying yes to one's gay identity and its Source is the foundation of subsequent integration for the gay male. The movement is from awareness (apprehension and appraisal) through acceptance toward integration (affirmation and application). No client can authentically integrate a new perspective or disposition in his or her life without the prior moment of a free assent in which the client radically affirms the appraised directive as "for me" in relation to the gracious and meaningful Mystery we name God. Without this affirmation, the new disposition or perspective is built on sand; it becomes a willful striving or a new behavioristic conditioning.

Only Peter can say this yes. The counselor cannot do it for him. Howard, however, can suggest the motivations of religious meaning that can support Peter's surrender. Howard can encourage Peter as he wrestles with this angel throughout the night of crisis (Gn 32:26–29). He can stand by Peter in this hour of decision so crucial for the rest of his life journey toward spiritual wholeness and psychological health. The choice is Peter's. It must not be assumed that because he sees gayness as a positive identity that he will assent to and assume this identity. The new identity is still largely in the realm of the unknown. To choose it freely is to risk the unknown, and risk generates fear. It is possible that, having ventured two steps toward freedom, Peter can walk three steps back into self-depreciation. He can reject the new directive of self-goodness or, more typically, experience paralysis in relation to it. That is, he will never really embrace and assent to it. The challenge for the pastoral counselor in this moment of the process is to shepherd the freedom of the client, to encourage conscious choice, and to offer his support as Peter surrenders to the divine mystery.

For wise integration of a newly affirmed gay identity into the whole context of one's life and commitments, the process of application must occur. This is often a long search and struggle. Usually only the first steps of it take place within a formal pastoral counseling situation.

In a sociohistorical situation charged with conflict and ambivalence in regard to homosexuality, positive and life-giving incarnation of one's affirmed gay identity will never be easy. Part of Howard's task is to help Peter realize and accept this so that he will not suffer disillusionment and consequent regression when he confronts the obstacles to integration in his own life and culture. He can encourage in Peter the conviction that no human or spiritual integration is possible without taking our share of "hardships for the sake of the gospel, relying on the power of God" (2 Tm 1:8, *NJB*).

Central to the task of application will be a cycle of strategic appraisals as to how Peter can best live as a gay man. Many of the issues involved in this movement toward integration will already have been explored in previous sessions, but now they take on a more urgent focus: "Fine, I'm gay and I'm okay, but now what do I *do* about it?" A host of questions present themselves. For instance, what about gay culture as such in its heterogeneous shapes? Like any culture, gay culture is both fallen and graced. The mature person participates in it with discrimination. Does being gay mean I will frequent places of gay socialization like bars, discos, gay community centers? Should I join Affirmation, the gay outreach group of the Methodist church? Again, how public shall I go? There are various stages of coming out that Peter may go through and probably should start trying while still in counseling. There is coming out to oneself, to a few trusted others, to family and all or most of one's friends. Finally, some gay people are called to a more public coming out, for example coming out as both gay and Christian in public forums such as writing, public speaking, public leadership in gay organizations, and so on. Each gay man is unique in this regard. He must find modes of application that are congenial, compatible, compassionate, and for which he is competent.

The criteria for application parallel those for the act of appraisal. The difference is that there is the "trying." Peter tries out different behaviors and strategies in his attempts to incarnate his identity as a gay man. Ideally, he does this within the stratum of values represented by his faith commitment. In practice, however, the counselor may have to stand by and witness behaviors he does not understand or agree with—casual and uncommitted sex, for example. The educated counselor will realize that this is common among gay men for many reasons. Chief among them are the alleviation of loneliness and protest against the oppressive dictates of the normative culture of heterosexuality. The counselor will not condemn or disapprove of such behaviors. His or her task is to challenge the client toward integration of sexual identity with the client's deepest values and commitments, especially the vocation to love that each human has received in the core of his or her being. No one is perfect in loving. The pastoral counselor shepherds the client's attempts to test and apply his newly affirmed gay identity. The counselor walks with the client in this process. As parents do not scold children for stumbling as they learn to walk, so the counselor does not disapprove when inappropriate behaviors are engaged in. The counselor continues to walk with the client and helps him stand up again when he stumbles or falls into inauthenticity or dissonant applications.

Pastoral counselor and client thus move together through the interpenetrating cycles of apprehension, appraisal, affirmation, and application. These structures and dynamics of the counseling session must always be kept in balance in a climate of freedom and disciplined spontaneity. It is all too easy to fixate on one or two at the expense of the others. For instance, Peter and Howard could spend many months getting in touch with Peter's experience (apprehension) and never think carefully through (appraisal) the meaning of the experience for human and spiritual growth. Or, they could gloss lightly over the range of Peter's experience and do all kinds of interpretive work before Peter has fully explored and come home to the truth of his experience. The subtle and deep act of affirmation or surrender might be passed over in favor of fixated attention on Peter's attempts to apply his new identity in functional behaviors. What matters in the pastoral counseling setting, as always, is mature balance on the part of the counselor, who must make wise decisions about when to engage in each of the four processes in service of the psychological and spiritual growth of the gay client.

Conclusion

We have attempted to portray the cultural and ecclesial situation from which the gay male comes for pastoral counseling. We saw that it is a conflicted context both objectively and subjectively for the gay man himself. For an accurate understanding of the gay male, the counselor will see him as embedded in this wide sociohistorical conflict.

Pastoral counselors will educate themselves in regard to the possible theological and ethical assumptions about homosexuality. They will be in touch with their own intellectual and emotional assumptions about persons with homosexual orientations. If they cannot counsel the gay male toward acceptance, affirmation, and positive incarnation of a gay identity, counselors ought to refer the gay male to someone who can serve his wholeness and health. There is no shame here, no accusation of incompetence. There is the simple recognition that pastoral counselors cannot counsel everybody. They should be aware of both their gifts and their limits and humbly accept them.

Once undertaken, the pastoral counseling contract with the gay male has at least a twofold purpose. First, the counselor will assist the client in the movement toward a radical self-affirmation as a gay man whose gayness is part of his creation in the very image of God. Second, counselors of gay men commit themselves to foster the wise integration of the affirmed identity in the total context of the client's life-field, including his relationship with the mystery of God that permeates this field.

Finally, we explored basic structures and psycho-spiritual dynamics that serve the purposes of pastoral counseling of gay men: apprehension of directives from the life-field, mature appraisal of the meaning of those directives concerning gay experience, support for the affirmation, and application of consonant directives for human and spiritual growth.

For the gay male, pastoral counselors can be midwives of a new identity and integration. It may seem shocking that part of their pastoral mission, which the Christian tradition has called the *cura animarum* or "the care of souls," may include helping bring homosexual persons out of the closet. But that is only because the theory and practice of ministry have been in part misshaped by cultural prejudices for centuries. The light of the authentic Judeo-Christian tradition invites all believers to come out of the closets of oppression and fear into the freedom of grace, wherein all people have been created to love with their unique orientations and gifts. Being gay is a graced orientation and a gift to church and society. Pastoral counselors stand in awe of this particular vocation as they assist gay people in their passage from darkness into light.

Notes

1. Freud, for example, taught that all humans are inherently bisexual; each sex is attracted to members of the same sex as well as to members of the opposite sex. This is the constitutional basis for homosexuality, although in most people the homosexual impulses remain latent. Whether hetero- or homosexuality gains ascendancy depends to some extent upon early conditioning factors in family and society (Hall and Lindzey 1978 p. 57). Denial of one's homosexual capacities often leads to *homophobia,* which is irrational fear of and consequent prejudice toward persons who are primarily homosexual. Often homophobia implies unconscious rejection or loathing of one's own latent homosexual tendencies and potential.

2. See the parallel with Bernard Lonergan (1972). Lonergan discusses "transcendental method" in theology and relates it to the exercise of the transcendent operations of the distinctively human spirit through its faculties of mind and will: experiencing, understanding, judging, deciding, and communicating.

References

Barth, Karl. 1961. *Church Dogmatics.* Vol. 3. Edinburgh: T. & T. Clark.

Boswell, John. 1980. *Christianity, Social Tolerance, and Homosexuality.* Chicago: University of Chicago Press.

Congregation for the Doctrine of the Faith. 1986. "The Pastoral Care of Homosexual Persons." Rome: 1 October 1986. *Origins: NC Documentary Service,* vol. 16, no. 22 (November 13, 1986).

Crompton, Louis. 1974. "Gay Genocide: From Leviticus to Hitler." Address delivered to the Gay Academic Union. New York University (November 30).

Duberman, Martin, Vicinus, Martha, and Chauncey, Jr., George, eds. 1989. *Hidden from History: Reclaiming the Gay and Lesbian Past.* New York: Penguin Books.

Freire, Paulo. 1982. *Pedagogy of the Oppressed.* Trans. Myra Bergman Ramos. New York: Continuum.

Gadamer, Hans Georg. 1975. *Truth and Method.* Trans. Garrett Barden and John Cumming. New York: Seabury.

Horney, Karen. 1950. *Neurosis and Human Growth.* New York: W. W. Norton.

Hall, Calvin S., and Lindzey, Gardner. 1978. *Theories of Personality.* New York: John Wiley and Sons.

Lonergan, Bernard. 1972. *Method in Theology.* New York: Herder and Herder.

McNeill, John J. 1976. *The Church and the Homosexual.* Kansas City: Sheed, Andrews and McMeel.

Merton, Thomas. 1961. *New Seeds of Contemplation.* New York: New Directions.

Nelson, James B. 1978. *Embodiment: An Approach to Sexuality and Christian Theology.* Minneapolis: Augsburg.

Nugent, C. Robert, and Gramick, Jeannine. 1982. *A Time to Speak: A Collection of Contemporary Statements from U.S. Catholic Sources on Homosexuality, Gay Ministry and Social Justice.* Mt. Rainier, Md.: New Ways Ministry.

Pittenger, Norman. 1977. *Gay Lifestyles: A Christian Interpretation of Homosexuality and the Homosexual.* Los Angeles: The Universal Fellowship Press.

Tracy, David. 1981. *The Analogical Imagination: Christian Theology and the Culture of Pluralism.* New York: Crossroad.

van Kaam, Adrian. 1979. *The Transcendent Self.* Denville, N.J.: Dimension Books, 1979.

——. 1983. *Fundamental Formation.* New York: Crossroad.

——. 1985. *Human Formation.* New York: Crossroad.

——. 1987. *Scientific Formation.* New York: Crossroad.

Whitehead, Evelyn Eaton, and Whitehead, James D. 1984. *Seasons of Strength: New Visions of Adult Christian Maturing.* New York: Doubleday.

Wicks, Robert J., Richard D. Parsons, and Donald E. Capps, eds. 1985. *Clinical Handbook of Pastoral Counseling.* New York: Paulist Press.

For Further Reading

Conn, Joann Wolski. 1989. *Spirituality and Personal Maturity.* New York: Paulist Press.

Fortunato, John E. 1983. *Embracing the Exile: Healing Journeys of Gay Christians.* New York: Seabury.

Gonsiorek, John C., Ed. 1985. *A Guide to Psychotherapy with Gay and Lesbian Clients.* New York: Harrington Park Press.

Moses, A. Elfin, and Hawkins, Robert O., Jr. 1982. *Counseling Lesbian Women and Gay Men: A Life Issues Approach.* St. Louis: C. V. Mosby.

Tripp, C. A. 1975. *The Homosexual Matrix.* New York: McGraw Hill.

SECTION III
THE CHALLENGES AND OPPORTUNITIES OF LIFE STAGES

As we navigate through the choices and decisions to be made in our adult life, we sometimes find ourselves in need of pastoral support, either as the result of the normative pressures of our life-stage or because of the resultant conflict from some of our life choices. The chapters contained in this section address a number of unique needs experienced by adults as they cope with the life crises presented during the adult years.

Chapter 11, "Midlife Transitions in Men and Women," provides an exploration of the theories and research addressing midlife transitions. Margaret Gorman provides the reader with an insightful review of contemporary research surrounding the tasks of midlife. Further, she provides a convincing argument for the pastoral opportunities that are presented during midlife transitions. Those in this period of life, notes the author, "whether they voice it or not may well be yearning for deepening of their spiritual dimension," and as she clearly notes, responding to this yearning is the ministry of the pastoral counselor.

In Chapter 12 Paul Giblin presents both the grim realities and the faith-filled hopes of marriage in the 1990s. Giblin suggests that marital conflict of the repetitive and nonproductive type is clearly the inverse of marital spirituality. Further, it is his thesis that reducing such conflict clearly invites opportunity for spiritual growth. Giblin, evoking incarnational theology, describes the opportunity of marriage as one of encountering God in the person of one's partner. He also provides a model and useful guidelines for assisting couples in the move from conflict to growth in the spirit and in love.

The reality is that for many the conflict described by Giblin unfortunately does not result in spiritual growth, but rather in the termination of the relationship. The increasing rate of divorce has created another challenge and opportunity for those in pastoral counseling:

providing care and support for the single parent. In Chapter 13 David Blackwelder presents an encompassing look at various stressors affecting single parents in the 1990s. He builds on the theological principles of love, forgiveness, suffering, stewardship, death, and resurrection to provide a developmental model aimed at facilitating singles in the process of rebuilding their identity. From his review of the literature and his own experience as both single and pastor, Blackwelder argues as well for the value, need, and necessity of parish-based pastoral intervention with single parents.

Margaret Gorman, R.S.C.J.

11. Midlife Transitions in Men and Women

Donald Capps (1985) gave an excellent adaptation of the Levinsonian model as a basis for pastoral counseling for middle adults which emphasized a "transformed narcisissm." Around that time many articles and books were written on midlife in men and women (Baruch and Brooks-Gunn 1984; Roberts and Newton 1987; Hunter and Sundel 1989; Alexander and Langer 1990; Fiske and Chiriboga 1990). Despite the increase in studies of midlife, only the last two books referred—and then indirectly—to the role of religion and spirituality as an important component in midlife. For a consideration of the religious development of both men and women in midlife, Jung and Maslow give greater consideration than do more recent studies. Those who base their suggestions for pastoral counseling on Jung also emphasize the spiritual dimension (Brewi and Brennan 1982; Brewi 1988; Studzinski 1985).

Where the earlier studies of midlife (following Levinson) emphasize the negative aspects of these years, this article will consider middle age as rich in possibilities for growth, especially in the spiritual dimension.

> Midlife is a period of many more positives than negatives. Research findings . . . have shown, for example, that many middle-aged people are self-confident, assertive, outgoing, generous, nurturant, dependable and warm. . . . There is no significant decline for the majority of middle-aged persons in their physical, psychological, social intellectual, or cognitive functioning. Most middle-aged people are neither stagnant nor stodgy, and they are not experiencing a "midlife crisis" (Hunter and Sundel 1989, p. 282).

After reviewing the broad history of current studies on adult development with attention to the presence or absence of reflection on religious development, I will examine the research comparing the adult development of men and women. The final section will examine more recent psychological theories that do consider the religious component of adult development and therefore might enrich the perspectives of pastoral counselors.

Overview of Adult Development Theories and Research

Carl Jung

One of the earliest writers on lifelong psychological development was Carl Jung (1933), to whom Daniel Levinson (1978) admits his indebtedness. In Jung's very short essay "The Stages of Life" lies the seeds of most of the future reflections on midlife. Jung compares the course of human life to the course of the sun:

> In the morning it [the sun] rises from the nocturnal sea of consciousness and looks upon the wide bright world. . . . At the stroke of noon the descent begins. And the descent means the reversal of all the ideals and values that were cherished in the morning (Jung 1933, p. 106).

This passage forms the basis for his delineation of the development of human life.

The central theme is that the qualities or interests in the first half of life will be changed into the opposite qualities in midlife. Thus older women become more masculine and more autonomous.

> A man consumes his large supply of masculine substance and has left over only the smaller amount of feminine substance which he must now put to use. . . . It is the other way around with women; she allows her unused supply of masculinity to become active" (Jung 1933, p. 107).

This can cause havoc with marriages, "for it is not hard to imagine what may happen when the husband discovers his tender feelings and the wife her sharpness of mind" (p. 108).

Of equal importance, according to Jung, is the shift from concern with outer role prescriptions to concerns about one's inner life:

> The significance of the morning undoubtedly lies in the development of the individual, our entrenchment in the outer world, the propagation of our kind and the care of the chil-

> dren. . . . Whoever carries over into the afternoon the law of the morning must pay for so doing with damage to his soul (p. 109).

The cost of concentration on development of the ego and consciousness of the outer world in young adulthood is very great. It must be followed in the second half of life by the development of the self and the bringing to consciousness more of the primordial images in the unconscious.

Jung pointed out the narrowness of the standards of the first half of life, which emphasize success in social roles:

> Its [society's] prizes are always given for achievement and not for personality. . . . We are forced to limit ourselves to the attainable (p. 102). . . . We wholly overlook the essential fact that the achievements which society rewards are won at the cost of a diminution of personality (p. 104).

During midlife Jung says we must face our shadow—our capacity for evil and our finiteness (Neumann 1969, pp. 137–47; Brewi and Brennan 1982, pp. 94–98). Because of the need to recognize and accept one's finiteness, middle age could be a period of rich and profound growth in one's relation to the Infinite. This is also why Jung says that the concerns in midlife are about the growth of the inner life of meaning and less about success in roles.

Abraham Maslow

Maslow also claimed that the religious or spiritual dimension is an essential component of each human being. In the preface to the revised version of *Religion, Values and Peak Experiences* (1970) he writes: "If I were to summarize both the book and my remarks in this Preface I would say it this way: Man has a higher and transcendent nature and this is part of his essence" (p. xvi). Later on he linked acknowledgment of the religious dimension to psychological health:

> It is increasingly clear that the religious questions themselves—and religious quests, the religious yearnings, the religious needs themselves are perfectly respectable scientifically, that they are rooted deep in human nature. . . . As a matter of fact, contemporary existential and humanistic psychologists would probably consider a person sick or abnor-

> mal in an existential way if he were *not* concerned with these "religious" questions (p. 18).

In fact, he implies that mature adults, perhaps those in middle adulthood, should be and are concerned with religious questions:

> Indeed these serious people are coming so close together as to suggest that they are becoming a single party of mankind, the earnest ones, the seeking questioning, probing ones. . . . The other party then is made up of all the superficial, the moment-bound . . . those who are totally absorbed with the trivial . . . those who are reduced to the concrete, to the momentary, and to the immediately selfish. Almost, we could say, we wind up with adults, on the one hand, and children on the other (p. 56).

Erik Erikson

Erik Erikson (1950) presented an epigenetic model of human development in eight stages. There are five stages from birth to adolescence and three for adulthood. While there has been no empirical evidence of epigenesis (that a certain strength develops at each period and is retained and developed in succeeding periods), there is evidence that throughout our lives the characteristics or strengths that he described—trust, autonomy, initiative, competence, identity, intimacy, generativity, and integrity—are essential characteristics for mature adulthood.

Contrary to the accepted view in the United States that autonomy is indicative of maturity, Erikson describes generativity and care as the key characteristic of middle adulthood. In some way this link to the larger society may be similar to Jung's model of turning inward in middle age to link up with the archetypes of the collective unconscious.

Daniel Levinson

Perhaps the most influential of all those investigating adult development is Daniel Levinson (1978; 1990). He is less influenced by Erikson and more by Jung. While his earlier book emphasizes the notion of the midlife crisis, he recently has clarified his distinction between crisis and transition:

> In contemporary usage, the term *transition* is generally given connotations of both opportunity and risk, whereas *crisis* usually has more negative connotations of danger and

> disruption. Partly for this reason I use *transition* as the most general term for a basic process of structural change and *crisis* for a particular kind of transition, one that is relatively painful, tumultuous, or problematic. . . . The theory of life structure development gives equal weight to the *structure* (i.e., the periods of building and maintaining a life structure and the *transitions* (i.e., the periods of questioning and modifying the structure) (Levinson 1990, pp. 45–46).

From his qualitative study of ten executives, ten blue collar workers, ten novelists, and ten biologists, he posited five eras in life: childhood; adolescence (to age 22); early adulthood era (17 to 45 years); middle adulthood era (40–65 years); late adulthood (age 65). Within those years he proposed five transitions: early adult transition (from ages 17 to 22); the age 30 transition (28 to 33); the midlife transition (40 to 45); age 50 transition (50 to 55); and the late adult transition (60 to 65).

Despite the criticisms of many, he maintains that these structures and transitions transcend culture, gender, and race: "This sequence of eras and periods holds for men and women of different cultures, classes, and historical epochs" (Levinson 1990, p. 44).

> There are wide differences in the kinds of life structures individuals build and in the changes they make during transitional periods. My findings indicate, however, that the timing of the periods in life structure development varies only minimally across cultures, classes and genders (p. 52).

Levinson recently has expanded his description of the three major development tasks in life structure development: termination, individuation, and initiation:

> First one must terminate the past; finally one must initiate a new life. In between as a basis for change is the work of individuation. . . . All three tasks may contine throughout a transitional period (p. 46).

He conceives "of individuation in part as the resolution of four polarities . . . Young-Old, Destruction-Creation, Masculine-Feminine, and Attachment-Separation" (p. 48).

Although Levinson uses the Jungian term *individuation*, he admits that he has steered "a course somewhere between the single-factor emphasis of some investigators (Erikson, Jaques, Neugarten) and the tremendously complex approach of Jung" (Levinson 1978, p. 196). For Jung, individuation means the realization or growing consciousness of all aspects of the self, particularly the unconscious aspects. "My life is a story of the self-realization of the unconscious" (Jung 1961/1965, p. 3). Levinson does not refer in depth to the unconscious, but there are similarities to Jung's archetypes of the unconscious, the shadow, the animus and anima, the Puer/Senex or Young/Old in his polarities (Levinson 1978, pp. 209–44).

However, where Jung (1957/58) and his followers (see Brewi and Brennan 1982; Brewi 1988; Studzinski 1985) link recognition of the shadow with the growth of a genuine religious sense, Levinson never refers to the faith or religious dimension. Although Levinson did describe the institutional membership of the forty men, he never asked the role of faith or meaning in their lives. Jung had distinguished between creed and religion:

> A creed gives expression to a definite collective belief, whereas the word religion expresses a subjective relationship to certain metaphysical extramundane factors. A creed is a confession of faith intended chiefly for the world at large and is thus an intramundane affair, while the meaning and purpose of religion lie in the relationship of the individual to God (Jung 1957/58, p. 31).

Thus Jung saw that midlife, with its recognition of the shadow, can be an occasion for deepening one's relationship with God. Although he saw this recognition of the shadow as necessary for deepening human relationships, it can be assumed that he would apply it also to relationship with God. "The perfect has no need of the other but weakness has for it seeks support" (Jung 1957/58, p. 117).

Levinson also missed the opportunity to see that, since midlife adults question the strict role conformity of early adulthood, this phenomenon could also have religious implications. Jung, on the contrary, saw the danger of immersion in one's roles: "These identifications with a social role are a very fruitful source of neurosis" (Jung 1983, p. 95). According to Jung, the power to resist the pressure of role prescriptions is also religious: "The individual who is not anchored in God can offer no resistance on his own resources to the physical and moral blandishments of the world" (Jung 1957/58, p. 34).

While other studies also see midlife as a search for meaning and a recognition of one's limitedness (Neugarten 1968; Gould 1978), there is no reference to the possibility that these phenomena might open the middle-aged person to growth in his or her spiritual dimension and relationship with God. Recently, however, Fiske and Chiriboga (1990) presented the results of a twelve-year longitudinal study 216 lower-middle-class white males and females from San Francisco, ages 17 to 58 in the beginning of the study. In examining change and continuity they included an assessment of the goals and values of the adults studied. They grouped the goals and values in this way:

> Goals: achievement, social service, and growth
> Positive values: philosophical/religious
> Negative values: hedonism
> Neutral values: people; ease and comfort (p. 217).

They wished to discover which values and goals changed over the course of the twelve years. The results indicated that the religious dimension was considered the most important value by each subgroup, with little change over the twelve years. The majority were religious rather than philosophical (pp. 217–18). The authors believe that Jung's theory that the second half of life balances out the goals of the first half was exemplified in the results. The oldest men valued achievement less and interpersonal relationships more while the oldest women valued achievement goals more than interpersonal goals (p. 241).

Others who chose the more comprehensive Jungian perspective (Brewi and Brennan 1982; Studzinski 1985) also referred to midlife as a period of growth in the spirit.

Adult Development of Women

Donald Capps (1985), working from a Levinsonian perspective, pointed out that one of the tasks of middle age is to develop the "narcissistic dream" of young adulthood into the "transformed" narcissism of middle adulthood (p. 215). In fact, Capps holds that reappraisal of the dream is "a central, perhaps the central focus of pastoral counseling for middle adulthood." However, since Levinson confined his study to males, the question must be raised: Is this true of women? Four doctoral dissertations (cited in Roberts and Newton 1987) examined women according to the Levinsonian paradigm and found considerable differences between the dreams of young women and those of young men. Only Droege's dissertation (cited in Roberts and Newton 1987) explored women in midlife transition, but Roberts and Newton concluded:

> Although the timing of the periods and the nature of the developmental tasks appeared to be similar, the ways of working on the tasks as well as the outcomes achieved were different (p. 154).

The four components of Levinson's model of early adulthood were dream, mentor, occupation, and special woman. These components were explored in these dissertations with the exception that relationship with special man was substituted for special woman. A total of thirty-nine women were studied. Roberts and Newton reported that while men's dreams "tended to incorporate an image of independent achiever in an occupational role," the dreams of women were "fundamentally different" and the majority had "split dreams" (p. 157). Only seven women had individualistic dreams, while twenty had dreams that concerned both occupational and relational elements.

Middle-aged women also structured their lives around dreams consisting of both individualistic and relational components. Droege's data suggest that although women attempt to emphasize the more individualistic components of their dreams in middle adulthood, the relational aspect continues to influence the choices they make beyond the midlife transition.

While more studies of women are needed, the evidence from these four dissertations points to the fact that pastoral counseling for women in middle adulthood may not be exactly what Capps proposed for men: "If the Dream of early adulthood is grounded in the desire for self-direction, the Vision of middle adulthood is the freedom to grow into the likeness of God" (Capps 1985, p. 243).

The vision may be the same but the emphasis may be different since the relational aspect is already there for most women and their dreams in young adulthood are more complex:

> For those women who emphasized occupational goals during their 20s—38% of the total number of subjects—the search for marriage partner and the establishment of a family or a community of friends gained equal if not top priority at around 30. For those women who chose to emphasize marriage and motherhood—47% of the total number of sub-

> jects—a developmental transition at around 30 was marked by a shift to more individualistic goals and a psychological separation from the husband (Roberts and Newton 1987, p. 162).

The remaining women (15%) could not order their priorities and suffered emotional crises in the early adult transition. More research into women's lives is needed.

Around the same time as these dissertations were being written, more studies on women were published. Not all can be covered here, but one study coming out of the Wellesley College Center for Research on Women is indicative of the omission of the faith dimension in the lives of both men and women. In an effort to answer the question, *What is well-being all about for women?* the authors (Baruch, Barnett and Rivers 1983) gave a two-dimensional picture of well-being.:

> We found a strong relationship among self-esteem, control over one's life and levels of anxiety and depression. . . . We were able to identify the first dimension of well-being which we called "Mastery" . . . related to the doing side of life, the instrumental side. We found a similar strong relationship among three other measures of well-being: happiness, satisfaction and optimism . . . giving us our other dimension "Pleasure." Pleasure is closely tied to the feeling side of life—the quality of one's relationship with others (p. 18).

While these two dimensions are, of course, important components of well-being, the question about a faith or meaning dimension of well-being is omitted. The authors conclude that at least by middle adulthood the women who were involved in a combination of roles—marriage, motherhood, and employment—were the highest in well-being despite warnings about stress and strain (p. 247).

It is probably safe to make the generalization that few studies include the faith dimension in the exploration of women's development. However, a recent doctoral dissertation on women's faith development explored the growth of women's faith as a result of being exposed to biblical feminism (Cripe 1989). The study is limited to twelve self-identified biblical feminists (no ages given) who are members of the Evangelical Women's Caucus. These women were early embedded in creed and relationships, "having been taught that womankind's place was in subjection to men" (p. 8). They were then exposed to biblical feminism. An ideology which some might think would stimulate excessive autonomy in the sense of questioning institutional creeds and practices. However, instead of developing extreme individualism, "integrative relationality" resulted, according to the author. Six trends emerged: spiritual depth and sensitivity, intellectual challenge and stimulation, self-concept issues, relational orientation, commitment to social action, and concern for integration of feminism with other life issues (p. 12). Two of these themes, relationship with God and self-concept need to be explored because they address the concern about the integration of a growing sense of autonomy with the relational aspects.

Significantly, a "relational" response to God is central to all references in this spirituality.

> The transition, for example, impacted the women's view of God in ways that deepened close contact with the Divine: a developed sense of God's acceptance of each as a person and a woman, an increased awareness of God's imminence [sic] and intimacy and a freeing affirmation of feminine spiritual imagery. For none of the respondents is God any longer a transcendent or far-removed figurehead (p. 12).

A more positive self-concept was developed as a result of exposure to biblical feminism, and this also improved the quality of important relationships (p. 13). Thus these women integrated their newfound autonomy with relationality. Gilligan (1982) has already pointed out that women reach midlife with a different perspective than men, based on their knowledge of human relationships:

> Since the reality of connection is experienced by women as given rather than as freely contracted, they arrive at an understanding of life that reflects the limits of autonomy and control. As a result, women's development delineates the path not only to a less violent life but also to a maturity realized through interdependence and care (p. 172).

While these studies are very limited, they may help pastoral counselors see that the model of male adult development should not be univocally applied to women, and that relationship and autonomy can be integrated within adults but differently for men and women. In the former case, autonomy or agency needs to be mitigated by and integrated with relationality or communion, while for women, relationality needs to be "de-embedded" strengthened by and integrated with autonomy. This reflects Kegan's interindividual stage, described by Conn (1985, pp. 37–57) and further developed by Kegan himself (Souvaine, Lahey, and Kegan 1990).

More Recent Views of Adulthood

More recent views of adult maturity are beginning to include the spiritual dimension. The theories of Erikson and Levinson emphasize a linear progression that is universal, predictable, and stable, with the goal of fitting into society. Weick proposes a growth task model, which "conceptualizes growth as a cluster of developmental tasks that form cyclical themes in individual lives" (Weick 1989, p. 237). The cluster of tasks can be uniquely arranged by each individual at different periods of adulthood. The tasks go beyond egocentric concerns. Under work they include productivity and creativity; under love they include intimacy and nurturance.

> The fifth task, transcendence speaks to the human capacity to develop beyond the intellectual, physical, and social limits accepted by culture. It is best described as the spiritual dimension because it calls people to explore beyond known and familiar realms of being (pp. 238–39).

To counteract the extreme individualism portrayed in *Habits of the Heart* (Bellah, et al. 1985), Weick states these principles as foundational:

1) All human beings grow and develop within the context of community.
2) The idea of community embraces interlocking circles of connection among all human beings and, ultimately, all forms of life and matter (p. 238).

It is in the formulation of the task of transcendence that Weick specifically addresses the faith dimension:

> In the task of transcendence, personal power is joined with the power of others to express a common goal or ideal. It may be expressed in service to the community, in religious commitment, or spiritual practices. Transcendence is more than altruism, although it may have this component. It is primarily an expression of a broader definition of power—

> one that attempts to life mankind to a higher plane of awareness (p. 240).

Weick points out that the current emphasis on success in work and human relationships often gives rise to disillusionment, especially at midlife when people realize that "life has not been what they were led to expect" (p. 244). She questions the expectations given society and points out they may be misguided and should be critically examined. In her growth task model, in midlife "one of the elements of intimacy may be the turning inward to discover who one is beyond a self defined by social roles" (p. 247)—a task already described by Jung. As for transcendence, it can be equated with the presence of organized religion or it can engage us "in the expansion of our view of the world into the spiritual realm" (p. 248). Weick urges counselors to be aware of these tasks and to help others to develop their own powers in the best way for each one.

While not referring to a religious dimension explicitly, it is the thesis of Maas (1989) that midlife should be a period of social responsibility:

> The essence of social responsibility is . . . twofold. First it involves a person's sense of obligation. The obligation is to work on behalf of or otherwise contribute to the general welfare beyond self-interest. The obligation is based on a keen awareness of one's group membership—ultimately the human race—and of human interdependence in society. Having obtained by the middle adult years some of the advantages of such interdependence, a middle-aged person should be ready to make some repayments. . . . The second component of social responsibility involves . . . capabilities of fulfilling an obligation or trust. . . . At this time of life, the middle-aged become especially crucial links in responsive environments, in supportive networks needed for attachments or collaborative communities important not only in helping but also in modeling and developing reciprocity in others (p. 260).

While Maas emphasizes social responsibility in middle adults, those familiar with Kohlberg's work will remember his stage 7, which he posited as proposed reflection not on the question *What is moral?* but on the question, *Why be moral?* (Kohlberg 1973a, b; 1974; 1981; 1984; 1987). In a posthumous article with Robert Ryncarz he addressed the same topic and indicated his concern with the religious or spiritual dimension of adulthood. As before, he points out that the question *Why be moral in a world that is unjust?* implies a further question, *Why live?*, which is a question about the meaning of life:

> I have posited a purely metaphorical notion of a Stage 7 as pointing to some meaningful solutions to these questions that are compatible with rational science and rational ethics. The central characteristic of all these Stage 7 solutions is that they involve experience of a non-egoistic or non-dualistic variety. The logic of such experience is sometimes expressed in theistic terms, but it need not be. Its essence is the sense of being a part of the whole of life and the adoption of a cosmic as opposed to a universal humanistic (Stage 6) perspective (Kohlberg and Ryncarz 1990, p. 192).

So Kohlberg joins the growing number of psychologists (including Jung, Maslow, and Weick) who recognize the spiritual dimension that develops strongly in middle adulthood.

Summary and Conclusions

This exploration of both theories of midlife transitions and research on persons in midlife transition has resulted in certain common insights:

1. Some psychologists (Jung, Brewi and Brennan, Studzinski) would agree that in midlife characteristics and concerns emerge that are the opposite of the characteristics and concerns of the first half of life.
   a) men become more concerned about relationships and less concerned about achievement, while many women, especially homemakers, become more concerned about achievement and less concerned about relationships;
   b) in the first half of life both men and women are more concerned about outer matters (work, family, success, conformity), whereas in the second half of life men and women are more concerned about inner meaning.
   c) whereas in the first half of life the questions are on what is right or *how* to act, in the second half the questions raised are *why* to be moral and *why* live? (Kohlberg).

2. In middle adulthood many adults come to the realization of the limitation of being human—being finite, mortal, and imperfect.

3. Recently models of adult development have included transcendence or the spiritual dimension as well as social responsibility, moving adults away from narrow concerns for self to concerns for social justice and the interdependence of all humankind (Maas, Weick).

4. Despite the fact that studies of middle adults, beginning with Levinson (1978) and going on through the research in the 1980s, ignored the spiritual dimension, the evidence both from recent and older theories of adult development as well as from some empirical research points to the possibility that middle adults—both men and women—are both capable and yearning for growth in the spiritual dimension of their lives. Pastoral counselors should be aware that persons in this period of life, whether they voice it or not, may well be yearning for a deepening of their spiritual dimension. However, because men and women face this era with different early experiences, there must be awareness that women need to develop their sense of self (and perhaps biblical feminism can help), while men need to develop their relational side and sense of social responsibility.

References

Alexander, C. N., and Langer, E. J. eds. 1990. *Higher Stages of Human Development.* New York: Oxford University Press.

Baruch, G., Barnett, R., and Rivers, C. 1983. *Lifeprints: New Patterns of Love and Work for Today's Women.* New York: McGraw Hill.

Baruch, G., and Brooks-Gunn, J. 1984. *Women in Midlife.* New York: Plenum Press.

Bellah, R. N.; Madsen, R.; Sullivan, W. M.; Swidler, A.; Tipton, S. M. 1985. *Habits of the Heart: Individualism and Commitment in American Life.* Berkeley: University of California Press.

Brewi, J. 1988. *Celebrate Midlife: Jungian Archetypes and Mid-life Spirituality.* New York: Crossroad.

——, and Brennan, A. 1982. *Mid-life: Psychological and Spiritual Perspectives.* New York: Crossroad.

Capps, D. 1985. Pastoral Counseling for Middle Adults: A Levinsonian Perspective. In Wicks, Parsons, and Capps, *Clinical Handbook of Pastoral Counseling,* pp. 213–44.

Conn, J. W. 1985. Spirituality and Personal Maturity. In Wicks, Parsons, and Capps, *Clinical Handbook of Pastoral Counseling,* pp. 37–57. New York: Paulist Press.

Cripe, J. A. 1989. "Integrative Relationality: Themes of Transition in Women's Faith Development." *Journal of Women and Religion* 8:1–20.

Erikson, E. 1950. *Childhood and Society.* New York: W. W. Norton.

Fiske, M., and Chiriboga, D. A. 1990. *Change and Continuity in Adult Life.* San Francisco: Jossey-Bass.

Gilligan, C. 1982. *In a Different Voice: Psychological Theory and Women's Development.* Cambridge, Mass.: Harvard University Press.

Gould, R. L. 1978. *Transformation: Growth and Change in Adult Life.* New York: Simon and Schuster.

Hunter, S., and Sundel, M., eds. 1989. *Midlife Myths: Issues, Findings and Practice Implications.* Newbury Park, Cal.: Sage Publications.

Jaques, E. 1965. "Death and the Mid-life Crisis." *International Journal of Psychoanalysis* 46:502–14.

Jung, C. G. 1933. *Modern Man in Search of a Soul.* New York: Harcourt Brace Jovanovich.

——. 1957/58. *The Undiscovered Self.* New York: New American Library.

——. 1961/1965. *Memories, Dreams, Reflections.* Translated by R. and C. Winston. New York: Vintage.

——. 1983. *The Essential Jung* (selections by A. Storr). Princeton: Princeton University Press.

Kohlberg, L. 1974. "Education, Moral Development and Faith." *Journal of Moral Education* 4:5–16.

——. 1981. *Essays on Moral Development: The Philosophy of Moral Development.* Vol. 1. San Francisco: Harper & Row.

——, and Powers, C. 1981. "Moral Development, Religious Thinking and the Question of a Seventh Stage." In Kohlberg. *Essays on Moral Development,* pp. 311–72.

——, and Ryncarz, R. 1990. "Beyond Justice Reasoning: Moral Development and Consideration of a Seventh Stage." In Alexander and Langer. *Higher Stages of Human Development,* pp. 191–207.

Levinson, D. J. 1990. "A Theory of Life Structure Development in Adulthood. In Alexander and Langer, *Higher Stages of Human Development,* pp. 35–53.

Levinson, D.; Darrow, C.; Klein, E.; Levinson, M.; and McKee, B. 1978. *The Seasons of a Man's Life.* New York: Knopf.

Maas, H. S. 1989. "Social Responsibility in Middle Age: Prospects and Preconditions." In Hunter and Sundel, *Midlife Myths: Issues, Findings and Practice Implications,* pp. 253–71.

Maslow, A. H. 1970. *Religions, Values and Peak-Experiences.* New York: Viking Press.

Neugarten, B. L. 1968. *Middle Age and Aging.* Chicago: University of Chicago Press.

——. 1979. "Time, Age and Life Cycle." *American Journal of Psychiatry* 135:887–94.

Neumann, R. 1969. *Depth Psychology and a New Ethic.* Translated by E. Rolfe. New York: Harper & Row.

Roberts, P., and Newton, P. M. 1987. "Levinsonian Studies of Women's Adult Development." *Psychology and Aging* 2:154–67.

Souvaine, E., Lahey, L. L., and Kegan, R. 1990. "Life After Formal Operations: Implications for a Psychology of the Self. In Alexander and Langer, *Higher Stages of Human Development.*

Studzinski, R. 1985. *Spiritual Direction and Midlife Development.* Chicago: Loyola University Press.

Weick, A. 1989. "Patterns of Change and Processes of Power in Adulthood." In Hunter and Sundel, *Midlife Myths: Issues, Findings, and Practice Implications,* pp. 235–52.

Wicks, R. J., Parsons, R. D., and Capps, D. E., eds. 1985. *Clinical Handbook of Pastoral Counseling.* New York: Paulist Press.

Paul R. Giblin

12. Marital Conflict and Marital Spirituality

This chapter proposes that marital conflict of the repetitive and non-productive sort and marital spirituality are the direct inverse of each other. That is, the dynamics of conflicting couples' feelings, thoughts, and behaviors bear a remarkable resemblance to, yet are the direct opposite of a marital spirituality. If this hypothesis is demonstrated and accepted, then marital spirituality, like other "spiritualities" (e.g., twelve-step programs), could serve as a powerful intervention moving couples from destructive conflict to the presence of trust, open communication, and acknowledgment of differences.

The term *spirituality* is increasingly evident in various domains—popular publications, twelve-step programs, academic and professional training programs. Its meaning is flexible and often differs according to context. An initial discussion of its anthropological, experiential, non-dogmatic use as a *marital spirituality* is warranted.

An incarnational theology views God as source of all reality, before and beside us in our daily efforts to love, to make responsible decisions, to identify what we most deeply want, to make meaning of and seek direction in our lives. Human beings are hearers of the word, inherently open to and hungry for God's self-communication. God is encountered on both the inward journey, while listening for the "still small voice," and the outward journey, in the context of relationship. For marital partners the outer journey is the encountering of God in each other. The journey is neither quick nor easy. Marital partners inevitably engage their own as well as their partner's "dark side," "sin," "shadow side," "sore points," and "woundedness." Marital conflict presents partners with a significant opportunity to reexamine beliefs and behaviors about self and other. It also provides partners with a unique locus for encountering God. "Where the action in a person's life is, God is most present and active" (Hart 1989).

The term *marital spirituality* is thus intended to refer to more than prayer, church activity, and/or religious exercises. It is intended to encompass the many ways that marital partners continually struggle to communicate, accept, forgive, celebrate and give meaning to their joys and sufferings. It is the same anthropological understanding found in both Schneiders and Brocollo:

> Spirituality is the experience of consciously striving to integrate one's life in terms not of isolation and self-absorption but of self transcendence toward the ultimate value one perceives (Schneiders 1989). Spirituality is how I cope with life . . . the attitudes and behaviors towards self, other, God and the world (Brocollo 1990).

Marriage Today

What is the contemporary cultural context for marriage? What are the reciprocal influences between culture and marriage? While a comprehensive response to these questions is beyond the scope of this essay, a brief examination of four points is necessary.

First, the cultural context is clearly that of change. A decade ago Jonas Salk (1981) characterized the times as a critical moment in history and human evolution. He argued that the values, attitudes, and behaviors that brought us to the current time (EPOCH A: competition, independence, power, win/lose philosophies, short-range cost/benefits analyses) are not adaptive for future times (EPOCH B: where survival needs will demand collaboration, interdependence, consensus, win/win attitudes and behaviors, long-range perspectives). Salk's optimistic belief is that the EPOCH B values and behaviors will prevail. Whether we agree with his predictions or not, change is a major element of our social context. Changing roles for men and women, high divorce rates, greater mobility and decreasing contact with extended family, decreasing involvement with organized religion and neighborhood are well-documented examples of our shifting cultural landscape (Bellah 1985; Greeley 1989; Helgesen 1990; Wallerstein and Blakeslee 1989). The augmentation of Epoch B values and behaviors would both support family life and mitigate those factors that have undermined marriage.

Second, the traditional systems of extended family, church, and neighborhood were primary buffers to deal with change. They offered in ritual, story, and symbol a sense of meaning and direction in life. Rituals provided a sense of identity, continuity, and healing, particularly in the context of transition. Contrary to the findings of a recent New York Times/CBS New poll (1990), which indicated that 80 percent of family members eat dinner together on week nights, family rituals appear to be a diminishing resource for many people today (see Imber-Black 1988 and Giblin for discussions of the necessity of healthy family rituals).

Third, contemporary culture is described as addictive, out of touch with its deeper needs and wants, resorting instead to substances, habits, and/or other forms of denial and escape (May 1988; Schaef 1987). Faced with the dual challenges of accepting our finiteness/humanity and responding to the call to creativity/divinity, we live in considerable fear and denial (Becker 1973). Preoccupation with careerism, materialism, constant change, and innovation serve to mask our deeper questions, disappointment, and experience of the "poverty of affluence" (Wachtel 1983). It is not surprising then that the spiritual/psychological questions *What do you ask/want?* and *How do we make meaning of our struggles?* are at the very heart of pastoral marital therapy.

Finally, the sources of marital conflict are numerous at multiple systems levels. As mentioned above, the origins may be at macro systems levels, including work, political, social, economic influences on marriage. Stress associated with finances, career, household responsibilities, and with management of individual, couple, and parental time provides fertile ground for conflict (Curran 1985). At the micro level, partners themselves have unrealistic expectations, lack marital vision or goals, lack essential coping skills, and are undifferentiated from family of origin.

Marital Conflict

While couples conflict for a host of reasons, the elements of their conflict—their feelings, thoughts, and behaviors—tend to be predictable and have common patterns. Like any system, these elements tend to be interrelated and interdependent. That is, feelings are influenced by interpretations, assumptions, and predictions, which influence behavior, communications, interactions, which in turn influence feelings and thoughts. Elements overlap within and between partners resulting in a lack of clarity about beginnings and ends; for example, one partner hears criticism when the other was seeking information. Each partner brings to the interaction his or her own feelings and images from previous interactions.

Most marital therapies describe conflict in terms of a specific element: unrealistic expectations (Sager 1976), faulty attributions (Epstein 1982), the power of negative thinking (Beck 1988), "imago transference" (Hendrix 1988), anger management (Mace 1982, 1983), and absence of marital vision/goals and relational skills (Stuart 1980). In contrast, Feldman (1979, 1982, in press) has sought to integrate psychodynamic, behavioral, and systems approaches in developing his model of individual, marital, family assessment and intervention. Feldman's "integrative multi-level model" works with both intrapsychic (feelings and thoughts) and interpersonal (communications, skills, behavioral interactions) origins and reinforcers of problems. Lazarus (1981) and Nichols (1988) provide related comprehensive models.

AFFECTIVE ELEMENTS

A cluster of feelings, usually beginning with anger, characterizes marital conflict. Conflicted feelings of anger, shame, guilt, sadness are experienced as "the enemy" and are defended against, often by splitting them off from the self and projecting them onto one's partner: "He is the bad one"; "She is the angry one." The partners may feel defensive, protective, out of awareness, reactive, or drained of energy.

Mace (1983) clearly illustrates the development of marital conflict. As partners move beyond high idealism and infatuation they experience the need to deal with important differences and concomitant disappointment and frustration. Differences between partners become threatening to one or both as they experience themselves as powerless, not listened to, and unable to articulate their wants. A resultant sense of fragmentation and low self-esteem leads to reactive anger. Mace defines anger as the "first outpost of the defense system of the ego," indicating impending threat or displeasure.

Feldman (1979) examines the more unconscious dynamics of "nonproductive marital conflict." He, like Mace, indicates that conflict is directed toward reducing marital intimacy. That is, where love draws partners together, anger/conflict guarantees greater autonomy. Based on both research and clinical practice, Feldman identifies five types of intimacy anxiety: fear of merger and loss of self; fear of exposure, inadequacy, inferiority; fear of being attacked; fear of one's aggressive, destructive impulses; and fear of abandonment and loss of the other. Thus, beneath a strong, angry stance, partners have touched deeper fears, wishes, anxieties, and/or threats to the ego and sense of self.

Chronic marital conflict generally stems from unresolved family-of-origin issues, that is, "debits," "undifferentiation," "childhood wounds/imago transference." Essential psychological tasks of childhood necessary for healthy adult functioning and especially the capacity for intimacy sometimes fail to be completed within the family of origin. As adults, partners marry persons of similar levels of differentiation or undifferentiation. Mate selection is powerfully and unconsciously influenced by efforts to rework those unresolved issues; we tend to be attracted to and marry partners that replicate the positive and, in particular, the negative traits of our primary caretakers. In cases of chronic marital conflict partners remain excessively dependent upon and need to control the partner in order to maintain a wounded and fragile sense of self. The old trauma is used to sustain a defensive equilibrium or homeostatic balance between and within spouses.[1]

COGNITIVE ELEMENTS

What happens to the thinking processes of couples with considerable martial conflict? Along with unintentional and unconscious defending against painful and threatening feelings, partners' cognitions predictably narrow and distort. Partners selectively perceive the negative in the other and the good in the self, highlighting differences between self and other, attributing blame and ill motivation to the other. Partners' "automatic thoughts" or "internal communications" are typically characterized by cognitive distortions that Beck (1988) has listed as tunnel vision, selective perception, overgeneralization, polarized thinking, magnification, personalization, mind reading, and a tyranny of "shoulds." Such distortions result in all-encompassing negative expectations and beliefs about self, other, marriage, change, and perhaps therapy (Epstein 1982; Sager 1980).

Partners' views of reality, time, and the other narrow and distort. Time-past and time-present fuse as, with remarkable swiftness, partners retrieve past grievances and add these to present interactions. Images of self and other are fashioned and clung to tenaciously. Data that might qualify, challenge, or expand these perceptions tend to be missed.[2]

BEHAVIORAL/INTERPERSONAL ELEMENTS

Partners' inner worlds of conflicted emotions and thoughts play out in the interpersonal arena of communications, efforts to solve problems, and interaction styles in typical patterns. Interactions are characterized by blaming, name-calling, put-downs, complaining and counter complaining, placating, or denial. Communications are characterized by less than adequate self-awareness, unwarranted certainty about what the other is saying, misunderstanding, failure to seek clarifications, withholding positives, high exchanges of negatives, and efforts to punish the other (Gottman 1976; Miller 1988).

Conflict resolution is more typically instinctual, that is, fight, flight, submit, or freeze (Heitler 1990) rather than face-to-face, collaborative problem solving. Conflict is viewed as win-lose, interests are mutually exclusive, and the need is to change the other. Problems are often unclearly defined; person and problem become indistinguishable. Anger and fighting, agreement and acknowledgment are also indistinguishable.[3]

Conflict Resolution: Psychological and Spiritual

The major task of this chapter is to describe and compare repetitive, nonproductive marital conflict and marital spirituality. Indeed it is often the painful context of seeing themselves conditioned by unproductive family patterns that gives life to questions of meaning and transcendence encompassed by a marital spirituality. The pastoral counselor is thus in a unique position by virtue of training in theology/spirituality and psychology to offer help at the level of finding meaning and purpose in the couple's struggle as well as help based on theories of human behavior. The pastoral counselor calls forth personal meaning and dignity and helps to restore self-esteem. The couple then learns to lower defenses, to enter into conflicted feelings, to view their lives from an expanded perspective, and to relate in a more loving, differentiated, and satisfying manner.

There are many spiritualities evident today, for example Ignatian, Buddhist, twelve-step, New Age, and so on. Common elements in all of these include God as central to and pervading life; progressive distancing from less free, less aware ways of being toward increased freedom; charity and love as primary values by which life is guided; importance given to living the present moment, with mindfulness, thankfulness, forgiveness; acceptance of suffering as part of life; transformation of suffering through love in relation to God.

The marital spirituality described here is identified as experiential and Christian. Such a spirituality flows from experience of marital and family life in dialogue with Christian tradition (Boyer 1988;

Leckey 1982; Hart and Hart 1983; Rossi 1990; Wright 1989). Such a spirituality holds much in common with less explicitly Christian spiritualities (Fields 1984; twelve-step programs).

AFFECT: FROM DEFENSIVENESS TO OPENNESS

Through such interventions as the genogram, letters to or visits with the extended family, inclusion of the family in marital therapy sessions, "Imago workup," dreams, and other insight techniques that lead each partner to understand present affect in relation to past and family of origin, the mystery of a couple's woundedness can be uncovered. The couple is enabled to acknowledge and understand the frustrated longings each partner brought into the marriage. They can be helped to lower defenses and befriend their feelings of anger, fear, and anxiety, to listen to and learn from each partner's feedback, especially criticism. Partners become more aware of and less reactive to their own feelings and increasingly willing to acknowledge the partner's feelings.[4]

Where marital conflict is characterized by defensiveness and protectiveness, marital spirituality calls partners to openness, acceptance of one's brokenness, and vulnerability. In psychological terms Becker (1973) describes the challenge of recognizing and moving beyond denial to embrace the fears associated with both limitations/finitude and hunger for the divine/infinite. In scriptural terms partners are called to enter into the "darkness," bringing to light all that is concealed and in need of healing. Marital partners become "light bearers bringing light to all that is hidden and illuminating within us the dark corners that we'd rather not poke around in" (Leckey 1982).

One starting point of marital spirituality is the knowledge and acceptance of one's own and one's partner's "brokenness," "woundedness," "sore points," "shadow"—inherent elements of the human condition. In twelve-step programs the first step includes acknowledgment of one's powerlessness and the unmanageability of one's life. In the Ignatian exercises the first week emphasizes human sinfulness or, more important, the human need for God.

A marital spirituality calls partners *not* simply to release their anger, "be not afraid," or "not to worry." The call is to lower one's defenses, enter into the painful hurt, anger, disappointment, and communicate these feelings to both one's partner and God. Self disclosure, attentive listening, mutual sharing of vulnerabilities become spiritual moments. Doing this first with God, perhaps in prayer or in journaling, may facilitate doing the same with one's partner. Mystic

Frank Laubach (1937) relates his listening to God: "The talking you do to me is essential. . . . Talk a great deal to me. Let others talk a great deal to you, appreciate everything fine they say and neglecting their mistakes."

Mistakes made and learned from become primary stepping stones on the marital and family spiritual journey (Rossi 1990). Marital conflict provides a singular opportunity to facilitate self and partner healing. As partners learn to acknowledge each other's painful emotions without becoming reactive, and respond to each other's deeper needs and wants, which surface only in marital conflict, they facilitate both partners' healing (Hendrix 1988). For Christians the acceptance of darkness, brokenness, and woundedness is aided by the knowledge and experience of God's unconditional acceptance.

COGNITION: FROM CERTAINTY TO TENTATIVENESS

Cognitive dimensions of marital therapy encourage partners to move firmly held perceptions, assumptions, and interpretations into more tentative status, awaiting more extensive data gathering as well as examination of their cognitive distortions. Couples learn to modify unrealistic expectations and to challenge irrational myths and beliefs, especially regarding anger, conflict, and the ideal mate/marriage. Partners learn to block "automatic thoughts," put-downs of both self and partner, "exits," and fantasies that carry the self out of the relationship and its related painful emotionality. More positive "self-talk" and images of self and other are substituted. The cognitive approach underlines the power of expectations, beliefs, predictions, perceptions, and images as source of healing as well as dysfunction.

Where marital conflict is characterized by egocentric, limited perspectives, which focus on the "little picture," and tenacious believing in the certainty or truth of one's perceptions, marital spirituality calls partners into viewing "the bigger picture," seeing self, other, suffering, and conflict through God's eyes. Successful marital therapy helps partners grasp this broader perspective, a context perhaps influenced by several generations of hurt in respective families of origin or by ethnic differences. Marital spirituality expands the picture further. *Who is my partner in God's eyes?* becomes a daily lived question. The Hoblitzelles (in Fields 1984, p. 39) speak to the cognitive/behavioral dimensions of marital spirituality suggesting that partners

> acknowledge that you have a sense of karmic destiny. Respect the divine longing in one another. Accept the relationship as a central part of your spiritual path. Look at difficul-

ties as a training. Have faith in the process of growth and change in your partner as well as yourself. Keep before you the vision of your partner's true self—especially when it is lost to view.

Stuart, Worthington, and Hendrix all conceptualize marital therapy as necessarily beginning with a positive image of marriage and one's partner. A partner's relationship with God can clearly inform this vision.

Cognitive behaviors that follow from a marital spirituality include: 1) forgiving and accepting self and other. Laubach's observation is particularly pertinent for couples in conflict: "This conscious, incessant submission to God has proved extremely difficult. Yet I must start over now and succeed. This philosophy that we can begin all over instantly at any moment is proving of great help" (Laubach 1937, p. 23); 2) embracing images of self and other as seen by God, that is, "putting on the eyes of Jesus" counters the more natural tendency to focus narrowly and negatively; 3) interrupting marital conflict to ask not only what each partner really wants at this moment —the answer to which is most often out of their awareness—but asking further what God wants, expanding the context of inquiry; 4) accepting that "the truth" is less likely a sole possession than a lived reality created between partners in open, honest, hopeful exchange and accepting also that "the truth" as in righteousness or "who is right" is far less important than the person and relationship involved. With repeated practice the cognitive behaviors of openness, acceptance, forgiveness, and hope can become a way of life. Spirituality calls partners to increased self-knowledge and responsibility for sharing and responding to each other's needs.

BEHAVIOR: FROM REVENGE TO FORGIVENESS

From an open, accepting perspective partners learn to exchange behaviors in a more mutually satisfying manner, to communicate more skillfully, and to resolve their conflicts effectively. These positive changes are born of increased self-awareness and willingness to take responsibility for one's wants, needs, feelings, thoughts, and behaviors. Change comes from increased willingness and ability to encourage one's partner to self-disclose, to seek clarification when in doubt, and to attend to the positives in the other.

Partners learn to maintain separateness from each other's anger and criticism, to resist being entangled by the other's projections/anger/criticism, and to distinguish between agreement and acknowledgment. Partners become more sensitive to the need for time and space to resolve difficult issues and more willing to provide for each other's wants and needs. Partners learn that different people see the same event differently, and that acceptance of differences is the beginning of conflict resolution. With the knowledge that they were loved first by God, partners move to a "change first" stance, willing to commit to relationship change independent of the partner's reciprocity, free from the if-then contingency typical of marital conflict. Therapeutic interventions designed to promote these behavioral changes often include tracking of behavioral "pleasers and displeasers," establishing "caring days," using the "powergram" (Stuart 1980), communication and conflict resolution exercises (Miller 1988), role play, role reversal, anger containment (Hendrix 1988), and self-instructional training (Meichenbaum 1985).

Where marital conflict emphasizes opposing interests and competition, spirituality emphasizes mutuality of needs and cooperation. Paradoxically, the losing of self is also the finding of self, and seeking to meet the partner's needs is essential to meeting one's own needs. Where conflict emphasizes egocentrism and defensiveness, spirituality emphasizes softened egos, interdependence, and vulnerability. To strike back and return wound for wound is natural; to respond by withdrawal, submission, or freezing is instinctual (Heitler 1990). To pause for face-to-face cooperation and collaboration is both human and divine. Rollo May indicates that "real freedom is the ability to pause between stimulus and response and in that pause choose" (in Miller 1988). Spirituality, like marital therapy, is about freedom and generating pauses.

Behaviors that flow from a marital spirituality include the repeated practices of forgiveness, acceptance, and thanksgiving. Partners need to pray for each other's growth, confidence, recognition of gifts, and decision-making. The good that partners elevate is the good they find. The ambiguity, ambivalence, confusion, and mystery they surely encounter become either stumbling blocks or "spiritual training grounds," depending on their perspective. Wright (1989) provides the helpful observation that while prayer is a central element to a marital/family spirituality, "if sitting still is not something that you or your family do well, there is another way to grasp the mystery. The key is giving thanks. . . . Acquiring the spirit of gratitude serves to heighten our awareness of God's gift, of the is-ness of things" (p. 194). Marital spirituality moves partners into the depth and breadth of each other and the broader world, the "is-ness of things," as opposed to the self-fashioned and limited reality generated in conflict.

Marital spirituality creates a healthy triangle, with God as the third person of the relationship. God is gift, grace to both the individuals and the marriage. One's relationship to God informs one's relationship to spouse, and one's relationship to spouse informs one's relationship to God in the love, thanksgiving, communications, exchanges, and forgiveness experienced with each other. Relationship with the transcendent gives vision to the marriage, transforming an egocentric perspective, informing decision-making, facilitating reconciliation, and liberating desire and the freedom to choose.

Marital conflict presents partners with danger and potential. Partners can enter into the pain, hurt, anxiety, and disappointment, befriending these difficult emotions instead of defending against them. Partners can transform their thinking, opening themselves to a broader understanding of self and other. Partners can listen to each other's complaints, criticisms, and hurts, hearing them not only as request for change and healing, but as a recognition of the need for relationship with God. As partners recognize their need for not only the other, but for community and for God, then each will help the other to grow and in so doing facilitate his or her own healing. It is particularly in relation to the transcendent that partners develop the counter-cultural attitudes and behaviors of a marital spirituality. Table 1 presents a comparison of the attitudes and behaviors characterizing marital conflict with those characterizing marital spirituality.

IMAGING MARITAL SPIRITUALITY

What is the value of an image? Behaviorist Arnold Lazarus (1981) indicates that before we can change a behavior we first need an image of what the change looks like. Research by Andrew Greeley (1980) points to a direct relationship between religious imagery and marital satisfaction. How then might religious or spiritual imagery be employed in the service of the cognitive component of marital therapy? While a thorough answer to this question is beyond the scope of this chapter, a brief sampling of images is offered.

Leckey (1982, 1987) provides a series of helpful images. *Journey* and *pilgrim and pilgrimage* describe the progressive, "already and not yet" dimensions of journey both inward and outward. Partners are *light bearers,* bringing light to all that is hidden, illuminating the

Table 1
A Comparison of Marital Conflict and Marital Spirituality

CONFLICT	SPIRITUALITY
Fear, anxiety, defensiveness	Openness, humility, acceptance
Reactivity, energy drain	Vulnerability, weakness
Certainty, data closure	Freedom, goal-directed activity
Conflict as burden, negative	Tentativeness, humility, learning
Suffering as failure	Conflict as growth opportunity
Judgment, past remembered	Suffering transformed to intimacy
Take for granted	Forgiveness, live present moment
Blaming, complaining	Thanksgiving, attitude of gratitude
Positioning, competing	Responsibility
Exclusive thinking/differences	Cooperation, mutuality
Rehearsing	Inclusive thinking/similarities
I-we inclusiveness	Attentiveness, listening
Hopelessness/negativity	Much bigger world
	Hope, trust

well-defended, hidden "shadows" we would rather deny. Partners are *icons*, seeing in and through each other "God's abiding love that is richer beyond all imagination." Partners are *friends* or *spiritual friends* with whom one's spirit is attached and entrusted without fear or hiding.

PASTORAL APPLICATIONS

How do pastoral counselors encourage and facilitate a couple's development of a marital spirituality, clinically and/or preventively? The following are brief suggestions concerning the role of silence and solitude; scripture study; community; prayer, journal writing, meditation; spiritual direction; and bibliotherapy.

SILENCE AND SOLITUDE

Creating both time and space is essential in order to listen for the still, small voice within, for the God who is at our center. "One of the greatest favors partners can do for each other is to guard and provide silence and solitude for each other (Leckey 1982, quoting Rainer Maria Rilke)." Boyer (1988) provides excellent discussion of the importance of marital/family space concerns.

SCRIPTURE STUDY

Parish liturgy is an essential place for encouraging couples to befriend the scriptures. A dialogue homily that involves sharing of experiences of living the word is a strong support for marital spirituality. Reflections on what is personally attractive and/or problematic in the reading, and its theological and social message, can foster a deeper integration.

COMMUNITY

It is difficult if not impossible for a couple to maintain spiritual growth without the support of other couples and individuals. A couple's prayer group, marriage enrichment group, or base Christian community becomes church, the place to break open the scriptures, to know and be known in deep ways, to discern gifts and vocations. It is in community that social action and justice dimensions generally surface; it is also where partners learn to move away from the cultural addictions that bind deeper needs and desires (Leckey 1982; May 1988).

PRAYER, JOURNAL WRITING, MEDITATION

Taking time for prayer and meditation are obvious elements of marital spirituality. Journal writing is a common spiritual exercise. The "Ten and Ten" of Marriage Encounter—ten minutes writing then ten minutes sharing reflections—is a powerful exercise. Journal writing particularly in the context of marital conflict can provide a cooling-off moment, a time to pause and consider what is really desired in the situation, a time to expand perspective.

SPIRITUAL DIRECTION

As interest in spirituality continues to surge, and as programs training spiritual directors continue to develop, hopefully new attention will focus on marital spirituality and the couple as "directee." Perhaps such direction will occur in the context of group, lay movements such as Christian Family Movement (CFM) and parish base communities.

BIBLIOTHERAPY

Spiritual reading can be a powerful adjunct to marital therapy and enrichment. Reading and shared discussion within and between couples generates growth and learning. In addition to the references already mentioned, the following are excellent resources: Donnelly (1979), Fields (1984), Garland and Garland (1986), Whitehead and Whitehead (1984, 1989).

Notes

1. See Bowen 1978, Hendrix 1988, and Scarf 1987 for excellent descriptions of these dynamics.
2. Beck 1988, Epstein 1982, and Sager 1980 are excellent resources describing the cognitive dynamics of marital conflict.
3. Excellent resources that describe the behavioral and interpersonal dynamics of marital conflict include Fisher and Ury 1981, Gottman, et al. 1976, Heitler 1990, Miller 1988, 1989, and Stuart 1980.
4. Feldman 1982, Hendrix 1988, McGoldrick and Gerson 1985 are excellent resources clarifying this approach to marital therapy.

References

Beck, A. 1988. *Love is Never Enough.* New York: Harper & Row.
Becker, E. 1973. *Denial of Death.* New York: The Free Press.
Bellah, R., et al. 1985. *Habits of the Heart.* New York: Harper & Row.
Bowen, M. 1978. *Family Therapy in Clinical Practice.* New York: Aronson.
Boyer, E. 1988. *Finding God at Home.* New York: Harper & Row.
Brocollo, G. 1990. *Vital Spiritualities: Naming the Holy in Your Life.* Notre Dame, Ind.: Ave Maria Press.
Curran, D. 1985. *Stress and the Healthy Family.* San Francisco: Harper & Row.
Donnelly, D. 1979. *Learning to Forgive.* Nashville: Abingdon.
Epstein, N. 1982. "Cognitive Therapy with Couples." *American Journal of Family Therapy* 10, 1: 5–16.
Feldman, L. 1979. "Marital Conflict and Marital Intimacy: An Integrative Psychodynamic-Behavioral-Systemic Model." *Family Process* 18 (March): 69–78.
——. 1982. "Dysfunctional Marital Conflict: An Integrative Interpersonal-Intrapsychic Model." *Journal of Marital and Family Therapy*, 8: 417–27.

——. 1992. *Integrating Individual and Family Therapy.* New York: Brunner/Mazel.

Fields, R., et al. 1984. *Chop Wood Carry Water.* Los Angeles: J. P. Tarcher.

Fisher, R., and Ury, W. 1981. *Getting to Yes.* New York: Penguin Books.

Garland, D., and Garland, D. 1986. *Beyond Companionship: Christians in Marriage.* Philadelphia: Westminster.

Giblin, P. November, 1991. "Family rituals". *PACE* 21: 70–73.

Gottman, J., et al. 1976. *A Couple's Guide to Communication.* Champaign, Ill.: Research Press.

Greeley, A. 1980. *The Young Catholic Family.* Chicago: Thomas More Press.

——. 1989. *Religious Change in America.* Cambridge, Mass.: Harvard University Press.

Hart, K., and Hart, T. 1983. *The First Two Years of Marriage.* New York: Paulist Press.

Hart, T. 1989. "Counseling's Spiritual Dimension: Nine Guiding Principles," *Journal of Pastoral Care* 43, 2 (Summer): 111–18.

Heitler, S. 1990. *From Conflict to Resolution.* New York: W. W. Norton.

Helgesen, S. 1990. *The Female Advantage: Women's Ways of Leadership.* New York: Doubleday.

Hendrix, H. 1988. *Getting the Love You Want: A Guide for Couples.* New York: Harper & Row.

Imber-Black, E., Roberts, J., and Whiting, R. 1988. *Rituals in Families and Family Therapy.* New York: W. W. Norton.

Laubach, F. 1937. *Letters by a Modern Mystic.* Westwood, N.J.: Revell.

Lazarus, A. 1981. *The Practice of Multimodal Therapy.* New York: McGraw Hill.

Leckey, D. 1982. *The Ordinary Way: A Family Spirituality.* New York: Crossroad.

——. 1987. *Laity Stirring the Church.* Philadelphia: Fortress Press.

Mace, D. 1982. *Love and Anger in Marriage.* Grand Rapids: Zondervan.

——. 1983. "Training Families to Deal Creatively with Conflict." In *Prevention in Family Services: Approaches to Family Wellness* edited by D. Mace. Beverly Hills: Sage Publications.

May, G. 1988. *Addiction and Grace.* New York: Harper & Row.

Meichenbaum, D. 1985. *Stress Inoculation Training.* New York: Pergamon Press.

Miller, S., et al. 1988. *Connecting with Self and Others.* Littleton, Col.: Interpersonal Communication Programs.
——. 1989. *Connecting Skills Workbook.* Littleton, Col.: Interpersonal Communication Programs, 1989.
New York Times/CBS December 12, 1990. "Even in the Frenzy of the 90's Dinner Time is for the Family."
Nichols, W. 1988. *Marital Therapy.* New York: Guilford Press.
Roberts, W. 1988. *Marriage: Sacrament of Hope and Challenge.* Cincinnati: St. Anthony Messenger Press.
Rossi, A. 1990. *Can I Make A Difference: Christian Family Life Today.* New York: Paulist Press.
Sager, C. 1976. *Marital Contracts and Couple Therapy.* New York: Brunner/Mazel.
Salk, J., and Salk, J. 1981. *World Population and Human Values.* New York: Harper & Row.
Scarf, M. 1987. *Intimate Partners: Patterns in Love and Marriage.* New York: Ballantine Books.
Schaef, A. 1987. *When Society Becomes An Addict.* San Francisco: Harper & Row.
Schneiders, S. 1989. "Spirituality in the Academy." *Theological Studies* 50: 676–97.
Stuart, R. 1980. *Helping Couples Change.* New York: Guilford Press.
Teyber, E. 1989. *Interpersonal Process in Psychotherapy.* Pacific Grove, Cal.: Brooks/Cole.
Wachtel, P. 1983. *The Poverty of Affluence: A Psychological Portrait of the American Way of Life.* New York: The Free Press.
Wallerstein, J., and Blakeslee, S. 1989. *Second Chances.* New York: Ticknor and Fields.
Whitehead, E., and Whitehead, J. 1984. *Marrying Well: Stages on the Journey of Christian Marriage.* New York: Doubleday.
——. 1989. *A Sense of Sexuality: Christian Love and Intimacy.* New York: Doubleday.
Wright, W. 1989. *Sacred Dwelling: A Spirituality of Family Life.* New York: Crossroad.

For Further Reading

Eisler, R. 1987. *The Blade and the Chalice.* New York: Harper & Row.
McGoldrick, M., and Gerson, R. 1985. *Genograms in Family Assessment.* New York: W. W. Norton.
Worthington, E. 1989. *Marriage Counseling.* Downers Grove, Ill.: InterVarsity Press.

David Blackwelder

13. Single Parents: In Need of Pastoral Support

The situation of the single parent offers a unique challenge and opportunity for the parish pastor, pastoral care-giver, and pastoral counselor. For generations pastors have offered care and counseling to parents following the death or divorce of a spouse. Due to the spiraling rate of divorce in America, the reality of the divorced single parent has become a major focus for pastoral care and counseling ministry.

According to the 1980 U.S. Census Report, the current divorce rate in this country is at the 50 percent point, double the rate in 1960. In 1980 12.2 million children lived with a single parent, one in five children in America. The Bureau predicts that after 1990 over 50 percent of the children born in this country will live some portion of their childhood with a single parent (Garfinkel, p. 166).

This chapter will address the phenomenon of single parenting, offer a pastoral counseling model for working with the single parent, and suggest a number of practical resources in understanding the process and ministering to the single parent in our society.

Even though the primary target audience for this presentation is the parish pastor, pastoral care-giver, and pastoral counselor, much of the material presented will be of interest and relevance to individuals directly involved in the single parent experience (especially in the rebuilding phase).[1]

Single Parent Dynamics, Circumstances and Complexities

For the pastoral care-giver and pastoral counselor to respond appropriately to the single parent, it is vital to understand the complexity of the single-parent phenomenon and context. The origin of the single-parent status is varied. Most typical are: 1) the death of the spouse (lengthy illness, sudden and unexpected death, suicide, or accident). Naturally, initial pastoral care is responsive to the unique circumstances of the death and initial shock period of the single parent, children, and extended family; 2) a mutually agreeable divorce and child custody arrangement. Even though this is not a common reality, when it is there are often fewer hysterical overtones to the initial negotiations and settling-in experiences; 3) A highly emotional and polarized fight over a divorce, division of property, and child custody. In such situations, the mediator role of the pastor is of foremost importance; 4) never-married single parents. Typically here the pastoral relationship is established in religious services such as baptism, circumcision, or education, or at a financial, personal, or family crisis point for the single parent.

The many varieties of custody arrangements for the children of divorce affect the emotional status of the single parent and the pastoral approach of choice. *Mutual or joint custody*—the shared responsibility/custody of children by former spouses—has increased since the 1970s. The reasoning behind such arrangements ranges from a defensive "I won't give up by baby" to adult attempts to parent the children mutually. There are glowing reports of spectacular success in such joint custody (see Blau 1990), where through behavior modification former spouses "act adult for the sake of the children" and cooperate in mutual parenting. As ideal as such successes may seem, it is my clinical experience that true mutual or joint custodies are short-lived in their effectiveness, and that one spouse eventually becomes the custodial parent.

Another custody arrangement is *single custody by the mother with visitation rights for the former husband.* This remains the most common custody arrangement in the United States today. However, *single custody by the father with visitation rights of the former wife,* virtually unheard of twenty years ago, is growing significantly in this country due to modernization of divorce and custody laws in most states. From current literature on this subject, there is a marked similarity in the contextual dynamics for the single custodial parent, both male and female.

Certain divorce circumstances merit custodial care of the children of a divorce being allocated to a *family or state-appointed guardian.* Such arrangements often cause both parents to experience the noncustodial parent reactions of loss and grief.

The unique characteristics of the varying custodial arrangements are often the source of complicated and heated dynamics between former spouses and the extended families of the involved children. The pastoral counselor needs to be aware of such implications, especially in the early stages of divorce adjustment when the system of custody, care, parental input, and responsibility is being molded.

There are a number of common realities, complexities, and dynamics present for the custodial parent which are of interest and impact for the pastoral care-giver.

The single-parent reality demands many role changes. Most notable is the sole responsibility (real or perceived) for the child/children. The instinctive yet unrealistic need to be mother and father for the children is especially heavy for some single parents.

Grief is the universal and overriding reality for the single parent and children of divorce or parental death. The loss of coparenting, the loss of the person of the spouse, the loss of couple identity—these are but a few of the significant losses leading to the phenomenon of grief and mourning.

The complexity of responsibilities thrust upon a single parent are often overwhelming. Despite financial assistance (sometimes withheld by the noncustodial parent) and part-time assistance with the care of the children, the single parent often experiences alone the total responsibility for self, children, family, and home.

Frequently the single mother needs to work outside the home for financial support for herself and children. This necessitates child-care arrangements and time away from the children, often a significant time, energy, and emotional drain on the single parent. Current literature is quite mixed in the evaluation of the effect of such situations on the overall welfare of the children of single parents.

It is generally accepted that parenting is difficult under the most ideal circumstances of a two-parent family, economic stability, health, and so on. Parenting in the single-parent circumstance is even more difficult. Most studies of single-parent families indicate that grief exacerbates both children and single-parent frustrations, fears, and acting out, making parenting and family relations more difficult (Simenauer 1982, p. 299). According to Simenauer's research, the majority of single parents named their greatest asset and pleasure as their children—and the greatest source of difficulty as their children! Such paradoxical feelings and perceptions toward the children is a common complexity for the journey of the single parent.

Nichols (1988, p. 241) states that 85 percent of divorces are not mutually agreeable; therefore there is a large probability that the single custodial parent may feel victimized in the role of single parent. Victimization is an unfortunate yet common denominator for female single parents, and a phenomenon of significant import for the pastoral counselor.

Counseling and therapy seem like unreasonable and unrealistic luxuries for many single parents. With the pressures and responsibilities of single living, working outside the home, child care, financial stresses, continual conflict with the ex-spouse, and complex single-parent responsibilities, the single parent may instinctively enter a survival mode of living. In such a situation he or she is tempted to avoid counseling investment. (This is especially true for the welfare single mother.)

Guilt feelings are often present for the single parent despite the realities of the particular situation. The assertive spouse often experiences guilt after seeing the reality of divorce for himself or herself, for the ex-spouse, and for the children. The single parent may struggle with guilt over failure of the marriage, over failure to reconcile, or over the abnormality perceived in the single-parent phenomenon.

"Games" are common to the single-parent divorce situation, due to the very adversarial nature of the process. Conscious and unconscious games are often played by parents and children, with the inherent win-loose results wreaking havoc on all.

Morawitz (1984, pp. 13–22) suggests several dilemmas and pitfalls of the single-parent situation that merit the consideration of the pastoral counselor: 1) A child is seen as the embodiment of the absent parent. 2) A parent "marries" the child. Weiss (1979) (p. 66–96) claims that research shows that *most* single parents replace the absent spouse with a relationship with one of their children (pp. 66–96). 3) A child is seen as an overwhelming burden. 4) Perspective is lost in the struggle for survival. 5) Guilt impedes effective functioning. 6) Reentry into the social scene is experienced as a return to adolescence. 7) The single parent becomes excessively dependent on the family of origin. Morawitz suggests that the counselor be alert to these familiar pitfalls in developing therapeutic strategies and relationships with single-parent families.

Obviously, no listing of common dynamics is complete. Neither can it cover all unique situations. The above represent some of the most typical contextual realities for the single parent having custody of the child or children.

Theological Implications

There are numerous theological realities that directly impact the single parent, the context of the single-parent family, and the counseling relationship in these situations. As is often the case, theology is a rich resource for the pastoral counselor, for the pastoral counseling process, and potentially for the single parent involved. I will address some of the most basic relevant areas of theological implication, with several references to the Christian point of view in which I live and function. However, it should be noted that most of the following theological principles are found in Judaism and several other non-Christian world religions as well as in Christianity. If the pastoral counselor or client orientates to other theological systems, these other systems should form the basis for theological reference and resource.

Love

A theological grounding in love is extremely relevant to the single-parent situation. Eric Fromm's *The Art of Loving* contains principles that have direct bearing on the complicated love dynamics often present in the context of the single parent situation. The most fundamental love dynamic of divine love penetrating the human situation is present in virtually every pastoral counseling relationship, though often a stumbling block (or growing edge) for persons experiencing loss, grief, suffering, and the difficult rebuilding experiences of single parenthood. I have found that a most basic Christian textual reference to the eternal and unconditional love of God in the midst of difficult life situations is Paul's declaration in Romans 8:38–39; "For I am certain of this: neither death nor life . . . nothing already in existence and nothing still to come . . . will be able to come between us and the love of God, known to us in Christ Jesus" (*NJB*).

Jesus' Great Commandment—You shall love your neighbor as yourself—is a profound and central truth for the counseling relationship and for persons experiencing brokenness, loss, and the need to restructure their lives and world. However, this most basic axiom often becomes a complicating factor for persons who misunderstand the commandment. In my pastoral ministry I have discovered many misinterpret the commandment as "You shall love God first, your neighbor second, and (if any love is left) love yourself."

This is an erroneous reading of Christ's words, which causes some to miss the validity and need for self-love. Fromm and others contend that the Great Commandment clearly speaks of the "three in one" phenomenon of reflective love. God's eternal and unconditional love is the base and source of love in which persons respond in faith and reflect that love to themselves and all who are their neighbors. Love is therefore seen as a continuum rather than a hierarchy of love steps with oneself on the bottom rung. Based solely on the scriptural truth of God as the source of Love, a clearer reading of the Great Commandment is "You shall love God ('faith') as the source of Love, and in reflection of that Divine love you are enabled also to love your neighbor ("even your enemy") as you love yourself."

Note that the key word is *as*. Christ did not say "before" or "instead of". When single parents learn such an understanding of love, many are able, sometimes for the first time, freely and fully to love themselves, rather than continuing in the familiar avoidance of self love, fearing selfishness. Fisher and others contend that self-love in the sense of the Great Commandment is essential in the grief and rebuilding process of the single parent journey. John Powell, clinical psychologist and theologian, writes:

> If a person does not love himself or herself there is not much that can make such a person happy. There will always be the inner struggle, the inner loneliness, the unavoidable sadness. It is likewise true that if someone does not love others, that person will not be loved by others and will be condemned to live in a small and lonely world. Finally, if someone goes through life without a love relationship with God, much of the meaning of life and the motivation for a life of love will be lost.

My pastoral experience is filled with persons (including single parents) who, when discovering this love truth, are enabled to receive divine love and self-love in a new and energizing way. This continuum of love reality not only penetrates the individual's life but opens new horizons of reflective love in relationships with the Divine and persons in their world. I am continually impressed by references in secular clinical literature of this love continuum in psychotherapy.

Forgiveness

Theologically and psychologically, forgiveness of God, self, and others is a central reality in the single-parent context as well as in the therapeutic change involved in healing and rebuilding. By no more coincidence, the continuum and reflective principal of love (above) is present and active in the miracle of forgiveness. One of Jesus' descriptions (not prescription) of forgiveness is "Forgive each other as readily as God forgave you" (Eph 4:32, *NJB*). One in a faith relationship with God experiences the eternal and unconditional forgiveness of the Divine, which may be reflected in Divine forgiveness for self and others.

In my pastoral experience with single parents I have witnessed the miracle of the continuum of reflective forgiveness as it has profoundly and personally touched individual lives and often those related to that individual. When an individual truly experiences the forgiveness of the Divine, he or she is often empowered to forgive self and even to forgive the other spouse or deceased spouse.

Secular clinical literature on the subject regularly notes the profound role of self-forgiveness and forgiveness ("letting go") of the other in the positive working through of grief and rebuilding after loss. Theologically we understand the central and unique source of such forgiveness as the Divine.

Suffering

Inherent in the single-parent phenomenon is the reality of suffering. Religious authors, philosophers, and secular theorists have struggled with the mystery of suffering for ages. In the scriptures and the current literature on the phenomenon of suffering in a psychological and psychosocial perspective, there is a common theme: Suffering can be endured; and in time, suffering may positively enhance one's life and character. Scripture is rich in its proclamation of hope in the midst of suffering, and in the potential of growth and faith through the suffering process. The Hebrew Scriptures' recurring message for the Jewish people of God's eternal presence and promise of victory echoes through the chronicles of suffering and lamentations of this band of God's people.

The Christian Scriptures are grounded in the victory of suffering as seen in and shown through God's own suffering and victory in his Son's atonement. Personal and careful reading of Christ's suffering journey can become a model for hope for individuals suffering in the present. St. Paul proclaims the wisdom of God through the suffering of Jesus, which so often seems like "foolishness" to humankind, and yet through the eyes of faithful experience does make sense and is the source of the believer's redemption and growth through suffering (1

Cor 1:18–25). John Powell (1984, chap. 8) magnificently describes what he terms "a Christian attitude . . . a healthy and profitable way of looking at suffering":

> Pain is the teacher, constantly suggesting a lesson whenever the pupil is ready to listen (Zen proverb). Certainly the most life-transforming insights of my own life have been connected with and have grown out of some experience of pain. Suffering always teaches us something and often invites us to change and grow; "When the pupil is ready, the teacher will appear." Meanwhile, be patient. Love the questions and live in trust. Someday I shall share all the answers and all my secrets with you. Over and above the smoke of our dreams and delusions stands the loving but lonely figure of Jesus. In back of him, casting a long shadow, is a tall cross. The cross to most of the people in our world is a stumbling block, a madness to be avoided. But to us who believe that there is in suffering the challenge of metanoia, the invitation to life transformation and personal growth, suffering is a valuable teacher. Thank God for pain. Jesus seems to be asking our generation, "Can you drink from the chalice of suffering with me? Can you trust me?" And then Jesus says softly, as his did two thousand years ago, "Whoever does not his carry his own cross and come after me cannot be my disciple!" (Luke 14:27).

Stewardship

The challenge and reality of stewardship is found in the theology of most world religions. The possibility of responsible and mature stewardship of the gift (even suffering) of life is endless. Despite the rarity of secular psychological theorists' use of this term, I find in most therapeutic modalities of growth the reality of the challenge of stewardship in life. To view the life of the single parent as a challenge of stewardship is often a most positive and helpful perspective.

Death and Resurrection

Physical and existential death is a central aspect of the single parent's journey. Resurrection, rebirth, and new life potentially play a central role in the process. Christianity and other theological perspectives contain personal assurances of existence beyond the human finality of earthly death. Such assurance is potentially of great comfort and meaning for the widow or widower following the death of a spouse; for example,

> I am the resurrection.
> Anyone who believes in me, even though that person dies, will live (Jn 11:25, *NJB*).

The death and resurrection experience is equally relevant to the single parent working through the death experience of divorce and the resurrection and new life potential of rebuilding as a single and free person.

There are many theological realities which are clearly applicable to the situation of the single parent. I believe that the most fundamental are love, forgiveness redemptive suffering, stewardship, and death and resurrection. I find it fascinating that the reality of each of these theological principles is widely respected and utilized in so-called secular and humanist schools of psychotherapy. The duality of love and forgiveness, the redemptive potential of suffering, the dynamic of death and resurrection, and responsible stewardship of life are frequent references in theoretical and clinical practice in the non-theological world. My contention in this matter is that the growth and change potential of these realities is evidence of the existential existence of such powers in the world and human life. Those of us with theological orientation name these realities and attribute the Source as the Divine. Named or not, attributed to God or not, the universal truth and power of these realities is abundantly clear in the transforming growth in persons' lives as they work through the challenges of single parenting.

Counseling and Therapy Approaches with Single Parents

There currently exist over two hundred modalities of counseling and psychotherapy, many of which have direct application for the contextual situation of the single parent. I would like to note briefly the most typically used models in this area of assisting persons in a single-parent life situation.

Grief Work

Grief work is central to the task of assisting individuals, couples, and families live through nature's healing process of mourning.

Though there are unique characteristics of "death grief" (physical death of the spouse) and "love grief" (divorce), the counseling process is remarkably similar in both. With the knowledge and understanding of the natural grief process, including the unique manifestations of grief in each individual situation, the counselor invites, encourages, and enables the griever to address his or her mourning in a safe and accepting atmosphere.

Nichols (1988) suggests that grief work permeates the entire single-parent phenomenon and is the central focus of therapy from initial shock to the stabilization of life, family, and life networks, that is, completion of the mourning process (pp. 244–46). It is interesting to note that Nichol's five divorce stages of grief (pp. 244–45) are the very same as Sanders's death grief steps: shock, awareness of loss, conservation and withdrawal, healing, and renewal (Sanders 1989, p. 46).

Osterweis (1984) suggests these skills as necessary for the caregiver in working with the bereaved: attentive listening; continuing relationship with the bereaved; empathy with the bereaved; personal coping (grief) skills; observation skills; appropriate referral resources; and knowledge of bereavement dynamics and patterns (in Nichols 1988, pp. 222–23).

Behavior Modification

There is an abundance of popular and practical models for living through death and divorce grief, and for creatively living through the post-grief stage. Such models appear in written form (e.g. Krantzler 1974), in seminars and workshops, through individual counselors and psychotherapists, and in popular magazines. Blau (1990) described such an upbeat, modern, "adult," and practical approach in an article that described the actions and lifestyle of participants (under the guidance of psychotherapists) who successfully worked through the post-divorce trauma by "acting adult" in their individual and family lives—including such activities as holiday and vacations spent with present spouse, children, step-children, former spouse's new family, and so forth. Such models often offer instant (but rigid) scripts for resolution of the single-parent dilemma, and they continue to receive glowing reports from participants and the press.

Leibermann suggested a "guided mourning" process in which mourners were directed to confront the deceased and say "goodbye" (in Sanders 1989, pp. 227–28), thereby enabling them to move beyond grief. Reports of instant success were widespread.

Growth and Developmental Approaches

The primary thrust of the growth or developmental model comes after the shock and settling in of the single-parent continuum. Among the theorists advocating this intentionally working through the stages from shock to establishment of a new life as a single parent are William Nichols and Bruce Fisher.

Virginia Satir (in Fisher 1987, p. 1) describes divorce as "metaphorical surgery," which affects all areas of one's life including deep emotional feelings of despair, disappointment, revenge, retaliation, hopelessness, and helplessness. She describes the post-shock period as analogous to "convalescence after surgery." The growth and developmental models address this process of recovery and healing.

Fisher (1987) describes fifteen "building blocks" during the restructuring period that follows divorce; Satir suggests that most are also true for widows and widowers as well. Fisher's first level contains areas of initial growth and development which I contend are essential in the grief/mourning process: denial, loneliness, guilt, rejection, grief, and anger. These stages are most typically addressed in the grief counseling described above.

Fisher continues his building-block metaphor with a four-tier pyramid of areas for cognitive and emotional evaluation and restructuring in the rebuilding process after death/divorce of a spouse (p. 4):

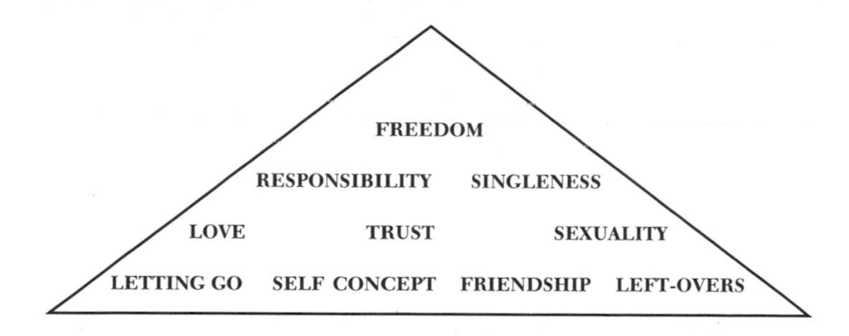

Fisher's contention is that following such an intentional journey ("mountain climb") through the stumbling blocks of grief and the building blocks (above), the formerly married person achieves "freedom," a state where one has the freedom to be oneself, to choose one's lifestyle, friends, and lovers. This is similar to Maslow's hierarchy of needs-development into self-actualization.

Fisher and others holding such a developmental-growth approach offer the assistance of self-help workbooks, seminars, and workshops teaching the model; support group discipline in following such a process; and encourage individual therapy using the model (s). Most theorists claim that such a process requires discipline as well as objective feedback and guidance. In other words, it is virtually mandatory for the single parent to obtain outside assistance in his or her journey.

Other examples of such evaluation and restructuring are Capps's restructuring goals in Wicks is *Clinical Handbook of Pastoral Counseling* (1985); Spencer's *Life Changes* (1990, pp. 169 ff.), with ten steps for living with change; Nichols's (1988) "tasks of the post-divorce stage (pp. 237–38), moving from the mourning stage to securing appropriate stabilization of one's social network; and Morawetz's *Brief Therapy with Single Parent Families* (1984, pp. 22–28), which describes the developmental process for the single parent *family* as moving from "aftermath" to "realignment" to "reestablishment" to "separation."

Nichols points to a study of Piercy and Sprenkle in summarizing the developmental model:

> The therapist's role during the postdivorce stage has been described as that of facilitating the growth of the divorced persons as autonomous individuals who form stable lifestyles, helping them to develop social relationships that are independent of the former love relationships, and, often, helping them to deal with issues pertaining to their children. To this should be added the task of helping the clients to complete the mourning process (in Nichols 1988, p. 246).

Family Systems Approach

By definition the family system model for the single-parent situation relates to the entire family system of the individual: the broken family, family of origin, extended family, and new single-parent family.

Anita Morawetz of the Ackerman Institute of New York has written a comprehensive clinical text examining the single-parent phenomenon and therapy for the single parent family entitled *Brief Ther-*

apy with Single Parent Families (1984). In her introduction she writes, "The absent parent is recognized as playing an important role in all families, and the way this absence has been handled usually provides the key to therapy (p. xviii). The systems approach is focused on enabling the family to structure a new family system around the reality of the missing parent. Morawetz sees the initial interview in the systems approach to the single-parent family as a microcosm of therapy in this specific situation. She offers a clear systems model with helpful clinical examples, as well as specific and detailed strategies and goals for therapy. I find the most helpful aspect of this approach in its reminder of the single-parent context and the complex systemic implications for individuals and family responses to the single-parent status (see Morawetz 1984, chap. 4).

Individual Counseling Approaches

The central figure in the single-parent situation is the individual widow, widower, or divorced spouse. Individual models of therapeutic intervention include the analytic, cognitive, rational-emotive, and insight approaches. Typically the individual single parent is the pivotal individual in the new family constellation. If willing to invest in an individual counseling or psychotherapy journey, he or she is most able to affect his or her own life and the lives of any children and extended family.

Traditional psychoanalytic approaches, including object relations, cognitive restructuring, reality, and insight therapy often provide the approach of choice in addressing the needs of the single parent. The underlying principle of these approaches is that *if* the individual in the central position as single parent grows in cognitive and emotional understanding of his or her situation and is guided in a restructuring of his or her new life without a spouse, that person will serve as the foundation for the growth, change, and development of the single-parent family.

Networking and Support Groups

Sanders (1989) reports on the 1984 research of Parks and Raphael, which clearly indicates that professional counseling is *not* needed by all grieving persons. This research shows that the most universally beneficial assistance to grieving persons is found in support groups and in networking with persons who have lived through similar circumstances.

My own professional experience with single parents supports this theory. Many individual single parents who are not inclined to participate in counseling or psychotherapy for financial, stigma, or inclination reasons respond well to the care and guidance of persons or support groups of individuals who have experienced similar grief and readjustment. Regionally and nationally there are many single-parent support groups, devoted to assisting persons at this point in life. Some of these groups offer significant personal support; others are thinly disguised social or dating clubs.

Pastoral Counseling Opportunities in Ministering to the Single Parent

Due to the unique characteristics of the situation of the single parent, there are a variety of opportunities for the parish pastor, pastoral care-giver, and pastoral counselor to be involved in serving the single parent prior to the crisis of death/divorce, during the loss crisis, and in the rebuilding period beyond grief. I propose a pastoral counseling model based on several presuppositions:

1) The parish and parish community is the base of this model. In the late 1960s the National Institute of Mental Health found that the local church was the primary source of assistance for persons seeking help in personal and family crisis. Howard Clinebell claims that 47 percent of persons seeking help first turn to the local congregation. Based on these statistics, and the opportunities present in the local community, the pastoral care team is in a central position to serve the needs of the single parent, the family, and extended family. The parish pastor is also in a unique position to serve as base coordinator for services to the single parent.

2) This model defines "parish community" in the manner of the Roman Catholic tradition and Lutheran Church in America (former) 1970 definition holding that the parish responsibility for a local congregation is to those persons holding membership in the congregation as well as persons not affiliated with the church living in the community of that local church. Therefore, the single parents of any parish community are potential clients for the involvement of pastoral care and counseling in that community.

3) This model is clearly growth and development centered, as opposed to a model viewing the single-parent phenomenon as dysfunctional or pathological. The growth potential for the single parent

and single-parent family through the crisis, grief, and rebuilding transition offers a significant opportunity for the pastoral counselor.

4) This is an integrated model, supporting the cooperation of pastoral, theological, psychological, and social service resources in response to the needs of the single parent. Significant emphasis is placed on the interdisciplinary integration and networking of resources for the benefit of the single parent, often guided by the parish pastor in collaboration with other helping persons in the community.

5) I suggest an "assertive" pastoral care approach in the parish based ministry with the single parent. There are many opportunities for a pastor assertively to offer himself or herself in service to the single parent at virtually every stage of the process of growth and development, even without a traditional invitation being extended. Beginning with such entry into the life or family of the single parent, the pastor becomes a known and trusted helper and referral resource.

6) This model is grounded in the assumption that virtually all single parents are assisted in their journey by caring others, but not necessarily by professional care-givers. The process of living through grief and rebuilding a new life as a single parent is one that demands a caring and objective helper in the journey. Often the pastor, pastoral care-giver, or pastoral counselor is in a position to offer such care to the single parent.

The Process

Typically the single parent experiences a process which begins with the crisis of loss (death or divorce of spouse), leads into a period of grieving, and concludes with a period of establishment of the new single life. Each individual process is unique in timing and sequence and particularly in regard to the depth of investment in the stewardship disciplines of the process.

Nichols (1988, pp. 237–38) suggests these tasks of the post-divorce stage, which I contend parallel those of the post-death stage for the widow or widower: completing the mourning process; achieving a stable identity as a single, formerly married person; achieving a new perspective on life and an appropriate orientation to the future; completing the restructuring of relationships with children, former spouse, and family; securing appropriate stabilization of a social network.

Morawetz suggests phases of development of the single-parent family, which I suggest apply to the individual single parent as well:

—Aftermath: period of movement, adjustment, emotion following death/divorce.
—Realignment: adjustment to physical, emotional, economic, and social change necessitated by death or divorce.
—Reestablishment of social life of the family, extended family, single parent dating.
—Separation: the parent and child/children achieve independence and interdependence (Morawetz 1984, pp. 22–28).

There are numerous configurations for the relationship of the single parent to the pastor, pastoral care-giver, and pastoral counselor. The most common is the single parent as individual, with separate consultations with the children and others in the family. Often individual pastoral care offered to the single parent leads to other pastoral care and counseling opportunities with the entire family or with others in the family network.

Couple or conjoint pastoral counseling is often the approach of choice, especially when the couple is at odds regarding custody, child welfare, or divorce responsibilities. The pastoral counselor may serve as mediator and negotiator in such situations.

Direct pastoral care assistance, most often during the crisis period, brings the pastor into contact with the single parent, children, and the extended family. Family pastoral counseling is often requested or required, especially when the single parent believes that the entire family is reacting to the situation in a manner which merits intercession. Morawetz and systems theorists hold that *every* single-parent situation merits a family approach.

Pre-marriage pastoral counseling for the single parent and future potential spouse brings the element of remarriage or new marriage into the single-parent dynamic, as well as a new person in the single-parent family system. Such counseling merits attention as a subject of its own.

Morawetz (1984) offers a helpful list of potential client assumptions in single-parent counseling. She suggests the counselor be aware of the single-parent client's perceiving the counselor as rescuer, judge, decision-maker, replacement for the absent spouse, or substitute parent for the single-parent child (p. 53).

Pastoral Entry Points into the Single-Parent Life Situation

I believe that in parish based pastoral counseling there are numerous "entry points" into the life and situation of the single parent, which give opportunities for the assertive pastor or pastoral counselor to serve the single parent throughout the entire process. Entry points are of critical importance in working with single parents due to the inherent resistance often found in such situations and the reluctance of some to be open to religious or "church" professional care.

Pre-Crisis Opportunities

At the onset of a spouse's terminal illness, the pastor has a natural entry point with pastoral care and counseling to individuals and family, which often sets the stage for future relationships. Families availing themselves of Hospice care come into direct pastoral care as a matter of course.

Marriage counseling with a couple experiencing marital difficulties is a frequent opening for continued pastoral counseling after separation is accomplished. I am currently involved in a four-year counseling relationship which began with marriage counseling and has continued through the process of divorce. It currently involves the single parent and children in the rebuilding process.

Divorce mediation is a clearly defined and demanding entry point for the pastoral counselor. Frankly, this is not one of my most cherished tasks, primarily due to the fact that most couples enter mediation because it is less costly than the fees of two attorneys. The process often reminds me of an autopsy. Nonetheless, mediation sometimes evolves into a pastoral counseling relationship with one or both of the spouses.

Pastoral involvement in a couple's life prior to the death or divorce crisis paves the way for pastoral care involvement when the single parent phenomenon develops. One of the recurring blessings of parish ministry for me has been the natural entry point into persons' lives during crisis, based on previous pastoral relationships in the family.

Crisis Opportunities

The pastor is directly involved in pastoral care with the family in time of death and often establishes an identity in this role which leads naturally into a continuing pastoral counseling relationship. Similarly, a pastor may pursue the single parent in conjunction with the crisis of divorce, which naturally leads to pastoral association in the periods following.

One of the most common entry points for the pastoral counselor is by way of the children of the single-parent family. Children act out their grief in crisis in ways that concern some parents, who then may turn for assistance to the pastoral care-giver.

Some pastoral counselors are requested to assist couples in legal and child custody mediation. Such mediation can lead to future involvement with the single parent.

Intense emotional need during the crisis of death or divorce may cause the single parent to seek out the pastor or pastoral counselor. Most referrals I have received as an agency-based pastoral counseling specialist have fallen into this category.

Finally, financial and practical need often bring parish community single parents to the pastor, who through physical assistance may open the door for pastoral counseling opportunities with the family.

Opportunities During the Post-Crisis Rebuilding Period

As a parish pastor for twenty-five years, I discovered that pastoral counseling opportunities with single parents often evolve from routine parish activities. Sermons, community speeches, special services, seminars, workshops at the church, and congregational newsletters provided the incentive for some single parents to seek out pastoral counseling. Exposure, identity, and assertive openness to assist persons in need offer entry points for the single parent to become involved with a pastoral counselor.

When a single parent expresses difficulty in the grieving process or in establishing a functional new life as a single, there is often a move to obtain help from a professional. The network within a congregation and parish community leads many to the church to find such help.

Pre-marriage counseling (for a second marriage after a death or divorce) or wedding arrangements bring the single parent and prospective new spouse into contact with the pastor or pastoral counselor. Such contact can lead to the consideration of the grief process and to a rebuilding discipline not previously attempted. However, it is my experience that single parents entering prematurely into another marriage relationship often are deaf to suggestions of such evaluation and rebuilding.

Children and parenting needs are major incentives for the single parent to seek out pastoral counseling. If children do not successfully work through their own grief (separate yet related to the parent grief) or find it difficult to adapt to the new single-parent family, they will often exhibit behavior that is troublesome to parents, school, and community. Such acting out of children is a major motivation for some single parents seeking counseling. In such cases the request for counseling is "for the child." Family systems theorists believe that most cases of such acting out reflect the triangulation of child, single parent, and absent parent.

Individual and family crises which take place during the period of reestablishment often bring the single parent to the pastoral counselor for the first time. A significant illness, financial loss, major acting out by a child, and other life crisis may bring enough imbalance to the family so that outside help is requested for the first time.

Chronic difficulty in financial matters relating to the ex-spouse and unresolved child custody issues can involve the pastoral counselor in mediation with the formerly married couple; they may also be entry points into further work with the single parent.

A desire for insight into the former marriage and breakup is the motivating entry point for a few single parents. I have worked with several formerly married couples who have met with me for the sole purpose of receiving feedback from each other, regarding their relationship, in the safe discipline of a therapy setting. Occasionally I find the single parent who enters the counseling relationship to gain insight, growth, and understanding.

It should be noted that clinical skill is required of the pastoral counselor in accurately identifying and addressing the real problem and need of the single parent, who may enter into the counseling relationship through any of the above routes. Pastoral counselors need continually to be aware of the challenge to delve below the surface in the single parent's presenting problem, as well as to offer the single parent the opportunity to pursue the counseling relationship beyond the entry area of concern and need.

The Model: Development and Evolution

I offer the following as a comprehensive pastoral counseling approach to working with the single parent. I am using the Bruce Fisher *Rebuilding* model in the section on rebuilding because this model addresses the most universal elements in this process.

Crisis Period

The parish pastor, parish based pastoral care-giver, and pastoral counselor have regular opportunities to become involved with potential single-parent situations prior to the actual crisis or at the point of crisis itself. Pastoral care with the terminally ill spouse, followed by care through the death and funeral is a natural entry point for the pastoral care-giver. Often prior to the divorce crisis, the pastoral counselor is called upon for marriage counseling or mediation with the couple. Such involvement may lead to a continuing pastoral counseling relationship with the single parent at the crisis point and following. Pastoral care skills are also required in a ministry of presence and support during the actual crisis period.

As mentioned previously, the children of the single parent are often the precipitating factor in bringing the single parent to the pastoral counselor for assistance. The pastoral counselor may be requested to intercede on behalf of the single parent with a school that has registered concern about the child's work or behavior.

In addition to the typical pastoral presence and support in crisis, it is often appropriate for the pastor to become involved in some practical areas of assistance with persons in love-shock and death-shock. Such personal and practical help often lays the groundwork for further pastoral relationship with the single parent. Typically, such urgent practical matters need to be addressed prior to entrance into a cognitive and emotional growth process. The care-giver often is in a position to assist the single parent in survival and coping skills and in accessing faith resources, which are of particular meaning to the person in crisis.

Period of Grief and Mourning

The most basic responsibility of the pastoral counselor in assisting the single parent in grief is in thoroughly understanding the psychodynamics of grief. With such an understanding the counselor attends with the griever in a posture that is INVITING . . . URGING . . . ENABLING. With the conviction that grief is God's (nature's) healing process following loss, the counselor participates with the griever in openness to the process in the specific grief development of the individual.

Often entry into the grief process is difficult for the single parent due to the magnitude of practical responsibilities inherent in the situation—living needs, child care, economic pressures, working outside the home (sometimes for the first time), and care for the children as a single parent. Such responsibilities, coupled with well-meaning admonitions such as "You need to carry on for the sake of the children," sometimes cause single parents to repress their grief and view their own mourning as a luxury—to be done only if time permits. The pastoral counselor is in a position to invite such a single parent into the normal grief process as a fundamental healing journey beneficial to all concerned.

Sanders (1989) notes that "frequent church attenders were more likely to respond with higher optimism and social desirability [after a death-shock or love-shock], *but* with more repression than average of the bereavement responses" (p. 140). This phenomenon challenges the pastoral counselor to offer the invitation into grief for the church member with special and diplomatic assertiveness.

In my parish pastoral care ministry as well as in my specialized pastoral counseling work, I have found Granger Westberg's book, *Good Grief*, of immense value to single parents in the grief period of transition (Westberg 1962). In his simple yet profound work Westberg clearly describes the normalcy of the grief process, including the anger so many find difficult to face. Over the years I have given over two hundred copies of *Good Grief* to grieving persons—and frequently those reading it have stated that it was most helpful, that it "made me feel normal!"

Bruce Fisher's basic foundational layer of the rebuilding blocks for the single parent includes denial, loneliness, guilt, rejection, anger, and grief (Fisher 1987, p. 4). I contend that this is clearly the grief and mourning layer of the process, and is indeed foundational prior to the single parent's consideration of the journey of rebuilding a new life.

It is important to note that grief counseling is emphasized in most theological curriculums as well as in clinical pastoral training for clergy and lay. Because of this, single parents have a wide selection of resources in addressing their grief with the assistance of parish pastors, pastoral care-givers, and specialized (lay and clergy) pastoral counselors.

Coordination of Care, Collaboration, and Referral

I purposely place the role of pastoral coordination, collaboration, and referral in the heart of this suggested model because of my conviction that this is the most pivotal pastoral skill in assisting the single parent through the journey from crisis to new life. The parish pastor is literally on the front lines of contact with the single parent in the congregational community and parish community at large. Because of this unique opportunity, the pastor is in a position to minister directly to the single parent and to follow the individual through the entire process, often including referral and consultation with other caregivers in the community network.

Marowetz (1984, pp. 326–34) offers an excellent overview of the pastoral counselor as intermediary and advocate for the single-parent family during the developmental process. The parish pastor and pastoral counselor need to be aware of and connected with referral resources in their community. With such knowledge—and the willingness to refer—the pastoral counselor is able to collaborate with or refer to specialized resources relevant to the single-parent situations. These include legal, social service, educational, medical, psychological, psychiatric, financial, vocational, religious, and support network resources.

Rebuilding

When the single parent successfully works through the unique and individualized grief experience, it is such a relief that some feel the journey is completed. The reality is that much more work is required before the single parent is able to function effectively and comfortably in his or her new life and world. Inviting single parents into a rebuilding process requires significant finesse on the part of the pastoral counselor. Entrance into a rebuilding stage is often facilitated through involvement in a church or community growth program. The parish pastor, pastoral care-giver, or pastoral counselor may suggest such a growth experience for the single parent. Frequently such involvement is combined with individual care and counseling.

Fisher (1987) offers a comprehensive overview of the vital issues to be addressed in the single parent's journey toward freedom and new life. It must be emphasized that there is no inference of sequence in Fisher's model, only the suggestion that such blocks need to be worked through on the road to healing and new life as a single parent, so they become building blocks rather than stumbling blocks.

Letting Go

The difficult experience of letting go is the subject of numerous current works in the addictive and compulsion fields of psychology. For the single parent to move ahead into a new single life, it is necessary for him or her to relinquish the past couple reality and truly own the single state. Prolonged grief (in death-shock) and victim-based connection with the ex-spouse (love-shock) impede the developmental process toward healing and independence. Letting go is universally necessary for the single parent in this process, yet it takes place in unique ways and sequence for each separate individual. My own personal experience of letting go was quite sudden and somewhat dramatic. As a single parent I found myself frantically dating with the blatant purpose to "find a wife and mother for my children." Fortunately, as I now understand, I was not successful. One evening after a dinner date I returned home, paid the sitter, and sat down to process the events of the evening. I discovered the *only* positive element of the evening was that I didn't have to fix dinner and do dishes! This realization hit me so profoundly that, with the caring guidance of the pastoral counselor with whom I was working in therapy at the time, I let go of my unrealistic search for wife and mother and entered a period of chosen single-parent existence. This experience remains a benchmark in my own journey. After that night I was free to live, work, play, parent, and function as a single and independent human being—free from my own compulsive hunt—to be single *or* to enter freely into a loving relationship with another woman.

Self-Image and Concept

Understanding and addressing one's self-image is crucial in the rebuilding experience of the single parent. The single parent has lived through significant role changes due to the new life brought on by death or divorce of a spouse. Such change naturally causes one to wonder, "Who am I?" Almost universally the single parent experiences some degree of "victimization" in the process, which clearly affects self-image. Even though there are testimonies of victimization for the single parent who was rejected by the former spouse, I find many examples of such victim self-concept among widows and widowers, and in the script of the assertive divorcing single parent. Fortunately, in current co-dependency literature there is a wealth of helpful material on victimization. Self-concept is a vital building block that merits the careful attention of the pastoral counselor in working with single parents.

Friendships

The loss of friends in the single-parent scenario is significant. Often in a death-loss single parents actually loses a good friend, often their best friend. Even in divorce the single parent loses a partner with whom they have shared some degree (even if dysfunctional) of friendship.

Some single parents describe the exodus of former "couple friends" after death or divorce occurs. Numerous reasons and causes are cited for the break, which often complicates the natural loneliness of the single parent. Fisher (1987) strongly urges the single parent to pursue *new* friendships as a single in a single world, not only as a gap-filler for loss, but as a tangible relationship step toward rebuilding a new and realistic single life (p. 113).

Leftover Issues

Fisher (1987) contends that all single parents have significant leftover issues, unique to each situation, from the previous marriage and life. These need to be honestly worked through so as not to become impediments to the new life of the individual. Such leftovers can trigger deep, lifelong scripts or issues that the single parent may never have addressed, further hindering the movement to freedom, independence, and new life.

My experience is that such work with a single parent demands a great deal of diagnostic and invitational finesse on the part of the counselor.

Love

The reality of love is complicated under ideal circumstances. The experience of love for the single parent is typically traumatized through death-shock or love-shock. That trauma must be respected and addressed in a loving and caring way, so that the single parent can be open to new, fresh, and unincumbered love.

Fisher emphasizes the vital need for healthy self-love in the rebuilding process (pp. 130 ff.), which I believe clearly stems from the reflective love of the Divine through us. For the single parent, reentry into the realm of love is a fragile experience, meriting careful and loving attention by the counselor.

Trust

Trust is often shattered for the single parent, the result of "being left" by a deceased or divorced spouse. The residual scars of rejection and real or perceived abuse undermine trust of self and others. In a healthy counseling relationship or in a new and adult relationship with a friend trust may be reestablished in the process of rebuilding.

Sexuality

Sexuality is one of the most fragile yet vital aspects of the rebuilding process for the single parent. Simenauer (1982) interviewed singles regarding their sexual attitudes and behavior in the first year following the death or divorce of their spouse. Typically sexuality was more of a pressing issue for the divorced than for widows or widowers. In the divorce scenario, sexual dysfunction often precedes actual separation and divorce, heightening the biological and psychological need for sexual activity and expression and affecting the self-image of the divorced single person as a sexual being. Many divorced single parents become victims of their own sexuality in the early stages of grief and rebuilding. A key to assisting creatively the single parent in the sexuality building block is in differentiating between sexual involvement and interpersonal intimacy. Carefully addressed, the reality of sexuality can become a positive building block for the single parent.

Simenauer devotes a significant section to the complex practical realities of sexual behavior and activity within the context of the single parent world.

Responsibility

Fisher (1987) appropriately describes the vital aspect of realistic adult responsibility in the restructuring of the single parent life. Ideally, the single parent assumes appropriate responsibility for his or her past, intentionally using realistic approaches to address those areas of the past which merit amendment. Hopefully the single parent turns then to the appropriate adult responsibility for his or her life as a single individual who happens to be in a responsible parenting position. Such a process is often lengthy and difficult, yet essential in the path toward freedom.

Singleness

By definition the single parent is indeed single. However, some single parents view themselves as victims who have had the single state thrust upon them without their permission. Singleness, no matter what the individual origin, can be experienced as independence, which is a marked experience of both freedom and responsibility. The key is in the single parent's acceptance of the single state as a chosen situation as well as a positive and desirable position in life.

Pastorally and clinically it is essential that the single parent enter and experience the single independent state prior to involvement in a new romantic relationship of interdependence potentially leading to another marriage.

Freedom

Fisher (1987) holds that the state of freedom resulting from careful development through each of the building blocks is the "top of the mountain climb" for the single parent. In such a state the single parent is indeed free to "be" and to chose in his or her new life. I find Fisher's ultimate state of freedom similar to Maslow's point of "self-actualization," where the individual has worked through the developmental stages of need-growth and has arrived at a state of congruency and actualization with himself or herself and the particular world situation he or she has chosen. However, I propose that there is even higher ground for the single parent to climb in the ongoing journey into the meaning of life.

Beyond Freedom: Depth-Existential Therapy

Following the counseling journey through grief to freedom, some few single parents accept the therapy invitation to continue in a "depth-existential" experience with the pastoral counselor. Such a journey (in the model of Rollo May, Irwin Yalom, and James Bugenthal) offers the single parent an unique opportunity for insight and growth in regard to the meaning of his or her own existence. Sanders (1989, p. 227) offers a brief comprehensive overview of this process. I find that the majority of clients with whom I have worked in depth-existential therapy have been single parents who have accepted the invitation to continue therapy in this mode, following the counseling from grief to freedom.

Miscellaneous Related Issues

Support Groups and Networking

Spencer (1990, chap. 12) offers a good overview of support systems for the single parent. Congregations and church agencies offer support groups for people who are single, widowed, or divorced.

Denominational programs such as the Roman Catholic program "New Life," offer both support groups and educational program for the particular circumstances of single parents. Church-related groups offer seminars, workshops, and programs geared for the specific needs of single parents. An excellent example is "Fresh Start" of Wayne, Pennsylvania (Church of the Savior, 651 N. Wayne Ave.), which offers a three-day seminar, carefully developed and theologically based, for singles; a support network and continuing education in congregations; and a transition/rebuilding model for single parents and their children. Pastoral counselors need to be aware of such resources in the community for potential referral of single parents. Counselors also need to be cautioned that some so-called single-parent programs are in fact thinly disguised social dating schemes.

Networking, or matching single parents with others who have previously gone through similar experiences, is one of the most beneficial referral practices for pastoral counselors. My own experience is that many single parents have been most helped by association with another person who has walked their path before. Networking training for single parents is an opportunity to prepare a bank of such persons in the church and community.

Single Mothers in Poverty and on Welfare

Garfinkel (1986, p. 1) states that in 1973 over half of all single mothers in America were below poverty income level or on AFDC welfare. There are a number of explanations for this phenomenon: lack of financial support from the ex-husband; lack of vocational skill training and experience during the mothering period at home; and discrepancy in male and female salaries in the work place. Garfinkel describes the economic plight of single mothers and their children on welfare. For the pastoral counselor the harsh reality of this is that many single mothers are so involved in survival that they do not have the "luxury" of the grief process or the privilege of disciplined rebuilding so essential for new life as a single parent. My own pastoral experience with poverty level single mothers was that they were willing to "use the system" (the pastor), but not to trust him or her or the "system." This made pastoral care and counseling for growth and development virtually impossible with single mothers on welfare.

In light of the almost overwhelming nature of this aspect of the single-parent phenomenon, I suggest two primary responses of the church and pastoral care-givers: 1) aggressive pastoral care in the parish community, seeking out poverty level single mothers, offering direct physical assistance, and praying that such an entry point of pastoral counseling might lead to some deeper assistance; and 2) support of the church's ministry of advocacy for single mothers and their children in poverty, especially on the local and state level. Garfinkel (1986) offers a helpful summary and recommendation section for community and government response to the economic plight of such single mothers.

Legal Concerns

The very nature of the situation of single parents involves the surviving spouse or divorced parent in numerous legal matters. The pastoral counselor is often asked to become involved in legal wills as well as divorce litigation; he or she needs to be prepared appropriately in this area.

My own pastoral and counseling experience has been that the most frequent potential for subpoena from the courts is in regard to testimony regarding divorce and child custody. In researching the twelve cases in which I have testified in divorce or custody situations, I discover that every one has ended in pastoral or clinical disaster! My experience, and that of several professional colleagues I interviewed on this subject, is that due to the harsh adversarial nature of such court involvement, sharp polarity develops, and after the court appearance the persons involved terminate relationship with the counselor as a result of his or her involvement in their legal fight.

Tressler Lutheran Services offers an optional form for couples entering counseling, which emphasizes the growth motive of counseling and requests new clients to waive the right of calling the counselor for legal testimony. Such a waiver might be legally challenged; however, it has served well in discouraging couples from considering legal testimony by their counselor. Because of my own experience, I strongly suggest that pastoral counselors avoid legal involvement in divorce cases.

The Single Parent Considering Marriage (Again)

One entry point for the pastor or pastoral counselor into the life of a single parent is at the point of request for clergy participation in a new marriage. If no disciplined grief/rebuilding work has been done by the single parent, there is a remote possibility that the pastoral invitation into counseling will be accepted. In such cases of premarital consultation for the single parent I always offer counseling, yet find that the acceptance rate is less than 10 percent.

It is widely agreed that a single parent considering remarriage is best served as truly single and independent prior to entering into the interdependence of a new marriage. Additionally, it is advisable for the single parent to have completed the grieving process and addressed the "old business" of the former marriage before embarking on a new marriage relationship. Most pastors realize, however, that in such cases the power of new love and hope often supersedes such rational and responsible actions. Nonetheless, it is my contention that a clear invitation and admonition to consider pre-marriage counseling is an opportunity and obligation of the clergy in such situations.

Subjectivity and Countertransference

The subjectivity of the pastoral counselor in working with single parents is of vital importance. As is always the case, the counselor's feelings and attitudes regarding marriage, death, divorce, singleness, single parenting, and remarriage may potentially enrich the counseling relationship with empathy and understanding, but they also endanger the process if countertransferential realities unconsciously affect the relationship. Both merit careful monitoring by the pastoral counselor in professional supervision.

In counseling with single parents, it is of vital importance that the counselor be fully aware of his or her thoughts, feelings, and opinions in these related areas often broached in the counseling experience with single parents. Often, if the counselor has actually experienced death or divorce of their spouse and has successfully worked through the process, such an experience may be a strong empathetic asset to the counseling relationship. Some contend that a divorced pastoral counselor is not "qualified" to do counseling with divorcing persons. My own experience (and that of a majority of professional colleagues) is that a pastoral counselor who has adequately worked through his or her own divorce is particularly suited for such work. The greatest potential danger of transference and countertransference in counseling with single parents is found in the counseling pairing of different sexes. Frequently the single parent client relates to the counselor of the opposite sex as a caring, accepting, and loving friend or parent figure. Properly handled, such transference can be an enriching part of the counseling growth. Occasionally the counselor becomes involved in a natural countertransferential response to the single parent. Unless skillfully handled this can lead to improper and unethical behavior with the single parent client. In such cases, immediate professional consultation and supervision is required to address the counseling relationship at such a crucial point.

Conclusion

The pastoral care-giver and pastoral counselor are in strategic positions in the community to offer practical assistance, pastoral care, pastoral counseling, and pastoral psychotherapy to the growing population of single parents in America today.

The grassroots location of the local congregation, the propensity of single parents to seek assistance from the church, the numerous potential entry points for pastoral counseling with the single parent, and the growing knowledge and skill of pastoral counselors in this area of care lend themselves to a major opportunity for broad-based pastoral care for this segment of our society.

Note

1. I lived as a single parent for several years in the early 1970s, experiencing this unique yet increasing status of life of which I write. I will make some personal references to my own journey throughout this chapter; I hope the reader will find them enriching rather than distracting. My primary awareness in preparing this chapter was the rediscovery of the universal dynamics of the single parent life, yet the absolutely unique characteristics of the journey for each of us walking this special path in life.

References

Blau, Melinda. 1990. "Divorce, Family Style: How to Make Splitting Up Easier on the Children." *New York* magazine, October 8.

Fisher, Bruce. 1987. *Rebuilding.* California: Impact.

Garfinkel, Irwin. 1986. *Single Mothers and Their Children.* Washington, D.C.: Urban Institute Press.

Krantzler, Mel. 1974. *Creative Divorce.* New York: New American Library.

Morawetz, Anita. 1984. *Brief Therapy with Single Parent Families.* New York: Brunner/Mazel.

Nichols, William. 1988. *Marital Therapy.* New York: Guilford Press.

Osterweis, Marian, et al., eds. 1984. *Bereavement: Reactions, Consequences, and Care.* Washington, D.C.: National Academy Press.

Powell, John. 1984. *The Christian Vision.* Allen, Tex.: Argus.

Sanders, Catherine. 1989. *Grief . . . The Mourning After.* New York: Wiley Interscience.

Simenauer, J. 1982. *Singles.* New York: Signet.
Spencer, Sabina. 1990. *Life Changes . . . Growing Through Personal Transition.* California: Impact.
Weiss, Robert. 1979. *Going It Alone: The Family Life and Social Situations of the Single Parent.* New York: Basic Books.
Westberg, Granger. 1962. *Good Grief.* Philadelphia: Fortress Press.
Wicks, R. J., Parsons, R., and Capps, D., eds. 1985. *Clinical Handbook of Pastoral Counseling.* New York: Paulist Press.

For Further Reading

Bridges, William. 1980. *Transitions.* Reading, Mass.: Addison-Wesley.
Gardner, R. 1979. *The Boys and Girls Book About Divorce.* New York: Aronson.
Gullo, S., and Church, C. 1988. *Loveshock: How to Recover From a Broken Heart and Love Again.* New York: Simon and Schuster.
Landgraf, John. 1982. *Creative Singlehood and Pastoral Care.* Philadelphia: Fortress Press.
Levenson, D. 1987. *The Season's of a Man's Life.* New York: Knopf.
Oates, Wayne. 1976. *Pastoral Care and Counseling in Grief and Separation.* Philadelphia: Fortress Press.
Peppler, Alice. 1982. *Single Again, This Time With Children.* Minneapolis: Augsburg.
Rice and Rice. 1986. *Living Through Divorce.* New York: Guilford.
Sheehy, G. 1976. *Passages: Predictable Passages of Adult Life.* New York: Dutton.
Vogel, Linda. 1975. *Helping a Child Understand Death.* Philadelphia: Fortress Press.

SECTION IV
THE CHALLENGES AND OPPORTUNITIES OF THE DE-VALUED AND ABUSED

The reality of a loving God, who created each and every person in a loving likeness, is for many not enough to sustain their own self-acceptance or self-love. The chapters within this section point to the many threats to self-love and self-worth. There are threats coming from within (e.g., dysfunctional guilt and depression) and threats from without (e.g., abuse and neglect). The need for the loving presence, the need for pastoral care, is never more evident than with those who suffer such abuse and such loss of self-love.

Carroll Saussy's essay, "Pastoral Care and Counseling and Issues of Self-Esteem" (Chapter 14), provides a look at the factors affecting self-esteem. Saussy's research and personal clinical experience support the notion that beneath a person's low self-esteem is a lack of faith in one's value and possibilities, a lack of faith in oneself. From this perspective, the author suggests that in ministering to those of limited self-love, pastoral counselors can help them articulate the ideology that shapes their world and rewrite their world-view in support of their own intrinsic value and beauty.

In Chapter 15, William Sneck provides an analysis of the toxic and facilitative forms of guilt often experienced by those whom we counsel. Sneck distinguishes between shame and guilt and notes that rather than simply attempting to reduce the shame and guilt our clients experience, pastoral counselors need to discern when such feelings are an effort of the psyche to stir the person toward "healthier," more ethical living. To this end Sneck offers the reader specific counseling guides for integrating the guilt experience within a life of growth toward true freedom.

When the absence of self-love and the presence of guilt and shame are maximized, one often experiences the darkest night of the soul—depression. Howard Stone provides an insightful look at depression (Chapter 16) and the need for a pastoral response. Through an extensive review of the literature, Stone provides a comprehensive look at the causes and course of this devastating condition. The clear identification of the ways in which depression affects feelings, thinking, physiology, and behavior provides those in pastoral care with a clear set of benchmarks for identifying its presence. Further, Stone suggests practical steps to take in ministering to those with mild and moderate depression.

Continuing the theme of the section (attack on self-love), Chapters 17, 18, and 19 address the destructive effects of abuse from without. Sharon Cheston characterizes childhood sexual abuse in Chapter 17 as an epidemic so devastating and destructive to human growth that it is imperative for pastoral counselors to respond with competence in faith and love. Cheston describes both the diagnostic presentation and symptomatology of childhood sexual abuse, as well as directives for treatment planning. Cheston makes it extremely clear that healing for victims of childhood sexual abuse requires long-term therapy wherein life assumptions, faith in a supreme being, meaning of life, and the role of evil are all targets of discussion and growth. Cheston provides a six-stage model of the healing process, a treatment model that aids the victim to forgive, to reconcile, and to recognize the grace in his or her life.

Marie Fortune and James Poling expand our discussion of attack from without in Chapter 18 by reviewing the massive personal and social suffering of victims of a variety of forms of sexual and domestic violence. The authors challenge each of us to consider the silence which has been historically characteristic of the church's response to such abuse. They call for a "courageous" and "assertive" response on the part of the church to abusers in its midst, noting that we must respond in the face of the reality that some among us exploit and damage others. To this end they provide six principles to guide the church in its response to abuse.

This sections ends with a look at a form of psycho-emotional abuse that is as destructive as the more dramatic forms of sexual and domestic violence, yet often goes unnoticed due to its subtlety. In Chapter 19 Eileen Gavin discusses the damaging effects of psycho-emotional abuse. Anything but trivial, psycho-emotional abuse is presented as the prototypical form of child maltreatment. In her presentation the author provides the reader with a clear, operational look at the various forms psycho-emotional abuse takes and suggests steps we need to take to prevent and treat such abuse.

Carroll Saussy

14. Pastoral Care and Counseling and Issues of Self-Esteem

Definition of the Problem

People who seek pastoral counseling are often struggling with a dysfunctional or dissatisfying relationship (in many cases with an abusive relationship). Beneath the relational issues the counselor generally uncovers a chronic problem with low self-esteem. Yet these same people who have a low opinion of themselves usually articulate faith in a loving God, who created and sustains the universe; belief in Jesus Christ, God-with-us, as the cosmic and personal redeemer; faith in the presence of the Holy Spirit in their lives; and assent to the claim that the faith community into which they have been received through baptism is the nurturing, graced body of Christ. They also hold the belief that human beings are made in the image of the holy God. At the same time they all too frequently see themselves as unworthy or unlovable people who do not deserve genuine, sustained happiness in life. One possible explanation for the paradox might be that conflicting images of God are at work in their psyches, and these cancel out the God of love.

Still other Christians claim that self-esteem is incompatible with Christianity, that Christians are first and foremost unworthy sinners —"not OK" in the eyes of God—whose task it is to humble themselves in submission before the throne of God. Sin is regarded as something to be punished, not a condition to be healed. In contrast, Rita Nakashima Brock (1988) calls sin "a sign of our brokenheartedness, of how damaged we are, not of how evil, willfully disobedient, and culpable we are" (p. 7). A theology of submission and obedience, which keeps God in "his" heaven and God's creatures in a constant state of repentance, fosters an overemphasis on one's private relationship with an angry, exacting Deity. A God who does not want human beings to enjoy profound self-acceptance and self-esteem is incompatible with a God of love, a God in love with the universe.

Several years of research on this issue led me to the suspicion that what some people call "faith in God" or "faith in Jesus Christ" might be an escape from faith in one's self. Many people believe there is a close relationship between faith in God and the capacity to cope with life, as well as between their religious faith and their self-esteem. Undoubtedly a pastor has often heard remarks such as those written on a self-esteem inventory which I distributed within a seminary community: "God has pulled me through difficult times"; "Self-esteem follows when one gives all problems to the Lord"; "You come to realize that even when times look hard, you can do all things through Christ"; "God can make everything all right." One wonders what the individuals were thinking and feeling and doing when God took over their lives in this way.

What many women and men call faith in God is an escape from establishing a foundational belief in their value and destiny and in their own innate capacity to respond to the challenges of life. Faith is too often used as a life preserver for people who are not sure they can really swim. Many TV evangelists have connected religious faith with material success, cures, and personal aggrandizement. Often people who fill the Christian churches talk about the connection between their religious faith and the experience of success or cures or special protection from illness or death. Far fewer speak of discovering the incarnate Deity in themselves, of finding themselves empowered to respond to their own problems.

My study of self-esteem moved from using a pencil and paper inventory with both women and men to more in-depth research with a volunteer group of twenty-one women. At the same time I concentrated on the remarkable writings of feminists exposing the damaging effects of patriarchal society on women's lives. The book *God Images and Self Esteem* (Saussy 1991) weaves the stories of the women in my study into an exploration of the development of self, the role of God images in one's self-concept, the dimensions of self-esteem, and concrete plans for enhancing self-understanding and self-esteem. When I was asked to contribute to this handbook, I planned to use one of the chapters from the book, which was then in the making. That plan changed as I worked through the manuscript reflecting on how an audience of women and men might best profit from my work. While their struggles surely may differ, both women and men are up against gender assumptions that play havoc in their personal development, weaken their faith in themselves, and it goes without saying, diminish their self-esteem. While women in patriarchy surely have a distinct set of challenges to face in order to affirm themselves as men's equals, many of the conclusions I drew about women apply to men as well.

Thesis

Religious faith in the goodness of life, most often expressed in terms of a loving Deity who creates and sustains the world, is only complete when it builds on personal faith in the intrinsic value and beauty of the believer, that is, *faith in self.* In other words, religious faith does not contribute to self-esteem unless it grows out of and along with faith in one's abilities, in one's innate worth, in one's capacity for intimacy, out of and along with faith in what has been called one's *true self* (Miller 1981, p. 32). When a person lives out of a true self, faith in Deity cannot be an escape from faith in self. Whereas when a person lives out of a *false self,* or an adapted self who acts according to other people's expectations, faith in Deity is easily an escape from faith in self. False self escapes into false deity. Religious faith that is built on faith in one's true self provides powerful motivation to join in the struggle to liberate anyone who is not free to enjoy such fullness of faith.

A sub-thesis is that women especially need more inclusive images of Deity than traditional religions have offered in order to appreciate fully the faith claim that women and men are profoundly holy, that as equals they image God.

Clarification of Terms

Faith

The word *faith* is used here to include both the act of believing and the content of that belief. In other words, faith is both a *process* through which a person understands, values, and responds to life, and *content* or truth claims, which are also in process. Faith is both a human experience and a transcending experience that is often called religious, but which is in fact profoundly human.

Human faith is belief in one's value and in the possibility of genuine relationship; it is the gift a child receives as a result of "good enough" parenting.[1] *Religious faith* is a gift or grace that empowers a person to believe that a transcending power or being creates and sustains the universe—that the Holy is with us. Faith is a response or surrender to the gift of both human and religious faith, and a life process that enacts the gift. Faith in the Holy results in a way of life in which one's beliefs inform or shape one's way of seeing, acting, and being in the world.

Erik Erikson (1963) roots the capacity for foundational trust and for religious faith in the earliest months of human life. The ability to trust in another and in oneself is the result of a satisfactory resolution to the *trust versus mistrust* core conflict central to the first two years of life. Erikson's stages of human development describe the emergence of new capacities at chronological ages or stages. The first capacity is the capacity to *trust:* to trust that a nurturing parent will continue to respond to the infant's needs and trust that the infant will continue both to express need and connect with her or his care-giver. The development of the capacity to trust results as much in a trust in oneself as a trust in one's parent(s). The faith process, then, begins at the beginning. James Fowler (1981) studies the progression of faith through stages, from an infant's primal trust in one's parents, self, and world through to the universal love of a person radically open to reality. Each stage represents a more mature, differentiated perspective in which people become increasingly aware of both their interconnectedness with all of life and a selfless concern for justice and love for all.

The content of one's faith includes both theological claims and psychological claims about human life and one's place in it. What is too often overlooked by theologians and psychologists is the central significance of a person's earliest self-understanding as well as the internalization of primitive God imagery to his or her faith in self, in others, and in Deity. This chapter places major emphasis on self-understanding and God imagery and their impact on self-esteem.

Self

The *self* is a concept which defines what is most personal and unique about an individual. The self includes the body, mind, and spirit; abilities and limitations; and repressed and remembered experiences both positive and negative—bodily experience, relational experience, cultural experience, religious experience. People are themselves, some combination of the true self and false self. The *true self* is the unique "experience of aliveness" (Winnicott 1987, p. 148) discovered at the deepest level of the human psyche; it hints at the realistic possibilities of who a person might become. The *false self* is either an idealized image of who one ought to become, which others have held up as one's agenda, or a negative image of the failure others have predicted one will become.

Self-Esteem

Self-esteem is a concept used to measure a person's thoughts and feelings about himself or herself. *Esteem* comes from *estimate*, and indeed people estimate or evaluate themselves repeatedly. They form opinions about their bodies, intellects, talents, behaviors, performances, and their capacity to develop and sustain intimate relationships. Much of this ongoing evaluation is automatic and unconscious.

Self-esteem is multilayered and complex. I find it useful to distinguish between the self-esteem with which an infant who has received good enough parenting springs into childhood and the self-esteem that grows out of the processes of socialization, namely between *foundational self-esteem* and *secondary self-esteem*. Foundational self-esteem is always based on the emerging *true self* or authentic expression of feelings, sensations, and needs. Secondary self-esteem builds on that foundation. However, when there is little foundational self-esteem—an "as-if personality" (Miller 1981, p. 12)—a defensive secondary self-esteem can be built on the sham foundation of the *false* or "as-if" *self*. Thus secondary self-esteem can be either authentic or counterfeit. When secondary self-esteem supports the true self it is genuine. When secondary self-esteem represents an adaptation to the demands of the false self, it is defensive or counterfeit.

Secondary self-esteem achieved through good relationships and the reworking of one's faulty self-understanding can be remedial. That is, weak foundational self-esteem can be shored up when an adult is helped through authentic, respectful relationship(s) to recover his or her lost child or true self. Recovery would include the validation of authentic feelings, sensations, and needs. The result of such confirmation can be *good enough true-self esteem*.

Dimensions of Self-Esteem

Self-esteem is a complex disposition that is related to at least six major experiences: 1) parental acceptance; 2) an ideology (an understanding of human life and one's place in it) which fosters self-esteem; 3) satisfying relationships; 4) competence; 5) passion for life; and 6) self-acceptance.

The first of these is clearly the most crucial, namely, parental acceptance, love, and esteem of the infant and child. The component most crucial to the effective pastoral care of women and men struggling with self-esteem issues is *ideology*, that is, the belief system out of which a person comes to understand and evaluate herself or himself. What follows is a brief discussion of the major experiences relevant to self-esteem. Because of its importance to the pastoral care and counseling of persons suffering from low self-esteem, ideology will be explored in greater detail after the other five experiences.

Parental Acceptance

Unconditional acceptance is demonstrated through physical and emotional availability and the *respect* the parent shows for the child's full range of feelings. *Respect* is perhaps the key word in conveying the kind of acceptance that I am describing. Acceptance which includes unqualified respect for the unique possibilities and budding personality of this child allows the child to develop its *true self*. The true self, elusive because it is always in the process of becoming, begins to emerge with the authentic expression of feelings, sensations, and needs, which later become the authentic expression of ideas and emotions. The primitive capacity to feel one's needs and communicate them is the earliest sense of self, one's "experience of aliveness." When the expressed need is accepted, the true self begins to unfold. When the expressed need is rejected, the true self is violated. The damaged true self is then protected and hidden by the *false self* with its defensive feelings and needs. If parents set the agenda for who or what the child is to become, insisting on certain feelings or behaviors and forbidding others, the *false self* defends the child from the parents' judgment and thus assures their acceptance. The false self accommodates to parental needs, losing touch with authentic wants and needs, and is rewarded for making the adaptation. The "as-if personality" silences the true self, keeping it in a state of noncommunication (Miller 1981, p. 12). Absolute acceptance of the child as the child discovers and expresses herself or himself results in what I call *good enough foundational self-esteem*. Without a healthy supply of it, the child suffers a deficiency which will play havoc with her or his self-evaluation. Low self-esteem will continue unless the person, through some form of therapeutic process or an extraordinarily respectful relationship, or perhaps through the experience of belonging within a faith community, comes to an understanding of the deficit and experiences radical acceptance and respect. Persons with good enough foundational self-esteem are like those William James (1961) called once born believers. They may go through life with a minimal amount of self-doubt or self-rejection. The twice born need to be re-created, some of them many times over, through genuine mutual relationship. People who did not receive adequate positive parenting have a hard time being convinced of their intrinsic worth.

Relationships

Self-esteem builds on the capacity to develop and sustain mutually satisfying relationships, without which one remains unknown and disconnected. The sense of significance essential to self-esteem comes only through relationships that are based on mutual respect and acceptance. Social expectations have made it difficult for both women and men to enjoy relationships in which they can develop and express their true selves.

Women have most often been seen as those who carry major responsibility for relationships within the family. In fact, patriarchy requires that women take major responsibility for children and home and family life. Women's capacity for intimacy and nurture and the structures men have put in place have resulted in the social expectation that women fill an assigned role, a role that is generally seen as less valuable than the role of their male counterparts and as more powerful than it is. Miriam Greenspan (1983) suggests that "without an adequate conception of how motherhood is shaped by the patriarchal rule of the father in the family, the extent of a mother's power over her children is both wildly overestimated and severely misunderstood" (p. 18). In other words, mother is not the all-powerful figure children see her to be but an oppressed woman held accountable for major social responsibilities that ought to be shared by parents who are co-equals in all aspects of family and social life. For husband, children, and doctor, executive women become wife, mother, nurse, and secretary. Women have learned to sacrifice their own wants and needs and possibilities to "better serve those they love." In the process women can so lose touch with their abilities that they no longer have a sense of what they want in life apart from fulfilling their roles as helper, wife, and mother.

Men too suffer from patriarchal expectations that limit their freedom to develop the side of themselves that society has called feminine. They are often less willing or able to express deep emotion; less inclined to be nurturing in adult relationships, especially with other men; less likely to allow themselves to be vulnerable in relationships. Daniel Levinson (1978) concluded from his extensive study of forty men that very few of them had close friendships apart from their spouses. For both men and women to enjoy good enough self-esteem they need open relationships in which they can discover and accept and express themselves freely about their thoughts, feelings, dreams, and fears.

Recent feminists writers have offered constructive insights into addictive or co-dependent relationships, helping people understand when relationships turn into self-defeating attachments (Schaef 1986, 1987; Beattie 1987). A co-dependent relationship is one in which an individual defines herself or himself primarily in terms of the other person. Co-dependent persons have little sense of meaning or value in their own life except that which comes through this relationship, around which they focus all of their energy. Without the relationship, co-dependent people are afraid they would have no sense of self. For women and men to come to faith in themselves, their relationships must include both a sense of *attachment* to and *separateness* from the other. That is, they must know that they live only in relationship to others, but not define themselves solely in terms of a particular relationship.

Competence

Competence is understood as an individual's experience of achievement and success in meeting personal and social goals and expectations. The sense of competence begins as soon as the child tries to work with the things and ideas that fill its world: from building blocks to spoons and forks; from the alphabet and numbers to sand castles and bicycles; from examinations to driver's licenses.

Children and adults need confidence in their ability to learn what needs to be learned in order to function competently in their world. The most well-loved child will struggle to maintain self-esteem if she or he cannot meet the normal expectations of teachers and other significant adults in life.

Children with learning disabilities, especially when the problem goes undiagnosed, suffer with feelings of inferiority and failure. Competence normally includes an ability to perform in the school's recreational and athletic programs, to experience one's body as coordinated and able. When children suffer from a physical disability, their self-esteem will be influenced by the way in which both peers and adults relate to them. The child may be perceived as a whole person with differing abilities than its classmates, for example. On the other hand, the child might be labeled handicapped or disabled and isolated from the temporarily able-bodied in the group. If society would recognize that this is a thoroughly relational world, those differently abled might be perceived as sister or brother, and the community made more effectively aware that it shares responsibility for the child's well-being.

Competence is intimately connected with the next component of good enough self-esteem: vocation or passion. It is often through the discovery of one's particular competencies that a person feels called or moved to pursue a particular goal or purpose.

Passion for Life

Passion for life is often related to a sense of vocation or purpose. Passion for life comes with discovering something worth knowing, worth doing, worth working toward. In studying the life structures of his research group of middle-aged men, Levinson calls this the "Dream" (Levinson 1978). However, the dreams he describes in the lives of the men he studied are primarily ambitions to reach a certain rung on the ladder of success, success measured in terms of financial reward or social prestige. My understanding of dream is akin to the concept of vocation or calling, perhaps more accurately described as a *passion,* something that mobilizes energy and enthusiasm and becomes a positive structure in one's life. Generally people do not feel good about themselves if they have not discovered a meaning or purpose that transcends their own wants and needs and personal satisfaction.

Such meaning or purpose takes different shape and form at different phases of a person's life. In other words, the focus of one's passion or vocation can evolve over a lifetime. Children begin dreaming about what they want to be and do when they grow up. Sometimes these dreams are realized and fill a life with direction and purpose. More often the dream or sense of call takes new directions as life progresses. Perhaps a sense of vocation or passion is more easily grasped in considering its opposite: meaninglessness and apathy. When nothing seems worth learning or doing or worrying about, a person bogs down in depression and loses any sense of self-worth. Life is experienced as a gigantic burden one faces with little fascination or reward. Helping a person move from apathy to engagement is no small task. The vocation or call may come through the power of respectful listening; it may be heard as one truly hears and responds to the pained voice of a person in need.

The component of secondary self-esteem which can be realized only when other components are present is self-acceptance. Self-acceptance is possible because a person has enjoyed respect within relationship. Such people have an understanding of their world and their place in it as competent, passionate persons. The concept of self-acceptance is close to the concept of self-esteem, yet distinguishable enough to warrant separate discussion.

Self-Acceptance

Self-acceptance is used here in a specific way. It refers to the acknowledgment of one's physical and psychological givens as well as one's heritage—one's body, mind, emotion, spirit, and all that comes with being this particular person within this particular family in this particular time and place. Self-acceptance requires a realistic perception of those physical and psychological givens, a difficult task because so few people perceive themselves as others perceive them.

The self-accepting person develops a trust in her or his inner experience, which requires a realistic understanding of the true self. That is, a person pays attention to what she or he is feeling, checks out intuitions and thoughts with friends she or he has come to trust, and acts out of her or his best insights. Acceptance is used here to underscore that each person must come to a practical, honest recognition and endorsement of his or her very real embodied givens. The demands of the false self, magnified by society's conventions, can make such radical self-acceptance extremely difficult.

All of the components or experiences that account for good enough self-esteem are interrelated. One's ideology or world-view, which begins at the very beginning and affects development throughout life, is centrally important to faith in self and self-esteem.

Ideology and Its Influence on Self-Esteem

An Infant's Ideology

Within the first few years of life an ideology or cosmology takes shape in the child's psyche that will result in the child feeling free to develop creatively her or his capacities, gifts, interests, *or* in the child's sensing an obligation to adapt to the needs and desires of its primary caretakers. More likely, the child will both appropriate the parents' world-view and the parents' hopes for the child's place in that world *and* at the same time find room in that cosmology for her or his unique contribution to "the scheme of things."

From the moment of birth an infant is compelled to connect with the most important person in the universe. Mother is eager for the same connection. While the relationship between two individuals is indeed underway, at birth the infant is unable to distinguish itself from its mother or primary care-giver. Only gradually does the infant come to a primal understanding of being separate from its all-important provider, the center of its universe. (After birth the father may play the role of center of the infant's universe. However, in our society the mother continues to take primary responsibility for the infant and later the child.) Thousands of small interactions will take place over hundreds of days before the infant comes to an elementary sense of itself as separate from this powerful sustainer.

To simplify what is in fact a complex, psychodynamic process, one might say that every exchange or encounter between mother and infant has both an objective and subjective side. The objective side is what takes place "out there" between mother and child. But the event that takes place on the outside is also experienced internally by both mother and child. The encounter may be perceived subjectively in markedly different ways. For example, a mother responds to her infant's need as she perceives it. Subjectively, her response is colored by whatever emotions she feels at the time that she cuddles, nurses, cleans, or dresses her infant. The infant's subjective perception of mother is also colored by the physical and emotional sensations the infant is experiencing on the inside. The infant's psyche is busily dealing with mother's gestures and words and tone of voice. Each of the interactions with mother is remembered as mostly rewarding or mostly frustrating, at times totally rewarding or totally frustrating. Some part of the infant takes in some part of mother. For example, the infant may have a felt need to be stroked and cuddled; the mother's warm, tender response is tucked away in the infant's memory bank: content, lovable me and comforting, tender mother. On another occasion the hungry infant is not satisfied by mother's breast or bottle and cries itself into a desperate rage: hungry, lonely me and cruel, rejecting mother. Since the infant is so critically dependent upon the good mother for survival, it protects itself from these negative memories by splitting them off from the good memories and repressing them or erasing them from consciousness. Splitting the infant's internal world into fragmented memories is a protective strategy which the infant unconsciously uses for survival. While both the infant's unmet need and the mother's negative response are repressed together, the infant carries a vague, unconscious memory that she or he is bad, for it is safer to consider oneself bad than to reject one's life source. Repressed experiences result in the infant's unconscious rejection of herself or himself: bad me. The British "object relations" school of thought calls these introjected perceptions of mother/other and self "internal objects." I choose to use the word *memory* instead of *object*.

Psychologists have used the word *mirroring* to describe the mother-child interaction in which the mother, through eye contact and absorbed presence to the infant, gives the child a sense of being seen, recognized, and understood. The baby seeks the mother's face in order to know who she or he is (Winnicott 1971). Whatever the mother is feeling inside is projected onto the child, and whatever the child sees on its mother's face is internalized. In other words, a delighted mother visibly reflects her delight in her presence to her baby; a brokenhearted, despairing mother reflects pain and desperation. Both mother and infant find themselves mirrored in the face of the other. The process is contaminated by the mother's emotions to the extent that the child is not allowed to find itself in the mother's face. Instead of a cluttered, self-absorbed face, in better circumstances the child might have found a transparent, child-focused face. Enormous power is in the hands of parents, and in the earliest months in the hands of the primary nurturer: "Our earliest relationships can steal our true selves or mirror them back to us" (Brock 1989, p. 50).

Respectful affirmation of the child in its vulnerable infancy is all-important to the child's ability to be its true self and experience foundational self-esteem. Otherwise the child senses that it must comply to mother's or father's blatant or subtle demands and pursue a false self. Through the mirroring process an ideology is in the process of formation, a world-view that informs the child as to what is expected of it, that gives the child a sense of its place in mother's and father's lives and in the world.

Ideology Beyond the Home

While the parents give a child a sense of the world and the child's place in it, there is a universe beyond the home where the child must learn to live. The family world-view needs to be tested, developed, integrated, and owned or replaced as the child comes to understand human life and society and how he or she fits in. Siblings and other relatives, friends, teachers, pastors—many people continue to contribute to one's self-understanding and values, which in turn shape self-esteem. Social institutions of every kind also contribute to ideology. Media, advertising, theater, school, church, the business world, all are constantly impinging upon the world-view of individuals with messages about who they are and should be, messages about both possibilities and limitations, messages about what is valuable, worth pursuing, necessary if they are to feel attractive.

In *God Images and Self Esteem* I include vignettes from in-depth interviews with twenty-one women. In preparation for the interview the women were given open-ended questions that provided a focus to the session. These questions helped the women get in touch with the ideology of their childhood as well as their current understanding of the world and their place in it (Saussy 1991).

A. Recall messages from parents, siblings, teachers, other significant adults, childhood and adolescent girlfriends and boyfriends; peer groups at various ages; close women and men friends; church, media, literature, health professionals; experience, study, reflection:

   1. What significant messages come up for you about who you "should" be and/or who you are? At which stage of your journey were those messages most influential?

   2. Are you conscious of conflicts you experienced between the ideology included in the messages you received and your capacity or desire to live it? How did you resolve the conflict?

B. When have you felt most alive, most engaged in life, most in touch with who you are and what you value?

C. What images of Deity and religious experience stand out for you: in your childhood, adolescence, young adult life, middle adult life? Are female images of Deity valuable to you?

The final question about God images proved to be of central importance to many of the women in the study and only deepened my conviction that more inclusive God imagery, namely female images of Deity, are conducive of greater faith in self and self-esteem for many women. However, before dealing with theological words and images, an exploration of the primitive God images of infancy is in order.

God Images and Ideology

Of central importance to faith in self and self-esteem is the place that primitive God images formed in the early months of life—as well as the theology and God language which dominate in institutional religion—play in the ideology out of which persons value or disvalue themselves.

In her ground-breaking work on the formation of God images Ana-Maria Rizzuto (1979) explains how early interaction with parents, which results in both positive and negative memories or representations of oneself and one's parents, provides the primal stuff that get worked into God representations or God *imagos.* These images may or may not be compatible with later ideas about God introduced by parents, religious educators, or theologians and artists who try to express in religious symbols and imagery their conceptions of the sacred in human life.

In the language of the object relations school of thought out of which Rizzuto works, children rely on memories (or internalized objects)—namely, internalized aspects of their parents and themselves —to help them function in their world. A memory of mother or father, stored along with memories of the child having been loved by the parent, sustains the child during the absence of the parent.

Sometimes concrete objects such as a blanket, a stuffed animal, a piece of clothing, are used as *transitional objects.* The objects help the child bridge the gap between inner perceptions and memories and outer reality, as well as between the private parent-child world and the world peopled by other family members and even strangers. The clutched blanket or toy is truly security-evoking. Strengthened by memories of caretakers and armed with a special symbol of powerful providers, the child moves about in what is called *transitional space.* Transitional space refers to the time of psychological progression from a private inner world of infancy to an expanding outer world of childhood. Children around the age of two or three populate their transitional space with an abundance of fascinating creatures—God among them (Rizzuto 1979).

Many memories and experiences go into early God images: characteristics of the parents, of siblings and other relatives, the good experienced in ourselves and others, the religious and intellectual culture of the home, and circumstances present in the child's life. Illustrating how particular incidents can influence a God representation, Rizzuto says:

> A striking example could be an impressive summer storm after the child has had his first conversation with his mother about God. The child may experience the storm as God's personal show of frightening power or anger. In one of the

> cases studied, the opposite experience, of being under God's protection, was triggered by the equally irrelevant circumstance of finding a penny in the street after the child had asked God to provide for him (p. 45).

Rizzuto helps answer a question raised in the introduction to this chapter, that is, why faith in a loving God can fail to result in positive self-esteem. She distinguishes between God representations or internalized *imagos* and the rational ideas about God (theology and dogma). A third level of experience contributes to one's God conception, namely the God convictions one holds as the result of religious experience. Self-esteem is related to all three levels of God imagery: unconscious God representations formed through the child's interaction with parents, ideas about God learned through socialization, and the experience of God in one's life. The unconscious representations of God and self may have the strongest impact on *good enough self-esteem.*

Early images or representations of parent and self are invariably distorted. These images shape early God representations. When negative images predominate, they can so reduce people's ability to believe in themselves that anything they learn about God in later life seems unbelievable. However, faulty representations can be reshaped consciously in adult life through relationships in which a person is realistically perceived and treated with respect. Through a positive relationship a person can be helped to move away from the poor self-representation which led to the pursuit of *false self* and toward a realistic self-representation that encourages the expression of the *true self.* Parallel to that accomplishment one is able to leave behind a negative God representation which results in the creation of a *false God* and to move toward a positive God representation which allows one to discover the *true Deity.*

God images are multi-layered and complex. In addition, permeating all the layers are the effects of a patriarchal mindset, which have dramatically influenced every aspect of human life, including God imagery.

God Images in Patriarchal Society

The only society that anyone raised in Western civilization has ever known is a patriarchal society. The word *patriarchy* applies to any society in which the father is the supreme or final authority and in which wives and children are legally dependent upon him. In patriarchal societies descent and inheritance are reckoned in the male line. One might take issue with the claim that the only society known to Western people is a patriarchal one and point out specific cases and even whole subcultures in which the mother is effectively the head of the family. However, a man's (legal) financial responsibility for his family, as well as descent and inheritance coming through the male line, would apply even in cases where a matriarch rather than patriarch actually dominates an individual or extended family. In addition, the family or subculture ruled by females is itself immersed in a larger patriarchal society in which the majority of elected and appointed leaders are men and in which men are more highly valued than women. In other words, patriarchy is so pervasive that it could be used as a synonym for the broadest use of the word *society.*

At the heart of patriarchy, as the definition suggests, is the hierarchical position of sovereign males over dependent females. When patriarchal value judgments are projected onto a supreme being, Deity is automatically imaged in male terms. While there are female images of Deity in the Hebrew Scriptures—God imaged as mother (Isaiah 66:13), as a woman giving birth (Isaiah 42:14), as midwife (Psalm 22:9), as mother bird (Luke 13:34), as the female personification of Wisdom (Wisdom 6—8)—these images have been eclipsed by the dominant male imagery.

The central point to be made here is that gender assumptions are pervasive in patriarchal societies. Gender assumptions pervade the parent-child relationship; cultural attitudes toward the role of women in society influence the way parents raise both their sons and their daughters. Gender matters slant religious beliefs; an exclusively male God perpetuates a male-dominated hierarchy. Gender distortions may even contaminate the positive lived experiences which teach people most intensely and persuasively about God. A woman convinced of her second-class citizenship can easily find herself in worship seeking "crumbs from the master's table" (Mark 7:28). A husband may be confused because he does not want his wife to regard him as she "regards the Lord" or submit to him "in everything" (Ephesians 5:21–24). On the other hand, he may *expect* such submission from his wife, who is rewriting her ideology and rejecting the oppression in Paul's directives in Ephesians. As long as one gender is seen as subordinate, the other dominant, the gender assumed "inferior" suffers injustice and often practices self-rejection. The gender assumed "superior" suffers from ego inflation. And as long as gender assumptions are projected onto the God of faith, the patriarchal hierarchy will continue. God is male and male is God.

The truth is that monotheism *as we have known it* has distorted and reduced our awareness of the mystery of Deity in our lives. The distortion and reduction has been especially harmful to women. Monotheism as we have known it has primarily meant the worship of a male God. Yet everyone needs to discover her or his unique expression of the Deity, and many women are conscious that the traditional images of a male God in the Christian churches block that discovery.

No single metaphor or image of Deity, no combination of images of Deity is large enough. And yet embodied people seek images or metaphors to express the incomprehensible, mysterious, both transcending and immanent Deity. Better to recognize the Deity in what is known and experienced than to use only abstract language that names a power beyond knowing. Like Jesus, and at his invitation, we can find the presence of God in the earth and air and fire and water; in the miracle of nature; in inquisitive minds and loving hearts that meet in relationship; in children's cries and laughter; in adults' tears and moments of ecstasy; in the immediacy of the poor and homeless; and in the passion of the inspired. We find the one God in the stories of God-with-us revealed in the Hebrew Scriptures and in the remarkable life of the prophet Jesus reported through the gospels. Better that we come to expansive images of a monotheistic Deity than settle for a hierarchical God, Father, Lord, King who dominates our universe and helps patriarchy keep women in a subordinate position. The simple fact that a male word, *God,* is accepted in most parts of our patriarchal culture as a gender-inclusive word, but the female word *Goddess* is deemed pagan, speaks to the distortion of our language and concepts of Deity. *God* refers to male deity; Goddess to female deity. Perhaps most men and many women are unable to use the word *Goddess* to name the presence of the Holy One. Yet perhaps everyone would agree that *Goddess* connotes aspects of Deity that *God* does not evoke.

While the incomprehensible Deity is neither male nor female, the first mention of God imagery in the opening book of the Hebrew Scriptures is that both male and female human beings *image* Deity.

> God created humankind in the image of Godself; in the image of God, God created them; male and female God created them (Genesis 1:27).

An obvious way to keep alive the scriptural claim that women image Deity is to keep alive a female metaphor of Deity. Many may yearn for the day when all gender-specific language of Deity will be balanced by symbols of the other gender as well as by powerful genderless images. Meanwhile, a growing number of women feel the need for female concepts in order to reclaim the truth that they too image the Holy One.

In summary, ideology, or one's conception of reality, of the world, and of one's place in the scheme of things, has a powerful influence on how one esteems oneself. An ideology includes self-understanding, values, faith claims—all that goes into a philosophy of human life. Ideologies designed and supported by a patriarchal society must be rewritten if women are to leave behind notions of second-class citizenship and if men are to live in right relationship to women. Ideologies designed and supported by a patriarchal church must also be redesigned if the church is to be true to its mission of fostering a community of justice and love among equals. That rewriting can begin with every pastor offering genuine care or counsel.

A Brief Summary of the Research with Women

The trap that most ensnared the women in my study was the assumption that if they could be good enough to win the *unqualified approval* of another, they would achieve their goal in life. Being good enough, however, came to mean achieving perfection. "Perfect" was often used in the interviews. Only perfect performance would give them the sense of having some control over the approval they needed from another. After all, perfection leaves no room for disapproval. As long as one needs perfection in order to arrive at unqualified approval, she must live in anxiety that the imperfection she well knows to be part of her life might be discovered. Feminist therapists Polly Young-Eisendrath and Florence Wiedemann write that they "have never encountered a woman in therapy who did not believe she was hiding a secret flaw that others would eventually discover" (1987, p. 31). Arriving at perfection in order to meet with unqualified approval took different forms for the different women in the study. For one woman perfection was assumed to be gained through acceptance by everyone; for another perfection required consistent success in whatever she attempted; for one perfection necessitated that she have a body other than the one she had; for still another perfection meant making an emotionally wounded parent happy again or saving her parents' troubled marriage. As many as sixteen of the twenty-one women expressed some form of a drive for approval, a drive always related to a false need to comply to the expressed or assumed demands of another.

A second major theme that was evident in the study was *gender/sexual abuse.* The abuse took several forms: physical sexual abuse, verbal abuse of a woman's (child's) body, and the psychological and social abuse a lesbian experiences because society does not support what she experiences as her nature, her true self.

I use the combined term *gender/sexual abuse* in describing the oppression of the women in the study in order to connect physical and psychological abuse of a sexual nature, the battering of a woman's body as well as the domination of women by men. My claim is that *any denigration of a female body or of the female gender is a form of sexual abuse.* Insulting words or harmful behavior related to a woman's body or gender, especially when the verbal message or inappropriate behavior is directed toward a woman who is in a subordinate position to the male or female offender, is sexual abuse. A claim is made here that all sexism is sexual abuse. What is generally called sexual abuse is generally a greater evil than destructive words. However, such hideous abuse would not be as widespread as it is if society did not continue to support the domination of women by men, which includes the control of a woman's body and the false ideology about the appearance of that body if it is to be deemed desirable.

The National Coalition Against Domestic Violence reports that at least once every fifteen seconds a woman is being battered in the United States. This statistic is based on a 1986 report by the Bureau of Justice. The report estimates that three to four million women are beaten in their homes each year by husbands, ex-husbands, and lovers. That figure includes only those crimes which received police or medical attention. There are over twelve hundred battered women's shelters in the United States, which served over 375,000 women and their children in 1987.

I contend that there is a connection between those dreadful statistics and attitudes toward the female body that show up early in a young girl's life. Messages that a child's body does not meet with a parent's approval or with the standards of other significant people in the child's life are heard as strong statements of rejection. To criticize or reject a child's appearance is to tell the child that she (or he) should have a body that she does not have—which sends the message that the child should be someone she is not. Unconstructive criticism of a child's body is an evil that can destroy a children's faith in her or his true self and weaken resistance to physical, sexual abuse.

Finally, the two lesbian women in the study suffered a particular kind of abuse. The truth is that no one really knows why a vast majority of human beings are oriented toward persons of the other sex for genital sexual fulfillment and a minority toward persons of the same sex. Some within that minority have a double or bisexual orientation. Yet without sufficient knowledge, society—and centrally religious institutions which have become the ethical "spokespersons" for that society—has dictated that the dominant orientation is what God and nature intended. The orientation of the minority has been labeled unnatural, debased, evil, sinful.

The mirroring, the modeling, the messages within the home and beyond the home, all reach a consensus: one's true self is a heterosexual self. The infant is immersed within patriarchal society's major story line: boys and girls grow up to be husbands and wives who raise more boys and girls and then become grandfathers and grandmothers. The girls need the boys because the boys are primary persons; the girls are secondary and therefore incomplete. Gay men are a threat to some straight men because straight men assume that one of the "queers" takes the place of a woman. Gay men also threaten straight men who are frightened of their own homosexual desires. Lesbian women are an abomination to straight men because women are supposed to need men to be complete. As Miriam Greenspan (1983) says:

> One of the most radical aspects of lesbianism, and the most threatening aspect for men, is that lesbians choose one another as *primary persons*—in defiance of the cultural message that women are not persons (in the males sense) at all (p. 214).

Like so many of their sisters and brothers living in a homophobic society, the women in the research group grew up terrified that something was amiss in their psyche and body: an attraction to persons of the same sex. To continue to repress these thoughts and feelings constituted the repression of the true self and pursuit of the false self.

Pastoral Response: Effecting Good Enough Self-Esteem

The focus of this chapter has been primarily on understanding the dynamics of faith in self and self-esteem in human life: understanding how foundational self-esteem grows out of early parent-child relationships; understanding that the deepest meaning of faith in oneself is of a piece with faith in God/dess who makes life Holy; understanding how images of Deity influence the way a people perceive themselves; understanding the factors that shape secondary self-esteem; understanding the interrelationships among people's self-concept, God concept, and the ability to believe in and value themselves.

The shift now is from understanding to *understanding actively,* that is to enacting one's understanding of the meaning of human life and of one's place in the scheme of things. In some cases the enactment will amount to developing competencies important to self-esteem. The focus is on practice, on actually designing ideology which supports faith in self and self-esteem, and acting out of an ideology which recognizes and enhances the beauty and power of human beings. The question to keep in mind is how pastors can be helpful to those ready to design and appropriate a new ideology.

It is not always easy to determine whether belief in the dignity and beauty of a person comes before the person changes her or his patterns of behavior, or whether patterns of behavior change before a person truly believes in her or his dignity and beauty. Whether behavior is shaped by attitudes or attitudes follow behavior has been a prolonged debate in psychology. People who believe in insight therapy claim that once a problem is understood, the person is able to do something about it—that is, the enlightened person can change self-defeating behavior. Unless the problem is understood, habits of self-defeating behavior continue, making change more and more difficult. In other words, the *Aha*! experience or insight comes first.

Behaviorists see the process in reverse. Once people change their characteristic ways of responding, behaviorists believe, their attitudes automatically change. It matters not whether the cause of the problem is understood. Act in a way conducive of self-esteem, and self-esteem will follow. For persons who are not only trying to redesign their understanding of human life and their place in it, but are also trying to put that new ideology into practice, both insight and behavioral change are necessary. Both insight and behavioral change allow a person to gain faith in herself or himself and to develop good enough self-esteem.

Psychologists Richard Bednar, Gawain Wells, and Scott Peterson (1989) clearly vote for behavioral change as the key to high self-esteem. The central conclusion they draw from years of research and clinical practice is that self-esteem is achieved if a person chooses coping over avoidance when faced with conflict involving anxiety and fear. Furthermore, they point out that what results from the coping is not as important to self-esteem as the fact that the person faced the conflict rather than avoiding it. To be able to say, "I didn't succeed but I sure gave it my best try," is what is most important. If people initiate changes in their characteristic ways of responding to unwelcome experiences, they will feel better about themselves, even if their attempts at a new response fail to achieve the desired effect.

For example, a woman who never confronts her parents when they make excessive demands on her time, for example, may say no to a particular demand which she believes to be unreasonable. She does not want to comply to their request or demand. Her aim is to be true to herself and respect her feelings—as well as her time and energy—and at the same time sustain a connection with each of her parents. She wants to alter her relationship to them without either alienating them or cutting herself off from them. Her parents may react angrily to her unusual response and put immediate distance between themselves and their "unappreciative and disrespectful" daughter. The daughter would probably have very mixed feelings about her behavior. She might be saddened by her parents' abusive remarks as well as haunted by guilt feelings because she has made them angry. Yet while she may feel hurt and be bothered by nagging guilt, she might at the same time be convinced that she made the right choice. She feels better about herself for initiating a change in her life-long pattern of being compelled to say yes to all of her parents' demands. In saying no she begins to dismantle the false self which says she is lovable only if she is compliant and attentive to her parents' wishes, and to move toward a more honest expression of her true self. Her parents may or may not get over their disappointment that their daughter has changed the family system.

Bednar, Wells, and Peterson (1989) describe coping as "a growth oriented process in which personal development is the inevitable result of facing, understanding, and resolving conflict situations" (p. 83). In the context of this chapter the word *confronting* is more appropriate than *coping*. *Coping* implies putting up with obstacles or adversity and maintaining oneself in the process. *Confronting* implies challenging oneself or a person or situation because a practice or expectation ought not be "put up with"—the situation cries out for change. Confronting, then, is the process through which people both rewrite the patriarchal ideology that has governed their lives and put into practice their new convictions about themselves and their place in the world.

Bednar, Wells, and Peterson call the opposite of coping *avoidance*, "a process we engage in that allows us to cling to our childish ideals by not facing those unpleasant psychological realities that can expose the fraud and faults in our idealistic self-conceptions" (p. 74).

In the language of this chapter, *avoidance* is a process in which a person engages that allows her or him to cling to the demands of the false self and seek self-esteem through conforming to the expectations of others.

What is needed to effect a move from the recognition of an ideology which promoted a false self to the enactment of an ideology which recognizes and insists on pursuit of the true self? To do so requires a concrete plan of action, which always involves insight and understanding. The plan of action begins with a genuine, open, honest relationship with at least one other, in some cases a spouse or partner, in some cases with a professional counselor or therapist, in some cases with a support group. In relationship one recognizes the social, political, and religious context in which both women and men live and consider the impact patriarchy has had on their development. They confront the dysfunctional aspects of their ideologies—talking through the messages which distorted their sense of self and recognizing the true strengths which are there to be claimed once the road blocks are removed. For example, a woman has been told by a mother who bought into patriarchy's denigration of women that what society has called female qualities—nurturance, bonding, care—are really weaknesses. This mother wants her daughter to be tough, aggressive, competitive. The daughter needs a new ideology that supports her true self. She is indeed a nurturing, compassionate, caring woman, but has fought against those gifts. In another case, a man believes he has to make more money than his wife or he will lose her respect, his self-respect, and the respect of anyone who knows that his wife is the major breadwinner in the family. He gave up his passion to work in a low-paying service organization because he knew he would not be able to match her income. He too needs a new ideology.

Developing faith in self requires that women and men break the habit of conforming to patriarchal notions of who they should be. Patriarchy has socialized women to be docile, subordinate, dependent—over-functioners in the home and under-functioners in "the world." They must also claim with genuine pride the values society has typically assigned to women as second-class values: nurture, care, responsibility, empathy, cooperativeness, mutual relations. Patriarchy has socialized men to be strong, dominant, independent, over-functioners in "the world," and underfunctioners in the home. They must also claim with genuine pride the values society has taught them to leave to women: nurture, care, responsibility, empathy, cooperativeness, mutual relations. Women and men must break their covenant with patriarchy.

Women and men must also break covenant between their false self and a false God (Jordan 1986, p. 30). The Deity who creates and loves the world is not an "Ultimate Patriarch" who has a design on every aspect of a person's life (which gets translated by lesser patriarchs as the "will of God"). Nor does the Deity seek obedient children who relate to the Holy One as to a parent who knows best what "his" children should do. Rather God/dess seeks ongoing, vital incarnate relationships with thinking, feeling, choosing, passionate people who, under the inspiration of the Spirit within, co-create their lives day by day. To enact one's belief that religion is essentially a vital relationship with the Holy One is to live a profoundly creative spiritual life, including prayer and reflection, living worship, and community engagement. This kind of spiritual relationship results in a continuation of the struggle for equality and justice and love that set the agenda in Jesus' life. Like Jesus, women and men inspired by the Holy One confront themselves and other people and institutions day by day, repeatedly asking how best to respond to the challenges of life. The question in a given situation is not so much, "Where is God's will?" Rather, the question becomes "God/dess, what do we do with this challenge?" Women and men need to continually rethink and rework their understanding of God's will and God's presence in their lives. They are not only children of God; they are co-creators with the God/dess of their own lives and of their communities.

Enlightened women and men need expansive ideologies that recognize at every level of human life that they are images of the Holy One and are one another's equals. They need to support one another in putting into practice what they believe about their dignity and power. Together they can not only discover themselves and one another in patriarchal society, but they can look forward to the day when patriarchy will be a thing of the past.

> Now this [God] is the Spirit, and where the Spirit of [God] is, there is freedom. And we all, with unveiled faces, reflecting like mirrors the brightness of [God], all grow brighter and brighter as we are turned into the image that we reflect; this is the work of [God] who is Spirit (2 Corinthians 3:17–18).

Summary

Pastoral care-givers and counselors need better to understand and more effectively to respond to persons seeking ways of increasing their self-esteem. Beneath low self-esteem is a lack of faith in one's value and possibilities—a lack of faith in self. People seeking a minister's help often articulate claims about a loving God who creates and sustains the universe, but are themselves unable to receive that loving acceptance at the deepest level of their being; they are unable to love themselves. Religious faith in the goodness of life is only complete when it builds on personal faith in the intrinsic value and beauty of the believer, that is, *faith in self.* Religious or spiritual faith does not contribute to self-esteem unless it grows out of and along with faith in one's *true self.* When a person lives out of a true self, faith in Deity cannot be an escape from faith in self. Whereas when a person lives out of a *false self,* or an adapted self who acts according to other people's expectations, faith in Deity is easily an escape from faith in self. False self escapes into false deity.

Self-esteem is a complex disposition that is related to at least six major experiences: 1) parental acceptance; 2) an ideology (an understanding of human life and one's place in it) which fosters self-esteem; 3) satisfying relationships; 4) competence; 5) passion for life; and 6) self-acceptance. One can distinguish between the *foundational self-esteem,* which results from good enough, respectful parenting received during the first few years of life, and *secondary self-esteem,* which grows out of successful relationships and accomplishments throughout one's life. Persons lacking foundational self-esteem most often need therapeutic intervention that amounts to an experience of reparenting. Pastoral care-givers can assist in the process by helping people build secondary self-esteem. They can help persons suffering from low self esteem articulate the ideology that shapes their world and rewrite that world-view in support of the true self.

What has too often been overlooked is the central significance of a person's earliest self-understanding as well as the internalization of primitive God imagery to a person's faith in self, in others, and in Deity—and thereby to one's self-esteem. God images formed in the early months of life, as well as the theology and God language which dominate in institutional religion, play a central role in the ideology out of which people value or disvalue themselves.

Self-esteem is also built or torn down by gender assumptions. Gender assumptions pervade the parent-child relationship—cultural attitudes toward the role of women in society influence the way parents raise both their sons and their daughters. Gender matters slant religious beliefs; an exclusively male God perpetuates a male-dominated hierarchy. The gender assumptions embedded in one's ideology are critically important to self-esteem.

The term *gender/sexual abuse* is used to describe the oppression of women in order to underscore the connections among physical and psychological abuse of a sexual nature, the battering of a woman's body, and the domination of women by men. *Any denigration of a female body or of the female gender is a form of sexual abuse.* The abuse of women would not be as widespread as it is if society did not continue to support the domination of women by men, which includes the control of a woman's body.

Developing faith in self and thereby increasing self-esteem requires that women and men break the habit of conforming to patriarchal notions of who they should be. Through confronting themselves and the persons and structures that dominate their lives, they both rewrite the ideology that has governed their lives and put into practice new convictions about themselves and their place in the world.

Notes

This essay is an altered and condensed version of the author's book *God Images and Self-Esteem: Empowering Women in a Patriarchal Society* (Louisville: Westminster, 1991).

1. The term "good enough mothering" was used by D. W. Winnicott to describe adequate parenting that allows the child to arrive at a realistic sense of self (Winnicott 1987, p. 145; St. Clair 1986, pp. 70–71).

References

Beattie, Melody. 1987. *Co-Dependent: No More.* Center City, Minn.: Hazelden.

Bednar, Richard; Wells, Gawain; and Peterson, Scott. 1989. *Self-Esteem: Paradoxes and Innovations in Clinical Theory and Practice,* Washington D.C.: American Psychological Association.

Brock, Rita Nakashima. 1988. *Journeys by Heart: A Christology of Erotic Power.* New York: Crossroad.

——. 1989. "And a Little Child Will Lead Us: Christology and Child Abuse." In *Christianity, Patriarchy, And Abuse: A Feminist Critique,* edited by Joanne Carlson Brown and Carole R. Bohn. New York: Pilgrim Press.

Erikson, Eric. 1963. *Childhood and Society.* New York: W. W. Norton.

Fowler, James W. 1981. *Stages of Faith.* New York: Harper & Row.

Greenspan, Miriam. 1983. *A New Approach to Women and Therapy.* New York: McGraw Hill.

James, William. 1961. *The Varieties of Religious Experience.* New York: Collier Books.

Jordan, Merle. 1986. *Taking on the Gods.* Nashville: Abingdon.

Levinson, Daniel J. 1978. *Seasons of a Man's Life.* New York: Knopf.

Miller, Alice. 1981. *The Drama of the Gifted Child.* New York: Basic Books.

National Coalition Against Domestic Violence, 1012 14th Street NW, Washington, D.C. 20005.

Rizzuto, Ana-Maria. 1979. *The Birth of the Living God.* Chicago: University of Chicago Press.

Saussy, Carroll. 1991. *God Images and Self-Esteem.* Louisville: Westminster.

Schaef, Anne Wilson. 1986. *Co-Dependence: Misunderstood—Mistreated.* Minneapolis: Winston Press.

——. 1987. *When Society Becomes An Addict.* Minneapolis: Winston Press.

St. Clair, Michael. 1986. *Object Relations and Self Psychology.* Monterey, Cal.: Brooks/Cole.

Winnicott, D. W. 1971. *Playing and Reality.* New York: Basic Books.

——. 1987. *The Maturational Processes and the Facilitating Environment.* London: Hogarth Press.

Young-Eisendrath, Polly, and Wiedemann, Florence. 1987. *Female Authority: Empowering Women Through Psychotherapy.* New York: Guilford Press.

William J. Sneck, S.J.

15. Guilt

> Thoroughly wash me from my guilt
>   and of my sin cleanse me.
> For I acknowledge my offense,
>   and my sin is before me always (Ps 51:4–5).
>
> If we say, "We are free of the guilt of sin,"
>   we deceive ourselves; the truth is not to be found in us (1 Jn 1:8).
>
> Little children,
> let us love in deed and in truth
> and not merely talk about it.
> This is our way of knowing we are committed to the truth
> and are at peace before him
> no matter what our consciences may charge us with;
> for God is greater than our hearts
> and all is known to him (1 Jn 3:18–20).

The complex human emotional and cognitive experience of guilt is hinted at if we position these scriptural passages side by side. The psalmist cries out for purification as while struggling under the burden of admitted sinfulness, a weight that seems never to leave consciousness. The people in the first chapter of 1 John did not know the term *rationalization,* but their effort to deny their guilt encounters the sting of the author's rebuke. This same writer in the third chapter seems to have a compassionate understanding of neurotic guilt, for he hints that his counselees' consciences are hyperactive, their hearts out of tune with God's truth, their inner peace destroyed because of too great a sensitivity to possible wrongdoing. His therapeutic suggestion involves attention to deeds of love rather than endless talking and needless focusing on inaccurate inner mental states. Repentance, rationalization, reexamination: these are only three of the myriad responses humans employ to deal with guilty thoughts and feelings. In an effort to sort through these and countless other responses to this pervasive human reality, I shall sample some of the current literature on guilt to provide a hint at the contrasting perspectives on interpretation and understanding; secondly, I shall offer a simplifying—but I hope not simplistic—pastoral focus on guilt in the phrase "loved sinner"; finally, I shall elaborate some implications for treatment and ministry to the guilt-free and the guilt-ridden.

Interpreting Guilt

During the summer of 1990, while I was researching this chapter, the sad news came of the death of Dr. Karl Menninger, that towering genius of American psychiatry, an intellectual grandfather to me, since he taught my teachers. Despite their affection for "Dr. Karl," I vividly recall their reaction to the publication of his *Whatever Became of Sin?* (1973). One roguishly suggested that Dr. Karl should see himself for therapy, since he published such a book! Like my teachers, many mental-health professionals automatically react to guilt as "the enemy," unhealthy always, and to be eradicated. Menninger warns us against our cultural error: sin exists, and we'll never succeed in talking ourselves out of the resulting guilt. Perhaps more than any other author, Karl Menninger made it respectable to entertain multiple viewpoints on guilt and to respond to it in a more nuanced way than was the case before his courageous essay.

Playwrights, novelists, and philosophers, however, successfully avoided the narrowness and blinders that psychologists somehow fell prey to. John Carroll (1985) attempts a socio-historical review of writers treating the emotion of guilt and its impact upon humankind. In contrast to many mental-health workers, Carroll quotes with approval Nadezhda Mandelstam's pithy summation, "A sense of guilt is a man's greatest asset" (p. 1).

Carroll traces evolution into complexity in Shakespeare between Macbeth and Hamlet:

> Already with Hamlet the simple traditional moral world of Macbeth is left behind. Macbeth killed, felt guilt, and his guilt destroyed him. Hamlet is a modern man in that his guilt is an essential part of his being: before he has done anything he is guilt-hounded, and paralyzed from doing what he has to do by anxieties of whose cause he has no inkling (p. 2).

Carroll reminds us of Raskolnikov in Dostoevsky's *Crime and Punishment,* another guilt-hounded person "in search of a cultural form to guide action that might give him release from his torment" (p. 3). Guilt stalks Joseph K. in Kafka's *The Trial.*

American literature studies guilt too: Nathaniel Hawthorne's *The Scarlet Letter,* Herman Melville's *Moby Dick,* and William Faulkner's *Absalom! Absalom!* recreate the inner torment of the guilt-obsessed.

Friedrich Nietzsche's *The Genealogy of Morals* takes as its central theme the role of guilt in the development of civilization and characterizes guilt as "the most terrible sickness that has ever raged in man" (p. 4). Sigmund Freud (1930), unlike some of his disciples, viewed guilt as coursing "through the main arteries of the social body, both as life-blood and poison" (p. 4).

Carroll (1985) introduces the ethnological distinction between shame-cultures and guilt-cultures, and with this division let me caution the reader to inquire mentally of each author consulted how he or she defines or describes these two closely related phenomena. In an encounter with shame, one has failed to live up to a goal of one's ego-ideal. Shame can either involve or be independent of another's gaze. For example, I can be applauded for an artistic, professional, or business accomplishment, but still be interiorly ashamed because I didn't put my best effort into the achievement. Guilt, on the other hand, results from a violation of a dictate of conscience. While an adult's conscience may be mature and may supply rational directives, its psychological roots are laid down in the child's experience of guilt before parents whose love it no longer deserves because of an infraction of one of their dictates. I may experience thoughts and feelings of both shame and guilt. In more technical language, shame and guilt each function at cognitive and affective levels.

Helen B. Lewis (1971) wrote a whole book on the painful and unhealthy varieties of these two states called *Shame and Guilt in Neurosis.* From the psychoanalytic perspective she contends that "the superego is sometimes apprehended as the sense of guilt, and sometimes as the shame of failure to live up to an ego-ideal" (p. 495). Whether or not one wishes to embrace the psychoanalytic perspective or to employ that terminology, one can understand the "superego" to be that aspect of ourself which experiences shame and guilt. Lewis suggests that there are many more variants of shame-feelings than there are of guilt-feelings; namely humiliation, embarrassment, chagrin, shyness, humiliated fury, mortification. Furthermore, there is an affinity between shame and depressed feeling, and an affinity between guilt and obsessive thinking. Thus she tends to locate shame in the affective realm and guilt in the cognitive: "Shame is a painful or negative emotion; guilt is not necessarily an emotion, but something more objective, a failure of duty, delinquency, an offense" (p. 64).

I would argue that a more accurate description of human experience of these two realities, shame and guilt, finds them operating at both levels, thought and feeling, and that both may manifest healthy and pathological variants. It is perhaps because guilt and shame are never fun or pleasant that many therapists and counselors instinctively want to reduce shame and guilt rather than patiently inquire whether such thoughts and feelings are an effort of the psyche to stir the person toward healthier, more ethical living. In other words, shame and guilt both have unhealthy and healthy manifestations on the emotional and cognitive levels.

Shame Examples

Healthy Emotional: A young married woman is enjoying a business lunch with a male co-worker. Coincidentally, a cousin of hers drops into the restaurant and is seated at an adjoining table. In making introductions the young woman feels herself blushing, much to her surprise.

Healthy Cognitive: Chatting later that day with her cousin, the woman wonders aloud about her blushing and its meaning. She thinks that perhaps her shame at being seen socially with another man may indicate an inappropriate searching for something she has felt ebbing recently from her marriage but has not talked about with her unsuspecting spouse.

Unhealthy Emotional: A male high school teacher with excellent educational credentials enjoys a successful reputation among his students and colleagues both in the classroom and in extracurricular endeavors. Yet he confesses one day to a close friend that he feels like the Wizard of Oz, who, behind the fireworks and machinery, is a manipulator of impressions, naked, scared, and alone.

Unhealthy Cognitive: Invited to reflect on this feeling by his friend, the teacher admits having more than occasional thoughts that he is no good: as a teacher, as a person, as anything.

Guilt Examples

Healthy Emotional: An engineer with several youngsters in college and many years of commitment to his firm is assigned to work on a weapons system commissioned by a Defense Department contract. Though hardly a "peacenik," he is aware of his church's teachings on nonviolence and feels divided within himself when he tries to silence his unease about his new project with reminders of his children's educational needs.

Healthy Cognitive: Counseling with a sympathetic cleric helps the engineer clarify his own views about the weapons project: that his continued participation on the weapons team is morally objectionable, but his material circumstances are causing confusion as to a next step.

Unhealthy Emotional: A parent has tried her best to transmit her values and religious tradition to her children, but three of the four, while leading basically decent lives, no longer go to church or keep all God's commandments as she understands them. She is consumed with sadness and remorse, and wonders how she went wrong in rearing her kids.

Unhealthy Cognitive: Every time this mother reads gloomy newspaper editorials on crime statistics and the breakdown of modern civilization, she blames herself as a bad mother for contributing to the current moral malaise.

Although this paper focuses on guilt, let us look at one more phenomenological description of the interaction of shame and guilt so as to understand better their interplay:

> Guilt is the process of judging or condemning one's behavior, thoughts, or words. This process automatically produces feelings of shame and grief. These feelings motivate and regulate the individual's response to his/her impulses, a condition which eventually contributes to the development of the individual's personality. Shame is the feeling evoked after the individual had interiorly made a judgment of the self's violation of a standard value or norm of conduct.
>
> . . . Guilt also produces a sense of grief or "loss." The awareness of the transgression brings about shame which in turn results in a loss of self-esteem. This loss of self-esteem could also generate fear of losing a love object whom the individual wants to please (Agudo 1980, pp. 17–18).

The above examples and citations reveal the complex interweaving of thought, feeling, health, and unhealth between shame and guilt. Perhaps better than any other author, John Bradshaw (1988) has successfully analyzed the contrasting dynamics of shame and guilt. Following Erikson (1963), Bradshaw locates the origin of shame earlier developmentally than the rise of guilt. During Erikson's second psycho-social state (age fifteen months to three years), the task confronting the developing child is to strike a balance between autonomy and shame/doubt. As children learn to walk and explore, they must separate from their primary parental figures—with whom they have established, it is hoped, a relationship of trust during the first stage. Touching, tasting, testing limits, youngsters develop a healthy sense of shame and doubt, of boundaries beyond which they may not safely go. As Bradshaw explains:

> In itself, shame is not bad. Shame is a normal human emotion. In fact, it is necessary to have the feeling of shame if one is to be truly human. Shame is the emotion which gives us permission to be human. Shame tells us of our limits. Shame keeps us in our human boundaries, letting us know we can and will make mistakes, and that we need help. Healthy shame is the psychological foundation of humility. It is the source of spirituality (Bradshaw 1988, p. vii).

Shame, however, becomes toxic and dehumanizing when it gets transformed into a state of being, into one's whole identity. To suffer shame as an identity is to believe that one's being is blameworthy and flawed, that one is at bottom defective as a human being.

Again according the Erikson (1963), the third stage of psychosocial development is the polar balance between initiative and guilt, which is ordinarily faced between the third and the sixth year. Like shame, guilt appears in healthy and toxic forms. Healthy guilt is the emotional core of our conscience. Guilt is the painful feeling we suffer when we are aware of having done something we believe is wrong, or failed to do what we know is right. Again, following Bradshaw:

> Guilt presupposes internalized rules and develops later than shame. . . . Guilt is developmentally more mature than shame. Guilt does not reflect directly upon one's identity or diminish one's sense of personal worth (p. 17).

Having attempted distinctions between guilt and shame, we now consider guilt more closely and focus on differences between healthy and toxic forms of guilt.

Healthy Guilt versus Toxic Guilt

Before losing ourselves in a welter of descriptions and distinctions, it may help to state simply that healthy guilt is to be promoted and toxic guilt to be combatted. When a guilt-tinged thought or emotion is experienced *before* an action, one should be encouraged to obey one's conscience if the guilt is discerned to be healthy. If healthy guilt *follows* a behavior, one should make amends interpersonally, and intrapersonally one would wisely seek healing through repentance. If, however, the guilt is considered toxic, one should resist acting in accord with its peremptory dictates and endeavor to remove the cause of the guilt through prayer, reflection, counseling, or spiritual direction. These "treatment" suggestions will be further developed below, but they are presented now before consideration of the dynamics of healthy and unhealthy forms of guilt.

Healthy guilt may be considered an aspect of our response to our own and our community's values. One's response to violation of a value may be proportionate or disproportionate to the objective seriousness of the wrong done. Healthy guilt is experienced when the intensity of the emotion or self-critical thoughts is coordinated with the depth of evil as evaluated by a rational consensus of wise members of the community. Thus, in American society, differing degrees of guilt would be judged of appropriate and proportionate intensity if one felt somewhat guilty for losing one's temper in a heated argument; felt more guilty for making a sexist or racist comment in ordinary conversation; felt very guilty for attacking someone's reputation out of jealousy; suffered extreme guilt after participating in a bank robbery. Were a person's sense of guilt minimal or lacking after a bank heist, that person's sense of responsibility could fairly be judged disproportionate to the wrong done, and suspicion of an antisocial personality disorder would be raised. On the other hand, were one to endure extreme pangs of self-recrimination for occasional loss of temper, such a person's sense of guilt could be considered disproportionate to the wrong done, and other signs of neurotic anxiety in his or her behavior might be manifest. Thus a useful check on the healthy or toxic nature of guilt would consist in its proportion or lack thereof to the objective degree of evil done or anticipated.

Yet an objection might be raised at this point: in the discussion above, reference was made to a "rational consensus of wise members of the community." Must one always look outside oneself for validation rather than within?

Nothing could be further from the truth. While one's culture and community remain important reference points, adhering mindlessly to the status quo brings the danger of conformity rather than personal-ized, individual growth. No, one must rather chart one's course by one's inner light, discern one's path by following the inner voice of conscience. Along with Glaser (1971), we want to suggest that conscience-based morality generates principles for joyous living whose violation yields healthy guilt, whereas superego-based morality undergirds toxic guilt.

Glaser describes conscience as the preconceptual recognition of an absolute call to love, and thereby to co-create, with God, myself as my genuine future. Put another way, conscience is the non-verbal insight into a radical invitation to love God in loving my neighbor, and thereby to become abiding love. A "good conscience" is to be understood "as the pre-conceptually experienced harmony existing between the ultimate ground of reality, the created values, and that existence which I am, co-created by my free act" (Glaser 1971, p. 31).

By contrast, according to Glaser, the dynamic of the superego derives from a frantic compulsion to experience myself as lovable, not from the call to commit myself in abiding love. The commands and restrictions of the superego do not arise from any sort of perception of the intrinsic right or wrong of the action envisioned. *The* source of such commands/prohibitions can be positively characterized as the desire to be approved and loved, or negatively as the fear of loss of such love and approval (p. 33).

Reflection on one's own and one's clients' experiences of guilt enables us further to delineate the differences between conscience-based and superego-based morality, and the emotions/cognitions deriving from each. Genuine conscience is extraverted in the sense that one's thematic center is the value that invites; self-value is concomitant and secondary to this. Superego is introverted in that a person's thematic center is a sense of one's own self-value (p. 38).

Conscience is dynamic; it is an awareness of and sensitivity to value which develops and grows, a mind-set that can function accurately in new situations. Superego is static; it does not grow or learn. Because superego cannot function creatively in a new situation, it merely repeats basic generalizations.

Conscience is value-oriented. The value or disvalue is perceived and responded to, regardless of whether authority has ordered or not. Superego is oriented to an authority figure. Rather than perceiving and responding to a value, superego salutes authority's commands blindly.

Conscience weighs the importance of individual acts as a part of a larger process or pattern. Superego concentrates on atomized units of activity as its focus.

Conscience is future-oriented and creative. Conscience interprets the past as implying a future and helps to structure this future as a better future. Superego is past-oriented and primarily concerned with cleaning up the record with regard to past misdeeds.

Conscience expresses the need to repair by structuring one's future orientation toward the value in question, a process that includes making good past faults. Superego urges only that one be punished and thereby deserve reconciliation.

Conscience accepts the gradual process of growth that characterizes all dimensions of genuine human development. (A biologist friend once commented, "All real growth in nature is slow. The only rapidly growing entity is cancer!") Superego demands the rapid transition from severe isolation and guilt feelings to a sense of personal value achieved by confessing to an authority figure.

Shifting our focus somewhat from conscience and superego to the experienced actuality of guilt, both healthy and toxic, we can offer further differentiating notes.

Healthy guilt is accompanied by a realistic, non-exaggerated conviction of one's personal responsibility for the wrong done. A person acting from such a conviction ceases to blame parental influence, teachers' deficiencies, lacks in upbringing, material poverty, peer influence, psychological determinisms, and so on. Unhealthy guilt tries to rationalize itself out of existence by projecting blame on the other, like Adam blaming Eve and Eve blaming the serpent in the biblical account of creation. An illustrative sports analogy demonstrates the attitudes described. When a basketball referee calls a foul, the mature player raises his right arm and two fingers, takes the penalty, and the game goes on. Symbolizing toxic guilt, the self-righteous player disrupts the rhythm of the game by denying the referee's call, starting an argument, and generating mayhem.

Again looking to the cognitive realm, we may speak of healthy guilt's realistic confrontation with one's deliberate malice, principles violated, laws broken, values betrayed. Clarity and honesty suffuse one's self-knowledge. Actions taken or avoided are judged by one's evolving inner standards of righteousness. Unhealthy guilt, however, shifts the interior dialogue from actions to self-image: a person will harangue himself or herself as blameworthy, bad, evil, unworthy of

God's concern or human companionship. Concomitantly, remorseful self-hate is stirred up, and emotions churn in self-destructive ways leading to depression and sometimes to despair. Of course, the opposite psychopathic variant is also possible: society, the church, my family, my victims are to be blamed, but surely not myself. With Judas such a person queries, "Is it I, Lord?" (Matthew 26:25).

If the person is a Christian, healthy guilt will be accompanied by a sense of a need for a Redeemer and will serve as a stimulus for compunction, contrition, a desire for reconciliation and inner peace. Unhealthy guilt closes such a person in on himself or herself—like the naked Adam and Eve, the person fears the presence of the God who had walked with him or her in the cool of the evening. Instead of stimulating gentleness of heart, toxic guilt produces hard-heartedness, lack of trust, self-condemnation swinging back and forth to self-pity.

Healthy guilt culminates in forgiveness sought and received and results in new depths of trust in oneself and security in the restored relationship with the offended beloved. Toxic guilt fosters avoidance of even the desire for forgiveness, and the afflicted spirit plummets to new depths of self-centeredness and morbid introspection.

Biblical examples of healthy guilt include Peter and the prodigal son. After thrice denying Jesus, Peter received the pained glance of his Lord, went out, and wept bitterly (Luke 22:61–62). According to an ancient oral tradition in the Christian community, Peter's tears were so copious that his face ever afterward bore the marks of their furrows, even to the end of his life. Yet Peter's honest self-confrontation led to his reconciliation with himself, his God, and his community so that he assumed its leadership and died a martyr's death. As an exercise leading to understanding of the various points made thus far, the reader is invited to reflect on the description of healthy guilt and to keep in mind Peter's fall and restoration.

Similarly, the operation of healthy guilt is neatly summarized in the brief phrase that evokes the mental state of the prodigal son sitting among the pigs and comparing his situation with that of the servants back home in his father's house: "Coming to himself, he said . . ." (Luke 15:17). Healthy guilt functions as a "mid-course correction" throughout life and invites us back to the path to genuine selfhood from the tangential sidetracks of selfishness, self-indulgence, and self-centeredness.

A brief reference has been made to Judas as an exemplar of toxic guilt. For the prodigal son and Peter, guilt led to life. For Judas, guilt turned a man away from repentance, from reconciliation with his friend, Master, and Lord, and spun him into suicide.

The clarity provided by these examples is diminished somewhat by their being polar opposites from one another and from the situation of most ordinary guilt-enduring Christians, directees, and clients. "I'm no St. Peter," someone might reflect, "and I'm still living and breathing, so I haven't met Judas's fate either." To render these personages useful, we might arrange them on a continuum with Peter at the healthy end, Judas at the toxic nadir, and the prodigal son somewhere in the middle, but closer to the healthy zenith:

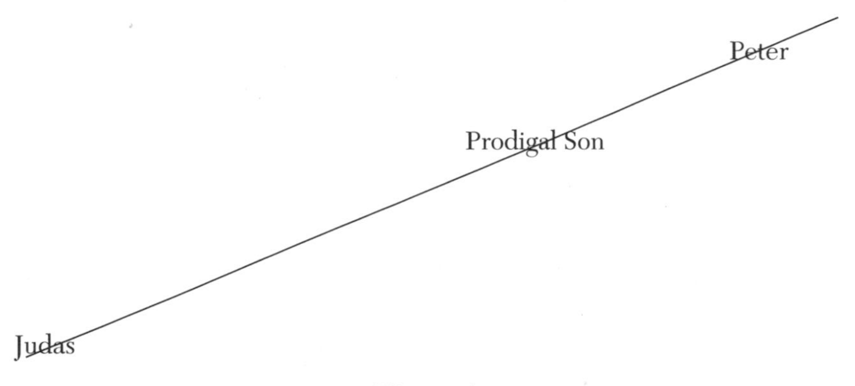

Figure 1.
Exemplars of Healthy versus Toxic Guilt

We should have less difficulty in identifying with the prodigal son than with either of the other two.

Figure 1 illustrates another important point: in order to sharpen the conceptual differences between conscience-based and superego-based morality, and between healthy guilt and toxic guilt in the discussion above, each antithesis was sketched as starkly as possible. Within real human beings, however, both elements of the dichotomy are present in varying degrees. For example, genuine conscience has been characterized as extraverted/value-centered and superego as introverted/self-focused. One could imagine using Figure 1 with "value-centered" at the top and "self-focused" at the bottom, and understand oneself to be gravitating along this continuum at different growth-moments and in various situations of one's moral life. One hopes always to be moving toward the healthy pole, but past habits, present tensions, and neurotic patterns pull one toward the toxic pit. The function of pastoral counseling lies in assisting the client to strive earnestly toward experiencing and interpreting guilt in a healthy mode.

Now that we have attempted to describe guilt's various phenomenological expressions and to distinguish it from shame, another similar but subtly different reality, we move toward providing the counselor some means for dealing with or healing guilt in one's and one's clients' development.

One's Identity as a "Loved Sinner"

From my experience in pastoral counseling and spiritual direction, *the* most useful way to nudge people into a stance of healthy, conscience-based guilt consists in inviting them to experience and claim one's identity as a *loved sinner.*

Either half of this dichotomy by itself proves one-sidedly inadequate to foster growth. Stressing only sinfulness in the style of traditional "fire and brimstone" preachers may succeed in scaring the simple into doing good for a while (at best), but such motivation does not last and leads instead to a heightened sense of unworthiness and inability to please God, fellow humans, or even oneself. Pounding away at sinfulness may galvanize a negative self-image, depression, despair, and in the worst case suicide, as with Judas.

Alternatively, counselors seek to repair the damage of an excessive sin-consciousness by inviting their clients into an awareness of how much they are loved by God and by significant others. Such a therapeutic strategy is praiseworthy and is rewarded with relief from neurotic guilt-feelings and with genuine progress in self-acceptance. Yet, in one way or another a pastoral counselor wants to assist the client in integrating the human ontological reality of sinfulness into his or her self-image. Ignoring this challenge produces the "smile-button personality," one of those annoying, naive persons who feel forced to grin constantly and to ignore or deny the dark side of life's sufferings, people who routinely greet others with a "Praise the Lord!" (if they are overtly religious), or "I'm just great; how are you?"

Human nature, human identity is expressed in the phrase *loved sinner.* Since "the truth shall make you free," only when a client can fully accept the dynamic tension between intrinsic lovableness and simultaneous sinfulness can he or she be empowered to remove the boulders along life's path strewn by guilt, and to journey toward mature human living. I am a sinner who can honestly admit that painful fact to myself, but I also experience the love of Christ and his Father, the love of friends who know me as I really am, and perhaps most difficult of all, the genuine love of myself.

As I grow in self-realization, in self-identification as a loved sinner, I normally endure experiences of guilt over what the Greeks called *hamartía.* This was their word for sin, but its root meaning is instructive; in archery, when one missed the mark, failed to hit the bull's-eye, one committed a *hamartía.* So too in living, when one fails to live up to an internal ego-ideal, a societal standard, or an interpersonal commitment, one is guilty of *hamartía,* of missing the mark. The psychopath thinks and feels nothing of the objective wrong done or contemplated. The neurotic is burdened with excessive self-recriminations and shifts the sense of evil from the deed to the doer. The loved sinner apologizes, makes amends, seeks forgiveness, and changes the behavior in the future.

One never fully achieves or finally arrives at total self-appropriation as a loved sinner, just as one never completes self-development and maturity or claims entire self-mastery. Rather, these goals are asymptotic because of the human capacity for the infinite. It is the privileged and exciting role and vocation of the pastoral counselor to facilitate a client's gradual movement toward these maturational milestones. Whatever theoretical perspective from psychology guides a pastoral counselor's interventions and therapeutic interactions—psychodynamic, behavioral, humanistic-existential, cognitive—clients will integrate guilt in a growthful way to the degree they accept themselves as loved sinners.

Although this task is made easier if the client lives from a religious vision, the model can be adapted for one who follows a secular or humanistic philosophy of life. Sin, *hamartía,* is interpreted as a violation of humanly embraced values (rather than as an offense against divine law or a rupture in one's relationship with a personal God); unconditional love will be remembered from familial, or interpersonal, or therapeutic relationships (rather than from God). With both the religious and the secular client, it is incumbent upon the pastoral counselor to reincarnate and model such accepting love through unconditional positive regard and non-judgmental interactions.

Having sketched a portrait of an objectively healthy person as a loved sinner, we shall consider various techniques and approaches in dealing with guilt.

Ministry to the Guilt-Free and the Guilt-Ridden

Before we proceed, a quick caveat needs to be introduced in conjunction with the immediately previous remark about providing unconditional love and presenting oneself non-judgmentally. In treating someone suffering the antisocial personality disorder (known colloquially as a psychopath or sociopath), one does both the client and society a disservice, even an injustice, by behaving overly permissively. Because such a person seems incapable of experiencing guilt at either the emotional or the cognitive level, it is useless to search for, much less try to stir up, a sense of guilt. A behavioral or cognitive approach may prove useful in helping such a client contract to set limits to his or her behavior, to structure concrete goals for living, and to make plans for interacting with family, community, and society. Perhaps the most important lesson to impart is that actions have consequences. For such a client, the pastoral counselor serves primarily as teacher.

For most other clients, especially those overly burdened by guilt, a different approach is in order. Following what has been outlined thus far, we seek to make way for healthy guilt and to join the client in resisting toxic guilt. Concretely, and on the cognitive level, such a process entails educating the conscience to develop a personally appropriated scale of values that integrate individual insights, vocation, religious tradition, societal norms duly examined, and so forth. Simultaneously, one seeks to learn the ways of the superego by reflecting on irrational interior commands and urgings, especially through paying attention to personal behavioral patterns that are unfulfilling, diminishing, inappropriate, and of a compulsive quality. One needs to cultivate a similar reflective awareness focused on one's feelings around guilt, so that they may influence behavior and decisions if they are adjudged healthy and may be neutralized if they are discerned to be toxic. Such is the pastoral counselor's guiding philosophy to be shared with the client and worked at. What about some tactics for imparting this philosophy/viewpoint/lifestyle?

The best educational approach known to this writer for imparting a healthy approach to human/spiritual living is a personal experience of the *Spiritual Exercises* of St. Ignatius Loyola. This involves a series of meditations and prayers made under the guidance of a director who assists the directee in reorienting his or her life around the love of God. After being wounded at the battle of Pamplona (1521), Ignatius was converted from a life of soldiering to embracing God's will. As part of his pilgrimage he spent ten months in a cave at Manresa in Spain and wrestled with the Spirit. He recorded his struggles in a diary and later formalized them in a manual for directors, the *Spiritual Exercises,* so that others could benefit from his insights. These *Exercises* are

> a book of meditations which can exercise and stretch the human spirit to such a creative, blessed compliance with God's Love that the Spirit of God in Jesus becomes the energizing vision for a person's whole life. . . . The acknowledgement of God's love as creative source and glorious goal of all reality, though initiated by God and grace, will only have its formative effect as it becomes actual experience for this person now, however much struggling, doubting and testing may have preceded such an abandonment to the truth. . . . Once the principle and foundation of God's faithfully continuing love has been established, the First Week (Ignatius calls each of the four parts a Week) of the *Exercises* brings an experience of one's sinfulness in all its reality and mysteriousness. It is God's love, seriously experienced, which reveals and shows up a person's own sinful lack of love and basic self-absorption. Without a sense of God's carefully intimate love, this vision of sin could be destructive. But in God's love, the humiliating shame of acknowledging one's sin leads to the exhilarating experience of a forgiveness more pervasive and thorough than could have been imagined. The beauty of a crucified savior becomes a source of chastened confidence, humble joy and zealous thanksgiving. This experience in the *Exercises* becomes a life-long process: God's loving forgiveness disciplining our sinfully unruly hearts to mature freedom in the Spirit. After such an experience, Jesus crucified is always known by a weak, sinful creature as a source of healing, hope and confident humility (Aschenbrenner 1982, pp. 2, 4, 6).

Although these sentences capture, to some extent, the transformative dynamic of the *Exercises,* reading the manual will not produce the vision; the meditations must be prayed through under guidance and incorporated into one's life. One can make the *Exercises* either in the quiet of a retreat center or as an ongoing practice in daily life. Though the tradition of making and directing the *Exercises* stems from Roman Catholicism, today both Catholics and Protestants direct and make the *Exercises*. I heartily recommend this experience to pastoral counselors and their clients alike.

Two meditations in the *Exercises* illustrate how guilt and personal sinfulness are dealt with. During the First Week Ignatius recommends a meditation to review one's personal sin-history. Because Ignatius allows great freedom for the director to modify and adapt the points of meditation for the exercitant, I shall share an approach suggested by a colleague, James Maier, S.J., and used by me with great profit. The exercitant is instructed to imagine going on a picnic with Jesus. During the meal in a meadow by a river, a series of barges floats by on which are visualized tableaus of scenes from the exercitant's life. The exercitant asks Jesus to recount his interpretation of and reaction to the scenes presented. In this way the Lord tells the retreatant's story with an objectivity and compassion that heals guilt and short-circuits the mutterings of the superego. Through such an imaginative exchange the exercitant learns the place of guilt, repentance, and forgiveness, and is brought to forgive himself or herself and to make constructive resolutions for change.

In the meditation that culminates the First Week, the retreatant goes before Jesus hanging on the cross and ponders three questions: What have I done for Christ? What am I doing for Christ? What will I do for Christ? In the ensuing conversation, or "colloquy" as Ignatius terms it, exercitants are always profoundly moved by healthy guilt as I have been describing it here; by gentle self-acceptance because they sense acceptance from the Crucified; by insight; and by courageous resolve to make changes in their lives.

Even if one has not made the *Exercises*, these two meditative reflections can be assigned to a client who leads a prayer-life and with whom a counselor can converse explicitly within a religious framework.

Another assignment that can assist a client to work through guilt from within a religious perspective is an imaginative, prayerful exercise that I developed for my workshop on the "hard emotions" (hurt, anger, guilt). The counselor could encourage the client to think and pray with pen in hand so that the experience could be retained and perhaps reviewed with the pastoral counselor.

Emmaus Walk Exercise

Goals: To work through some area of guilt

To seek self-understanding

To experience the Lord's and one's own forgiveness

Approach: Invite quiet into your heart, mind, and spirit.

Prayerfully read Luke 24:13–35.

Imagine the path through the Judean countryside where the two friends walked conversing.

You are one of those persons.

The friend with you is someone you have hurt.

Speak honestly with your friend about what you did, what your friend did, how you each feel now—do not shy away from
 unpleasant feelings
 angry feelings
 the pain of recollection
 the deeper underlying basis of
 your union

Christ comes along and joins you in your walk.

You and your friend share fully and deeply with Christ what you have been discussing.
 What do you tell Christ?
 What does your friend say?
 What does Jesus say?

As a follow-up to this meditative reflection, advise the client to ritualize her or his guilt and eliminate it by writing on some aspects of the pain he or she wants to remove from life, from memory, from the relationship with Christ and the friend. Then let the client go outdoors, burn the paper, and bury or scatter the ashes. This seemingly simple action turns out to be deeply moving for all types of people:

the uncomplicated and the sophisticated, the unlearned and highly educated. It never seems gimmicky, artificial, or contrived.

Suppose the client is not very religious, or even is turned off by religion. At least the first and the third imaginative exercises could still be used in a modified way. In the "barges" exercise the client could be accompanied on the picnic by someone from whom he or she has experienced unconditional love. Such a person could be a close friend, a grandparent, or even the therapist. The important point is that the life-story and sin-history should be narrated by someone *other* than oneself, since superego intrusions can easily be triggered in solitary rumination.

The "Emmaus walk" exercise could similarly be adapted by having a mutual friend appear on the walk, and inviting that friend's objectivity, compassion, and esteem for the unreconciled companions. The client could be asked to articulate potential changes: in thoughts and feelings about the self, about guilt, about the offended party, and in terms of behavior as well.

Further insight can be gleaned from Ignatius's *Spiritual Exercises,* specifically from the section entitled "Rules for the Discernment of Spirits," a set of very practical directives for interpreting and responding to diverse movements of the mind and heart. Ignatius proposes that one use a different criterion than the instinctive pleasure-pain rule for following up an idea or feeling. Rather than allowing myself to be swayed by its effect on me right now—avoiding something because it makes me feel bad, or going toward an imagined delight—Ignatius recommends a self-transcending pause to note whether the proposed inner course of action tends toward or away from God in its outcome. (It might be observed in passing that Ignatius's world-view included the Holy Spirit and evil spirits who could and did affect humans' inner and outer life. Whether or not one accepts Ignatius's ontology of the spirit world, his subtle approach and concrete suggestions are useful.) Here are his words:

> 1) In the case of those who go from one mortal sin to another, the enemy is ordinarily accustomed to propose apparent pleasures. He fills their imagination with sensual delights and gratifications, the more readily to keep them in their vices and increase the number of their sins.
>
> With such persons the good spirit uses a method which is the reverse of the above. Making use of the light of reason, he will rouse the sting of conscience and fill them with remorse.

> 2) In the case of those who go on earnestly striving to cleanse their souls from sin and who seek to rise in the service of God our Lord to greater perfection, the method pursued is the opposite of that mentioned in the first rule.
>
> Then it is characteristic of the evil spirit to harass with anxiety, to afflict with sadness, to raise obstacles backed by fallacious reasoning that disturb the soul. Thus he seeks to prevent the soul from advancing (Ignatius Loyola 1951, p. 141).

Here Ignatius provides a framework for understanding guilt and for deciding whether or not to be influenced by it. Guilt is interpreted as growth-producing if it leads us back to God from our evil habits; growth-retarding if it thwarts our progress in holiness and obstructs our relationship with God and humankind.

In the first rule just cited Ignatius introduces the case of someone caught in a habit of sin and wrongdoing. "From one mortal sin to another" need not describe only the total blackguard, but anyone who in some areas of life is blinded by self-seeking. The "Sunday Christian" who oppresses his or her employees comes to mind, or the pious but racially prejudiced preacher, or the "perfect" parent whose children emerge as socialized conformists with crushed or rebellious spirits. The interior life of such clients may be described as calm and peaceful, with delight taken in their usual way of proceeding. Yet should the nagging rebuke of conscience stir in such a person, the pastoral counselor will want to rejoice and to help the client attend to the unsettled nature of the discomfort so that a change may be embraced. Such clients may come to counseling to be rid of what they view as needless, annoying guilt. The pastoral counselor must work with them to see whether indeed the striking employees need dialogue rather than confrontation; whether they should welcome a person of color to their neighborhood rather than organize the opposition; whether as parents they need to balance societal expectations against a growing guilty sense that they are causing distress in their youngsters.

The second rule applies to a different sort of person. Here delicacy of conscience and sensitivity to morality is in evidence, and the relationship with God guides behavior. The "evil spirit" or one's own lingering psychological unhealthiness—however one ultimately names the reality, the experience is what counts—produces anxiety, sadness, fallacious reasoning, disturbances in the soul, or what here has been called toxic guilt. Superego morality generates unease, and when it has been determined that the guilty thoughts and feelings are indeed toxic, the pastoral counselor brings from the armamentarium of psychological techniques of intervention a means recommended and sanctioned by the theory to which he or she adheres. A Freudian, for example, may decide to seek insight into the causes of the toxic guilt by reviewing the client's relationship with parents during early childhood. A Jungian may ask the client to personify the guilt and to write out a dialogue by use of active imagination. A cognitive-behaviorist may teach thought-stopping techniques to terminate guilt-tinged ruminating. An existential therapist may explore with the client the significance of guilt within the context of a developing sense of the meaning of the client's life. (I am not seeking here to convey a notion of mindless theoretical eclecticism, but rather to demonstrate briefly that most theoretically grounded techniques of pastoral intervention can be used within the psycho-spiritual, philosophic-theological perspective developed within this chapter.)

Further Concrete Suggestions

Let me conclude with some examples that can flesh out all the theoretical principles elaborated above.

For persons bent on personal psycho-spiritual growth, guilt can appear in many disguises:

- the guilt of failing to attend to someone—or saying too much;
- the guilt of stealing a few moments for myself when there are so many unmet needs around me;
- the guilt of enjoying a balanced diet when millions go to bed hungry;
- the guilt of saving time for prayer when so much work is undone;
- the guilt of overwork and skipping prayer (Kelley 1980, pp. 88–89).

Some feel guilty about stuffing themselves with food, but not about ignoring others at the meal. Some feel guilt over masturbation, but not from working eighteen hours a day. Guilt arises for being a workaholic or for not being more of a workaholic. Guilt surfaces for not measuring up, not doing enough, not achieving enough, or not being successful enough. There are those who feel guilty for saying no or for giving in too easily; for setting limits or for making themselves too available; for taking a stand or for going along with the majority. Others may blame themselves for taking time off, for resting, for not filling every moment of the day with useful activity. Some take themselves to task for expressing anger, others for not expressing anger and being "Mr. Nice Guy." Some feel guilty for being too cognitive in their approach to life, and others for appearing too emotional (Bilotta 1980, p. 103). From just this short list of daily situations, it appears that almost any behavior, thought, feeling, *or its opposite* can become grist for the guilt mill! Thus the importance of discerning rationally just what stance toward living and acting fits each individual's scheme of values.

The thoughts, feelings, and behaviors just catalogued can be self-imposed expectations, but they can just as easily derive from expectations of others. Such expectations can push us to act contrary to our goals and our perceived best interests. Expectations, however, can descend into manipulation when family members, working colleagues, or advertisers appeal to our guilt and to our natural instinct to avoid it. Pastoral counselor can assist their clients to sort through such efforts at control and domination. The spoken or implied criticism and judgment of our actions get conveyed through the frowning condemnation, the silent treatment, the cold shoulder, the walking away in a huff, the glare that kills: all are intended to generate guilt for the purpose of altering our behavior. Such manipulation implies a threatened withdrawal of affection or approval. This kind of threat provides quite powerful leverage over others unless they are very sure of themselves and confident in their identity. Only free assent changes the expectations and manipulations of others into personal obligations. We should assent only when such expectations coincide with our own life's direction. Counselors can support and strengthen their clients' free choices by helping them explicitate their identity and values, and discern whether or not to comply with others' expectations (Bush 1980, pp. 42–43). Clients will thus be empowered to respond to that part of each person that is always worrying what "they" might be thinking of me. "They" might include parents, children, co-workers, employers, policemen, waiters, or even passing strangers! Coaching clients to apply rational analysis to such essentially irrational reactions does much to alleviate toxic guilt.

Here is a suggested strategy for handling guilt feelings and freeing ourselves from their tyranny. First, do not *do* anything, since interpreting guilt emotions is less a matter of doing than of awareness.

Sit with these feelings and even try to befriend them. Once we learn that we can stand the feelings, we are ready for some exploration. The next move is detective-like, that is, to chase down their origin: Who or what event occasioned them? What are the implicit "musts," "oughts," and "shoulds"? Bring as much of their irrationality into consciousness as possible. Refuse to act out the guilt feelings or to try feverishly to eliminate them. Such essentially useless activity becomes repetitive and strengthens their control over us. Regard guilt feelings as temptations to renounce freedom and responsibility. If we can isolate those circumstances and situations that cause us guilt, we can determine to deal with them differently next time. We can interpret our feelings of guilt as signs of our lack of personal freedom. Accordingly, we can accept them as a challenge to grow, to root out determinisms, and thus to become more fully ourselves.

When guilty thoughts or feelings become too powerful to be handled by ourselves, we may discuss them with someone we trust. Sharing guilt occasions objectivity and reduces the feelings to manageable intensity.

Since guilt feelings are basically self-centered, another remedy is to turn our attention outward. The focus of our attention should be redirected from our internal state of soul to an interest in our neighbor and in God. Almost every uncomfortable state can be alleviated by assisting someone else, or by prayer (Bush 1980, pp. 47–49).

The following considerations may assist efforts to "befriend" one's guilt. Guilt may be personified as an important guide to my life, or as a helpful teacher if I am willing to struggle to permit it to reveal its lesson to me and to learn from its meaning. The experience of guilt can serve as an invitation to pause and reflect on who I really am and what my life's goals are. Guilt may question me about how I have been dealing with myself and others. Have I been responding to myself and others as gifts of God? Guilt can remind me to be my truest self. If I strive to befriend my guilt experiences, perhaps they will direct me along my journey to God. Guilt may be a gentle, quiet whispering that I am in danger of *betraying* my identity. On the other hand, if I listen to this still, small voice, I have an opportunity to *remember* who I am (Bilotta 1980, pp. 120–21; 123).

As a companion in our daily lives, guilt helps us to become more aware of our humanness and can connect us to our growth and development in a truly authentic way. It orients us to reality. It empowers us to experience ourselves as men and women deeply involved in a lifelong task of psycho-spiritual growth into genuine wholeness. It warns us against our tendency to become insensitive or ego-inflated. It reminds us simply and powerfully that we are human, that we are not God (Franasiak 1980, p. 143).

Note

All scripture quotations in this chapter are taken from the *New American Bible.*

References

Agudo, Philomena. 1980. "Guilt: Its Effect on Wholeness." In *Guilt: Issues of Emotional Living in an Age of Stress,* edited by Kathleen Kelley, pp. 17–32. The Fifth Psychotheological Symposium. Whitinsville, Mass.: Affirmation Books.

Aschenbrenner, George A. 1982. *The Jesuit University Today: An Introduction to the Ignatian Vision in Higher Education.* Scranton, Penn.: The Scranton Journal.

Bilotta, Vincent M. 1980. "Guilty: For Betraying Who I Am." In Kelley, *Guilt: Issues of Emotional Living in an Age of Stress,* pp. 101–23.

Bradshaw, John. 1988. *Healing the Shame That Binds You.* Deerfield Beach, Fla.: Health Communications.

Bush, Bernard J. 1980. "The Critical Eye." In Kelley, *Guilt: Issues of Emotional Living in an Age of Stress,* pp. 35–49.

Carroll, John. 1985. *Guilt: The Grey Eminence Behind Character, History, and Culture.* London: Routledge and Kegan Paul.

Erikson, Erik. 1963. *Childhood and Society.* New York: W. W. Norton.

Franasiak, E. J. 1980. "When Enough Is Not Enough: Affirmed Sufficiency and Guilt." In Kelley, *Guilt: Issues of Emotional Living in an Age of Stress,* pp. 137–44.

Freud, Sigmund. 1930. *Civilization and Its Discontents.* London: Hogarth Press.

Glaser, John W. 1971. "Conscience and Superego: A Key Distinction." *Theological Studies* 32: 30–47.

Kelley, Kathleen E. 1980. "Let Tomorrow Take Care of Itself." In Kelley, *Guilt: Issues of Emotional Living in an Age of Stress,* edited by Kathleen E. Kelley, pp. 87–99. The Fifth Psychotheological Symposium. Whitinsville, Mass.: Affirmation Books.

Lewis, Helen B. 1971. *Shame and Guilt in Neurosis.* New York: International Universities Press.
Loyola, Ignatius. 1951. *The Spiritual Exercises of St. Ignatius.* Edited by Louis J. Puhl, S. J. Chicago: Loyola University Press.
Menninger, Karl. 1973. *Whatever Became of Sin?* New York: Hawthorn Books.
Nietzsche, Friedrich. 1967. *The Genealogy of Morals.* New York: Vintage.

For Further Reading

Books:

Dyer, Wayne W. 1976. *Your Erroneous Zones.* New York: Funk & Wagnalls.
Houselander, Frances Caryll. 1951. *Guilt.* New York: Sheed and Ward.
McKenzie, John Grant. 1962. *Guilt: Its Meaning and Significance.* New York: Abingdon.
Metz, Johannes, ed. 1970. *Moral Evil Under Challenge.* Concilium: Theology in the Age of Renewal. Moral Theology, vol. 56. New York: Herder and Herder.
Reik, Theodor. 1957. *Myth and Guilt: The Crime and Punishment of Mankind.* New York: G. Braziller.
Segundo, Juan. 1974. *Evolution and Guilt.* Maryknoll, N.Y.: Orbis Books.
Smith, Roger Winston, ed. 1971. *Guilt: Man and Society.* Garden City, N.Y.: Anchor Books.
Soboson, Jeffrey. 1982. *Guilt and the Christian: A New Perspective.* Chicago: Thomas Moore Press.
Tournier, Paul. 1962. *Guilt and Grace: A Psychological Study.* New York: Harper.
Westphal, Merald. 1984. *God, Guilt and Death: An Existential Phenomenology of Religion.* Bloomington, Ind.: Indiana University Press.

Articles:

Aden, Leroy. 1984. "Pastoral Counseling and Self-Justification." *Journal of Psychology and Christianity* 3, 4: pp. 23–28.
Banmen, John. 1988. "Guilt and shame: Theories and Therapeutic

Possibilities." *International Journal for the Advancement of Counselling* 11, 1: 79–91.

Belgum, David. 1985. "Guilt." *Counseling and Values* 29, 2(April): 128–40.

Bruun, Christine V. 1985. "A Combined Treatment Approach: Cognitive Therapy and Spiritual Dimensions." *Journal of Psychology and Christianity* 4, 2: 9–11.

Goldberg, Carl. 1988. "Replacing Moral Masochism with a Shame Paradigm in Psychoanalysis." American Psychological Association Annual Convention: Infantile Anxieties, 1987. *Dynamic Psychotherapy* 6, 2: 114–23.

Goldman, Harriet E. 1988. "Paradise Destroyed: The Crime of Being Born: A Psychoanalytic Study of the Experience of Evil." *Contemporary Psychoanalysis* 24, 3(July): 420–50.

Marks, Malcolm J. 1988. "Remorse, Revenge, and Forgiveness." *Psychotherapy Patient* 5, 1–2: 317–30.

Nathanson, Donald L. 1989. "Understanding What Is Hidden: Shame in Sexual Abuse." *Psychiatric Clinics of North America* 12, 2(June): 381–88.

Schneiderman, Leo. 1988. "Two Types of Remorse in Psychotherapy." *Psychotherapy Patient* 5, 1–2: 135–45.

Shaw, Jeanne. 1988. "The Usefulness of Remorse." *Psychotherapy Patient* 5, 1–2: 77–82.

Switzer, David K. 1988. "The Remorseful Patient: Perspectives of a Pastoral Counselor." *Psychotherapy Patient* 5, 1–2: 275–90.

Vanderwall, Francis W. 1986. "Guilt, Jesus, and Spiritual Counseling." *Studies in Formative Spirituality* 7, 2(May): 253–66.

Watson, P. J., Morris, Ronald J., and Hood, Ralph W. 1988. "Sin and Self-Functioning: I. Grace, Guilt, and Self-Consciousness." *Journal of Psychology and Theology* 16, 3(Fall): 254–69.

——. "Sin and Self-Functioning: II. Grace, Guilt, and Psychological Adjustment." *Journal of Psychology and Theology* 16, 3(Fall): 270–81.

Howard W. Stone

16. Depression

Depression can be a spiritual disorder. The "dark night of the soul" that many experience was described at length by the early Christian mystics. Their expressions of the absence of God, the doubt, and the loss of meaning in religious ritual and service are akin to many symptoms of what we now call depression.

During any given year, according to a study for the National Institute of Mental Health (Beck 1979, p. 1), 15 percent of all people in the United States between the ages of 18 and 74 will have significant depressive disturbances. In addition, 75 percent of all those hospitalized in a psychiatric hospital will report depression as part of the total cause of their treatment. Since depression strikes especially during the adult years, when vocations are important and children are being reared, it not only affects the individual but also has a major impact on marriage, the family, the church, the work place, even society. It is the "common cold" of mental, emotional, and spiritual disorders.

For the melancholic, depression leads to disturbance of relations with significant others. For the mystic, for the deeply religious, it is the most important relationship that is affected: the relationship with God.[1] Further insight into depression as a spiritual plight comes from a study of the vice *accidie*, one of the seven deadly sins now frequently translated as sloth. It may help our understanding of the melancholy that creeps into a person's relationship with God and ultimately causes some people to leave the church. The term *accidie* (also known as acedia or akedia) has gone through considerable transformation of meaning throughout the centuries. At first it was used to describe something that affected only hermit monks; in the Middle Ages accidie was applied to all Christians.

Evagrian Ponticus (fourth century A.D.) was the first to describe accidie clearly. Evagrian belonged to a community of ascetic monks living in widely scattered individual huts on the Egyptian desert near

Alexandria. He (Wenzel, 1967, p. 5) described accidie as a demon that plagued hermit monks:

> First he makes the sun appear sluggish and immobile, as if the day had fifty hours. Then he causes the monk continually to look at the windows and forces him to step out of his cell and to gaze at the sun to see how far it still is from the ninth hour, and to look around, here and there, whether any of his brethren is near. Moreover, the demon sends him hatred against the place, against life itself, and against the work of his hands, and makes him think he has lost the love among his brethren and that there is none to comfort him. If during those days anybody annoyed the monk, the demon would add this to increase the monk's hatred. He stirs the monk also to long for different places in which he can find easily what is necessary for his life and can carry on a much less toilsome and more expedient profession (in Wenzel 1967, p. 5).

Elsewhere in his work Evagrian (Wenzel, 1967, p. 5) described other traits of accidie as listlessness, psychic exhaustion, monotony, boredom, dejection, and so forth.

> In the end accidie causes the monk either to give in to physical sleep, which proves unrefreshing or actually dangerous because it opens the door to many other temptations, or to leave his cell and eventually the religious life altogether (in Wenzel 1967, p. 5).

The remarkable similarity between Evagrian's description of accidie and a contemporary understanding of depression cannot be missed. Accidie, at least as it was understood by the Egyptian desert monks, was a form of melancholy that affected one's relationship with God. A staleness in this relationship and in religious practices frequently led the monk to avoidance of the ascetic observances, to a feeling of general malaise and sleeping away time, or ultimately to escape from the community and sometimes from the church.

I do not believe these states—described by mystics as the dark night of the soul and by the ascetics as accidie—are particularly uncommon. Certainly they are not the exclusive problems of a past age or of the full-time monastic. They are common to human experience, albeit magnified by the religious's concern with absolute reality. Indeed accidie appears to be like depression, but with unique characteristics arising from its association with the absolute. It is, to use Morton Bloomfield's term, a "dryness of the spirit" that can affect one's whole being (1952, p. 96).

On an average this dryness of spirit will be felt by fifteen of every one hundred adults in churches this year. How will the depressed worshipers respond to the sermon I am preparing for Sunday? Will they sense any hope? Will they even be in church? Is a depressed church member able to experience hope, or only despair? Is depression tantamount to lack of faith and therefore sin? When I speak in the sermon of the trinity of virtues—faith, hope, and love—how can the depressed individual who lacks hope, has little faith in God, others, or self, and feels as if no one cares, make sense out of my words? Even more, what do these words mean when the very person speaking them is despairing? How can the depressed minister speak of faith and hope?

An Ancient Malady, A Contemporary Disorder

We have seen that melancholy or depression did not appear suddenly on the scene in recent times. Throughout recorded history one can find descriptions of depression and explanations (both psychological and environmental) for its cause. The book of Job tells of one man's immense melancholy. In the depths of his despair Job could not imagine that his life would ever improve. He turned his anger from his parents toward God: "God's terrors stand paraded against me" (Job 6:4). He describes his agony:

> I am nearly blind with grief
> and my limbs are reduced to a shadow. . . .
> My days are over, so are my plans,
> my heart-strings are broken (Job 17:7, 11, *NJB*).

From the earliest recorded descriptions of depression to the present, there has been considerable confusion concerning what depression is and how it develops. Under some circumstances, such as bereavement, depression appears to be a very natural response. Just as there is normal and pathological grief, so there is normal and morbid depression. In seventeenth, eighteenth, and early nineteenth century Britain, for example, it was considered romantic and somewhat fashionable to be overcome with melancholia. There always have been "tortured" artists and melancholic poets. In fact, for those who are unhappy with the way they are living their lives, depression may be the signal that something is wrong and may provide the very impetus needed for positive change. For the grieving it is a necessary stage in the healing process.

Melancholy, the historical word for depression, literally means "black bile" (one of the chief humors, or body fluids, which in ancient Greece was believed to come from the kidneys or spleen and which produced depression, irritability, or gloominess). Hippocrates wrote of depression some twenty-five hundred years ago: "Melancholics develop their illness when the blood is contaminated with gall and mucous; their mental state is disturbed, many even become mad" (in Tellenbach 1980, p. 5). In his discussion of one patient, Hippocrates stated, "Stupor accompanies her continuously; loss of appetite, sleeplessness, loss of initiative, attacks of rage, discontent, expressions of melancholy affect" (ibid.). Hippocrates did not equate momentary bouts of loneliness or feeling blue with melancholy, but "if feeling of fear or sadness continues for a long time, the suffering is melancholic" (ibid.).

Debate over the causes of depression—whether it is based environmentally (on psycho-social factors) or physiologically (especially on genetic, biochemical, and neurological predispositions)—has continued for centuries. It would be difficult to argue successfully that environment alone or physiology alone causes depression. In the estimation of many, it is the most organically based of emotional disorders. Many individuals who seek counseling cannot identify what has triggered their dysphoria (a generalized depressed feeling of ill-being, the opposite of euphoria). Others may report physical symptoms such as sleep disturbance and fatigue without knowing their causes, without being aware that they are depressed, or even without feeling remarkably sad or "down." In yet other cases, a seemingly trivial environmental event will set off or be associated with a deep depression. One woman I counseled had to be hospitalized for depression after her husband announced he had bought a dirt bike. She had been wanting a new sofa.

It appears that some people are more physiologically biased toward depression than others. For them, a less potent precipitator is required to trigger melancholy than for others. You or I may respond to a scowl and angry words from a colleague with the thought, "He is just out of sorts today"; for another the same event can be the beginning of a downward spiral of self-recrimination, self-doubt, social isolation, and pervasive despair. The difference is not necessarily one of relative mental health.

A very legitimate question, in this case, may be "If depression is organically based, shouldn't the individual be given anti-depressant drugs rather than counseling?'' The answer is an equivocal yes and no. Beck's research (1979, p. 2) suggests that various forms of antidepressants are at least somewhat helpful for 60 to 65 percent of individuals, but that 35 to 40 percent cannot be helped by drugs and many others are unwilling to take medication or suffer from side effects that preclude their use (Beck 1979, p. 2). Counseling can be of benefit regardless of whether one's depression is due to environmental factors or a physiological predisposition, and whether or not antidepressant medications are used.

Traits of Depression

Depressives as a group report a number of typical characteristics. It is highly unlikely that any one person would exhibit all of these symptoms. One may experience ongoing exhaustion and difficulty speaking with others, and yet have no headaches or sleep disturbance. Another may feel immense sadness, a loss of satisfaction in what previously had been desirable activity, and frequent bouts of crying, but no other signs of depression.

It is important to keep in mind that some of these symptoms also are characteristics of physical diseases. For example, a client I saw several years ago who described low mood, constant exhaustion, diminished appetite, weight loss, and ongoing marital strife. He had a history of depressive episodes, but the rapid weight loss and his general "out of sorts" feeling suggested to me that his problem might be more than just depression or marital difficulties. I recommended a physical examination, which revealed that he had cancer and needed immediate surgery. It is clearly important to refer any individual with more than just mild depression to a physician for a thorough medical evaluation.

The characteristics of depression fall into four categories: affect, or emotions; behavior; physiology; and cognitions. Accidie is not a fifth category but is the whole of which the four are the segments.

AFFECT

The depressed often feel dysphoria, a pervasive state of feeling sad, "blue," or "down" most of the time (except in the case of manic depressives, who can have wide swings of mood from euphoria to depression). The depressed may suffer guilt and anger, although the anger usually is aimed at themselves. They think of themselves as failures. They feel unable to do anything about their situation; everything seems hopeless. Their spiritual life may become stale, and it may seem as if God no longer has any interest in them. Joy is replaced by melancholy, and they may find themselves crying frequently and for no apparent reason.

BEHAVIOR

Depressed individuals lose satisfaction in doing things and experience a generally lowered activity level. Put more simply, they do less. They engage in fewer spontaneous moves like calling a friend to go out to a movie. Those who previously enjoyed hobbies like sailing, eating out, or cycling, no longer get a "kick" out of such activities. They even lose motivation for undertaking the mundane tasks of living. They may spend more time sitting, staring into space, idly watching TV, leafing through magazines, or napping. When they do practice spiritual disciplines such as worship and prayer, they do so without vibrancy. Often they abandon spiritual activities altogether. (Remember Evagrian's comments on accidie.)

Associated with a lower level of activity is the tendency to avoid or escape from the usual pattern or routine of life. When I am depressed, my daily activities seem useless, boring, and devoid of meaning, and I have my "hit the road" fantasies. I want to throw a sleeping bag and fishing tackle into a truck and take off for the lakes or the mountains. I do not want any constraints; I want to get up when I want, fish when I want, sleep when I want, and do whatever I feel like at the moment.

Many depressed individuals experience increased dependency. Those who feel helpless and hopeless rely more upon others for what they feel unable to provide themselves. At the same time, the depressed frequently experience a loss of emotional attachments—both the desire to be related to others and, because they have withdrawn from people, the actual opportunity to be related. What is more, when they do interact, they tend to have interpersonal problems. It may be difficult for them to be assertive, or at the other extreme they may easily erupt into a destructive rage.

Depressed individuals have impaired abilities to cope with practical everyday problems. One who normally can replace a washer in a faucet, find a lost mitten for a child, or deal with a mixed-up order at a catalog store now finds these tasks insurmountable.

PHYSIOLOGY

Physiological retardation, or slowing of movements, can accompany depression. (A severely depressed individual may sit in a corner and not move all day!) For me, an early indication of the onset of depression is my tennis game. I simply cannot move my body around the court as fast as usual, and I tend to let the hard shots go by.

Retardation of speech patterns is a common sign. Depressed persons may speak slower and at a lower pitch, and the severely depressed may speak in a flat, lifeless monotone, if they speak at all. There also is a general feeling of exhaustion or fatigue, even after periods of rest. Those who are depressed tend to feel tired all the time; they lack the energy to do those things that would help them combat their melancholia. Some have difficulties with headaches, constipation, or diarrhea. There can be a loss of appetite; the joy has gone out of eating, and, in fact, food may seem tasteless. Others may eat large amounts of food but without pleasure. There also can be a loss of interest in sex, which the severely depressed experience as an intrusion into their private world.

Finally, many depressed individuals experience sleep disturbances. Insomnia is one form, especially waking very early in the morning and being unable to get back to sleep. On the other hand, like the monks suffering from accedia, there are depressives who sleep more than usual, as much as fourteen to sixteen hours or more each day. I have counseled several people who would fall asleep at one or two in the morning, wake up just long enough to get their children off to school, and then sleep again until moments before the children arrived home.

COGNITIONS

Depression affects individuals' thinking; they tend to distort and misinterpret reality. In this regard Beck (1967, pp. 255–61) speaks of "the primary triad," or the three major disturbed thought patterns of a depressed individual—the viewing of events, self, and the future in an idiosyncratic manner. The depressed perpetually interpret events in a negative way, conceiving of their interactions with the world—and with God—as defeat, disparagement, abandonment, and deprivation. Neutral and even positive transactions with other people are seen as failures. Cognitively, the depressed evaluate their own *selves* lower or of less value than when they are not depressed (lowered self-esteem). They commonly indulge in blame (of self or other) and self-criticism, followed by feelings of guilt. When compared to others, they find themselves wanting. They also tend to be indecisive and may spend immense amounts of time trying to make a choice, often looking for the "perfect" solution or the "right" path. They view the future negatively. They have a vision of hopelessness, of a future that will bring only continued suffering and pain, of being trapped. To them, time most emphatically does *not* heal all wounds.

It is my experience that depressed individuals also experience God in the same negative and hopeless manner. Although faith is certainly not based on cognition alone, the depressed tend to be especially troubled by doubts or lose their faith in God entirely. They have difficulty saying with the psalmist, "My hope is in the Lord." A steadfast faith that has remained unshaken through many earlier adversities, even tragedies, can crumble under the weight of depression.

The cognitive set thus described sometimes leads to thoughts of suicide. If it seems that life consists of unending and unabated suffering, suffering which is due to one's own defects, a person may view death as beneficial not only to self but also to friends and family.

Background and Assessment

Depression is not a momentary bout of sadness, but a response that can affect the total organism—cognitively, physiologically, affectively, and behaviorally. Because it is not a simple phenomenon, it is rarely easy to care for. It seems to have a multiplicity of causes and a number of ways in which it reveals itself. Therefore the helping response must be tailored to each individual's particular situation, grouping of symptoms, and severity.

The extent of true depression customarily is categorized as mild, moderate, or severe. In *mild* depression, the individual may feel sad or blue, a feeling that fluctuates considerably and may even be absent at times. Or the individual may be unaware of feeling especially sad but may experience a loss of interest in work or hobbies, some insomnia, and/or relatively moderate but uncharacteristic fatigue or restlessness. The dysphoric feeling can be relieved temporarily or permanently by outside stimuli, such as a compliment, a joke, a vacation, or a piece of good news. Other symptoms are often relieved by such things as regular, strenuous exercise, a reevaluation of goals, appropriate dietary changes, and so forth.

The *moderately* depressed individual's dysphoria tends to be more pronounced and more persistent; it is less likely to be influenced by attempts to offer cheer. Any immediate relief of this condition is temporary, and treatment can be expected to take some time. The dysphoria frequently is at its worst in the morning and may lighten somewhat as the day progresses. Cognitive, physiological, and behavior symptoms are likewise more resistant to simple solutions.

The *severely* depressed are apt to feel relentlessly hopeless or miserable. Persons experiencing agitated depression often state that they are beset with worries. In Beck's study (1967, p. 17) 70 percent of severely depressed persons said that they were sad all the time and could not snap out of it; that they were so sad it was very painful; or that they were so sad they could not stand it. Severe depression is also more likely to slow people down to an extreme, to cause debilitating exhaustion and passivity, to impede seriously their relationships and their normal functioning.

It is obvious that some depression is so severe that hospitalization and medication are needed, yet the majority of individuals encountered by the pastor are only mildly depressed and can be offered skillful and much-needed help. Such pastoral care is not second-class treatment but is precisely the quality of care that is required. It does not take place exclusively in counseling sessions and is not offered only by the pastor; it also includes the response of the priesthood of all believers, incorporating the depressed one into the community of faith.

Let us say that a person who claims to be depressed or who has many of the symptoms of depression has walked into the minister's office for the first time, asking for help. At the outset it is important for the pastor to discern whether the person in fact is depressed or has some other configuration of emotions or possibly a physical illness. Since both the experience of depression and its precipitators vary considerably from individual to individual, the minister must learn the specific ways in which the client is experiencing the dysphoria and what might be causing or exacerbating it.

It is also necessary to determine the extent and severity of the depression. Degrees to which melancholic persons are depressed are quite variable. (The episodic and transitory "blues" most of us experience are not, clinically speaking, depression. Uncomfortable as those hours or days are, they are not of significant degree or duration.) As a rule of thumb, ministers ought to see only mild and some moderately depressed individuals, referring the more severely depressed to mental-health professionals. However, both minister and congregation can offer significant pastoral *care* to seriously depressed members who are in and out of psychiatric hospitals throughout their lifetimes.

The first meeting with the depressed client should involve some history taking; the establishment of a relationship and building of rapport; ventilation of emotions concerning specific problems; and assessment of the depression's severity, especially to determine whether the client is so severely depressed as to require medical attention or possibly hospitalization. The minister who is uncertain about the severity needs to refer the individual for psychiatric evaluation.

The minister should remember that grief is not the same as depression, even though a grieving individual usually will be depressed for a period of time and inadequate resolution of grief can bring on long-term depression. There are major differences between depression that is a normal part of grief and significant chronic or acute depression (Stone 1972, pp. 31–34). Grieving people most frequently describe *bouts* of depression that come and go with decreasing intensity and frequency after a loss. The depressed, especially the moderately or severely depressed, are less likely to have episodic bouts and are more likely to find no relief for days, months, even years.

Early in the counseling process it is helpful to communicate that pastor and parishioner are a pair of sleuths who must investigate the depressed person's thinking, emotions, and behavior. This investigation is the equal responsibility of the client, who in the future ideally will take on the majority of the assessment task. In a collaborative fashion minister and parishioner ask the following questions about the depression to ascertain its severity and to discover what strengths and coping abilities are available.

1) *What immediate difficulties are impeding functioning?* For example, if the person's marriage is disintegrating, the first intervention may focus in this area. If he or she is suicidal, this must be addressed first. Or the person may have been laid off, or fired, or passed over for a promotion—a career crisis—which seems to have precipitated the depression. If so, that's where intervention can begin.

2) *What are this person's strengths?* Each individual has many skills, abilities, and resources that may have been temporarily forgotten or undervalued and need to be rediscovered. This can be accomplished by helping the person to remember good or successful experiences from the past and to review how he or she functioned differently in those positive situations.

3) *Are the symptoms primarily behavioral, physiological, cognitive, or affective?* Referring to the four symptom areas discussed earlier, it is valuable to identify a clustering of symptoms so that treatment methods can be aimed toward those areas which seem most debilitating.

4) *What practical first steps can be taken to help turn this depression around?* Both the minister and the parishioner may have a long-range vision for the person's life, but the complete task often is too much to tackle. They need to come up with some realistic first steps that can stop the slide into deeper depression and initiate the journey out.

In addition to answering these questions, the minister can use a number of standardized inventories to considerable advantage in ascertaining the extent and depth of the depression: Beck Depression Inventory (1967, pp. 186–207), the Zung Self-Rating Depression Scale (1965, pp. 63–70), the Raskin Rating Scale for Depression (1970, pp. 163–73), and the Hamilton Rating Scale (1969, pp. 56–62).

The assessment process may itself accomplish a great deal; indeed, some depressed persons need only this one encounter with the minister to allow some catharsis and problem-solving. Such persons will not desire or require any further visits. If an individual finds more than one visit necessary but is not sufficiently depressed to require medication, medical help, or hospitalization, the minister can follow one of two approaches. One course involves one to three additional visits that focus primarily on sustenance, allowing discussion of difficulties and imparting some strength and self-esteem to the individual through the minister's presence and support. During such sustaining sessions, a few relatively small changes in habits could be suggested (such as exercise or a change of diet). The other option is to begin a process of care that will most likely take longer, will strive for more significant change on the part of the client, and will use several of the methods described in the next section of this chapter.

Depressed persons who come to the pastor for help usually do not arrive saying, "Pastor, I feel depressed." People who are depressed tend to go to physicians describing back problems or sleeplessness rather than depression; they go to marriage counselors complaining, "My husband is insensitive to my needs," rather than speaking of their melancholy; they go to the minister with their guilt or spiritual struggles rather than with a recognizable identification of depression. The minister must listen for depression lurking behind somatic complaints, a troubled marriage, or dryness of the spirit. Many of the depressed do not speak directly of their pain. In fact, many depressed individuals do not ask for help, and it may be friends or family members who tell the minister of this person's trouble. A visit from the pastor usually is required, and in such situations the pastor's position, as one who can and traditionally does visit people in their homes, is unique among professional care-givers.

Risk of Suicide

If it appears during the process of assessment that a person may be suicidal, some additional steps must be taken. One does not need to be depressed to threaten, attempt, or commit suicide, but a significant number of depressed individuals do all three. Beck (1967, p. 57) found that the suicide rate for depressives is 36 times higher than for the general population, and at least three times higher than for either schizophrenics or alcoholics. Ideas of suicide occur at one time or another in 75 percent of depressives, and at least 15 percent make the attempt (Fairchild 1980, p. 33). These statistics reveal a population at risk.

A helpful way to "listen for" the lethality of suicide risk in depressed clients is to use the following criteria. These criteria should not be used as a checklist but they should be internalized, with the answers gained informally but clearly from the potentially suicidal person. They serve as a proximate way to determine the possibility that someone will commit suicide (Stone 1991).

Age and Sex: Over half of completed suicides are men, but women attempt it more frequently. The threat of suicide increases with age, especially in the case of men. All talk of suicide, however, must be treated seriously.

Suicide Plan: The plan is the most critical element in assessing suicide risk. The pastor will need to determine how specific the plan, how lethal the method, and how available the means for putting the plan into effect. The answers to these questions generally will require direct questioning of the depressed person. Some means of committing suicide are more lethal than others—a gun more than tranquilizers, for example, or a full bottle of barbiturates more than a handful of aspirin. If a person has a very specific plan, has spent time thinking in detail about how he or she will go about it, has selected a lethal method, and has the means readily available, there is a very serious suicide risk.

Stress: Most serious threats of suicide occur when an individual has experienced a loss or potential loss such as death, divorce, illness, or retirement. If the stress is extreme and the individual has a specific suicide plan, then a very active response is required.

Symptoms: The completion of the suicide act can come as a result of several different emotional states. The most serious is the depressive-agitated state, in which the person feels emotionally depressed but is simultaneously tense and active and therefore has the energy and determination to complete the act. Furthermore, a depressed person who is also an alcoholic, drug abuser, homosexual, or sexual deviate has considerably higher than average suicide lethality.

Meaning and Religious Involvement: Strong religious beliefs and regular involvement with church provide both emotional support and social constraints against suicide. However, it is important to remember that even highly religious people do commit suicide.

Resources: It is essential to identify relatives, friends, church members, co-workers, and others who are available to assist the suicidal individual. Although the depressive probably feels "nobody cares," there usually are more resources available than the individual realizes. In the case of a depressed person who appears suicidal and is immobilized or unwilling to talk frankly with others, the pastor is in a position to tell these resource persons about the suicide potential so they can become involved and actively communicate their caring. If the one considering suicide has few personal resources, the pastoral carer can call on members of the church to reach out and provide support.

Lifestyle: A stable lifestyle is indicated by such things as consistent work history, long marriage and family relations, and absence of past suicide activity. Unstable individuals may exhibit chronic alcoholism, job-hopping or marriage-hopping, character disorder or psychosis, frequent unresolved crises, and so on. Chronic suicide threats happen only among unstable personalities, but acute suicidal gestures may occur among people with stable as well as unstable lifestyles.

Communication: Communication is vital; depressed individuals who have stopped communicating with others may have given up hope and are more likely at least to attempt suicide. Indirect nonverbal communication (such as making a new will, giving up prized possessions or favorite activities, etc.) rarely reaches the notice of mental-health professionals and can be difficult to discern. Family and friends, along with the minister and members of the congregation, may thus be the only ones to notice such signs of distress.

Health: The pastoral carer should find out if a depressed and possibly suicidal individual has (or fears) a serious disease such as cancer, impending or recent surgery, or chronic illness. Individuals who have or believe they have a terminal illness may seek suicide as a way of coping.

None of the above criteria, except for a specific and lethal plan, is necessarily dangerous when taken alone, though all are more serious in the case of a depressive than with one who is not depressed. It is important to gather information and look at the whole picture to see if a pattern is beginning to form.

A basic underlying rule in dealing with even the hint of suicide is: *Take all ideas about suicide seriously.* People who makes statements like "Life isn't worth living anymore" or "There is no way out" should be asked directly if they are thinking of taking their own life. Discussing it will *not* cause someone to do it; talking about suicide, in frank and specific detail so that assistance can be offered, is *much better* than ignoring it. Once again, if anyone is even suspected of being suicidal, the pastoral carer must take it seriously and, if necessary, contact mental-health professionals or a crisis center immediately.

Pastoral Counseling Methods

Several methods for the treatment of depressed individuals are presented below. Each focuses especially, though not exclusively, on one of the four characteristics of depression (affect, behavior, physiology, and cognition). These techniques are drawn from a variety of psychological schools, from the field of pastoral counseling, and from the history of pastoral care and spiritual direction. All, in my experience, have been helpful responses to depressed persons. The reader will readily observe that a number of these methods can relieve more than one characteristic of depression. A review of "outcome" research studies indicates that the best treatment often incorporates methods that target more than one symptomatic cluster. For example, cognitive and behavioral methods can be used together. In some cases the inclusion of antidepressant medications gives even more effective results.

The list of methods presented is in no way complete, and the discussion will of necessity be brief. No minister or counselor would ever use *all* of these methods. I suggest that ministers select ones which appear most beneficial for the people they encounter. It is helpful for the minister to have a confident grasp of at least two techniques that apply to each of the four areas of depression.

METHODS OF AFFECTIVE INTERVENTION

We know from research done on the process of psychotherapy that significant symptomatic relief occurs between the

> time a patient enters a waiting room and the time he or she leaves after being interviewed by a clinic secretary; thus, it should not be surprising that some patients with mild depressions can be sufficiently helped through the clarification, catharsis, and hopefulness of an evaluation interview (Lieberman 1981, p. 244).

Lieberman is suggesting that for some people, depression can be turned around simply through the *expression of emotion* and the *discussion of the problem.* The empathy, warmth, and hope that a minister offers may be sufficient to help them with their melancholy. In this understanding environment they can say what previously only could be thought; they can put into words those feelings that once had seemed too powerful to express. Sometimes the depressed are afraid to talk with friends or family about what troubles them, and so a whirlpool of ruminations swirls around within them. With mild but reasonably acute depression, the expression of such feelings may be not only beneficial but also sufficient.

The *expression of anger* also can be very helpful. Some psychological theorists view depression as anger turned inward. Venting this anger may serve as a motivator and energizer to action. Beck has pointed out,

> Being angry is not only more pleasant than being sad, but has connotations of power, superiority, and mastery. . . . Nonetheless, the expression of anger is often regarded negatively by the [person] and may provoke other people; thus it is not a reliable vehicle for improvement (Beck 1976, p. 296)

Beck also states that "talking about how miserable and hopeless they felt and trying to squeeze out anger often seemed to accentuate the [person's] depression; their acceptance of their debased self-image and pessimism simply increased their sadness, passivity, and self-blame" (p. 263). Indeed, in the name of "love," some very well-meaning Christians have invested many hours listening to depressed individuals and running to their beck and call, and to an extent perpetuating their depression. *Repeatedly* talking with people about their depression and sympathetically listening without urging them toward action may amount to offering a stone instead of a loaf. Many melancholic individuals are so preoccupied with negative thoughts that further introspection—though possibly resulting in some short-term good feelings—tends to aggravate the pervading dysphoria. In my practice, the ventilation of feelings has been effective primarily with acute but not severe depression, and then only in the initial stages of care.

Resignation is another affective method. One of the tasks of the bereaved in the weeks and months after the loss of a significant relationship is learning to let go, to release their attachment to the dead. A natural part of the grief process is a recognition that one can no longer have what once was precious, that one now must live life within the loss. Resignation is beneficial for melancholics who worry about what might happen in the future, or whose expectations are out of proportion to their skills and abilities. Such helpless feelings may actually be realistic; the depressed may, indeed, lack the abilities, skills, or wherewithal to obtain the outcomes they desire. Resignation involves finding more realistic expectations for themselves, for the world, and for others; changing some of their unrealistic assumptions or expectations; choosing alternative goals to work for; and discovering new sources for meaning in life. It does not involve resigning oneself to helplessness, however; on the contrary, encouraging people to acquire whatever new skills they need to cope with a loss is vital.

Another technique, from the psychological school of psychosynthesis, is the use of *dis-identification,* or *self-identification,* exercises. Roberto Assagioli (1965, p. 22) maintains that "We are dominated by everything with which our self becomes identified. We can dominate and control everything from which we dis-identify ourselves." I have found his technique of dis-identification to be helpful for people who are very self-critical. The purpose is to help them dis-identify themselves from their negative emotions, thoughts, or desires, recognizing that they have them but are not defined by them. They are ultimately to see themselves as infinitely precious to God, even though they may have difficulty believing it. The clients are instructed to relax (relaxation techniques can be used if needed) and then to dis-identify with their body, emotions, and intellect through detailed imaging of an internal dialogue. (e.g., "I have a body, but I am not my body. I have an emotional life, but I am not my emotions or feelings." "I have desires, but I am not those desires." "I am lonely much of the time, but that loneliness is not me." "I have depressed feelings, but I am not those feelings.") They are urged—first in the session and then in practice on their own—to use these formulas with anything they falsely identify as their *selves,* such as their "role," their depressed feelings, their own self-image, their sins, their misdeeds, and so on. Finally, a positive assertion is introduced, such as, "I am a child of God: I am an infinitely worthful person." Clients are to practice the dis- and self-identificatory statements for ten or fifteen minutes twice a day in a relaxed position with their eyes closed, imagining the mental dialogue. This ritual dis-identification is helpful only with mildly depressed individuals who are generally healthy but desire greater directedness and control over their lives—especially those who feel they are dominated by particular feelings, thoughts, objects, or individuals.

The affective technique of *diversion* is especially helpful with individuals who find a certain part of the day (typically the morning) or week especially difficult, a time their depression seems most pronounced. Clients are urged to plan diversionary tactics for such times. For example, every morning a retired man who lived alone felt very depressed and had difficulty facing his work around the house. The method he developed to deal with his depression was to get up early, finish all his chores by 8 A.M., and leave the house until noon. "Getting out of the house" did not always mean going to some other location; it could mean nothing more than pulling weeds in the backyard or sitting in a lawn chair and reading. His morning diversionary tactics were, in my assessment, one of the major aids in coping with his depression—especially at first, until other methods also could be employed.

Urging depressed persons to *tell a friend* about their feelings is a technique which is particularly helpful for those who carry their anguish close to their breasts. Such individuals are urged to express their pain, in small or moderate "doses," to significant other people. By so doing they may be enlisting the support and sustenance of people who probably were not aware of their inner pain. Unfortunately, *A Prairie Home Companion* notwithstanding, there are no "Powdermilk Biscuits" to "help shy people get up and do what needs to be done" when they are depressed. I have not had much success in helping very shy, depressed individuals to share themselves with others unless I was able to involve them in supportive group situations. Small existing groups within the congregation (such as a choir or ongoing Sunday school class) or specially created "sharing groups" can be beneficial. Otherwise, it can be *very* difficult helping depressed, reclusive individuals to pour out their heart to others.

The opposite extreme, however, is more common in my experience: those who wear out their family and friends with incessant talk of their sadness, irritation, and anguish. These individuals can be helped by setting limits on *excessive expressions* of their melancholy. When sharing their suffering to others, typically they invest even more time focusing on the bad feelings and thus become more depressed. Furthermore, such behavior usually is repellant to friends and relatives who might otherwise serve as a significant support system.

BEHAVIORAL METHODS OF INTERVENTION

Melancholic individuals tend to see themselves as ineffective. It is, therefore, extremely important for them to be *active*, in order that they have the opportunity to see themselves being productive. This usually requires two counseling processes. The first is helping depressed individuals structure into their lives a number of activities in which they can be effective. The second is helping them look at what they have already done (or are presently doing) and recognize their own competence. The latter calls for cognitive techniques, which will be discussed later. Since most depressed people resent attempts to prod them into activity, the pastoral carer needs to be very creative in choosing the methods of assistance and the incentives to be used. Other depressed individuals see all of life as a big *either/or*, and their expectations are so elevated that they could not achieve them even if they were not depressed. The minister can use cognitive techniques to help them trim such expectations.

Assisting the depressed to become more active typically requires a series of "homework" tasks. Ideally homework is negotiated between pastor and parishioner rather than "assigned" in an authoritarian manner. (In cases where the depression is quite deep, several of the first assignments may have to be prescribed. Later, such clients can take a more active part in determining the tasks they will do outside of the actual counseling sessions.) It is helpful to have the clients write down precisely what homework they have agreed to do, and at what time. I request those who are very withdrawn or are significantly distorting reality to read the assignments back to me, making sure we agree on what the homework is to be.

It is vital for depressed individuals actually to *do* their homework, thus taking the small steps that lead to success. If the depression is advanced, some of the early assignments need to be quite small and easily achievable. These people do not need another failure! Too large a task may become another insurmountable obstacle.

Some of these first assignments may seem inconsequential, even trivial, but to the depressed they may be very rigorous. The minister's task is to determine that clients are not attempting too big a jump, one at which they are likely to fail. For example, the man who needed to get out of the house every morning agreed first to weed the garden, and then the yard. From lying in bed or sitting around the house all day it was a big step to spend an hour weeding. Successfully accomplishing this led him to further, more difficult tasks.

Depression is a vicious circle in many respects: a reduction in activities and positive interpersonal interactions leads to depression; the more depressed people feel, the less motivated they are to involve themselves in activities which might have positive outcomes, which leads to even greater depression; and so on. This spiral can turn positive, however, and homework assignments are a key to the reversal. Improved performance in activities and interpersonal relationships leads to improved self-esteem and self-evaluation, which now increases the motivation to do even more, which leads again to improved performance, and so on.

Several researchers (Lewinsohn 1978, p. 125) have described "mood related activities" that can be helpful for depressives. Their investigation—and my own experience—has found that individuals who do the following types of activities feel better and are less depressed than those who do not do them:

• Interpersonal activities in which the depressed individual feels appreciated, accepted, valued, esteemed, and liked (for example, a depressed amateur radio operator shows his equipment to some interested "novices," a lonely single makes a point of being among people who are enjoying a mutual good time, or an elderly widower finds others who show interest in his ideas and hobbies).

• Activities in which the depressed individual can demonstrate competence, independence, and adequacy (for example, taking on a special project at work, beyond the normal requirements of the job, which allows creativity and independence).

• "Fun things," that is, activities that contain intrinsic pleasure—or would, when the depressed person is not melancholic (for example, going out for dinner at a fine restaurant, lying on the beach, going to a favorite sporting event, or taking a drive in the country to see the autumn colors).

• Activities that give the client a sense of meaning in life. Most depressed individuals have difficulty finding any sense of purpose for their existence. Victor Frankl (1963) suggested that those who are able to make some sense out of life—even in a concentration camp, as he was—have less tendency to be depressed and more energy for carrying on the tasks necessary to existence. He pointed out that meaning is not something that comes to one spontaneously, but something that each individual has to carve out, strive for, seek. In the concentration camp those who did not find meaning did not survive.

Unfortunately, many depressed persons, *because* of their depression, simply will not do these activities. Being pushed too quickly will only strengthen their resistance. It may be useful to search together for activities—however insignificant they may seem to the helper—which the person *can* realistically accomplish.

A purpose of homework assignments, then, is to help people make some sense out of their existence and gain some meaning in life. Depressed individuals must ascertain what might be potentially meaningful for them, and begin to do those specific activities (e.g., doing grounds work at the church or volunteering to tutor a child with reading problems). Sometimes the only way to determine what will be meaningful is to begin acting and then reflect on what has been done.

Several factors potentially can hinder the performance of these activities:

- Depressed persons frequently exhibit a lack of serious care in choosing activities. They may just fall into undertakings in which they have little interest, rather than selecting what might give them enjoyment, meaning, or a sense of adequacy.
- The feeling of pressure from tasks left undone can be another hindrance to performing activities. For example, I find this pleasure-destroying anxiety common among depressed students who have difficulty enjoying a movie or reading a novel because they cannot help thinking about all the homework that has yet to be done in the semester. During the last few days of the term this is appropriate, and they should be studying; but four, six, or even eight weeks into the semester, they cannot expect to complete all of the term's requirements before relaxing!
- Sometimes the precipitators of a depression (significant crisis, loss, or change) remove the availability of quality activities. This is especially true of pleasurable relationships with friends. For example, in grief research carried out a number of years ago, I found that widowed middle-aged spouses immediately lost half of their friendships, especially with other couples, when their mates died. Those friends could have been a very important source of comfort.
- Anxiety or stress also can affect both the performance of activities and the enjoyment of pleasurable events. Persons under significant stress are less likely to experience enjoyment in what they do, especially if they are depressed (Lewinsohn 1978, pp. 154–56).

The following suggestions for the scheduling of homework may help overcome such hindrances. The depressed need to recognize that *doing* the activity is most important, not necessarily what they will accomplish.

• Sometimes what a person is able to accomplish is determined as much or more by external factors than by internal ones. (For example, it may be generally helpful to learn assertiveness, but one's employer may be afraid of such behavior and make things more difficult.)

• Many depressed individuals have a tendency toward either/or thinking and believe they have to do every iota that they have planned; if not, they feel even worse and assume their time and effort was wasted. It is beneficial for the minister to aid in trimming expectations and keeping things in perspective.

• Sometimes it is beneficial to help clients, especially the more severely depressed, schedule their daily activities. Each evening before bed or the first thing in the morning, they write out an hour-by-hour schedule of the day ahead. For those who are quite depressed, accomplishing a few basic maintenance activities around the house is a giant step forward.

Another behavioral method is *teaching specific social skills.* This is crucial with those who have been depressed on and off for an extended period of time. Research indicates that the depressed tend to seek out fewer social events and interpersonal contacts than non-depressed individuals, initiate fewer contacts with new people, and perform less skillfully in interpersonal and social interchanges. They also describe themselves as less comfortable in social situations, often sensitive to being ignored or rejected and yet not performing the required social niceties. They also may lack skill in being assertive. Part of the minister's task is to help them learn whatever social skills they need and develop the assertiveness they lack.

Such social training may be done in many ways; the minister's approach is really up to his or her own creativity. Some methods that have been helpful for me include:

• Model ways of socially interacting with people.

• Role-play specific social events that are especially threatening to the depressed individual.

• Give didactic instructions on some of the niceties required in social occasions.

• Encourage the person to join a church group which will be especially supportive, empathetic, and open to new members. (Be aware that some church groups are closed and unreceptive to new people, especially if the new members are somewhat reclusive and depressed.) Sometimes it is helpful to make contact with one especially helpful, empathetic member who will assist the client's entrance into the group.

- Involve the person in a sharing group or group therapy.
- Suggest assertiveness training or social skills classes taught at a local community college.

A final behavioral method is asking clients to *keep a journal* of their activities. Frequently, depressed persons are unaware of how many events in their lives *do* give them a sense of meaning, pleasure, and confidence, or some sense of mastery and competence. In addition, the daily record of activities helps the minister continue to plan new activities and assists in the honing and refining of present ones.

METHODS OF PHYSIOLOGICAL INTERVENTION

There are fewer techniques available to the minister to cope with physiological symptoms. Obviously the major physiologically effective technique is the use of *medications*, and a few comments on their application might be helpful. Two of the drugs commonly used to treat depression are tricyclics and lithium carbonate. The first is actually a group of antidepressant medications; it includes Tofranil (imipramine), Sinequan, Elavil, and others. It was mentioned previously that 60 to 65 percent of melancholic individuals demonstrate a definite improvement when treated with a tricyclic antidepressant drug. These drugs do not provide immediate relief, as aspirin does, but have a cumulative effect requiring a period of time, usually one to four weeks, before benefits are observed. Most physicians believe that antidepressant drugs, unlike common tranquilizers such as Valium and Librium, are not habit-forming (though there is always the possibility that future research will reveal otherwise).

The second drug, lithium carbonate, has had almost miraculous effects with some severely depressed individuals, especially the bipolar types such as manic-depressives. Lithium, a salt that already exists in the blood of all normal people, was first used for the treatment of the manic phase, or "high," in the mood swings of manic-depressives. Research is presently underway to determine its benefits for depression. So far, the results have not been as dramatic as with the manic phase, but there is hope for its potential.

Some depression is *precipitated or exacerbated by drugs.* A number of those who come to the pastor with depression may be seeing several physicians for various complaints and obtaining medications from each of them. Unfortunately, such people often fail to tell every physician of the other drugs they are taking and may use as many as a dozen different drugs which can be interacting with each other. In such situations it is very important to send these persons to *one* of their doctors to take inventory of the medications they are taking or (my preference) to a psychiatrist or other physician who will evaluate the total constellation of their drugs, be in contact with the other physicians, and determine if there are any inter-drug complications.

Medications such as Reserpine, a drug for the treatment of high blood pressure, can produce depression as a side effect. So can birth control pills. If depression is triggered by a drug, the physician needs to find another medication which will not produce that side effect—or decide whether the benefits of a particular drug are being eclipsed by the side effect of depression.

Depression is complicated in some cases by the use of some more readily available drugs, especially alcohol and caffeine. Alcohol is a depressant and, though possibly giving some short-term relief, will only heighten the melancholy. I customarily urge depressed clients to abstain from alcohol totally or trim down to a couple of drinks each week—and never drink alcohol when they are feeling noticeably depressed. (This also goes for illicit drugs.)

Caffeine found in coffee, tea, many soft drinks, chocolate, diet pills, and the like seems to affect depression in some people. It gives a momentary "up" followed by a greater "down." Caffeine and sugar, in excess, act as drugs, causing overstimulation of the pancreas, resulting in higher insulin output, which causes low blood sugar levels, irritability, and possibly depression.

A number of depressed persons have their most difficult period in the morning. Many people routinely begin their day with several cups of coffee, toast, and a glass of orange juice (which is surprisingly high in simple sugar). At midmorning they may add two or three more cups of coffee or a cola and a doughnut or Danish. So, in the five hours or more after the deprivation of food during a night's sleep, they have ingested primarily sugar and caffeine. Instead, beginning the day with protein and complex carbohydrates—no doughnuts, sweet rolls or other simple sugars, and no caffeine beverages—can be a way for some people to help trim wide mood swings in the morning. For one recent client of mine, diet changes and the addition of regular exercise were all she needed for significant change in the depression, and only one counseling session was required. The client did not have any exceptional situational precipitators for her depression—outside of the normal stresses and strains of life—but was in need of some physiological problem-solving.

I usually do not use any particular techniques to address loss of desire for food or sex, since neither tends to bother most depressed individuals. A physiological symptom that *is* of great concern to many depressives is *sleep disturbance,* and it is experienced by a majority of mild, moderate, and severely depressed individuals. Such difficulties may consist of early morning waking, difficulty in falling asleep, or the kind of restless sleep from which one awakens feeling as if one never really slept. Most individuals will regain their typical sleeping patterns after the depression has lifted. There are some suggestions the minister can make to help them sleep better in the meantime:

- Suggest that they use the bed (in effect, the bedroom) *only* for sleep and sex. It is not a good idea for people with sleep disturbance to lie in bed while they watch television, read for long periods of time, or study.
- If they are not sleepy, they should not stay in bed. When depressed people lie awake in bed, they may obsessively rehearse their negative thoughts. It is far better for them to get up and do something constructive. The occasional loss of a night's sleep is not harmful and may help them sleep better the next night.
- Interpret to depressed individuals that they actually get more sleep than they think. Many who believe they were lying awake all night actually slept a good deal, but part of their negative thinking is to believe they are not sleeping.
- Encourage them to become active during the day. Individuals who spend most of the day sitting, reading, watching TV, and napping, will not be inclined to sleep at night. It is better to be as physically active as possible and not to take naps.
- Regular exercise can be very helpful, except in the last two hours before sleep, because it can serve to stimulate and energize as well as relax.
- A fixed bedtime routine can cue people that it is time to sleep. One such routine might begin with a warm bath before watching the ten o'clock news, followed by a period of quiet meditation and prayer (possibly using some relaxation exercises), followed by a light carbohydrate snack.
- Emphasize that anyone with sleeping problems should always avoid stimulants—such as tea, coffee, chocolate, caffeinated sodas, and so on—prior to going to bed.
- Train in relaxation techniques. Frequently (though not always), learning to relax physiologically also causes the mind to slow down, and obsessive negative thoughts quiet down as well. Some cassette relaxation tapes can be very helpful in this task.

A final physiological technique for the care of depression is *exercise*—especially cardiovascular exercise. Long before jogging was in vogue, researchers found that people who performed regular cardiovascular exercise (at least three times a week) had less depression and less anxiety than did those who were sedentary. One difficulty with exercise is getting people—especially depressed people—to do it regularly. Therefore a crucial step is to help the depressed individual find an exercise activity that brings some modicum of enjoyment as well as the cardiovascular benefits.

Exercise is beneficial in several ways. It obviously helps people to get in better shape physically and thus feel stronger and more energetic, and it has the additional benefit of giving people a sense of accomplishment. Here is something that they *can* do, and it introduces some discipline into what usually is a haphazard life. Discipline gives a sense of self-control to depressed individuals, who tend to feel they have no control over anything.

COGNITIVE METHODS OF INTERVENTION

The depressed sometimes have an ever so subtle shift in their cognitive mental organization. Certain thoughts begin to predominate to the extent that the individuals regard themselves, their experiences, and their futures in a negative way. Misconstructions and misperceptions follow these basic, faulty information-processing errors. Theorists on the cognitive components of depression have described six typical ways in which depressed individuals cognitively misconstrue their experience in a negative way.

1) *Arbitrary inference:* The depressed draw inferences that are counter to supportive evidence or in absence of such evidence.

2) *Selective abstraction:* The depressed focus on one minor aspect while ignoring the more crucial features of a situation, and they view the whole situation through this one detail.

3) *Overgeneralization:* As the term indicates, depressives can reach sweeping conclusions about themselves, their worth, and their ability to perform based on a few isolated incidents.

4) *Magnification and minimization:* Melancholic individuals do not perceive events accurately but tend to blow small, negative occurrences out of proportion and render their positive accomplishments insignificant.

5) *Personalization:* The depressed may take responsibility for negative external events when there is no basis for such a connection.

6) *"Either/or" thinking:* The absolutist, dichotomous thinking of depressives categorizes all they do into opposite positions: perfect or

wholly defective, all or none, beautiful or ugly, immaculate or filthy, and so forth. Since depressives can never fit the "good" (perfect) category, they see themselves as "bad" (defective).

Most cognitive theorists believe that childhood experiences serve as the basis for forming negative beliefs about oneself, the future, and the external world. These negative cognitions frequently are latent, but they are brought to life by specific external precipitators that are dynamically analogous to the original experiences that created the negative attitude. Most depressives are not negative about everything but tend to be especially sensitive to certain categories of stimuli, or "triggers," that set the negative thinking in motion.

Techniques have been designed to change these learned negative cognitions and to teach a new set of reality-based beliefs. In fact, Arnold Lazarus believes that "the bulk of psychotherapeutic endeavors may be said to center around correction of misconceptions" (Lazarus 1972, p. 165), which may either precede or follow actual change of behavior.

How does one change another's cognitions? It is not easy! Ministers, who are trained in pastoral care and counseling and also have a background in theology and philosophy, are probably the best equipped of all helping professionals to enable people to change their beliefs.

Cognitive restructuring is the name used for the process of helping persons to see the world more realistically and to change unfounded beliefs, misconceptions, and expectations. The recent philosophical emphasis on the conscious objective experience draws extensively from the works of Kant, Heidegger, and Husserl. The historical church generally has acknowledged (though post-1950's pastoral counseling practice sometimes has not) that our beliefs about the future, self, others, the world, and God greatly affect how we act. Cognitive psychological theorists recognize this as well, but state it in non-theological terms.

The method of changing cognition as outlined below is one I have described elsewhere in greater detail (see Stone 1980, pp. 31–44). It includes the following steps:

1) *Assessment:* One of the first tasks of ministers and clients is to try to understand the core negative assumptions or misconceived beliefs that the depressed hold about themselves, God, and the world.

2) *Teaching/Learning:* It is important to help depressed individuals change their erroneous beliefs. Exposing cognitive misconceptions is the easy part of the process; relearning is much more difficult.

It can be facilitated by an explanation of how people develop faulty information-processing mechanisms or irrational beliefs.

3) *Practicing:* The depressed need to move from education about their negative misconceptions to the actual practice of catching themselves. Clients recognize their own cognitive distortions and reformulate their thinking in more reality-based ways. At first they may not catch their cognitive misconceptions right away, sometimes not for several days. They are urged, when suddenly overcome with a wave of depression, to stop and mentally move backward to find the trigger of the depression and to identify their automatic, unrealistic thoughts and beliefs.

Additional methods that can aid in the process of changing cognitions include the following:

In *cognitive rehearsal* clients image themselves going through all of the steps involved in a certain activity, and then discuss specific roadblocks and potential conflicts that might occur while actually doing the activity. They report all irrational thoughts that occur and attempt to correct these cognitive misconceptions. Clients are urged to pay special attention to every detail and then to work out strategies for carrying out the activity in real life. They imagine the activity several more times to discover any additional cognitive misconceptions and to begin feeling comfortable with the step-by-step process required for carrying out the act. The minister needs to be aware that individuals who are quite depressed may have difficulty concentrating and their minds may wander. Patience and gentle urging are called for.

Thought stopping, best used together with other techniques, teaches clients *mentally* to shout the word "Stop!" whenever obsessive and upsetting thoughts come to mind. They begin by vocalizing it (in fact, screaming it) aloud and gradually work to saying it subvocally. Whenever negative ideas appear, they silently yell "Stop!"—and the ruminations do stop. I urge clients to practice thought stopping two times a day for ten or fifteen minutes a time the first week after learning the technique. Frequently they can gain quicker control over their intrusive negative thoughts by purposely bringing them to the fore and then practicing their banishment, rather than waiting for them to occur. Once the skill is developed, thought stopping can be used by clients to banish troublesome thoughts whenever they crop up.

Worry time is scheduled for some depressed people who find themselves so overwrought with worry that they spend every counseling session and many hours each day obsessed with their troubles. In a fifty-minute counseling session, I may suggest that ten to fifteen minutes of the session (usually the opening minutes) be given over to the venting of their problems, and the rest of the session to working on changes to be made in their lives. When this technique is used by clients at home, the idea is not to avoid completely thinking about troubling subjects, but rather to gain some control over them, to decide exactly when and how much time will be devoted to them. For example, a client may choose a half-hour period for worrying each day, say from 4:15 to 4:45 P.M.; he or she is not to do anything else during that time except worry. The purpose is to free the remaining waking hours from lugging about this load of worries and problems.

The *blowup technique* asks clients to exaggerate their disturbing negative thoughts to such an extent that they no longer seem so awesome and may even appear ridiculous, ludicrous, or humorous. This method can be enhanced by having clients close their eyes and image a troublesome situation in which such negative thoughts may occur. Then they are to exaggerate mentally the whole situation while describing in the first person what they are thinking, feeling, seeing, and experiencing. (It should be noted, however, both with thought stopping and with blowup, that terminating negative thoughts does not necessarily bring about positive ones—especially in more severely depressed individuals. It is necessary for the depressive to learn new, positive reality-based thoughts.)

The *alternative technique* is especially useful for individuals who systematically bias all their interpretations of stimuli and events in a negative way. The pastor explains to the clients the six cognitive information-processing errors that people frequently make. Together they discuss specific experiences, coming up with explanations and interpretations of the events other than the ones previously formed. The task for the depressed individuals is to recognize their negative biases and substitute more accurate interpretations of their experiences. This technique serves as a basis for problem-solving. Clients consider and plan alternative ways of handling problems based on a new interpretation of the circumstances.

Reattribution, a cognitive method somewhat similar to the alternative technique, helps depressed clients correctly assign blame or responsibility for negative events that happen to them. Working together with the pastor, the depressed discuss selected events in their lives, applying the rules of logic and common sense as well as a sound understanding of ethics to a variety of negative incidents; they try to determine realistic responsibility for them. The goal is not to absolve themselves totally but to note the multitude of outside factors that can contribute to any negative event. Reattribution greatly helps individuals lift the weight of self-reproach, search for ways of salvaging troublesome situations, and prevent recurrences. It can help parishioners to accept responsibility for *real* guilt but *not* take blame for imagined sins. Reattribution of major negative events (such as divorce or the death of a child) can be followed by the historic pastoral methods of confession, forgiveness, absolution, and amendment of life. The pastor should be alert, however, for a dangerous pattern which Roy Fairchild suggests many Christians learn: "They [the depressed persons] move from guilty feelings to atonement to attempted redemption by placating and obeying, by overworking, by denying themselves pleasure, and by subtle self-sabotage or clear self-destruction" (Fairchild 1980, p. 33).

Recent tendencies in the church to minimize or even ignore sin except as part of some global social issue are an immense loss for depressives seeking help. Most feel they are very sinful and have done wrong (and indeed *are* sinful and *have* done wrong). The minister who does not believe in sin or offers grace too glibly and cheaply does not take the depressed or their experience seriously. To the degree that this occurs, the depressed are left alone to grapple with their gnawing guilt, unaided by the religious professional.

Spiritual direction, not only a cognitive technique but also a historical pastoral care method which continues in practice today—especially in the Catholic and Anglican communions—is another useful instrument for change. Depressed persons tend to be very self-absorbed. Most of their thoughts center on themselves or on how they relate to other people or events. Spiritual direction allows them to develop and extend their relationship to God, to focus on what is ultimate, beyond themselves.

There are a great variety of spiritual exercises, some of which I have covered in greater detail elsewhere (Stone 1988, pp. 92–123). One that I have found helpful for depression uses certain selections of scripture (especially psalms, or certain portions of the gospels such as the parables). Clients first read a passage completely, then line by line they focus and reflect on what the passage says to them. This method's value for depressives is that they are not dwelling on their own problems, but rather are concentrating on what the word is saying to them. With those who are greatly distorting their experiences, I first go over the passages in the counseling session, where we have a chance to talk about them together, and I help them catch distortions in their interpretations. For example, the person who thinks forgiveness is only for others can be urged to apprehend what is freely offered to all, irrespective of how heinous their sin may appear. For less troubled individuals this method can serve as an excellent homework task.

One caution in the use of spiritual direction: some depressives may use spiritual direction as one more excuse for pulling away from other people. Be careful that the uses of scripture, prayer, meditation, contemplation, or the offices do not become an additional excuse for people to retreat from daily life. For the depressed, spiritual direction ideally is a way in which they enter into a positive outside relationship with the Ground of their being.

Conclusion

I am always impressed by the enormous impact melancholy can have upon individuals. Depression usually does not wriggle and squirm, act out and disrupt class, even rob a bank. It is more likely to sit quietly in the corner, not wanting to be a bother to anyone. In its quietness it often goes unnoticed until the silence becomes so deep that problems are impossible to ignore—like deterioration in job performance, reclusiveness, marital difficulties, even suicide. Understanding that depression affects feelings, thinking, physiology, and behavior gives the minister a clearer focus on the variety of ways it can manifest itself.

This chapter has offered a number of methods that can be used to offer care to the mild and moderately depressed persons whom the minister encounters in the parish. Since depression is so often a quiet phenomenon, the parish pastor more than any other helping professional is in a position to see and to offer help. With such pastoral initiative, those who are "down" can be reached before they fall into more severe depressive states.

The church as a caring community can provide light that helps the depressed find their way out of the cavern of despair and returns them to a life of meaningful service; as they shed some of their own pain, they are called in turn to help alleviate some of the individual agonies and global pains of this world. Meaning, for the mature Christian, is based on service and on a realistically positive attitude toward life that relies on "the One who strengthens me" (Philippians 4:13, *NJB*).

Note

1. The terms *melancholy* and *depression* are used interchangeably in this chapter.

References

Assagioli, R. 1965. *Psychosynthesis.* New York: Hobbs, Dorman and Company.

Beck, A. T. 1967. *Depression.* New York: Harper & Row.

———. 1976. *Cognitive Therapy and the Emotional Disorders.* New York: International Universities Press.

———, *et al.* 1979. *Cognitive Therapy of Depression.* New York: Guilford Press.

Bloomfield, M. 1952. *Seven Deadly Sins.* East Lansing, Mich.: Michigan State College Press.

Fairchild, R. W. 1980. *Finding Hope Again: A Pastor's Guide to Counseling Depressed Persons.* New York: Harper & Row.

Frankl, V. 1963. *Man's Search for Meaning.* New York: Washington Square Press.

Hamilton, M. 1969. "A Rating Scale for Depression." *Journal of Neurology, Neurosurgery, and Psychiatry* 23: 56–62.

Lazarus, A. 1972. *Behavior Therapy and Beyond.* New York: McGraw-Hill.

Lewinsohn, P. M., *et al.* 1978. *Control Your Depression.* Englewood Cliffs, N.J.: Prentice-Hall.

Lieberman, R. P. 1981. "A Model for Individualizing Treatment." In *Behavioral Therapy for Depression,* edited by Lynn Rehm, p. 244. New York: Academic Press.

Raskin, A., *et al.* 1970. "Differential Response to Chlorpromazine, Imipramine, and Placebo: A Study of Sub-Groups of Hospitalized Depressed Patients." *Archives of General Psychiatry* 23: 163–73.

Stone, H. W. 1972. *Suicide and Grief.* Philadelphia: Fortress Press.

———. 1980. *Using Behavioral Methods in Pastoral Counseling.* Philadelphia: Fortress Press.

———. 1988. *Word of God and Pastoral Care.* Nashville: Abingdon.

———. 1991. *The Caring Church: A Guide For Lay Pastoral Care.* Louisville: Westminster/John Knox Press.

Tellenbach, H. 1980. *Melancholy.* Pittsburgh: Duquesne University Press.

Wenzel, S. 1967. *The Sin of Sloth: Acedia in Medieval Thought and Literature.* Chapel Hill, N.C.: University of North Carolina Press.

Zung, W. W. 1965. "A Self-Rating Depression Scale." *Archives of General Psychiatry* 12: 63–70.

Sharon E. Cheston

17. Counseling Adult Survivors of Childhood Sexual Abuse

> An enemy is in deadly pursuit,
> crushing me into the ground,
> forcing me to live in darkness,
> like those long dead.
> My spirit is faint,
> and within me my heart is numb with fear (Psalm 143:3–4).

When I began working as a professional counselor in 1976, I knew that some children were sexually abused and that I might meet an adult at some time in my work who had been sexually abused as a youngster. In my first position I was given a case load of ten people: eight woman and two men. By the end of six months I discovered that three of the women had been sexually abused as children and one of the men had recently sexually molested his daughter. The end of that first six months marked the end of my naiveté as a therapist concerning sexual abuse. Currently, a preponderance of my cases are adults who were sexually abused as children. While I recognize that those in therapy are not a representative sample of the total population, the research indicates that one out of three women and one out of seven men were victims of sexual abuse by the age of eighteen (Bass and Davis 1988). However, researchers and clinicians assert that the above ratios may not account for all instances of childhood sexual abuse owing to the fact of low reporting rates, which are underscored by the use of repression as a method of dealing with the pain, and the lack of reporting of covert sexual abuse.

Low reporting rate as compared to actual occurrences has its roots in isolationism. Up until recently whatever occurred in a family was considered to be no one else's business. Therefore abuse and neglect were not dealt with by outside agencies except in extreme circumstances. Today, every state in the nation has a law protecting children from having to endure any physical or sexual abuse or neglect once it is reported. Nevertheless, there is still a reluctance on the part of many people to report child abuse, in part because there is a fear of accusing an innocent person who may suffer because of the accusation and in part because we tend not to believe children (Rencken 1989). In addition, children are reticent about revealing the abuse, often not wanting to be the cause of furthering family problems. Thus abused children sublimate their safety needs to maintaining peace, a pattern that often continues into adulthood. Most pastoral counselors and other helpers wait until they have a level of certainty before reporting suspected child abuse. In cases where the suspicion is true, the child is being tortured with no hope that it will end. Interestingly enough, if a stranger were accused or suspected of the molestation, there would be public outcry against the crime and the criminal. Also the police and social services would be criticized for not moving fast enough. But if a father is accused then there is more hesitancy to protect the child and criticism of the same agencies if they move too fast.

Pastoral counselors are in ideal positions to effect change. Clients who are victims of childhood sexual abuse need a holistic approach that addresses not only cognitive and affective changes but also deals with values, faith, and existential issues.

Causes of Low Reporting Rates

> Look on my right and see—
> there is no one who recognises me.
> All refuge is denied me,
> no one cares whether I live or die (Psalm 142:4–5).

Repression is one of the most utilized defense mechanisms by those who are victims of sexual abuse. Due to the very nature of repression many victims do not have any recollection of having been abused or only vague images or bodily sensations that they do not understand. If a victim enters therapy, where it is safe to express suspicions, then some of the repression may lift and the memories may begin to revive. However, many men and women remain unaware of the abuse while manifesting symptoms of other mental and physical disorders which may or may not become the impetus to enter therapy.

Finally, there is much unreported covert abuse that is discounted or minimized. Some victims attempt to laugh it off as the "dirty old man" issue; some victims claim that they would be criticized as having a too active imagination; others insist that the abusive behavior was accepted by the entire family even if they felt uncomfortable about it. The many cases of unreported sexual abuse means that in the future we, as therapists, will be dealing with many more victims who become adults and have the pain of childhood still hanging around their necks like albatrosses.

Definitions

Different authors have attempted to capture the effects of child abuse by defining concretely the necessary terms. However in the last twelve years the definitions have shifted directions several times and will continue to change as researchers and experts attempt to establish universally accepted terms.

Currently, *child sexual abuse* refers to an activity between a child under the age of eighteen and an adult in which the child is passively or actively used to gratify an adult's sexual needs. Some authors also include in their definitions of child sexual abuse any abuse that occurs to one under eighteen by someone five years older even if that person is another child or adolescent. For the purpose of this chapter, child sexual abuse is defined as any sexual activity involving a child and another person who is at least five years older than the child and in which there is an unequal distribution of power so that the abused child cannot protect himself or herself from the abuse.

Incest is one type of child sexual abuse where the perpetrator is in a protective or parental role to the child (Lew 1990). The word "protective" in Lew's definition is so general as to include teachers, babysitters, pastors, and so on; I will restrict the definition for the purposes of this chapter to close family members. All others who abuse children will be considered to be in an abusive non-incestuous relationship.

Sexual abuse can involve a myriad of overt and covert activities which an adult or older child can force on a child. Some of these activities include:

- Being touched in sexual areas
- Being shown sexual movies
- Being forced to listen to sexual talk
- Being made to pose for sexual photos

- Being subjected to unnecessary medical treatments that involve sexual areas
- Being forced to perform oral sex on an adult or other child
- Being raped or penetrated with objects
- Being fondled, kissed, or held in such a way as to make a child feel uncomfortable
- Being physically punished in a sexual manner, such as being forced to disrobe to receive a beating
- Being ritualistically tortured in a sexual manner
- Being made to watch sexual acts or look at sexual parts
- Being bathed in a intrusive way
- Being ridiculed about the body
- Being encouraged into sexual activities
- Being told that his or her worth as a person is only for sex
- Being forced into child prostitution or pornography

The words *victim* and *survivor* have been widely debated in the literature. I dislike the word *survivor* for the very reason that others find the word helpful. Lew (1990) uses the word to refer to someone who is not being abused today but was abused in the past. The word has a more upbeat positive ring to it than *victim*. Lew (1990) states that a victim is a victim during the abuse but a survivor after the abuse ceases. I contend that the word *survivor* is a euphemism that obscures the reality of the pain and the role of victim. In addition, when the sexual abuse ceases the victim continues to be victimized psychologically, physically, spiritually, intellectually, and socially. As one victim stated, "I was a victim then and I am a victim now. Everything I do is colored by the fact that I was sexually abused. I may get better but I'll never get over it. Time alone does not heal all wounds." Even if a victim were to enter counseling and become able to deal effectively with the abuse, the word *survivor* would be too limiting because victims want to do more than survive, they want to thrive. As the comedian (and sometimes philosopher) George Carlin asserts, let us not use psycho-babble to cover up excruciating pain and trauma.

The word *abuser* refers to the adult who abuses a child. Several authors also use the word *perpetrator* (Rencken 1989; Lew 1990). Here the words will be used interchangeably. *Covert sexual abuse* is sexual abuse ensconced in teasing, joking, punishment, bathing, teaching personal hygiene activity, or imparting sexual information. Covert sexual abuse is kin to passive-aggressive behavior. In passive-aggressive behavior one is aware of the aggressive intent but cannot prove it through the words or actions used. In covert sexual abuse the child is aware of the sexual innuendo and feels uncomfortable or even abused but cannot prove it because the abuser can claim that he was only teasing, bathing (and his hand slipped), and so on. Because of the covert nature of the abuse, the child may grow up feeling abused, crazy, or bad for suspecting that she was abused. The subtlely creates confusion, dysthymia, or major depression and anxiety. (Because 90 percent of all victims are female and 90 percent of all abusers are male, I use in this chapter the feminine pronoun to refer to victims and the masculine pronoun to refer to abusers, thus avoiding the cumbersome he/she, him/her structure.)

Covert sexual abuse includes behavior such as leering; physically punishing in a sexually confusing manner; joking repeatedly about sexual matters; performing personal hygiene tasks on children where the child feels uncomfortable; treating a child as if she is more sexually mature than she is; tickling, goosing, or touching that makes the child feel uncomfortable; talking frequently about genitals; asking the child to undress under the pretense of giving medical help; massaging the child in a sexual way; walking around naked and calling attention to bodily parts; interrogating the child about sexual exploits; and using derogatory sexual words to describe the child.

One final note concerning definitions is needed. It is beyond the scope of this chapter to cover child sexual abuse comprehensively. If you, as a pastoral counselor, are going to work with victims, then it is imperative for you to know the correct names of all the bodily parts that are involved in sexual abuse as well as the various DSMIII-R (American Psychiatria Association 1987) diagnostic labels used to identify perpetrators' and victims' psychopathology. For a more complete set of definitions I refer you to Robert Rencken's book *Intervention Strategies for Sexual Abuse* (1989).

Society and History

Child sexual abuse is rooted in the concept that children are the property of their parents and as property can be treated as the parents wish (Lew 1990). This concept places children at the bottom of the power ladder and increases the risk of children being exploited, manipulated, or abused. While laws are being introduced to change this balance of power so that children are protected, society and individuals do not change attitudes quickly. Despite what the various laws state, we are still living in a male-controlled society where children are bearing the burden of inequitable power and are at high risk of being abused by (predominantly) males who feel they have the right to violate a child's personal boundary and receive no punishment (Rencken 1989). In addition, Rencken (1989) asserts that we are living in a sex-negative society where sex is used to sell products and where we see sex as an area for exploitation. This leads to a supportive atmosphere in which sexual abuse can thrive.

However, despite the above concern that our society does not protect a child against sexual abuse, anthropologists and historians have discovered that there is a taboo against incest in every society throughout recorded history. Freud investigated incestual relationships trying to find some precedent in prehistoric cultures and found a preponderance of prohibition of incest (Freud 1950). With such strong proscriptions concerning incest, why is there such a proliferation of sexual abuse? Rencken (1989) states that the "why" question needs to become a "how" question. *How* does sexual abuse happen? To understand this complicated issue, we need to take a look at the various components that make up sexual abuse.

The Abuser

> Whoever misgoverns a house inherits only the wind (Proverbs 11:29a).

People who sexually abuse children come from every socioeconomic class, profession, culture, race, religion, and gender (Bass and Davis 1988). However, research shows that abusers tend to be male more than female. Female victims were abused by men 95 percent of the time, and male victims were abused by men 80 percent of the time. While these statistics show that women are much less likely to be the sexual abuser, Rencken (1989) contends that woman do abuse and should not be overlooked. My experience has been that women are more likely to be involved in covert sexual abuse connected to the role of mothering and nurturing. Because of the abuse-nurturing connection, the victim will hesitate to call the mother's activity abuse; to do so negates the nurturing which is so needed and valued.

Within the family structure fathers, step-fathers, grandfathers, and uncles are those who tend to be identified as the abusers, with step-fathers being five times more likely to be the perpetrator than natural fathers. Outside the family anyone who has the trust of the child and who has the opportunity to be alone with the child can take advantage of the situation and abuse. The abusive stranger frightens all of us but makes up a small minority of the sexually abusive situations. The abuser is more likely to be a person whom the family, child, or society tends to know well and trust.

Secrecy

> For nothing is hidden but it will be made clear, nothing secret but it will be made known and brought to the light (Luke 8:17).

Secrecy is the glue that keeps sexual abuse in place (Lew 1990). The perpetrator must be careful to assure the maintenance of the secret of the abuse. Therefore the perpetrator needs to ensure that the child cannot or will not tell anyone about the abuse. The abuser may use threats, cajoling, or fear tactics, such as telling the child the perpetrator would go to jail, to keep the child quiet. Another tactic that has been reported by victims as most convincing is the threat that if she tells then she will not be believed, will be called a liar, and will suffer rejection from the rest of the family. In addition, the perpetrator needs to find a time that is safe from interruptions and seduce the child into cooperating by being passive. He may do this by convincing the child that the sexual abuse is love and affection, by calling on family loyalty, by threatening to hurt the child if she doesn't cooperate or by threatening the child with isolation from others.

Diagnostically, abusers tend to be socially alienated, hostile persons who have peculiarities of thought, a rigid superego, and are guilt-ridden. On Axis I of the DSM-IIIR (American Psychiatric Association 1987), they usually meet the minimum criteria for depression or dysthymia. Their Axis II diagnoses are inclined toward the dependent personality and passive-aggressive disorders with some antisocial traits (Rencken 1989).

The Family

> And if a household is divided against itself, that household can never last (Mark 3:25).

The family in which abuse occurs tends to be one that is isolative, rigid, controlling, and traditional (Finklehor 1979; Herman 1981). Despite the fact that they depend on clear power structures, these families devalue communication and therefore are less cohesive than healthy families (Alexander and Lupfer 1987). Also, while there is a boundary between parent and child in healthy families, there is a disregard for the same boundary in abusive families (Rencken 1989). This boundary distortion manifests itself in four ways that allow for sexual abuse to occur.

First, the father is usually a dictatorial, possessive parent who has ultimate control over the family and sees himself as having the right to abuse everyone in the family. The mother is placed on the children's side of the power structure and cannot protect the children from the father because she has no power.

A second way that boundaries become distorted is if the father is immature and irresponsible. In this scenario the father joins the children in opposition to the power of the mother. He becomes the children's peer, and since sex is usually accepted among peers, sexual abuse can occur and seem justifiable to him.

The third family structure that can lead to incest is the step-family. In a step-family the incest taboo is weaker because the step-parent sees the child as not his. Therefore, with the incest taboo lifted, the step-parent can defend his action to himself.

Finally, the family that encourages the child to act as a pseudo-adult allows the child to cross the generational boundary and become an adult. This, once again, places the child in the same power camp as the adults and decreases the protection of parent/child dichotomy that is necessary to keep sexual abuse from occurring (Rencken 1989).

The Victim

> It is never the will of your father in heaven that one of these little ones should be lost (Matthew 18:14).

The victim of childhood sexual abuse is typically a female child between the ages of four and twelve. While boys are also victims, they make up a small percentage. Further, society tends to dismiss this abuse because males are supposed to be strong, confident, and not victims. The little boy is expected to deal with it as a little man and not whine or complain. So he develops a facade and buries the pain. He can become macho and join the perpetrators, or he can become emasculated, receive little support, and thereby stay a victim. The boy has one other alternative; that is, he may vow to prevent abuse from happening to another and become a protector of children. However, he still runs the risk of being seen as not manly (Lew 1990). In addition, sex between an older female and younger male is usually ignored, discounted, or seen as romanticized fantasy of positive conquest or "scoring." To change this attitude helpers must create an atmosphere of recognizing sexual abuse for what it is: an exploitive, manipulative, unequal relationship that destroys children's sense of right and wrong, trust, faith, self-esteem, and normal psycho-sexual development. Instead, sexual abuse instills guilt, shame, fear of intimacy, depression, social isolation, alienation from God, negative body image, and traumatic coping style. In addition, becoming a victim of sexual abuse can set the lifelong pattern of seeing oneself as a victim.

Signs and Symptoms of Sexual Abuse in Children

Young children (less than seven years old) who are being sexually abused tend to regress, have nightmares, act as if they are being terrorized, express uncontrollable rage, withdraw from people of the same sex as the abuser, or have atypical knowledge about sex for their age group (Rencken 1989).

Older children who have not yet reached puberty may exhibit signs of acting out, withdrawal, running away, substance abuse, poor peer relationships, poor academic achievement, or hypervigilance (Rencken 1989).

The adolescent who is being sexually abused is more likely to attempt suicide, runaway, withdraw, develop an eating disorder, develop antisocial traits, cease attending church, and resist the treatment system (Rencken 1989).

Adults who were victims of childhood sexual abuse have the feeling that there is something wrong with them. They lack trust in self, others, God, and the world; they fear intimacy. These victims feel cheated out of a childhood and now feel cheated out of life. Because they were betrayed by a significant adult other, they tend to be needy in relationships or establish a series of intense but volatile interpersonal relationships. Reality can be so distorted for some of the victims that they have developed methods of coping that appear crazy to others. Those adult victims who were abused by someone outside the family usually manifest the same but diminished symptoms if they are believed and supported by the family. However, if the family does not support and try to understand at the time of abuse then the child learns that she cannot rely on family or adults and may feel victimized all over again.

Coping Styles of Those Who Were Sexually Abused

The child who is sexually abused is experiencing a trauma that needs to be reduced immediately and handled in the future as the child develops. Because of the severity of the trauma an equally severe coping mechanism must be employed by the child. The child may use a form of dissociation by leaving her body so that the abuse happens to the body but not to the mind. This ability to dissociate is a God-given gift to the child and is reported by many survivors of automobile accidents, the Holocaust, and war. This coping mechanism is somewhat akin to the use of anesthesia during an operation, where the body experiences pain during surgery with the mind not remembering anything of the procedure (Bass and Davis 1988).

Dissociation can take a number of forms from numbing, to out of body experience, to creating another personality that flees the pain. Numbing is a process by which the client experiences a "not real" feeling. One client described it as a ringing in the ears followed by a sense of tunneling where the body feels as though it is falling away from the scene. She said that she was still aware of people, time, and space, but it was as if she had been doused in novocaine.

Out of body experiences actually feel as if the child has left her body and floated to another place; thus she avoids experiencing the trauma. Interestingly enough, some children retreat to a corner of the same room to watch the abuse. Others fly out windows to visit other places and do not know what is going on back at the body.

The most severe form of dissociation is the famous multiple personality. In this case the child escapes her body by creating another person who experiences the abuse while the child retreats into her mind with whatever part of her is left. It appears that once a child learns to split off another personality to take the abuse, the child can form new personalities easily and can use this coping mechanism in other situations. One personality suffers the abuse, another holds the rage, another becomes the innocent child, while still another becomes seductive. Each personality has a position paper from which she plays out her role and each personality serves the group by handling emotions and memories that are too traumatic for the whole victim to handle. The best example of how this works is the alter who becomes the seducer. When a child is abused, her body may react with some feelings of pleasure. To the child this is incomprehensible and horrifying, so a personality is created to feel these sensations that are unacceptable to the child, relieving the child of the need to deal with the sensual feelings.

Clients who use dissociation as a coping mechanism usually feel and fear that they are crazy. Helping them to see that dissociation is God's gift that *keeps* them from going "crazy" is a powerful step toward healing.

Another commonly used coping mechanism is minimization. This mechanism allows the victim to diminish either the effects of the abuse, the amount of abuse, or the reason behind the abuse. This typically co-dependent trait gives the victim a chance at not having to face the power of the entire situation. It is a way of shutting down emotions and denying the total impact of the abuse. Clients say: "He just fondled me." "It only happen once." "He couldn't help it. He was drunk." In some ways minimization is a more powerful defense than dissociation because with dissociation comes a feeling of or worry about being crazy that can serve as an impetus to enter therapy and work on the painful issues of sexual abuse. Minimization keeps the pain in abeyance and allows the client to function on a day-to-day basis. This defense against pain works well; only when it breaks down does the client usually face the pain. Breaking through minimization takes time, trust, and courage for the client willingly to experience the pain. One client likened the process to what Christ went through when he voluntarily put himself on a cross to be painfully crucified in order to live again. She said that to face the pain, all the pain, meant to confront a crucification experience in order to obtain a new promise. It is critical to see the promise in the pain, but it does not guarantee that the client will willingly proceed.

Repression is thc ultimate coping mechanism to deny the abuse that occurred. Those victims who are able successfully to repress the abuse have no memory of the traumatic incidents. However, the effects of the abuse linger in symptomology that yield Axis I + II diagnoses. In addition, many victims experience chronic physical problems that are related to the abuse or the stress of the repressed material. While the mind has the ability to repress successfully information that it chooses not to accept, the body does not have the same ability. As one client said, "I have no memory of any abuse, but when my husband touches my breasts I know I was abused because my entire body shudders." Later, the client was able to break through the repression and remember her abuse. Some clients who experience the feeling that they were abused and who have no memory worry that they are "making it all up" or are overreacting to their bodily sensations and intuition. Bass and Davis (1988) confirm what I have found, however; suspicion tends to lead to confirmation. In other words, clients do not remember abuse and then find out that they were in error. So when a client suspects or feels that she was abused as a child, I treat her as if she was abused and wait for her to feel safe enough to begin remembering. If abuse took place, sooner or later the client will begin having at least flashes or impressions of the abuse scenario.

Denial of feelings is another means of coping and is somewhat similar to minimization. However, this defense does not minimize the abuse; rather, it denies that there is any emotion or pain surrounding the situation. The client usually says, "Yes, it happened. So what. It didn't affect me." The irony of the above statement is that it is usually said while the client is sitting in a pastoral counselor's office in the midst of severe problems. But there is no connection in the client's mind between the abuse and the succession of patterns over her life where the client has had problems. One male client who said something similar proceeded to tell me that he could not form lasting relationships, that he always feels that he has to be perfect and hypervigilant, that he is an alcoholic, that he has such intense emotional pain that he cannot function, and that he feels suicidal. However, he still maintained tenaciously that he had no feelings about the abuse.

Developing a facade is a common means for a victim to protect herself from being hurt by others or from having others find out too much about her. As a coping mechanism it becomes a way of life that sometimes the victim does not even notice. But a facade, especially a heavy one that is used to cover the pain of abuse, is exhausting to maintain. One client reported that her facade had become so much a part of her that she felt that she had simply gained a hundred pounds of weight and had become used to having it. These facades serve the purpose of protection but actually get in the way of the formation of genuine relationships. This form of distancing can take several forms. There are comic, tragic, polyanna, academic, angry, blustery, placating, dare-devil, childish, aloof, and do-gooder facades, just to name a few.

When sexual abuse occurs the normal developmental tasks are interrupted or distorted for the victim. Some children respond by becoming fixated at a certain developmental stage, while others skip stages and become overly adult for their years. The child who becomes fixated usually regresses slightly to a time just before the abuse started. The purpose of the fixation is to stay developmentally at a point before the abuse so that she does not have to emotionally live through the abuse. As adults, these clients react to situations in an immature, sometimes frightened manner that seems inconsistent with their age and status. Children who skip developmental stages appear and act too mature for their years, but there is a gap in their development so they appear oddly fragile in their adult demeanor. These children try to skip over the developmental stages where the abuse occurred, but in doing so, they also skip the completion of developmental tasks and do not acquire the necessary skills with which to approach life. One other purpose for maturing rapidly is so that the child can become more self-sufficient and not have to rely on the abusive or other non-supportive adults.

Most children who are sexually abused turn to some form of self-defeating behavior. That behavior by its very activity makes them feel better but then leads to more problematic behavior. Children who were sexually abused can also sublimate their pain into socially acceptable, creative avenues that on the surface appear quite adaptable while still serving to layer positive on top of negative experiences. While this defense is a healthier approach to life than turning to drugs, sex, or binging, the victim still feels empty, hurt, or angry. Some of the more popular sublimation activities are humor, art, music, religiosity, work, and helping others. It is no wonder that many members of the helping profession were abused children who now desire to help others.

Coping mechanisms do not make victims healthy, but they do allow victims to live day by day creatively clinging to a semblance of normalcy. When coping mechanisms fail or do not develop, then victims develop severe mental illnesses such as psychoses; make suicide attempts; become addicted to drugs, alcohol, or gambling; turn to crime as a lifestyle; develop life-threatening eating disorders; use compulsive sex to meet intimacy needs; lie compulsively; mutilate themselves; or begin abusing others.

Treatment Plans

> Though my father and mother forsake me, Yahweh will gather me up.
> Yahweh, teach me your way,
> lead me on the path of integrity because of my enemies (Psalm 27:10–11).

The focus of this chapter is primarily on adults who were abused as children and who are now looking at the pain and suffering that they have experienced and are experiencing so that they may be free of their past trauma and become healthier in their present and future relationships, including their relationships with themselves and God. Pastoral counselors who are working with children and their families who are currently in the midst of discovering, confrontation, and legal ramifications are referred to other books on this subject (see the bibliography at the end of the chapter).

Adults who were sexually molested as children present myriad symptoms such as recurrent recollections, generalized anxiety; sexual dysfunction; depression; self-blame; poor self-esteem; dissociation; somatization; phobic avoidance; repeated victimization; sense of shame; contempt for either men or women, whichever was the non-abusive adult; fear of either men or women, whichever was the abusive adult; overvaluing of the abusive sex; adolescent acting out; extreme responsibility as professional caretaker; passivity; promiscuity; impulsiveness; self-injuriousness; post-traumatic stress; inappropriate guilt; religious defection (Shearer and Herbert 1987).

On Axis I victims usually qualify for dysthmia, major depression, and generalized anxiety disorder. In addition, they can also be dependent on substances or have eating disorders. On Axis II victims frequently fit the diagnostic criteria of either borderline, dependent, passive aggressive, paranoid, antisocial or obsessive-compulsive personality disorder. However, since trauma, depersonalization, and chaos are the underlying causes of all personality disorders the sexually abused victim may meet the diagnostic criteria of any one or many different personality disorders. The personality disorder is born out of an attempt to cope with an intolerable childhood. And since children do not process information as adults do, their perception and subsequent interpretation of the chaos lead them to develop coping mechanisms that work for them as children but do not work for them as adults. Because of their fear, mistrust, and depression/anxiety, these children are also not able to learn new coping styles as they mature. Thus the victims are rigidly fixated not only at a specific developmental phase but also in a mode of reacting that is debilitating as an adult.

In addition, these victims often have numerous Axis III complaints, which are over-represented by gynecological, urinary, and oral diseases and conditions.

The faith dimension of adults who were sexually abused feels as confusing to the victims as their multi-axial diagnosis. Some victims cling to their childhood God with a tenacity that appears slightly too retentive, while other victims give up on God totally, surmising that since God did not answer their cries for help as a child then God must not care. Most victims retain some faith but look for *the* answer and end up changing churches frequently and dabbling in cultish type activities from time to time. However, as with all their relationships —which tend to be too intense or absent—these religious relationships cycle through a pattern of intense commitment, attachment, disillusionment, and abandonment.

The typical adult client who was sexually abused as a child is a female, in her thirties to forties. She enters your office as if your are her last hope. She appears depressed except when she is anxious and presents a multiplicity of problem areas. She might have flashes of memory that she has always kept at abeyance and is highly resistant to your questions about these flashes. You like her and see something painful in her eyes that tugs at the core of you as a counselor/minister. She loves the fact that you listen to her and strokes you for your kind attention and empathy. You have great expectations that she will get better. However, she has the capacity to be as resistant as she is charming, to be as manipulative and seductive as she is open and honest. She acts as if she trusts you completely but then three years later reveals startling important data that has "slipped her mind." If she meets the criteria for any of the Cluster B personality disorders, she will have a problem respecting boundaries, and when confronted with boundary issues will claim that you do not care. If she stays with you after the first major confrontation surrounding boundary setting, she will probably stick with the therapy. (There will be more about boundaries later in this chapter.) Expect that at the precise moment that she is getting better, there will be a crisis that she claims has thrown her back to "day one" of counseling. Expect to hear horrendous stories that seem to be scenes from a Stephen King movie or at least a tabloid-type newspaper. Except to feel overwhelmed, incompetent, and enraged at times.

While I know that I am painting a pretty grim picture, working with these victims is also very rewarding. They do make progress and when they begin to remember their abuse and connect the early childhood abuse with their current problems, they can move very quickly toward health. It is at this point that they became sponges, soaking up any wisdom, encouragement, and affirmation that you give them.

If the client is a male, the above description is still applicable. However, the male victim tends to be more rigid, obsessive-compulsive, and emotionally shut down. Men tend to remember but suppress the memory, while women tend not to remember by repressing the memory. Men are more inclined to be antisocial and angry at society, the world, and others, while women are more apt to turn the anger inward.

The Therapeutic Process

> God is both refuge and strength for us,
> a help always ready in trouble;
> so we shall not be afraid though the earth be in turmoil (Psalm 46:1–2a).

The healing process requires long-term therapy with an experienced pastoral therapist. I also believe that for a victim to heal, her faith must be an issue that is brought into the therapeutic process. This does not mean that the client must be religious or belong to a religious organization. It means that the life assumption, faith in a supreme being, the meaning of life, and the role of evil must be food for discussion and growth if the client is going to move toward health.

There are six stages to the healing process. Stages 1 and 2 must precede Stages 3 through 6 but the final four are fluid allowing the client to move in and out of the stages as each feeling, issues, memory, or thought is dealt with.

The Stages of Healing

> With Yahweh on my side I fear nothing;
> what can human beings do to me? (Psalm 118:6).

Stage 1: The Decision to Heal: Taking the Risk (Bass and Davis 1988)

Perhaps it seems obvious that this would be the first step toward health. In fact, it could be argued that this is the first stage of all therapy. Yet when dealing with the trauma of child abuse, the client will attempt to elude the topic by trying to deal with the symptoms rather than the underlying cause: the chaotic, harmful, childhood environment. Making the decision to heal requires psychological fortitude and the ability to risk looking at the very painful experiences that the client has been trying to avoid for years. This decision can only be made in an atmosphere of trust. The relationship between the pastoral counselor and the victim is the most critical part of this stage.

When a child's personal, physical boundary is violated by a trusted adult, that child develops a lack of trust in others. This lack of trust also extends to God, the ultimate parent. As the abuse continues, the child begins to turn lack of trust to distrust. Throughout the rest of the developmental phases the child greets every situation, both hostile and friendly, with mistrust. She may even believe that she knows more than the others who care for her. When this victim enters therapy she is operating from a vantage point of distrust. The therapist is now asking the client to trust, and this is almost impossible to do without a great deal of time, effort, testing, and risking. Further, abuse usually occurs when there is only one other person present—with a great deal of secrecy, behind closed doors and with an unequal distribution of power. Therapy occurs behind closed doors, with secrecy (confidentiality), and only one other person present. There is also, from the client's point of view, an unequal distribution of power. Looking at the similarities, one can see why the act of entering counseling and building trust in a stranger is a difficult task for a victim of sexual abuse. Since trust is not easy at the beginning of a therapeutic relationship for a victim, it is important that the pastoral counselor take the time to build the relationship slowly, expecting setbacks and many acts of testing the relationship.

Making the decision to heal also involves the decision to face a great deal of pain. This may include remembering previously repressed incidents, facing intolerable facts about significant others, feeling rage, losing control, or understanding patterns of behavior. Therefore it takes courage as well as trust to make the decision to heal. Clients need to hear and believe that they deserve to be healthy, that they can have hope, that they can be better, that it is never to late to take the risk of health, and that the road to health is difficult but they are worth it (Bass and Davis 1988). Pastoral counselors can assist these victims' struggles by using an active person-centered approach with a lot of affirmation and confirmation that they will not be alone. It is critical not to move too fast, push too hard, or become impatient, because others have pushed, become impatient, and moved too fast previously and clients run from this type of pressure. The important stance is that this time they can have all the time they need, they will not be abused, and they can begin to have a trusting relationship with at least one other person.

Stage 2: Acknowledging the Reality of the Abuse

After clients grapple with the difficult decision to heal, they must begin the process of healing. In and of itself the decision to seek mental health is a step toward healing as any co-dependency and dependency self-help group will attest. However, taking the next step is a terrifying look at reality, and for many victims this step will often send them reeling back to question their decision to work on their childhood sexual abuse. One client told me that making the decision to enter therapy as akin to making the decision to marry. The real work comes after the wedding, and no one can prepare you for how difficult the work is. In fact, many newlyweds do run back home wondering if they made the correct decision.

At this point in the therapeutic process clients fall into three categories: they have total recall of the horrific events; they have some pieces of memory, impressions, or suspicions; or they have no memory of the abuse, but have some of the symptoms described earlier.

Clients who have memory of their past abuse may appear, at first glance, to be the easiest to work with in Stage 2; however, having memory may mean that they have also developed excellent, resilient defenses to deal with the memory. Clients who have vague suspicions or no memory usually employ one major defense, repression, and when that one defense wavers, the client is bombarded with memory and does not have coping mechanisms in the form of accessible defenses to deal with the crises. While this is a dangerous time for the client, it is a highly effective time for moving the client toward health.

Clients with memory will state that they have faced the reality of the abuse and are ready to move on "to do something about it." It is at this moment that the counselor needs to consider the timing of this wish for health. If the client has memory of the abuse and has not "done something about it," why is she choosing to work now? The answer to this question may be a hint of how the client has not faced the reality of the abuse.

Facing the reality means that the victim was emotionally, physically, intellectually, spiritually, and interpersonally scared. It also means that her entire life has been somehow affected by the abuse, and that she probably was cheated out of a part, if not all of her childhood. It further means that the victim has carried the burden of what someone else did and that someone may be a very significant, beloved person to the client. Acknowledging the reality means to acknowledge waste. In addition, clients may acknowledge the *fact* that they were abused but not acknowledge the extent, the intensity, or the effect of the abuse.

This stage assists the client in facing the abuse as a part of her childhood. To do this the client needs slowly to piece together the abusive circumstances. The pastoral counselor must listen carefully because while children are excellent observers they are poor interpreters. In this stage the client only needs to concern herself with the facts: time frames, incidence, persons involved, and the effects. While this is excruciating work as the pain begins to surface, the counselor must focus on helping the client to deal with the reality of the abuse and not the pain at this point. What many victims have discovered is that once they begin outlining the abuse, they break down and cry, and the therapist jumps in and rescues them by telling them that it is OK or they do not have to remember anymore. Thus, the victims never face the full reality of the abuse and are defended from moving into Stage 3, where they do face the pain.

Stage 2 is not only the fact-finding stage but also the denial-reducing stage. Victims should be gently reminded that they are victims of sexual abuse whenever they begin to forget or minimize the abuse. In some ways this process is similar to the acknowledgment process that must occur in the alcoholic who says, "Yes, I know I drink too much and have to stop." What she has not said is "*I am an alcoholic.*" Even after the reality is established and the alcoholic can indeed state that she is an alcoholic, there are many times when the alcoholic will slip into denial and, for example, attend a gathering of heavy drinkers in a bar and claim only to have drunk soft drinks. Alcoholics need to be reminded that they are alcoholics and cannot put themselves in tempting situations where heavy drinking occurs and the pressure to drink is great. Sexual abuse victims who face the reality of their abuse also slip into denial and repeatedly place themselves in abusive or harming situations. In addition, these clients tend to be very critical of themselves. When they regress or do not progress as they wish they will begin carping about their lack of progress, their poor motivation, and their inability to move quicker toward health. It is at this time that the clients need to be reminded that they are victims of sexual abuse and have years of ingrained patterns of behavior and responses that will not abate easily. When these clients "forget" or minimize their reality, the therapist needs gently to confront the denial, confirm the sexual abuse, affirm the victim, and ask her to join the therapist in the process.

Clients with glimpses of memory, impressions, or suspicion will be open to exploring the incidents that lie at the root of their vaguest memory but will also feel a great deal of fear and trepidation at taking on the mammoth job of remembering. They will be torn between the desire for health and the pain of finally remembering what happened. Many years ago I learned about the approach-avoidance syndrome, but nowhere is it more evident than in dealing with sexually abused clients who have vague impressions of a horrific ordeal. These clients respond to a variety of techniques which can enhance memory.

While these relaxation techniques can seem to be too behavioral or "trendy," they are very beneficial for clients who are filled with anxiety and defenses which impede memory. The various techniques are easy to teach and transferable to outside of the therapeutic hour. The key to the efficacy of relaxation is practice. The client must practice the chosen technique, and the counselor must reinforce the practice with in-session use. I find that sometimes I tend to leave it totally up to the client to rehearse the technique because I do not wish to take up valuable session time with "just" relaxation. However, the reinforcement potential and the power of relaxed defenses which come as a result of in-session use is catalytic to further memory. (Readers are referred to other resources on the various techniques but my personal favorites include three deep breaths, muscle contraction and release, deep muscle concentration, guided imagery, and prayer.) Each client will respond differently to each technique. The key is to find the one or two that resonate with the client and reinforce the daily use.

While relaxed, the client is freer to experience increased memory because relaxed defenses are lower allowing some repressed material to surface. The use of guided imagery can approximate the same result, except that with guided imagery the therapist can escort the relaxed client to various places or times through the use of images. My experience with guided imagery has been powerful, especially when I was able to tap all the senses, not just the visual sense. The smell of bacon frying, the sound of a pet cat purring, or the feel of the rug underfoot can bring potent memory images back to the client.

Prayer also helps the client who has vague memories. Because prayer involves both a higher power and the client, the client does not feel as isolated or alone. With some relaxation techniques the client can become afraid that the reviving of memories will paralyze her when no one is around to help. Prayer seems to evoke a protected feeling with clients that reduces the fear. If they have memory while praying, they feel less alone and able to cope. A combination of relaxation followed by guided imagery and then prayer allows the client to have all the benefits of the various techniques at this stage. Relaxation lowers defenses and puts the client in control. Guided imagery enhances the memory and crystallizes impressions. Prayer invokes a higher power, a letting go, and a feeling of love and safety.

The client with no memory can utilize all of the above techniques, but my experience has been that she usually requires a different sort of intervention in the form of hypnosis or a combination of hypnosis and guided imagery as in the David Grove style (1989) of invention. The clients with glimpses of memory can also take advantage of the techniques listed below but I usually start out with the techniques that utilize the conscious activity first and than move slowly into the more unconscious-tapping activities. With the use of hypnosis or deep relaxation clients often remember enough to affirm their suspicions. This gives them a foundation of information from which they can understand their pathology. At this point they then move into Stage 3. However, some clients with no memory may at this point in therapy decide that they do not want to know anything about the abuse. This escape route was mapped out years ago through the use of repression and needs to be respected. There is, however, a technique that has been developed by David Grove (1989) that allows the abused client to surface the pain without necessarily surfacing the memory. He calls this technique "Healing the Wounded Child Within." The technique is described briefly below in Stage 3, but the reader is referred to the original work for this effective but intricate technique.

Stage 3: Facing the Pain

Facing the pain means breaking the silence of the secret so that it can be brought out into the counseling session affectively. Stage 2 deals more with the intellectual understanding of the abuse while Stage 3 moves into the deeper realm of "knowing" emotionally and the pain of grieving. Stage 3 can be spontaneous, as with a client who called me at 11:00 p.m. from a heated swimming pool where she had been swimming laps. The client, whom I will call May, had no memory of sexual abuse, yet she suspected that something was wrong. After several weeks of relaxation and swimming in a heated pool, she had a flash of memory of her father raping her at eight years old. Prior to the flash of memory, May "knew" that she had been abused intellectually, but the memory now deepened her knowledge into the emotional pain of "my daddy raped me." The grieving was primitive, cleansing, and health producing. We stopped talking about the abuse and began to just sit with it. Hour after hour May cried, grieved, prayed, laughed, remembered, and hurt. There was no more talking around the subject. The silence of doubt, denial, intellectualization, and repression was lifted.

The use of techniques to break down the dam that holds back the "knowing" were described in Stage 2. The techniques of Stage 3 are difficult to call techniques. They are so basic to good therapy that they are themselves the foundation of pastoral counseling.

Listening—When a client is in the kind of pain that May was in, the best way of helping is just to be with her and listen. My temptation was to jump in and rescue or console or move forward. However, the current moment is important at this stage. The "what" of the conversation is background noise. The pain is the only sound. Allow the catharsis to wax and wane naturally, which may mean that you will have to allow for some extra time for the session.

Silence—The gift of silence with a client at this point is precious. Do not be afraid of it. Silence will serve you well in Stage 3. *Do not rush* moving to the next feeling or stage. Allow the client to set the pace; you provide the drag to keep her from moving too fast.

Do not use interpretations or insights that you may have had. There is plenty of time later for this.

Prayer—While I do pray with a client when the client requests it, I frequently use silent prayer in Stage 2 without the client knowing it. I feel at these times that the client and I are sitting in an evil place and a blessed place all at the same time. My prayer is usually for patience, healing, discernment, and the gift of love.

Don't do anything, *just be* there experiencing the moment.

When the client appears to be moving away from the pain, bring her back gently until she does not seem to be fleeing from the pain but moving naturally toward health.

Once the client does not fear or recoil from the pain, but is facing it, experiencing it, and embracing it, then she will begin to move into Stage 4. This cannot be rushed because if the client moves too quickly, then the defenses of suppression, intellectualization, and denial may be used and the healing will not be complete.

Some clients fear this stage because they fear being out of control, or they fear that they may disintegrate. For clients who cannot remember the incidents or face the pain, David Grove's technique provides hope and healing.

Grove (1989) asserts that when a child experiences a trauma (T), the child becomes stuck at T − 1, which is Trauma minus 1 (minute, second, day). His theory implies that the child becomes fixated at T − 1 so she does not have to live through the impending trauma. The rest of the person minus a piece of child goes on to experience the trauma and then to grow up, but the adult is always missing a piece of herself. The child, therefore, never knows whether she survived the trauma. The anxiety, panic, or dread of the trauma and the trauma itself are unacceptable and incomprehensible to the child so she transforms them into metaphors expressed in terms of bodily symptoms and manifestations. Examples of typical bodily symptoms are a lump in the throat, a stabbing pain in the chest, or a balloon in the head. Through an Ericksonian-type hypnotic induction the child is spoken to and encouraged to emerge. As the child emerges the therapist begins a dialogue that includes slowing of speech, carefully constructed questions, and purposeful tracking that allows the child to use the trauma metaphor in a healing manner. In this way the child moves from T − 1 through T to T + 1, the time after the trauma. However, at no time is the child made to relive the trauma. She is instead given permission to mature the metaphor and thus mature herself. Grove believes that forcing the child within to relieve the trauma *is* child abuse, the second time.

I have found this technique to be extremely pastoral and powerful. As the metaphors emerge and mature, many clients (and their children within) identify a God or Christ metaphor that becomes the reconciler or the catalyst to move past the trauma to T + 1, the time after the trauma. The child then knows that she survived, and through the maturing of metaphors the child has freedom where once there was pain. The technique seems to blend person-centered imagery (not guided but followed) and gestalt approaches into an intricate but highly useful tool of health. Clients who fear reliving the trauma need not do so. The Grove approach is a way to unlock the fixation without being traumatized again (Grove 1989).

If mental images or recollection of past events occur, the child then begins grieving and accepting the trauma as a part of her. However, the key to the success of Grove's technique is that the client is never forced or encouraged to remember the trauma. If this does, in fact, occur then *the client* has decided to remember and experience the abuse. If the client does not remember, healing can and does occur as the physical symptoms, pain, and the identified metaphors are recognized, experienced, and matured.

While in Stage 3 and experiencing the pain of the sexual abuse trauma, the client can regress, flee the therapy, flee into health, or become depressed. This time in therapy becomes difficult as the pastoral counselor decides how much pain is too much. The client is often the best source of information concerning this dilemma.

I believe that the best way to help a client through this stage is to keep her informed about what to expect and to assure her that the feeling of "craziness" is normal. One client likened this stage to vomiting. She said that she kept trying to deny that she needed to vomit but as the pain increased she could not deny the pain. When she finally did vomit she was grateful for someone just to be there to assure that she did not hurt herself and to assure her that she would feel better once it was over. Once she experienced the pain, she found that she felt so much better that she wondered why she had waited so long and experienced so much distress before she "vomited" her pain.

Stage 4: Understanding and Gestating the Self and Experience

Stage 4 is a dynamic stage in which the client is helped toward wholeness. It is in this stage that the intellectual knowing, the emotional pain, the spiritual estrangement, the abused child, the adult, and social relationships begin the process of integration. However, the activities of this stage can occur throughout the therapeutic process. The key to knowing if you are working in Stage 4 is whether your client has the child readily available for work. This child has the need to be cared for by the adult client and by the therapist. The child could have any of the following misconceptions based on the abusive experiences:

- It is the child's fault that she was abused.
- She should be punished for noncompliance, yet she feels punished for cooperating.
- She feels sinful, unclean, damned to hell, and is therefore unlovable to God.

- She believes that she is evil or a "bad seed."
- She feels ashamed because there was an element of closeness which she enjoyed or because she felt pleasure, sexually arousal, or had an orgasm.
- She may have loved the abuser and feels that she has betrayed him by talking about the abuse and feeling all the emotions of the past.

The adult has carried those same misconceptions into the current relationship. Having the abused child within identify these misconceptions and the adult recognize that these misconceptions are emotionally still believed today begins an integration process of acknowledging the ingrained patterns of thinking and feeling which are destructive to the client's well-being. The job of the therapist is to introduce a new reality to the child and the adult and then to have the child and adult reinforce the new reality through exercises. For example, let us start with the first basic misconception: It is the client's fault that she was abused.

To the child, this is reality; to the adult, this is an internalized misconception that is based on the child's reality. First, we must understand whence this misconception came. The client will usually know that the abuser sent this signal to her, and because the client felt disgusted and ashamed at a very young age, the misconception was easy to internalize. In addition, if the child attempted to disclose the abuse to another and was told that the abuse was her fault, then the child's feeling of guilt was reinforced. While the above messages are overt, there are many more messages that are sent to the abused child which are covert. One young woman said that she was the least attractive of all the children and the only child sexually abused by her father. In addition, her mother singled her out as being the only child in the family who was "different." Whenever anything unpleasant happened to the client, her mother would state that the client deserved the misfortune. In addition, if the client did something wrong, according to her mother, then the client would be told that her behavior was typical of the type of person she was. This led the client to believe that there was something inherently wrong with her and that is why she had been abused. She often referred to herself as "the bad seed."

The next part of the challenge to the basic misconception is for the client to determine intellectually whether the feeling that she was at fault for the abuse has validity. It may take some time for the client actually to state that the abuse was *not* her fault. Next the client has to state, still in the intellect, who was responsible for the abuse; obviously the answer is the abuser. Once these facts are established, then the client must speak to her child and say, "None of this was your fault. You were just a child. It is an adult's absolute responsibility to refrain from abusing children (Bass and Davis 1988). Our abuser is 100 percent responsible for the abuse." This must be repeated over and over again in many different ways in order for the new facts to be internalized. Soon the client, with the therapist's help, will recognize new potentially abusive situations and learn to affirm that she does not have to be abused, that she does not deserve to be abused, and that she can and will avoid abusive situations. Then for each of the other misconceptions the client and therapist reconstruct new reality statements to challenge the old misconceptions.

A number of specific challenging statements and behavioral activities are listed below. These have been shown to assist clients with their ability to alter their misconceptions.

Client Misconception	*Challenging Statements or Behavior*
Abuse is the child's fault	1) See above. 2) Ask the client to watch other children who are currently the same age as client was when the abuse started. Question whether such a small child could be responsible for being abused. (Current media figures make grist for discussion.) 3) Discuss how unhealthy adults lie and deceive. (Current media figures make grist for discussion.)
Punished for noncompliance and punished by being passive.	1) Does a child the age she was when abused have the ability to fight off an adult? 2) Does a child have the emotional strength to stand up for self, risk the rage of the abuser, and risk the isolation from significant others? 3) Did she have any choices, as she saw it?

Sinful, unclean, damned, and unlovable by God.	1) Discuss what sin is, how a person is damned by God, and what makes a person unlovable by God. The answers of the child, and probably the adult, will not match the Bible's messages and most church doctrine. 2) Ask the client to justify the differences in her feelings and attitudes with the Bible's messages. This will help to integrate the child's misconception with the estranged spiritual dimension and the intellectual and emotional dimensions of the client. 3) Ask the client to role play with you. You play a sexually abused client while letting the client play the therapist. Often just hearing the words coming out of her mouth can help challenge the misconceptions.
She believes that she is evil or a bad seed.	1) Nature/nurture discussion is helpful here. If she looks at a baby, does she really believe that it could be a bad seed and deserves to be abused? Or is it a child who has the capacity to respond to love or abuse? 2) Discuss the difference between feeling the presence of evil because of something that happened, doing something wrong, or being evil. The differences can be potent discussion material.
Feeling shame because of feeling close, sexual arousal, or having an orgasm during the abuse.	1) Discuss with the client the natural reactions of the body to various stimuli (E.g. knee jerk reaction, or salivation at the smell of food).

	2) Help the client state in her own words that physical reaction to abuse is normal and natural just like emotional reaction is normal and natural.
Feelings of having betrayed beloved abuser by breaking the conspiracy of silence.	1) Discuss the abuser's lack of regard for your client's right not to be abused. 2) Discuss the client's right to seek help in a *confidential* relationship. 3) Discuss fear of disclosure and how the conspiracy of silence helps to protect the abuser while leaving the victim with no support. 4) Discuss the likelihood that the abuser has abused others and may continue to abuse others. 5) Discuss the right of the victim to cease being victimized.

One positive outcome from Stage 4 includes the child's integration into the adult. This does not mean that the child completely goes away, but that the child is accepted and loved by the adult. One way to encourage the feeling of acceptance is to use guided imagery and to have the adult rescue the child from the abuse and then to love, cuddle, and affirm the child within the adult.

Another outcome of Stage 4 is the client's beginning to trust herself. She will have learned skills in avoiding current and future abusive situation, how to deal with intrusive thoughts and feelings, how to relax and enjoy life, how to find the support she needs, and how to set limits and boundaries for self and others. This last outcome of Stage 4 is a key to further growth.

However, boundary setting must begin in Stage 1 when the client first contacts the pastoral counselor. At the beginning of counseling the therapist sets the boundaries regarding, time, place, appropriate behavior, intersession phone calls, honesty, and fees. This models for the client appropriate limit setting. The pastoral counselor then helps the client to define her own time, space, and rights, including the right to protect her own body and psyche from being abused, the right to say no, and the right to put herself first when appropriate.

Boundary setting does not have to be hostile, cruel, or harsh. In fact, for every defined boundary that is perceived as a no there is a disguised yes. When a client says no to abuse, she is saying yes to health. It is important that the client realize that a boundary may bring hostile reactions from those who are used to crossing boundaries, so the disguised yes must be identified and affirmed.

Stage 5: Dealing with Anger and Other Negative Feelings

Perhaps the postponement of dealing with angry feelings is causing some concern for the reader since abused clients have many unresolved feelings concerning their abuse. This stage does not mean that this is where we first experience negative feelings, only that this is where we deal with the harder feelings. Over the course of counseling a myriad of feelings will have emerged, been acknowledged, and subsided. This process continues for all of our lives. This stage, however, has more to do with the intense rage and bitterness that the client feels towards those who abused her or have not supported her. Anger feeds anger into a downward negative spiral. To deal appropriately with anger a client must first have some skills in dealing with other feelings and have some support systems which nurture and affirm her, including her own inner sources of strength. Unless a client has explored Stages 1 to 4, she has little chance of resolving anger and moving toward some resolution and reconciliation. One author even suggests that there is no reason to forgive, and that clients need not expect this of themselves (Bass and Davis 1988). I disagree in part. I do find forgiveness the most difficult part of therapy, but it is something that most clients eventually want for themselves (see forgiveness later in this chapter). However, many therapists get the client to express anger early, applaud (reinforce) the expression, and then call the client healthy because she has gotten in touch with her true feelings. I believe that there is a healthier way to manage oneself then just getting in touch with feelings. But first let us look at the getting in touch and expression of feelings which are hard to accept.

Anger, fury, and rage are felt when one is abused. Some clients reject these emotions as not applying to them. However, the more they reject them the more they play a part in the unconscious motivation of behavior. Therefore, never accept a client's word that she has no anger. Second, help clients recognize the difference between *expe-*

riencing an emotion and *acting* on that emotion. At this point the client may experience the insight that she may feel *and then choose how to react.*

Many clients are uncomfortable with feeling angry and therefore attempt to deny, stifle, and swallow their feelings. I encourage clients to sit still and feel the emotion. As they experience the emotion, anger waxes. Have the client continue to feel the emotion and as the feeling peaks, have them breath slowly; as the expression of the emotion becomes more evident encourage them to emote by crying, yelling, pounding a pillow. Support the anger as justified. Allow clients to continue until they become exhausted and the feeling wanes. Clients will feel tired but relieved.

After a client has experienced several episodes of rage in this safe manner, she will begin to feel less fearful of feeling rage and will be ready to learn how to express rage with others present. The key to expressing feelings to others is to express emotion in such a way as to feel positive about oneself and to avoid degrading another. Role play, rehearsal, letter writing, and empty chair techniques help to teach appropriate ways of expressing emotions. Group work can also assist in the practice of the newly acquired skills.

Stage 6: Resolution and Reconciliation

This stage is not simply forgiveness. This stage is akin to acceptance and rapprochement; it is an ongoing process that continues even after therapy is completed. It is in this stage that the victim needs to decide whether she is going confront the abuser, if he is still alive. In addition, the client will begin letting go in this stage. Topics of conversation revolve more around the here and how. Subject matter can include current relationships, career development, or parenting issues. There appears to be a letting go of the issues of abuse and an embracing of the client's current needs.

The first reconciliation that needs to occur is within the client herself. She needs to understand and forgive herself for anything she perceives that she did, felt, or thought at the time she was actively a victim and then later after the abuse ended. Clients often report feeling murderous rage and planning their perpetrator's demise. This leads to feelings of guilt and then inward rage. Learning that she can be human, vulnerable, and honest with herself will relieve much of the guilt. Going farther, the victim can then learn to love herself. This usually takes much time and cognitive restructuring. Too many therapists try to get a client to love and accept herself in the early stages of counseling hoping that this love will be a panacea for the sexual abuse. However, until the client has faced the abuse in some form, grieved over the loss associated with child abuse, and experienced all feelings including rage, the client cannot accept herself. Accepting and loving oneself includes physically taking care of oneself, emotionally caring for one's needs, intellectually using the gifts given to the fullest possible extent, establishing healthy relationships, and feeling spiritually connected.

Termination

Peace I bequeath to you,
my own peace I give you,
a peace which the world cannot give, this is my gift to you.
Do not let your hearts be troubled or afraid (John 14:27).

Termination occurs when the client has attained Stage 6 and feels that she can function and continue growing on her own. I recommended that termination occur slowly over a period of months with successively longer and longer periods of time between sessions. Remember that these client are particularly sensitive to rejection and abandonment, so letting go must seem like a natural process.

Therapeutic Techniques

Stage-specific techniques have been presented at each stage of the process of pastoral counseling. The following techniques are ones that I have found useful for all stages, and I tend to make use of them frequently.

BELIEVE YOUR CLIENT AND BELIEVE IN YOUR CLIENT

The absolute best help that you can give your client is the willingness to believe her stories, suspicions, impressions, and feelings. While there will always be times when you will have doubts as to the client's veracity, you need to show your client your willingness to hear and believe. This can be very difficult in the times of revealing the abuse and expressing feelings. Belief in your client is a person-centered stance that is paramount to the relationship. Few people ever believed in the client, and the client does not believe in herself, so if therapy is going to work the pastoral counselor must have faith in the client, in the process of counseling, and in the intervention of her Supreme Being.

DEVELOP TRUST

Victims of child abuse have learned to distrust everyone. You will be no exception. Even if a client who has been a victim of sexual abuse appears to trust you, an element of mistrust is always present. The act of mistrusting is one way the client has learned to survive. Expect that you will be distrusted, that you will be misunderstood, or that you will have your veracity questioned. Above all, remain calm and be honest and fair throughout your dealings with the client. If you make a mistake or error, own up to it and model for your client how to be responsible for your actions. If you are being unfairly accused, remain firm in your innocence but help the client look at why the accusation is being made. Do not dismiss the event, try to get the client to see your point of view, or become defensive.

PRAY

> Because of the Lord's great love we are not consumed, for His compassions never fail (Lamentations 3:22, *GNB*).

I find that these clients drain every ounce of energy I have to offer. I have the absolute need to pray for each of them and for myself. Many times I feel that I am flying into a snowstorm and have zero visibility. At times, clients wish for me to pray with them and when they ask I gladly respond. More often, though, I find these clients alienated from their faith and mistrustful of God. As they become healthier I usually find the right time to tell them that I have been praying for them and ask them to join me everyday in praying for themselves and for me. Timing is critical. Trust has to be high, progress must have been made, and the client needs to feel hopeful of further progress.

IDENTIFY AND AFFIRM THE CLIENT'S HEALTH

Even though clients come to counseling to work on their unhealthy selves, there are some healthy parts to these clients. Pastoral counselors must keep their clients' healthy sides always in plain view for themselves and their clients to see. Throughout the stages of therapy it is easy to focus on the abuse and its results and forget the areas of health that the clients bring.

SET LIMITS AND BOUNDARIES

Because many of the victims have significant Cluster B traits, if not full-blown personality disorders, boundary and limit setting is crucial to working with these clients. Boundaries were ignored or purposefully breached by their abusers; they therefore do not respect their own boundaries or others' limits. Sometimes they actively resent the boundaries that others have set. Your job to set reasonable boundaries and then respect them yourself and insist that your clients respect them too. Explain why boundaries are important to help utilize structure and energy to its maximum and to protect everyone from violating others' rights. Expect these clients to look for any way around a boundary but, as with small children, you need gently and lovingly to reiterate the need to respect the boundary. As each stage is entered expect that these clients will attempt to push boundaries to the limits over and over again.

ENCOURAGE GROUP WORK

Group work is the treatment of choice for adults who were sexually abused as children. My experience with these clients leads me to believe, however, that unless the clients are in at least Stage IV, they will not participate in such a way as to move toward health. Individual work is more effective in the early stages, but group work becomes a beneficial and important experience in the later stages.

Through group work clients are able to act out the different roles they played and then try out new methods of behaving. In addition, clients get support from others who have been abused and learn that they are not alone. This honest, experiential, and supportive environment will feel so different to the victim that at first she may rebel, runaway, or flee into health. These responses can be confronted by the group members effectively because of their own experiences. If a client is terminating from individual therapy and has not participated in group, then this is an ideal time to encourage the client to enter group.

Confrontation

The literature differs on the importance of confronting the abuser and breaking the conspiracy of silence with other family members (Bass and Davis 1988; Lew 1990). The positive outcomes of disclosing or confronting may include confirmation that the abuse did occur from another sibling, stopping a perpetrator from hurting another child, support from others for the client, an apology from the perpetrator, and ego strength for the victim because she has finally said "stop it." The negative outcomes of confrontation may be revenge, loss of family support, being called crazy or a liar, and denial.

Clients who wish to confront need to look carefully at their motivation and the possible negative outcomes. If a client decides to confront, she also needs to be prepared for the confrontation and rehearse the manner in which she will approach the abuser. She should be cautioned about the possible negative outcomes and be encouraged to stay in her adult without letting the abused child show. Frequently clients want a mediator to assist in the confrontation. I recommend that another pastoral counselor be selected so that your role as therapist remains clear. In addition, the client and counselor need to assess together whether there is any possible physical danger to the client if a confrontation should occur. Have the client ascertain what she has to gain or lose in confronting the abuser and whether she is healthy enough to lose other family members' support. Breaking the taboo of disclosing can shake up the client's life as well as the lives of other innocent family members.

I have had experience with clients who have had positive outcomes and negative outcomes, and with clients who have decided not to confront. I cannot say that clients who have confronted have had a better or quicker or more complete recovery than those who chose not to confront. The difference seems to be in a positive mental strength when making the decision and being prepared for whatever outcome occurs. Deciding not to confront or disclose is no crime and is no condemnation of a good prognosis if the decision is made from a position of strength (Bass and Davis 1988).

If the perpetrator has died, then the victim does not have to decide whether to confront the abuser but still may wish to disclose the abuse to the rest of the family. Do not be deceived that disclosing to a family without having to confront the abuser is easier. Family members have a great stake in maintaining their family image. Also, if the abuser has died, the relatives may have elevated the abuser to a pedestal. Therefore, preparation for and the decision to break the silence has to be done carefully even if only the family is to be confronted.

The victim can still bring some closure to the pain of abuse through confronting the perpetrator in absentia. Clients have found that letter writing, grave visitation, and role playing can bring the confrontation and resolution of which the client is desirous.

The Pastoral Dimension of Treating a Victim of Sexual Abuse

When a child is sexually abused, 90 percent of the time the abuser is well-known to the child as either a family member or a trusted person such as a teacher, minister, or babysitter (Rush 1980). Because of the caretaker role or trust relationship the child feels betrayed, confused, and mistrusting of authority figures. For children who are taught in church schools that God is a loving, parental figure, the child will soon develop a degree of mistrust in God who, in the child's mind, represents the supreme caretaker and authority. Many abused children end up leaving their church and losing faith because when they were being abused they cried out for help from God, and when the abuse did not stop, they felt abandoned by a cruel and uncaring God.

The job of the counselor is to aid the client in seeing ways that God has been supportive over the years. This activity may not be embraced by the client at first because of bitterness and pain, but as the client moves through the stages of therapy and is supported in feeling anger and hurt, she will begin to see some areas in her life where God has been active. One woman with whom I was working saw nothing that God had done for her. She still believed in God but had the image of a cruel, punitive God. Over the course of therapy she refused to discuss her faith which she called "nil." But then one day she was describing her youngest child as a "gift from God." I asked her to pause and reflect on the statement. She said, "God didn't rape me, my uncle did. God didn't make it happen, my uncle did. I just do not know if God was there when I was crying out for help." On further pondering she said, "God did answer my prayer for it to stop because it did stop one month later. I guess I forgot to ask God to make it stop *now*." As counseling continued, she saw many ways in which God's love was present in her life. One way was the wonderful escape she had in her out-of-body experience during the rape. She claimed that it was the only thing that kept her sane. Seeing her out-of-body experience as a blessing from God gave her the impetus she needed to say "thank you" in prayer. While she did not return to church immediately she did begin praying and reading inspirational books. She claims to feel more peaceful and reconciled to her supreme being.

Forgiveness

> Any bitterness or bad temper or anger or shouting or abuse must be far removed from you—as must every kind of malice. Be generous to one another, sympathetic, forgiving each other as readily as God forgave you in Christ (Ephesians 4:31–32).

Authorities differ over the need for forgiveness as a part of healing. Lew (1990) and Bass and Davis (1988) assert that forgiveness is not necessary for healing; in fact, they indicated that forgiveness can impede healing. "If you have strong religious ties, particularly Christian ones, you may feel it is your sacred duty to forgive. This just isn't true. If there is such as thing as divine forgiveness, it's God's job, not yours" (Bass and Davis 1988).

The perpetrator and others may even demand *forgiveness* and further demand that the child *forget* what happened. Fourteen years ago I worked with a father, mother, and daughter as the daughter attempted to express her feelings of anger at her father for having fondled her while he was intoxicated. The father stated that he was sorry; he expected to be forgiven and the whole incident forgotten. He asserted that if the daughter could not "forgive and forget," then she was harassing him, was certainly no Christian, and would go to hell for her inability to let go of the incident. The mother calmly sat and agreed with the father that her daughter was indeed a very unforgiving person and therefore was a religious hypocrite. This type of harassment of the victim is fairly common and teaches the abused child to ignore her feelings. It also teaches and reinforces that the perpetrator can do what he wishes and escape accountability. It is within this area that the many child abuse laws make sense. A victim is a victim because of the powerlessness of her position. She may say, "This is wrong." But as long as the perpetrator holds the bulk of the power, the victim will be subject to abuse. The child abuse laws make the act of abusing a child a criminal offense. This takes the responsibility off the child and puts it on the shoulders of society and its representatives. The perpetrator can demand forgiveness from the child and threaten the child if the child does not forget, but a court of law will not be so easily manipulated and will hold the abuser accountable for his actions.

The problem with the forgive and forget principle is that it has been misused and misinterpreted. Forgiveness means to give up resentment against or the desire to punish (Websters 1983). Forgiveness is not pity, exoneration, or absolution. Further, "forgiveness is not letting the abuser off the hook or accepting or minimizing the abusive behavior. It is letting go of the rage so that the pain does not continue to determine the future" (Lew 1990) *Forget* is an even more difficult word. To *forget* means literally to fail to recall or remember. To forget an event at will is almost impossible. The act of willing to forget would cause the person to remember. In addition, the act of forgetting that becomes denial and then repression is usually seen as a defense mechanism and unhealthy. Therefore, when a child is asked to forget, she is asked to do the impossible or the unhealthy.

Perhaps we need to change the phrase to "remit and omit." The word *remit* means forgive, but it also means to refrain from exacting payment and to submit for judgment or action to someone whose business it is to look after such things. *Omit* means to leave out. In this word we see the conscious ability that is missing in forget. The victim therefore does not need to forget, but rather consciously to omit the information or pain from determining her future.

Sandford (1988) disagrees with many writers by citing that forgiveness is freedom, a letting go. Remitting the behavior of another, pain, guilt, and rage to God allows the victim to move toward health. Sandford does note that this letting go can take a long time.

Personally, I find that both sides of this issue are near the target but off center. Lew (1990) as well as Bass and Davis (1988) believe that forgiveness is not necessary for health. I have found that forgiveness *early in treatment* is not necessary to become *healthier*. In fact, forgiveness too early can block health. However, later in Stage VI forgiveness is almost always necessary to obtain health. It is here that Sandford is correct. Forgiveness becomes freedom.

One type of forgiveness that is erroneously touted as being necessary in the therapeutic process is the forgiveness of self. In this instance forgiveness implies some guilt or responsibility that needs forgiving. The child of sexual abuse bears no such guilt or responsibility. Once again I recommend a substitute word. The words *exonerate* and *exculpate* mean to free from blame and declare guiltless. When a person spends years punishing herself for something that was not her fault, she does not need forgiveness, she needs exoneration! Liken this to a person who was jailed for a crime that he did not commit. If this person is proven innocent of the charge, he would not need to be forgiven; he would want and deserve to be exonerated and his good name cleared. The victim of child abuse needs the same consideration. In addition, rather than a punishing external force, the sexually abused person has a demoralizing, punitive internal force. This means that the client is her own worst enemy and may take months of deprogramming and cognitive restructuring. Using the word *forgiveness* underscores that there is something within the client that needs forgiving.

Grace

> I shall give the weary all they need and satisfy all those whose strength has gone (Jeremiah 31:25).

Victims of sexual abuse have trouble seeing grace in their lives. When people quote "I cried because I had no shoes and then I met a man who had no feet," the sexually abused victim feels like the man with no feet. For some, this leads into years of depression. Others turn to is drugs, repetitive self-abuse, or any number of other symptoms. These clients need to learn how to look at and count the graces which are predominant in their lives.

One young woman told me that she felt as if she were in the bottom of a well with only a pinpoint of light as a guide. Yet after a few months she was able to count her spouse, her child, her job, her best friend, and her recent success in school as loving gifts in her life. After many more months she could see where God had entered her life and changed it. Grace is usually not recognized until the pain has been felt and acknowledged. Then, as the pain subsides, clients begin to experience other positive emotions that lead to thankfulness and a recognition of where grace has become life-giving.

Reconciliation

> Come back to Yahweh your God,
> for he is gracious and compassionate,
> slow to anger, rich in faithful love,
> and he relents about inflicting disaster (Joel 2:13).

The entire life of a sexually abused child becomes one of alienation. She becomes alienated from the once trusted abuser, herself, others whom she sees as unprotective, God, and authority. During the therapeutic process the victim must address each alienated piece of herself as well as each person or group who are alienated. Each step becomes one of identifying the lost part or person, affirming the importance of the lost piece, accepting the part or person back into the self, and setting appropriate boundaries for how much importance the part of self or person will have in the victim's future.

For example, Freda had alienated all males from her life. She believed that the world was better off without them. She knew, however, that a world without men would end. And she also had to affirm that her experience was not every person's experience. She next looked at her male side and recognized its strength in her life and accepted that it is not maleness that is bad but abusive maleness that is bad. Finally, she embraced that males were OK, but that as a victim she needed to proceed carefully building any male friendships lest she fall back into the role of victim with another male. This process is a long one fraught with many setbacks.

Shame and Guilt

While guilt is a feeling that is experienced when someone has done something that she judges to be wrong, shame is a feeling of unworthiness about oneself just because of existing. The sexually abused person typically feels both inappropriate guilt and unjustified shame. But they feel both just the same. When Christian clients speak about Christ's death as taking away both the guilt and shame of the world, they mean everyone's sins except theirs. They even believe that their abusers are forgiven and blessed without feeling that they, the victims, are. Yet when challenged, they cannot cognitively justify their positions. They often end up saying, "That's just the way it is." Arguing or confronting does not work. What does work is prayer. "Some incest survivors report that prayer provides them with feelings of calm, comfort and connection with a strength that goes beyond themselves" (Lew 1990).

I encourage clients to pray for the love, grace, and forgiveness that God has given to others. I do not argue that they already have it. I follow their axiom: "If they don't feel it, they don't have it." Usually their prayer life has a rocky, hit-or-miss beginning, but I encourage them to keep at it. Sometimes I am amazed at the grace that is felt. In fact, I have watched my clients find grace in the most incredible situations. One client named Bill was always complaining that no one ever spoke to him in social situations. My efforts at getting him to see how he set up this self-fulfilling prophesy by withdrawing from others and that this was responsible for his social isolation met with massive resistance. One day at a professional football game a total stranger said to Bill, "Do you always look like you don't want to be where you are?" Bill was stunned, but he began to look at what he was doing in social situations. Someday I may write a book called *God's Graces in the Most Unusual Places.*

It is roughly at this point that clients begin to feel the freedom to talk about their anger at God for abandoning them so many years ago. This is a rough moment. Clients are likely to feel that because they expressed their anger, resentment, and sense of betrayal at God, they are going to be struck dead, or worse, a loved one will be harmed. They are sure that they are going to hell. Some of this response will be in direct relation to how the pastoral counselor reacts. If the counselor's reaction is loving acceptance and affirmation of the strong feeling, the client is more likely to breath a sight of relief, feel a little less afraid and more hopeful, and to express other tabu feelings.

Conclusion

The mental-health profession is citing childhood sexual abuse as an epidemic. Pastoral counselors may be seeing up to 90 percent of their client population as being victims of sexual abuse, even though some of their clients may be unaware of their past abuse. It is therefore imperative that pastoral counselors understand as much as possible about the symptomatology of and treatment planning for those who are victims of childhood sexual abuse. In addition, the prophylactic issue for today's children is an extremely important task for all pastoral counselors. The contribution of pastoral counselors to the entire problem of sexual abuse is significant because childhood sexual abuse raises many issues of faith. Secular counselors may address well the issues of sexual abuse, but they often ignore the faith dimension so critical to the healing process, which must integrate the various personal dimensions: intellectual, physical, social, emotional, and spiritual.

> Yahweh then said, "I myself shall go with you and I shall give you rest" (Exodus 33:14).

Resources

Adults Molested as Children United, P.O. Box 952, San Jose, CA 95108 (408)280-5055. Focuses on Self-Help Treatment

C. Henry Kempe National Center for the Prevention and Treatment of Child Abuse and Neglect. 1205 Oneida St., Denver, Co 80220. (303)321-3963 Focuses on child abuse treatment, research and training.

Incest Recovery Association 5200 N. Central Expressway Suite 209, Dallas, TX 75206 (214)373-6607 Groups, information and training for professionals.

National Coalition Against Sexual Assault. 8787 State Ste., E. St.

Louis, IL 62203 (618)398-7764. Professionals supply services and Information.

P.L.E.A. Box 22 Zia Rd., Sante Fe, NM 87505 (505)984-9184. Focuses on male survivors of incest.

Survivors of Childhood Abuse Program, 1345 El Centro Ave. P.O. Box 630 Hollywood, CA 90028. 1-800-422-4453. Research, training and education and referrals.

Survivors of Incest Anonymous (SIA), P.O. Box 21817, Baltimore, MD 21222-6817; (301)282-3400 Self-help groups for survivors of incest based on a 12-step program for both women and men 18 years and older.

Survivors Network Newsletter % Crawford. 18653 Ventura Boulevard #143 Tarzana, CA 91356.

Voices in Action, Inc., P.O. Box 148309, Chicago, IL 60614; (312)327-1500 National network of incest survivors and supporters of survivors; referral service; survival packet of resource material; newsletters and national conferences.

Note

Unless otherwise indicated, scripture quotations in this chapter are taken from *The New Jerusalem Bible,* copyright 1985 by Darton, Longman & Todd, Ltd. and Doubleday, a division of Bantam Doubleday Dell Publishing Group, Inc.

References

Alexander, P. C., and Lupfer, S. L. 1987. "Family Characteristics and Long-Term Consequences Associated with Sexual Abuse." *Archives of Sexual Behavior* 16: 235–45.

American Psychiatric Association. 1987. *Diagnostic and Statistical Manual of Mental Disorders,* 3d ed., rev. (DSMIII-R). Washington, D.C.: American Psychiatric Association.

Bass, E., and Davis, L. 1988. *The Courage to Heal.* New York: Harper & Row.

Finkelhor, D. 1979. *Sexually Victimized Children.* New York: The Free Press.

Freud, S. 1950. *Totem and Taboo,* translated by James Strachey. New York: W. W. Norton.

Grove, David. 1989. *Healing the Wounded Child Within.* Edwardsville: David Grove.

Herman, J. 1981. *Father/Daughter Incest.* Cambridge, Mass.: Harvard University Press.
Lew, M. 1990. *Victims No Longer.* New York: Harper & Row.
Rencken, R. H. 1989. *Intervention Strategies for Sexual Abuse.* Alexandria, Va.: AACD.
Rush, F. 1980. *The Best-Kept Secret.* Englewood Cliffs, N.J.: Prentice-Hall.
Sandford, Paula. 1988. *Garlands for Ashes: Healing Victims of Sexual Abuse.* Tulsa: Victory House.
Shearer, S. L., and Herbert, C. A. 1987. "Long-Term Effects of Unresolved Sexual Trauma." *AFB* 36 (October).
Webster's 20th Century Dictionary of the English Language, Unabridged. 1983. New York: Simon and Schuster.

For Further Reading

Bell, A., and Weinberg, M. 1978. *Homosexualities.* New York: Simon and Schuster.
Butler, S. 1985. *Conspiracy of Silence.* San Francisco: Volcano Press.
Finkelhor, D. 1984. *Child Sexual Abuse.* New York: The Free Press.
Russell, D. E. 1986. *The Secret Trauma.* New York: Basic Books.

Marie M. Fortune
James Poling

18. Calling to Accountability: The Church's Response to Abusers

A girl in the youth group tells the pastor that her father is pressuring her to have sex with him.

Raped by the leader of a neighborhood boy's club, a ten-year-old boy tries to commit suicide.

A member of the congregation is hospitalized because her husband beat her.

Sexual involvement with several female parishioners leads to a pastor's dismissal from his charge.

Stories that only a few years ago were unusual have become commonplace. Increasing numbers of pastors and congregational leaders are coming face-to-face with survivors of physical and sexual abuse who are in need of the healing ministries of the church. Fortunately the church is beginning to respond, and there are resources, including articles in this volume, for counseling victims (Fortune 1982; Pellauer 1987; Sgroi 1982; Bass and Davis 1988; Ledray 1986; Caesar and Hamberger 1989). Still, much more needs to be done.

For every victim who is trying to escape a private hell, there is a perpetrator who has taken advantage of the victim during a period of vulnerability. As more and more victims come forward, pastors are discovering perpetrators of abuse in their congregations and in their local communities. While it is not useful to be overly fearful of offenders, the increasing prevalence of physical and sexual abuse places upon Christian leaders an imperative to confront this issue. *Specifically, the church can minister to victims by being willing to deal with abusers.*

However, the church's mistaken understanding of God's love for all people has sometimes led Christian leaders to tolerate rather than to stop abusers. Providing nurturing concern and healing resources is an appropriate response for victims of violence. However, for perpetrators the most loving response may be the development of systems of accountability and consequences that stop their destructive behaviors.

For a congregation to face the reality that one of its own members, or even its own pastor, may have sexually or physically abused an adult or child can be devastating. At the point of disclosure by the victim(s), there are many temptations for a church to play the Priest and Levite, passing by the wounded person on the side of the road:

THE TEMPTATION OF DISBELIEF

Abusers often are respected members of the church and community. They teach Sunday School or chair the Board of Trustees or preach the sermon every Sunday. They are often well-known and liked; their public persona is totally contrary to the image of a sex offender or wife beater. To believe that such a person is responsible for the abuse of another brings us face-to-face with our own failure of judgment. This reluctance to believe has made the church slow to respond to the victims and survivors in its midst. In our naiveté about the behavior of abusers, we may inadvertently contribute to the silence which perpetuates suffering for many.

THE TEMPTATION TO PROTECT THE CHURCH'S IMAGE

Sometimes a church's reluctance to believe that one of its members or its pastor is an abuser arises out of its desire to protect its own image in the community. Even if there has been some private acknowledgment, there is often public denial or minimization. This refusal to deal openly with the reality of victimization is excruciating for victims who have come forward. It is yet another denial of their experience. It also allows the abuser to continue to minimize or deny responsibility.

THE TEMPTATION TO BLAME THE VICTIM

The most common reaction to those who disclose that they have been victimized by sexual or domestic violence is to blame them for it. Churches are notorious for thinking that victims brought the destruction on by their own behaviors. As long as the church persists in blaming the victims, it can avoid holding the abuser accountable.

THE TEMPTATION TO SYMPATHIZE WITH THE ABUSER

This temptation is in tandem with blaming the victim; it focuses on the pain which the accusation causes the abuser, the possible damage which will be done to the abuser's career, and so on. Again, it ignores the real issue: this person is responsible for harm done to another. Thus the abuser avoids accountability for the harm done.

THE TEMPTATION TO PROTECT THE ABUSER FROM THE CONSEQUENCES OF HIS OR HER BEHAVIOR

This temptation leads to the avoidance and secret-keeping which so often accompany any disclosure of abuse in a church setting. It also underlies a pastor's avoidance of reporting abuse to law enforcement. Some pastors seem to believe that their primary responsibility is to prevent a church member from ever encountering law enforcement. Unfortunately, the protection from consequences only further supports the abuser's minimization and denial of responsibility, which are not in anyone's best interest.

THE TEMPTATION OF CHEAP GRACE

If and when a congregation does acknowledge that a member or pastor is an abuser, there is an immediate move to forgive and forget. Not only is this bad psychology, it is even worse theology. It has no basis in either Hebrew or Christian scriptural teaching. The purpose of judgment is always to bring someone to confession and from confession to repentance. The substance of repentance is always "a new heart and a new spirit" (Ezekiel 18:31). Repentance always begins with acknowledgment to oneself, to one's victim or victims, and to one's community of responsibility for harm done. Jesus outlines the basics of accountability in the gospels: "If your brother does something wrong, rebuke him and, *if* he is sorry, forgive him. And if he wrongs you seven times a day and seven times comes back to you and says, 'I am sorry,' you must forgive him" (Luke 17:3–4, emphasis added). Cheap grace shortcircuits the process that the abuser needs in order to repent.

A group of twenty-five incest offenders sat in a circle during their treatment. They said, "Tell the clergy for us that they should not forgive us so quickly." Each of them upon arrest had gone to the minister and had been prayed over, "forgiven," and sent home. Each of them said it was the worst thing that could have been done. That cheap grace allowed them to continue to deny responsibility for their abuse of others. It in no way facilitated their repentance or their treatment.

If there is any hope of stopping physical and sexual abuse, leaders of the church need to join social workers, police, lawyers, psychologists, and judges in educating the public and developing systems of accountability. To this end this chapter summarizes research on physical and sexual abusers and suggests some principles for stopping them.

What Is Abuse?

Anne Ganley (1989) separates spouse abuse into four categories. We are applying these categories more broadly here:

PHYSICAL VIOLENCE

This is the most overt form and includes slapping, punching, kicking, pushing, throwing objects at a person, using a weapon, and so forth. Obviously this form has the highest probability of causing serious injury or death.

SEXUAL VIOLENCE

Included here are rape (marital, acquaintance, or stranger), child sexual abuse (incest or molestation), and sexual harassment and exploitation (in the work place or in a professional relationship).

PSYCHOLOGICAL ABUSE

This is a persistent pattern of psychological pressure or brainwashing with the intent of instilling fear in the victim in order to control his or her behavior. This form of abuse includes verbal humiliation, threats, manipulation, and coercion, usually over a period of time.

DESTRUCTION OF PROPERTY AND PETS

This form, which is common in the family setting, carries a psychological dimension. There is always an explicit or implicit threat toward the victim in the damage to property or pets: "This time it is the china; next time it will be you."

These types of behaviors can occur between family members, between acquaintances, coworkers, friends, or least often, between strangers. They are most likely to occur between men and women, but also can occur between men or between women. They can occur between persons of every age. They are most likely intraracial but can be interracial. They occur in public and in private.

Abusers are persons who use aggressive and/or manipulative behaviors to enhance their position of dominance in order to coerce or control another person for the abuser's own purposes. Abusers may use physical force, emotional assaults, psychological pressure, threats, and/or social privilege and position to exploit the vulnerability of another in order to control (as is the case with batterers and most rapists) or to seek sexual gratification (as is the case with molesters).

Abuse can occur between any two persons; regardless of who is the abuser and who is the victim, it is a matter to be taken very seriously. But those persons most likely to exploit the vulnerabilities of others are those with the resources—the power—to do so. In a patriarchal society this means that abuse is most likely to be male to female and adult to child. Men of color, who exercise less power due to race and class, still retain the privilege of gender within their own racial and class groups. Male violence against women and children in our society is not merely an individual experience but a social issue because it is socially sanctioned in many ways.

> Madison, Wis. (AP)—Amos Smith was sentenced to 14 years in prison for sexual assault yesterday despite his attorney's argument that violence against women is acceptable in American society. His attorney, Roger Merry of Belleville, argues that Smith, 30, should not be sent to prison "for being a victim of culture." "Hostility toward women, I think, is something that is culturally instilled in men," Merry said. "It's part of our culture that has been for hundreds of years, that violence against women is not unacceptable" (*Seattle Times*, September 1, 1982).

Thus in dealing with individual male abusers who have victimized women and children, we are dealing not only with an individual's misconduct or pathology but with an entire set of social, cultural, and religious beliefs which serve to justify and support his conduct (Poling 1991).

Identifying these *behaviors* as abusive helps us identify those who engage in these behaviors as abusers, which then allows us to address their need for accountability and possible treatment.

Types of Abusers

Clinical and sociological research has focused on categories of abusers: child molesters, rapists, batterers, and persons who use their profession and position to exploit others. (While there are women who abuse, research suggests that men are the most frequent perpetrators of interpersonal violence; cf. Lystad 1986; Gelles and Straus 1988). Because abusers are members of our churches and of the communities in which we minister, we must be able to recognize their behavioral patterns.

CHILD MOLESTERS

Child molesters sexually exploit children. Researchers estimate that 35–38 percent of girls under eighteen were molested by someone at least five years older than themselves (Russell 1986, p. 70) and 5–10 percent of boys under eighteen were molested (Finkelhor 1984, pp. 150ff.). This usually includes attempted or actual sexual contact, but can include exhibitionism, pornography, inappropriate sexual references, and other behaviors that are clearly destructive of children at various stages of development. The defining characteristic of child sexual abuse is the use of an adult's superior power over a child to obtain the adult's sexual gratification. Child molesters fit into several subcategories.

a. Some molesters abuse girls and boys within the family and within other situations of trust. Fathers, stepfathers, grandfathers, uncles, cousins, and trusted community leaders who molest children form the largest group of molesters, making the family and other intimate groups the most dangerous places for children. Coerced and/or manipulated, children are forced to comply with adult sexual desires and threatened with consequences if they don't keep the secret. Their confusion and terror is often made worse when other adults in the family respond ineffectively to their disclosures and deny them the help they need for healing.

b. Adolescent molesters are usually abused children who act out sexually in relation to younger boys and girls with whom they have contact. Because they themselves are often seriously damaged, both the adolescents and the children they molest need help.

c. Pedophiles, men who target boys and girls of specific ages for sexual abuse, sometimes develop sophisticated plans of manipulation and coercion to entrap children. Pedophiles are especially dangerous when they hide in trusted leadership roles such are pastors, teachers, and leaders of children's organizations. They are also dangerous because they have multiple victims, sometimes numbering in the dozens. Contrary to stereotypes about dangerous strangers, pedophiles are often known and respected persons whose social position protects them from suspicion. They are predominantly heterosexual in their adult relationships, even though they may molest young boys. They are often protected because boys are less likely than girls to report sexual abuse and because men who have been abused as children are slow to report their childhood trauma. Both of these hesitations are rooted in homophobia.

d. A small number of men brutally rape and sometimes murder children they do not know. Because of their especially gruesome nature, these cases often receive notorious attention from the press and public. Men in this category form a very small percentage of all molesters, yet the group often receives the most attention. The public hysteria about child rapists and murderers actually may serve to protect the majority of molesters, who are known and trusted members of families and churches.

RAPISTS

Rapists engage in coercive and exploitative sexual behaviors. Because rape also describes the sexual abuse of many children, this group overlaps with molesters. In a classic study A. Nicholas Groth defines rape as "all nonconsenting sexual encounters, whether the victim is pressured or forced" (Groth 1979, p. 4). Social pressure and physical assault are two primary methods that rapists use to coerce sexual activity.

> In pressured situations, advantage is taken of a person's vulnerable status, so that refusal to engage in sexual activity may have serious social, economic, or vocational consequences. . . . The defining characteristic in forced assault is the risk of injury or bodily harm to the victim should she refuse to participate in sexual activity. Her physical safety is placed in jeopardy (Groth 1979, p. 3).

It is difficult to estimate the prevalence of rape because our understanding of what constitutes it is changing so quickly. In a landmark empirical study of 930 women Russell (1982) shows the prevalence of attempted and completed rape. Of her sample, "forty-four percent (44 percent) of the 930 women interviewed had been subjected to at least one rape or attempted rape in the course of their lives, but . . . 8% of the entire sample, which includes women who had never been married, had been raped by a husband" (p. 64).

In trying to understand rapists, Groth suggests a distinction between an anger rape and a power rape. "In some cases of sexual assault, it is very apparent that sexuality becomes a means of expressing and discharging feelings of pent-up anger and rage. The assault is characterized by physical brutality" (Groth 1979, p. 13). In the power rape,

> "it is not the offender's desire to harm his victim, but to possess her sexually. Sexuality becomes a means of compensating for underlying feelings of inadequacy and serves to express issues of mastery, strength, control, authority, identity, and capability. His goal is sexual conquest, and he uses only the amount of force necessary to accomplish his objective" (p. 25).

A third pattern is sadism, in which the pain and torture of the victim is used for sexual gratification (p. 44).

Given this background, we can differentiate between types of rapists according to whom they victimize: men who rape women and children within the family (brothers, uncles, cousins); men who rape within marriage and other intimate relationships; men who rape dates and acquaintances; men who rape strangers.

BATTERERS

Batterers inflict harm upon women and children in their families. Gelles and Straus (1988) estimate that 25 percent of married women will be abused sometime in their marriage (p. 104). Men Stopping Violence, an agency for treatment of batterers, estimates that 50 percent of all men are violent or threaten violence with intimates at one time of another (Bathrick et al., p. 1). The physical abuse of children is almost universal. "A national study of 2,143 intact families with children aged 3–17 found that . . . 8% were kicked, bitten, or punched, about nine times per year; 4% were beaten and this occurred about six times per year; and 3% had a gun or knife used on them" (Lystad 1986, p. 56). Sibling violence is also widespread, as well as physical abuse of elders. Physical abuse can coexist with sexual abuse and rape; batterers can also be child molesters and rapists (Lystad 1986, p. 57).

One type of batterer physically, psychologically, and sexually abuses his wife or lover. Clinicians who work with wife batterers believe that the abusers act primarily out of an expression of the need for power and control. Feeling entitled to dominate wives or girlfriends, such men are willing to enforce their dominance with physical abuse. Highly dependent, often emotionally isolated from others, they try to control and possess their spouses. "One of the common expectations of a man who batters is that his partner must be available to him, when, where, and how he wishes her to be. When, for whatever reason, she isn't there for us to meet our needs, we act as though we will do anything to get her back" (Bathrick et al., p. 32).

Another type of batterer physically abuses children. Sometimes he batters both wife and children, and sometimes he batters one or more children.

> The most widely accepted incidence figures are those prepared by the National Committee for the Prevention of Child Abuse, which estimates that over 1 million children are "seriously abused" and 2,000–5,000 deaths occur in the United States each year. In other words, it believes that 2 to 2.5 percent of the families in this country engage in physical child abuse (Cicchetti and Carlson 1989, p. 48).

Physical abuse of young children is the one area in which gender issues are less clear.

> Gil found females to be responsible for the abuse in 51% of the cases and males in about 48%. Because children generally spend the vast majority of their time with females, however, such data may actually indicate that women are less likely to victimize children than are men (Cicchetti and Carlson 1989, p. 52).

Abusers in the professions betray client's trust. In *Is Nothing Sacred?* Fortune reports a detailed case study of a pastor who manipulated and coerced over a dozen women in his parish into sexual relationships under the cloak of his religious office. When the women went to congregational and judicatory leaders with complaints of pastoral misconduct, the church was inept in understanding and dealing with this breach of ethics. The pastor's crimes were never made public, and he was able to escape the consequences of his behavior (Fortune 1989).

In one of the first books on the subject of sexual misconduct by men in other professional relationships, Peter Rutter coined the phrase "sex in the forbidden zone" to describe men in power who betray women's trust:

> Almost 80 percent of the women I spoke with had an incident to recount about having been approached sexually by a man who was her doctor, therapist, pastor, lawyer, or

> teacher. In about half of the cases, an actual sexual relationship took place, with disastrous results. Those who did not become sexually involved reported feeling outraged, confused, or sickened by the man's erotic innuendos in ways that forever compromised a once-vital relationship. The 20 percent of women to whom this had never happened all knew two or three other women to whom it had (Rutter 1989, pp. 11–12).

While this is a heuristic rather than a scientific study, it is suggestive of the growing wisdom of clinicians that sexual abuse by professionals is not unusual and that the ethical standards for such misconduct must be reexamined. The underlying pattern of abusing power in order to exploit the vulnerabilities of others is clear. Even though such behavior is not illegal in many places, it surely is unethical by Christian standards. The church needs to focus much research and other resources on this issue.

Principles for Intervention with Abusers

When the church and its leadership are willing to hear a victim's disclosure of abuse, they are then called upon to intervene on behalf of the victim. The Hebrew tradition of hospitality is one mandate for action. The hospitality tradition called upon the community as a whole to protect the widow, the sojourner, and the orphan. These were the persons in the community who had the least resources and were most vulnerable to exploitation by others. In our communities surely victims of sexual and domestic violence are vulnerable and in need of our assistance.

Both Hebrew and Christian traditions place heavy emphasis on justice as the proper response to injustice and harm done to others. From the prophets to the gospels we hear a word of judgment for those who cause harm to innocent people (e.g. Luke 17:1). That word of judgment is the basis of accountability for abusers from which may come confession and repentance and ultimately restoration to the community. The ultimate concern of our faith is genuine healing and restoration. But Jeremiah cautions against the pretense of healing:

> Without concern they dress my people's wound
> saying, "Peace! Peace!"
> Whereas there is no peace (Jeremiah 6:14).

It is our task within the church to face the reality that some among us exploit and damage others among us, and that as a faith community, in concert with the wider community, we have the resources to confront this evil with justice and bring genuine healing in its wake.

The goals of our efforts are as follows (Fortune 1991):

Goal #1—protect the vulnerable from further abuse [hospitality];

Goal #2—call the abuser to accountability [confrontation, confession, repentance];

Goal #3—restoration of the relationship (between victim and abuser) *if possible* [restitution, healing]. Often this restoration is not possible. The harm is too great, the damage too deep, the resistance of the abuser to change too formidable. If not possible, then mourn the loss of that relationship and work to restore the individuals [comfort for the grieving]. There is always a sense of grief, loss, and anger for the victim who was denied a genuine, healthy relationship because of the abuser's treatment.

The important thing for any pastor or lay leader to understand about these goals for intervention is that they are in chronological order. Goal #3 is the most worthy goal, but it cannot be accomplished until goals #1 and #2 are complete. The successful completion of these two goals is the most effective means to helping achieve goal #3.

In order to be effective in roles of pastoral care with abusers, the following principles should guide our efforts.

1. The church's first priority must be the safety of and pastoral care for victims of abuse (see Fortune 1982; Pellauer et al. 1987; Sgroi 1982; Bass and Davis 1988; Ledray 1986). The first priority, whenever a pastor learns about physical or sexual abuse, must be the protection of those who are most vulnerable, the victim or victims. While this principle should be obvious, experience has shown that sympathy often goes first to the perpetrator, especially if he is a respected leader, because his reputation reflects on the identity of the community itself.

Those terrorized by physical or sexual violence are in danger and least able to protect themselves. Unless there is intervention, disclosure alone almost never ends the abuse, and the victim continues to be in danger. Safety can be enhanced if there is no contact between perpetrator and victim in the immediate crisis. All future contact must be based on the needs of the victim assessed with the help of trained care-givers. The victim must receive whatever medical care, crisis intervention, financial support, safe housing, and counseling necessary for creating a new context for living. Adequate care for victims is the first step in stopping abusers.

2. *In order to stop abusers, church leaders must use wider community structures of accountability* (Bathrick et al.; Sgroi 1982; Groth 1979; Barnard et al. 1989). Clinical and legal research has shown that abuse does not stop unless the abuser is subjected to accountability and consequences. Since many forms of abuse are illegal, effective accountability usually requires legal action. The moral authority of the pastor alone is useful but often insufficient to stop the patterns of abusers. In confronting an abuser privately and accepting reassurances that things will change, a pastor only enables the abuser to hide his or her actions better and to further threaten the victim or victims. As a result there is no accountability in the community. In fact, rather than effecting any real change, the pastor may have inadvertently warned the abuser to lie low until the crisis blows over. Referral for counseling alone is likewise ineffective because there is no motivation for the abuser to tell the truth to the counselor about what has happened (Isely and Isely 1990, p. 96).

In spite of the best intentions expressed by an abuser ("I'll never do it again. . . ." "I've found the Lord. . . ." "I'll go to counseling. . . ."), it is virtually impossible for true repentance—a fundamental change of self—to take place without expert help and a structure of accountability. If we carry a genuine concern for the well-being of the abuser, our best pastoral intervention is seeing that he or she is held accountable in a community or church structure with the power to enforce participation.

This often means that the pastor to whom a disclosure of abuse is revealed either by a victim or through the confession of an abuser should *assist* in reporting this allegation to the appropriate legal and/or church authorities for further investigation and possible action. *If the report involves the abuse of a child, the pastor should report on behalf of that child immediately to the state child protection service.* Some states legally require ministers to report child abuse, while others do not. Regardless of the law's requirement, our pastoral mandate to protect the vulnerable from further harm requires that we act immediately to bring to bear all possible resources to assist that child (Fortune 1988). Some states also provide for reporting abuse of the elderly and of persons with developmental disabilities. These persons are also extremely vulnerable to abuse and need our assistance.

In the case of an *adult* victim or survivor who chooses to report an abuser to either secular or church authorities, our pastoral task is to assist that person with support and information. In other words, it is finally the choice of that adult whether to report or confront the abuser, and that adult should decide the terms of his or her action.

Making such reports are often difficult for pastors or church leaders, especially if they know the persons involved. Often there is a wish to provide pastoral care and referral for counseling before taking what seems like such drastic action. However, this only increases the danger for victims and may even block the perpetrator from the help needed to stop his or her destructive behaviors. What may seem to be harsh measures are actually the most appropriate and helpful forms of pastoral care for all involved.

3. *Church leaders must be able to combat the secrecy and deception that abusers use to hide their crimes.* When confronted, abusers will minimize, lie, and/or deny responsibility for their actions. All abusers depend on deceiving others about the nature of their behaviors. Child molesters threaten and manipulate their victims into silence. Batterers batter in the privacy of their homes while a "normal" facade is presented to the public. Rapists choose dark and private times and places to avoid confrontation. Abusive professionals use the privacy of counseling and other confidential settings to hide their exploitative behaviors.

Abusers often rely on the naiveté of Christians who believe that they would not lie to protect themselves from the consequences of their behaviors. Church leaders who would confront abusers must be alert to this web of lies even in those who hold positions of trust within the community. When scandals emerge, Christians sometimes find it hard to face their own gullibility and complicity.

4. *The church must not allow a misuse of confidentiality to prevent it from acting to intervene in situations of abuse* (Fortune 1988; Bullis 1990a, 1990b). The purpose of confidentiality in the religious setting is to provide a safe place for victims to understand their suffering without the voyeuristic glare of the community's judgment. Because people are fragile and need confidence in their healing relationships, trust must remain a cornerstone of all religious and secular counseling. But counselors experienced in working with abusers agree that the rules of confidentiality must not jeopardize those who are least able to protect themselves. Confidentiality is too often equated with secrecy; that is, pastors incorrectly believe that keeping a confidence means keeping a secret. Secrecy is the key to a pattern of abuse; the abuse thrives on secrecy, and the only way to assist the abuser and the victim is to break the silence which sustains the secret. Confidentiality means that one does not share information received in

confidence without legitimate reason, for example, to seek consultation or to report suspected abuse. In seeking consultation from another professional it is not necessary to disclose names in order to get help on how to deal with people. In reporting child abuse it *is* necessary to disclose names of those involved.

Some denominations retain the privilege of the seal of the confessional for their clergy. A pastor, while respecting the primacy of this seal, can still intervene. If, under the seal, a penitent confesses to abusing another, the pastor can direct the penitent to report himself or herself to the authorities. If the abuser refuses, there is nothing the pastor can do to help the abuser, but the pastor can continue to assist the victim.

Rarely does the disclosure of an abusive situation occur in the formal confessional setting. It is more likely to come in counseling or conversation and most often from the victim rather than from the abuser. This information then is not subject to a confessional seal, and hence the pastor is free to report. The right of children and women to protection from physical and sexual violence overrides the value of secrecy. In fact, inserting accountability for destructive behaviors into a counseling relationship is often the most healing intervention a counselor can make with a perpetrator.

5. *In order to stop abusers church leaders must work cooperatively with other professionals.* It should be obvious by this point that most pastors and church leaders are not qualified to confront and stop abusers by themselves. Rather, the stubbornness and severity of this problem require the concerted effort of many community agencies and authorities. Pastors need to know the resources in their local communities and must be willing to cooperate with them in appropriate ways. Every community has a network of social workers, psychologists, and legal agencies that specializes in intervention, counseling, and prevention in situations of abuse. Rape counseling centers can provide information and advocacy for rape victims. Battered women's shelters have expertise in providing safe havens for women and children in danger. Child protection agencies and family courts have authority to protect children by intervening in families. Finally, the police and criminal courts can bring misdemeanor and felony charges for some forms of abuse. One of the marks of adequately trained professionals, including pastors, is their willingness to call upon or cooperate with the specialized resources needed to protect those who are vulnerable to abuse and stop those who are responsible.

The church sometimes has the mistaken notion that Christian

faith and community alone are adequate for all human problems. While problems of abuse have a spiritual and religious dimension, an adequate response to this manifestation of evil requires cooperation in the wider community.

6. *Churches must institute effective structures of accountability and consequences for leaders who abuse their power* (Fortune 1989, pp. 135–53). The church has a long, sad history of covering up the sins of men in powerful positions who abuse women and children. Pastors who are perpetrators have moved quietly to other congregations where no one has been warned of the danger. Clergy who have abused wives and children have been supported for the sake of family unity while their victims have been deprived of truth and resources for healing. Regional and national religious leaders have been excused for their violations of others while their victims disappeared from public view.

Churches need to reassess their own policies and procedures for identifying and dealing with abuse among their leaders. Persons with specialized training should be authorized to conduct timely investigations when complaints are filed against clergy. Procedures must be fair not only to those who are charged, but also to victims whose lives have already been damaged. Consequences must be severe enough that abusers will be held accountable and stop their destructive behaviors.

A note to ministerial professionals reading this: If you have been or are tempted to use your professional position for sexual contact with a parishioner or client, you should immediately seek help. Though you may not see the word *abuser* applying to your behavior, you must accept the truth that you are not the best judge. There are men and women in every community who are trained to help you evaluate the extent of your problem and begin a program of change and restitution. It is possible to change if you are willing to face yourself honestly and seek help.

Conclusion

This chapter suggests the need for a courageous and assertive response on the part of the church to abusers in its midst. In the face of the massive personal and social suffering of victims of sexual and domestic violence and in the face of a history of silence on the part of the church, this response is long overdue. Large numbers of children who have been sexually and physically abused carry lifelong consequences because of their trauma. Large numbers of women and some men have experienced some form of sexual or physical violation. As these victims come forward, their stories lead us to reassess our understanding of ourselves as Christian communities.

The six principles outlined above should guide the church in its response to the problem of abuse. The church must respond more aggressively to the danger facing women and children by providing victims with safety and needed resources for healing. It must call for better societal structures of accountability and consequences for abusers, inform itself on the role of secrecy and deception in abuse, reevaluate its practice of confidentiality, cooperate with other professionals and agencies, and institute internal structures of accountability for leaders of its own community. In sum, the church must be much better informed about the dangers of abuse and much more assertive in establishing its vision of justice and mercy for all persons.

Note

Unless otherwise indicated, scripture quotations in this chapter are taken from *The New Jerusalem Bible*, copyright 1985 by Darton, Longman & Todd, Ltd. and Doubleday, a division of Bantam Doubleday Dell Publishing Group, Inc.

References

Barnard, George, et al., eds. 1989. *The Child Molester: An Integrated Approach to Evaluation and Treatment.* New York. Brunner/Mazel.

Bass, Ellen, and Davis, Laura. 1988. *The Courage to Heal.* New York: Harper & Row.

Bathrick, Dick; Carlin, Kathleen; Kaufman, Gus; and Vodde, Rich. Nd. *Men Stopping Violence: A Program for Change.* Men Stopping Violence. 1020 DeKalb Ave., Atlanta, GA 30307.

Bullis, Ronald. 1990a. "When Confessional Walls Have Ears: The Changing Clergy Privileged Communications Law." *Pastoral Psychology* 39, 2 (November): 75–84.

———. 1990b. "Child Abuse Reporting Requirements: Liabilities and Immunities for Clergy." *Journal of Pastoral Care* 44, 3 (Fall): 244–49.

Caesar, P. Lynn, and Hamberger, L. Kevin, eds. 1989. *Treating Men Who Batter: Theory, Practice, and Programs.* New York: Springer.

Cicchetti, Dante, and Carlson, Vicki, eds. 1989. *Child Maltreatment.* New York: Cambridge University Press.

Finkelhor, D. 1984. *Child Sexual Abuse.* New York: The Free Press.

Fortune, Marie. 1982. *Sexual Violence.* New York: Pilgrim Press.

———. 1988. "Reporting Child Abuse: An Ethical Mandate for Ministry." In *Abuse and Religion,* edited by Horton and Williamson. Lexington, Mass.: Lexington Books.

———. 1989. *Is Nothing Sacred? When Sex Invades the Pastoral Relationship.* New York: Harper & Row.

———. 1991. *Violence in Families: A Workshop Curriculum for Clergy and Other Helpers.* New York: Pilgrim Press.

Ganley, Anne L. 1989. "Integrating Feminist and Social Learning Analyses of Aggression." In Caesar and Hamberger, *Treating Men Who Batter.*

Gelles, Richard, and Straus, Murray. 1988. *Intimate Violence.* New York: Simon and Schuster.

Groth, A. Nicholas. 1979. *Men Who Rape.* New York: Plenum Press.

Isley, Paul, and Isley, Peter. 1990. "The Sexual Abuse of Male Children by Church Personnel: Intervention and Prevention." *Pastoral Psychology* 39, 2 (November): 96.

Ledray, Linda. 1986. *Recovering from Rape.* New York: Henry Holt.

Lystad, Mary, ed. 1986. *Violence in the Home.* New York: Brunner/Mazel.

Pellauer, Mary, et al., eds. 1987. *Sexual Assault and Abuse: A Handbook for Clergy and Religious Professionals.* New York: Harper & Row.

Poling, James. 1991. *Abuse of Power: A Theological Problem.* Nashville: Abingdon.

Russell, D. E. 1986. *The Secret Trauma.* New York: Basic Books.

Russell, Diana. 1982. *Rape in Marriage.* New York: Macmillan.

Rutter, Peter. 1989. *Sex in the Forbidden Zone: When Men in Power—Therapists, Doctors, Clergy, Teachers, and Others—Betray Women's Trust.* Los Angeles: J. P. Tarcher.

Sgroi, Suzanne, ed. 1982. *Handbook of Clinical Intervention in Child Sexual Abuse.* Lexington, Mass.: Lexington Books.

Eileen A. Gavin

19. Words Can Never Hurt Me? The Psychological/Emotional Abuse of Children

A familiar saying that is part of the American folk culture of childhood provides the context for this paper. It goes like this: Sticks and stones will break my bones, but words can never hurt me. One can scarcely deny the first part of the saying. But what of the second part? Because young children have not developed the skills or the backlog of experience that might enable them to disregard negative appraisals of themselves, they are much less able than are mature adults to find that "words can never hurt me." This paper will focus on the various forms of psychological/emotional abuse of children, often communicated through negative appraisals, in the hope that doing so will identify and perhaps prevent or at least alleviate some risk conditions.

Psychological/emotional abuse is more subtle and difficult to identify than physical abuse. Nevertheless, it ought to be recognized, especially because it appears to be the prototype of child abuse. After briefly introducing this topic, this chapter will aim to define and specify psychological and emotional abuse and relate it to major approaches to child maltreatment. Next it will attempt to explain why understanding and assisting children who experience emotional/psychological abuse has been problematic. It will attempt to link emotional/psychological abuse to the broader literature on child development and then more specially to development of a sense of self and emotional attachment. Next it will address emotional/psychological abuse by sharing evidence from a prospective project that helps to clarify origins and consequences of psychological and emotional abuse of children. Finally, it will share the main lines of a pastoral approach to prevention and intervention of psychological/emotional abuse of children, some features of which may be helpful to some readers.

Introduction

Psychological/emotional abuse is anything but trivial. I see treatment of children, as many others also do, as an important moral barometer of society. When viewed as the prototypical form of child maltreatment, psychological/emotional abuse merits serious consideration. It may be hard to acknowledge and face the presence of psychological/emotional abuse in a "highly-developed" country such as the United States. Nevertheless, for the sake of children who deserve the "right to life, liberty, and the pursuit of happiness," and for the common good of society as well, it is best to admit that it occurs. A recent estimate indicates that 12 percent of those below the age of eighteen suffer some form of psychological illness (Toufexis 1990, p. 47). No doubt, many of these children have experienced psychological/emotional abuse. Lamentation, however, does not go far enough. Study and intervention are also needed.

Ever since the Battered Child Syndrome first became publicized (Kempe et al. 1962) physical child abuse has received considerable attention. In recent years sexual violence against children has also been in the spotlight. The less frequently emphasized dimension, psychological/emotional abuse, merits more attention than it has received, particularly since it serves as root of other forms of abuse. Unfortunately, vagueness of criteria for identifying or even ascertaining the presence of psychological/emotional abuse (Kinard 1987, p. 223) has sometimes discouraged people who might otherwise be in a position to prevent or alleviate it. Because the phenomenon has often been hard to identify, a next step has frequently been to ignore or deny its occurrence.

Efforts to Define Psychological and Emotional Abuse of Children

Defining and identifying psychological/emotional abuse is certainly more difficult than specifying physical or sexual abuse of children. Yet even physical and sexual abuse has been fraught with definitional problems that reveal no consensus. Specification of an act as "abusive" or "violent" frequently requires and reflects a social judgment. What some unequivocally appraise as physical abuse—for instance, spanking as a preferred policy to socialize a child—others may (however erroneously) view as occurring "for the child's own good." Of course, other actions, such as inducing burns in a child, signal unequivocal abuse. Yet the dynamics that prompt the abuse may be debated. Because psychological/emotional abuse leaves no palpable scars, explicit definition and unequivocal identification can be very difficult to establish. Moreover, in socioeconomic groups that do not usually receive public social services, its incidence may be underestimated. Nevertheless, difficulty in defining and identifying psychological/emotional abuse and in pinpointing its etiology does not negate the fact that it occurs all too frequently. It seems wise, therefore, to acknowledge it rather than pretend things are otherwise. Because psychological/emotional abuse can result in outcomes quite devastating to psychological development of young children (Egeland and Erickson 1987, p. 115) a good working definition of psychological/emotional abuse is needed.

One reason for shutting one's eyes to the reality of psychological/emotional abuse may be that some proposed definitions of psychological maltreatment of children universally imply censure and blame of an adult or adults responsible for the child. For instance, J. Garbarino defines psychological maltreatment as "a concerted attack by an adult on a child's development of self and social competence, a pattern of . . . destructive behavior" that takes forms of rejecting, isolating, ignoring, terrorizing, or corrupting the child (Garbarino 1987, p. 7). Assignment of blame has become, in this case, part of the definition of psychological maltreatment. However, parental ignorance or other limitations rather than unqualified viciousness of the perpetrator may be involved in many instances of psychological maltreatment. For instance, the child of an insecure adult may be treated unwittingly as a pawn in a power struggle. The child is the loser in this case even though the parent is not deliberately undercutting the child's fragile sense of self and may, in fact, claim otherwise. Because many victimizers have themselves been victims, it may be wise to bracket the issue of blame while attempting to identify psychological/emotional abuse. Assuming responsibility for the child who is suffering, however, must be faced head on.

Study of forms of child maltreatment (which include but go beyond psychological/emotional abuse) reveals that they are quite heterogeneous. They cannot be described by a "unitary construct with a simple definition, a single etiology, or a single set of consequences." Instead, they testify to a "complex, multifactored set of syndromes with multiple manifestations, etiologies, and possible sequelae" (Rizley and Cicchetti 1981, p. vii). Even psychological/emotional abuse takes on varied "faces." For instance, parents of children who suffer psychological/emotional abuse may be neglectful, hostile, verbally abusive, psychologically unavailable (Egeland and Erickson 1987, p. 113) or may show express more than one mode of treating a child, including at times physical abuse. For this reason I propose this provisional, "working" definition of psychological/emotional abuse: *A child's not generally experiencing responsive and sensitive caretaking, with the result that the child comes to see himself or herself not only as devalued but as not valuable.* Neglect that ignores the child's needs is a form of psychological abuse as well as care that directly and characteristically discounts the child's needs (such as chronic verbal abuse that attacks the child's sense of self). The proposed definition includes psychologically unavailable care-giving, that is, detachment and lack of involvement or pleasure with regard to the child's activity, while nonetheless taking care of the physical needs of the child. Chronic lack of responsivity to the child as a person differentiates psychological/emotional abuse from occasional lapses in optimal care that are part and parcel of being imperfect humans.

Why Relatively Little Progress Has Been Made So Far

Not long ago Rizley and Cicchetti observed:

> We know next to nothing about child maltreatment. We have very little systematically collected, scientifically acceptable information about the antecedents, manifestations, sequelae (developmental, social, legal, and so on), treatment responses, or intergenerational transmission of maltreatment. . . . The existing literature is riddled with the views, opinions, and idiosyncratic orientations of a variety of disciplines, including psychology, pediatrics, social work, and law. While there are attempts to present comprehensive models of maltreatment, generally these efforts represent only a pretheoretical orientation. . . . Often they are silent about one or more of the issues of etiology, transmission, sequelae, or differential treatment response.
>
> Moreover, research in the area has been plagued with methodological problems and theoretical misconceptions, resulting in an accumulation of diverse and even contradictory findings, which have contributed less than they might have to the clarification of the problem or the identification of its causes or consequences. We know very little about the efficacy of therapeutic programs, about the types of professionals who might most effectively provide services, or about the type of professional training needed. In addition,

> while many prescriptions have been suggested for eradicating the conditions that encourage child maltreatment, there are few substantive empirical data on which to base social policies to address the problem (Rizley and Cicchetti 1981, p. vii).

Fortunately, some recent progress offers promise for prevention and treatment of psychological/emotional abuse of children. Various earlier approaches to understanding child maltreatment (including psychological/emotional abuse) have at times been helpful as well, though no program taken alone has been quite sufficient to the task. For instance, Parke and Collmer (1975) cited a variety of approaches to child maltreatment, including the psychiatric model, sociological model, social-situational model, and child-based model. The psychiatric model has focused mostly on personality characteristics of abusive parents and on child-rearing histories of abusing parents. The sociological model has emphasized cultural attitudes that promote child abuse such as various stressors, including poor housing and substandard living conditions; unemployment; poverty, especially in relation to large families; ordinal position of the child in the family; family-community relationships, with social isolation seen as a contributing factor to child maltreatment; and so on. The social situational model has explored how conditions such as punitive child-rearing and inconsistent discipline are related to child maltreatment. It has also emphasized conditions that maintain maltreatment, such as justification of abuse, minimization of abuse, shifting responsibility, blaming the victim. The child-based model has focused upon the relatively high incidence of abuse among children with particular characteristics; for instance, children with low birth weights, children with special needs, later-born children from large families whose presence may precipitate family crisis.

Although each of these approaches has contributed something to knowledge of antecedents of psychological/emotional abuse of children, all have deficiencies when adopted exclusively. For instance, the sociological model, which has correlated child maltreatment with low socioeconomic status, has a hard time dealing with underrepresented (because often "invisible" and therefore unreported) child maltreatment in upper socioeconomic strata. Certainly the middle and upper socioeconomic levels of society are not free from child maltreatment as talks with psychiatrists who work with economically "privileged" people will attest. Therefore, a careful search for antecedents and correlates of psychological maltreatment of children would assist identification of such treatment. An important recent project, for instance, has demonstrated that parents who maltreat their children differ from adequate caretakers in "their lack of understanding of the complexity of social relationships, especially caretaking, and their feelings about meeting the needs of another person" (Pianta, Egeland, Erickson 1989, p. 205). Becoming alert to these signs may help to prevent or alleviate psychological/emotional abuse of children.

A Fruitful Context for Approaching Emotional/Psychological Abuse

Because child maltreatment (emotional/psychological abuse) is enormously complex and sometimes occurs along with other forms of abuse, studying it requires a "multifactorial perspective, whereby the multiple influences of a variety of risk and protective factors are considered simultaneously" (Pianta, Egeland, and Erickson 1989, p. 210). Also important is careful reflection upon available knowledge. This, in turn, can prompt appropriate remedial or preventive action.

Emotional/psychological abuse will profit from being nested in a "something more" theoretical context. At times a complex context may prompt conclusions that initially resemble a koan, with some aspects apparently at odds with one another. No doubt lack of comfort associated with arrival at ambiguous conclusions has led some researchers to despair over ever discovering what goes into psychological/emotional abuse. Investigation of psychological/emotional abuse calls for use of "sophisticated and multicontextual developmental measurement techniques and complex developmental models." Theories and research strategies must deal with "four types of heterogeneity: in type of maltreatment, in etiology, in sequelae, and in treatment response" (Rizley and Cicchetti 1981, p. vii). Theory and research strategies must also be able to deal with ongoing change in relationships between child and caretakers.

Because maltreated children share characteristics with other people of their age and developmental level, research and reflection must mesh with pertinent child-development literature (particularly literature that pertains to characteristics children usually reveal at particular levels of development, attachment literature, and literature that addresses the development of self and self-concept).

Developmentally, for instance, two-year-old children characteristically have begun to express a sense of autonomy. They often show an exaggerated insistence on doing things for themselves in their own way, a fact that coexists with an imperfectly consolidated and therefore quite fragile sense of self. Unless the two-year-old's bid for autonomy is understood as characteristic of children at that level of development, the child's behavior may be badly misinterpreted and may, therefore, prompt a battle of wits. In real life settings, finding an appropriate balance between socialization practices that are in the best interests of the child while allowing expression of the child's nascent autonomy is not easy to achieve. However, parents who understand and acknowledge well-documented principles of child development are in a better position than are ill-prepared parents to be sensitive to the child's needs. On the contrary, expecting more mature behavior of a child than that child can "deliver" is likely to prompt resentment. This in turn may trigger pervasive and long-lasting psychological/emotional abuse. Surely lack of understanding of a person's level of development does not serve the child's best interests.

Although absolutizing a single principle, such as attachment, is insufficient to account for the quality of a child's development, evidence that flows from research on attachment is significant for understanding adequate care of children as well as the psychological/emotional abuse that children sometimes experience. Attachment theory arose from three "parents": ethology, developmental psychology, and psychoanalysis (Karen 1989, p. 39). The late John Bowlby, British psychoanalyst, is generally credited as originator of attachment theory (Karen 1990, p. 39). Another psychoanalyst from the same time period, Rene Spitz, found that orphanage infants who lacked loving attention and a positive relationship with the caretaker failed to thrive and sometimes even died. He wondered whether results he had read in accounts of experimental research with monkeys might in fact reflect "abnormality" that results from lack of permanent ties with other monkeys. After communicating this speculation to the late experimental psychologist Harry Harlow, Harlow went on to explore the dimensions of "mother love." His early research identified the unexpected importance of contact comfort. Later Mary Ainsworth found in her research with infants and young children that children who develop secure relationships with their caretakers fare much better than children who do not.

Recently, a prospective, longitudinal study of relationships with their children of more than 250 mothers believed to be at risk for maltreatment because of economic hardship, youth of mothers, and frequently unplanned pregnancies, that is, multiproblem families that lived in often chaotic and disruptive environments (Pianta, Egeland,

and Erickson 1989, p. 218) is providing important empirical information about psychological/emotional abuse in relation to attachment and related child-development issues. This prospective research project, the Minnesota Mother-Child Interaction Research Project, offers an important advantage over retrospective examination of outcomes in selected people who have suffered emotional/psychological abuse. For one thing, it reveals antecedents and correlates that actually predict psychological/emotional abuse. This longitudinal Minnesota project has already collected extensive material through the early school years that bears upon characteristics of mothers and of their children who have suffered psychological/emotional abuse. It also provides data concerning child-parent interaction and environment (Pianta, Egeland, and Erickson 1989, p. 218). Because many of the mothers considered to be at risk for maltreatment of their children have in fact provided adequate care for their children, these parents constitute a control group from the same "at risk" population. Comparison of the control group with abusive parents from the same population reveals some striking differences that appear even during pregnancy and shortly after birth; for instance, in contrast to the control group,

> maltreating mothers . . . did not make basic preparations for their babies' births. . . . Even in the hospital immediately after the babies' births, these mothers showed less interest in their babies (as judged by nurses) than did mothers who subsequently provided adequate care. Prenatal assessment indicated that mothers who later maltreated their children also differed from mothers who provided good care in that the former did not know what to expect of their babies in terms of behavior and development milestones, and, very importantly, they lacked understanding of the psychological complexity of their child and their relationship with their child (Egeland and Erickson 1987, p. 118).

These findings send important signals that could lead to prevention of psychological/emotional abuse in some cases and to early identification in others. The investigators also found that abusive mothers, in contrast to mothers who provided adequate treatment, tended "to interpret the child's behavior in terms of their own needs and feelings rather than in terms of the reality of the situation" (Egeland and Erickson 1987, p. 118).

A parent's expressions of verbal abuse are certainly not conducive to the child's development of a healthy sense of self. Erickson and Egeland, for instance, found that at forty-two months, children who had been verbally abused differed from adequately cared for children in showing relatively low self-esteem and low self-control. Emotionally neglected children from the same population (who had psychologically unavailable caregivers) registered more noncompliance, poor self-control, high dependence, negative emotion, and varied and extensive behavior problems (including nervous signs and self-abusive behavior) than children from the same population who received adequate care (Erickson and Egeland 1987, Table 1).

A Pastoral Approach for Ministering to Children Who Have Suffered from Psychological/Emotional Abuse

From childhood to the present I have greatly admired Popeye, that great fictional philosopher whose views about the primacy of the person mark my pastoral approach. Certainly Popeye's conduct (rough and ready, non-impeccable manners) may leave something to desire. I have heard him described as grossly undersocialized. To me, however, this "writing off" of Popeye misses what is central to him. Popeye celebrated the primacy of the unrepeatable, unique person. For this reason, I suppose, I see his view as central to my own pastoral approach. His "I yam what I yam cuz I yam what I yam" continues to inspire my admiration. He refused to lose himself for the sake of pleasing others. He refused to eliminate what was special about him, to compromise and mirror someone else's approved view of "the right kind of person," which would have rendered him less a genuine and centered person and more a colorless "generic" personage. My pastoral approach is also grounded in a view of human nature that includes more than the influence of heredity and environment. I also acknowledge what I consider to be the personal regard that God has for each and every human being. Because of this spiritual outlook, I tend also to consider my ministrations to others as God-given, as not coming solely from me. In addition, I believe that all human beings, as loved by God, are intrinsically valuable, just as they are unique. I certainly appreciate and make use of my natural and developed gifts. Not the least of these gifts has been opportunities to pursue and develop my knowledge of psychology. I exercise my gifts mostly as a psychologist who teaches and advises undergraduates. I believe that the people I teach share in these gifts, and that they in turn may offer fresh and even unique gifts that find expression in their own pastoral work.

Theory that meshes with the best I know not only from study of psychology but also from other ways of knowing (theological, philosophical) is part of my pastoral contribution to the understanding of psychological/emotional abuse. Presenting pertinent available evidence and attempting to share it with the people who come into my life is a major interest. Background that pertains to children who have experienced psychological/emotional abuse is one expression of sharing. I realize, for instance, that children who have experienced psychological/emotional abuse often view themselves as not counting for much. Of course, it is necessary to remember that the same appearing behavior does not always have the same dynamics. Nevertheless, a child's failure to put her best foot forward—I am thinking of one who has chronically experienced psychological/emotional abuse—often becomes better understood by relating the behavior (and knowledge of the child) to available research on psychological/emotional abuse. For instance, some psychologically abused children may feel a need to try, more than do other children, to get someone to realize that they exist or that they matter (which, of course, is true). They may make their point through behavior disorders, distractibility, and so forth. In such cases a principle espoused by the late Carl Rogers, which greatly resembles the outlook of Popeye, is helpful. Rogers endorsed the principle of unconditional positive regard for a person. This principle, properly applied, can help to redress the discounting of self that children who have known psychological/emotional abuse have experienced. They, like all people, benefit from recognition of their intrinsic and unrepeatable worth as persons, with accomplishments taking second place.

I am reminded of the straits of a school child whose teacher, one of my former students, came to me recently, in desperation. The child has been consistently verbally abused, sometimes ignored, regularly devalued for his views and even for his very being. His parents, according to my former student, see him as a nuisance and as a "problem" who is always in the way. The young teacher, a very gentle, caring person, told me that she has tried her best to identify activities that the child does well, and she has made efforts to compliment him whenever she has noticed "appropriate" actions. She has reinforced such behavior, as behaviorists would say. However, she discovered to her dismay that well-deserved compliments did not really seem to help this child. For instance, after the young teacher had complimented the child for a fine drawing he had produced, he scribbled over it and tore it up. I encouraged the teacher to continue to work toward gaining for the child the best of therapy and also to encourage therapy for his entire family. I also told the young teacher that the child's experiencing years of feeling discounted would not be overcome overnight. Unfortunately, the child's family continues to see him as "the problem" disrupting their lives. I have encouraged the young teacher to continue to support the child unconditionally as an unrepeatable person and to focus more on that reality than on his accomplishments. Her work with the child is ongoing.

Available evidence now suggests important ways to prevent or at least reduce often-overlooked (because frequently subtle) forms of child abuse, such as verbal berating or lack of responsivity to the child's needs (as in psychologically unavailable parenting). Current evidence also suggests some hopeful knowledge that may help to break the cycle of abuse. It has long been recognized that many abused parents in turn abuse their children. Nevertheless, repetition of the abuse cycle is not universal, not an ironclad sentence or prophecy. One prospective study, for example, reported that a third of mothers who were themselves abused as children were able to break the cycle of abuse and provide adequate care for their children (Egeland, Jacobvitz, and Sroufe 1988). The parents most able to break the abusive cycle were significantly more likely than those who failed to break the cycle to have participated in therapy at some time in their lives. They also tended to have less abusive and more stable and emotionally satisfying relationships with a mate (Egeland, Jacobvitz, and Sroufe 1988). These results suggest that therapy for abusive parents has been quite successful in reducing abuse of children. Often the abusive parent has been victim and victimizer (Pianta, Egeland, and Erickson 1989, p. 247). Egeland (1988) cautions, however, that no single risk factor predicts abuse with full accuracy. The fact that many parents who were abused as children provide good quality care for their own child supports this conclusion.

Can anything be done to identify parents at risk for abuse of their children before the abuse occurs? Based upon research gained from a prospective, longitudinal project designed to study the development of high-risk children who do or do not actually experience abuse (it includes a control group of children from similar backgrounds of poverty and high stress) Egeland and Erickson propose a program of preventive intervention with high-risk mothers beginning during the last trimester of pregnancy (Egeland and Erickson 1987, p. 118).

Intervention late in pregnancy offers promise for breaking the cycle of abuse, as described earlier. Maltreating mothers are less likely than mothers who treat their children adequately to lack knowledge of what to expect of their babies by way of behavior and developmental milestones. They also lack understanding of the psychological complexity of the child and their relationship with the child (Egeland and Erickson 1987). Major goal of the preventive program that Egeland and Erickson suggest is that of helping the mother understand the child's behavior. A second goal is that of helping high-risk mothers to become better perspective caretakers, people who are sensitive to what the infant is experiencing and thus able to respond appropriately to the infant's cues and signals (Egeland and Erickson 1987, p. 118).

Mothers targeted for the preventive intervention program would receive help with concrete child-care tasks, such as feeding, dressing, and play. Discussion of videotapes of the mother's actual interactions, along with meetings with other mothers who have infants of similar ages, provide part of the program (Egeland and Erickson 1987, p. 119). Summarily, an extensive, continuing program during the first years of the child's life even extending from the last trimester of the pregnancy shows promise for fostering healthy future development of children otherwise likely to suffer psychological/emotional abuse.

Tapping a community's resources (for example, through foster grandparenting volunteer programs, through discovery of retired psychologists who might contribute their services to a valuable volunteer program) could help to launch a relatively inexpensive effort that could enhance the lives of children at risk for psychological/emotional abuse while enriching the lives of the volunteers as well. In these ways forms of child abuse that are most subtle and hardest to identify may in some measure be mitigated or prevented.

References

Egeland, B. 1988. "Breaking the Cycle of Abuse: Implications for Prediction and Intervention." In *Early Prediction and Prevention of Child Abuse,* edited by K. D. Browne, C. Davies, and P. Stratton. New York: John Wiley and Sons.

———, and Erickson, M. F. 1987. "Psychologically Unavailable Caregiving." In *Psychological Maltreatment of Children and Youth,* edited by M. R. Brassard, R. Germain, and S. N. Hart, pp. 110–20. New York: Pergamon Press.

———, Jacobvitz, D., and Sroufe, L. A. 1988. "Breaking the Cycle of Abuse." *Child Development* 59, 4: 1080–1088.

Erickson, M. F., and Egeland, B. 1987. "A Developmental View of the Psychological Consequences of Maltreatment." *School Psychology Review* 16, 2: 156–68.

———, Egeland, B., and Pianta, R. 1989. "The Effects of Maltreatment on the Development of Young Children." In *Theory and Research on the Causes and Consequences of Child Abuse and Neglect,* edited by D. Cicchetti and V. Carlson, pp. 647–84. New York: Cambridge University Press.

Garbarino, J. 1987. "What Is Psychological Maltreatment?" In *When Children Need Help: A Special Report,* edited by Lewis P. Lipsitt. Prepared for the Brown University Child Behavior and Development Group. Providence, R.I.: Manisse Communication Group.

Karen, R. 1990. "Becoming Attached." *The Atlantic Monthly* (February): 35–70.

Kempe, C. H.; Silverman, F.; Steele, B.; Droegemueller, W.; and Silver, H. 1962. "The Battered Child Syndrome" *Journal of the American Medical Association* 181, 1: 17–24.

Kinard, E. M. 1987. "Child Abuse and Neglect." In *Encyclopedia of Social Work,* 18th ed., edited by A. Minahan, vol. 1, pp. 223–29.

Parke, R., and Collmer, C. 1975. "Child Abuse: An Interdisciplinary Analysis." In *Review of Child Development Research* 5, edited by E. M. Hetherington, pp. 509–90. Chicago: University of Chicago Press.

Pianta, R., Egeland, B., and Erickson, M. F. 1989. "The Antecedents of Maltreatment: Results of the Mother-Child Interaction Research Project." In D. Cicchetti and V. Carlson, *Child Maltreatment,* pp. 203–253. New York: Cambridge University Press.

Rizley, R., and Cicchetti, D., eds. 1981. *Developmental Perspectives on Child Maltreatment.* San Francisco: Jossey-Bass.

Toufexis, A. 1990. "Struggling for Sanity: Mental and Emotional Distress Are Taking an Alarming Toll of the Young." *Time* (October 8): 47–48.

SECTION V
PROBLEMS, CHALLENGES, AND OPPORTUNITIES OF THE ADDICTED

Addictions and dependencies in various forms, and with many victims, are almost a sign of our times. The chapters contained in Section V all investigate the devastation inflicted on victim, family, friends and community as a result of addictions. In Chapter 20 Paul Mickey provides a view of the multi-determined nature of bulimia and anorexia. While presenting an excellent review of the diagnostic criteria and therapeutic regime employed with eating disorders, the unique value of the essay lies in the special caution aired to pastoral counselors working with bulimic and anorectic clients. The already complicated diagnostic and intervention process appears, according to Mickey, further complicated by the fact that pastoral counselors typically represent an ideological system easily associated with scrupulosity and perfectionism and are therefore especially vulnerable to therapeutic entrapment and "burnout" while counseling those with eating disorders. The theme of "therapists beware" is clearly identified and needs to be heeded.

The issues confronting the pastoral counseling of psychoactive substance abusers are described in the essay by Paul Lininger (Chapter 21). As with the previous authors, Lininger offers the reader an in-depth review of the current state of knowledge regarding the whats, whys, and hows of the problem. The literature review along with the clinical examples provide an excellent base for any pastoral counselor to begin to understand the individual effects and consequences of psychoactive substance abuse and the differentiating criteria for co-morbid psychiatric disorders. But beyond the excellent scientific review, Lininger also focuses on the special need and role to be played by pastoral counselors. He notes that pastoral counselors, unlike any other mental health professional, bring a richness of a holistic perception of persons as body, mind, emotion, and spirit and an accompanying familiarity with the deep substantive issues of life and death as well as a willingness to cry out in prayer to the One without whom none of us could be free of our addictions.

Chapter 22 extends the previous discussion by looking at the very significant impact alcohol has on the other victims of alcoholism: the adult children of alcoholics. Rachel Callahan and Rea McDonnell provide a look at the extensiveness of the problem, along with its many varied forms of manifestation. While sharing some common patterns, most adult children of alcoholics are unique in their pain. The authors note that pastoral counselors need to be versed not only in the knowledge of addictions but even more so in family dynamics. Further, as pastoral counselors, the authors note that we need to be prepared to offer unconditional positive regard, hoping to make up some of the original deficits in parenting.

The final chapter of this section (Chapter 23) addresses an old, yet growing concern among those who minister to the addicted: the addiction of gambling. In this chapter Joseph Ciarrocchi details the nature, course, and impact of pathological gambling. The crisis for many pathological gamblers is, as Ciarrocchi points out, that although creating major occupational, financial, legal, health, and family problems, their gambling has often not been seen by the professional community as a problem. All too few in our society recognize it as the devastating problem it actually is, and fewer yet are prepared to provide assistance. Ciarrocchi calls upon pastoral counselors to step in and fill this void of therapeutic support.

Paul A. Mickey

20. Bulimia and Anorexia: Signs of the Times

Bulimia nervosa and anorexia nervosa share five factors in their multi-determined nature that have complex interactions of negative self-image, family dynamics, psychomythology, social dysfunction, and ideational rigidities. This makes both the diagnosis and therapeutic intervention difficult and cumbersome. In religious settings proper intervention is further complicated beyond the techniques and settings available to the field of psychopathology because the pastoral care-giver represents an ideological system easily associated with scrupulosity and perfectionism and is especially vulnerable to therapeutic entrapment and burnout while counseling those with eating disorders.

History

The clinical symptomatology of anorexia and bulimia is relatively recently derived in medical literature. Efforts among British, French, American, German, and Italian medical historians to report on cases of anorexia nervosa and bulimia nervosa have come under more critical scrutiny as these clinical disorders receive more notoriety in the United States. Habermas traces the psychiatric history of anorexia and bulimia and makes a clear distinction between "primary" and "secondary" eating disorders. Of special interest to the pastoral care-giver are the various accounts of fasting and food deprivation among women for religious reasons: 1) some women restrain their food intake in attempts to follow the late-medieval ascetic model in detaching themselves from worldly pursuits and strengthening their spirituality. Comparable ascetic practices are the self-constraints of sleeping on stone, isolation from others, and self-mortification; 2) post-medieval women are known for living without eating as a further statement of their religiosity because of the symbolic value of the food; and 3) the general practice of religious fasting (Habermas 1989, p. 260). These practices may have appearances similar to anorexia, but they provide a religious or secondary function, whereas the primary diagnostic category for the anorectic is "delusional fear of being or becoming too fat despite a state of emaciation" (Garfinkel and Garner 1982). A concern about weighing too much and not being presentable has both religious and social etymology but clinically needs to be seen as "secondary anorexia" (Bruch 1973).

Characteristics of the anorectic patient's symptoms, which classify them as a psychiatric disorder, include the patient's overactivity in denial of illness, the secretiveness of losing weight, giving other explanations for a refusal to eat, and a delusional fear of obesity along with "cases of compulsive overeating and induced vomiting evolved in connection with anorexia nervosa" (Habermas 1989, p. 270). Anorexia and bulimia may have been present for a long time, but the delusional concern with exaggerated weight characteristic of the bulimic has added diagnostic credibility to what constitutes primary anorexia nervosa. The increased sophistication of diagnostic criteria for anorexia nervosa and bulimia nervosa are reflected in the changes of the DSM III-R (American Psychiatric Association 1987, p. 67).

In the change in the diagnostic criteria for bulimia one notes the requirement of frequency of binge eating and the obsession ("persistent over concern") with body shape and weight. Not until the DSM III-R does bulimia nervosa receive official nomenclature. For the psychopathology of anorexia nervosa to be present, the principal feature is a "morbid fear of becoming fat." In exploring the history of nineteenth-century anorexia, Joan Brumberg focuses attention on the Victorian family and particularly its controlled world of the middle-class women with attention on "love and food." Therefore "food refusal was the ultimate passive/aggressive rebellion of the female child who had few other means to protest against the extensive restrictions and limitations of microcosm of Nineteenth Century patriarchy (Brumberg 1988, p. 379).

Once the more stringent DSM III criteria of chronicity and frequency was added in DSM III-R, bulimia was observed in 1 percent to 3 percent of women in the college-age group (Mitchell 1986, p. 91). Less than 10 percent of the reported cases of bulimia related to males. "The cardinal feature of bulimia is binge-eating . . . with patients with bulimia not uncommonly consuming 5,000–20,000 calories during eating binges. . . . Many described entering an 'altered state' while they are ingesting food." Mitchell further notes, "Most patients

Table 1
DSM III-R Criteria For Bulimia Nervosa

A. Recurrent episodes of binge-eating.

B. A feeling of lack of control over eating behaviors during the eating binges.

C. Regular practice of self-induced vomiting, use of laxatives or diuretics, strict dieting or fasting, or vigorous exercise in order to prevent weight gain.

D. A minimum average of two binge-eating episodes a week for at least three months.

E. Persistent overconcern with body shape and weight.

Table 2
DSM III-R Diagnostic Criteria For Anorexia Nervosa

A. Refusal to maintain body weight over a minimal normal weight for age and height, e.g., weight loss leading to maintenance of body weight 15% below that expected; or failure to make expected weight gain during period of growth, leading to body weight 15% below that expected.

B. Intense fear of gaining weight or becoming fat, even though underweight.

C. Disturbance in the way body weight, size, or shape is experienced, e.g., the person claims to "feel fat" even when emaciated, believes that one area of the body is "too fat" even when obviously underweight.

D. In females, absence of at least three consecutive menstrual cycles when otherwise expected to occur (primary or secondary amenorrhea). (A woman is considered to have amenorrhea if her periods occur only following hormone, e.g. estrogen, administration.)

end up institutionalizing the bulimic eating pattern into their everyday routine. . . . The foods most commonly ingested are those high in fat and/or carbohydrates which can be easily ingested and do not require much preparation such as ice cream, doughnuts, and candy. Immediately after binge-eating, most bulimic individuals self-induce vomiting. They then feel a strong sense of guilt and dysphoria" (p. 92). Mitchell also reports on an associated feature of bulimics, "a high rate of depression in the first-degree relatives of patients with bulimia. . . . Bulimia can be regarded as a 'substance abuse' disorder which is analogous to abuse of alcohol or other drugs (and substances). [This] appears to be a useful construct for understanding some of the features of bulimia" (p. 95). Additionally, gastrointestinal problems may well develop as well as dental erosion and irregular menses, but "profound amenorrhea associated with anorexia nervosa is rarely seen if patients are of normal weight" (p. 97).

Diagnostic Factors

Vanderheyden, Fekken, and Boland (1988) identify five factors associated with the anorectic population: restraint, general psychopathology, depression, anxiety, and negative self-image. I have modified those factors to place them in a more pastoral perspective: 1) negative self-image, 2) family dynamics, 3) psychopathology, 4) social dysfunction, and 5) ideational perfectionism. Following the lead of Vanderheyden I submit that for theological as well as psychological purposes these five orthogonal dimensions are common problems to those who suffer anorectic disorders and are commonly associated with the population groups that suffer from these disorders, but they are not unique to bulimia or anorexia.

Negative Self-Image

One of the developmental problems associated with anorectics is the disturbance of body image that is especially acute during the adolescent process, when normal developmental separation from parents and family should be occurring. Several investigators have hypothesized an interrelationship of appropriate adolescent separation from parents, distress in body image perception, negative self-image, and the genesis of eating disturbances. At a time when normal developmental progress would suggest differentiation and separation from parents, disturbances in differentiation and definition of one's person from parental influence have a high correlation with the difficulty and distress associated with finding one's identity, especially that of body boundaries. Where differentiation between parents and child does not exist, one may expect to find lack of definition and positive boundary images for the adolescent child.

David Zakin discovered "the lack of a significant correlation between these measures (body image and emotional separation) suggests that they may independently contribute to the development of eating disorders" (Zakin 1989, p. 415). Zakin's research suggests that there may be independent variables closely associated with eating disturbances. He concludes, "The results suggest that women less emotionally independent from their parents, more dissatisfied with their bodies, and evidencing a less stable sense of self are more likely to manifest eating disturbance" (p. 415).

Another area of negative self-image is sexual orientation. Where confusion exists between one's identity, self-image, and perceived sexual orientation the effects of the confusion, anxiety, and negative self-image over sexual conflict are contributory factors to anorectic conditions. Van Strien and Bergers conclude:

> When the variance of anxiety and negative self-concept and femininity scores are partialled out, femininity no longer contributed significantly to emotional and external eating. This indicates that the contribution of femininity to both types of eating behavior is due mainly to anxiety and negative self-concept associated with female stereotypes. This is in line with the hypothesis that negative emotions and lack of adaptive coping behavior associated with female sex role status may lead to the consumption of food as a noneffective response to difficult situations and negative emotions (van Strien and Bergers 1988, p. 99).

The authors hypothesize further that women who have an appropriate or balanced concept of androgyny or who have appropriated and integrated developmentally appropriate concepts of femininity and masculinity are less susceptible to anorectic conditions. The implication is that the more pressure a woman experiences from parents, social settings, or peer groups to conform to a rigid female stereotype—often exaggerated among college and adolescent populations—the greater the anxiety, negative self-image, and likelihood of acting out the conflict with eating disturbances.

Where negative self-image, boundary, and differentiation confusion exist, one can anticipate some highly disturbed reactions. Ferguson and Damluji conducted a study of twelve patients who fulfilled the DSM criteria for both anorexia nervosa and schizophrenia. Symptoms examined were "feeling empty, autism, ambivalent, amotivational, anhedonic, decreased sexual contact, promiscuity (episodic), poor judgment, drug abuse (episodic), deterioration from previous level of functioning" (Ferguson and Damluji 1988, p. 348). This study concluded that the perceptual disturbances in their sample reveal negative systems, which make the disorder harder to treat, rather than positive symptoms, in which direct delusional affect can be pharmacologically treated:

> The sense of self gives a normal person a feeling of individuality, uniqueness, and self-direction and was disturbed in our patients. This loss of ego boundaries was seen in their extreme perplexity about their own identity. The eating disturbances appeared in many ways to organize their life and give them a sense of identity, if not a meaning to their existence. Profound ambivalence led to a virtual cessation of goal-directed activity and was present in all of the patients along with a marked decrease in reactivity to the environment, a reduction in spontaneous activity, and bizarre mannerisms, both when eating and other times (Ferguson and Damluji 1988, p. 350).

Among the anorectic patients included in this study, there was a marked deterioration from previous levels of functioning that persisted over a period of six months or longer. These findings suggest that the severity of eating disorder disturbances can be quite significant and that the negative symptomatology, that is, a withdrawal from social interaction in contrast to the positive symptomatology of heightened interaction through delusional systems, proves to be even more difficult to treat because of the complex therapeutic interventions required.

While few males (5–10 percent of anorexia nervosa patients) are considered anorectic, Andersen and Mickalide (1983) report that most research has focused on affected females. Franco et al. (1988) found that the males most at risk for eating disorders were body builders because of the "narcissistic investment of the body." The researchers found three male subgroups most at risk with a negative self-image and overcompensation by undue attention to body mass, definition, and appearance: body builders, long-distance runners, and homosexuals. The emphasis among these male population groups places emphasis on body and physical appearance and approaches the levels of inappropriate attention that place them at higher risk for eating disorders (Katz 1986; Herzog et al. 1984).

Fairly common is the dynamic that negative self-image plays itself out in over-restricted dietary constraints. Van Strien (1989) concludes that women most susceptible to eating disorders have a "relative absence of masculine traits" (p. 461). In his sample base, taken from a religious residential community, where the correlation between dieting and dissatisfaction with figure were positively correlated with actual body mass, the primary variable was the actual overweight of the women in the residential community in contrast to the typical college or university female student, where ideal body size is related more directly to sexual stereotypes, fear of failure, and an idealized body size. Among the van Strien female non-college students, dieting and dissatisfaction with figure were more appropriately self-diagnosed than among female college students.

Family Dynamics

Because anorectic symptomatology generally exhibits itself in crucial transitional and developmental stages (adolescence and college-age), the issues of attachment/detachment, transition, control, separation anxiety, and significant others play a crucial role in the diagnosis of those with eating disorders. Because the family is "the major creator and sustainer of the characteristic intrapersonal and interpersonal behavior of the individual, it mediates attitudes to eating and the other appetites" (Rakoff 1983, p. 29). Research indicates that the determinants of "the obsession with looking thin" and the "need for control" are crucial variables with a specific vulnerability to defects in generational, appetitive, cultural, religious, and emotional expressions of warmth (p. 38). By examining family, culture, and the "democratization of a concern for fashion" among a broader base of the population, one may hypothesize that the increase of eating disorders, while clinically restricted to more aristocratic families a century ago, now comes under the influence of the Eriksonian concept of adolescent moratorium as the dominant rite of passage for America. The modern transition from childhood to adulthood is more ambiguous and problematic; youth are made to "feel dependent" for an increasing sizable portion of the population. Family controls, definition, and influence are at their minimal during adolescent college years. This coupled with the deterioration of the intact family and the rise of the entertainment and female sports figures who stress thinness, according to Rakoff, has contributed to a "pathology of appearance" among the current adolescent female population. An adolescent girl may "treat her body as her corseted Victorian ancestor might have—the raw material for existential sculpture" (p. 38).

In a discussion of the applicability of the major tenants of Bowlby's attachment theory for anorectics, Armstrong and Roth (1989) observe:

> In view of its implications for the understanding of eating disorders, it is important to note that anxious attachment (characterized by chronic separation distress) has a variety of psychological consequences, most notably phobias, low self-reliance, and susceptibility to separation depression (p. 143).

Following on the Bowlby assertion of a direct connection between the quality of one's attachment and the general attitude toward the environment, the authors postulate that where heightened "anxious detachment" exists, patients are unable to distinguish between brief, everyday, appropriate leave takings and more permanent and disastrous breaks in relationships. Separation distress for those suffering from eating disorders suggests that,

> Lacking or misperceiving their own resources, the anorexic or bulimic excessively depends upon the resources of significant others in order to feel safe and secure. This underlying sense of basic inadequacy and helplessness, coupled with insecure neediness, is the hallmark of anxious attachment (Armstrong and Roth 1989, p. 145).

The problem does not originate with the eating disorder, but the authors look at the families of origin and characterize them as being disorganized and conflict-ridden, with parents so caught up in their own chronic struggles for stability in intrafamilial dynamics as well as external relations that parents "cannot be relied upon to consistently perceive and meet their children's need for security. The bulimic may learn from such experiences to expect that others will similarly be unavailable or insensitive when called upon for support. She turns this [insecurity] to binging, then, as a readily available method of self-soothing when threatened" (p. 145).

Armstrong and Roth compare the results of several research studies of families of anorectics and bulimics. They conclude:

> Self-report and direct observation methodologies portray the families of bulimic and anorectic-bulimic patients as being relatively unsupportive, detached, conflictual, hostile, disorganized and non-nurturant. . . . The anorectic family profile is quite different. . . . In marked contrast to the bulimic, these families have a tendency towards overt conflict avoidance, enmeshment, and overprotectiveness (Armstrong and Roth 1989, p. 152).

Thus, while family dynamics are important, the research indicates that two different patterns of familial conflict emerge: the bulimic comes from a family characterized by hostility, detachment, and disorganization; and the anorectic comes from a family where enmeshment and inappropriate over-nurturing and over-protectiveness are key characteristics.

Psychopathology

I have already suggested that negative self-image, complicated by conflicted familial interaction patterns of the anorectic patient and the resultant attachment anxiety, exhibits itself in significant psychopathology. Prather and Williamson suggest that psychopathology exists in a "continuum of severity, with the binge-purger group showing the highest levels of psychopathology, and the binge-eaters and clinical obese showing significantly more distress than the two control groups (non-bulimic obese presenting for treatment for obesity and normal control subjects)" (Prather and Williamson 1988, p. 177). That significant psychopathology exists among anorectics is demonstrated by a number of studies. Strober and Katz (1988) review earlier findings suggesting that "depression is prominent in the clinical presentation of both anorexia nervosa and bulimia nervosa. Reports of its frequency vary considerably, ranging from 20% to 100%" (p. 81). The authors conclude, "It appears that depressive states of varying intensity foreshadow the onset of symptoms of anorexia nervosa and bulimia nervosa in a significant proportion of patients" (p. 84).

In a study exploring the "clinical correlates of personality disorder in bulimia nervosa," Yates, Sieleni, and Bowers (1989) conclude that a personality disorder is prevalent among bulimics of normal weight and conclude that "since personality disorder reflects a link to major depression and bulimia, we may be measuring the effects of an already documented link between major depression and bulimia" (p. 476). In addition to these two studies numerous other researchers, including Garfinkel and Garner (1982) and Russell (1979), link depression to morbidity with eating disorders, especially bulimia.

Lingswiler, Crowther, and Stephens (1989) reinforce previous research "suggesting that negative mood states may precipitate binge episodes for bulimics" (1989, p. 537). Further, that "both bulimics and binge eaters also report experiencing significantly greater negative moods prior to their nonbinge episodes than normal controls report prior to their eating episodes suggests either that negative mood states may generally precipitate eating in eating-disorder populations or that negative mood states may be more characteristic of these populations independent of food and eating" (Lingswiler, Crowther, and Stephens 1987).

Others have suggested a high correlation of borderline personality disorder with anorectic patients. Cooper et al. (1988) employed the psychiatric symptomatology (SCL-90 and Eating Disorder Inventory [EDI], and the Diagnostic Survey for Eating Disorders [DSES]) with ten patients. The researchers discovered that borderline patients often experience elevation of hostility, uncontrolled temper outbursts, frequent arguments, and heightened levels of irritation, but the borderline eating disorder patient did not differ from the general population on the hostility scale. The distortion of borderline patients can approach psychotic levels, whereas the eating disorder patient with some borderline characteristics did not show an elevation on the psychoticism scale of the SCL-90. The borderline personality disorder characteristics associated with eating disorder patients reveal the psychopathology of the borderline eating disorder group through self-report, "Patients experience themselves primarily as passive, avoidant, insecure, and filled with self-doubts as well as distrustful and suspicious of others" (p. 48). The evidence suggests that anorectic patients, when categorized as borderline personality, distort life not in the direction of increased hostility or cognitive distortions but rather in the more passive direction of distrust, self-loathing, hopelessness, and social isolation (Cooper et al. 1988).

A study by Torem collaborates the findings of Cooper et al. in reporting on the disassociative statements by anorectic patients that move more toward self-loathing than hostility:

> "I don't know why I do it. I am so confused. It is not like me."
>
> "A part of me wants to binge and then throw up and another part of me hates it and is just plain disgusted."
>
> "Whenever food is put in front of me, I automatically become frightened like a little kid. I know I need to eat, but it's like the Devil gets into me."
>
> "When I binge, it feels so strange, as if I am in a daze. I don't know what comes over me" (Torem 1985, p. 149).

The psychopathology of anorectic patients can present serious psychiatric as well as medical complications. Zucker has detailed a number of medical concerns for the bulimic and anorectic: nutritional state, metabolic state, musculoskeletal system, neurological complications, cardiac complications, dental complications, gastrointestinal complications, endroendocrin complications, and reproductive complications (Zucker 1989, pp. 28–35).

Social Dysfunction

The social functioning of anorectics comes under tremendous stress. Some of that stress occurs through cultural conditioning, some through the stress process of eating disorders that produce cognitive dysfunctioning, and finally, some are seen in an inability to act appropriately when confronted with food in a social setting. Sarah Gilbert comments on several aspects of Western culture that compound the anorectic propensity. Food supplies are abundant to the West. Most food items can be bought with high levels of fats and carbohydrates. As the Western culture becomes more sedentary, the need for high caloric intake continues to lessen (Gilbert 1986, p. 5). Another cultural factor adverse to the anorectic is the neutral to positive value on stout to obese women in underdeveloped communities, where obesity is a sign of fertility (p. 6). In professional class Western culture, however, there is a prejudice against people who are overweight. Therefore those who are obese or fear themselves becoming obese perceive "themselves as less worthy of respect than are other people" (p. 8). Ironically, in the less-developed societies emphasis is placed upon vegetarian diets, whereas Euro-American culture exhibits a "contradictory habit of marketing high fat, high sugar, high calorie, high salt and low fiber foods as rewards for success" (p. 9). Western culture in general sets impossible standards of perfection for diet, body mass, muscle definition, and social performance. The anorectic is caught in a bind that runs counter to the prevailing cultural patterns and increases the felt conflict.

Corroborating the Gilbert studies on cultural factors, Cattanach and Rodin examine the effects of acute stressors, stress-event sequences, chronic and chronic-intermittent stressors, and mediators of stress upon anorectics and poor coping processes. The anorectic's obsession but ineffective struggle with self-control, the lack of social support, and the personality characteristics of anorectics make them socially less able to cope with stressors. "In addition to depression, elevated levels of anxiety are commonly reported by bulimic women, along with guilt, worrying, poor concentration, and nervous tension. The anxiety experienced by bulimics has been linked to their anticipated lack of control" (Cattanach and Rodin 1988, p. 83). Their inability to make appropriate differential appraisal of stressful situations contributes to their impaired coping processes (p. 84). Finally, these researchers point to two vulnerability factors mitigating against anorectics coping with stress: "those of an etiological nature and those of a maintaining nature" (p. 86). They advocate examining more carefully the social dysfunction of the anorectic's particular attention to deficiency in appraisal, coping, control, and social support.

Where cultural pressures abound and ineffective coping with stress is a concomitant dysfunctional response, one may expect, as Strauss and Ryan report, an elevation of a cognitive dysfunction among anorectics. From the Cognitive Error Questionnaire [CEQ] and other related evaluatory instruments, they report, "Logical errors do appear to be a prominent feature in anorexia nervosa, particularly in the restrictive subtype, but not in normal-weight bulimia or subcultural eating pathology" (Strauss and Ryan 1988, p. 25). However, they warn that the cognitive slippage and restrictive logical functions are not seriously debilitating and that most anorectics perform within normal limits within the cognitive spheres. The researchers did, however, discover that "both affective measures (CEQ TDI) detected significant dysphoria and depression in all four eating disordered groups. . . . The findings suggest that cognitive dysfunction is in evidence in anorexia nervosa, although not on all indices" (p. 25). In examining ego functioning and ego boundaries among those with eating disorders, Norring et al. (1989) found significant personality variables related less to the level of pathology than to the style of functioning (p. 617). Their summary follows the findings of Rybicki and Lepkowsky (1987) that the bulimics "appear to be more extroverted, more capable of realistic social perception, more socially adept, more aware of subjective discomfort, and more prone to acting out behaviors" (p. 617). They concur with McLaughlin, Karp, and Herzog (1985) and Rybicki and Lepkowsky (1987) that anorectics and bulimics share in "deficits and self-directed autonomy, but the anorexics use a rigid overcontrolling ego style to compensate for it, whereas bulimics were more impulsive in their ego styles" (p. 617).

A variety of responses to social stressors in the daily environment, particularly those related to food ingestion, set off fairly predictable and dysfunctional reactions on the part of anorectics.

Ideational Perfectionism

Among anorectics, the "drive for thinness" exemplifies an ideological rigidity seen equally among anorectics and bulimics. The particular pathology may take different behavioral manifestations such as perfectionism, submission, loyalty, and supreme cooperativeness among anorectics, and mania, impatience, impulsiveness, and disorganization among the bulimics. The drive toward thinness, body weight control, the excessive thinking about weight and thinness manifest themselves in what is commonly known as *monoideistic fixation*.

Among those in religious groupings or in religious communities including ordained clergy, the threat of monoideistic fixation may be underscored in cultural and communal settings. One such study was a longitudinal study of anorexia nervosa among sixty-six kibbutz anorectic patients (forty restrictors and twenty-six bulimics) for a period from four to ten years (Kaffman and Sadeh 1989). In addition to the issues that relate to anorexia nervosa as a monoideistic illness the common denominator is the "continuous preoccupation with a restricted ideational theme" (Kaffman and Sadeh 1989, p. 45). Obsessive brooding renders the subjects unable to modify the dieting processes. This incapacity eventuates in the subjects brooding over dieting that proximates hypnotic trance with the precipite consequence of diminished volitional control. The authors claim that "cult recruits and anorectics seem to be cast from the same mold . . . all of whose energies go into the monothematic engagement with a concomitant decrease of interest in the outside world. . . . Certainly, one cannot dispel the false beliefs held by a member of the 'totalist' cult, a paranoid, or an anorectic patient by simply disputing the irrational element of the delusional thinking" (p. 47).

Many of those deeply and profoundly committed to religious ideation may in fact share the similarity and personality profile suggested by Kaffman and Sadeh: an emphasis on monoideistic thought, an obsession with the conformity to the standards and boundaries of the group, an obsession with right thoughts about religion, social behavior, sex life, and sex role, and in the case of the kibbutz women, obsessional thoughts about body weight. The emphasis upon perfectionism and scrupulosity especially among the more conservative and orthodox groups of Protestants, Roman Catholics, and Jews, suggests a distinct similarity of personality style if not personality type of anorectic patients and the type of support group organized around a monothematic world-view in tightly cloistered or quasi-cult religious groups.

For some, the ideological rigidity that anorectic patients bring to their lives is no more than an obsession with thinness that passes with advancing adolescent years. However, if a strong commitment to a religious ideational system persists and reinforces monoideistic fixations, there may be other factors involved in the disorder. Consequently, changes in rigidity of religious beliefs may also be a source of therapeutic intervention appropriate for "deprogramming" adherence under the power of manipulative groups or under the ideological power of the drive for thinness. This remains a very fruitful area for additional exploration and research.

A recent article that comments on the "drive for thinness" offers the thesis that some of the underlying cultural supports for developing the anorectic patient may be shifting: "During the last 25 years the idealized feminine form has been a gaunt, emaciated look, and the achievement of this appearance by young women has been symbolic of discipline, success, attractiveness, and health" (Johnson, et al. 1989, p. 652). The authors further argue that, "perhaps as a reaction to AIDS, the 'pursuit of strength' is replacing the 'drive to achieve thinness' as a mechanism by which young women attempt to demonstrate mastery, success, and physical beauty. There is an unprecedented interest among women in body-building techniques and endurance sports such as marathons, triathalons, and other forms of highly demanding physical exercise" (p. 652).

If the authors are correct in their hypothesis of the overall cultural effects of body building and the pursuit of strength among young women, we should expect a diminishment of the anorectic patient as well as a decrease in the monoideistic fixations. If that is the case we may, if the pursuit of strength is not a reaction formation to the pursuit of thinness, see the mainline denominations become more attractive to those who do not posture themselves ideologically in an asectic religious form. Concomitantly, dare we expect a diminishment in cultic and quasi-cultic activity in religious settings?

The drive toward success, perfection, and total control may—as a result of cultural shifts, therapeutic intervention, and medical problems like AIDS—provide a means by which the anorectic disorders will be less prevalent than they were when bulimia nervosa first was introduced into the DSM III in 1980.

Treatment Protocols

Because bulimia and anorexia have complex psychological, physiological, cultural, familial, and ideational genesis, treatment must utilize a multidimensional approach to address the multideterminant etiology of the disorder. Because so many variables interplay, therapeutic intervention is particularly subject to treatment refusal as an intense form of resistance (Goldner 1989, p. 299). Sufferers of primary bulimia and anorexia may suffer delusional responses comparable to schizophrenics endeavoring to elude enemies (p. 301). Because death is an imminent threat of anorectic behavior, therapeutic intervention carries with it perplexing legal as well as therapeutic problems. In an effort to reduce treatment refusal, Goldner suggests several therapy protocols: 1) seek to engage in a sincere and voluntary alliance, 2) identify reasons for refusal, 3) provide careful explanation of treatment recommendations, 4) be prepared for negotiation, 5) allow the person to retain autonomy, 6) weigh risk versus benefits of treatment imposition, 7) avoid battle and scare tactics, 8) convey balance of control versus noncontrol, 9) ensure methods of treatment are not inherently punitive, 10) involve the family, 11) obtain legal clarification and support, 12) consider legal means of treatment imposition only when refusal is judged to constitute a serious risk, 13) consider differential treatment in chronic anorexia nervosa, and 14) conceptualize refusal/resistance as an evolutionary process (pp. 303, 304).

Because anorectics, in their obsession with eating, become prisoners of their illness, they often exhibit dysmorphophobia. A dysmorphophobic 24-year-old woman who in her perfectionistic behavior became obsessed with the size and shape of her nose and resisted all efforts to ensure her that her nose was absolutely normal represents the typical reaction of deep feelings of insecurity at the body level

(Pantano 1989, p. 703). These intensely negative feelings are isolated and limited to one part of the body and often associated with recovery from anorexia nervosa.

Other problems complicating treatment of anorexia and bulimia are the distorted perception of time and fluctuation of subjects' "subjective clocks" due to the stress of the eating disorder. Faulkner and Duecker (1989) suggest that the obsession with eating speeds up one's internal clock rate so that the patient perceives that mealtime arrives quicker than those with a stabilized internal clock rate (p. 249).

Recent research by Jaffe and Singer (1989) suggests that eating disorders may be more prevalent among young children than realized. Likewise Hsu and Zimmer (1988) suggest that eating disorders may also exist among the elderly and may have been confused with early stages of Alzheimer's previously (p. 137). Likewise, research on the clinical features of eating disorders among males suggest that the recovery rate for females is better than males who suffer from eating disorders (Oyebode, Boodhoo, and Schapira 1988, p. 123).

Additional problems for therapeutic intervention were noted by Calam and Slade (1989). They assert "that there is a significant association between unwanted sexual experience and eating problems" (p. 391). Because eating disorders are not restricted to physiological or medical problems, they dramatically affect the family relations. They tend toward social dysfunctions in part because anorectics tend to have "low efficacy expectations" and therefore tend to withdraw from conflict which, in a marriage or highly emotional interpersonal relationship, further disturbs interpersonal relationships, especially with members of the opposite sex (Van Buren and Williamson 1988, p. 740). Bulimic patients, in their obsession for weight control, further complicate their lives and their physiology with their excessive use of "diet pills, diuretics, laxatives, and the drug ipecac which is used to induce vomiting" (Mitchell, Pomeroy, and Huber 1988, p. 211). The researchers are concerned because ipecac increases the risk of cardiomyopathy. Treatment has to take into consideration the abusive uses of various drugs and their effects on electrolyte abnormalities, gastrointestinal disorders, and potential heart risk.

An additional complicating factor for therapy is reported in a study by Bennett, Williamson, and Powers (1989) in an investigation of the relationship between bulimia nervosa and resting metabolic rate. It was determined that "severe bulimics had lower resting metabolic rates than less severe bulimics and normals who did not differ"

(p. 417). The research has not made it clear "whether decreased metabolism is a precursor or a consequence of bulimia" (p. 423).

Research indicates that short-term group therapy for females suffering with bulimia is effective, and that the patients attribute a high level of importance to both vicarious learning (observing how other group members improve) and hope (observing other group members actually improve). The overall benefits of homogeneous groups are positive. Hobbs et al. (1989, p. 632), Johnson and Connors (1987) stress the value of psychodynamic psychotherapy with an emphasis on development issues. Their research indicates that insight-oriented psychotherapy is a preferred long-term intervention. The researchers believe that behavioral interventions may improve the symptoms but fail to change the underlying problem.

Others believe that the best possible treatment for bulimia and anorexia is effective pharmacological intervention. Pope and Hudson (1985) strongly favor the treatment of bulimia through pharmacotherapy and give little credence to the value of psychotherapy whether cognitive-behaviorally or insight oriented.

When hospitalization is required, several researchers believe that hospitalization should be sustained only long enough to return the patient's weight to within 95 percent of ideal body weight (IBW). See Rockwell (1986, p. 15) for a fuller discussion of individual and group treatment patterns. Larocca (1986), in which Rockwell's essay appears, is an excellent resource for developing therapeutic skills.

Finally, researchers reported positively on Overeaters Anonymous [OA] (Malenbaum et al. 1988). Their finding was that the group support in OA achieves high rates of abstinence among participants with distinct improvement in morale, positive state of mind, and increased success of behavioral control of the disease. Likewise accolades are handed out to BASH (Larocca 1986).

Therapists Beware

The personality profile of the anorectic and bulimic patients with tendencies toward perfectionism and scrupulosity displays keen attention to details of social and physical attractiveness. The patients endeavor to stabilize difficult situations but often with minimum skills and conflict resolution. Thus they represent a particular challenge for therapists. The underlying difficulties for bulimics and anorectics for the therapist who is a pastoral care-giver is the unusual susceptibility of the care-giver to the stresses and demands of working with anorectic patients.

In order not to become enmeshed in the psychopathology of the anorectic or bulimic, the therapist needs to be especially vigilant for burnout. Rubel (1986) reports on stages of burn-out of therapists: "1) The first stage of burn-out consists of zealous enthusiasm for work fueled by high optimism and unrealistic expectations, 2) therapists discover some of the harsher realities of their job, when they discover their work will never be a substitute for satisfying outside activities, and 3) the move from a relatively vague sense of dissatisfaction to more disturbing feeling of futility" (p. 234).

Rubel cites various causes of burn-out: 1) stressful working conditions, 2) frustrating psychopathologies and client expectations, and 3) personal qualities and unrealistic expectations of therapists (pp. 237–42). His suggestions for "managing burn-out" encourage the therapist to design strategies that will: 1) improve working conditions, 2) accept inherent frustrations in working with anorectics and bulimics because the disorders are so hard to treat, and 3) correct the therapist's unrealistic expectations to cure the problem (p. 242).

Unless the therapist can maintain his or her own clinical distance from the circumstances and the personalities of bulimics and anorectics, the result is not only professional burn-out but a disservice by refusing to set limits to those suffering from anorexia nervosa and bulimia nervosa. One might summarize the warning for the therapist as, "physician heal thyself"—in order to be free to intervene appropriately in the lives of anorectics and bulimics.

References

American Psychiatric Association. 1987. *Diagnostic and Statistical Manual of Mental Disorders,* 3d ed. rev. Washington, D.C. Referred to in text as *DSM III-R.*

Andersen, A. E., and Mickalide, A. E. 1983. "Anorexia Nervosa in the Male: An Underdiagnosed Disorder." *Psychosomatics* 24: 1066–1074.

Armstrong, J., and Roth, D. M. 1989. "Attachment and Separation Difficulty in Eating Disorders: A Preliminary Investigation." *International Journal of Eating Disorders* 8, 2: 141–55.

Bennett, S. M., Williamson, D. A., and Powers, S. K. 1989. "Bulimia Nervosa and Resting Metabolic Rate." *International Journal of Eating Disorders* 8, 4: 417–24.

Bruch, H. 1973. *Eating Disorders: Obesity, Anorexia Nervosa, and the Person Within.* New York: Basic Books.

Brumberg, J. 1989. "Fasting Girls: The Emergence of Anorexia as a Modern Disease." *International Journal of Eating Disorders* 8, 3: 377–81.

Calam, R. M., and Slade, P. D. 1989. "Sexual Experience and Eating Problems in Female Undergraduates." *International Journal of Eating Disorders* 8, 4: 391–97.

Cattanach, L., and Rodin, J. 1988. "Psychosocial Components of the Stress Process in Bulimia." *International Journal of Eating Disorders* 7, 1: 75–88.

Cooper, J. L.; Morrison, T. L.; Bigman, O. L.; Abramowitz, S. I.; Blunden, D.; Nassi, A.; Krener, P. 1988. "Bulimia and Borderline Personality Disorder." *International Journal of Eating Disorders* 7, 1: 43–49.

Faulkner, K. K., and Duecker, S. J. 1989. "Stress, Time Distortion, and Failure to Recover among Obese Individuals: Implications for Weight Gain and Dieting." *International Journal of Eating Disorders* 8, 2: 247–50.

Ferguson, J. M., and Damluji, N. F. 1988. "Anorexia Nervosa and Schizophrenia." *International Journal of Eating Disorders* 7, 3: 343–52.

Franco, K. S.; Tamburrino, M. B.; Caroll, B. T.; Bernal, G. A. 1988. "Eating Attitudes in College Males." *International Journal of Eating Disorders* 7, 2: 285–88.

Garfinkel, P. E., and Garner, D. M. 1982. *Anorexia Nervosa: A Multidimensional Perspective.* New York: Brunner/Mazel.

———, Moldofsky, H., and Garner, D. M. 1980. "The Heterogeneity of Anorexia Nervosa." *Archives of General Psychiatry* 37: 1036–1040.

Gilbert, S. D. 1986. *Pathology of Eating* London: Routledge and Kegan Paul.

Goldner, E. 1989. "Treatment Refusal and Anorexia Nervosa." *International Journal of Eating Disorders* 8, 3: 297–306.

Habermas, T. 1989. "The Psychiatric History of Anorexia Nervosa and Bulimia Nervosa: Weight Concerns and Bulimic Symptoms in Early Case Reports." *International Journal of Eating Disorders* 8, 3: 259–73.

Herzog, D. B.; Norman, D. K.; Gordon, C.; Pepos, M. 1984. "Sexual Conflict and Eating Disorders in 27 Males." *American Journal of Psychiatry* 141: 898–990.

Hobbs, M.; Birtchnell, A.; Harte, A.; Lacey, H. 1989. "Therapeutic

Factors in Short-term Group Therapy for Women with Bulimia." *International Journal of Eating Disorders* 8, 6: 623–33.

Hsu, L. K. G., and Zimmer, B. 1988. "Eating Disorders in Old Age." *International Journal of Eating Disorders* 7, 1: 133–38.

Jaffe, A. C., and Singer, L. T. 1989. "Atypical Eating Disorders in Younger Children." *International Journal of Eating Disorders* 8, 5: 575–82.

Johnson, C., and Connors, M. E. 1987. *The Etiology and Treatment of Bulimia Nervosa* New York: Basic Books.

Johnson, C., Tobin, D. L., and Lipkin, J. 1989. "Epidemiologic Changes in Bulimic Behavior among Female Adolescents over a Five-year Period." *International Journal of Eating Disorders* 8, 6: 647–55.

Kaffman, M., and Sadeh, T. 1989. "Anorexia Nervosa in the Kibbutz: Factors Influencing the Development of a Monoideistic Fixation." *International Journal of Eating Disorders* 8, 1: 33–53.

Katz, J. L. 1986. "Long Distance Running, Anorexia Nervosa and Bulimia: Two Cases." *Comprehensive Psychiatry* 27: 74–78.

Larocca, F. F. E., ed. 1986. *Eating Disorders—Effective Care and Treatment.* St. Louis, Mo.: Ishiyaku EuroAmerica.

Lingswiler, V. M., Crowther, J. H., and Stephens, M. A. P. 1987. "Emotional Reactivity and Eating in Binge Eating and Obesity." *Journal of Behavioral Medicine* 10: 287–99.

———. 1989. "Antecedents to Eating Episodes in Bulimia and Binge Eating." *International Journal of Eating Disorders* 8, 5: 533–39.

Malenbaum, R.; Herzog, D.; Eisenthal, S.; Wyshak, G. 1988. "Overeaters Anonymous: Impact on Bulimia." *International Journal of Eating Disorders* 7, 1: 139–43.

McLaughlin, E., Karp, S., and Herzog, D. 1985. "Sense of Ineffectiveness in Woman with Eating Disorders—A Clinical Study of Anorexia Nervosa and Bulimia." *International Journal of Eating Disorders* 4: 511–23.

Mitchell, J. 1986. "An Overview of the Bulimic Syndrome." In *Eating Disorders—Effective Care and Treatment,* edited by F. F. E. Larocca. St. Louis, Mo.: Ishiyaku EuroAmerica. pp. 89–101.

Mitchell, J. E., Pomeroy, C., and Huber, M. 1988. "A Clinician's Guide to the Eating Disorders Medicine Cabinet." *International Journal of Eating Disorders* 7, 2: 211–23.

Norring, C.; Sohlberg, S.; Rosmark, B.; Humble, K.; Holmgren, S.; Nordqvist, C. 1989. "Ego Functioning in Eating Disorders: Description and Relation to Diagnostic Classification." *International Journal of Eating Disorders* 8, 6: 607–21.

Oyebode, F., Boodhoo, J. A., and Schapira, K. 1988. "Anorexia Nervosa in Males: Clinical Features and Outcome." *International Journal of Eating Disorders* 7, 1: 121–24.

Pantano, M. 1989. "A Case of Dysmorphophobia Following Recovery from Anorexia Nervosa." *International Journal of Eating Disorders* 8, 6: 701–4.

Pope, H. G., and Hudson, J. I. 1985. *New Hope for Binge Eaters: Advances in the Understanding and Treatment of Bulimia,* rev. New York: Harper & Row.

Prather, R. C., and Williamson, D. A. 1988. "Psychotherapy Associated with Bulimia, Binge Eating, and Obesity." *International Journal of Eating Disorders* 7, 2: 177–84.

Rakoff, V. 1983. "Multiple Determinants of Family Dynamics in Anorexia Nervosa." In *Anorexia Nervosa: Recent Developments in Research,* edited by Padraig Darby et al., pp. 29–40. New York: Alan R. Liss.

Rockwell, W. J. K. 1986. "A Critique of Treatment Methods for Anorexia Nervosa." In Larocca, *Eating Disorders—Effective Care and Treatment,* pp. 11–31.

Rubel, J. B. 1986. "Burn-out and Eating Disorders Therapists." In Larocca, *Eating Disorders—Effective Care and Treatment,* pp. 233–46.

Russell, G. F. M. 1979. "Bulimia Nervosa: An Ominous Variant of Anorexia Nervosa." *Psychological Medicine* 9: 429–48.

Rybicki, D., and Lepkowski, C. 1987. "Assessment of Anorexia Nervosa and Bulimia Using the Millon Clinical Multi Axial Inventory." *BASH Inc. Monthly Magazine* 6: 194–96.

Strauss, J., and Ryan, R. M. 1988. "Cognitive Dysfunction in Eating Disorders." *International Journal of Eating Disorders* 7, 1: 19–27.

Strober, M., and Katz, J. L. 1988. "Depression in the Eating Disorders: A Review and Analysis of Descriptive, Family and Biological Findings." In *Diagnostic Issues in Anorexia Nervosa and Bulimia Nervosa,* edited by D. M. Garner and P. E. Garfinkel, pp. 80–111. New York: Brunner/Mazel.

Torem, M. S. 1986. "Eating Disorders and Dissociative States." In Larocca, *Eating Disorders—Effective Care and Treatment,* pp. 141–50.

van Strien, T. 1989. "Dieting, Dissatisfaction with Figure and Sex Role Orientation in Women." *International Journal of Eating Disorders* 8, 4: 455–62.

———, and Bergers, G. 1988. "Overeating and Sex-role Orientation in Women." *International Journal of Eating Disorders* 7, 1: 89–99.

Van Buren, D. J., and Williamson, D. A. 1988. "Marital Relationships in Conflict Resolution Skills of Bulimics." *International Journal of Eating Disorders* 7, 6: 735–41.

Vanderheyden, D. A., Fekken, G. C., and Boland, F. J. 1988. "Critical Variables Associated with Binging and Bulimia in a University Population: A Factor Analytic Study." *International Journal of Eating Disorders* 7, 3: 321–29.

Yates, W. R., Sieleni, G., and Bowers, W. A. 1989. "Clinical Correlates of Personality Disorder in Bulimia Nervosa." *International Journal of Eating Disorders* 8, 4: 473–77.

Zakin, D. 1989. "Eating Disturbance, Emotional Separation, and Body Image." *International Journal of Eating Disorders* 8, 4: 411–16.

Zucker, P. 1989. "Medical Complications of Bulimia." In *The Bulimic College Student: Evaluation, Treatment, and Prevention* pp. 27–40. New York: The Haworth Press.

For Further Reading

Brownell, K. D., and Folreyt, J. P., eds. 1986. *Handbook of Eating Disorders: Physiology, Psychology, and Treatment of Obesity, Anorexia, and Bulimia.* New York: Basic Books.

Hornyak, L. M., and Baker, E. K., eds. 1989. *Experiential Therapies for Eating Disorders.* New York: Guilford Press.

Stunkard, A. J., and Stellar, E., eds. 1984. *Eating and Its Disorders.* New York: Raven Press.

Szmukler, G. I.; Slade, P. D.; Harris, P.; Benton, D.; Russell, G. F. M.; eds. 1986. *Anorexia Nervosa and Bulimic Disorders: Current Perspectives.* New York: Pergamon Press.

Thoma, H. 1967. *Anorexia Nervosa,* translated by G. Brydone. New York: International Universities Press.

Paul D. Lininger

21. Pastoral Counseling and Psychoactive Substance Use Disorders

> God grant me the serenity to accept the things I cannot change, Courage to change the things I can, And wisdom to know the difference.
>
> —The Serenity Prayer

What a strange way to begin to speak of addictions, namely, with a prayer! At least to the novice in the field of addictions it might appear to be a surprising introduction. Yet millions of individuals have uttered those same words today to their Higher Power asking for whatever they need this day to make it, one day at a time, one step at a time. Millions of individuals who are dependent or co-dependent are willing to become vulnerable through the opening of their minds and hearts, not knowing where today's journey will take them. In unison they cry out in prayer to One whom they need this day to live.

A chapter about addictions is a chapter dealing with life, love, and creativity, for it is a chapter about human beings. And if one believes that the beginning of all true life is a prayer—a communication of creative love, a fulfillment of the Genesis prayer, "Let there be light. . . . Let the earth produce every kind of living creature. . . . Let us make man in our own image (Gn 1:3; 1:24; 1:26)—then the Serenity Prayer speaks from the heart of one who has known the depth of pain and misery in human life, the web of addiction. The prayer-filled utterer is asking God for serenity, "a spirit of tranquil clarity and oneness"; acceptance, "a spirit of agreement"; courage, "a spirit that enables one to face danger with self-possession, confidence, and resolution"; and wisdom, "a spirit of understanding of what is true, right, and lasting."

In the vast field of addictions, one runs smack into the presence of the mystery of evil in human life with its contagious, manipulative pull and accompanying domineering lie in an atmosphere of denial. It muddies much, destroys many, and leaves remnants of its presence behind to be cleaned, nurtured, and restored by one's self and others. This source of pain in human life is not new to the modern world but has persisted in every era of humanity since the effects of botanical or manufactured highs were first realized. It has presented an enticing allure of relief from what one feels and knows to be true, that life is difficult. It allows momentary relief and then pulls tight as its web encircles and snares a prey. The addictive process fulfills what Heraclitus observed centuries ago: "The limits of the soul you cannot find, whatever path you may walk on; it has such a deep nature" (Heraclitus, *Fragments*).

Addictions have no favorites. They render their presence directly or indirectly. And they come in all shapes and sizes: a parent, spouse, child, teenager, lover, friend, neighbor, classmate, teacher, doctor, religious leader, pastoral counselor, or therapist. The pain, misery, and sorrow of such complicated issues have left few unscathed of their unbalancing effects on mind, body, emotions, or spirit. By their nature, addictions and compulsive disorders create victims and victimizers out of the afflicted and affected. Whether the person, or the one loved, happens to be an alcoholic, a drug addict, a gambler, a rebellious teenager, a workaholic, or a neurotic parent the addiction web tightens into a stranglehold of pain and misery.

Yet, the picture is not only doom and gloom. There is yet life to be fulfilled in hope. "Tell me, because it is the right time (the Kairos), that these things are discovered" (Sophocles, *Oedipus Rex*). "Spirit of Christmases Yet To Come are these images of what must be or what will be . . . (Dickens, *A Christmas Carol*). The field of addictions is a rich fertile area of therapeutic intervention especially for the pastoral counselor. It is a vivid opportunity to rejoice, empathize, and celebrate the incarnation, passion, and resurrection themes of the scriptures.

In this chapter the wish is to focus on therapeutic care for individuals of addictions. For the purpose of clarity and limitation, the aim will be targeted on the addictions of substance abuse inclusive of both alcohol and drugs. Why? Simply put, these areas are more in this author's field of competence. Although much of what will be raised or said might possibly be generalized to numerous other addictive disorders, the intention is to stay within a specific realm of psychoactive substance use. There is no effort to present a definitive statement concerning substance abuse. It is a very active field of clinical and research intervention with new insights and data being produced continuously. Instead, this is an effort to present some information, reflection, and stimulation to further the inquest of pastoral counselors into the vast field of substance abuse and other addictions.

Pastoral Counseling Includes Substance Abuse Therapy

The word addict or addiction comes from the Latin "addictus"—given over, i.e. one being awarded to another as a slave—and "addicere"—to award to (ad = to; dicere = to say), that is, to pronounce, to adjudge. The American Heritage Dictionary (1985) defines *addict* as "to devote or to give oneself habitually or compulsively to something." This devotion takes on many forms in its ensnarement of an individual, encompassing mind, body, emotion, and spirit. To treat only a singular dimension without recognition of the need to treat the whole person is to jeopardize the lasting, enriching effects of any treatment intervention.

Bill Wilson, one of the founders of AA, was greatly influenced by Jung and Jungian psychology in the treatment of alcoholism. In fact, the influence is somewhat mythological in AA history. Jung had treated a patient known in AA literature as Roland H. He was a successful American businessman who had come to Jung for treatment of his alcoholism. He had undergone a seemingly successful Jungian analysis with the master himself and had left Zurich certain that he was cured. He felt that he had such deep self-understanding that he would never again have trouble with booze. In a short time he returned to Jung, drunk and in despair. Jung told him that there was no hope. Roland H. asked if there was none at all, and Jung replied that only a major personality reorganization driven by a powerful emotion—in essence, a conversion experience—could save him. Roland H. left, still in deep despair, but Jung's words had touched something within him.

He did what AA would later call "hitting bottom," and in his despair he reached out for help. He did indeed have a conversion experience, joining the Oxford Group, an upper-middle-class revival movement popular in the 1920 and 1930s. He became and remained sober. The Oxford Movement espoused a set of "spiritual steps," which their members followed. These steps became the basis of AA's Twelve Steps. Roland H. spread the good word to his friend and fellow alcoholic Ebby Thacker, who also became sober. Ebby in turn went to visit his drinking buddy, Bill Wilson, who was drunk. Ebby told Bill the story of meeting Roland and joining the Oxford Movement. Bill Wilson entered a hospital to dry out, where he experienced some sort of "peak" or mystical experience. When he left the hospital, he too joined the Oxford Movement and remained sober.

Bill gradually pulled away from the Oxford Movement, although he borrowed a great deal from it. He began to work with alcoholics on his own. Shortly thereafter he joined with another alcoholic, Bob Smith, whom he had helped to become sober, and AA was born. Ebby Thacker didn't make it; he died in Rockland State Hospital of alcoholism. Many years later Bill Wilson wrote to Jung telling him the story, and Jung replied that Roland's "craving for alcohol was the equivalent on a low level of the spiritual thirst of our being for wholeness, expressed in medieval language: the union with God. . . . You see "alcohol" in Latin is "spiritus" and you use the same word for the highest religious experience as well as for the most depraving poison. The helpful formula therefore is: *spiritus contra spiritum*." In the language of self-psychology, the cure lies in the merger with an omnipotent self-object (Levin 1987).

There are numerous theories and treatment protocols for alcoholism and substance-abuse psychiatric disorders—the disease model, the behavior model, the self-control model, and so on. Implicit in some theoretical models of addiction are such items as control, mortality, disease, responsibility, and others. Pastoral counselors do well to become familiar with these various theories in order to understanding the dynamics of a psychiatric substance disorders.

There is another important component in working with substance-abusing clients. They elicit reactions from any mental health professional or anyone involved in the care-giving profession. Being with another who has used or is actively using a mood altering substance has an impact. A pastoral counselor needs to be attuned to his or her inner world in encounters with these clients. One way to be in touch is to ask some vital questions: Where have I personally encountered substance-abusing individuals? Perhaps it has been with myself, an immediate family member, a close friend, or colleague. Chances are, given the statistical presence of substance use in this culture, that there will not be an individual who has not had some personal experience with the problem. Another important dimension is how a pastoral counselor has learned to sit with a client who is hurting. When I hear a client broach the topic of substance use or when I elicit information concerning addictions, what happens? Do I recoil in disbelief, quickly change the topic, and move out and away (moving-on)? Or do I listen, reflect, and elicit further information about the substances involved and their impact both in the past and present life circumstances of this particular client? Either approach will elicit a transference from the client but also a substantial amount of countertransference from the counselor.

Pastoral counselors need to deepen their knowledge base of psychoactive substance-use disorders and possible therapeutic interventions if they are to assist individuals on their journey. Progress through the implementation of scientific research and clinical interventions have had an impact on the understanding and treatment of substance abuse and related substance-abuse problems. Today's knowledge base requires not only a recognition of the biological parameters of addiction with a focus on the substance and its pharmacological effects but also therapeutic reflection concerning one's personal or theoretical presumptions about addictions (Marlatt and Gordon 1985).

Enriched by the knowledge gained through these approaches, pastoral counselors can then enrich their therapeutic interventions with an approach which focuses on treatment and spiritual enpowerment of an individual. Therapeutic intervention is not just a set of rules or steps to be followed automatically but rather on a much deeper level involves a conversion experience—a kenetic experience of self-emptying in order to be filled, a *maranatha* of waiting and yearning, and finally a new birth into a fulfillment of a new reality. It is the experience of Paul on the road to Damascus, which begins with a sudden burst of illumination which frightens, overwhelms, and energizes the Apostle of Faith, motivating him into some movement of change. And then commences the second dimension of that same experience, namely, the long, drawn-out, less dramatic experience of slow change in values and perspectives. It then becomes a lifelong experience of renewal and new birth beckoning one forward to new heights and mountain tops of human experience, occasional plateaus, or to lows of uncertainty and valleys of fear. Conversion is a journeying experience on the road of life. It is the journey of faith, hope, and love not made alone but in the company of another. To traverse this journey with another who suffers the pain and frightening effects of substance abuse as a pastoral counselor is to model the salvific plan of the scriptures—to journey with another who is called out of darkness into a wonderful light. The imperative, therefore, in rendering therapeutic care to a substance-abusing person is not to cure but to care. Caring in this sense is both a difficult and arduous task.

As pastoral counselors become more numerous in the mental health field through the multiplication of training and skill development institutes and programs, they will have more and more influence on the therapeutic care of a substance-abusing population. In a recent study of the graduates of Loyola's pastoral counseling program (Lininger 1990), 36 percent of the program's graduates reported a counseling specialization in the area of substance abuse or therapeutic intervention with individuals in recovery—AA, NA, ACOA, and others. One can only imagine how that survey might look if those who selected other specializations, such as individual, family, or marital counseling, were asked about how often they have encountered substance abuse or its effects with clients in clinical settings. Substance abuse affects society as a whole and leaves its mark in so many ways that no one in today's world appears to be left unscathed directly or indirectly.

Statistically Speaking

Pastoral counselors undoubtedly will encounter substance abuse as they expand their presence in the field of counseling and begin or continue working with multiple societal groups. The following is not intended to scare the reader or to distract from the topic of addictions. Rather, it is a means to explore some of the far-reaching effects of substance abuse and to enforce the idea that pastoral counselors will be drawn into this web of human destruction.

Between 80 percent and 90 percent of the population of the United States drink at some time during their lives, and 30 percent to 40 percent of these may develop some temporary alcohol-related problems. Drinking problems which go beyond temporary alcohol difficulties and meet the criteria for alcoholism, a diagnosis indicating pervasive and persistent alcohol-related life problems, afflicts 10 percent of adult men and 3 percent to 5 percent of adult women at some time during their lives, with an even higher rate among patients attending medical clinics. The importance of genetics in the vulnerability toward alcoholism is supported by evidence from family, twin, and adoption studies in humans. First, the familial nature of alcoholism has been documented for more than one hundred years. The risk appears to increase with the number of alcoholic relatives and the closeness of the genetic relationship (Schuckit 1985). The statistics on the general population's use and dependence on substances other than alcohol, such as heroin, cocaine, LSD, PCP, and prescribed medications such as valium, xanax, dilaudid, and so on, are only roughly estimated. For instance, in the city Baltimore there are an estimated twenty-five thousand to forty thousand opioid-dependent persons in need of treatment and only about thirty-five hundred publicly funded programs for treatment intervention.

Consider some harsh statistics of the United States Bureau of Justice. In 1979 almost a third of all inmates of state prisons (274, 564) said they had drunk very heavily just before they committed the offense for which they were convicted. Twenty percent of the inmates said that they drank very heavily every day the entire year before they entered prison. About 16 percent had at some time been enrolled in an alcohol treatment program. Habitual offenders and persons convicted of assault, burglary, and rape were more likely to be very heavy drinkers than other prisoners. Whites, American Indians, and inmates aged eighteen to twenty-five were especially likely to be very heavy drinkers (BJS 1983). Another 1979 census (304, 844) revealed that 33 percent of persons serving time in state prisons reported having used drugs regularly—once a week or more often for at least a month. An estimated 100,000 prisoners had used major drugs—heroin, illicit methadone, cocaine, LSD, or PCP—regularly before their most recent arrest. These results represented a 7 percent increase of all inmates who were under the influence of a drug at the time of the time of the offense (Innes 1988). By 1986 the number of state prisoners had grown to 465, 383, of whom more than 35 percent—close to 140,000—used one or more of the major drugs regularly before arrest, and over a quarter of a million reported using other drugs, primarily marijuana or hashish, regularly (Wish and O'Neil 1989). Inmates were more likely to report they were under the influence of cocaine at the time of the offense than in earlier surveys (Innes 1988). Almost 80 percent of inmates had used drugs at some time in their lives; 52 percent had used a major drug. White inmates and female inmates were somewhat more likely than others to have been regular users of major drugs at some time in the past. In a Washington, D.C., study designed to use arrestee drug test results to forecast community drug problems (Wish and O'Neil 1989) it was reported that the percentage of arrestees who tested positive for any drug climbed from 50 percent in April 1984 to about 70 percent in June 1988. During this same period increases occurred in the city's drug-related emergency room episodes, overdose deaths, property crimes, homicides, and child abuse reports.

The above statistics might appear to be too brutal for some readers who might be trapped into thinking these are definitely not the type of clients they will choose to be involved with. People are not born as criminals, and not all offenses are freely chosen human acts. They can represent the inevitable pitfalls of losing control over one's activities and behaviors. People are people and, given the right time or circumstance, are capable of anything.

Drunk driving may appear less serious to many. However, it is a serious crime and has had significant consequences for a multitude of individuals, families, and communities. Drunk driving is a serious crime in its prevalence and its consequences. DUI or driving under the influence of alcohol is the general term for drivers who operate a motor vehicle after having consumed an intoxicant such as drugs or alcohol. DWI or driving while intoxicated refers to individuals who drive while legally intoxicated on a substance such as drugs or alcohol. The legal limits are defined by state law as a specific concentration of alcohol in the blood. In 1986 there was about one arrest for driving under the influence of an intoxicant for every eighty-eight licensed drivers. The National Highway Traffic Safety Administration estimates that perhaps as many as a quarter of a million persons were killed in alcohol-related motor vehicle crashes over the last ten years. More than 650,000 persons are injured in such crashes every year. The annual cost in property damage, medical costs, and other costs of drunk driving may total more than $24 billion (Greenfield 1988). Between 1970 and 1986 arrests for DUI increased nearly 223 percent, while the number of licensed drivers increased by 42 percent. Arrest rates for DUI were highest among 21 year olds and reached their peak in 1983 with a rate of one arrest for every thirty-nine licensed drivers of that age. Since 1983 most states have phased in new laws raising the minimum age for the purchase and sale of alcoholic beverages to twenty-one. The drop of legal sale of alcohol to those under the age of twenty-one, however, does not reflect a lowering of use of either alcohol or drugs by this same population. In fact, the trend appears to be escalating in the opposite direction. In 1986 more than 158 million persons held driver's licenses in the United States, nearly 86 percent of the population age sixteen and over. During the same year the FBI estimated that nearly 1.8 million arrests were made by state and local police agencies for driving under the influence of an intoxicating substance. The same year, 46,056 motor vehicle fatalities occurred; about 40 percent were probably alcohol related according to the National Highway Traffic Safety Administration. Prior to their arrest for DWI during the same period of 1986, convicted offenders had consumed a median of six ounces of pure alcohol (about equal to the alcoholic content of twelve bottles of beer or eight mixed drinks) in a median of four hours. About 26 percent consumed at least ten ounces of pure alcohol (equivalent to twenty beers or thirteen mixed drinks).

The prevalence of arrests for DUI must be viewed in the context of the levels of consumptions of alcoholic beverages in the United

States. In 1985 the per capita consumption of alcoholic beverages was 27.6 gallons. This was greater than the per capita consumption of coffee (25.9 gallons per U.S. resident) and milk (27.1 gallons) and was exceeded only by the consumption of soft drinks (45.6 gallons). The annual consumption of alcoholic beverages based only upon the population age twenty-one and older would equal about 34.5 gallons of beer, 3.5 gallons of wine, and 2.5 gallons of liquor per person. However, individual patterns of consumption vary. It has been estimated that a third of the adult population accounts for 95 percent of the alcohol consumed and 5 percent of the adult population accounts for half of the consumption (Greenfield 1988).

Substance abuse has had and continues to have a serious impact on society and represents a distinguishable threat to individuals and communities. It creates innocent victims and victimizers, who are themselves victims. It assists in the escalation of violence, which may be organized or episodic, as well as criminal activity such as robberies, thefts, or burglaries. This menace undermines the health (mental, physical, emotional, and spiritual), economic well-being, and social responsibility of substance abusers. It is hard to stay in school, hold a job, or care for a child when one is spending all one's energy, finances, or efforts thinking about or being overwhelmed by the need to get high. The families and friends of the substance abuser pay a dear price as their resources, both mental and physical, are strained or drained by obligations which may include care for the substance user or responsibilities that the substance user has abandoned. Society as a whole also pays a great price for the presence of substance abuse in diminished family support, economic losses related to lost work production, health-care problems, legal issues, and the costs of community activity and involvement.

Meanings

Definitions are important when one speaks about a set of clinical concepts central to the discussion of substance abuse. Some of the following definitions are borrowed terms, which this author credits to Marc A. Schuckit, M.D., who in turn admits to having borrowed from a wide variety of standard texts and published studies in an attempt to blend them into a readily usable framework.

A *drug of abuse* is any substance (note that alcohol is a drug) taken through any route of administration that alters the mood, the level of perception, or brain functioning. Such drugs include substances ranging from prescribed medications to alcohol to solvents. All these substances are capable of producing changes in mood and altered states of learning.

Drug abuse is the use of a mind-altering substance in a way that differs from generally approved medical and social practices. When the continued use of a mind-altering substance means more to the user than the problems caused by such use, the person can be said to be abusing the drug.

Dependence, also called *habituation* or *compulsive use,* connotes a psychological and/or physical need for the drug. Psychological dependence is an attribute of all drugs of abuse and centers on the user needing the drug in order to reach a maximum level of functioning or feeling of well-being. This is a subjective item almost impossible to objectively quantify and thus is of limited usefulness in making a diagnosis. Physical dependence indicates that the body has adapted physiologically to chronic use of the substance, with the development of symptoms when the drug is stopped or withdrawn. There are two important aspects to physical dependence: a) *tolerance* is the toleration of higher and higher doses of the drug or the need for higher and higher doses to achieve the same effects; b) *withdrawal* or an *abstinence syndrome* is the appearance of physiological symptoms when the drug is stopped too quickly (Schuckit 1990).

Drug Classification

In order to clarify what types of psychoactive substances are being discussed, it is helpful for the reader to know some of the drug classifications. The intention is not to give an exhaustive list of details about each drug class and the successive effects of use. The drugs discussed here all affect the brain or the central nervous system (CNS). There are myriads of compendiums available to assist mental health professionals in their understanding of the pharmacological effects of these substances. Any pastoral counselor would do well to purchase one or more of these volumes; especially recommended is the Physicians' Desk Reference (PDR). Specific drug actions depend on the route of administration, the dose, the presence or absence of other drugs, and the client's clinical condition.

CNS depressants depress the excitable tissues at all levels of the brain. This depressant class of drugs includes alcohol, hypnotics, and anti-anxiolitic drugs (valium, xanax, librium, barbituates, qualudes, and seconal). CNS stimulants stimulate brain tissues through the blockage of the actions of inhibitory nerve cells or by the release of transmitter substances from the cells, or by direct action of the drugs themselves. This stimulant class includes amphetamines, speed, crystal meth, dexadrine, ritalin, cocaine, and crack. Related to this group are caffeine and nicotine. Opiate analgesics (narcotics) are used to decrease pain; they include morphine and other alkaloids of opium and synthetic derivatives. The opioids include almost all painkilling medications, that is, darvon, codeine, percodan, demerol, heroin, methadone, and talwin. Marijuana contains the active ingredient tetrahydrocannabinol (THC). Today's research does not consider marijuana a harmless drug. Hallucinogens (psychedelics) have the predominant effect of producing hallucinations, usually visual in nature. They have no medical usefulness. Hallucinogens include such drugs as PCP ("angel dust"), LSD, mescaline, peyote, psilocybin, and mushrooms. Inhalants are various substance used by the consumer to alter the state of consciousness, producing primarily dizziness and confusion. Inhalants include glues, solvents, aerosols, nitrous oxide, amyl/butyl nitrate, and a number of household/garden products. Over-the-counter drugs are also taken by abusers to help induce feelings of light-headedness and euphoria. This class includes substances sold without prescription for treatment of constipation, pain, nervousness, insomnia, and other common complaints. The sedative or hypnotic medications are the most frequently abused because they contain antihistamines, which are desired for the effects. Steroids, ever present in the body-building culture or physical mystic, are another example of substances used and abused for their euphoric effects, with potentially devastating consequences. This is a simplistic breakdown of some of the drug classifications. Enrichment and development of one's knowledge of these substances is encouraged.

Assessment Affects Treatment

There are many important elements to consider when a pastoral counselor enters into a therapeutic relationship with a client who is currently or is vulnerable to becoming an abuser of substances. Many assessment tools have been proposed for the proper assessment of a client's substance-abuse history and the degree of impairment. There are pros and cons offered for each system of evaluation. Also, because a pastoral counselor's graduate studies and professional development training may have overlooked this important dimension of client assessment, it would benefit his or her professional development of any pastoral counselor to become familiar and comfortable with the utilization of at least one professional instrument. A chapter dealing with addictions would be derelict of its responsibilities to the reader if some sort of evaluation and assessment instrument or technique were not discussed.

Many theories have been advanced to explain why individuals abuse alcohol or drugs. Different theories have stressed social, cultural, economic, genetic, and pharmacological factors as the central causes of a psychoactive substance use disorder. Family pathology, peer pressure, and individual psychopathology have also been reported as casual factors. It would be appropriate to presume that all of these factors play an important part in the development of substance-use problems in at least some individuals, and substance abuse in most individuals is determined by a combination of influences including those mentioned and many left unmentioned.

A pastoral counselor is faced with the arduous task of attempting to assess and evaluate the behavior of a particular client. Any observable behavior bears the impact of more than what is on the surface. A client's behavior may be affected by current life circumstances. An individual's predisposition also needs to be considered. What individual vulnerabilities are present, such as heredity, physical factors, illness, and family environment, including sexual or physical abuse. Ecological predispositions include peer group pressure, activity, culture, community, and school; these possibly influence a client's behavior. Finally, opportunities and situations have a powerful effect on behavior; items such as access to drugs or alcohol, and potential celebrations with peers or family members where there is direct or indirect insistence on drinking or drugging behaviors.

Finding out "what is what" is the difficult task of any mental health professional. This author has found it useful to collect a comprehensive history of each client, paying specific attention to the presence and impact of substance use or abuse on the individual's personal development, social interaction, and current life problems. Generally, when working with a substance-abusing client, the therapist does not enjoy the luxury of having an extended period of time to collect a comprehensive history of the client's history. These clients most often present for treatment in the midst of crisis and generally bolt from treatment when they have experienced some symptomatic relief—the family tension subsided, the boss didn't say anything the next day, or they've apologized again and everything is all right. The following psycho-social interview of a client is designed to elicit the most client information and data in a brief period of time. The therapist is in control of the interview and can ask for further elaboration at any time. However, the therapist should be aware that this is a primary assessment of the client's need and will be expanded upon during ongoing therapeutic involvement with the individual. The information originally given might even change during ongoing therapy. The interview is based on the Phipps Psychosocial Assessment procedure utilized in the Johns Hopkins Hospital, Department of Psychiatry.

In an open and non-judgmental atmosphere the mental health professional, who in this case happens to be the pastoral counselor, will ask about a client's unique personal history. This requires a deep sense of reverence, respect, and dignity. Regardless of what one might hear as a client relays the circumstances of his or her life experience, be aware that operative in the mindset of this person is a feeling of immense shame and a damaged self-esteem.

A. Client's Chief Complaint

1. Who is this person?
2. Why has he or she come to see you now?

B. Client's Family History

1. Start with the client's parents: married, separated, divorced, never married?
2. Then, for each parent individually: age, education, general health, the cause of death if deceased, personality, quality of relationship to the client, any history of substance abuse or other psychiatric disturbance.
3. Siblings: same as #2.
4. Family's social position and home atmosphere. Was there any history of physical or sexual abuse in the family?

C. Client's Personal History

Health:

Date of birth, place, mother's health during pregnancy, length of pregnancy, type of delivery, any birth complications, general health as a baby, developmental milestones, childhood behavioral abnormalities, any childhood illness, injuries, or accidents requiring medical treatment?

Education:

Age school begun and finished, highest grade completed, grades including the best and worst years, any special classes for the gifted or learning impaired, quality of client's relationships with peers and teachers, truancy or suspensions or expulsions, other behavioral problems? Summarize educational strengths and weaknesses.

Occupation:

Age of client's first job, number and type of different positions held prior to age eighteen, number and type of different positions since age eighteen, the longest period of regular employment and the position held, nature of any warnings and reasons for any suspensions, firings, or job abandonment (were any of these drug related?), current employment status, the length of current employment, client's degree of satisfaction with current employment?

Legal:

Summarize any illegal activities the client may have been involved in *prior to* age fifteen and note whether the client was arrested or would have been arrested if caught, any periods of court involvement, probation, incarceration in detention centers and the reasons. Note if any of the client's activities involved drugs or alcohol use. Was the activity while the client was intoxicated, attempting to get high, or while in detoxification from any substance? Summarize any illegal activities since age fifteen and note whether arrested or not, any periods of incarcerations, parole or probation, and current legal status. If the client is on probation or required to report to a court officer, find out the probation or parole officer's name.

Sexual History:

For females: age at menarche, pattern, problems, last period. For males: age at puberty, any associated problems?

Sexual inclinations and practices; how did the client acquire sexual information, masturbation experience, age at first sexual intercourse, sexual orientation, number of sexual partners, safe-sex and contraception practices? Level of the client's satisfaction with his or her sexual life. As this history is collected remain attuned to whether or not the incidences and practices reported involved any substance use.

Dating History:

1. Age the client started dating, number of relationships, longest period a relationship lasted, reasons for breakups occurring before the age of fifteen? Were breakups substance related either by the client or by the partner?
2. Number and length of dating relationships since age fifteen

and the typical reason for their ending. Note the longest sexually monogamous relationship.

3. Summarize the quality of current dating relationship (length of time, current problems). Does the client's significant other abuse any substances? Does the partner know about the client's substance abuse? Summarize any strengths or weaknesses in the client's current relationship.

Marital History:

1. Current marital status and number of prior marriages, length and reasons for any separations or divorce. Was substance abuse involved by the client or the spouse?
2. Summarize the quality of the current marital relationship (length of time, current problems). Does spouse abuse any substances? Does spouse know about the client's substance abuse? Summarize any strengths or weaknesses in the client's current relationship.
3. If client has any children (from present or previous relationships), note ages, general health and psychological adjustment, any substance use, and, if living elsewhere, level of the client's involvement.

D. Social/Recreational Activities

1. Social relations (number of close friends, frequency of contact, extent to which these relationships represent positive or negative influences for the client). Note any recent changes in these relations.
2. Client's interests, including type and amount of time typically involved. Note any changes.
3. Client's self-attitude: realistic or unrealistic? chronically self-conscious or self-doubting? grandiose? etc.
4. Client's ambitions and current goals.

E. Religious Affiliation

1. Client's religious affiliation, experience, family and personal milieu and religious practices.
2. Client's self-reported spirituality and its impact on their life experience.
3. Client's degree of satisfaction with current religious or spiritual experience.

F. Strengths and Weaknesses

Client's assessment of their own strengths and weaknesses.

G. Medical History

1. List past and current major surgeries, accidents, illness and medical care. Note age and any substance-use relationship.
2. List any medications currently prescribed for the client.

H. Psychiatric History

1. Ages, locations, lengths, reasons, types, medications, individual or group therapies, outpatient or inpatient care.
2. Note any recent hospitalizations or concurrent outpatient mental health care and type of treatment.

I. Substance Abuse History

1. Summarize any substance use including both alcohol and drugs (e.g., age of onset for all substances reported, routes of administration, changes in patterns of use, age of onset of life problems, and incidents).
2. Duration and types of outpatient, inpatient, or long-term residential treatment (e.g., detox, pharmacological intervention, half-way house, AA, NA, etc.).
3. Note any episodes of abstinence for three months of longer and differences in client's issues during those periods. Stated reasons for relapse.
4. Summarize frequency and/or amounts for all substances used by the client in the past thirty days.

J. History of the Present Illness

1. What has been happening in the most recent past for this client? Why has he or she come to treatment at this time? What symptoms or problems are being exhibited? How does the client interpret the recent events?

K. Summary and General Assessment

1. Include a summary of the client's current mental state: general presentation, behavior, speech, sample of talk, mood, delusions, illusions, hallucinations, obsessions, compulsions or phobias, any suicidal or homicidal ideation.
2. Include a brief cognitive assessment (e.g., Mini-Mental State Exam or Quick IQ Test).

L. Treatment Plan Recommendation

Psychoactive Substance Use Disorder

Having ascertained a comprehensive psycho-social assessment of the client, where does a therapist turn next? The main objective now is to evaluate the client for an actual psychiatric diagnosis of substance abuse, whether that be alcohol or non-alcohol dependence/abuse. Alcoholism or any substance abuse diagnosis in itself is not a personality disorder, nor is it a manifestation of another psychiatric condition. Rather, it is a primary disorder, characterized by drinking or drugging to a point at which the user and the environment are seriously damaged. It is a disease insofar as it is compulsive and not under the control of the user (Levin 1987). It is a chronic illness; left untreated its symptoms and characteristics as well as physical effects will only worsen. Personality disorders are certainly associated with alcoholism and substance abuse, but they are not themselves the psychoactive substance abuse disorder, however much of the substance use may be a futile attempt to treat a personality disturbance. Substance abuse, both alcohol and non-alcohol, is likewise an independent diagnosis of any other DSM III-R Axis I diagnosis, and it requires a developed skill for a therapist to rule out other concomitant psychiatric disorders. Obviously, the more a counselor learns about substance-use disorders and their accompanying intoxication and withdrawal effects, the more he or she should be able to differentiate between various symptoms and psychiatric disturbance. The substance abuse, the drinking or drugging, must be addressed before the client can improve or find the inner strength needed to deal with other psychiatric problems.

The American Psychiatric Association in its most current edition of the DSM III-R contains a category of "Psychoactive Substance Use Disorders." In this category substance-use disorders are classified according to their severity as either "substance abuse" or "substance dependence." Since the DSM III-R definitions of psychoactive substance use disorders are comprehensive, they are cited in their entirety:

PSYCHOACTIVE SUBSTANCE DEPENDENCE (DSM III-R)

A. At least three of the following:

(1) substance often taken in larger amounts or over a longer period than the person intended;
(2) persistent desire or one or more unsuccessful efforts to cut down or control substance use;
(3) a great deal of time spent in activities necessary to get the substance, taking the substance, or recovering from its effects;

(4) frequent intoxication or withdrawal symptoms when expected to fulfill major role obligations at work, school, or home, or when substance use is physically hazardous;
(5) important social, occupational, or recreational activities given up or reduced because of substance use;
(6) continued substance use despite knowledge of having a persistent or recurrent social, psychological, or physical problem that is caused or exacerbated by the use of the substance;
(7) marked tolerance: need for markedly increased amounts of the substance in order to achieve intoxication or desired effect, or markedly diminished effect with continued use of the same amount;
(8) characteristic withdrawal symptoms;
(9) substance often taken to relieve or avoid withdrawal symptoms.

B. Some symptoms of the disturbance have persisted for at least one month, or have occurred repeatedly over a longer period of time.

C. Severity: Mild, Moderate, Severe.

D. Remission: In Partial Remission—some use and some symptoms in past six months; In Full Remission—no use or use with no symptoms during past six months.

PSYCHOACTIVE SUBSTANCE ABUSE (DSM III-R)

A. A maladaptive pattern of psychoactive substance use indicated by at least one of the following:
(1) continued use despite knowledge of having a persistent or recurrent social, occupational, psychological, or physical problem that is caused or exacerbated by use of the psychoactive substance;
(2) recurrent use in situations in which use is physically hazardous.

B. Some symptoms of disturbance have persisted for at least one month, or have occurred repeatedly over a longer period of time.

C. Never met the criteria for Psychoactive Substance Dependence for this substance.

The criteria for a psychoactive substance-use disorder are clearly delineated by the DSM III-R but the difficulty for any counselor is eliciting the necessary information from a client. Again, this can be accomplished by a counselor with the assistance of some evaluative tools. Perhaps the reader will find it useful to utilize the following evaluative questions to assist diagnosis of a psychoactive substance-use disorder for a client. The questions are based on the Structured Clinical Interview for DSM III-R: SCID (Spitzer 1990) and are proposed as suggestions to assist the therapist. It is recommended that a counselor seek some additional training and skill development in the area of psychoactive substance use with an emphasis on evaluation and diagnosis.

PSYCHOACTIVE SUBSTANCE-USE DISORDER EVALUATION

A. Alcohol Dependence or Abuse

1. Rule out questions:
    1. What are your drinking habits like? How much do *you drink?*
    2. Was there ever a period in your life when you drank too much? Has alcohol ever caused you problems? What problems did it cause?
    3. Has anyone ever objected to your drinking? Why?

2. If the client acknowledges problems or excessive drinking, then proceed:
    1. Did you often find that when you started drinking you ended up drinking much more than you were planning? What about drinking for a much longer period of time than you were planning?
    2. Did you try to cut down or stop drinking alcohol? Did you ever actually stop? Or how many times did you try to cut down or stop altogether? Did you want to stop or cut down? Is this something you kept worrying about?
    3. Did you spend a lot of time drinking, being high or hung over?
    4. Did you ever drink while doing something where it might have been dangerous (driving, child-care, operating some

work equipment, etc.)? How about attempting to do or missing something important while you were drinking, intoxicated, or hungover? (going to school, to work, to an appointment, etc.)?

5. Did you drink so often that you started to drink instead of working or spending time at hobbies or with your family or friends?
6. Did your drinking cause problems with other people, such as with family members or people at work? Did your drinking cause you psychological problems, such as getting depressed, or physical problems? Did it make a physical problem worse? Did you keep on drinking anyway?
7. Did you find that you needed to drink a lot more in order to get high than you did when you first started drinking? How much more? Did you find that when you drank the same amount, it had much less effect than before?
8. Did you ever have the shakes when you cut down or stopped drinking? Was it so obvious that other people noticed?
9. After not drinking for a few hours or more, did you often drink to keep yourself from getting the shakes or becoming sick?
10. For how long a time were you having these symptoms?
11. When did you last have problems with alcohol?

B. Non-Alcohol Psychoactive Substance Dependence or Abuse

1. Rule out questions:
   1. Have you *ever* taken any drug to get high, to sleep better, to lose weight, or to change your mood? (Refer to the earlier mentioned drug list for classification of drugs.)
   2. How often would you say you used that drug in a one month period?
   3. Did you ever get hooked or dependent on a prescribed medication?
   4. Did you ever take much more than was prescribed?
   5. Are you using any medications now? drugs?
   6. Was there ever a period of at least six months when you were using a lot of different drugs at the same time? During that period did you always have a drug of choice? (Polydrug Use)

2. If the client acknowledges use or excessive drugging, then proceed: (*Remember to ask about each drug class independently.*)
   1. Did you often find that when you started using you ended up

using much more than you were planning? What about using for a much longer period of time than you were planning?

2. Did you try to cut down or stop using alcohol? Did you ever actually stop? Or how many times did you try to cut down or stop altogether? Did you want to stop or cut down? Is this something you kept worrying about?
3. Did you spend a lot of time using, being high or hung over?
4. Did you ever use while doing something where it might have been dangerous (driving, child-care, operating some work equipment, etc.)? How about attempting to do or missing something important while you were using, intoxicated, or hungover (going to school, to work, or an appointment)?
5. Did you use so often that you started to use instead of working or spending time at hobbies or with your family or friends?
6. Did your using cause problems with other people, such as with family members or people at work? Did your using cause you psychological problems, like getting depressed, or physical problems? Did it make a physical worse? Did you keep on using anyway?
7. Did you find that you needed to use a lot more in order to get high than you did when you first started using? How much more? Did you find that when you used the same amount, it had much less effect than before?
8. Have you ever had withdrawal symptoms, that is, felt sick when you cut down or stopped using (drug)? What symptoms did you have? (Note the characteristic withdrawal symptoms for drug class.)
9. After not using for a few hours or more, did you often use to keep yourself from getting sick with (withdrawal symptoms)?
10. For how long a time were you having these symptoms?
11. When did you last have problems with (drug)?

Case Studies

Case 1

The following is a case presentation utilizing the above stated assessment and evaluation. The intention is to assist a counselor in understanding the degree of information which can be made available in a timely fashion for clinical therapeutic intervention on behalf of a client. The client in this case is enrolled in a hospital based clinical treatment program. The client's current drug use and symptomatic clinical presentation was to be assessed and evaluated. If necessary, a psychiatric consultation would be sought. The total evaluative process including both assessment and diagnosis was completed in ninety minutes.

Chief Complaint:
Client is a 37-year-old married white male who is the father of one seven year old son. Client is employed full-time in a general factory position. Client sought treatment after a recent psychiatric hospitalization for a drug overdose and possible suicidal attempt.

Family History:
Both of the client's parents are living and have been married about forty-three years.
Father: Client's father is sixty years old, a retired factory worker, who is described by the client as currently having some medical problems related to "heart valves." Client is unsure of medical diagnosis and current medical treatment. Father has an eighth grade education level. Client describes his relationship with his father as "poor" and "not close." His father was a "strict, often cruel disciplinarian who would have his children kneel on hard peas for punishment." Client denies any psychiatric problems or treatment for his father. Client reports his father "occasionally used alcohol" and denies any problems associated with ongoing use, including discipline practices.
Mother: Client's mother is also sixty years old, in good health, and currently is employed part-time as a sales clerk. Client denies any substance use or psychiatric problems for his mother. Client describes the relationship with his mother "a strong supportive relationship . . . someone I could always count on, even today."
Siblings: Client is the second oldest of five children (three brothers, one sister). Client's older brother is forty years old, married, no children, employed full-time, has a history of alcohol related problems, and is considered "cold and distant" by the client. Client's younger sister is thirty-four years old, divorced with two children, unemployed, has a history of drug problems, notably significant PCP use, and has little contact with client. Another brother is thirty-two years old, employed full-time as general laborer, was born prematurely, and attended special education classes for developmental problems. He is married with no children and has alcohol related problems.

Client's youngest brother is thirty years old, married with three children, unemployed, has a history of psychiatric problems and treatment (client not sure of diagnosis), is positive for a history of drug and alcohol related problems, and has legal problems related to drug use.
Maternal Grandfather: Positive history for alcohol abuse and related problems.
Maternal Uncle: Described as having "close relationship" to client during developmental years. Positive history for alcohol abuse and related problems.

Personal History:
Client was born April 10, 1953, product of a full-term vaginal delivery without complications. General health as an infant and young child was good. Reached developmental milestones without complications.

Education History:
Client attended Catholic grammar school for grades one through eight. He was considered a B+ student. Switched to public school for the beginning of ninth grade. He began using drugs while in the ninth grade and began experiencing declining grades, increased problems with peers and teachers; was suspended 3×'s for fighting; initiated fights "usually related to his small stature" at least 1× per week. Remained in public school till end of tenth grade. In the eleventh grade client was remanded to juvenile court and charged with being "incorrigible" and was placed in a "training school." Spent nine months in a youth center and then six months at forestry camp. Client then returned to regular school system but "just quite attending" due to frequent fighting and truancy. Client received a GED at age twenty-five, while in jail. Client has recently enrolled in a community college but has not chosen a specific degree field. He is attempting to "see if he likes and can handle school."

Occupational History:
Client was first employed at age fifteen with his favorite uncle in general construction work. Lost job due to drug use. Till age of twenty-two client held a number of part-time positions generally lasting a few months and left jobs or was fired due to drug related problems. Longest employment episode was four years as a factory employee; left employment due to being arrested on drug related charges. Currently employed as a machine operator in a manufacturing plant. Client feels "OK" about current employment but is not

satisfied and would prefer an employment opportunity "with more personal reward such as working with kids."

Legal History:
Prior to age fifteen client had legal problems which began after he started using alcohol, i.e. car theft, stealing, vandalism, and fighting. Client during same period ran away from home with the intention of not returning four times, and on one occasion "bought a bus ticket to California." Charged with being "incorrigible" and sent to youth center and forestry camp for fifteen months.

After age fifteen, client has a history of illegal activity for B&E, stealing, theft, drug sales, etc., all related to drug use. Client has been arrested four times: age twenty-two, drug charge, possession, received probation; age twenty-three, drug charge, possession, probation; age twenty-six, drug charge, possession, sentenced to two years in jail, served nine months, paroled; age thirty-three, disorderly conduct and assault, alcohol related, fined $100; currently, no charges or probation.

Sexual History:
Sexually active at age thirteen. First sexual intercourse was at age fifteen. Has had five sexual partners in his lifetime. All sexual activity has been heterosexual. Denies any homosexual involvement including during period of incarceration.

Dating History:
Began dating at age thirteen. Client's longest monogamous relationship was with his current wife. They have been together twelve years and have been married nine years. Client describes the marriage as a "good and supportive relationship." They have one child, a son who is seven years old. Client describes his relationship with his son as close.

Social/Recreational Activities:
Client enjoys bowling with coworkers on a weekly league. Most other social activities are family oriented, such as shopping, eating-out, or visiting with extended family members. Considers himself very active with son, especially in his school events. Complains of needing "more couple events with wife."

Special Interests:
Enjoys doing jig-saw puzzles, reading, and watching sporting events on TV.

Ambitions/Goals:
"To be a good father and husband; go to college and get a degree; and to get out of the labor field and into a more enjoyable type of job like working with kids."

Religious Affiliation:
Client says he believes in God and does pray in an informal manner. He feels something is lacking in that expression of his spirituality, but for right now any organized religious expression is out of the question. Client is a non-practicing Roman Catholic. His son does attend Catholic school. Client says at times he would like to be more involved in his religion but feels unmotivated to attend due to feeling "they are always preaching judgment with little understanding of the problems in life people really have."

Self-Perceptive Strengths/Weaknesses:
Strengths equal "positive thinking, trying to be my best, and enjoying putting forth effort into things." Weakness is "drug use and trying to stay off altogether."

Medical History:
Client experienced a torn leg cartilage and head injury at seventeen years old. Received 175 stitches in his head due to the injury. Has had no physical problems related to that accident. A few years ago client noticed an increase in stomach problems with cramping and nausea and was evaluated for possible ulcer. The diagnosis was negative. Current health is "good" except for the symptoms related in history of present illness section. Client is on no medications.

Psychiatric History:
Client was seen one time by a psychiatrist at age thirteen for evaluation due to behavioral problems. At age thirty-seven, client was hospitalized at a state-run psychiatric facility after a drug overdose. He was seen and evaluated by a mental health professional immediately after discharge and referred to ongoing clinical drug treatment program.

Substance Abuse History:
Client began using alcohol at age twelve. At age thirteen client began using marijuana, barbituates, inhalants, and stimulants (other than cocaine). At age fifteen client began using cocaine, hallucinogens

(PCP), sedative-hypnotics (valium), and narcotics (heroin, dilaudid, percodan). At age thirty-six client began using other nonprescriptive over-the-counter medications, notably sleeping pills.

Substance Abuse Diagnosis:
Client met criteria for the following psychoactive substance abuse disorders:
Alcohol Dependence—Severe—In full remission
Sedative—Hypnotic Dependence—Severe—In full remission
Opiod Dependence—Severe—Current
Other Nonprescription Substance Dependence—Current Cocaine Abuse

Drug Treatment History:
Client has been in substance abuse treatment five times in his lifetime. First three treatment episodes were abstinence modalities including detoxification and rehabilitation of twenty-eight days. Fourth episode was a methadone detox modality. Fifth episode was methadone maintenance.

History of Present Illness:
Client reported he began using over-the-counter nonprescription sleeping pills about nine months ago to help him sleep. Client reported at that time he was experiencing increased sleeping problems due to work-related stress. Client's use of sleeping pills escalated from recommended dose levels to five to eight tablets per day. Client began experiencing increased family and marital problems with continued escalation of drug intake. Client's sleeping pill use escalated to ten to sixteen tablets per day for a period of last ninety days prior to drug over-dose. In the last thirty days prior to overdose, client reported using sixteen to twenty tablets per day.

On the specific day of the drug overdose, client reported remembering he was experiencing increased tension with his spouse about his pill use and family problems. He argued with his wife and choked her during the argument. Immediately after the incident he left the house, drove to the pharmacy, and purchased two packages of sleeping pills (thirty-two tablets). Client returned home and consumed the thirty-two pills in a suicidal attempt. He was found unconscious on the bathroom floor by his wife.

He was taken to the emergency room for treatment. His stomach was pumped, and his condition evaluated. On the following morning he was transferred to a state psychiatric facility for ongoing in-patient care. Client remained hospitalized for one week. Client denies use of any illicit or over-the-counter medications since discharge from in-patient care.

Client also reported that his wife has been using over-the-counter diet pills to help control her weight gain problems. He reports being disturbed by his spouse's refusal to be involved in his current drug treatment.

Likewise, client noted he has experienced increased caffeine consumption since his discharge from in-patient care. Reports daily consumption of at least three pots of coffee daily and about three ten-ounce bottles of caffeinated beverages daily.

He now reports he has been experiencing increased dizziness, increased numbness in head and hands, nightmares, increased feeling of jitteriness and tremors, orthostatic hypotension, constipation, and marked insomnia since discontinuing sleeping pill use.

Mental State Exam:
Client is about 5′5″ tall and weighs 135 lbs. He appears much younger than his stated chronological age. He was neat, appropriately dressed, and interactive with good eye contact through out the interview. He reported experiencing decreased sleep with marked periods of insomnia, appetite loss without weight gain or loss but "has been trying to force himself to eat more." Energy level has decreased with feelings of "being tired quickly." Decreased concentration, which was noted in client's ability to complete successfully a jig-saw puzzle. Poor memory, which client excused as related to lifelong memory problems since involvement in chronic drug use. Sporadic psychomotor agitation which has been noticed by others. Reported decreased libido and decrease in sexual performance due to "generally being distracted during sexual activity and loses desire." Speech: normal in rate, rhythm, and tone. Self-attitude is "pretty good . . . looking forward to the future." Mood is "somewhat depressed . . . and more emotional at times when thinking about all that has happened in these last months." Denies thoughts of death. Denies hallucinations, illusions, delusions, obsessional-compulsive behaviors or suicidal/homicidal ideation.

Mini Mental Status Exam: 30

Treatment

The client whose case history was just reviewed is indeed in need of positive treatment intervention. But where does a pastoral counselor begin?

The following outlines the process that was used and the philosophy which motivated treatment intervention. This approach to the treatment of substance abusers is based on two assumptions. First, it is assumed that the underlying causes which motivate substance abuse exist in the present. Understanding an individual's past is both helpful and necessary in understanding the evolution of the client's belief systems and patterns of behavior that are presently maladaptive. The immediate emphasis, however, is on changing the current behavior before proceeding with any necessary treatment interventions for co-morbid psychiatric diagnoses or problem solving. The counselor working with an actively using individual does not have the luxury of waiting several weeks to collect a self-reported history of a client. Waiting would seem to be an injustice to client treatment when an immediate intervention is necessary and recommended. The focus of treatment intervention at this phase of the therapeutic relationship is geared primarily on identifying and challenging maladaptive belief systems and behaviors that exist in the present and on improving skills and changing present life circumstances. Crisis intervention has a way of breaking through many of the walls that generally take weeks for a client and therapist to dismantle.

Second, it is assumed that whatever the underlying causes of an individual's substance abuse, the individual's substance abuse will diminish as the client becomes more effective in dealing with the normal and abnormal problems of living and more proficient at learning constructive ways of satisfying basic physical and emotional needs.

If stabilization and clinical improvement are desirous in the care and treatment of any client, then the primary treatment goal in working with a client who is using psychoactive substances is to affect the client's current behavior. Namely, the imperative is to stop the current pattern of use. The successive goals to be met will continue to deal with other principal goals and secondary treatment areas, such as:

Employment: Employment is beneficial in many ways provided that income, job satisfaction, and opportunities for advancement are consistent with the client's abilities and aspirations. A job structures time, helps combat boredom, promotes self-esteem through economic self-sufficiency, and provides for potential social opportunities with others who are not substance users. To obtain a satisfactory level of employment some clients will need to go to school or obtain training.

Interpersonal Relationships: Long-term abstinence from psychoactive substance use is unlikely for clients who maintain social contacts with people who are actively using either alcohol or non-alcohol substances, even occasionally. Healthy relationships with nonusers are a vital source of support for individuals attempting to remain abstinent.

Living Accommodations: It is important that a client's living accommodations provide adequate space, privacy, and a reasonably attractive living environment. It is of even greater importance that they be located away from environments in which drug use occurs. There is evidence that exposure to even the surroundings in which they once used psychoactive substances can induce cravings in former users. Many clients have experienced relapses which occurred simply because they ran into an old friend who offered them a "taste."

Recreation: Hustling for drugs has been described as an exciting and challenging occupation, and many addicts have rated the satisfaction involved in buying and hustling as equal to the satisfaction of the actual drug "high" itself. It has also been noted that many clients who get their drug use under control and obtain good jobs subsequently become bored and apathetic. In most instances these clients appear to have developed little in the way of social or recreational activities to provide them with the stimulation and excitement they once experienced hustling drugs on the streets or in a bar.

Family Life: Some recent studies have found that addicts tend to maintain unusually close contact with their parents and, in many instances, continue to live with a parent well into adult life. Wherever possible clients should be encouraged to establish healthy relationships with family members. However, it must be recognized that existing relationships may not necessarily be supportive of growth to maturity in the client and some intervention may be necessary in order to make the family's influence a constructive one. Where clients remain in regular contact with parents, spouses, or siblings, these relatives should be enlisted in the treatment process so that the counselor can be aware of their positive and negative influences on the client, capitalizing on the former and working to diminish the latter.

Self-Esteem: While positive accomplishments in the areas mentioned above will increase self-esteem and self-confidence, most clients require assistance to help them use more recent accomplishments rather than the failures and negative behaviors of the past as the basis for self-evaluation. Typically, clients continue to evaluate themselves negatively long after desirable changes in behavior and achievement warrant a more positive self-assessment. Families are notoriously slow to recognize and reinforce clients when they begin to do well. This is not surprising in that families have usually seen such improvements in the past only to be disappointed by yet another relapse. However, it is also true that family members sometimes have their own reasons for not wanting the client to become healthy. In any event, it is common for clients who are beginning to do well to find that their families are more inclined to dwell on their past negative behaviors than to recognize the merit of their present behavior.

There is no simple formula for increasing self-esteem, although common sense suggests that self-esteem will not increase unless the client substitutes positive behaviors for the negative behaviors which have decreased self-esteem in the past. Success in any legitimate endeavor tends to increase self-esteem, although changes in self-esteem may lag far behind actual achievements.

Unfortunately, low self-esteem causes clients to expect failure, so that they either do not try new endeavors (jobs, school, etc.) or they try but give up quickly. Counselors should be alert to the fact that many clients feel profoundly pessimistic about their ability to succeed at anything. It will take consistent and continuing support for such clients to try and to keep trying, even when they are doing well and experiencing success.

Client Responsibility: By their seemingly hopeless presenting features clients very often indirectly entice a counselor into taking responsibility for them. A counselor is well advised to recognize and deal with this countertransference issue before it enters into the treatment process. Emphasis is on the client, even a small amount at a time, to attempt to bring about constructive change in his or her life. Clients are held responsible for their actions and are expected to put forth the necessary effort. If a counselor enters into a therapeutic contract with a client, then the prescribed contract is binding on both individuals if its therapeutic effect and value is to be felt. Remember that manipulation of individuals and situations is a primary component of substance abuse. Because substance abusers experiences in their families and in later relationships have been marked by inconsistency and unpredictability, the consistent setting of limits is a fundamental part of the treatment process. Even termination from therapy, which might be viewed by some as a negative impact or too harsh, may actually be a very positive intervention on behalf of a client.

The client mentioned in the extended case study received a total medical evaluation and psychiatric consultation to rule-out any concomitant illness or disorder. In the final determination the client was viewed as suffering from the protracted withdrawal effects of the nine month history of over-the-counter sleeping pill use, which was being exacerbated by his continued excessive caffeine use. The severity of withdrawal symptoms from any psychoactive substance are measured by the amount of drug taken and the period of time over which the drug was used. Education therapy was the chosen modality of intervention. The client's symptomatic complaints would continue for at least a few weeks. He needed to be aware of the CNS effects of his continued use of a substance over a long period of time and what withdrawal effects were to be expected. The client was also informed that the chronic use of a tolerance-inducing drug (caffeine), which has a moderate to rapid elimination rate, makes that compound a good candidate for producing physical dependence as manifested by biochemical, physiological, or behavioral disruptions occurring upon termination of drug administration. It was hoped that by explaining what a substance does while in the system and noting what phenomenological effects were to be expected with cessation of the drug use the client would have a better understanding of his symptoms, management of his ongoing care, and a more trusting relationship with his counselor.

The client was asked to cease all caffeine consumption and to chart the withdrawal effects he noticed and to note when he felt they had cleared. The client did experience some real anxiety about ceasing his caffeine intake, and when he stopped he noted increased headaches, lethargy, fatigue, facial flushing, and orthostatic hypotension. After a few days he noted a change in his other symptoms as well, leading to eventual extinction of their presence. The client remained abstinent from all substances of abuse.

The client was also informed that if there were no changes in the target symptoms he had presented within an acceptable time frame then his treatment protocol would be reevaluated. Having the client be an active participant of his care helped utilize another significant therapeutic intervention known as *mastery.* Mastery through small calculated growth steps helped boost his self-perception from one of self-defeatism to self-enpowerment. He showed an increased self-pride and confidence in his ability to reach some of his goals.

He was then able to begin to move on to some of the deeper counseling issues—self-esteem, self-image, marital problems, personal choices, and growth. As he began to challenge his own questions of life the client more than once came close to relapse of his substance use. And assessing for possible relapse criteria is essential to the work of therapy. He is currently in therapy and making positive strides. Along with individual therapy the client has become active in a self-support group—Narcotics Anonymous (NA). Group support and dynamics are a vibrant aspect of substance abuse treatment in order to help break through the denial and manipulative components of these disorders. The more components of care or treatment services used in the treatment of these clients, the better the chances are for the outcomes to be positive.

Conclusion

Pastoral counselors add an important dimension to the mental health profession. They utilize their professional training as a counselor coupled with a belief of human existence which validates people's spiritual dimension. As mental health professionals they are very active in the therapeutic care and treatment of individuals, families, and groups in which they utilize a wide spectrum of therapeutic interventions. Substance abuse, whether involving the drug known as alcohol or use of another class of psychoactive substances alone or in conjunction with one another, is a powerful and growing problem in this culture. The effects of these substances are chronic and devastating not only to the individual user but to the extended societal circles of family, significant others, friends, and the community as a whole. The effects of substance abuse are a strong component of many other therapeutic issues, such as physical abuse, sexual abuse, marital problems, adolescent behavioral problems, and childhood developmental problems. Based on the frequency of these issues in therapy, it appears inevitable that individual users or co-dependent persons are going to seek out the professional assistance of a pastoral counselor. Having a good knowledge base of the individual effects and consequences of psychoactive substance abuse and the differentiating criteria for co-morbid psychiatric disorders which may or may not be concomitant is an important asset to any pastoral counselor. Evaluation and assessment skills concerning psychoactive substance-abuse disorders will enhance a pastoral counselor's insight in determining a treatment plan for an individual client. Hopefully, the more counselors learn about substances and their effects, the better therapeutic care and interventions will be given.

Perhaps pastoral counselors need to be encouraged to go one step further and to focus their professional skill development and services directly in the substance abuse field. With their wealth of experience and background pastoral counselors would be bringing an additional dimension of service unlike any other mental health professional to the field of psychoactive substance use—the richness of a holistic perception of persons as body, mind, emotion, and spirit, and an accompanying familiarity with the deep substantive issues of life and death. In the field of substance-use disorders pastoral counselors would exhibit the qualities of a degree with a difference.

References

BJS (Bureau of Justice Statistics). 1983. "Prisoners and Alcohol." U.S. Department of Justice Publication. Rockville, Md.: Drugs and Crime Data Center.

Brooner, R. K. 1991. Southeast Baltimore Drug Treatment Program Procedural Manual (unpublished).

Greenfield, L. 1988. "Drunk Driving: 1983, 1986, and 1987." Bureau of Justice Statistics. Rockville, Md.: Drugs and Crime Data Center.

Innes, C. 1988. "Drug Use and Crime: State Prison Inmate Survey, 1986." Bureau of Justice Statistics. Rockville, Md.: Drugs and Crime Data Center.

Levin, Jerome D. 1987. *Treatment of Alcoholism and Other Addictions.* Northvale, N.J.: Jason Aronson, Inc.

Lininger, P. 1990. "An Outcome Study of the Graduates of Loyola's Pastoral Counseling Program Since Its Foundation in 1976 to 1988." Ph.d. diss. Baltimore, Md.: Loyola College. [*Alumni/ae Survey of the Pastoral Counseling Program at Loyola College*, UMI, 36-3580102]

Marlatt, G. Alan, and Gordon, Judith R. 1985. *Relapse Prevention.* New York: Guilford Press.

Schuckit, Marc A., ed. 1985. *Alcohol Patterns and Problems.* New Brunswick, N.J.: Rutgers University Press.

———. 1990. *Drug and Alcohol Abuse: A Clinical Guide to Diagnosis and Treatment*, 3d ed. New York: Plenum Medical Book Company.

Spitzer, Robert L. 1990. *User's Guide for the Structured Clinical Interview for DSM III-R: SCID.* Washington, D.C.: American Psychiatric Press.

———, Williams, J. W.; Gibbon, M.; and First, M. B. 1990. Structured Clinical Interview for DMS III-R: SCID-P, Version 1.0, Patient ed. Washington, D.C.: American Psychiatric Press.

Wish, E. D., and O'Neil, J. A. 1989. "Drug Use Forecasting." National Institute of Justice. Rockville, Md.: Drugs and Crime Data Center.

For Further Reading

Charken, M. R. 1989. "Prison Programs for Drug Involved Offenders." National Institute of Justice. Rockville, Md.: Drug and Crime Data Center.

Wurmser, Leon. 1981. *The Mask of Shame.* Baltimore, Md.: Johns Hopkins University Press.

Rachel Callahan, C.S.C.
Rea McDonnell, S.S.N.D.

22. Adult Children of Alcoholics

Description of the Problem

Unlike some of the other topics in this handbook, the issue of recovery from damage done to those who grew up in alcoholic families is not only a new focus of study. It has become a veritable industry. Self-help books for adult children of alcoholics, grandchildren of alcoholics, and adult children of dysfunctional families abound. This is a topic on which the reader is apt to discover more books on the best-seller shelves than on the shelves of a graduate school library. The ACoA (Adult Children of Alcoholics) movement is less than a decade old, and it is still conspicuously absent from the professional journals of pastoral care and counseling. *Psychological Abstracts* includes the category "adult offspring" but not "adult children of alcoholics."

Over the past decade the problem has been articulated and redefined in various areas of study. Originating in work done with families of alcoholics in recovery, early writers describe some of the rules (Black 1981; Gravitz and Bowden 1985). Growing up in families in which rules of "Don't talk. Don't trust. Don't feel" and roles of "hero, scapegoat, mascot, lost child, placator" are inflexible, the young child learns early to invest in a false self. This false self is rigidly maintained for the sake of balance and cohesion in a family system made chaotic by the abuse of alcohol. The cardinal defense of the alcoholic family—denial that anything is wrong or painful, let alone abnormal—often keeps the family bound in dysfunctional patterns of thinking, feeling, communicating, and behaving. Thus addictions studies use some of the insights from family studies to assess and understand the dynamics of the alcoholic family.

The Dysfunctional Family System

Using a family root system or genogram (McGoldrick and Gerson 1985) is an efficient way to collect a fair amount of useful information.

By gathering both demographic and functional data the pastoral counselor can examine the family context. It is important to be able to situate an individual's story both in terms of historical context and in terms of any particular ethnic scripts. By gathering data for a multigenerational family system the counselor can see at a glance whether there are any particular patterns within the family. Patterns of abuse, whether chemical or physical, frequently repeat across generations.

In collecting data it is useful to see who in the family fulfills particular roles over the generations, for example, caretaker or problem person. In a dysfunctional family roles are often rigid and fixed. Those who have worked with adults who grew up in alcoholic families can identify some fairly consistent roles. Wegscheider-Cruse (1981) notes four of the typical roles:

THE FAMILY HERO

This child, who functioned as the super-reasonable one (sometimes called the "parentified child"), is often perfectionistic, overachieving. This person carries the family banner and helps maintain the outer facade that all is well.

THE SCAPEGOAT

This child is frequently the identified patient in a troubled family. Playing a complementary opposite role to the Hero, this child unites the family through failure and acting out of hostility. In a sense the scapegoat is the family lightning rod, drawing fire, attention, and distracting from the alcoholic's disease.

THE LOST CHILD

This child is almost invisible both in the family and in school. Sometimes comforted by a very rich life of fantasy, the child tries to maintain the balance in the chaotic system by "disappearing."

THE FAMILY MASCOT

This child uses humor and entertainment to lighten the family tension. By making the family laugh the child attempts to dispel some of the anxiety trapped within the family system.

Black (1981) simultaneously identified similar roles, calling the hero the "responsible one"; the scapegoat the "acting out child"; the lost child the "adjuster"; and also describing the "placator," that is, the child who is the little social worker, responsible for keeping family emotions on an even keel.

Roles closely parallel some of the dysfunctional patterns of communication specified by family therapist and theorist Virginia Satir (1972). In gathering family data it is useful to identify the patterns of communication within the family and between generations. Examining patterns of closeness and distance and evidence for enmeshment is important because typically in a dysfunctional family boundaries are an important issue. Lacking a clear and cohesive sense of self, parents can inadvertently use children as extensions of themselves. In that process they may not be respectful of the boundaries of the children as individuals. In its most blatant form the violation of boundaries in an enmeshed family appears as sexual and physical abuse. Emotional intrusiveness, such as reading children's diaries and letters, also violates children. In distanced families, on the other hand, personal boundaries are so rigid and nonpermeable that children feel, and often are, uncared for. For example, a workaholic parent, a "neat-nik" parent, a severely depressed parent, or an alcoholic parent does not give children respect either.

A genogram should also lift up some data about conflict management within the family. People have different ways of managing conflict. Some use distance, others blame, yet others scream. Within families, individuals frequently form triangles, often unconsciously, in order to defuse conflict. By bringing a third party into the conflict, tension between two persons can appear to be more manageable. When triangles are cross-generational and involve children, they can be very damaging to a child.

When dealing with the adult child of an alcoholic the pastoral counselor has to be particularly sensitive to the family's major defense of denial. Even blatant abuse of alcohol is not considered to be a problem. John, a young man, highly anxious, compulsively workaholic, denied that his father was alcoholic but then went on to describe how it was to try to talk to his dad. "We had to approach Dad sometime between his fifth and seventh drink. Before that we couldn't go near him because he would be too uptight, and after that we couldn't talk to him either." Caught in some old stereotypes about alcoholism, John believed that because his father went to work every day he could not possibly be an alcoholic.

Addictions Studies

The impetus and much of the vocabulary of the ACofA movement derives from the field of addictions study. More practical than theory based, this movement has grown out of the experience of working with families of recovering alcoholics. Adult children of alcoholics often wrestle with their own addictive processes. Many struggle with substance addictions: food, drink, or alcohol; others struggle with compulsive gambling or sexual behavior or patterns of work.

A common phenomenon in alcoholic families is co-dependence, variously defined by writers in the field of addictions study. Schaef (1986) summarized these various writings and identified co-dependence as a generic disease process found in every level of our addictive society. Characterized by the denial of any addictive process, co-dependence is a disease of the incomplete self. As a relationship addiction it hooks individuals into unhealthy, damaging relationships. Instead of knowing and claiming one's own gifts, needs, and wants, the co-dependent attempts to control relationships by caretaking. Not only "de-selfing" in the supposed service of others, the co-dependent, through impression management, needs a kind of "photo opportunity" to feel any self-worth. Popular writers (Beattie 1987) offer practical insight about how to recognize and change such behaviors. Their best-seller status attests to their resonance with great numbers of individuals. Al-anon, for spouses of alcoholics, has mothered this movement for the healing of the self. Adult children, co-dependents all, profit from that particular twelve-step program.

Individual Psychological Issues

Often the pastoral counselor meets an individual in pain rather than a family in distress. What are some of the signals that suggest the client is an adult child from a troubled family? Many of these signs cluster around "self" issues.

Too often the adult child suffers from an incomplete sense of self. "Doing" is a more reliable indicator of self-worth than "being." Because of the chaos in an alcoholic family, too often the mothering person is not able to attend adequately to the child in the crucial developmental period of early childhood. During the first three years of life, when a solid sense of self is built through processes of bonding, basic trust may be disrupted. Because the initial attachment to the mother is symbiotic and pre-verbal, the child absorbs her feelings of anger, anxiety, or disgust. Early pre-verbal experiences get lodged in the infant's feeling memory. These memories are both intense and, in a kind of infant time, are eternally now, forever. Consequently the adult client often experiences and is ashamed of unreasonable fear, anxiety, rage, grief. He or she worries about engulfment by a significant other and/or abandonment. Afraid of and unskilled at intimacy, the client experiences feelings of shame, guilt, and depression in and about relationships. An inordinate attachment hunger drives many an adult child. If this deficit in bonding, the age-appropriate symbiotic attachment to the mothering figure has occurred, the adult longs for and may compulsively seek inappropriate substitutes.

If the deficit occurs a little later, during toddler-time, then what Bradshaw (1990) describes as "oppositional bonding" happens. When the child cannot be his or her true self but must act or be in a certain way to win or sustain parental approval, the child very early develops what Miller (1981) describes as the "as if personality" and what Winnicott (1965) earlier described as the "false self." The false self increasingly relies on external approval. Being deprived of approval, applause, or attention can precipitate feelings of emptiness and fragmentation. Frequently overachieving, this adult child needs to look good and is exquisitely vulnerable to feelings of shame and embarassment when criticized. The same perfectionistic and grandiose expectations that he or she has of self are usually but covertly also required of others and the world in general. Consequently, the person is extremely vulnerable to feelings of hurt and is frequently disappointed, sometimes to the point of rage, with daily reality. Requiring all-or-nothing perfection, the person is unable to be nourished by the juice and joy of ordinary life. Johnson (1987) summarizes this plight this way: It becomes more important to look good and think well of self than to feel good.

In addition to feeling issues which are legacy of the "holes in the heart"—these early deficits in parenting—there are also some cognitive distortions which characterize the experience of the adult child. Burns, in *Feeling Good: The New Mood Therapy* (1980), popularized some of the earlier work of Ellis (1962, 1975) and Beck (1979).

Again lodged in a very early childhood phenomenon called splitting, a dividing of reality into all good or all bad, the adult child often continues the child's view of the world and thinks in *all or nothing* terms. Another cognitive distortion of adult children is *catastrophizing*. A catastrophizing person assumes and vividly imagines an awful outcome to a situation, generating enormous internal anxiety. ACoAs have often learned how to worry as children, not only from the codependent parent's modeling but because catastrophe really did happen at home, sometimes daily. Learning not to expect the worst can be taught, however (Burns 1980).

Personalization is another common cognitive distortion of ACoAs. Children often feel responsible when something bad happens. "If only I were good/brighter/neater/. . . then maybe Mother or

Daddy wouldn't need to drink." We cannot create feelings in another person and certainly cannot cause the disease of alcoholism in a parent. But too often adults who have grown up in a dysfunctional family are taught to believe they are responsible for the family's ills: "You kids are driving me to drink."

In addition to the cognitive issues briefly referred to above there are a number of common affective issues shared by ACoAs. Early encouraged to stifle and deny feeling, very often the ACoA is most aware of a frozen, numbed sadness. Sometimes experiences of abuse or chaos are so traumatic that memories with their associated feelings of terror, rage, shame, grief, or despair need to be repressed for the sake of survival. But in the course of healing, as will later be described, strong feelings can surface. Shame in the core of one's being needs reworking. Anger, sadness, anxiety, fear, and guilt are only a few which often surface.

In summary, the breadth of defining the problem of the adult child of the alcoholic keeps expanding as ACoAs name and claim and share their plight. Broad streams from family systems theory, addictions study, and psychodynamic and cognitive psychology converge in this phenomenon, which in some ways has become greater than the sum of its parts. Is it a movement which will peak and fade or does it in fact give vocabulary and healing community to a vast number of individuals? We believe it is the latter, although as in any venture of self-improvement, it can suffer from excess and pull individuals too deeply into self-absorption. Part of the co-pilgrimage of the pastoral counselor is to facilitate more growth than self-absorption.

Pastoral Focus

When an adult who has grown up in a family troubled or even fractured by alcoholism (or by premature death or illness or divorce or . . .) comes for pastoral counseling, some lynchpins of healing are already in place. First, there is an awareness that healing happens in community. The adult child, whatever the past family role, depends on the community in the person of the counselor. To admit the need for another's help is crucial for the hero-responsible one. To come into the light of another's care is a major act of trust for the lost one. To take pain seriously enough to make an appointment is already a first step toward healing for the family mascot. To stop acting out so as to look in with the support of a counselor indicates the scapegoat's readiness to face reality. Because disease and rupture have happened in the first community, the family, we can expect healing and wholeness to happen also in community.

Second, because such an adult chooses a *pastoral* counselor, we can more freely use stories of faith and symbols of spirituality in leading our client to healing and wholeness. Alcoholism is both a family disease and a dis-ease with God. It follows that those in the alcoholic family might need some healing of the heart's life with God. The underlying spirituality of the Twelve Steps is foundational for release for addicts and for those shaped in their formative years by addicts. Twelve-step spirituality springs from the New Testament—that we are powerless to save ourselves (Rom 5); is reiterated in Ignatius Loyola's "principle and foundation"—that God is God and we are creatures, dependent always on God; is secularized by Ernst Becker (1973) in his Pulitzer prize-winning *Denial of Death*—that our limits and mortality challenge us to accept, individually and as a society, that we are finite. "We admitted . . . our lives had become unmanageable . . . a power greater than ourselves could restore us to sanity . . . (and) made a decision to turn our will and lives over to the care of God." These first three of the Twelve Steps cut through the addict's grandiosity, whether secret or overt, and through the family defense of denial.

Not only has family disease probably distorted the image of God for our clients, but our religious institutions have sometimes compounded the problem with their mentality and morality. Preaching and teaching about love, perfection, the will of God, and self-denial often fed abusive ways of relating in the alcoholic family (Callahan and McDonnell 1990, pp. 61–73). Sometimes church leaders themselves have been abusive of power, and in local or diocesan relationships have unwittingly mimicked the dysfunctional family system.

To focus on just one issue which the pastoral counselor can raise and probably should raise, there is the client's image of God. Other religious issues may fall into place if the client can re-image God through adult experiences of love and fidelity. Our first image of God is formed during the exploratory period of childhood, ages two to four years. Of course, it is shaped by our experience of our parents' (or parent's) care and protection—or lack thereof (Rizzuto 1979). If, in a two-parent family, the alcoholic parent has enthroned the bottle as God and the co-dependent parent has worshiped, often in fear and trembling, the alcoholic as God, the child's image of God is undoubtedly distorted.

Yet often, the co-dependent parent particularly will rely on religion and prayer for solace. One woman tells of being continually urged by her mother as a youngster to pray for her father's release from alcohol. As the girl's first communion day approached, her mother's urgency mounted to near panic: "God listens to little children. You *must* get Daddy to stop drinking when you take communion." First communion day brought no miracle. The child was cross-examined about her prayers for Daddy, then scorned by her mother for not being good enough to win God's help.

God imaged only as parent is problematic. The inconsistency of an alcoholic father, if the child learns to call God Father, not only sets up the child for compulsive adult behaviors, but also leads to profound mistrust of God. Replacing the father image with a mother image usually does not help for long.

The mother may have been alcoholic, but at best she was co-alcoholic in her "de-selfing" attitudes and behaviors. Many of our clients use the childhood defense of splitting: the alcoholic is all bad, the non-drinking parent all holy. The prime image of God for the youngster, even for many adults, is then the "good parent." In therapy that idol crashes as both parents become demythologized. Professor Merle Jordan considers the "taking on of the gods" as the task of the pastoral counselor (1986). When the client begins to understand that the alcoholic "is a good person with a terrible disease" (McConnell 1986) the co-dependent's pedestal is often lowered. For any of us, ACoA or not, a sign of maturity is the realization that our parents are not gods. Healing happens when our splitting into all bad and all good is drawn into the unified whole of *real* persons—parents with mixed motives, gifts and virtues, faults and even evils.

If we do indeed take on these parental gods and God created in their image, how can we help clients re-image God now as adults? The Muslims have one hundred names for God; devout Hindus recite one thousand names for God; the Jewish scriptures are rich with images; Jesus not only called God Father but Shepherd, Farmer, Housewife. We have encouraged clients to let images of God "bubble up" from their unconscious where "the Spirit personally makes our petitions for us in groans that cannot be put into words" (Rom 8:26). In this free association anything is acceptable: the rich and sensuous, the angry and violent. One client burst out, calling God a "God-damned fool," as her images of God freely surfaced. She then sobbed as a terrible boulder in her heart moved.

It may be helpful then to invite clients to listen to God's name for them. One burly law enforcement officer reported with tender, trembling awe: "God knows my name, and it's not asshole." God had corrected his dad's vicious name, which of course the client had internalized for some forty years.

If the first name God reveals to Moses in Exodus 3:14 seems distant, "I am who am," at least it is a name which affirms existence, simple being. John Bradshaw (1988) has coined a term for a major defense against core shame: adult children become "human doings," frantically hoping to win parental and divine approval in all their relationships. The God who simply *is* can serve as an antidote for the "human doing," inviting the adult child simply to claim a right to personal existence.

Moses asks to see God's glory, and God lets him see God's beauty. God passes by calling out a new name. It is not enough that God is. God is "Yahweh, Yahweh, God of tenderness and compassion, slow to anger, rich in faithful love and constancy" (Ex 34:6). "Love" is the Hebrew *hesed,* a kindness and care which is merciful, tender, abundant, extravagant, and unconditional. "Faithfulness" is the Hebrew *'emet,* a devotion which is steady, consistent, forever. This double attribute of God, *hesed w 'emet,* is hymned throughout the Jewish scriptures, especially in the psalms. It is translated into Greek as "grace" (*hesed*) and "truth" (*'emet*), which comes through Jesus Christ (Jn 1:17). It is embodied by our compassionate (*hesed*) and faithful (*'emet*) high priest, Jesus (Heb 2:17). It is also our mission to embody God's love and faithfulness so our clients can begin to re-image God as steady and deeply caring. As God's healing flowed through the attention, the eyes, the touch, the listening of Jesus, so we continue his own mission (Callahan and McDonnell 1987).

To do that most effectively, of course, we need some clarity of self-awareness, some acceptance of our own pain and scars from home. We also need some overview of how family dynamics, myths, and shame; fears of both intimacy and abandonment; feelings repressed, oppressed, and depressed continue to skew adult thinking and acting. We need not only to know (dia-*gnosis*) the pain but how to minister to the pain-filled. Of course, the more we have had our relationship with God healed and deepened, the more at ease our clients will be to re-image God and let God's healing soak into them.

Ministering to ACoA

Adults who carry open wounds and/or scars from childhood often look to a minister to facilitate a healing of their hearts. Any pastoral person can listen with compassion as the adult gets in touch with long denied, buried pain. Some degrees of early childhood damage however require more therapy than the parish minister or a twelve-step program can offer. Ministers without specialized training in psychotherapy may have to refer these more seriously hurt people to a professional mental health worker while maintaining a relationship of pastoral care with the person. Monthly sessions, no longer than an hour, can assure the ACoA that he or she is not abandoned by the church (and read, "God").

Ministers whose pastoral care is most helpful are those who have examined their own needs to rescue or fix; their own prejudices regarding alcoholism, child abuse, and expression of emotions; their own ability to maintain professional boundaries, accepting human limits; their sometimes overarching need to escape conflict by pushing for forgiveness. Forgiveness of one's parents, family, and self is not an act of the will (although it may pose as such) but God's gift (Patton 1985). God gives when gifts can be received; for the neglected, rejected, or abused child that readiness may come after a lifelong process of healing. Long into the healing process, all a client may be able to do is to pray for the gift of forgiving.

Instead of preaching the need to forgive to the victim, ministers could well point out various forms of child abuse from the pulpit. Many parents "discipline" with cruelty (Miller 1981, 1980) and believe this is what God wants. Jesus, on the other hand, is enraged and hopes a mill stone drowns anyone who harms a little one (Lk 17:2)!

For the more professionally trained minister, the pastoral counselor, undoubtedly the first service we offer is reparenting for the adult client. Even if only one parent was alcoholic, both parents were preoccupied by alcohol, and the child was not properly parented. Should the client assure the counselor that indeed the co-dependent was a model parent, we know better—yet the client will discover that much later. Because many ACoA have a need to rush, to make order out of chaos, we will have to assure them that it took ten or seventeen years to crush them. It will require time for healing.

Reparenting calls for unconditional positive regard, a steady devotion, attentive care. The counselor mirrors the client so the client's own self is validated. As the mother looks at the newborn, in their mutual contemplation basic trust is meant to be birthed. But this child often has found no delight in its mother's face; thus a kind of deep, respectful, contemplative regard of the client can fill a major deficit. Many ACoAs will barely be able to return that look, so ashamed are they even to be seen. Echoing, assuring the client that both content and feeling are heard and received, validates and reinforces any self-expression, thoughts, feelings, desires, and needs. Not only is a child from an alcoholic home usually not grounded in trust (do not trust, do not feel, do not talk) but often is not grounded in being. "Do not be," we would add to the ACoA theorists' triad of cardinal rules.

Another rule in such a family is usually, "Do not need." Legitimate dependency needs of an infant, toddler, and child are ignored, even mocked, leaving not only a hole in the heart (Callahan and McDonnell 1991) but shame at any feeling of neediness. Sometimes the terror of being exposed as dependent shapes a macho, super-responsible, compulsive personality.

A piece of parenting is also teaching and coaching. Because ACoAs only guess at what is normal in relationships, we may have to teach about emotions, the distinction between feeling and acting on emotions, and expressions of feeling which are appropriate. We may even have to offer a basic vocabulary for emotions; they may not have words for what they feel, but pre-verbal memories will haunt them until they can say what troubles them. Cognitive therapy to straighten crooked, negative thinking can be taught, as can self-affirmations to be repeated throughout the day.

Because the family of origin was so troubled, ACoAs may need coaching in how to relate with family, friends, authorities, and co-workers. They may need to practice and report on limit setting, whether in caring, volunteering, overworking. They can role-play saying what they mean, leveling (Satir 1972), practicing conversations which, because communication was so skewed in their homes, loom out of proportion as huge confrontations. We can invite them to say no when they mean no; to assert their legitimate needs and rights; to ask directly for what they want; and eventually to share a range and depth of feeling outside the safety of our office.

All the while, we may be frustrating in gentle and kind ways the client's need for instant gratification. Deprivation has opened chasms of hunger: for touch, extra time, special attention, speedy results. Our professional boundaries may be tested.

Unless the ACoA is somehow forced into counseling, this client will be his or her harshest critic and judge. It will be helpful to retrain an ACoA from instant internal self-judgment—"I am good/bad; this anger is justified; this violent feeling is evil, and so on—to curiousity instead—"I'm feeling violent, how interesting! I wonder how that happens now? Is it triggering a memory? My, what a deep feeling! I *have* felt this before. Let me explore this." The client often needs to talk and talk and our listening non-judgmentally allows the wound to drain.

After basic trust Erik Erikson posits autonomy as the child's next task. If the toddler cannot establish itself as separate, shame results. Shame is encoded in the toddler and then triggered in the adult by needs, wants, hopes, feelings, hungers (Kaufman 1985; Bradshaw 1990). "I *am* deficient; I do not even deserve to exist" may well be an ACoA script. These clients often fight for their place in the universe by frantic doing, working, pleasing, achieving. They will be hypervigilant for our approval, will hope to be our best client (whatever that means!), will want to do therapy right, be right, get it right this time. It is important, while offering a steady care, not to applaud too loudly lest we reinforce this false self (Winnicott 1965; Miller 1981). They need to rely on their own interior acceptance rather than continuing to look outside themselves.

The ACoA client reports a success in maintaining a personal boundary. "Great!" we exclaim. A double bind for us. We have just reinforced their external referenting (bad) and have spoken emotionally, spontaneously (good). We will have to trust our own self, our intuition, our timing. Our spontaneity and making mistakes can help to heal the perfectionistic client. "My mother was 100 percent right, so I never learned that an adult could make a mistake, let alone admit it. I cover up all the time, and I am mortally tired," a client reports.

We may become mortally tired as the true self of the client emerges. There will be mess, strong emotions, a period of almost clinging dependency. Good-enough parents can expect nothing less (Winnicott 1965).

As ACoAs learn to attach to us they are grieving the babyhood and the childhood which they missed. Not only have mistrust and shame distorted their infancy, but guilt (vs. initiative, according to Erikson; vs. playfulness, spontaneity, creativity of the preschool child) marks them as well. Indeed, all Erikson's stages of normal development—industry, identity, intimacy—have been sabotaged. Even in midlife generativity is skewed for the ACoA. In their one and only life the moment of childhood, of perhaps young adulthood as well, has passed. We reparent and teach them to care for their inner child (Napier 1990).

One further—and central—resource for pastoral counselors is God, literally a re-source. Whoever believes in (trusts) Jesus, "From his heart shall flow streams of living water" (Jn 7:38). Jesus' humanity with its limits, emotions, mistakes, approachability, and vulnerability has helped clients learn to appreciate their own limited, frail, and feeling humanity. Psalms, expressing a range and depth of passion, give permission to ACoAs to be real in prayer, in relationship with God. The Jewish scriptures portray a very passionate God who asks for our passionate response. The laments encourage clients to cry "*Lamah?*" (Why?). Our God is a God who hears the cry of the poor, who heals the brokenhearted and saves (not rescues, as it has come to mean in English, but from the Hebrew *yesh:* to give space and time, to set free in the open) those who are crushed in spirit.

Our God is a God who talks. God feels, God talks in so many varieties of self-revelation, God trusts. Conversation with God, letting Jesus look at us humbly and tenderly, is a way of prayer taught by Teresa of Avila and a way of healing for the ACoA. Her compatriot, Ignatius of Loyola, taught that our neediness and dependency and imperfect creaturehood are unconditionally accepted and delighted in by God. God invites us to be, need, feel, talk, and eventually trust. Trusting God is that faith which alone saves. Trusting a pastoral counselor may thus, for the ACoA, be a first step in and toward the "glorious freedom as the children of God" (Rom 8:21).

Summary

Just as each alcoholic's disease takes a unique course toward destruction, so offspring and families are unique in their pain, their surviving and their healing. Most adult children of alcoholics (and those from other dysfunctional families) are characterized by an overarching need for control springing from a profound mistrust of themselves and others. Most are rooted in a shame which signals emptiness, a lack of self and self-esteem. This may lead either to a "de-selfing," giving up one's own legitimate needs, wants, feelings, thoughts, and decisions so as to maintain a relationship, no matter how demeaning, or, on the other hand, to a grandiosity which covers shame with a frantic need to perform, achieve, maintain center stage lest the deficit at the core of one's being is discovered.

Because they are taught, overtly or covertly, that they are deficient as human beings, ACoAs often are ashamed to feel, let alone own and/or talk about neediness, desires, or their emotions. They are either terrified of depending on another lest they be engulfed or abandoned, or they cling desperately. Either stance indicates a codependency, a disease characterized by the incomplete self seeking to stuff the hole in the heart. Of course, problems with an appropriate and adult dependence lead to problems with intimacy in which adults learn to depend and be dependable in free and flexible ways.

Many adult children will identify themselves at once. However, the chief ACoA defense, denial, will undoubtedly lurk. Denial, which usually pervaded the entire family of origin, is often compounded by strong doses of intellectualization.

Each diagnosis of an ACoA will be unique, ranging from schizoid, borderline, or narcissistic character disorders to dependent, obsessive-compulsive, histrionic traits. Because truth in an alcoholic family was so skewed, cognitive distortions too range in severity. Anxiety and depression are two frequent affective disorders which might lead the ACoA to self-medicate with, for example, alcohol, food, shopping, and so on. Thus it is important to assess past and current addictions of the client.

Therapeutic considerations include some knowledge of addictions and even more understanding of family dynamics. A genogram helps to uncover both family facts *and* feelings as the client talks about discoveries, memories, puzzlements. Group therapy may be indicated since the family, the first group, may have been and continues to be too painful a place for healing. However, if the counselor can invite the family of origin and/or (at separate times) the client's current family for some sessions, the client can be coached to speak directly, practicing more level ways of communicating, setting boundaries, caring, and confronting.

Primarily the pastoral counselor offers unconditional positive regard, hoping to make up some of the original deficits in parenting. The incomplete self of the ACoA can discover wholeness and self-esteem by claiming needs, feelings, desires, and talking about them. As ACoAs learn to trust not only the counselor but life, they thereby surrender, day by day, a grandiose, god-like, and sadly delusional control; as ACoAs learn to trust themselves, they can reach out, risk, and assert appropriately. The counselor, while not encouraging the perfect performance of the false self, does assist the ACoA to explore truth within and about himself or herself.

One seasoned pastoral counselor, working more frequently now with clients "in recovery," reports that he is dealing more directly with spiritual issues. As pastoral ministers we represent the healing community of the church. Yet we can distinguish the spirituality of the Twelve Steps from a defense of organized religion. Instead, we "take on the gods"—whether the false self and/or the parents of our clients. Helping ACoAs to accept both self and parents neither as demons nor as gods but as real, human persons, leads them to the truth which sets free.

References

Beattie, M. 1987. *Codependent No More.* New York: Harper & Row.

Beck, A., et al. 1979. *Cognitive Therapy of Depression.* New York: Guilford Press.

Becker, E. 1973. *The Denial of Death.* New York: The Free Press.

Black, C. 1981. *It Will Never Happen to Me.* Colorado: Medical Administration.

Bradshaw, J. 1988. *Healing the Shame That Binds You.* Deerfield Beach, Fla.: Health Communications.

______. 1990. *Homecoming.* New York: Bantam Books.

Burns, D. 1980. *Feeling Good: The New Mood Therapy.* New York: Signet.

Callahan, R., and McDonnell, R. 1987. *Hope for Healing: Good News for Adult Children of Alcoholics.* New York: Paulist Press.

______. 1990. *Adult children of alcoholics: Ministers and the ministries.* New York: Paulist Press.

______. 1991. *Wholing the Heart.* New York: Paulist Press.

Ellis, A. 1962. *Reason and Emotions in Psychotherapy.* New York: Lyle Stuart.

______. 1975. *A New Guide to Rational Living.* Englewood Cliffs, N.J.: Prentice-Hall.

Gravitz, H., and Bowden, J. 1985. *Guide to Recovery.* Holmes Beach, Fla.: Learning Publications.

Johnson, S. 1987. *Humanizing the Narcissistic Style.* New York: W. W. Norton.

Jordan, M. 1986. *Taking on the Gods: The Task of the Pastoral Counselor.* Nashville: Abingdon.

Kaufman, G. 1985. *Shame: the Power of Caring.* Cambridge, Mass.: Schenkman.

Marlin, E. 1987. *Hope: New Choices and Recovery Strategies for Adult Children of Alcoholics.* San Francisco: Harper & Row.

McConnell, P. 1986. *Adult Children of Alcoholics.* San Francisco: Harper & Row.

McGoldrick, M., and Gerson, R. 1985. *Genograms in Family Assessment.* New York: W. W. Norton.

Miller, A. 1981. *Drama of the Gifted Child.* New York: Basic Books.

______. 1980. *For Your Own Good.* New York: Farrar, Straus, Giroux.

Napier, N. 1990. *Recreating Your Self.* New York: W. W. Norton.
Patton, J. 1985. *Is Human Forgiveness Possible?* Nashville: Abingdon.
Rizzuto, A. 1979. *The Birth of the Living God.* Chicago: University of Chicago Press.
Satir, V. 1972. *Peoplemaking.* Palo Alto: Science and Behavior Books.
Schaef, A. 1986. *Co-dependence.* San Francisco: Harper & Row.
Wegscheider-Cruse, S. 1985. *Choicemaking.* Pompano Beach, Fla.: Health Communications.
Winnicott, D. W. 1965. *The Maturational Processes and the Facilitating Environment.* Madison, Conn.: International Universities Press.

Joseph Ciarrocchi

23. Pathological Gambling and Pastoral Counseling

Definition and Description of Pathological Gambling

Scope of the Problem

Approximately one to three persons in one hundred have a gambling problem in the United States according to even the most conservative population surveys (Volberg and Steadman 1989). To put this figure into perspective, it is as common a disorder as schizophrenia or manic-depression.

Almost all indicators suggest that the problem will only increase as gambling achieves greater public acceptance as a recreational activity. Some form of gambling is now legal in forty-eight out of fifty states in the United States, and one trade publication estimates that in 1988 210 billion dollars were wagered legally in the United States (Christiansen 1989). In 1974 61 percent of the United States adult population gambled, while current estimates are that over 80 percent gamble legally with amounts increasing more than one thousand percent in the past fifteen years (Lesieur and Rosenthal 1990). Gambling is legal in over ninety countries as well. Furthermore, estimates indicate that the amounts wagered illegally equal amounts wagered legally. One survey of gamblers in treatment found the average amount of indebtedness to be ninety-two thousand dollars (Politzer, Morrow, and Leavey 1985).

Numbers alone can never fully reveal the human dimension to the problem. The following cases represent typical scenarios caused by the disorder which the pastoral counselor is likely to encounter:

1) An older semi-retired working-class man makes a routine call to his bank to clarify the lack of interest calculated in his quarterly statement for an eleven thousand dollar account. With great sacrifice

the money was set aside for his children, to help them in early marriage with housing and other burdensome start-up costs for today's young couples. He discovers the bank made no error; he has a balance of $128. His wife depleted the account by forging his signature on withdrawals over the past six months to play the lottery.

2) A mother I interviewed on the CBS news show *60 Minutes* whose husband was a pathological gambler described sitting on the kitchen floor cradling her two-year old while laborers hired by the finance company removed all her furniture and refrigerator. She and her husband were both college graduates with professional jobs, and their only possession was a small kitchen table. She describes sitting on the floor blankly wondering what to do with her last dollar bill—whether she should buy peanut butter or toilet paper.

3) The wife of a financially successful attorney with three small children desperately rummages the house for any available cash to pay chronically overdue household bills. The telephone has been turned off; they are three months behind in their mortgage; it is the middle of winter and she just received notice that the heat will be turned off today. While searching through her husband's suit pocket she discovers ten thousand dollars in cash. She confronts him later, "You told me you had no money for bills." "That's right," he retorts, "that was my gambling money."

How is it that otherwise decent, caring people allow their lives to reach such a state where they inflict such pain on themselves and loved ones? To readers who are knowledgeable about alcohol and drug abuse the patterns and characteristics of pathological gamblers will have a familiar ring. Alcohol and other drugs are well known to create horror stories equal to or worse than the ones cited here. The interesting and challenging feature of gambling is that it represents a *purely psychological addiction.* No external agent enters the body (alcohol, drugs, food); there is no intense physiological experiences (sex, for example). The activity alone is capable of generating the compulsive behavior.

While no external agent alters the body's physical state, there is some evidence that gambling addiction generates powerful internal states. A study conducted by researchers at the National Institute of Drug Abuse found that the described emotional state of pathological gamblers when winning is indistinguishable from the emotional state of cocaine or stimulant addicts when using their drug of choice. If winning at gambling creates euphoria equivalent to cocaine for some, then the reinforcing and potentially addicting power of gambling is more understandable.

The environmental characteristics of the condition further complicate treatment and resolution. No matter how addicted to alcohol or other drugs an individual is, the addicting substance itself is not essential to carry out one's every day affairs. Money is, however. Having money available continually is equivalent to an alcoholic carrying a flask. Naturally this represents an enormous difficulty for the gambler who sincerely wishes to stop—and for family members who have to develop creative ways to work around this essential need for currency.

Discerning the Pathological Gambler

The American Psychiatric Association codifies mental disorders by symptoms in *DSM III-R* (American Psychiatric Association 1987). The following criteria for pathological gambling represent those currently being considered for its next revision (*DSM IV*) and differ only modestly from earlier versions.

1) *Mental preoccupation with gambling.* The person spends a good deal of time thinking about gambling, ways of betting, and how to improve his or her chances, and in efforts to obtain money in order to gamble. I recall one recovering gambler in treatment who, despite remaining abstinent, could not look at license plate numbers without calculating combinations of 21 for Blackjack.

2) *Increasing the amount wagered to achieve the desired excitement.* For those familiar with substance abuse this criterion parallels the concept of tolerance, that is, the need to consume more to get the desired effect. The gambler has an analogous experience of needing to wager more to achieve euphoria. Obviously the amounts wagered are relative to and limited by the person's access to money. The amounts initially wagered and the absolute ceiling a gambler achieves will differ depending upon whether the person is chief executive of a large corporation or a homemaker taking household expense money to bet the lottery. The method of gambling also enters into the tolerance issue. Some forms of gambling are on a pay-as-you-go basis (lottery, horse racing, bingo), whereas other forms allow one to establish credit (casino gambling, illegal sports betting with a bookmaker, financial gambling). Credit forms of gambling tend to generate a fantasy experience for the gambler since he or she does not see any actual money exchange. Gamblers tend to increase wagers more rapidly for these forms of gambling. As the financial risk increases so does the gambler's sense of excitement—and the occasional win reinforces

the thrill of anticipatory success. Some observers of the irrational wagering behavior of severely addicted gamblers interpret this behavior as the gambler's "desire to lose," or being "hooked on the action itself of gambling," making winning or losing irrelevant. I have never been impressed with these interpretations and would maintain with others that the gamblers are hooked on the anticipation of winning—or at a minimum, their recollections of that experience.

3) *Irritability and agitation when not able to gamble.* Again the parallel for substance abuse here is the concept of withdrawal. The pathological gambler experiences something similar. While it does not have the intense physiological symptoms of substance-abuse withdrawal, the psychological discomfort is quite marked. The gambler may exhibit restlessness, jitteriness, racing thoughts, easily triggered anger, as well as the physical and psychological symptoms of anxiety. The depression and agitation sometimes require brief intervention with pharmacotherapy. This state of unrest leads to various strategies to resume gambling. One often repeated story is the husband purposely insulting his wife's cooking to generate an argument to justify leaving the house to gamble.

4) *Gambling as a form of relief from negative feelings or problems.* This parallels a phenomenon in the alcohol field termed "relief drinking." Gambling in this sense provides relief from negative emotional states or provides an intense activity which is so absorbing that the gambler forgets pressing concerns. One could muse on the similarities between gambling and playing golf in terms of each's ability to cause dissociation. Many golfers describe having their attention so absorbed on the little white ball that they would be oblivious to a nuclear explosion.

I have been acquainted with at least a dozen professional men whose problem gambling started during stressful phases in their careers. Gambling provided an escape for these highly successful individuals; it did not have the hassles associated with exercising, relating to anyone, or ingesting any mood-altering substance. This relief feature also reflects a pattern common for women. Women's gambling careers—similar to women's alcohol patterns—typically begin later than men's, and typically also started as a means of coping with some developmental crisis, such as bereavement, retirement, or role conflict (career versus family, etc.).

5) *"Chasing" losses.* Sociologist and gambling expert Henry Lesieur titled his field study of compulsive gamblers *The Chase* (1984), a lucid and straightforward story of fifty compulsive gamblers. According to Lesieur and other experts "chasing" involves

the most reliable and distinguishing characteristic of pathological gamblers. Chasing is a gambling pattern which "doubles up" or "throws good money after bad" in an attempt to recoup loses. A gambler down five hundred dollars on a football game bets one thousand dollars on the next to get even. Naturally if one persists in such high-risk patterns the law of averages dictates rapid financial disaster. Few gamblers can sustain long periods of chasing without incurring serious social problems. This is the equivalent of continuous cocaine use. Ordinary life does not sustain either. Not all problem gamblers reach this phase before needing or seeking help, and it may be useful here to consider one description of the "natural life" of pathological gambling to see how chasing fits into it.

The person in the mental health field most responsible for generating professional credence in the identification and assessment of pathological gambling was psychiatrist Robert Custer (Custer and Milt 1985). While working with alcoholics in a Veterans Administration hospital, Custer was approached by members of Gamblers Anonymous to provide consultation. Eventually his interest in the disorder led to his co-founding the first formal gambling treatment program with psychologist Alida Glen, residing at the Brecksville, Ohio Veterans Administration Hospital. Custer identified several phases in the development of pathological gambling.

a) *Winning Phase.* This phase is characterized by the so-called "big win." Many pathological gamblers in their gambling history can trace back to a significant win early in their gambling careers. This is usually a substantial amount—something in the neighborhood of a half year's income. Such a win tends to be associated with multiple successes at gambling and perhaps sets the stage psychologically for reinforcing the expectation of gambling as the royal road to an easy fortune.
b) *Losing Phase.* Gradually, as with all gambling endeavors, statistical odds are "with the house," so to speak, and the gambler starts to lose more regularly than win. This phase truly separates out those who are able to walk away and "cut their losses" from those who maintain the illusion that their fortunes will change. By definition the pathological gambler persists in gambling despite mounting losses.
c) *Desperation Phase.* This is the stage characterized by chasing losses with observably irrational betting patterns. The gambler's behavior in this stage is frantic and may appear truly manic although this is no authentic manic-depressive

disorder. In addition to massive financial losses, this stage usually leads to severe social dysfunction and often illegal behavior.

Not all gamblers proceed through these stages in an orderly fashion, and some shift back and forth between stages. At times the outsider may not easily discern the gradual shift from one stage to another, and labeling the particular stage is less important than assessing the negative consequences of the gambling itself.

6. *Deceiving others regarding the extent of gambling.* This deception includes outright lying to significant others to conceal the degree of gambling involvement. Gamblers lie to explain away questionable social activities, friendships, work patterns, health issues, romantic encounters, other addictions and, of course, financial management. Naturally this creates a negative response from others and partially explains the next indicator.

7. *Gambling causing significant problems in important relationships, marriage, educational endeavors, occupation; or results in the loss of any of these.* This indicator summarizes the all-important "social consequences" criterion, which is a hallmark in determining the severity of an addiction for any compulsive behavior pattern. This indicator suggests how the gambling behavior is now so compelling that it markedly interferes with social adjustment. Simply put, nothing matters more than the addicting behavior.

8. *Engaging in illegal behavior to procure money for gambling.* Theft, forgery, embezzlement, fraud, or misappropriation of funds are common. In a Gamblers' Anonymous Survey 20 percent (out of 150 members) had a history of criminal arrests, while in a survey of 250 gamblers treated at Taylor Manor Hospital nearly 40 percent had criminal arrest records (Ciarrocchi and Richardson 1989). The issue of committing illegal acts to finance gambling often has important treatment implications. Some gamblers clearly have antisocial personality disorders (ASP) and as such ASP is usually associated with a criminal career. More often, however, gamblers seeking help on their own or through family members are not antisocial. They more closely resemble non-criminals in terms of overall values and past history of social responsibility. The urgency to gamble results in many illegal acts to obtain money to maintain gambling behavior. In this way they resemble substance abusers in that once the addiction is brought under control criminal behavior ceases. The presence or absence of ASP is quite important because ASP has an extremely poor prognosis with almost no known effective treatment. Pathological gambling, on

the other hand, has a recovery rate at least as reasonable as substance abuse, if not slightly better. Assessing ASP is important as it can at least suggest parameters to the intensity of treatment. At the beginning of treatment, however, it is often extremely difficult—even for experienced clinicians—to diagnosis ASP in conjunction with an active gambling problem.

To family, friends, and colleagues the ingenuity of the gambler to create schemes to raise money is amazing, if not inspiring. The pathological gambler uses the trust inherent in close relationships to satisfy the need for money. Significant others are usually shocked and appalled when the truth comes out. Furthermore, many pathological gamblers have charming personal characteristics which further allow them to defraud others. While substance abusers also steal and obtain money illegally, the degree of surprise among family members is usually not the same. Common stories include missing bank accounts, forged checks, loans taken out in other people's names (second mortgaging a home without a co-owner's consent is a common example), or attorneys, bankers, and stock brokers pilfering client accounts. Since many gamblers are deceitful in the early stages of recovery, it is frequently difficult to assess accurately the meaning of antisocial behavior. I can recall several instances of clients misleading me, some even after twenty or more sessions. In one case the fact that the recovering person was a school teacher probably resulted in my not keeping a high enough index of suspicion through repeated relapses. When he finally "came clean" with me and revealed the full extent of his illegal involvement, the most I could offer was a referral to an attorney. The diagnostic dilemma of an antisocial personality is sometimes put succintly by GA members: "Are you dealing with a gambler who steals or a thief who gambles?" The accurate answer to that question may help determine the best use of limited mental health services in individual cases.

9. *Requiring one or more persons to give money to remediate a financial crisis caused by gambling.* In the gambling treatment field this indicator is termed a *bailout.* Pathological gamblers often have several bailouts in their careers. Some never stop having them. The problem gambler naturally seeks out sources for debt relief and, depending on the resources or determination of family and friends, will go on seeking bailouts indefinitely. We have known cases of pathological gambling from wealthy families who are continually bailed out and probably will never seek treatment. Others have few resources available and rapidly deplete their supply of potential benefactors. This may induce them to resort to criminal activity. This indicator

demonstrates the critical importance of working with families or significant others for comprehensive treatment of the disorder; consider the wasted effort of treating a gambler who knows that when he blows his next pay check he can successfully plead with his parents for money. Pathological gamblers are also adept at using the bailout scenario for their own purposes. For example, they will prey on family concerns about the gambler's physical safety if they do not pay back their illegal loan sources. Despite indoctrination from grade B movies and television crime series, the overwhelming majority of bookmakers use decidedly nonviolent means to collect debts. Indeed, it is more usual to nurture a relationship with an active gambler. Families require a great deal of support from clinicians and/or self-help groups to disengage from this type of manipulation. Often spouses come to their senses when children go in need or household essentials (utilities, rent, and so on) are ignored. Parents or elderly relatives may be especially vulnerable to loans for a real or imagined crisis. Educating the family provides a further challenge given the gambler's frequent lack of truthfulness about his or her potential bailout sources in the early stages of treatment.

In summary, these proposed *DSM IV* guidelines suggest that persons exhibiting at least four of the nine indicators fall into the classification of pathological gambler. The counselor needs to appreciate, however, how difficult this assessment can be when all of the data are unavailable, which often happens due to the gambler's denial and/or dishonesty. Interviewing family, friends, or employers is often essential to making a diagnosis. One drawback of the current as well as the proposed diagnostic criteria is that they lack a category of "gambling abuse," which would parallel a similar problem in the alcohol or drug abuse dimension. Just as there are individuals who can abuse alcohol without necessarily being alcoholic, this author believes there are individuals who can abuse gambling without necessarily being pathological gamblers. However, the treatment field has not progressed to put forth established criteria to make this distinction.

Another tool for assessing pathological gambling is a brief questionnaire called the "South Oaks Gambling Screen" (SOGS). The SOGS takes only a few minutes to fill out and is quickly scored. It has been widely used to assess rates of pathological gambling in the general population (Volberg and Steadman 1989), substance abusers (Ciarrocchi 1991b; Lesieur, Blume, and Zoppa 1986), and adolescents (Lesieur and Klein 1987). It is an excellent screening tool which the counselor needs to supplement with interview, but obviously requires honesty on the part of the client when filling it out.

Treating the Pathological Gambler

Special Features

Possibly no other mental health problem has as limited treatment resources as pathological gambling. This feature severely limits the availability of professional treatment resources or a network of conveniently located self-help groups. The reasons for these limitations are extensive and well beyond the scope of this chapter. The major reasons are a) the disorder's relatively recent professional recognition as a mental health problem, b) almost total absence of publicly funded treatment programs, c) nonrecognition of the disorder as a reimbursable psychiatric disorder by health insurance carriers, and d) lack of training regarding diagnosis and treatment of this disorder across every discipline of mental health providers.

The result is that concerned persons utilize clinicians who learn about the disorder as they attempt to treat it—not a desirable situation. The gambling treatment field today probably approximates the alcoholism treatment field of perhaps forty years ago with regard to knowledge, public awareness, number of treatment providers, and established programs. When gamblers and their families discover a sympathetic treatment provider, they are immensely relieved. (Addresses and phone numbers of select resources and referrals are included at the end of this chapter as a starting point for seeking assistance.) Large numbers of people with gambling problems are currently underserved by the few existing programs. Population surveys which identify pathological gamblers in the general community (Volberg and Steadman 1989) repeatedly find much higher rates for women and racial minorities with the disorder than are found in treatment settings. For example, in the state of Maryland women comprised approximately 41 percent of pathological gamblers (Volberg and Steadman 1989), yet in our treatment program located in the same state at Taylor Manor Hospital only 8 percent treated are women (Ciarrocchi and Richardson 1989). This contrasts dramatically with substance abuse programs, which also treat far fewer women than men. Substance-abuse population studies, however, confirm that rates of female substance abusers are truly less, whereas for pathological gamblers rates are almost equal between men and women. Furthermore, since the gambling careers of women differ from men—typically starting later in life and being associated with developmental crises, women gamblers are more likely to end up in general psychiatric treatment for anxiety or depressive disorders.

While this help may be beneficial, if the gambling problem is not identified and resolved recovery is unlikely to endure.

Self-Help Groups

The first resource available is Gamblers Anonymous (GA), a self-help program modeled closely on the Twelve Steps of Alcoholics Anonymous (AA). While not as large as AA, GA has strong followings in most major cities. Its central office will help concerned people locate meetings across the United States and other countries. GA itself is similar to AA in philosophy and traditions. For GA members abstinence from gambling is considered essential, and gambling is viewed as a disease over which one is powerless. The group support helps provide the motivation to stop gambling and to deal with the inevitable adjustment to long-term recovery. A unique feature of the GA program involves the concept of restitution. One aspect of the AA program is called "making amends," wherein the recovering person attempts to redress wrongs inflicted on persons during his or her alcoholic period. GA adds a twist to this concept through the notion of restitution. The recovering gambler is expected to pay back—to the degree reasonable—debts to others. This program feature builds in two important components to the recovery process. The first involves a component of social responsibility. Too often gambling has obliterated social conscience and restitution is a step toward rehabilitating it. Second, restitution often takes years to accomplish—indeed in some cases it is essentially impossible—yet paying even a token amount regularly provides a continual reminder of the devastation created by the disorder. This awareness certainly aids recovery, especially as the acute urge to gamble dissipates over time, possibly generating a sense of false confidence.

Another unique feature of GA is the "pressure relief" meeting. Since financial problems are paramount in early recovery, they often create an incentive to gamble in hope of another "big win." GA members, when requested, will sit down with a member (and spouse) having serious financial problems and to assess the member's financial condition as well as develop realistic payment plans and income-generating strategies. The member brings in records of income, debts, and other financial obligations, which senior members review and make recommendations.

In my experience the GA community has always welcomed interest from professional health care providers and pastoral counselors. Members are usually eager to educate the community about their programs and welcome inquiries to their published phone numbers (see Appendix). The pastoral counselor is well placed in the role of gatekeeper/referral source to GA and, with experience, can provide the pastoral/spiritual dimension to GA members who wish to pursue these interests outside the formal structure of GA. As our experience with AA has taught us, the recovery process frequently awakens or reawakens in the addicted person the need for a spiritual connection which was either underdeveloped or squashed during the addiction phase. Some may wish to reconnect with a church or synagogue, yet wonder about acceptance since their gambling exploits may have taken on a public dimension resulting in embarrassment or shame. GA membership and exploration of the guilt dimension with a pastoral counselor often facilitate reconciliation.

Outpatient Treatment

The most common treatment modality for pathological gambling after self-help groups is outpatient treatment. Although information on this issue is limited, most pathological gamblers probably end up receiving treatment from clinicians who are not specialists in pathological gambling treatment. In this situation counselors must rely on an ability to listen carefully, to appreciate addictive disorders, and to read about the disorder or seek consultation.

Those who work regularly with pathological gamblers would agree that several core issues specific to the disorder need to be addressed in addition to providing what professional therapists term standard quality care. Standard care, of course, involves adequate assessment of all relevant problems, adherence to ethical standards, and providing appropriate levels of empathy and support to create the necessary atmosphere for change.

Crisis Intervention Model

The counselor who faces a typical gambler presenting for help has an experience similar to William James's apt phrase for the infant's experience at birth, "a blooming, buzzing confusion." So many aspects of the gambler's life are falling apart simultaneously and at such rapid speed it is difficult to know where to begin. In addition to the objective difficulties, the counselor may not have the total picture from the gambler. This happens for a variety of reasons both practical and dynamic: denial, minimization, lack of trust, ambivalence about quitting gambling, fear of legal consequences, and often a belief that with just a little extra effort the gambler can work out any remaining problems. As a result the counselor often receives information piecemeal—session by session—sometimes only after collateral contacts with family, friends, employer, or attorney. Not infrequently in the early stages the gambler is still "in action," that is, if not actually gambling still doing a great deal of financial juggling and interpersonal manipulation to keep the house of cards from crumbling. In this stage the gambler often does not let the counselor in on the whole story because "it's all going to work out anyway." Gradually the truth emerges when the gambler realizes that the various schemes will ultimately fail and honesty is the only way to start the problem-solving process.

Accordingly, if the counselor conceptualizes this early stage of treatment through a crisis intervention model (see Callahan 1991) some of the confusion lessens. Therefore several immediate tasks emerge:

Abstinence Control. Obviously, the first goal is directed toward gambling cessation. An immediate referral to GA is the first order of business. GA involvement greatly aids the work of the counselor and enhances the prognosis for many clients. The next step is to do a situational analysis of the gambling behavior (e.g., Marlatt 1985). Counselor and gambler need to identify the situational determinants of the gambling behavior—the who, what, where, when, why, how often, and what does it feel like dimensions of the gambling behavior. This analysis will provide ideas for prevention, for example, situations to avoid; and necessary support systems, persons, places, or activities which will act as deterrants to gambling. The gambler draws up a daily schedule or routine which minimizes contact with high-risk situations.

A major effort toward abstinence control involves obtaining control of the addicting substance—in this case money or its equivalent. A number of the strategies would be labeled "stimulus control" procedures by learning theorists (Bandura 1969). Simplistically stated, if you wanted to overcome a late night potato chip binge habit, one stimulus control is not to buy potato chips in the first place. Stimulus control strategies as applied to gambling problems means removing access to money or its equivalent as much as humanly possible—and in some cases seemingly beyond what is humanly possible!

Abstinence control procedures include direct deposit of pay checks to a responsible family member or financial manager, taking away all credit cards, terminating access to bank teller machines, establishing bank accounts not in the gambler's name (or requiring a counter-signature), asking an employer to hold pay checks so that responsible family members may obtain them, closing out lines of credit or "open loan" accounts at banking institutions, and securing more tightly the access to retirement accounts, children's investments, savings bonds, stocks, or other securities. If there is a way for compulsive gamblers to obtain money they will find it. So the first order of business is to deny access. Family members are initially reluctant to think in such drastic terms, until they uncover some tragic financial scam. Abstinence control may also entail placing the gambler on a strict budget by doling out a daily living allowance instead of carrying substantial sums. At first this may appear degrading or humiliating; even angry spouses sometimes see this as pouring salt in the wound. If they believe this they will be open to manipulation and have difficulty maintaining necessary limits. These procedures and limit setting do not insure that gambling will not occur, but they provide environmental support and create an atmosphere conducive to recovery.

Resolving Financial Crises. In the initial stage of counseling the gambler and family are usually facing some financial crisis. Indeed, more often than not this is the driving force behind seeking help. Resolving the immediate crisis entails walking a thin line between assisting recovery and a bailout. *Bailout* is a perjorative term in the GA and treatment community; it stands for financial assistance that allows pathological gamblers to continue gambling rather than face the natural negative consequences of their behavior. Examples of bailouts include loaning money to gamblers to pay off gambling debts or even non-gambling debts that have resulted from the gambling lifestyle. As noted before, in the typical career of a pathological gambler many bailouts have occurred. In the beginning the gambler borrows from friends, employers, and relatives. As non-payment occurs only primary relationships such as parents, children, or spouses continue to loan money. The net effect of these bailouts is to prevent the gambler from hitting bottom.

Resisting a bailout, however, may be extremely difficult. An active pathological gambler is quite skillful at manipulating sympathy for his or her plight. How does a parent easily resist pleadings such as, "Mom, it's not for me but think of my wife and baby"? Or, how do concerned persons resist giving money when the gambler subtly suggests that if debts are not paid the "mob" will be looking for him? While no airtight rules exist, financial assistance should not result either in assisting the gambler to continue gambling or allow the gambler to avoid responsibilities. If there were a hierarchical decision tree, it might look something like the following: Step one—give no money at all; step two—if necessary, assist financially for treatment; step three—if desirous of assisting the victims of the gambler (family, dependents), ensure that the victims are helped directly rather than through the gambler; step four—if desired, assist financially with legal assistance.

The above suggests what *not* to do in resolving the immediate financial crisis. *Positive* steps include immediate budget planning for the next thirty days. The impact of the planning is usually to make immediate contact with creditors in order to enlist agreement to reduce minimum payments. This both establishes a good working relationship with potential enemies and buys some breathing space to work out of the financial tangle. The gambler or supporters from GA may need to contact betting creditors such as bookies or loan sharks to explain that no more gambling is possible, that this person has a problem with gambling and will make payments according to a reduced schedule. The gambler often exaggerates the degree of urgency to paying off bookmakers since this tends to generate financial assistance from worried family or friends. We regularly caution elderly parents, for example, not to deplete their retirement accounts to pay off bookies for fear of physical harm to their son or daughter.

We also caution against rapid repayment of specific gambling debts to illegal sources, such as bookmakers or loan sharks. Often the gambler feels driven to settle differences quickly. This strategy, however, directs a disproportionate amount of the family's financial resources to gambling losses alone. Other needs have priority, including legitimate debt obligations (for example, house, vehicles, legal loans) and other family obligations. Family members have suffered enough; prolonging their financial deprivation unnecessarily to pay off a bookie is both an injustice and aggravates the family's healing. This seems all the more so when rapid repayment is only in the interest that the gambler feel better about relieving the debt.

Since gamblers and their families are often temporarily destitute, the counselor may need to utilize crisis intervention skills such as assisting clients and families to obtain unemployment income, social welfare assistance, as well as food or medical assistance. Pastoral counselors are often likely to have an established referral/support network in place through church or synagogue.

Legal Crisis. Clinical and empirical evidence clearly demonstrates the high rate of legal problems for compulsive gamblers in treatment. One study (Ciarrocchi and Richardson 1989) found that 40 percent of gamblers in treatment had been arrested, 19 percent had served jail time, 20 percent had pending criminal charges and 31 percent had pending civil charges. This being the case, those seeking treatment will need an attorney almost as much as a counselor. Ideally, referrals should be made to attorneys familiar with pathological gambling. The local GA may be one source of such information. Attorneys knowledgeable about the disorder often do not exist, and it may fall to the pastoral counselor, with the client's permission, to work in a consultation-liaison manner with a client's attorney. Such a liaison is quite therapeutic since gamblers often give piecemeal information to professionals, and consultation minimizes the chances of "selective recall" by the gambler.

The breadth of the gambler's illegal activities is limited only by his or her ingenuity in generating money-making schemes. Common ones involve writing bad checks and obtaining loans fraudulently. Some steal from employers by misappropriating funds or illegal bookkeeping. Attorneys, accountants, or bankers "borrow" clients' funds to gamble. They may escape detection when winning but become exposed in the losing phase. For gamblers who are self-employed, tax problems lead to charges of failure to pay or the more serious charge of tax evasion. A small minority of gamblers seeking help are antisocial personalities lacking in social conscience. Fortunately, compulsive gamblers tend not to engage in violent crime to obtain money, although some lurid stories exist of crimes perpetrated by gamblers (for example, *Diary of a Jewish American Princess*).

Assessment of Immediate Risk. Various studies (Ciarrocchi and Richardson 1989; Custer and Custer 1978) indicate that nearly one gambler in five in treatment reports having made a suicide attempt. These data along with other sources noting high rates of depression in compulsive gamblers point to the importance of routine assessment for suicide in all pathological gamblers. Even though depression may be situational, the lack of perceived solutions may cause self-destructive acts. Assessment of suicidal potential must occur during the initial assessment of all pathological gamblers. When suicide potential appears high, appropriate crisis intervention strategies are required (see Callahan 1991). Furthermore, since co-addiction is also quite common in this disorder, assessment of the role alcohol and other drugs play must be a part of risk-management procedures.

Marital/Family Crisis. The stress associated with living with a pathological gambler equals and may even exceed that of living with an alcoholic or drug addict. Alcoholism, for example, generally develops slowly and families experience a steady erosion of emotional and financial support. Pathological gambling, on the other hand, often has precipitant stress that seems more comparable to natural disasters like fire, flood, or hurricane. One minute life appears comfortable and normal and the next the family has nothing. Dealing with this shock is quite traumatic and reinforces the venerable notion of calling addiction a *family disease*. The shock, fear, anger, shame, and depression which typically stun a gambler's family are natural and understandable. Research on gamblers treated in a psychiatric hospital reveals that spouses measured as high on psychological tests of anxiety, depression, and emotional upset as the hospitalized gamblers themselves (Ahrons 1989). In other words, *the spouse's emotional distress is indistinguishable from that of the psychiatrically hospitalized gamblers!* The level of support, therefore, needed by family members parallels the needs of the addicted gambler. My usual practice is to refer family members to Gamanon, a twelve-step support group for families and friends of compulsive gamblers similar to Al-Anon for alcoholics. There they obtain support and hear from others who have lived through similar problems.

The popular concept of co-dependence fits families of gamblers as well as alcoholics. They are susceptible to the same emotional traps as family members of substance abusers, and the spouses of gamblers are often adult children of alcoholics themselves. They may also benefit, in addition to Gamanon, from attending ACofA meetings for support and insight.

Therapy and/or self-help group membership for families are needed to provide education to the family members regarding bailouts, abstinence control strategies, budgeting issues, and setting priorities on debt repayment. These concepts are not self-evident, even for high functioning individuals, let alone for persons operating in the chaos of this active addiction. The counselor almost always needs to do some family work, however brief, to coordinate the complex treatment plan required by this disorder.

Similarly, even if family members affirm intellectually the necessary strategies for recovery, they often unwittingly sabotage their efforts due to intense negative feelings toward the gambler. Family members often find it impossible to contain their anger and resentment as the wreckage of the disorder, financial and otherwise, seeps more and more into consciousness. While the gambler knows the extent of the bad news all along, families learn in bits and pieces, and the accumulative effect is infuriating. Furthermore, the timetable for healing differs drastically for gamblers and family members. The gambler focuses on the immediate fixation of the need to gamble. As gambling stops the compulsive gambler believes, correctly, that he or she deserves praise. At approximately the same time the spouse is uncovering one fiscal nightmare after another. The gambler quickly labels the spouse critical and non-supportive, while the spouse can hardly contain his or her rage at the massive deception. Furthermore, this timetable continues to march out of harmony. As months or even years of abstinence continue the gambler feels deserving of even more accolades. As I frequently tell recovering gamblers and their families—with abstinence from alcohol a damaged liver can regenerate. Never, however, has a failed bank account spontaneously regenerated. Resentment grows as families realize that a permanent change in their standard of living has occurred in comparison to their peers. Vacations are canceled or trimmed; conspicuous consumption is out; dreams of sending kids away to college often die; and plans for a new car are postponed. In short, a total readjustment of family lifestyle is usually inevitable. Families may choose either to adjust to these new circumstances or remain permanently embittered—blaming the gambler and ventilating their hostility directly or indirectly. Again, this highlights the utility of directing family members to appropriate support groups.

Long-term Recovery Issues

In addition to dealing with immediate abstinence from gambling, the long-term focus of the recovery process should attend specifically to three areas. The first involves the problem of co-addiction. Gamblers, in my experience, as much as alcoholics or drug-addicted persons, tend to develop high rates of co-addiction, particularly with regard to alcohol. Ongoing counseling needs to monitor alcohol consumption closely and discuss prevention openly with the client.

Secondly, dysfunctional conditions may arise from anxiety or mood disorders. A certain percentage of recovering gamblers will have clear-cut anxiety disorders (panic attacks, phobia, generalized anxiety disorder) while still more may suffer from severe depression. A small number, but disproportionately high in terms of the general population, will suffer from manic depression (Bipolar Disorder). Such cases will involve referral to appropriate mental health specialists who may work in concert with the pastoral counselor. Addictive gambling sometimes masks an underlying psychological condition but can only be seen clearly once the dust settles and the client has a track record of abstinence.

The third area requiring focus is long-term personality growth. While there is not one all-encompassing "gambler personality," subsets of pathological gamblers have repeatedly observed personality characteristics. One subset commonly encountered is the gambler's sense of entitlement or, in psychiatric jargon, narcissism. Many gamblers tend to view reality with the perspective that they are entitled to receive life's benefits without regard to effort exerted. This extends to a life devoid of pain, easy money, and the esteem and affection of others. Although many people have similar desires what differentiates compulsive gamblers is their belief—or perhaps more an attitude—that the universe *owes* all this to them. Some argue that gamblers believe this because they have a distorted belief system where ordinary laws of behavior-consequences are suspended in their case. One needs to distort the laws of probability, for example, to engage in a compulsive gambling pattern. This belief of their specialness extends to other areas and may be equally self-defeating. This personality style requires much reflection and hard work to change and should occupy the later phases of recovery.

Pastoral Focus

Addictions have long been a focus for pastoral counselors, and some have made important contributions to the field in their own right (e.g., Clinebell 1978; Royce 1989). Many of the pastoral counseling themes operative for addictions apply as well to compulsive gambling (see Ciarrocchi 1984, 1987, 1991a). Nevertheless, certain pastoral themes emerge, specifically for gambling addiction.

Illness Versus Moral Lapse

While many still view alcoholism and drug addiction as moral weakness, public education has greatly increased society's understanding of these disorders as primarily health problems rather than sin. There is much less public acceptance of compulsive gambling as an illness and more likelihood of seeing it as a form of moral weakness. Furthermore, the general public is prone to label out-of-control-gamblers pejoratively. The upshot of the public's viewpoint is to make it more difficult for gamblers to accept an illness model as opposed to a moral one.

As recovery unfolds the gambler acknowledges many behaviors which are dissonant to his or her value system. These commonly include lying, cheating, stealing, fraud, ignoring the needs of family or friends, irresponsible work habits, and even sexual misconduct. The pastoral counselor creates an accepting relationship which allows the gambler to a) examine this behavior in the context of the addiction, b) seek forgiveness from those offended sincerely and honestly, c) reevaluate his or her personal standard of conduct to derive further motivation to remain abstinent, and d) formulate an understanding of past conduct in terms of his or her current relationship with God or a higher power. This last point may even evolve into a traditional religious ritual of forgiveness-seeking as practiced by a faith tradition.

For those familiar with the AA-modeled twelve-step programs the logical place to deal with such issues occurs when working on the Fourth and Fifth Steps. While this theoretically holds for gambling recovery programs as well, my experience indicates much less utilization of Fourth and Fifth Step work among recovering gamblers than with their substance-abusing counterparts. The pastoral counselor may suggest such work to the recovering gambler or be the facilitator directly of this work. Recovering gamblers usually welcome the attention of pastoral counselors, and there is a salutary and healing component to the pastoral counselor's interest. The recovering gambler often interprets this positively as a means of working through his or her own shame and guilt about past behavior.

Changing the Meaning of Money

Compulsive gamblers are not materialistic by the common sense definition; that is, one for whom all values are subservient to obtaining materialistic goods. Nevertheless, they often retain in the recovery phase behavioral features which appear materialistic. Some of these behaviors are vestiges of the gambling *persona*, a public presentation which a pathological gambler promotes to confuse the onlooker. For example, active pathological gamblers will not admit to chronic losing. To do so means having a bookie or loan source cut them off. To remain in action they must keep up an appearance of prosperity. Hence they engage in ostentatious displays—purchasing conspicuous items as gifts or personal possessions such as jewelry, clothes or expensive cars. They purchase such goods despite the priority needs for their limited disposable income.

This public image dies hard even in recovery. Often what emerges is emotional attachment to the *meaning* of money. For some gamblers money was the only symbol of affection they received in an impoverished childhood. Often they can recall the only positive exchanges with a parent as those associated with money. For some, the parents may have spent considerable money on the child but in a random or inconsistent fashion, usually as guilty reparation for their inattentiveness. For others, the lack of sufficient material goods as a youngster left strong feelings of deprivation. In these cases money comes to symbolize a solution to healing psychic wounds.

In short, gambling becomes associated with the emotional meaning of money. The pastoral counselor's task is to assess non-judgmentally the person's emotional meaning attached to money, to reflect this view back to the person, to question deeply with the person the negative impact of such a view, and to explore what alternative meanings are available. The pastoral counselor should appreciate that direct discussion of values will often backfire. Even compulsive gamblers committed to recovery have a hard time appreciating abstractions such as alternative values in the early phases of recovery. One must keep in mind that the prevailing mindset is that money will solve all problems. This mindset may even be more compelling in the early stages of recovery. It is difficult to identify problems in this phase that a sudden influx of money would *not* improve.

The challenge to the pastoral counselor, then, is to assist the person in seeing that this mindset is what actually results in his or her downfall, that in addition to other changes, a value-system shift will go a long way toward ensuring abstinence.

The practical effect of such a stance by the pastoral counselor can be envisioned in the following example. John, a pathological gambler abstinent for just a few weeks, presents the following set of family dilemmas: now that he has revealed the true extent of the family's financial crisis due to his gambling he no longer has the option of spending money to keep up the appearances of a normally functioning family. Instead, over the next year several radical cutbacks will be necessary: summer camp for the children is canceled, two weeks at the beach will become three days at best, four years away at a private college for his eldest daughter cannot occur, one of the two family cars will have to be sold, and piano lessons for his ten year old will also be canceled.

The pastoral counselor's assessment uncovers John's view that these items identify him as a "good provider," and he cannot feel positive about himself without this label. Further assessment reveals, however, that when gambling John spent very little quality time with either his wife or children, but they complained little since he always purchased activities for them. The pastoral counselor's role here would be to explore what is involved in the concept of "good provider." What are the true goods that children and family members need? Are they purchased commodities? Or, are they human gifts of interpersonal giving? If the latter, then perhaps John can come to a point of reformulating his self-definition as a good provider. If his self-definition is not changed at the core, he will remain vulnerable to gambling urges because his value system is consistent only with materialistic solutions. No one is better suited or better prepared to deal with the notion of values clarification than the pastoral counselor, particularly since the value the gambler places on money is self- and life-negating. Frequently, too, the pastoral counselor may need to intervene with family members in this process since they may have also incorporated the gambler's value system as their own.

Summary

According to even conservative estimates one to three persons in one hundred have a serious gambling problem. Gambling for these individuals creates major occupational, financial, legal, health, and family problems. The economic cost to society based on legal consequences alone are staggering. Within the last twenty years there has been a small but strong movement within the mental health community to view pathological gambling as a mental health problem and an addiction. Intervention efforts take the form of assisting the gambler to accept this out-of-control behavior as a problem, referring to self-help groups (Gamblers Anonymous), as well as making available both outpatient and inpatient treatment. Due to society's slow recognition of pathological gambling as a mental health issue the number of trained professionals is limited, and there are fewer still treatment programs. GA is available in many communities, and mental health professionals may need to learn about the problem through consulting GA. Outpatient treatment requires a crisis intervention model with attention directed toward abstinence control, financial restructuring, legal assistance when required, family intervention, and psychological risk assessment. Inpatient treatment is generally reserved for pathological gamblers with serious mental health issues in addition to gambling, for example, severe depression or manic behavior. The pastoral counselor has multiple avenues for approaching pathological gambling including pre-intervention, family support, coordination of available community resources, addressing the issues of moral lapses during the addictive cycle, and assisting the recovering person in confronting his or her personal value system regarding the emotional significance of money. It is expected that the adventurous pastoral counselors will make significant contributions to the healing process of pathological gambling just as this profession has in the substance-abuse field. A good example of this adventurousness and commitment is Monsignor Joseph Dunn, founder and first president of the National Council on Compulsive Gambling.

Resources

Gamblers Anonymous
Telephones for Major Areas

National Service Office
213–386–8789
P.O. Box 17173
Los Angeles, CA 90017

Consult your local directory if your area is not listed.

Phoenix, AZ
(602) 582–2089

Los Angeles, CA
(213) 260–4657

Sacramento, CA
(916) 447–5588

San Diego, CA
(619) 239–2911

San Francisco, CA
(800) 541–7867

San Jose, CA
(800) 541–7867

Calgary, CANADA
(403) 237–0654

Montreal, CANADA
(514) 484–6666

Toronto, CANADA
(416) 366–7613

Vancouver, CANADA
(604) 685–5510

Connecticut
(203) 777–5585

Washington, DC
(301) 961–1313

Miami, FL
(305) 447–2696

Atlanta, GA
(404) 237–7281

Chicago, IL
(312) 346–1588

New Orleans, LA
(504) 837–501

Boston, MA
(617) 739–7322

Springfield, MA
(413) 732–7854

Baltimore, MD
(301) 377–3889

Michigan
(313) 446–5144

Gamblers Anonymous
Telephones for Major Areas (continued)

Minneapolis, MN
(612) 922–3956

St. Louis, MO
(314) 647–1111

Omaha, NE
(402) 978–7557

Las Vegas, NV
(702) 385–7732
(702) 459–0864

New Jersey
(201) 756–1171

Long Island, NY
(516) 586–7171

New York City, NY
(212) 265–8600

Syracuse, NY
(315) 458–0085

Cincinnati, OH
(513) 244–9779

Cleveland, OH
(216) 771–2248

Oklahoma City, OK
(405) 525–2026

Portland, OR
(503) 233–5888

Philadelphia, PA
(215) 468–1991

Pittsburgh, PA
(412) 281–7484

Nashville, TN
(615) 254–6454

Dallas, TX
(214) 634–2095

Houston, TX
(713) 492–4611

Seattle, WA
(206) 464–9514

Spokane, WA
(509) 249–9158

Wheeling, WV
(304) 234–8161

ADVOCACY/REFERRALS

National Council
on Problem Gambling
445 West 59th Street
New York, NY 10019
(800) 522–4700

TREATMENT

Taylor Manor Hospital
Gambling Treatment Program
College Avenue
Ellicott City, Maryland
(800) 527–8238

Note

The author wishes to express his deep appreciation to Shelly Hare for manuscript preparation.

References

Ahrons, S. J. 1989. "A Comparison of the Family Environments and Psychological Distress of Married Pathological Gamblers, Alcoholics, Psychiatric Patients, and Their Spouses with Normal Controls." Ph.D. diss., University of Maryland.

American Psychiatric Association. 1987. *Diagnostic and Statistical Manual of Mental Disorders*, 3d ed. rev. Washington, D.C. Referred to in text as *DSM III-R*.

Bandura, A. 1969. *Principles of Behavior Modification*. New York: Holt, Rinehart and Winston.

Callahan, R. 1991. "The Ministry of Crisis Intervention." In *Pastoral Counseling*, edited by B. K. Estadt, M. Blanchette, and J. R. Compton. Englewood Cliffs, NJ: Prentice-Hall.

Christiansen, E. M. 1989. "1988 Gross Annual Wager." *Gaming and Wagering Business* 10, 8 (July 15).

Ciarrocchi, J. W. 1984. "Alcoholism." In *Psychiatry, Ministry, and Pastoral Counseling*, 2d ed., edited by A. W. Sipe and C. J. Rowe., pp. 363–78. Collegeville, Minn.: Liturgical Press.

———. 1987. "Addiction Counseling." In *The Art of Clinical Supervision: A Pastoral Counseling Perspective*, edited by B. K. Estadt, J. R. Compton, and M. Blanchette. New York: Paulist Press.

———. 1991b. *Rates of Pathological Gambling in Publicly Funded Outpatient Substance Abuse Treatment*. Manuscript submitted for publication.

———. 1991a. "Counseling with the Recovering Alcoholic." In Estadt, et al., *Pastoral Counseling*.

Ciarrocchi, J. W., and Hohman, A. 1989. "The Family Environment of Married Male Pathological Gamblers, Alcoholics, and Dually Addicted Gamblers." *Journal of Gambling Behavior* 3:257–63.

Ciarrocchi, J. W., and Richardson, R. 1989. "Profile of Compulsive Gamblers in Treatment: Update and Comparisons." *Journal of Gambling Behavior* 5:53–65.

Clinebell, H. 1978. *Understanding and Counseling the Alcoholic*. Nashville: Abingdon.

Custer, R. L., and Custer, L. F. 1978. *Characteristics of the Recovering Compulsive Gambler: A Survey of 150 Members of Gamblers*

Anonymous. A paper presented at the Fourth Annual Conference on Gambling. Reno, Nevada.

Custer, R., and Milt, H. 1985. *When Luck Runs Outs: Help for Compulsive Gamblers and Their Families*. New York: Facts on File.

Lesieur, H. R. 1984. *The Chase: Career of the Compulsive Gambler*. Cambridge, Mass.: Schenkman.

———, Blume, S. B., and Zoppa, R. M. 1986. "Alcoholism, Drug Abuse, and Gambling." *Alcoholism: Clinical and Experimental Research* 10:33–38.

———, and Klein, R. 1987. "Pathological Gambling Among High School Students." *Addictive Behaviors* 12:129–35.

———, and Rosenthal, R. J. 1990. *Pathological Gambling, 312.31: A Review of the Literature*. Paper prepared for work group on disorders of impulse control not elsewhere classified, American Psychiatric Association, DSM IV (February).

Marlatt, A. 1985. "Situational Determinants of Relapse and Skill Training Intervention. In *Relapse Prevention*, edited by A. Marlatt and J. Gordon. New York: Guilford Press.

Politzer, R. M.; Morrow, J. S.; Leavey, S. D. 1985. "Report on the Cost-Benefit/Effectiveness of Treatment at the Johns Hopkins Center for Pathological Gambling." *Journal of Gambling Behavior* 1:131–42.

Royce, J. 1989. *Alcohol Problems and Alcoholism*. New York: Macmillan.

Taber, J. I.; McCormick, R. A.; Russo, A. M.; Adkins, B. J.; Ramirez, L. F. 1987. "Follow-up of Pathological Gamblers After Treatment." *American Journal of Psychiatry* 144:757–61.

Volberg, R. A., and Steadman, H. J. 1989. "Prevalence Estimates of Pathological Gambling in New Jersey and Maryland." *American Journal of Psychiatry* 146:1618–1619.

SECTION VI
SPECIAL CHALLENGES AND OPPORTUNITIES FOR THE 1990s

Our final section presents articles that address a number of contemporary issues and concerns which appear to be taking center stage in the 1990s. In Chapter 24, David Foy, with the assistance of Kent Drescher, Allan Fitz, and Kevin Kennedy, presents a pastoral view of posttraumatic stress disorder. The legacy of Vietnam has given notoriety to the posttraumatic stress disorder; however, as the authors point out, PTSD is not restricted to the time or experience of war. In their review the authors acquaint the reader with the primary symptoms of PTSD; provide a model for discriminating normal trauma from pathological adjustment; and offer guides for appropriate pastoral responses aimed at facilitating the survivor's growth through the experience. A very poignant and helpful message contained within the essay is that pastoral care-givers need to beware, and be aware, of vicarious victimization. The authors note that persons who are exposed to the traumatic experiences of victims may experience the same destructive reactions. The authors suggest a number of specific strategies pastoral counselors can employ to reduce the risk of vicarious victimization. These recommendations are a must for those working with this population.

As an extension of this theme of posttrauma stress, Richard Parsons describes the extensive destruction reeked by one act of suicide on those who survive (Chapter 25). He provides an in-depth analysis of the various socio-psychological forces that exist and which encourage suicide survivors to deny and repress their grief, thus creating a pathogenic response to mourning. In addition to presenting a model for diagnosing pathogenic grief and suggesting steps to remediate and intervene with such pathogenic mourning, Parsons suggests a primary level of prevention which may serve as the pastoral counseling model of service delivery.

While appearing somewhat less dramatic than the previous forms of posttrauma response, for those in the midst of the stress of unemployment, the loss of one's job is certainly no less traumatic. In Chapter 26 Roy Lewis employs a grief model to understand the impact and process of a job loss. Through the use of a case analysis model, Lewis provides the reader with a clear, concise approach to the pastoral care of the unemployed. Since this pastoral area is in its infancy, the anecdotal tone of this paper is to be expected and points to the need for further attention on a number of levels both in the church and within pastoral counseling communities that minister to the unemployed.

Our final offering addresses one of the most devastating issues of the 1990s: ministry to those with AIDS. Walter Smith makes personal and real the very clinical data collected in the area of Acquired Immunodeficiency Syndrome. (Chapter 27) The temptation to depersonalize the syndrome as a way of alleviating our own anxiety is great. However, as well as providing a clinically sophisticated and pastorally moving view of AIDS, Smith challenges pastoral counselors to address their own personal and professional limitations when working with AIDS patients. Perhaps the most poignant section of the essay appears in the epilogue, in which Smith shares a story of a young man named "Matthew." In the days before the end of Matthew's life, he shares with the counselor his awareness that God truly does love him. In Matthew's own words: "God does love me and sent me an angel to bring me home. You've been that angel."

Matthew's experience is one of hope, one of love, and clearly one which is the essence of "the pastoral." For just as Matthew, and all of the other clients depicted throughout this volume, found the love of God through their encounters with the pastoral counselor, so too did those counselors who shared this information with us experience the love and face of God in their clients. Is it any wonder that even though pastoral counseling is such a demanding ministry, it has such great potential for those involved in it to experience, so directly and dramatically, the incarnational love of God every day?

David W. Foy
Kent D. Drescher
Allan G. Fitz
Kevin R. Kennedy

24. Posttraumatic Stress Disorder

Catastrophic experiences within the church family present pastors critical opportunities to minister to people made vulnerable by extreme adversity. Indeed, victims' feelings about how pastors and the church family respond to their needs in times of crisis often color their relationships with the church from that time on. Not only are trauma survivors' relations with the church affected by their experiences, their physical and psychological well-being is also challenged, placing them temporarily "at risk" for stress-related disorders. On a more positive note, evidence is accumulating which demonstrates that supportive behavior by caring members within victims' social circles can be important in reducing risk for stress-related disorders. Thus, pastors and others in the church family may serve vital roles in helping to prevent posttraumatic stress disorders (PTSD) in vulnerable members.

The purpose of this chapter is to acquaint pastors with current information about PTSD, including its primary symptoms and related traumatic experiences. Additionally, we will provide distinctions between "normal" traumatic crisis reactions and pathological adjustment to assist clergy in making screening assessments regarding the need for professional referral. Several theological implications of traumatic experiences will be presented, along with pastoral responses which may help trauma survivors to work through their experiences. Finally, an "anti-burnout survival kit" is offered for pastors who are heavily engaged in ongoing ministry to trauma survivors.

Definition of PTSD

Surviving a life-threatening personal experience often produces intense psychological reactions in the forms of intrusive thoughts about the experience and fear-related avoidance of reminders. In the first few weeks following a traumatic experience these patterns are found in most individuals and thus seem to represent a natural response mechanism for psychological adaptation to a life-changing event. Persistence of this reaction pattern at troublesome levels beyond a three month period, however, indicates that the natural psychological adjustment process, like mourning in the bereaved, has been derailed. At that point the psychological reactions natural in the first few weeks become symptoms of PTSD. In other words, PTSD may be seen as the persistence of a natural process beyond its natural time frame for resolution.

The cardinal features of PTSD are trauma-specific symptoms of intrusion, avoidance, and physical arousal. The primary requirement (Category A) is the presence of "an event that is outside the range of usual human experience and would be markedly distressing to almost anyone" (American Psychiatric Association 1987, p. 250). A life-threatening event, such as serious injury in a traffic accident, would satisfy this criterion, while the expected death of a loved one from natural causes would not. The current diagnostic system then groups PTSD symptoms into three additional categories. Category B includes the presence in some form of persistent intrusive thoughts and feelings. Recurrent distressing dreams or flashbacks while awake about the traumatic experience are examples. Category C represents the presence of avoidance symptoms associated with the trauma, such as avoiding driving following a severe traffic accident or fear of sexual relations following sexual assault. More subtle forms of avoidance would be general numbing of responsiveness or the absence of strong feelings about the trauma. Category D reflects the presence of symptoms of increased physical arousal and hypervigilance. Feelings of panic may be experienced in situations similar to the trauma; for example, combat veterans with PTSD may show powerful startle reactions to loud noises that resemble gunshots or explosions.

The medical history of PTSD can be traced back to studies of human reactions to trauma in the nineteenth century by German psychiatrists who discovered the similarities in the clinical courses of survivors of mining accidents and accidents which involved toxic exposure (Kolb 1988). Two major developments at that time stimulated investigations into what was then called post-traumatic neurosis. The initial spark of medical interest in the subject was ignited by a series of wars, including the Civil War in America and the two World Wars in Europe. Early conceptions of combat-related PTSD by physicians working with veterans of World War I presented it as "shell shock," a consequence of organic dysfunction rather than a psychological process. This formulation arose from use in World War I of both chemical agents and explosives of a power that previously had been unimaginable.

The second impetus was the emergence of social programs in several countries which began to provide compensation for work-related or military service-related disabilities. The early description of traumatic reactions as "compensation reactions" referred to a perceived rise in numbers of victims seeking restitution after the first compensations laws were introduced in Europe (Trimble 1985). This phenomenon presented an example of the tendency to relate symptoms of a trauma reaction to some process other than exposure to intense trauma itself.

While early views of posttraumatic reactions reflected the assumption that various types of trauma produced similar reactions, studies in the past twenty years have tended to be trauma-specific in their focus. Thus, labels for PTSD such as battle fatigue, rape trauma syndrome, and disaster survivor syndrome have developed in the literature (Foa, Steketee, and Olasov Rothbaum 1989). However, most recently, studies have shown similarities among several survivor groups, including combat (Foy, Sipprelle, Rueger, and Carroll 1984; Keane, Fairbank, Caddell, and Zimering 1989), rape (Neumann, Gallers, and Foy 1989), domestic violence (Houskamp and Foy, n.d.), childhood sexual abuse (Briere 1989; Lindberg and Distad 1985), childhood physical abuse (Ammerman, Cassisi, Hersen, and Van-Hasselt 1986), transportation accidents (McCaffrey and Fairbank 1985), and natural disasters (Green, Grace, and Gleser 1985).

Common elements of traumatic experience include being physically and psychologically overwhelmed by a life-threatening event which is beyond the victim's prediction and control. To understand such complex reaction patterns requires the integration of findings from both biology and psychology. Thus, current perspectives on the nature of PTSD include contributions from several approaches, including biological (Pitman 1989), behavioral (Keane, Fairbank, Caddell, Zimering, and Bender 1985), cognitive (Foa, Stekelee, and Olasov Rothbaum 1989), and integrative (Foy, Osato, Houskamp, and Neumann, n.d.).

From a biological perspective a number of studies in the past ten years have been conducted with Vietnam combat veterans with PTSD to examine their physiological reactions to combat trauma reminders or cues. Results from these studies have been consistent in showing large heart rate increases in most combat veterans with PTSD when they were exposed to combat cues. Other biological studies have also shown that combat veterans with PTSD have experienced changes in their central nervous systems so that they are overly sensitive to startle-producing noises. Studies are currently being conducted to determine whether these biological features are also applicable to PTSD associated with other types of trauma. Since these physical features of PTSD are almost universally described as painfully distressing in nature, this biological reactivity may be a critical element in the onset of social irritability and withdrawal in PTSD victims.

Contributions from behavioral psychology help in understanding how PTSD symptoms develop. Pavlovian conditioning occurs at the time of the trauma so that the overpowering feelings of life-threat and helplessness are paired with other cues present (which are not life-threatening). By this learning process these cues acquire the potential for evoking extreme fear when they are encountered later. The survivor also learns that escaping from these cues terminates the distressing fear. Planning life activities to avoid painful reminders, an example of instrumental learning, may become a preferred coping strategy since it reduces the painful exposure to trauma reminders.

From a cognitive psychology perspective, the meaning which the survivor attaches to the traumatic experience may play an important role in PTSD. Perceptions of helplessness associated with the traumatic experience may serve to immobilize survivors' more active coping efforts, thereby serving to maintain PTSD symptoms.

While these approaches are helpful in explaining possible mechanisms for the development of PTSD, they do not explain why some individuals exposed to intense trauma do not develop enduring PTSD symptoms. In order to address this issue an integrative approach is necessary which includes additional factors beyond biological reactivity, Pavlovian and instrumental learning, and symbolic meaning. In our integrative model of PTSD the experience of an overwhelming biological reaction during a life-threatening traumatic event lays the necessary foundation for the development of PTSD through behavioral and cognitive mechanisms of learning. However, other factors serve to mediate between exposure to trauma and the development of PTSD symptoms. Thus, an integrative approach to understanding PTSD includes the interaction between traumatic experiences and other non-trauma factors to account for the development or non-development of PTSD.

Non-Traumatic Factors Influencing PTSD Development

Much research has already established that the severity of exposure to traumatic events plays a primary role in the development of symptoms of PTSD (Foy, Sipprelle, Rueger, and Carroll 1984). For example, combat veterans who are wounded are at greater risk for PTSD than soldiers who saw limited combat without personal injury. However, other factors also serve to increase the risk or provide protection from the development of symptoms. Attributions or meanings that individuals assign to traumatic events may also influence the development of PTSD. Janoff-Bulman (1985) has shown that three basic life assumptions are often shattered by trauma. These are: 1) "I am safe," that is, self-invulnerability or, "It won't happen to me"; 2) "life is fair and equitable"; and 3) "I am a good person," that is, self-esteem from positive life experiences. A traumatic experience may cause shifts in these life assumptions toward extreme defensiveness. Inability to moderate "shattered" assumptions toward a more balanced view may worsen symptoms of PTSD in some victims (Foy, Resnick, Carroll, and Osato 1990).

Another influence involves previous life experiences, which may contribute positively or negatively to the development of PTSD symptoms. Events such as previous child physical or sexual abuse, severe marital or family dysfunction, and the presence of other life stresses at the time of trauma have been implicated in increasing risk for the development of PTSD. Conversely, protective factors such as strong social support before and after the trauma may act to prevent or diminish the severity of PTSD symptoms. In a related context it is interesting to note that there is some recent evidence that intrinsic religiosity, that is, religion as a central focus of life, may serve as a protective factor in reducing risk for developing PTSD or in moderating the severity of symptoms (Astin, Lawrence, Pincus, and Foy 1990).

Spiritual Challenges of Traumatic Experiences

The experience of trauma evokes intense emotions including rejection, betrayal, futility, alienation, estrangement, grief, guilt, shame, isolation, and withdrawal. While these emotional expressions are normal and expected, they may render the survivor temporarily more vulnerable in other areas. In particular, the experience of trauma may challenge the survivor's spirituality.

What are some of the most troublesome theological issues for those with PTSD? Perhaps the most common one concerns the problem of evil. The aftermath of trauma often produces reflection by both victim and helper on how and why the events occurred. Questions such as, "Why did this have to happen?" or, "How could a loving God allow such suffering?" are difficult to answer even for the best-trained theologian. Traumatic events have the power to shatter the most basic assumptions upon which people base their lives. The assumptions that life is basically fair and safe may be called into question permanently when traumatic events occur. Theologically, the idea that God cares for and protects individuals can be radically shaken by catastrophic events. Most victims are forced to reshape their thinking in some way to accommodate life-changing experiences.

Surprisingly, guilt and shame are also common emotional expressions by victims of severe trauma. If life is assumed to be ultimately fair, there may be a tendency to assign or assume unwarranted blame. Victims may blame themselves, especially if there is no readily available way to understand why the traumatic event occurred. "Survivor guilt" is a common emotional reaction in many types of traumas, exemplified when survivors ask themselves, "Why was I spared while others died?" Additionally, trauma victims often believe they should have done something to prevent the trauma from occurring, thereby blaming themselves for their actions or lack thereof. Self-blame may further be compounded through "secondary victimization," in which others hold victims responsible in some way for the events they have experienced. For example, in traumas like rape, incest, or physical abuse, some people assume that victims must have played a part in their own traumatization. Unable to comprehend or accept that anyone would perpetrate such terrible acts, these individuals may suggest that victims must have been overly seductive or provoked the abuse in some unknown manner. These assumptions may cause victims to be further traumatized, which in turn may increase their hesitancy to disclose to others.

Anger is another common response to trauma. Intense rage may be directed toward the event itself, the perpetrator of the event, and at others who do not seem to understand. Anger can also be self-directed when recovery is slow. Victims may commonly feel that "I should be able to get over this faster." This anger may further contribute to a sense of isolation and estrangement from others.

The Bible directly informs the religious community as to the kinds of responses it needs to make toward those who have been victimized by traumatic events. One scriptural theme emphasizes special concern for the weakest, most vulnerable members of society, often categorized as widows, orphans, and strangers. This directive seems no less relevant now since there is growing evidence that these individuals are most vulnerable to repeated victimization by human-induced traumas.

In the New Testament the church was assigned the task of caring for those in need: feeding the hungry, healing the sick, clothing the naked, and protecting the oppressed. The church is described as a community of mutual support, where individuals weep with those who weep and who bear one another's burdens. Thus, the religious community has a special responsibility by biblical mandate to care for the needs of those who have been oppressed by natural or human-made circumstances.

The Role of the Pastoral Counselor

Since the clergy represent the front lines of the mental health delivery system for many individuals, pastors are often the first contacts for parishioners in crisis. Pastoral counseling may serve as the sole professional resource for many who may never seek treatment from other mental health professions. Because of this key role, it is important that pastoral counselors be aware of the types of traumatic events which produce symptoms of PTSD. By recognizing risk in parishioners who have experienced these traumas, the clergy can take active steps to help in the crisis and thus reduce the risk for PTSD.

Though much research and public attention has been devoted to the difficulties many Vietnam combat veterans have had following the war, increasing evidence shows that many different types of traumatic events can produce PTSD. The most commonly known types of events are criminal assault, rape, transportation or industrial accidents, and natural disasters. Not only are the victims of such traumas at risk for developing PTSD, their family members, observers, police, and other help-providers may also be at risk for the disorder.

It has become increasingly clear that family violence presents the most frequent source of trauma through experiences such as childhood physical and sexual abuse, incest, and woman-battering. Because of cultural and family tabus against disclosing these experiences, many individuals suffer alone for years with symptoms of PTSD. Victims of such traumas are found in all segments of society, and among all socioeconomic groups, genders, ages, and races. Each of these individuals needs a place where there is no risk of being retraumatized, a place where to experience acceptance and nurturance. Since each church community includes individuals who, at some point, have been victims of traumatic experiences, pastoral counselors need to prepare themselves to assist these victims. Additionally, clergy need to also be aware of ways in which they could be affected by the traumatic experiences of others.

The Church's Response

When victims of personal assault, devastation, or loss seek comfort and support from people who share their faith, pastors can use their unique relationships to facilitate healing. By being knowledgeable about the ways in which traumatic events affect individuals psychologically, ministers can be prepared to give timely and meaningful help to individuals throughout the recovery process. One of the most significant contributions that clergy and the church can make to the recovery of persons, including those suffering from PTSD, is to provide a strong social support system to these individuals. Whether support is found among family, friends, or a formal support group, victims need others with whom they can disclose the events which have occurred without fear of misunderstanding, ridicule, or blame. A counselor should assess the physical and psychological resources which the victim has and be prepared to help find other needed supports as necessary within the community. Informal opportunities for the survivor to recount the story to others in a safe environment are often major parts of the healing process. Victims need to be able to process their experiences by talking about their feelings and by having the freedom to express a wide range of strong emotions about the events including rage, sorrow, hurt, and grief.

Recent research on the influence of social support on recovery from sexual assault shows that women with supportive networks cope much better with the assault and its aftermath than women without available support (Ruch and Hennessey 1982; Ruch and Chandler 1983). It is a cruel paradox that while persons suffering from emotional distress benefit from social support, this support frequently disintegrates or becomes severely strained following a severe trauma (Ellis 1983). This may be related to the fact that individuals with

PTSD are unable to relate effectively to others in their support system because of fear of disclosing the details of the trauma. Schwartz (1990) commented:

> Often the patient is fearful of expressing to others the nature of the trauma, not knowing what reactions to expect. This tends to increase the person's sense of isolation. In addition, patients who have flashbacks in association with loss of control, are frightening to others and are avoided by others. Last, many of these patients . . . have associated substance dependence and abuse problems. . . . Ultimately, through this type of behavior, the patient brings about from other people the rejection the patient had already expected to occur (p. 233).

Victims may find it difficult to talk about their traumatic events because when they "relive" them the experience comes flooding painfully back into memory. Avoiding people, objects, or events which serve as reminders of the trauma is, of course, one of the classic symptoms of PTSD. However, victims' experiences of isolation and feelings of estrangement may be due, in part, to accurate perceptions that other people are uncomfortable with their experiences and shy away accordingly. Often the support group itself resists the experiences of the traumatized person, particularly when the trauma is directly caused by human behavior. Thompson (1989), for example, noted that church settings may not be safe environments to initiate discussions about victimization through domestic violence and sexual assault since congregations may be unprepared or unwilling to acknowledge that the problem exists within the church community. Some church members may naively assume that spiritual maturity ensures universal psychological health. Such contentious attitudes may isolate trauma victims who have psychological difficulty in dealing with a traumatic event. Distressed individuals may leave the church or learn to hide their true feelings because of the implicit message that "true" Christians should be able to withstand trauma without distress. To better serve the needs of victims of traumatic events, the church needs to initiate and sustain support in a consistent, non-judgmental manner for members who have been victimized.

Pastoral counselors need to begin the helping process by normalizing the strong feelings survivors have about their traumatic experiences. Victims need to understand that it is common for ordinary events in daily life to serve as powerful reminders of their trauma and, consequently, to elicit strong feelings at seemingly inappropriate times and places. Flashbacks, fears, nightmares, and physical responses such as a pounding heart, sweating, and nausea can all be normal responses to everyday cues which serve as reminders of the trauma. The pastoral counselor can help survivors identify the types of reminders which produce trauma-related distress, thus helping prepare for future coping efforts.

Pastors and other church friends can particularly support survivors and traumatized individuals by recognizing that pain is often associated with "anniversary reactions," which many survivors experience each year. For example, the loss of a child in an auto accident may be especially painful to the surviving parents each year on the actual date of its occurrence because it is an inescapable reminder which may temporarily "re-traumatize" them. Accordingly, pastors can help by showing sensitivity to the emotional stress of trauma anniversary dates and by attempting to offer additional support during these times. Something as simple as a timely phone call or an encouraging note can be meaningful to a parishioner who is reexperiencing painful memories.

There are additional ways in which prepared pastors and lay counselors can help parishioners cope with the emotional pain of trauma. Several principles or guidelines are offered in Table 1 to assist clergy when dealing with trauma survivors (Bailey 1981; Dutton, n.d.).

Table 1 also represents a "bill of rights" for victims during the counseling process. The first principle, *non-judgmentality*, is the sine qua non of relationship building with traumatized persons. Hints of non-acceptance or blame in work or deed by the counselor may evoke strong feelings of helplessness or "re-traumatization" in the survivor. *Validation* refers to counselor acceptance of whatever emotional expressions the survivor experiences as normal and expectable, thus facilitating the necessary self-disclosure for trauma processing or working through to occur.

Pastoral involvement may range from minimal, as in providing temporary support during the crisis phase, to extensive, as in provision of counseling services to help resolve PTSD symptoms. An intermediate level of involvement would be represented by advocacy assistance with the legal or mental health system or providing a list of qualified therapists for psychotherapy referral.

Regardless of the particular role appropriate in each situation, pastors' attitudes and behavior toward survivors need to show a will-

Table 1
Principles for Pastoral Counselors Working with Trauma Victims

1. Non-judgmental acceptance and validation of the survivor set the psychological tone for helping.
2. Support, alliance, and advocacy are appropriate role expectations for the helper.
3. It is assumed that post-traumatic distress is primarily related to the traumatic experience(s), not personality or spiritual "weakness."
4. Willingness and ability to be exposed to the survivor's recounting of the traumatic experience(s) and consequences.
5. It is recognized that trauma transformation is a lifelong process.
6. Losses from traumatic experiences may not be compensable, but they can be grieved.
7. The right to self-determination is retained by the survivor.
8. Pastoral self-care is assured.

ingness to share in survivors' experiences of their trauma. This is actively promoted by application, both implicitly and explicitly, of the principle that assumes the "business" of trauma processing is the traumatic experience(s) and the consequences the survivor experiences. Further, since trauma represents a life-changing experience, the influence is expected to be profound and enduring. There is no time limit for trauma processing after which reminders are no longer potent. It is neither possible nor desirable for traumatic experiences to be forgotten.

In a similar vein personal losses suffered through trauma may be grieved, but they cannot be compensated or restored. Thus, the focus of trauma-related counseling is on facilitating the natural grieving process. In so doing counselors are mindful that survivors must retain the right to self-determination in order to regain control over their lives. Urges to preempt decision-making through the use of "shoulds" and "should nots" must be resisted.

Finally, pastoral counselors must be responsible for maintaining their own psychological well-being while ensuring that survivors' needs are uppermost in counseling relationships. Personal beliefs and attitudes toward the different forms of human-induced trauma—such as e.g. the Vietnam war, incest, domestic violence in wife-abuse and child physical abuse, and rape—must be explicitly acknowledged. Self-examination and possible modification of prejudicial attitudes will equip pastors to deal with powerful countertransference feelings, which may often be evoked in the course of trauma work.

If a trauma victim's symptoms seem to continue unabated despite good social support and the opportunity frequently to verbalize and express feelings concerning the event, it is appropriate to refer the individual to a trained professional who specializes in work with trauma. Relatively brief therapeutic interventions focused specifically on the traumatic experience can often provide relief from the painful physical and emotional reactivity that is a characteristic of PTSD, facilitating the natural healing process.

Helping the Helper: Avoiding Burnout

In addition to understanding ways in which the church can help trauma victims, clergy must also be aware of how they may be adversely affected by the traumatic experiences of those they seek to help. Vicarious victimization refers to signs and symptoms of traumatization which persons close to traumatized victims may experience. Specifically, persons who are exposed to the traumatic experiences of victims may experience the same numbing of feelings, avoidance patterns, intrusive thoughts and images, estrangement, and physiological reactions as those experienced by the trauma victims (Lindy 1988).

McCann and Pearlman (1990) expand on the concept of vicarious victimization by emphasizing the changes in thinking and feeling that occur as a result of both the external stress of dealing with trauma survivors and the unique psychological needs and cognitive patterns of the counselor. Disruptive and painful psychological effects may be experienced by persons who work with traumatized persons when helpers' cognitive schema are challenged by survivors' experiences. These schema include beliefs, assumptions, and expectations about the self and the world by which meaning is ascribed to experiences. Trauma disrupts basic assumptions in both survivors and helpers, such as beliefs in a meaningful, orderly world; that the self is safe and worthy; and that other people are trustworthy.

First, those who work with victims are often exposed to the many cruel ways that people deceive and betray each other. This may then, in turn, disrupt helpers' assumptions about trust, causing them to become cynical, distrustful, or suspicious of other people's motives. Second, helpers who work with trauma victims, particularly where threats or harm to innocent people have occurred, may have their assumptions about safety challenged and may experience a fear-related need to take precautions against such violations. In particular, individuals who work with victims of random violence or accidents may experience a heightened sense of vulnerability and an enhanced awareness of the fragility of life, especially if there are strong needs for security. Third, exposure to traumatic situations through survivors' memories may evoke concerns about pastors' own sense of power or efficacy in the world. In particular, those with high needs for power may be more adversely affected by the powerlessness reported by their parishioners. They may personally experience intense feelings of helplessness or despair about seemingly uncontrollable forces of nature or human violence (McCann and Pearlman 1990).

Pastors repeatedly exposed to the traumatic experiences of others may have their assumptions about causality or "why things occur" challenged. This may be particularly applicable for clergy who hold specific beliefs about the way in which God controls and orders the affairs of the world. Traumatized individuals may present direct challenges to religious assumptions about God's control of events through questions such as, "Why did this happen to me?" In order to deflect challenge to their own assumptions and to maintain their sense of order, religious helpers may try to redirect blame to the victim in order to "defend" God as the ultimate originator of the tragedy. Clergy may also experience an overall sense of disillusionment and confusion ("loss of faith") if their assumptions and beliefs are continually challenged by reports of traumatic experiences.

Pastoral counselors can reduce personal vulnerability for experiencing long-term negative emotional symptoms as a result of working with trauma victims. Above all, pastors need ongoing consultative relationships in which they can recognize, communicate, and work through their painful experiences in a supportive, confidential environment. This professional network of support is essential and must be readily available. Isolation from contact with other professionals who work with victims constitutes a major personal risk.

Pastoral counselors must understand how their assumptions and beliefs are disrupted or threatened through the course of their work and how their reactions to survivors may be influenced. As helpers discover their own salient need areas, they will be better able to understand their reactions to the experiences of their counselees. For example, pastors who have considerable concerns about safety may find it very stressful to work with victims of crime or rape; they might appropriately consider referring these cases.

Finally, pastors need to use positive coping methods to reduce some of the potential hazards of working with trauma victims. Some of the strategies which may be helpful include striving for balance between personal and professional activities; developing realistic outcome expectations; maintaining personal boundaries with trauma victims; giving themselves permission to experience fully any emotional reactions; and maintaining optimism and hopefulness in the face of tragedy (McCann and Pearlman 1990). Transcending the tragedy and pain of trauma to find positive meaning in the sharing of life experiences with "other strugglers" is the ultimate task of each trauma counselor.

Summary

Catastrophic experiences that provoke crisis reactions in survivors include combat, sexual and physical assault, natural disasters, transportation accidents, and catastrophic illnesses. Immediate reactions in survivors consistently include intrusive thoughts about the trauma, fear and avoidance of related memories and situations, and panic-like reactions to reminders of the experience. While almost everyone exposed to a traumatic experience will show temporary symptoms of a crisis reaction, not all survivors continue to be affected negatively by their experience. Within three months of the experience many survivors have shown positive signs of relief from intrusive thoughts and fears related to it. However, for some survivors these symptoms persist in the form of PTSD.

A primary factor for determining risk for PTSD is the severity of the trauma experience. Other factors which also influence disorder rates can be divided into "risk" or "protective" categories. Those individuals who have had previous traumatic experiences or who are under high stress from other sources may be more vulnerable for developing PTSD. Conversely, individuals who come from stable family backgrounds or who are well-supported throughout their traumatic experience by those in their social network may be resilient.

Pastors and other members of the church family may serve as important elements within survivors' social networks. Shame, rage, survivor guilt, and self-blame are common emotional reactions in trauma survivors which may present spiritual challenges. The pastor may be uniquely positioned to help survivors resolve those negative trauma reactions and their related theological issues.

Clergy who minister regularly to trauma survivors are especially vulnerable to "helper burnout." Risk for vicarious victimization in pastors serving trauma survivors can be reduced by regular use of collegial consultation whereby pastors' feelings and attitudes about the victims and their perpetrators can be processed.

References

American Psychiatric Association. 1987. *Diagnostic and Statistical Manual of Mental Disorders.* 3d ed. rev. Washington, D.C. Referred to in text as *DSM III-R.*

Ammerman, R. T.; Cassisi, J. E.; Hersen, M.; Van-Hasselt, V. B. 1986. "Consequences of Physical Abuse and Neglect in Children." *Clinical Psychology Review* 6:291–310.

Astin, M.; Lawrence, K.; Pincus, G.; and Foy, D. W. 1990. *Moderating Variables in the Development of PTSD in Battered Women.* Paper presented at the Society for Traumatic Stress Studies, New Orleans, La.

Bailey, L. 1981. "Women and Rape." *Pastoral Psychology* 29: 169–77.

Briere, J. 1989. *Therapy for Adults Molested as Children: Beyond Survival.* New York: Springer.

Dutton, M. A. N.d. *Psychological Trauma of Woman Battering: Assessment and Treatment.* New York: Springer. In press.

Ellis, E. M. 1983. "A Review of Empirical Rape Research: Victim Reactions and Response to Treatment." *Clinical Psychology Review* 3:473–90.

Foa, E. B., Steketee, G., and Olasov Rothbaum, B. 1989. "Behavioral/Cognitive Conceptualizations of Post-traumatic Stress Disorder. *Behavior Therapy* 20:155–76.

Foy, D. W.; Osato, S.; Houskamp, B.; and Neumann, D. N.d. "Etiology Factors in Posttraumatic Stress Disorder." In *Posttraumatic Stress Disorder: A Behavioral Approach to Assessment and Treatment.* Oxford, edited by P. Saigh. Pergamon Press. In press.

———, Resnick, H. S.; Carroll, E. M.; and Osato, S. S. 1990. "Behavior Therapy in Posttraumatic Stress Disorder." In *Handbook of Comparative Adult Treatments,* edited by M. Hersen and A. Bellock, pp. 302–15. New York: John Wiley and Sons.

———, Sipprelle, R. C.; Rueger, D. B.; and Carroll, E. M. 1984.

"Etiology of Posttraumatic Stress Disorder in Vietnam Veterans: Analysis of Premilitary, Military, and Combat Exposure Influences." *Journal of Consulting and Clinical Psychology* 52:79–87.

Green, B. L., Grace, M. C., and Gleser, G. C. 1985. "Identifying Survivors at Risk: Long-term Impairment Following the Beverly Hills Supper Club Fire." *Journal of Consulting & Clinical Psychology* 53, 5:672–78.

Houskamp, B., and Foy, D. W. N.d. "The Assessment of PTSD in Battered Women." *Journal of Interpersonal Violence.* In press.

Janoff-Bulman, R. 1985. "The Aftermath of Victimization: Rebuilding Shattered Assumptions." In *Trauma and Its Wake,* edited by C. R. Figley. New York: Brunner/Mazel.

Keane, T. M.; Fairbank, J. A.; Caddell, J. M.; Zimering, R. T.; Bender, M. E. 1985. "A Behavioral Approach to Assessing and Treating Post-traumatic Stress Disorder in Vietnam Veterans." In Figley, *Trauma and Its Wake,* pp. 257–94.

———, Fairbank, J. A.; Caddell, J. M.; and Zimering, R. T. 1989. "Implosive (Flooding) Therapy Reduces Symptoms of PTSD in Vietnam Combat Veterans." *Behavior Therapy,* 20:245–60.

Kolb, L. C. 1988. "A Critical Survey of Hypotheses Regarding Post-traumatic Stress Disorders in Light of Recent Research Findings." *Journal of Traumatic Stress* 1:291–304.

Lindberg, F. H., and Distad, L. J. 1985. Post-traumatic Stress Disorders in Women Who Experienced Childhood Incest. *Child Abuse & Neglect* 9:329–34.

Lindy, J. D. 1988. *Vietnam: A Casebook.* New York: Brunner/Mazel.

McCaffrey, R. J., and Fairbank, J. A. 1985. "Behavioral Assessment and Treatment of Accident-Related Posttraumatic Stress Disorder: Two Case Studies." *Behavior Therapy* 16:406–16.

McCann, I. L. and Pearlman, L. A. 1990. "Vicarious Traumatization: A Framework for Understanding the Psychological Effects of Working with Victims." *Journal of Traumatic Stress* 3:131–49.

Moss, D. M. 1979. "Near-Fatal Experience, Crisis Intervention and the Anniversary Reaction." *Pastoral Psychology* 28:75–96.

Ruch, L. O. and Chandler, S. M. 1983. "Sexual Assault Trauma During the Acute Phase: An Exploratory Model and Multivariate Analysis." *Journal of Health and Social Behavior* 24:174–85.

———, and Hennessey, M. 1982. "Sexual Assault: Victim and Attack Dimensions." *Victimol. International Journal* 7:94–105.

Schwartz, L. S. 1990. "A Biopsychosocial Treatment Approach to Post-Traumatic Stress Disorder." *Journal of Traumatic Stress* 3:221–38.

Silverman, D. 1977. "First Do No More Harm: Female Rape Victims and the Male Counselor." *American Journal of Orthopsychiatry* 47:91–96.

Thompson, C. 1989. "Breaking Through Walls of Isolation: A Model for Churches in Helping Victims of Violence." *Pastoral Psychology* 38:35–38.

Richard D. Parsons

25. Suicide Survivors: Intervention—Prevention—Postvention

"One Suicide but Five Deaths"

Suicide is a horrifying and almost completely incomprehensible act. Over the last twenty-five years suicide has risen dramatically, and in some populations (for example, among adolescents) the increase has been astronomical, being recognized as the second major cause of death among persons aged ten to twenty-five.

Self-destructive acts are among the major mental health problems in almost every nation of the world. Suicide has risen from twelfth among causes of death in the United States during the 1950s to eighth in the early 1980s (Official statistic from the National Center for Health Statistics, annual volumes of Vital Statistics of the U.S.).

Most researchers agree that even such dramatic and alarming statistics may be underestimations. The lack of a standard definition of suicide, the reluctance to classify death as suicide, and the various means of suicide that afford the opportunity to misinterpret suicide as death by accident (such as autocide) lend support to this hypothesized underestimation.

The statistics on suicide point to the tragedy of a life stopped in process. These statistics may even hint at the pain and anguish endured by the suicide victim and from which he or she may have been seeking relief. However, the statistics fail to show the lives which continue to be destroyed by this one act of suicide.

As many have noted, and thousands have experienced, suicide is a singular act with plural effects. "There are always two parties to a death; the person who dies and the survivors who are bereaved," wrote historian Arnold Toynbee (1969, p. 267). He continues: "There are two parties to the suffering that death inflicts; and in the apportionment of this suffering, the survivor takes the brunt" (p. 271).

Spouses, children, siblings, parents, and even coworkers feel the impact of this devastating act. While the "bomb" of suicide impacts all, it is the victim's immediate family members who are at true ground zero. It is family members whose dreams have been shattered, whose roles and responsibilities have now come under scrutiny, and whose reason for living may even be suspect.

It has only been within the last fifteen years that rising concern has led researchers to widen their focus beyond the cause and even the prevention of suicide to include the effects on suicide survivors. In his 1967 outline for the Center for Studies of Suicide Prevention (CSSP), Edwin Shneidman, co-founder of the LASPC, wrote, "A comprehensive suicide-prevention program should attend to the psychological needs of the stigmatized survivors, especially children who survive a parent who has committed suicide" (Schneidman 1967, p. 6).

While termed *postvention,* the support, the counseling, the assistance afforded as interventions for the survivors of suicide function as preventive measures, reducing the stress and negative impact suicide has on the survivors—and thus reducing their potential for further damaging the survivor.

Harvey Resnik noted that "given the present state of our knowledge about suicide proper postvention seems the most promising avenue toward reducing the large number of suicides that occur annually" (Resnik 1972, p. 177).

The research on this intervention—this prevention—this postvention with suicide survivors, is far from definitive and much of what we know comes from anecdotal clinical reports. It is a beginning, however, a beginning of which we as counselors, ministers, and mental health specialist must become fully aware. It is this beginning which will be the focus of this chapter.

Pastoral Counselor as Preventionist

I have previously argued for pastoral counseling to move to a primary prevention model of service delivery (Parsons 1985). Nowhere else can the value and need of prevention be so clearly demonstrated as in the inevitable impact of suicide on the survivors. And perhaps there is nowhere else that the role of a pastoral counselor is so clearly suited to provide preventive service as in working with suicide survivors. As will be demonstrated later within this chapter, suicide survivors are not only in need of the "healing" presence of a therapeutic listener, but are also in need of the message of love conveyed by Paul:

> For I am certain of this: neither death nor life . . . nor any created thing whatever, will be able to come between us and the love of God, known to us in Christ Jesus our Lord (Rom 8:38–39).

This therapeutic, loving presence, for which the pastoral counselor can serve as vehicle, will facilitate the psycho-spiritual healing so needed by the survivors of suicide, and serve not only as an intervention, but a prevention, postvention, to deter the possible negative effects of the legacy of suicide.

Levels of Prevention

A number of authors have distinguished between the various levels of prevention (primary, secondary, and tertiary) and while I have argued elsewhere (see Parsons and Meyers 1984; Meyers and Parsons 1985) that primary prevention is the most desirable, each level of preventive service has a value for the pastoral counselor.

Primary prevention can be defined as efforts designed to prevent the occurrence of a disorder in a particular population by promoting the well-being of all of those in that particular group or community. It is generally agreed that primary prevention is designed essentially to prevent the development of mental health disorders. Secondary prevention, however, is focused on problems which have already begun to appear. The goal of secondary prevention is to shorten the duration, impact, and negative effects of the disorder; that is, to intervene in such a way so as to prevent the occurrence of the "typical" cycle of the illness and thus prevent it from reaching a point of severity. The third level of service, tertiary prevention, includes those techniques designed to reduce the consequence of severe dysfunction after it has occurred.

As we discuss the unique nature of the grief experienced as a result of a suicide, it will become evident that interventions prior to suicide (primary prevention) and early in the grief process (secondary prevention) will clearly assist the survivor in avoiding or reducing the extremely negative impact of suicide survival.

Whether we call our helping actions intervention, prevention, or postvention, they are clearly needed and most certainly pastoral.

A History of Shame and a Shameful History

In an article on the history of the suicide survivor George Howe Colt (1987) describes, in great detail, an eighteenth-century engraving called "The Desecration of the Corpse."

The engraving is of the naked body of a young man which has been pulled through the streets of Paris by a spirited white horse. Colt describes the man lying face down, "his ankles roped together, his arms outstretched behind him, his fingers clawing the cobblestones" (p. 3).

Apparently the horse has come to rest and a crowd surrounds the body. The horror of the scene is further evidenced by Colt's description of the onlookers. He notes that "one women shrinks from the scene in horror, covering her face with her hand. A curly-haired child on hands and knees watches in open-mouthed terror. A bearded man, his fingers in his mouth, cringes in disbelief and a dog gingerly sniffs the corpse" (p. 3).

While the scene is certainly one of a horrible event, the real horror rests in the reason for this treatment of this man. According to Colt the young man had been "convicted" of suicide.

Degradation of the suicide victim has a long and appalling history. While we are more "civilized" today in our treatment of the suicide victim, our "civilized treatment" may not always be extended to the other victims of a suicide—the survivors.

Perhaps on closer inspection of the engraving described by George Colt, we might find the face of anguish, the expression of shock and disbelief, or the lines of unbearable guilt etched on the face of this man's wife, parents, or children. Suicide is an act of violence not restricted to the official victim. Shneidman (1969) noted that each suicide intimately affects at least six other people (p. 22). It is a case of one buried, but many more dead or dying.

As for our "convicted victim," it is not clear from the engraving or from Colt's description why he took his life. However, a review of the history of societal response to suicide—and to the other victims of suicide, that is, the survivors—makes very clear the consequence of his action.

Suicide as Crime

Historically, suicide was treated as a crime with moral and civil outrage. As such, much effort was given to the total desecration and post mortem humiliation of the victim, and often his or her survivors. For example, in addition to dragging the body through the streets, the body would be taken to a public square and hung upside down. Similarly, the victim was denied a proper burial with the body often tossed in the town dump. If the victim was a man of property, his property (and thus the inheritance of the survivors) was most often forfeited. In addition to destroying the physical remnants (body and possessions) of the offender, the practice typically included destroying the memory and the good name of the person. The practice was to defame the person's memory *ad perpetuam rei memoriam,* "to the end of memory" (Colt 1987, p. 3).

Suicide as Sin

These civil actions, as barbaric as they may sound, found support in the attitudes and practices of the early church. By the seventeenth century the church generally viewed suicide as a sin, which had to be punished.

While neither Hebrew nor Christian scriptures specifically prohibits or condemns suicide, incidents of suicide are described in each. In the Old Testament some descriptions almost present suicide as an honorable act: Samson's suicide as revenge against the Philistines (Jgs 16:23–31), or Saul's suicide as an act of honor (1 Sm 31:1–6). It is only in the New Testament's description of Judas's suicide that we begin to see the action as one of self-destruction, self-punishment, and a result of shame and lack of hope (Mt 27:5).

The sinfulness of suicide as viewed from the Judeo-Christian orientation appeared to rest on three foundations as explicated by St. Augustine and later expanded upon by St. Thomas Aquinas. The basic position was that life belongs to God and only God can terminate it (Gn 2:7). Further, suicide was viewed as a transgression against the fifth commandment, "Thou shalt not kill" (Ex 20:13). And finally, as Paul noted, individuals are the dwelling place of God; as such, suicide not only defiles the individual but also defiles God who dwells within (1 Cor 3:9–17).

The dilemma for early Christians and society's overseers was that the sinner—the criminal—was no longer available to amend for his or her wrongdoing. Thus the church and society imposed severe penalties not only on the victim's dead body and memory, but also on his or her family. The survivors were treated as an accessory to what was now a crime, and therefore needed to suffer the civil and moral consequences. The survivors not only had to endure the pain associated with such a tragic loss, but were also treated as hostages, held as "payment" for the victim's crime, an atonement for his or her sin.

Perhaps such ghastly treatment was an attempt to demonstrate by example what happens when one perpetuates such as "crime". It may be argued that this was but a primitive attempt at primary prevention, a warning and a deterrent to all those who considered suicide. A deterrent to future suicide victims aside, what was not considered was the potential devastation and destruction such a societal and church response had on the other victims of suicide, the survivors.

Suicide as Insanity

By the nineteenth century suicide was no longer considered a moral problem but rather an emotional or mental problem. The act of suicide became its own evidence of insanity. Viewed as an illness rather than a sin or a crime, the stigma associated with suicide, while not removed, changed.

With the perspective that the individual did not know what he or she was doing, most churches became sensitive to the pastoral needs of the family. Rather that desecrating or defaming the victim and his or her survivors, churches began to provide meaningful religious rituals that offered survivors the caring of a faith community. Suicide victims were permitted burial in consecrated ground and their property and possessions were no longer confiscated.

While certainly a more caring and pastoral position, survivors still experienced other forms of rejection, punishment, and stigmatization. Survivors traded the stigmas associated with criminal and sinful behavior for the stigmas and superstitions associated with insanity. Many believed that they themselves were doomed, if not to suicide, to insanity. And society's reaction to suicide as a social disgrace, while not as blatant as that of the seventeenth century, continued in subtle yet very destructive ways to place the survivors physical and mental well-being at risk.

Survivors of suicide were and continue to be denied free and honest access to the grieving process, a process which is essential if healing is to take place. Pastoral counselors, working from a preventive mode, need both to assist the bereaved overcome their self-admonitions against grieving and also to remove the subtle forces within the church community that repress the open, therapeutic expression of grief following a death by suicide. For pastoral counselors to assist in this healing process, they must first understand the nature of "normal" grief work and then the pathogenic impact suicide has on the grieving process.

Bereavement—The Potential for Healing

The death of a loved one is a great stressor; it evokes complex physical, psychological, and social reactions. These reactions taken together comprise what is known as the bereavement process. According to Hauser (1987) bereavement is a homeostatic process; it enables the bereaved to recoil, react, adjust to the loss, and then continue on with life. The emphasis is on continuing on with life, but quite often circumstances surrounding the grieving block the individual's movements through the stages of healing in order to accomplish this.

Stages of Bereavement

Bowlby and Parkes (1970) have investigated this homeostatic process in non-suicidal mourning and identified a number of predictable stages survivors go through in the process of reestablishing balance in their life. While depicted as a set of sequential steps or stages, bereavement and grief work do not proceed in a nice, neat, straight line. Rather, they resemble more a roller coaster with many twists, turns, and ups and downs. As care-givers to those in grief, it is important to understand the generalized schema in order not only to predict certain reactions but to prepare better for the type and form of intervention and support required. Regardless of the general framework from which we view grief work, we must remember that grieving is a highly individualized experience.

1. SHOCK

Following the death of a loved one, the individual absorbs the shock of the loss. Quite often denial along with a general numbness and sense of being overwhelmed are characteristic of this stage. This denial appears to function as a buffer, a shield to the ego, that protects the survivor from the full impact of the loss.

One of my clients, a forty-seven year old widow whose husband had died suddenly from a heart attack, described this experience vividly.

> The doctor approached us, and I know he said, "I'm sorry, but . . . ," but I really can't remember what else he said. I don't know where the next three days went. It didn't seem

> real. I know I went to the funeral home and out to the cemetery, but even now it doesn't seem real. It really was like I was watching a play and I was one of the actors. I kept thinking, he'll get up and take his bow, but I know he won't![1]

With time, this shield slowly gives way to increased intrusion from reality. The various demands and processes which need attention (such as the need to make funeral arrangements, attend the funeral, and so on), chip away at this denial until slowly and manageably the impact of the loss can be accepted.

2. YEARNING AND PROTEST

As shock and denial diminish, the active, open expression of sorrow begins to be manifested. The bereaved experiences a variety of emotional outbursts—tearfulness, anger, restlessness, tension, irritability intense yearning, and panic. The variations and intensity of the feelings give evidence to what has been called the *separation pain*. This is an extremely stressful time of anguish and disorganization in terms of living.

The bereaved may obsessively review the circumstances of the deceased's death and literally long for the person's presence. For example, a sixty-three year old retired man whom I counseled noted that he would find himself crying almost uncontrollably at unexpected times and places. He reported that he would just start to sob while grocery shopping or watching television. He also noted that he found himself sitting for what seemed like hours "day dreaming" and almost dazed, thinking about his wife of forty years.

3. DISORGANIZATION

The sense of yearning and loss eventually give way to a general malaise, a feeling of apathy and aimlessness. The emptiness experienced leads bereaved people to wonder and worry about the future and their redefinition of life. They may be overwhelmed by a sense of "What now?" The stress associated with letting go of the past life with the deceased and planning for a life without the person often results in the appearance of physical symptoms associated with stress (headaches, gastrointestinal distress, sleep disturbance, and others). The bereaved may also become preoccupied with the deceased and find that they are unable to concentrate or take the initiative in social situations. Rather than returning to their previous activities, hobbies, and friends, bereaved individuals may start to withdraw, remain in the house, and manifest what might be called a psychological living death.

Along with the depression, despair, and general dread about the future, the bereaved may experience feelings of hostility toward the deceased (for doing this to them) and subsequently intense guilt. Progress through this stage is often slow and may span years.

4. REORGANIZATION

The final phase of the grieving process requires that bereaved individuals relinquish the past and rebuild a life without their loved one. Such a rebuilding requires an alteration of their self-image, the development of new roles and behaviors, and even the establishment of new social networks. As one woman trying to start anew said:

> For thirty years of my life, over half of my life, I was Mrs. ______, and now I'm supposed to simply get on with it! OK, so I'm forty eight years old. People say I'm bright, attractive, but I haven't worked outside the home or dated for more than twenty years, I don't know how or where to go to meet people. For God's sake, I am not sure I can balance the checkbook much less get a job. I have so much to do, so much to learn, it's scary.

Such a reworking of self, is neither easy nor guaranteed. It is a process that even when successful may require a lot of time and support.

Grieving a Suicide

The normal grieving process is fraught with challenges and stumbling blocks. All mourners could use some psycho-spiritual support, some pastoral care. This need for support is significantly magnified when one considers the special experience of grieving following death by suicide.

While there is no quick and easy formula for assisting one with the grieving process—or any guarantee that any one individual will or will not have pathogenic reactions to the experience of a loss—the research (Cain and Fast 1972a; Hauser 1983) suggests that a number of factors have been associated with "successful" resolution of grief. These facilitative factors are almost always absent in the grieving process of a suicide survivor. With the absence of facilitating factors and the presence of increased stressors, it is not difficult to understand why suicide survivors have an increased risk of pathogenic grief response.

Cain and Fast (1972a) noted that a careful analysis of the inherent nature, context, and almost inevitable consequences of suicide gives strong indication of why the impact of a suicide may have pathogenic potential distinct from and well beyond the disruptive factors generally surrounding and following a death.

Hauser (1983) noted that the bereavement process appears more difficult when the death is sudden or unexpected. By definition, suicide is almost always unexpected and sudden. Because survivors were unable to prepare for the possible death, they were left without time nor opportunity to work on any unfinished business in the relationship. The suicidal act denied them any opportunity for closure with the deceased, and thus the suddenness and unexpected nature of the act of suicide accentuates the shock and disbelief. This alters the initial stage of grieving.

Hauser (1983) further noted that the grieving process is made more difficult when the death is violent or traumatic. The act of suicide, regardless of whether the means or mode was one of dramatic violence, is in itself both violent and traumatic. This trauma is accentuated for the survivor who discovers the victim. One can only imagine the pain and trauma for Mr. J, who arrived home from work one Friday evening expecting to leave early Saturday morning for a fishing trip with his three sons, when he opened the garage door and found his middle son, age nineteen, hanging from the rafters. The shock, the trauma, the haunting images make it more difficult to accept the death in order to move on through the grieving process.

In addition to the unexpected, traumatic nature of suicide other factors which Hauser (1983) has linked to unsuccessful or inhibited bereavement are clearly evidenced in many, if not most, deaths by suicide. Elements such as feeling responsible for the death; having a death accompanied by additional stressors; limiting permission to express one's grief and reducing social support for the bereaved; all these inhibit movement through the grief process. With these factors as a backdrop, it is not difficult to understand the added stress and trauma experienced by the bereaved of a suicide and the resultant increase in pathogenic response.

1. SHOCK FOLLOWING SUICIDE

The difficulty with surviving and "successfully" grieving a suicide is that one must accept two very traumatizing realities. First, suicide survivors must accept the death of their loved one, as do all who are in mourning. Second, and perhaps much more difficult, they must accept that the death was one of suicide (Seiden 1969). Without acceptance of both of these realities, movement through the grieving process will not be possible.

Denial is often the ego defense first noted in the initial stage of bereavement. For one to work successfully through grief, denial must give way to acceptance of the reality.

Suicide dramatically alters the life of the survivors. Plans and dreams fall apart; the life story is interrupted. The stress existing within the family prior to the suicide, along with the stress that results from the death, is only aggravated by the isolation and social stigmatization which often accompanies death by suicide.

Because of feelings of unacceptability and shame, survivors quite often attempt to conceal suicides. Denial, concealment, and refusal or inability to talk about the suicide tend to halt the mourning process. The conspiracy of silence which tends to surround a suicide sharply limits opportunities for catharsis. Family members consciously and unconsciously develop elaborate family myths regarding the nature of the death: "It was an accident," or "He had a long illness." These schemes emphasize the importance of denial and repression rather than acceptance of the grief. With such strong denial, movement through the healing process of grieving is all but eliminated.

In addition to the stress accompanying the death of a loved one, survivors of suicide often experience added stressors not typically experienced by mourners of non-suicide deaths. For example, consider the unpleasant meetings with police, who overtly or implicitly consider the alternative possibility of murder rather than suicide, or the contacts with sometimes hostile insurance representatives focusing on ways out of their policy payments.

These additional intrusions and additional demands tend to highlight the stigma associated with suicide. This stigma not only adds to the stress experienced by the survivors but often makes them unable to depend upon usual avenues of support to work through grief. Funerals are hurried and hushed, even to the point of not informing friends and relatives. "John didn't want to inconvenience anyone, even to the end!" Even church representatives may impede the opportunity to grieve by refusing to conduct burial services, or to do so only with much modification and compromise.

These added stressors and pressures encourage escape through denial and inhibit the healing movement toward acceptance.

2. YEARNING AND PROTEST/SUICIDE

In order for the next phase of the grief work to begin, survivors must freely experience their sorrow and the variations and intensity of feelings which accompany it. As noted above, such expression is often denied the bereaved of a suicide because their emotions are often repressed. The expression of even normal grieving has been confounded by the fact that they suffer under cultural confusion and stigmas surrounding suicide. They are encouraged to continue to deny and repress, not express.

Whereas it is most understandable and acceptable to feel intense sorrow at the loss of the loved one, all too often it is anger, not sorrow, which is first experienced by the survivor of a suicide. Intense anger is often directed at the victim for "giving up." Or the anger may be a direct result of the personal rejection implied by the suicidal act. Often, however, the pain of such rejection is too great to bear, and thus it is denied and only unconsciously expressed, again in the form of projected blaming. Under these conditions, the survivors' anger at the victim may be directed toward elements in the system which the survivors believe may have caused or contributed to the suicide. And finally, the expressed anger may be a manifestation of the survivors' unconscious transformation of guilt over not having prevented the suicide, with the guilt being projected in the form of anger onto a scapegoat.

In a culture that allows only sorrow, anger following a death is not only not understood but is often viewed unsympathetically and even punitively. This point is depicted in the self-accusation of one widow: "I looked at him—so peaceful—and I wanted to strangle him, to hurt him. I know it's stupid. For God's sake, he's dead. But I feel so angry, so furious. I am so ashamed for feeling like this. How can you be angry at someone you say you loved, someone who is dead? I must be horrible, God forgive me!"

The feelings experienced during this second phase of grieving are many and varied. In addition to anger many survivors of suicide experience a sense of relief. Because such a feeling following upon the death of a loved one is not socially accepted, the survivors often suppress the feeling and or again feel intense guilt about having it. The reality is that for most the sense of relief is not evidence of lack of love, but rather of the tension, the conflict that preceded this act. The suicidal death of an extremely troublesome child, or of an alcoholic and abusive parent or spouse will most likely be followed by a sense of relief. The danger is that many soften their memory of the abuse or the conflict and thus feel guilty over this "unacceptable" sense of relief that they experience.

Survivors of suicide most often share intense guilt as a common emotional reference point. As noted, they are guilty over feeling angry or experiencing relief, or because they failed to prevent the death. Survivors are often absorbed in obsessive thoughts regarding their own role in the precipitating events or the fact that in retrospect they see that they missed significant clues and should have acted differently.

The role of irrational guilt following bereavement has been amply recognized, but the ferocity of guilt in the survivors of a suicide is particularly striking. This guilt and the accompanying sense of blame redirects the grieving from a process of healing to a process of self-reprisal and even destruction.

The healing process is further inhibited by the lack of social support and the felt injunction not to discuss the suicide. Survivors of suicide often fail to share their experience, their thoughts, and their feelings. Such failure to share and openly experience the many, varied feelings denies suicide survivors the opportunity to check distorted fantasies against the realities of the suicidal act. Without such reality checks on the variety of gross misconceptions often experienced, suicide survivors have little hope of successfully resolving the irrational guilt or the angry reproaches they feel toward themselves or the person who committed the suicide. Thus they are unable to move from this stage of grief.

3. DISORGANIZATION/SUICIDE

In addition to the general apathy and aimlessness typically experienced in grief, bereaved suicide survivors often experiences self-pity and long-lasting depression. You will often hear this expressed in terms such as, "He killed himself, now he is killing me," or "I'll never get over it."

As with the previous feelings and experiences, this sense of hopelessness and depression is compounded by the general lack of support available to the bereaved of a suicide. Unlike more "typical" grievers, whose social support systems assist them to find meaning and direction in their lives, the bereaved of a suicide are often unable to depend upon the usual avenues for support in working through their grief.

The stigma still associated with suicide often results in survivors failing to find support from their social network. Quite often they experience network avoidance, gossip, and even finger pointing (Cain and Fast 1972b), which in term reinforces and perpetuates their sense of isolation, shame, and disequilibrium.

It appears that this massive avoidance, this lack of communication, this lack of free acceptance of the experience of grief with all of its various manifestations, virtually prevents the working through of mourning and therefore serves as the primary cause for dysfunctional, pathogenic responses to grief. Suicide survivors not only struggle through their grief work, but they often completely block successful grief work. The end result is the development of potentially self-destructive response patterns.

Pathogenic Grief Response

One set of pathogenic responses to grief involves attempts at completing avoiding the entire grieving process. Such survivors are pathogenic in that they inhibit free, open, and healing expressions of grief and thus stimulate grief manifestation through less than productive ways. Wolfet (1987) noted five forms of such grief avoidance.

Postponing occurs when the individual believes that if you delay your grief it will go away. However, the truth is that rather than dissipating, the grief builds up and comes out in other ways (depression, insomnia, destructive personal patterns, and so on).

Displacing occurs when the individual attempts to move his or her grief in other directions. For example, the displacer may begin chronically to complain about difficulty at work or in another relationship. He or she may appear agitated and upset at minor events, in general bitter toward life.

Replacing is the process by which the bereaved takes the emotions that were invested in the relationship and reinvests those emotions prematurely in another relationship. When another relationship is not available, the replacer may invest excessive energies into work, becoming a compulsive overworker, when there was no prior history of such behavior.

This was true of Mary, an elementary school teacher of eleven years. Following the suicidal death of her daughter, Mary began to "live at work." She would stay within her classroom until late into the evening, "preparing for *her* children and the next day." Mary began inviting some of the children in her class to stay and help her, even offering to take them to dinner with her as thanks for their assistance. Through counseling it became clear that Mary, who by her own description handled the death and funeral like a "little soldier," was now avoiding any possible reminders of the loss and attempting to find substitutes for her daughter in the work, and "her" children at work. Such replacement compounds the pain, confusion, and disequilibrium in one's life and needs to be confronted.

The fourth form of avoidance described by Wolfet (1987) is *minimizing.* Minimizing is the process by which the survivors take their feelings and through extensive rationalization attempt to reduce the significance and impact of these feelings. On the surface the minimizer looks good and appears to have rational answers to all that has happened. "He's with God, now," "At least she is no longer in pain," "But we had eighteen wonderful years together"—these could all reflect an attempt at avoidance through minimizing. Even though the surface looks and sounds good, feelings are building up and emotional strain will inevitably result.

Somatizing is the final form of grief avoidance. This is the process by which individuals convert their feelings into physical symptoms. The pattern may take the form of rather benign complaints, or it can take the form of a chronic pattern of multiple vague somatic complaints with no organic findings (somatization disorder). It is as if the survivors sense that such somatization legitimizes their need to be comforted, whereas their direct expression of grief following a suicide may chase people away.

While Wolfet's listing is certainly non-exhaustive, it is clear that such patterns of grief avoidance result in deterioration of relationships with friends and family; symptoms of chronic physical illness either real or imagined; and symptoms of chronic depression, low self-esteem, and chronic anxiety, agitation, restlessness, and difficulty in concentrating. While attempting to avoid the pain of grief, these attempts only serve to compound and extend the pain experienced.

In addition to such delay or avoidance patterns, suicide survivors appear to be particularly susceptible to a number of additional pathogenic grief responses (Cain and Fast 1972a, 1972b).

Pattern 1: In their study Cain and Fast (1972a) noted that many survivors attempted to resolve their unconscious conflicts and anguish over the loss of their loved one by re-engaging in a relationship as quickly as possible. Quite often these relationships were marked for failure, apparently neurotically determined.

Survivors would often remarry individuals who had evidence of chronic illness or gross physical handicaps. It is as if they were selecting individuals who needed nurturance as a way to redefine themself and their value in the face of the post-suicide guilt.

This was clearly the case with Tina, a thirty-nine year old widow with whom I worked. Following therapy Tina was able to explain the value of her remarriage following the suicidal death of her first husband; "Marrying Jack proved to me (and everyone else) that I was lovable. After all, he wouldn't have married me if I was the terrible person who would make somebody want to kill himself." Fortunately for Tina, the marriage to Jack did work out, but this is not always the case. In situations where the remarriage fails, survivors have additional "data" to support their guilt and feelings of unacceptability. This compounds the dysfunctionality of their grieving.

Pattern 2: The second pattern noted by Cain and Fast (1972a) was characterized as a plan for world rescue. These individuals identified with special interests and causes (cancer cures, grand economic designs, and so on), taking to these causes with unusual fervor. In the Cain and Fast research, the degree of their involvement proved pathogenic in that it deterred them from their normal functioning, interests, and responsibilities.

Pattern 3: The third form of dysfunctionality is much more direct in its form of self-destructive. Often survivors manifested openly self-destructive impulses and behavior, including suicidal ideation, attempts, and even "successful" acts.

Jack, age thirty-one, was a mechanical engineer. Within the last two years, he had three near-fatal car accidents. Through the course of therapy it was revealed that Jack often fantasized about his death. His imaging typically involved death at the hands of some dramatic and daring stunt, such as sky diving, car racing, or bungie jumping. In therapy Jack disclosed his thoughts about taking his own life, but felt that he was "too chicken" to ever do it. With time, Jack told his story. Jack was the youngest of three sons. His brother Al had a fatal car accident at the age of thirty, but Jack knew it wasn't an accident. On more than one occasion Al had shared with his younger brother the fact that he wished he was dead. Jack admitted that he never openly grieved for his brother; in fact, he had refused to go to his brother's funeral.

It appeared that the occasion of Jack's own thirtieth birthday, resurfaced the guilt and remorse he felt at not telling anyone about his brother's "death wish." Further, it appeared that his own dangerous actions were a dysfunctional attempt at self-reproach.

Pattern 4: Cain and Fast (1972a) found that for some of the survivors, reparation and undoing were not the choice of resolution. Rather, they used their new marital partner to assuage their guilt by playing out in the new relationship the complaints, grievances, and accusations previously held and belonging to the relationship with the suicidal partner. It appeared almost as if they were attempting to externalize and then master their own superego accusations.

Such a pattern was evidenced by Toni, a fifty-three year old widow. Toni remarried one year after the suicidal death of her husband. She and her new husband, Peter, entered therapy because of their almost constant fighting about his "always being out." Through the early sessions it became clear that Toni was distorting the reality of Peter's nights out. In fact, his evenings out were restricted to a once a week bowling league and once a month card club, to which she was invited. Through the sessions Toni consistently made reference to her first husband—how he, like Peter, never stayed home. On closer inspection it became clear that Toni was furious with her first husband, and that her first marriage had been characterized by continuous arguments over his tendency to go "out with the boys, and never take me anywhere." During the year following his death, Toni romanticized the relationship, having nothing but praise and warm feelings for how close they had been. She did not allow herself to accept or embrace her anger following his death and, as a result, looked for a "more acceptable" way to vent her feelings. The current marriage to Peter provided her with the opportunity to continue to play out that anger.

Pattern 5: The final pattern noted by Cain and Fast (1972a) appeared to involve the unconscious attraction to suicidal persons. One could speculate that such an attraction is an attempt at continued punishment and rapprochement or that it is a symbolic attempt to prevent the first event from having occurred. It is as if one is given another chance to stop the suicide.

Regardless of the hope or motivation, the reality is that connecting in such a relationship is not only a dysfunctional way to cope with the original guilt and remorse, but also exponentially compounds the survivor's stress, pain, and dysfunctionality, should this second relationship end in suicide.

A Model for Ministering to Survivors

The clinical data and an analysis of the pathogenic factors inherent in the consequences of suicide strongly suggest the need for post-suicide interventions with the bereaved. Conceptualizing grief work as occurring within a community context, a context which can exacerbate or facilitate healthy movement through grief—and which is also affected (positively or negatively) by the experience of the suicide and the grieving of the survivors—highlights the need for a prevention focus to our ministering. Whether we term it intervention, prevention, or postvention, facilitating movement through the grief process is essential.

While it is important to note that the grieving process is highly idiosyncratic and thus to avoid generalizations, there are still some common issues most suicide survivors need to address. As such, a general goal or aim for postvention is to help the survivors work through their feelings of grief, which invariably accompany a death. This includes the issues typically addressed within non-suicidal mourning, along with the special concerns so often aroused by suicide.

Tertiary Level Prevention

Quite often it is only after survivors have struggled with the grieving process and have experienced a degree of dysfunctionality that they seek the support of a pastoral counselor. With the focus on not only providing remediation but also assisting survivors to develop a more adaptive (preventive) coping style in the future, the pastoral intervention serves as a tertiary level of prevention.

Survivors of suicide may come to counseling through a variety of routes. Quite often they come for immediate assistance, a form of psychological first aid or crisis intervention. Others come only after exhausting all other means of coping and still finding the months or years since the suicide unbearable.

While both of these groups are clear as to the source of their life difficulty, some survivors may present themself as having difficulty with some other area of their life (a problem with a relationship, a child management problem, a work-related difficulty). On closer inspection it becomes clear that the unfinished nature of their grief is the issue which needs to be addressed.

Treatment with survivors of suicide is complicated by the tortured and erratic course of suicide grief. Some theorists have even suggested that it is better to wait up to a year before beginning an intervention since the shock, disorganization, and denial are so strong.

It has been my experience, and one supported by others within the literature (e.g., E. J. Dunne and Dunne-Maxim 1987) that suicide survivors who seek therapy after years of struggling with unresolved grief often present a number of recurring thematic issues. Quite often they will present as individuals who are "stuck" in a perpetual need to search (often physically as well as psychologically) for the reasons for the suicide. While understanding can be an element which facilitates their own closure, obsessional rumination often reflects their own denial and an attempt to defend via intellectualization. When such is the case, they must be confronted and encouraged to let go and move on.

A second theme often presented is that of being socially stigmatized. For example, consider the following case illustration. Albert was only thirty-one years old when his wife of five years committed suicide. Albert was seen in therapy three years after his wife's death. Initially he presented as someone who was depressed about his inability to make and keep friends. As the therapy developed, it became obvious that Albert's social isolation was self-induced and motivated by his own internalized negative attitudes toward himself. Albert felt that all of his old friends were avoiding him and that anyone he would meet would soon find out about the suicide and similarly move away from him. Through a number of cognitive debating exercises as well as in-vivo desensitizations these faulty beliefs were tested and reformulated (see Parsons and Wicks 1986). Albert was encouraged to begin to associate with old and new associates, and he soon found that his projected rejections never came to fruition.

Perhaps the most common theme reported in the literature is that of inexorable guilt. Survivors may express such guilt as self-reproach for not having done all that they could to prevent the suicide, or they may even project this guilt on to others in the form of anger. In working with a number of clients with intense non-suicide related guilt and anger, I have found the cognitive restructuring techniques effective and efficient strategy (see Parsons 1989).[2]

Secondary Prevention

Rather than waiting for the dysfunctionality to become fully manifested, the pastoral counselor may be able to intervene early in the grieving process in order to reduce the potentially negative impact of a pathogenic response at each stage of the grieving. Interventions occurring prior to full manifestation of a disorder and aimed at shortening the duration, impact, and negative effects of such pathogenic responses could be viewed as secondary prevention.

THE INITIAL STAGE OF SHOCK

It is clear that the most valuable thing the pastoral counselor can do at this stage of the grieving process is to be available to the survivor. The presence of a mental health professional, a counselor, or a minister immediately after the death can facilitate the family's expression of confusion and thus minimize subsequent unwillingness to communicate. As Herzog and Resnik (1969) reported, such early contact can serve as a needed and valued cathartic experience.

What is called for at this point is not so much directive interventions but crisis and supportive counseling. It is important to establish a compassionate tone for the grief process. During the initial shock stage it is especially important to present an atmosphere of both gentleness and understanding. Relationship skills (see Carkhuff 1969; Egan 1973) such as genuineness, warmth, unconditional prizing of the bereaved, and empathic understanding are essential during this particular phase of the grief process. It is not so important to "do for" or "do to" as it is to "be with" the bereaved.

Chilstrom (1989) noted that pastoral care is the vehicle by which God sends "listeners for the grief story," where the "telling and the retelling of details" will gradually help to ease the pain. The survivor needs emotional support and a large measure of reality testing. The presence of the counselor can assist the family to move from denial to acceptance of this death by suicide.

MOVEMENT THROUGH ANGER . . . GUILT . . . SHAME

As the survivors continue through the grieving they will be barraged by a variety of emotions, many of which they will find unacceptable, clearly not something one can admit. At this stage the helper needs to encourage expression of *all* feelings.

It is essential to convey a real sense of unconditional valuing or prizing for the bereaved and to offer a style of non-judgmental responding in order to allow them to express all their feelings, including their hostilities toward the deceased and even their own self-recriminations.

It may also be necessary to provide survivors' permission to express anger at God. Quite often the bereaved feel that such anger is sinful and its expression blasphemous. However, their anger is understandable given their perceptions of the "unfairness" of all that they are experiencing. The pastoral counselor can assist the bereaved to accept these feelings and to place their anger, their difficulty in forgiving God, in contrast to God's ability to always forgive.

Throughout the early stages of the grieving it is important to address the fact of suicide openly. This is not meant to imply that the suicide should be the focal point, but that the counselor must present a frank and undistorted view of reality. However, it is of very little therapeutic value to be argumentative or confrontational at this time. It is not so essential to point out minor omissions or commissions, which in our minds may appear to be of monumental importance. More than such intense reality checking, the bereaved need permission to embrace and accept all of their feelings along with the freedom to express these feelings as they wish.

SELF-PITY AND DEPRESSION

As the grief progresses survivors may become filled with self-pity. Quite often this stage manifests in severe depression with extreme anxiety and/or somatic involvement. The focus of the therapeutic intervention is to address the depression in such a way as to assimilate the grief and facilitate the survivors' growth through it.

One issue which needs to be confronted is survivors' irrational distortions of the reality surrounding the events leading up to the suicide as well as the import and impact of the suicide. Irrational beliefs and self-talk which defines their life condition as "hopeless," or "unbearable," and their self as "worthless" and "damnable" need to be confronted actively and debated (see Parsons and Wicks 1986; Parsons 1989).

The healing which results from successful navigation through the mourning process requires that the bereaved develop an honest, realistic regard for the circumstance of the death—and an honest, realistic appraisal of themselves.

SPECIFIC PASTORAL ISSUES

In addition to concerns and questions such as "Why did he (she) have to do it?" "What could we have done?" "What will I do now?" the bereaved may have anxiety and confusion around the issues of salvation and damnation for the victim.

Questions regarding the forgiveness of God, God's sense of justice, and the sinfulness of the act of suicide are questions to which the pastoral counselor needs to be prepared to respond. In order to deal adequately and therapeutically with these concerns the pastoral counselor needs to be able to identify his or her own feelings about, and theology of, suicide, death, forgiveness, and resurrection *before* entering the counseling relationship. It is hoped that the pastoral counselor will be able to give witness to the mercy, forgiveness, and love of God.

This author has found it helpful to assist the bereaved to understand the various factors which often cloud the judgment of a person committing suicide. Perhaps there was evidence of extreme pain, despair, depression, or dysfunctionality. From that perspective we might assume that it is unlikely that God would judge a desperate or ill action as immoral. It is also helpful if survivors can understand that we should not assume God's judgment is based on behavior performed under the influence of severe and debilitating illness rather than a person's life-time ledger of moral and immoral actions.

Hope is the cornerstone of all major religions, and forgiveness and mercy the message of a crucified and risen Christ. Hope—for themselves and for their loved one—is the therapy most needed for the bereaved of a suicidal death.

For all those wondering whether their loved one is happy or suffering, Jesus' prayer from the cross—"Father forgive them, they do not know what they are doing" (Lk 23:34)—is an invitation to trust in the Lord. It is this hope, this message of the risen Christ, which we need to reflect and affirm for the survivors.

There are a number of "non-counseling" activities which can prove therapeutic and have secondary preventive value. For example, it is helpful to involve survivors in planning the church services. Not everyone has to be involved or even attend, but the more involvement and participation the more readily they will accept the reality they are facing and the more readily the healing will begin. Making a ceremony out of the tasks of buying markers or developing plans for remembrances and perpetuation assists the family in both accepting and letting go, knowing that their loved one will be remembered.

Finally, as pastoral counselors we must accept that the grieving process does not end with the burial; it really only begins. Therefore it is important to maintain regular follow-up contact with bereaved. The roller coaster nature of the grieving process, especially when it is the result of suicide, requires that ministry to the bereaved become a long-term commitment.

Primary Prevention

Any steps which reduce the stress of the entire church community increase the competency and ability of the community members to handle stress. To develop a sense of church as a supportive, caring environment may actually function to prevent not only dysfunctional grieving, but even the act of suicide itself. All such efforts designed to prevent the occurrence of a disorder or dysfunctionality by promoting emotional well-being have been termed primary prevention.

The pastoral counselor should use the occasion of this tragedy as an opportunity to involve and educate the entire congregation on the phenomenon of suicide and the impact of suicide on survivors. (Be sure that any homily, lecture, or presentation be done with the permission of the bereaved and without specific reference to this incident.) Congregational growth and health can be stimulated by sharing the feelings commonly experienced by survivors (guilt, shame, embarrassment, stigma, anger, rage, shock, confusion, fear, anxiety, and social isolation) and encouraging the congregation to reach out and offer support to the survivors. Efforts to provide such community support provides secondary prevention to the survivors and may serve to reduce stress and a sense of isolation for others, which if unattended may evolve into a destructive, suicidal force. Thus such education and church community development has a high degree of primary prevention potential.

Conclusions

Clearly much has changed in the years since English law provided for the confiscation of the property of suicide victims and the disinheriting and stigmatizing of the surviving family members. However, societal attitudes toward survivors of suicide, if not overtly destructive, are still not uniformly supportive and helpful.

The potential pathogenic impact suicide has on the "other victims," the survivors, has only begun to receive the serious attention it and they deserve. The research describing the extent of the impact, its specific manifestations, and the recommendations for instituting programs of remediation and prevention has only begun. Much more empirical research is needed.

However, the bereaved, the survivors of suicide, cannot wait for the definitive research. They are in pain now. All too many are isolated from family, from society, and from their church at a time when they need the support and love which should be the hallmark of a Christian community.

The various social-psychological forces that exist and encourage denial, repression, and isolation need to be reduced, and survivors need to find the caring support they require to openly and honestly grieve.

The pastoral counselor who can walk with the bereaved—and encourage the local community to serve as a constant reminder of the living reality of Christ's love and forgiveness—intervenes, prevents, postvents, but most important, helps to heal all who are touched by the tragedy of suicide.

Notes

1. All case material has been modified to ensue anonymity.
2. The nature of this chapter doesn't allow for a full exploration of these techniques. Interested readers are referred to this article or the works of A. Beck or A. Ellis.

References

Bowlby, J., and Parkes, C. M. 1970. "Separation and Loss Within the Family." In *The Child in His Family*, vol. 1, edited by E. J. Anthony and C. Koupernik, pp. 197–216. New York: Wiley Interscience.

Cain, A. C., and Fast, I. 1972a. "The Legacy of Suicide: Observations on the Pathogenic Impact of Suicide Upon Marital Partners." In Cain, *Survivors of Suicide*, pp. 145–54.

———, and Fast, I. 1972b. "Children's Disturbed Reactions to Parent Suicide: Distortions of Guilt, Communication, and Identification. In Cain, *Survivors of Suicide*, pp. 93–111.

Carkhuff, R. R. 1969. *Helping and Human Relations.* 2 vols. New York: Holt, Rinehart and Winston.

Chilstrom, Corrine. 1989. "Suicide and Pastoral Care." *The Journal of Pastoral Care* 43, 3:199–208.

Colt, G. H. 1987. "The History of the Suicide Survivor: The Mark of Cain." In Dunne, et al., *Suicide and Its Aftermath*, pp. 3–18.

Dunne, E. J., McIntosh, J. L., and Dunne-Maxim, K., eds. 1987. *Suicide and Its Aftermath: Understanding and Counseling the Survivors.* New York: W. W. Norton.

Egan, G. 1973. *You and Me.* Monterey, Cal.: Brooks/Cole.

Hauser, M. J. 1983. "Bereavement Outcome for Widows." *Journal of Psychosocial Nursing and Mental Health Services* 21, 9: 22–31.

———. 1987. "Special Aspects of Grief After a Suicide." In Dunne, et al., *Suicide and Its Aftermath*, pp. 57–70.

Herzog, A., and Resnik, H. L. P. 1969. "A Clinical Study of Parental Response to Adolescent Death by Suicide With Recommendations for Approaching the Survivors." *British Journal of Social Psychiatry* 2, 3: 144–52.

Meyers, J., and Parsons, R. D. 1985. "Prevention Planning in the School System." In *Prevention Planning for Mental Health*, edited by J. Hermalin and J. Morall. Beverly Hills, Cal.: Sage Publications.

Parsons, R. D. 1989. "Forgiving-not-Forgetting." In *Psychotherapy and the Remorseful Patient*, edited by E. Mark Stern, pp. 259–72. New York: The Haworth Press.

______. 1985. "Prevention: A Duty, Responsibility, and Guiding Value for Pastoral Counseling." *Journal of Pastoral Counseling* 20: 37–46.

______, and Meyers, J. 1984. *Developing Consultation Skills*. San Francisco: Jossey-Bass.

______, and Wicks, R. 1986. "Cognitive Pastoral Psychotherapy With Religious Persons Experiencing Loneliness." In *Psychotherapy and the Lonely Patient*, edited by S. Natale, pp. 47–59. New York: The Haworth Press.

Resnik, H. L. P. 1972. "Psychological Resynthesis: A Clinical Appeal to Survivors of a Death by Suicide." In *Survivors of Suicide*, edited by A. C. Cain, pp. 167–77. Springfield, Ill: Charles C. Thomas.

Shneidman, E. S. 1967. "The NIMH Center for Studies of Suicide Prevention." *Bulletin of Suicidology* 1: 2–7.

______. 1969. "Prologue: Fifty-Eight Years." In *On the Nature of Suicide*, edited by E. S. Schneidman, pp. 1–30. San Francisco: Jossey-Bass.

Seiden, R. H. 1969. "Suicide Among Youth: A Review of the Literature." *Bulletin of Suicidology*, pub. #1971, pp. 1–51.

Toynbee, A. 1969. *Man's Concern With Death*. New York: McGraw Hill.

Wolfet, A. D. 1987. "Understanding Common Patterns of Avoiding Grief." *Thanatos* (Summer): 2–5.

For Further Reading

Cain, A. C., ed. 1972. *Survivors of Suicide*, introduction, pp. 5–33. Springfield, Ill. Charles C. Thomas.

Davis, J. M., Sandoval, J., and Wilson, M. P. 1988. "Strategies for the Primary Prevention of Adolescent Suicide." *School Psychology Review* 17, 4: 559–69.

______, Bates, C., and Velasquez, R. J. 1990. "Faculty Suicide: Guidelines for Effective Coping With a Suicide in a Counselor-Training Program." *Counselor Education and Supervision* 20: 197–204.

Hajal, F. 1977. "Post-Suicide Grief Work in Family Therapy." *Journal of Marriage and Family Counseling* 3, 2: 35–42.

Hill, W. C. 1984. "Intervention and Postvention in Schools." In *Suicide in the Young*, edited by H. S. Sudak, A. B. Ford, and N. B. Rushford, pp. 407–16. Boston: John Wright/P. G. S. Inc.

Lamb, F., and Dunne-Maxim, K. 1987. "Postvention in Schools: Policy and Process." In Dunne, et al., *Suicide and Its Aftermath,* pp. 245–60.

Resnik, H. L. P. 1970. "Center Comments." *Bulletin of Suicidology* 6: 2–4.

Rosenfeld, L., and Prupas, M. 1984. *Left Alive: After a Suicide Death in the Family.* Springfield, Ill.: Charles C. Thomas.

Rudestam, Kjell E. 1987. "Public Perceptions of Suicide Survivors." In Dunne, et al., *Suicide and Its Aftermath,* pp. 31–44.

Ruof, S. R., and Harris, J. M. 1988. "Decisive and Prepared Response After Suicide or Attempt Crucial." *NASP Communique* 16 (September): 12.

Roy Lewis

26. Pastoral Care to the Unemployed

It was six o'clock in the evening when the phone rang. Pastor Carroll picked it up and heard the voice of a parishioner.

"Reverend Carroll, this is Joan, I really need your help. Monday Dan got fired and he's really in a bad place. I don't know what to do for him. I've told him that everything will be OK and that he'll get a job soon, but all he does is feel sorry for himself and mope around the house. Can you come over and talk with him."

"Joan," replied Rev. Carroll, "losing your job is a very painful experience. Getting fired stinks. It is important that Dan and I talk. Can I come over tomorrow morning about nine?"

Without talking to Dan, Rev. Carroll knew from others in his congregation who had lost their jobs that this was a painful and difficult time. He knew that Joan's quick reassurance was probably not helping Dan. He needed time to mourn. Losing a job is like experiencing a death.

The next morning Rev. Carroll visited Dan and Joan. He spent an hour listening to Dan alone, and then he invited Joan in to help both of them reflect on what would be helpful in this crisis.

Dan was forty-three and had been doing well in his work as a manager in a large corporation for the last eight years. The company seemed to be doing well, and Dan felt secure. From time to time he had thought about looking for another job but decided against it.

It became clear to Dan, as he reflected on the last year, that he saw some warning signals that he might lose his job. He chose to ignore them. Dan was angry, fearful, in a time of shock and shame. He noted that his family was counting on him. What would they do to pay the bills if he didn't bring in money? Dan's father had always told him to be responsible and work hard. He remembered the stories his grandfather told him about coming to this country with nothing. His grandfather took any and every job he could find and worked hard. Maybe he should quickly get a job like his grandfather so that the family won't go under financially. Dan felt special pressure because his oldest son had just started college. "What will we do now?"

Clearly Dan was scared, angry, and anxious. He was beginning a grief experience. He told Rev. Carroll, "When I heard the news that I was laid off, it felt like I was fired. I was stunned and terrified inside. It was Monday morning. I was ready to start a good week of work. I immediately thought, How could they do this to me? How will I pay the bills? What will Joan think? How will I ever tell her I got laid off? My stomach was churning and my hands were cold as ice. It only took five minutes and it was over. I was let go after eight years."

Rev. Carroll asked Dan what happened because he knew from his experience and reading that there are usually four reasons people get fired. First, new management takes over the company and cleans house. Second, people get fired because of office politics; they took an unpopular stand on an issue. Third, the shifting economic picture makes job security an impossibility. There is no such thing. Fourth, a person may have been involved in a personality conflict with other people in the office or even with his or her immediate supervisor. As Rev. Carroll listened it became clear that Dan was caught in a new management take-over; the company was being "downsized." He was not "fired" or "laid off," according to the company. He was just part of a "downsizing" of the company. Dan *felt* fired. It felt as bad and as painful as other losses he had experienced. A common reaction to grief is to feel numb. But if a person stays numb a part of him dies. If Dan anesthetizes his feelings they will cause him even more problems. Rev. Carroll knew that to tell Dan that everything will be fine and that he shouldn't worry was to ignore the major grief that Dan is feeling and to abort the mourning needed for healing.

The story that Dan told Rev. Carroll is not uncommon. Most people are discharged during a quick, "come-into-my-office" conversation initiated by an immediate superior or a human resource manager. It is quick and painful (Koltow and Dumas 1990, p. 30). More and more companies in our nation are terminating people as a result of management take-overs.

Rev. Carroll realized that about 5 percent of his congregation had been terminated, fired, or laid off that year. In October 1990 the unemployment rate in the United States was projected to reach 6.5 percent or 8.1 million jobless in the next year. The current rate of unemployed in the United States was then 5.6 percent, or seven million people (Tritch and Smith 1990).

What Dan was feeling was appropriate. When a person loses his or her job, it is perfectly normal to have bouts of anger, depression, guilt, anxiety, fear, and despair. If these feelings and thoughts are not dealt with, some people may even experience some form of physical illness. Rev. Carroll knew that what Dan needed first was a safe place to express his feeling—someone to help him through the grief process.

It is frightening to realize how vulnerable and helpless we can be. Many people experience their sense of self-worth, self-esteem, and identity through what they do. They are what they do. Many of us live from paycheck to paycheck, so it is natural to be overcome with fear when we lose our job. In this sense losing a job is one of life's most difficult trials. When we lose our job and thus lose our self-esteem, we are ripe for feelings of shame. As with Dan, our parents and often grandparents have given us messages that we are to work hard and that being unemployed makes us bums, worthless people. This is not the case in our complex economy, where the shift in the price of oil in the Middle East can cause hundreds of companies to go broke and thousands to lose their jobs. We are not always in control, and it is clear that job security is a myth. When we lose our job, many things are out of our control. Our feelings of safety and security are threatened. There may be no one out there waiting to offer us another job.

When people lose their jobs, financial fears race through their minds. Seventy-five percent of those just-fired report that the loss of income was among the most difficult things to cope with after being terminated (Koltow and Dumas 1990, p. 40).

Research indicates that most people get fired on Monday morning, or if Monday is a holiday, on Tuesday morning. Fully 40 percent of people fired get the ax during one of these two times. The next most popular day and time for a person to get terminated is Friday in the afternoon, probably about closing time. This group represents 30 percent of those fired (Koltow and Dumas 1990, p. 23). Dan was fired on Monday morning. He was given an hour to pack up his things and leave. The only explanation he was given was that the company was having financial difficulty and that they were "downsizing" their work force. The manager was "sorry to do this."

When Dan reflected back with Rev. Carroll, he could see clearly that there had been warning signals. About a year before the company had been purchased by a larger company. New management arrived. He realizes now that they were evaluating and deciding whether this newly acquired company could or would make money for the parent company. The work environment changed, and Dan felt differently about working, but he couldn't put his finger on the problem. He had lost his passion for the work. He thought of taking some time to do career development and assessment but overrode that feeling with the thought that "everything will be OK. I'm a valued part of this company and have given it my all for eight years now." Thus Dan missed the internal and external warning signals. He decided not to explore other possibilities while he still had a job.

Dan was also able to identify an immediate sense of relief and a burst of elation because he had in fact sensed his termination coming. It was a relief to have it settled. Dan had enough sense about him to leave with style. He exited gracefully, thanking his secretary for her help over the years, his colleagues for their support and input. He was even gracious to his superiors. Yes, he felt angry inside, but he exited with poise, realizing that he might need them in the future for references and recommendations.

When Rev. Carroll left, Dan reflected on what had happened. He was mourning the loss of his job. He needed pastoral counseling to help him through the grief. Rev. Carroll had listened. He had asked Dan to retell the story of what happened. Dan began the process of identifying that he had experienced a death. Joan, his wife, realized that he needed support at this time and an opportunity to deal with the loss intellectually, emotionally, and spiritually. Dan needed her to assist him in the process of understanding its impact on the family. He needed her to help him deal with the old family message that his worth was related to his work. Dan thought he needed to be the provider. Joan was working, but they needed to spend some time reevaluating their current income and expenses so that Dan could have time to grieve, heal, and move on. Yes, it will be tight financially. They can make it.

Before the next visit Rev. Carroll thought a lot about Dan and Joan. He was very much aware that there is a cycle that persons who have been fired, laid off, or "downsized" go through. It was also clear to him and needed to be affirmed by him that, whether invited or not, God was in their presence. Dan believes in God; being fired doesn't change that. Rev. Carroll knew that his presence as pastor and counselor made it necessary for him throughout the process to invite Dan to reflect about God's presence at this time of pain and trial. The key to finding help from God is admitting that we need it. Dan was in the beginning stage of grief. He even felt angry with God. As he dealt with this, he was able to ask where God fits in and what God wants from him now.

Rev. Carroll knew that there are several very specific things that Dan needed to do immediately, and so he gave Dan several specific suggestions as they counseled through the grief. First, Dan needed to go to the local Unemployment Office to determine his eligibility. If eligible, he needed to register for unemployment. Dan wasn't sure about this. He didn't want a handout. Rev. Carroll helped him realize that it wasn't a handout but rather a fund that was available through the contribution of his employer and himself for just such emergencies. It would help him build a bridge over the present financial crisis. It was very important for Dan to contact his local unemployment office for services that would assist him at this time. The unemployment office has two branches. One pays benefits, and the other assists in a job search. Perhaps Dan also would be eligible under the Trade Adjustment Assistance Act of 1974, which assists persons whose jobs are terminated resulting from foreign competition. He might also find help in training under the Job Partnership Training Act. This information is all available through the local Unemployment Office.[1]

Second, Dan needed to get his resume in order. He hadn't upgraded it in years. He pulled out his old one and realized how outdated it was. In reviewing it he became more aware of his abilities and skills. At this time, Dan decided not to include a specific desired employment statement because he had an inner feeling it might change. Dan rewrote and printed his resume.

Third, Rev. Carroll suggested that Dan set up a specific workplace for himself, a place where he can use a phone and do what he needed to do to reflect, write, and market himself. It might be a room at home. Some churches have a room available during the day for those in job search.

Fourth, Dan needed to get his termination story straight. It wasn't clear whether the reasons he was given for his termination were the reasons his company and boss would give a prospective employer. He requested a letter of reference from his former employer, so that he could be sure what was being said. Rev. Carroll also suggested that one way to check on his reference was to have a friend call his former employer to be sure they were not going to give a negative reference.

Fifth, Rev. Carroll suggested getting an answering machine. "You don't want to miss a perspective employer's call." This made sense to Dan because he had friends who said they had called with important messages and couldn't reach him.

Sixth, Dan needed to get a business card printed. A card tells possible employers who he is, what he does, and where he can be reached. Cards are easily given out.

Seventh, Rev. Carroll asked Dan if he had a library card. Libraries are full of information. They offer a wealth of job-search related material, including the *Occupational Outlook Handbook,* books on resume writing, and specific groups such as professional associations and credentialing groups that can be of assistance in a job search.

Eighth, Dan needed to make sure his COBRA was in place. Since he had been covered by a company insurance plan, the Consolidated Omnibus Reconciliation Act of 1985 (COBRA) was important. In broad strokes, COBRA allows a person the option of purchasing continued health insurance coverage after a termination. In most cases, both person and dependents are eligible to continue insurance for up to eighteen months, providing the former employee was not fired for gross misconduct (Koltnow and Dumas 1990, p. 17). Dan made the arrangements to continue his coverage.

Ninth, Rev. Carroll suggested that Dan locate helpful organizations. The church had set up a group for support, encouragement, and specific help to men and women of the congregation in the same situation as Dan. This group meets twice a week at the church for the specific purpose of helping. The group provides support to the members through this difficult time of losing a job, finding a vocation, and securing the new position. Dan was invited to join (see Koltnow and Dumas 1990, pp. 10–22).

Rev. Carroll was aware that Dan needed specific suggestions at this time, but also that Dan was going through a number of specific stages of grief. William A. Borgen and Norman E. Amundson have identified distinctive patterns in the dynamics of unemployment (Borgen and Amundson 1987). The model they present is that the experience of unemployment is like an emotional roller coaster. Their conclusions indicate that there are specific stages that men and women go through from the time they are fired to the time they are either re-employed or repeat the pattern to a point of burnout and apathy (see Figure 1).

After the job loss, the first stage is the immediate sense of relief, followed very quickly by the stages of grieving suggested by Kübler-Ross (1969). These stages of grieving include denial, anger, bargaining, depression, and acceptance. It is important to note that people do not go through these stages in the same order or even go through all of them. Kübler-Ross suggests that most people experience facets of these stages.

This first stage in Figure 1 is the grieving process, which is necessary for all of us at the time of loss and particularly at the end of employment. Toward the end of the grieving process people experience an acceptance phase highlighted by the recognition that the old job is over and the job search must begin. At this point it is particu-

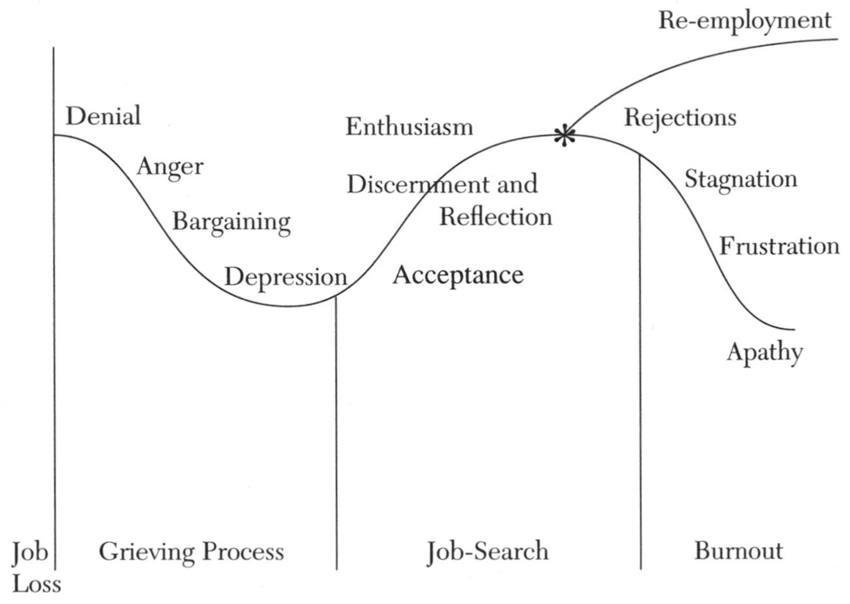

Figure 1.

larly helpful for the person to begin a process of discernment and reflection, which is the second stage. The third stage is the job-search phase, a job in itself. This stage begins with a great deal of enthusiasm and includes a process of advice and information interviews and the distribution of cover letters and resumes. Many end this phase through re-employment, which is the fourth stage. Others, however, enter a time of stagnation and frustration, which is a fifth stage. This fifth stage is a time of continued unemployment. Many soon run into difficulties given the current economic climate. Job searching forces us to face the harsh realities that getting a job is hard work. Those who continually run into rejection after rejection and unsuccessful interviews experience burnout. This burnout is fueled by extended periods of unemployment. When people find themselves in an extended period of unemployment that involves a sustained and unproductive job search, they may experience loss of personal power and feelings of helplessness may develop (Borgen and Amundson 1987, p. 181). The result is apathy and hopelessness. The person and the families now begin to adjust to the situation and accept a major change in lifestyle. They experience apathy, anger, helplessness, and confusion. To break free from this stage requires that the person recycle through

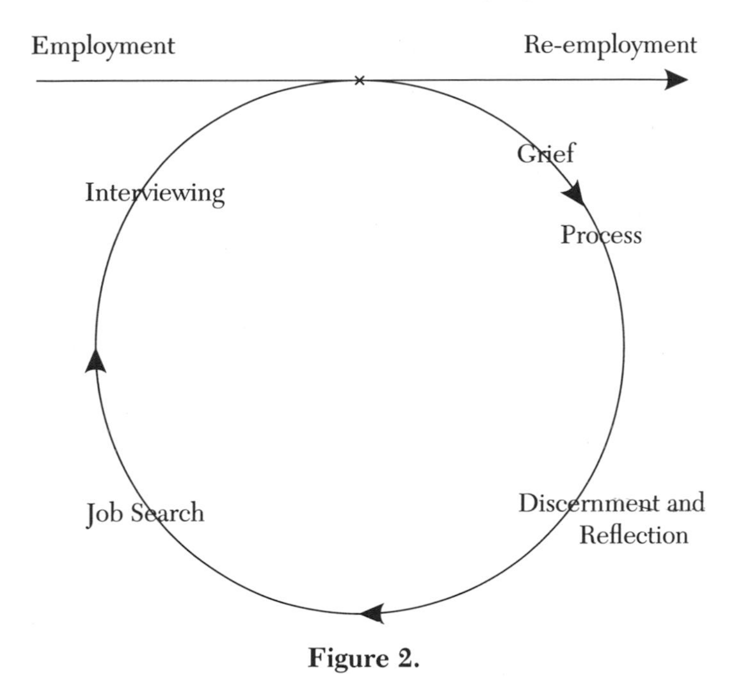

Figure 2.

the first four stages with the hope of breaking the cycle at the re-employment stage.

Rev. Carroll knows that he has to do grief counseling during the first stage. He does supportive and discernment counseling during the second stage. He will lend assistance during the job-search stage with specific suggestions and limited information. When Dan is re-employed, he will want to be there to help the family celebrate and give thanks. If Dan remains unemployed, he will need to assist Dan to break out of his apathy. Dan will then need counseling to begin the process again and move through the stages again. Supportive pastoral counseling will be needed for both Dan and the family.

Providing pastoral care and counseling to Dan immediately after his termination of employment required Rev. Carroll to do grief counseling. He was there for the mourning after. He listened to Dan's story and helped him express his feelings of anger, loss, denial, anxiety, and depression. Dan felt like he had entered an emotional roller coaster and became confused and "irrational". The loss of the job represented a significant emotional, physical, spiritual and identity loss. As time passed, Dan experienced a growing sense of loneliness. He tended to withdraw from his friends and his friends withdrew from him. His job loss raised their own fear and anxieties about their own job security. Rev. Carroll and the church group provides a person and place for Dan to be angry, express his fears and doubts, and have them accepted. Fear, anger, shame, and despair created a sense of stress in him. The pastor and the supportive congregation helped him put the stress into a manageable level. Rev. Carroll had already suggested that Dan do nine specific things. He now helped him through the grief. People handle getting fired differently but they all grieve. This is not the time to escape the reality of the pain and loss through alcohol and/or drugs. It is a severe crisis, and Rev. Carroll let Dan know that they both needed to recognize that this is the wrong time for drink or drugs.

There is a common temptation to feel lost, bereft, annoyed, and angry when fired, especially if the job is the source of the person's meaning and identity. Rev. Carroll was supportive of this, listening and assisting in helping Dan realize that he is not his work. Dan is far more than the greatest job in the world. Those who have lost their jobs need to face the question, "Who Am I, Really?" They should take the time to answer that question by writing a list of ten words that describe who they are (Reid 1971, p. 18). By doing this Dan was able to look beyond his identity as what he does but to who he really is. This may sound easy. It isn't. Getting fired, terminated, or laid off is a good opportunity to make the shift.

In doing grief counseling Rev. Carroll was aware that one aspect of grief is guilt. Dan began to tell him, "If I had only acted on this when I sensed it a year ago. If I hadn't waited until they fired me." These are the common phrases of guilt. Part of the pastor's job in this special form of grief counseling is to reflect with Dan on his part in his termination of employment. How was he bringing the situation to a head? What did he say to himself that overrode the natural instincts that he was aware of early in the process? At first Dan blamed others. He expressed anger that he was singled out. Most of this was projection. It was important for Rev. Carroll to help Dan delineate the difference between the aspects of his termination he had control over and the aspects he had no control over. He was not able to control the economy, the price of oil, or the decisions made by the president. He was not personally responsible for the sale of the company or the corporate decisions made to "downsize" his department. As Dan was able to see both the external causes and the internal perspective, he was able to move on. If he were to get stuck and adopt an internal perspective only and blame himself for the termination and negative circumstances, the result will be loss of self-esteem and continued wandering in grief and pain. However, Dan did play some part in his termination. He will also now play a major part in how he deals with the reality of the situation. The grief counseling process helped Dan express his feelings and pain. As he moved through the stages of denial, anger, bargaining, and depression to acceptance, he was ready to move to stage two.

Stage two is the recognition that getting fired, "downsized," or terminated is an opportunity. Sally Jessy Raphael, nationally syndicated TV talk-show host, radio personality, and author has been fired so many times, eighteen to be exact, that she's developed a philosophy of dismissal. She states, "Getting fired is a time to take assessment, to move in the direction you want to go. And as long as you have your hat in hand, I believe that you shouldn't try for less, but for more. More is as easy to get" (quoted in Koltow and Dumas 1990, p. 35). When Dan accepted the reality of being fired, he was ready to reflect on it as an opportunity and a new beginning.

Getting fired may provide a long-overdue opportunity to reassess likes and dislikes, reevaluate priorities, redirect energies, and claim a vocational dream. With Dan, as with all Christians, it is an opportunity to ask, "Is God at work here? Does God have a vocation for me?" This can be a time for intense discernment of God's calling and our vocational response. Losing a job opens us up to new possibilities and options and to remember again that God has something for us to do.[2]

"The very fact that you've been fired," Rev. Carroll told Dan, "may be a signal that you need to reassess your career choices and particularly reflect on this experience as an opportunity in which God is at work." Rather than encouraging Dan to rush out and get a job to reduce his financial and identity anxiety, Rev. Carroll suggested that Dan take the time to reflect, meditate, and explore vocational options. "If you could do anything you wanted and there was no chance of failure, what would be your vocational dream?" asked Rev. Carroll.

Dan took this thought home with him and over a three-week period began to refocus his thinking. He wrote, he thought, and he reflected. Who am I? What would make me happy and be both challenging and even fun? Where is God leading me in this? Dan knew that the first step in taking advantage of this opportunity was to look inside and begin to dream, to visualize the next career step. He invited God to be his partner in the process of claiming and identifying his bliss, his inner sense of self-actualized vocation.

To invite God into this process is to be open to God's call. The conclusion might be that Dan will do what he had been doing. He might be doing something else. Rev. Carroll supported this exploration knowing that a flexible personality can face his or her own pain, anxiety, anger, look it in the eye and find that it is not as unendurable as first suspected. Dan began to recognize that he had options, that he was not rigidly stuck in one type of job search. Rev. Carroll taught Dan to welcome options and choices. Flexibility is the key to success. This discernment process is a vital step in dealing with past vocational choices and future vocational options. Not to do this is to rush blindly into a lake while searching for a life preserver.

In this stage the purpose of Rev. Carroll's counseling was to be supportive, to be a listener, and to give specific suggestions. Dan was invited to use his inner resources and relationship with God through meditation and mental picturing. We often forget that God is a God of abundance, who walks with us and cares about us. As Dan put it, "My first reaction was to feel like a failure. I was laid off. It felt like the worst tragedy that could have happened to me. In that painful moment I felt I was worthless. Then I remembered with the help of Reverend Carroll that God is with me and I felt calm, focused, and determined to come out of this a winner. I realized that it could be an opportunity. I decided to trust God and the gifts and abilities that I know I have. I remembered the story of Jacob and how he wrestled with the angel. In discussing this with Reverend Carroll, I realized that Jacob came out of that struggle a winner, different, with a new sense of himself and his relationship to God and family. I plan to do that."

What started off as a feeling of failure and pain, getting laid off, was really an opportunity for a new beginning, a new life, and a vocation that brought meaning to Dan's life. He was learning to trust God, himself, and the abilities he has. Dan visualized and dreamed. "Given who I am and what my abilities are where will I serve God best and experience that sense of meaning and fulfillment I have been looking for?"

Dan, through his counseling with Rev. Carroll, began to put his dreams into words. He talked and talked some more. He shared his discoveries with his family. At times they were supportive and at other times they felt anxious and fearful of what his final decision might mean for them. He knew deep inside that he had already taken many steps toward securing a new vocation when he began reevaluating whether he was on the right career path before or whether this was the time for a change. He knew he was good at what he did. If he did something else it would be because it was the right next step for him and not because he was a failure. Dan realized that after dreaming and visualizing the dream, talking about it, and discussing it, he must act. He must seek to make real what he earnestly desired as the next vocational step.

Dan was now ready to move to the third stage, the job search. This can be a difficult and painful process, taking many hours and a great deal of determination. Rev. Carroll realized that Dan would need lots of support in this stage and decided to minister to him in three ways. First, he involved Dan in the support group. There were five people in the group, three men and two women. They had all been laid off, fired, or "downsized." Each was seeking to secure a new vocation and had found in the group people they could share common experiences with, gain support and encouragement from, and discuss how interviews went. The group was particularly helpful in role-playing interview situations, so that group members who had not been in the job-search process for a long time could develop better interviewing skills. The group discussed what was appropriate for the prospective employer to ask and what was not. They shared what they discovered. The group was also helpful as a clearing house for information.

Second, he encouraged Dan redo his resume to reflect his desired vocation. Dan presented his resume to the group and found their input helpful.

Third, Rev. Carroll suggested that Dan do advice and information interviews. These are short interviews with persons in the desired field. Dan began to develop a list of persons he knew who worked in his desired vocation. This list was derived from family, friends, his church friends, and Rev. Carroll. It wasn't until he sat down to make this list that he realized that he had more contacts than he thought. He then called all the contacts and asked to talk with them about what they do, how they enjoyed their work, what they didn't like, and what they had done to prepare themselves for the career. In general, Dan tried to gather as much advice and information about the vocation he desired to enter as he could. When an interview was concluding, he asked the person to recommend someone else that he might talk to. The group reminded Dan to follow up all advice and information interviews with a thank-you note. Two of the persons in the group received job offers as a direct result of these advice and information interviews.

This process worked especially well for Dan. With the help of Rev. Carroll he realized that he had always wanted to be a high school teacher. He was very good with math and science. Dan was especially gifted at working with the senior high youth group at the church. His advice and information interview were most helpful. Dan realized that he could be a high school teacher. He needed to go back to school for a year and secure his teaching certificate. After long conversations with his family and the counseling support of Rev. Carroll, Dan decided to enroll in the local college and fulfill a long-hidden dream to become a high school teacher.

Rev. Carroll realized that everything was going well for Dan, but that for some in his congregation the job search would be difficult and unsuccessful. Their continued unemployment will lead to further depths of despair, discouragement, anger, and pain. They will find themselves on a yo-yo, first being hopeful and searching, then spiraling down into despair, with feelings of worthlessness and isolation. In this repeated pattern they will need to rely more and more on the support of family, friends, the church community, and the supportive, guiding pastoral counseling of their pastor. They fall back, sometimes again and again, to the same feelings and grief that they experienced when they were first fired. Each time they will need the intervention counseling of the pastor to assist them in the grief, self-reflective/discernment, and job-search stages.

With these persons Rev. Carroll knows that a referral is in order. The Church Career Development Centers are good places to refer them. In such centers[3] people are assisted by professionals through five steps: clarification of outcome goals, self-assessment and discernment, career/vocational claiming, job search strategies, and assistance in job interviewing.[3] This is not a referral away but rather an opportunity for such persons to spend several days in self-reflection around vocational issues. When they return to the church and community, they will need the supportive pastoral counseling of their minister to help them make real what they have learned.

Rev. Carroll then sat down to review what had happened over the last five months from the first phone call from Joan to a time when Dan had made a decision to go back to school. He was aware that this was a relatively short period of time. Most people take an average of eighteen months from the time they leave a job until they secure another job. Dan will still have to do a major job search and secure a position after completing his schooling and certification. By then he will be in the field and his network will have increased and the college itself will help him secure placement.

Upon reflecting, Rev. Carroll was aware that he had ministered to Dan and Joan in some very significant ways. First, he accepted the loss of a job as a major crisis in the life of the parishioner and the family. Taking it lightly with quick reassurance would not have been helpful. Job loss is a serious and critical experience requiring pastoral care and counseling. Many persons are immediately referred by their employer to an out-placement agency. This is helpful but does not speak to the many emotional and spiritual issues that need to be dealt with. The out-placement agency can become a major help, but pastoral care and counseling is definitely needed. Rev. Carroll realized that Dan and the family needed the ministry and support of the church.

Second, people who lose their jobs go through a major period of grief and pain. Rev. Carroll was very familiar with this because of the deaths he had encountered in the parish. He was an expert in grief counseling with families and friends at the loss of a loved one. He realized the loss of a job was no different. A death had occurred. Dan and the family needed the same grief counseling. He knew how to do that.

Third, because the loss of a job was occurring with approximately 5 percent of his congregation, Rev. Carroll had already set up a support group for the unemployed. This group was a major focal point for Rev. Carroll's ministry and the ministry of the church to Dan and others like him. A group offers people support, input, information, and the true awareness that they are not alone. Since the natural tendency is for the unemployed to withdraw and for friends to withdraw from them, the group served many very important needs.

Fourth, Rev. Carroll gave Dan nine very specific suggestions. These suggestions focused Dan's energy and gave him something specific to do. These nine items are not always thought about in the midst of the crisis. Just as someone needs to make specific suggestions and even arrangements at the time of the death of a loved one, so at this time of the death of a job some caring person needs to give the grieving person specific suggestions. Rev. Carroll realized that these suggestions were helpful, but that they did not substitute for the grief counseling that was also necessary.

Fifth, it was important for Rev. Carroll to know the five stages that each unemployed person goes through: the grief process stage, the discernment and self-reflection stage, the job-search stage, the re-employment stage, and for some, the continued unemployment stage. Each stage required pastoral care and counseling. The grief stage required listening and supportive counseling. The discernment and self-reflective stage required prayer, encouragement in self-exploration, and inviting God into the process. The job-search stage required specific education, support, role play, and reflection. The re-employment stage invited celebration. For those who remain unemployed Rev. Carroll needed to be both supportive and listening, to invite the person to begin the process again, and to make a significant referral for career counseling and development.

It is clear that there is no such thing as job security. However, our faith invites us to be in continual communication with God to discern God's will for our lives in vocation. This is the ongoing ministry of both the pastor and the church.

Notes

1. Further information is available through state unemployment offices in the form of pamphlets.
2. For more details and an in-depth discussion of the spiritual and vocational aspects of career counseling, see Lewis 1990.
3. For additional information, contact the Northeast Career Center, Nassau St. at Cedar Lane, Princeton, NJ 08540.

References

Borgen, William A., and Amundson, Norman E. 1987. "The Dynamics of Unemployment." *Journal of Counseling and Development* 66 (December).

Koltow, Emily, and Dumas, Lynne S. 1990. *Congratulations! You've Been Fired.* New York: Ballantine Books.

Kübler-Ross, Elisabeth. 1969. *On Death and Dying.* New York: Macmillan.

Lewis, Roy. 1990. *Choosing Your Career, Finding Your Vocation.* New York: Paulist Press.

Reid, Clyde H. 1971. *Help! I've Been Fired.* Philadelphia: Pilgrim Press.

Tritch, Teresa, and Smith, Marguerite T. 1990. "Smart Moves for Tougher Times." *Money Magazine* (October).

Walter J. Smith, S.J.

27. Embracing Pastoral Ministry in the Age of AIDS

The Human Immunodeficiency Virus (HIV) has characteristics that make it terrifying: it seems uncontrollable, can infect anyone at any age, and is often fatal. Ignorance, prejudice, and uncertainty about the future course of this pandemic compound the challenges facing the entire corps of care providers, including pastoral counselors. In addition to awareness of the psycho-social issues affecting care, effective pastoral ministry to any person with HIV infection requires that the provider have a basic yet competent understanding of the underlying infection and of the diseases afflicting the person, their course and treatment.[1]

Persons living with HIV infection develop a specialized understanding of the various illnesses that comprise this syndrome. Many struggle to learn ways to live with an infection for which there is, at present, no permanent, definitive, curative treatment. It is not uncommon that the experiences of a life-threatening illness dominate their conscious thoughts and conversation. A pastoral counselor needs basic factual knowledge about HIV if he or she is to interact effectively with infected persons who either have become sick or who fear they will get sick.

Throughout our discussion, we refer to HIV infection and its related diseases rather than to the more common designation of Acquired Immunodeficiency Syndrome (AIDS). When reference is made to AIDS, it means the terminal result of HIV infection. This distinction has as much relevance for pastoral counselors as it does for physicians. Persons with HIV infection put a high premium on the terms used to describe their disease. Some associate the word *AIDS* with a hopeless, terminal condition. The same individual may view a diagnosis of HIV infection with fear, but also with a sense of hope. For this reason, sensitivity to language in speaking about HIV and the syndrome of illnesses related to this virus is important (AIDS Education Project of the American Psychiatric Association 1989).

In this chapter on pastoral ministry to persons with HIV infection and disease we shall review some basic data on Acquired Immunodeficiency Syndrome. To accomplish this, we shall reflect upon the three principal words that define this medical condition. Subsequently, we shall consider some psycho-social aspects of HIV that have bearing on pastoral counseling and comment upon opportunities for pastoral care of persons with HIV and their families. Finally, we shall suggest some ways to minister effectively in an age of AIDS.

Acquired Immunodeficiency Syndrome: Some Perspectives

Acquiring HIV Infection

AIDS is acquired through infection with the Human Immunodeficiency Virus (HIV). The virus is transmitted when HIV particles or infected cells gain access to another person's bloodstream. This transfer can occur in a variety of ways. Five principal routes of transmission have been identified. The first results from engaging in high-risk sexual behaviors, including vaginal, anal, or oral genital intercourse. A second route of infection comes from sharing improperly sterilized needles in intravenous drug use. A third source of infection is from an infected mother to her developing fetus, *in utero*. A fourth risk of infection to a breast-feeding infant comes from an infected mother's milk. The fifth route of HIV infection is from transfusion of contaminated blood or blood products. Since mid-1985 all donated blood is carefully screened for antibodies to the virus. It is important to note that the disease is *acquired*. For adults, this means that one is often responsible for getting it. Unfortunately, numbers of sexually active individuals, particularly adolescents, and persons using drugs continue to be infected with HIV even though much is known about the virus and how it is transmitted.

From the point of infection there is ordinarily an incubation period before a person develops an HIV-related disease and is diagnosed. Infected infants frequently become sick in their first or second year of life. Those over the age of fifty also have shorter incubation periods, between five and seven years. The majority of infected adults can remain ostensibly well for ten years. Apart from age, the length of the incubation period may be linked to the amount and virulence of the strain of HIV transmitted. Some individuals may be genetically more resistant to the virus than some others whose general health or body immunity may be compromised. The relatively long incubation period is a primary source of anxiety for many persons who know that they have been exposed to HIV.

Investigators are trying to understand the relationships between co-factors that may influence infection, incubation, and the clinical manifestation of disease. Issues such as general health, previous medical history, nutrition, exercise, environmental and economic variables, and a host of other related issues may have some significant role to play in explaining the wide variability among long-term survivors (see Callen 1990).

Pastoral care is not ordinarily focused on the issue of how or why a person has acquired the disease. However, the person with HIV may need to identify and discuss these issues. Non-judgmental dialogue with the pastoral counselor can help a person to process effectively these feelings and concerns related to incubation and survival.

The Basic Meaning of Immunodeficiency

AIDS is principally a disease of the body's immune system. The immune system relies on effective physical, chemical, and biochemical interactive barriers and is made up of a variety of cells whose function is to identify, isolate, and eliminate viruses, bacteria, and other foreign substances (antigens) from the body. The human body's immune system is designed in such a way that it is virtually impenetrable by threatening organisms. When the immune system recognizes a "foreigner," a number of specialized cells move into action.

Phagocytes are one of these defensive weapons. As its Greek name suggests, phagocytes have the ability to "eat" invading viruses, bacteria, fungi, protozoa, or worms, as well as any other debris that washes into the bloodstream. These cells are largely scavengers, whose purpose is to rid the body of any foreign material as well as dead tissue and degenerated cells. They play an indispensable role in immune system functioning. However, some of these foreign microorganisms, like HIV, have physical or chemical properties that make detection and destruction exceedingly difficult.

Lymphocytes, a specific subset of cells involved in these defensive immune functions are white blood cells that also patrol the body, alert to foreign invaders. These circulating lymphocytes routinely attack infected cells and prevent the invading microorganisms from reproducing themselves and migrating to other sites.

A class of lymphocytes are the T-cells, the "helper cells." Their specific function is to coordinate and manage the activities of the immune system. The T-cells stimulate the B-cells, which produce specific antibodies that attack, neutralize, or eliminate the invading virus or bacteria. Some have described T-cells as the watchdogs of the immune system. When the infection is under control, the CD8, or suppressor cells, call off the attack and the body returns to normal functioning.

Unfortunately, some of these foreign microorganisms, like HIV, have physical or chemical properties that make detection and destruction exceedingly difficult.

Viruses are incapable of independent life. A virus is nothing more than inert, organic material looking for a living cell in which it might reside. Only by invading a fully metabolized "host" cell can a virus become active, capable of reproducing its genetic material. A virus exploits the living cell it invades. It uses the host cell's metabolic machinery to make many more virus particles, which in time seek out other host cells in order to perpetuate the process.

HIV directly attacks the T-cells by invading the cells' structure, neutralizing their defenses, and rendering them ineffective. These helper cells are prevented from performing their infection-fighting functions. HIV can migrate freely within the body, proliferating within the T-cells it invades. These cells become effective partners with the enemy, HIV.

When the HIV invades the T-cells, it becomes part of the cell's DNA, the molecular chain containing the genetic information enabling cells to reproduce. We noted previously that during an incubation period the virus can remain dormant for a variable period of time. The only clear effect is that the T-cells are prevented from performing their normal defensive functions.

When the HIV is activated, stimulated perhaps by some specific triggers, which may include gender, genetic predisposition, physical and emotional health, and IV drug use, the virus does not waste any time reproducing itself and infecting other cells. The genetic components of HIV allow it to replicate itself a thousand times faster than many other kinds of viruses. The T-cells in which HIV has made its home become "factories" in which the virus reproduces. The original host cells are killed in the process. As the virus is released into the circulating blood it seeks out other T-cells, thus further debilitating the immune system and interrupting its important functions. The depletion of helper cells appears to precipitate immunological breakdown, and the symptoms of HIV disease probably result from this event.

The immune system of a person infected with HIV attempts to fight the presence of the virus and produces antibodies. However, these antibodies appear to be ineffective in neutralizing and destroying the virus. With a decrease in the number of T-cells, the immune system is unable to discharge its important defensive and regulatory functions. The person who is immunocompromised is thus unable to mount effective antibody reactions to new antigens and becomes vulnerable to a host of recurrent or new infections.

This description of the immunodeficiency resulting from exposure to HIV has symbolic relevance to pastoral care. An immunocompromised individual becomes defenseless. Immunodeficiency leaves a person feeling vulnerable, unprotected, under siege. The psychological and spiritual states of a person with AIDS frequently mirror the biological portrait of immunodeficiency. The biochemical characteristics of this disease can precipitate a number of related negative psychological and spiritual reactions. A person who feels defenseless looks for someone who will be supportive. Pastoral care has the potential to be this much needed source of support.

A person with HIV is vulnerable to subtle forms of rejection, real or perceived. An individual in a weakened physical state is prone to become disengaged, hopeless, and depressed, sometimes surrendering the will to fight, the will to live. While this is not a universal experience of persons with AIDS, the drama of human immunodeficiency can interpret the psychological and spiritual defenselessness some individuals feel.

A Syndrome of Diseases

In contemporary medical usage, a syndrome describes an aggregate of symptoms associated with any disease. When all of these symptoms are put together, they form the clinical picture of the disease. With a weakened immune system, an individual is prone to develop a variety of opportunistic infections which contribute to the clinical picture of this syndrome.[2] The term *opportunistic* is used to describe a wide range of illnesses. These illnesses are attributable to organisms commonly present in the environment, but threatening only to persons whose immune systems have been weakened. These organisms use the opportunity provided by the body's compromised defenses to gain a firm foothold.

A unique characteristic of HIV disease is the tendency for an infected person to develop many problems with the common denominator being the suppression of normal immune functions. Immunosuppression makes medical management difficult since the body is not effective in dealing with infections and cancers. Not only do the body's natural helper cells fail to fight off the HIV invader, but other viruses ordinarily living in check within the human body can express themselves as new, hostile forms of disease. Although the immune system is seriously impaired as a result of HIV infection, this does not mean that the individual is vulnerable to every infection.

One of the characteristics of this syndrome is that the HIV-infected individual appears to be particularly vulnerable to certain diseases. It will be helpful to discuss those life-threatening HIV-related diseases that pastoral counselors will most commonly encounter in practice.

Pneumocystis Carinii Pneumonia (PCP)

Among life-threatening opportunistic infections associated with immunodeficiency, Pneumocystis carinii pneumonia (PCP) is among the most common. Pneumocystis carinii pneumonia is caused by a yeast infection of the lungs by a single-celled parasite (protozoan). The parasite, Pneumocystis carinii, has been found in the lungs of animals and healthy humans. Although present, it does not flourish unless the immune system is significantly weakened. If the parasite is activated, it multiplies and consolidates the air spaces in the lungs in a honeycomb-like fashion. The initial manifestations of this disease are similar to other forms of pneumonia: dry cough, fever, and breathing problems. PCP occurs at least once in 60 to 80 percent of persons with AIDS.

Improved treatment and maintenance programs have increased survival rates for those who develop PCP. The pneumonia is responsive to a variety of antibiotic and other drug treatments, although none of these treatments eradicates the Pneumocystis organism. The possibility of recurrent infection is high because the immune system does not appear to recover. If the immunosuppression reversed, the infection would be checked in its progress.

With each successive bout of PCP an individual's chances for survival are decreased. Overall mortality rates for this infection have remained relatively constant with a 15 to 25 percent mortality for each episode. PCP continues to be the major cause of death in persons with AIDS.

Kaposi's Sarcoma (KS)

Kaposi's sarcoma is a cancerous tumor of the cells lining blood and lymphatic vessels. Apart from its association with AIDS, the cancer is not life-threatening. The cancer produces slowly developing lesions, disseminating on many body surfaces, most commonly appearing on the skin of the feet, the trunk of the body, on the head, neck, face, eyes, mouth, and throat. Lesions can also appear in the internal organs, such as in the gastrointestinal tract as well as on the lymph nodes.

The cancer is first visible when painless purple to brown colored, flat or raised, irregularly shaped blotches appear on or under the skin. Initially they look like ordinary bruise marks, but they do not disappear after a week or so. The lesions frequently are raised above the level of the surrounding skin and are hard to the touch.

Kaposi's sarcoma is rarely the primary cause of death for a person with AIDS. If the cancer appears in the throat or other internal organs, the threat to life increases. The treatments for these lesions with radiation and chemotherapies can be effective, but they can further suppress the immune system to such a degree that the treatments for KS may pave the way for other opportunistic infections.

From a pastoral counseling perspective, the disfigurement associated with this cancer, particularly on exposed skin surfaces like the face, neck, upper torso, and limbs can cause psychological distress for the person. The proliferation of lesions can disturb individuals who interact with KS patients and may become an obstacle to effective pastoral care.

Cytomegalovirus (CMV)

There are also a number of other viruses that can cause opportunistic infections in a person with HIV. Cytomegalovirus (CMV) is frequently encountered in persons with AIDS. The infection contributes to inflammation and destruction of the retina resulting in partial or total blindness. CMV also triggers seizures and dementia, and is associated with pneumonia, inflammation of the esophagus, and pernicious diarrhea.

Toxoplasmosis and Cryptosporidiosis

Another source of opportunistic infections is found in the family of protozoa. *Toxoplasma gondii* is one species of these protozoa associated with HIV-related disease. The *Toxoplasma gondii* parasite invades the central nervous system, triggering brain seizures, high fevers, and delirium, resulting in decreased levels of consciousness. Personality and behavior changes associated with this brain infection are often the most disturbing aspects of this disease. Some persons infected with this parasite become unable to speak.

Family members and those caring for an individual with HIV-related toxoplasmosis report difficulty in coping with the alterations in personality associated with this disease. The infection is one of the most treatable, but the treatments must be maintained for the life of the infected persons. The long-term use of drugs can have many undesirable side effects and can do additional damage to the immune system.

Cryptosporidiosis is another parasitic infection, virtually unknown in humans prior to the advent of AIDS in the early 1980s. The parasite, *Cryptosporidium difficile,* had been found in a number of animals and reptiles, but rarely in human beings. In the few human cases in which the parasite had been documented, the diarrhea resulting from infection was self-limiting. This is not the case when the parasite attacks a person with HIV. The diarrhea is sustained, high-volume, and life-threatening. This pernicious diarrhea results in a person being unable to absorb nutrients from food, contributing to severe loss of weight, dehydration, and malnutrition. Although there have been several drugs used to treat the cryptosporidium parasitic infection, none has proven to be effective in controlled human trials. The best that medications have been able to achieve is a reduction in discomfort associated with persistent diarrhea.

Mycobacterium Avium-Intracellulare (MAI)

Bacterial diseases are also related to HIV. One of this group of opportunistic infections is *Mycobacterium avium intracellulare.* The bacterium, MAI, is commonly found in the environment, for example, in dust, soil, water. Despite its ubiquity, it rarely causes disease in humans, except in those who are immunocompromised. The associated symptoms of MAI are similar to other HIV-related diseases: fever, weight loss, cough, reparatory distress, swollen lymph glans, abdominal cramping, and diarrhea. The lungs are usually affected, and the infection will frequently spread to the liver, spleen, lymph nodes, gastrointestinal tract, bone marrow, and brain. MAI is resistant to standard antituberculosis drugs, although some new experimental treatments are promising.

Summary of HIV-Related Diseases

We have described briefly a few of the more than eighteen fungal, viral, protozoal, and bacterial agents associated with opportunistic infections seen in persons with HIV disease. In addition, we spoke about a rare cancer commonly diagnosed in persons with AIDS. Many of these diseases cause neurologic impairments in addition to physical symptoms. These related neurological problems are often the most difficult for patient and care-giver alike. Higher cortical functions, such as thinking and remembering, are frequently disrupted. Emotional and behavioral changes, including disengagement from affectional bonds, lifelong personal and professional interests, and spiritual practices, as well as disturbances in gait and motor coordination are frequently noted. The person may also lose control over bowel and bladder functions, creating situations of added embarrassment and distress.

Pastoral Implications

We have begun our discussion of Acquired Immunodeficiency Syndrome with a survey of some of the basic clinical facts related to HIV. These basic issues help us to understand better the physical, emotional, and spiritual experiences of persons living with HIV. Pastoral counselors may debate the necessity and usefulness of knowing these clinical details. It is our contention that the pastoral care of persons with AIDS is enhanced when the pastoral counselor appreciates the physical, psychological, spiritual, and social concerns they share. For these reasons, it is important that pastoral counselors stay current as new knowledge about AIDS and its treatment are published.

We may conceptualize pastoral care as an essentially spiritual ministry. However, our efforts are enhanced to the degree we understand the ancillary concerns of the persons to whom we minister. As pastoral counselors we need to think about AIDS holistically. Our strategies for pastoral care hinge on how able we are to integrate effectively our knowledge about this new disease with our other experiences in ministering to persons with life-threatening illnesses.

Engaging in Pastoral Care with Persons with AIDS

AIDS has been experienced as a frontal attack on the death-denying character of our American culture. We are confronted continually with statistics and projections about this epidemic. By the beginning of this second decade, more than 150,000 cases of AIDS were reported in the United States, and more than 90,000 persons have died. It is estimated that there are more than 1.5 million persons in the United States infected with HIV, and more than 10 million worldwide.

Estimates for the next few years (1992–93) in the United States run from 265,000 cases to 450,000 cases. The proportion of gay or bisexual men is gradually representing a smaller proportion of the whole. Heterosexual IV drug users, their sexual partners, and the offspring of infected women account for an increasing proportion of the whole. The numbers of African Americans is increasing dramatically. While African Americans represent approximately one-eighth of the population of the United States, they account at present for almost one-fourth of AIDS cases in this country. Similarly, 7 percent of the United States population are Latinos, yet they account for 14 percent of all AIDS cases in the United States.

Alarming increases of HIV infections among minorities are related to IV drug use. Since IV drug use is the direct or indirect route by which many pregnant mothers are being infected with HIV, as many as 85 percent of all pediatric cases are seen among infants of color. In the first decade of this pandemic the proportion of women infected with HIV was relatively small, accounting for 7 percent of all cases reported in the 1987. By 1989 this percentage increased to 11 percent. It is expected that these percentages will continue to rise. African Americans account for more than half of cases of HIV+ women in the United States, and Latinos account for approximately 20 percent of infected women. Finally, the documented sexual activity among adolescents and the high incidence of cases of teen pregnancies and of sexually transmitted diseases, among which HIV is numbered, coupled with an average incubation period of ten years before the presentation of HIV-related symptoms, is a cause of grave concern to epidemiologists who are tracking the transmission of this virus. In short, we can look forward to a significant increase in the number of cases of persons in their late teen and early adult years unknowingly transmitting the HIV infection and developing AIDS in the next decade.

Thus, into the next century America will have to face the reality that deaths resulting from HIV infections will continue to rise. It is with this escalating medical and psychological crisis in mind that health care is preparing itself in order to meet effectively new challenges to provide counsel and care. It is within this same context that those involved in pastoral ministries within the churches and synagogues must prepare for the new demands they will inevitably encounter in increasing numbers.

In the natural history of medicine, AIDS is without parallel. It is a disease that has exposed many flaws in our social fabric. Because it is a severely stigmatizing disease, persons with HIV fear discovery, discrimination, rejection, and abandonment. The social and psychological stresses that compound the physical characteristics of HIV are significant, and effective management of these problems challenges all providers of care. We shall consider some of the specific problems pastors encounter in ministering to persons with AIDS and the significant others (spouse, parent, child, sibling, lover, friend) who are their primary care-givers.

In pastoral practice we are continually confronted with human struggles that demand a fresh examination of our thoughts, feelings, biases, prejudices, and fears. Pastoral care requires continual re-engagement with personal values, religious beliefs, and theologies.

Involvement in the pastoral care of persons with HIV raises its own particular set of questions. To work effectively with persons with HIV disease, pastoral counselors must be open to understand the world of the gay community and the communities of drug users and prostitutes, as well as the unique sociocultural features of the Black, Hispanic, and Native American communities. In addition, pastoral counselors must have special sensitivities to the mores of sexually active adolescents.

Unlike other life-threatening illnesses, persons infected with HIV or who develop symptoms related to the syndrome, experience stigma. Persons with HIV are not the only ones affected by social response to the disease; those individuals who become involved in providing care likewise are vulnerable to the negative reactions of others. It is important to acknowledge this social reality before embarking on a decision to assume a pastoral role in the care of a person with AIDS. Some counselors have reported the objections of their spouses, colleagues, and congregants to their pastoral involvement with persons with HIV. Despite strong evidence about how the virus is and is not transmitted, fear of infection can still exist among individuals exposed to persons with HIV. These fears and concerns about contagion and infection continue to be expressed, even in the second decade of this pandemic. A counselor must confront and reconcile any fears about becoming infected through contacts in ordinary pastoral care and must be ready to help others to allay their concerns.

In any helping relationship, it is important for the helper to pay attention to feelings he or she experiences toward the person seeking assistance. It is difficult to be effective in a helping relationship if one has strong negative feelings and judgments toward the individual seeking help. To attempt to provide care without attending to and resolving personal issues related to the individual is irresponsible. Sometimes helpers create more problems for the helpee than they solve. In medicine, these problems are termed *iatrogenic,* meaning they have their origin in the attitudes and behaviors of physicians toward their patients. The same phenomenon can exist in pastoral care, when a pastor's overt or covert hostility or negative attitudes can intensify a person's suffering.

Pastors and physicians share parallel responsibilities in relation to the provision of care for persons with HIV. Society presumes that doctors and religious professionals will provide care for all persons. In return for the special status that society accords physical and spiritual healers, it expects its physicians and pastors to be self-sacrificing. Acknowledging medicine's tradition of providing care to infectious persons, the American Medical Association says: "Not everyone is emotionally able to care for patients with AIDS" (AMA 1986). Not every pastoral counselor is emotionally able to care for a person with HIV. It is important to recognize this fact and make other provisions for the person's care. We rarely encounter a situation where a pastor overtly refuses ministerial assistance to a person with HIV. To do so would be scandalous and unacceptable behavior, not in keeping with one's public profession. What is more disturbing, however, is covert refusal.

The majority of persons with HIV for whom we care as pastors are young men and women. Many of these afflicted persons profess a valiant commitment to live despite the disabling aspects of HIV. Yet for the majority of these individuals, the disease proves to be a terminal illness. Their trajectories to death may be either slow or accelerated, but eventually most die. People in the health care professions who provide care for persons with HIV speak about their frustration in seeing so many promising young people become ill, struggle with a variety of recurring illnesses, progressively deteriorate, and ultimately die. These physicians, nurses, and other care providers become very involved with persons with HIV and with their families and friends. Inevitably bonding takes place. Where there is attachment, there will be experiences of loss and grief when the person dies. The deaths of persons with AIDS have a way of eroding a thin protective barrier and forcing us to come to terms with our personal mortality.

Health care providers not only describe their subjective experiences of burnout from working so hard to manage the multiple physical and emotional problems of persons with AIDS, but they also acknowledge the cumulative effect of working with so many people who die. Although they are dedicated to this work, a number of individuals find that they have to leave work with persons with AIDS because the confrontation with death proves to be too strong.

Dealing with the Experiences of Persons with HIV

Healthy psychological functioning depends upon the effective use of defense mechanisms. The principal purpose of psychological defenses is to assist a person to meet the challenges presented by a specific crisis. Denial is one of the more common of these defenses. It takes time to assimilate the facts and consequences about one's condition, especially when the information is that one has HIV or a disease that defines AIDS. It is understandable that a person may resist the medical facts, may plead diagnostic error, or may dispute the prognosis offered. After a while, denial often gives way to acceptance.

In healthy individuals denial is a temporary solution, not a permanent one. It is a transitional state, a bridge between the world as it is and the world as we would like it to be. The majority of people utilize denial as a temporary retreat while they better prepare themselves for engagement with the facts and consequences of their illness. Some pastoral counselors experience difficulty in dealing with persons who deny the reality of their situation. However, it is important to underscore the appropriateness, normality, and for a number of people, the necessity of denial. Denial may resurface a number of times in the course of ministering to a person with HIV, and to those who are their loved ones and care providers.

Denial operates in other ways as well, such as rejecting treatments and dispensing with taking prescribed medications. Because such individuals do not accept the seriousness of their illness, they can engage in injurious behaviors, including excessive drinking and other forms of substance abuse. They may not monitor diet and sleep habits, adding further stress to the body's ability to fight infection. If they are sexually active, they may continue to expose others to infection through unsafe practices.

Denial can be employed by family or friends as well. Admittedly, it is difficult to acknowledge that someone you love is seriously ill and may die. It is a fine line to walk between continuing to treat a person with AIDS as alive, while also recognizing and adjusting to the reality that the person may not survive as a result of this disease. There are situations in which a person with HIV, who is aware and accepting of the reality of his or her diagnosis, is faced with family, lover, or friends who are unwilling to accept the same reality. In essence, denial functions as a psychological block preventing open awareness of the life-threatening diagnosis and acceptance of the fact of death. By their words and behavior, others pretend that the evidence of the disease is not compelling and that the person with HIV will be able to conquer the illness. This pretense is different from a realistic attitude of hope and the desire to live, which will be discussed later in this chapter.

Living with a life-threatening illness requires that the person with HIV and those who are important members of his or her support network be able to experience the feelings which are catalyzed by the illness. Together they need to experience the losses that are a natural part of this process and be able to talk freely as the time of death draws closer. If a person with HIV is to engage positively in this process, he or she must feel support and acceptance from those who share this experience. If that support and acceptance is not perceived, then the person with HIV may feel isolated and vulnerable to fears of being abandoned.

Some pastors, in efforts to express positive support and to help maintain hope, become confederates in denial. They pretend either that the person is not as sick as he or she truly is, or they become allies with the denial of some important members of the family.

Anger is also a common, normal, and legitimate psychological defense of a person living with HIV. There are countless reasons which explain his or her anger. It is not necessary to chronicle these multiple sources of anger. Any person facing potential or certain death may feel anger. Such individuals see other people, comparable in age and life experience, who are well and alive. They may resent the perceived "wellness" in others, while hating the "illness" in themselves. For example, a gay man with HIV may become angry with a lover who is not sick.

In its Scandinavian and Icelandic origins, the word *anger* means "grief" and "sorrow." In pastoral and psychological practice it is not uncommon to discover underneath expressions of anger an individual's more painful experiences of loss, sorrow, and grief. In order to gain access to these more important feelings, it is essential that the counselor not react negatively to angry outbursts or attacks. Family members and caring friends acknowledge that one of the most difficult things with which they contend in assisting a person with HIV is dealing with expressions of anger. Anger is often targeted at those individuals who are most accessible and who are the closest supports to the sick person.

Caring for a person with HIV is demanding, both physically and emotionally. The task is compounded when the person whom you are assisting makes you the focused object of anger. The most natural response is to retaliate, to express anger in return.[3] Walking away from a person with HIV is one strategy. It helps to dissipate or diffuse negative feelings, provides perspective, and gives recovery time. However, it is important to interpret the walking away, since the person with HIV may read this behavior as abandonment. Perceived rejection or abandonment can intensify anger. When a person in need perceives being abandoned, he or she may also experience a weakening or loss of control, heightened anxiety, and real fears. Anger is one of the exterior masks behind which many frightened feelings play.

Pastoral counselors will encounter expressions of anger in caring for persons with HIV. Effective care is contingent upon a clear understanding of the genesis of the person's anger and what it means in the context of life-threatening illness. Pastoral care may be able to help the person to focus anger better. A pastoral counselor needs to find appropriate ways to respond to projections of anger directed either to the church or to his or her own person.

Persons with HIV display multiple levels of anger. Anger may be focused on the HIV itself, which surreptitiously has gained access to their bodies and silently and successfully begun to overwhelm the body's defenses. For example, they may make the virus the *enemy,* the focus of visualization exercises, using anger constructively in this way.

Persons with HIV may be angry at those individuals whom they suspect have been involved in transmitting the virus to them. They may be angry at medicine's inability to check the virus or cure the diseases that threaten their survival. They may be angry at the government bureaucracy for not making an adequate response to the AIDS pandemic by increasing the amount spent on research on HIV and its related diseases. Some persons perceive the government as an all-protective parent and are angry that the problem reached the magnitude it did before the government became seriously involved in the fight.[4]

Persons with HIV may be angry at pharmaceutical companies, which appear to be profiting unreasonably with drugs that have shown promising results in the management of HIV and its related diseases. Or anger may be focused on agencies like the FDA, which may delay approval and availability of promising new drugs.

Anger is often directed at God or the church. Or a person with HIV may be angry at himself or herself for becoming infected with the virus.

Clearly, it is not uncommon to find several sources of anger in a single individual with HIV.

It is never easy to encounter anger in the context of pastoral care or pastoral counseling. Pastors may be exposed to verbal abusiveness, aggressive and hostile accusations, sarcasm, and insult. It is difficult ministering to a person who is negative, withholding, or withdrawn. It is helpful to recall that a person with HIV has reason to be angry, and that anger may be one strategy the person utilizes in his or her attempt to cope with an HIV diagnosis. Anger is a common camouflage for the deeper pains of anxiety, fear, guilt, and grief. If a pastoral worker can patiently endure the vitriol of a person's anger, he or she may be in a strategic position to assist the person to deal with the more substantive needs which the anger is masking.

Ministering to the Psychosocial and Spiritual Needs of Persons with HIV

The physical aspects of an illness and the treatment programs used to manage it can overtax a person's energy reserves. Serious illness is also an emotional strain. It is important to be able to assess how the experience of illness is affecting a person's basic functioning, particularly psychological activities. At the bedrock of healthy psychological functioning are issues of safety, trust, and security.

Illness, by definition, upsets the balance of safety, trust, and security. Illness exposes an individual to potential dangers, doubts, and risks. It is important to assess how much an illness threatens these basic needs in order to determine how effective any form of interpersonal assistance will be.

HIV is perceived by many infected persons to be a very threatening enemy. Not only does the virus destabilize the functioning of the body's immune system, but its associated diseases can negatively affect basic psychological functioning. What relevance does this have for pastoral counseling? For an interpersonal relationship to be helpful, the person being assisted needs to experience the helper and the environment as trustworthy, safe, and secure. As noted before, it takes time, skill, and patience to establish these foundational experiences.

In working with a person with HIV the pastor will frequently encounter a weakening of the person's self-esteem. There are many things that affect self-esteem. A person's perceived inabilities to supply for his or her own basic physical and psychological needs can weaken self-esteem. In a culture where a person's worth is defined as a function of what he or she is able to do, disability related to disease can have profound effects on self-esteem.

Changes in self-esteem may be dramatic, but more often they are gradual, and sometimes imperceptible to others. Mental health practitioners are alert to issues that weaken self-esteem and work to help individuals maintain and improve their self-esteem. Since mental outlook has a significant role either in improvement in health and functioning or in the progression of illness, this is something that demands attention in the pastoral care of persons with HIV.

The physical care of a person with HIV can be so demanding and time-consuming that there may be less time available to identify and respond to psychosocial and spiritual issues. Competent pastoral care can respond effectively to these needs. In order to do this, the pastoral worker needs to understand how the diagnosis of HIV is affecting the individual's self-esteem. A few quick words of encouragement or some trivial cliche is rarely an adequate antidote to the HIV-related problems of self-esteem.

Providing pastoral counsel and care to a person with HIV is comparable to Jesus' ministry to the leper as recorded in the opening chapter of Mark's gospel (Mk 1:40–45). In the Jewish society of Jesus' day leprosy was the ultimate form of uncleanness. Lepers were excluded from participation in the community. They were thought to be a source of defilement for others. In the Marcan story the leper approached Jesus and begged, "If you will, you can make me clean." The evangelist focuses on the reaction of Jesus. Many texts translate Jesus' emotional response as "moved with pity." However, some commentators note that a more accurate rendition of Jesus' reaction is, "moved with anger." It is reasonable that when Jesus was confronted with a person whose illness had excommunicated him from others, he felt anger and indignation. The leper brought Jesus face to face with the powers of evil. The emotional response of Jesus, the sense of injustice he felt at the leper's social isolation, interpret his subsequent actions. The gospel writer tells us that Jesus touched him, a most unlikely thing since it meant Jesus himself was defiled by that physical contact. It was—and is—a gesture of acceptance, support, of solidarity with the afflicted. By that gesture, the text observes, the leprosy "left" him, as if the power of evil departed from him. Jesus' physical gesture of touch and his words helped restore the man to a rightful place in the community. Emphasis is not placed on the healing act itself, but on the indignation, understanding, compassion, and reconciliation of Jesus.

Some have referred to HIV and its associated diseases as a new form of leprosy. To be able to minister effectively to this new group of lepers requires a variety of helping skills. One of these skills involves making a competent assessment of the psycho-social and spiritual strengths and weaknesses of the person being helped. While it is clear that persons with HIV have physical stresses related to weakened body immunity, one should not assume that there is a parallel weakness in psychological or spiritual functioning. We shall consider some of the issues to which pastoral counselors should be sensitive in offering assistance to persons with HIV.

Initial contact with a person with HIV is important, both for the individual and for the pastoral counselor. For the person with HIV, it represents the establishment, reconnection, or continuation of relationship with a community of faith. For the pastoral care provider it provides an occasion in which to reach out, to *touch* a person. This mean to establish rapport, trust, and confidence, as well as to begin to assess what will be required further in pastoral care. Some pastors prematurely select resources they judge might be helpful, only to discover that the individual is indifferent, nonresponsive, or rejecting of such ministries. In some cases, the resources the pastor selects are disturbing, counterproductive, or damaging to the person in need. It is important that the proper resources be selected and utilized.

Some pastoral providers are inclined to begin a relationship by "doing" something, rather than by taking the essential time to establish a relationship, make a competent assessment of the person's needs and assets, and then beginning to help the individual choose the appropriate resources in order to respond to these needs. Taking the time to attend to the establishment of a relationship with the person with HIV is an indispensable prerequisite to any effective pastoral care ministry. The Who are you?, What do you have?, and What do you need? questions are indispensable. The establishment of an accepting and understanding relationship makes it possible for a pastor to begin assessing the person's inner resources.

It might be helpful to consider some specific areas a pastor may wish to explore with a person with HIV. A person with HIV may have had experience with the disease predating his or her diagnosis. Because AIDS is now well into its second decade, many people have firsthand knowledge and experience about the syndrome. Knowledge, however, is variable, and a person's perceptions of the disease will also vary. It is essential to know how the individual understands HIV, and how he or she is prepared to respond. A pastor needs a basic understanding of the person's perception of his or her illness.

Concerned about providing complex medical services, the psycho-social and spiritual needs of a patient may be neglected by some health care providers. A skilled pastor can respond to this deficit in care. In practice, most persons with HIV adjust to their diagnoses and life-threatening diseases; they do not develop extraordinary psycho-social problems. As noted earlier, many persons with HIV are positively committed to living a quality life. Persons with HIV make decisions in light of this goal of *living*. However, they do need understanding and support to realize this objective.

Stress

Coping with any life-threatening illness is inherently stressful. Stress may be evident on various levels of care: medical, physical, psychological, spiritual. Stress is defined as a person's emotional and bodily responses to demands that either approach or exceed the limits of his or her coping abilities. Because of the nature of opportunistic infections and immunodeficiency, a person with HIV lives with the ever-present possibility of a new threat or a new medical crisis, often occurring before the body has been able to recuperate or detoxify from earlier physical battles. This is a major source of stress for persons with HIV illness.

Stress also is evident on many levels of psychological functioning. How a person perceives, interprets, and understands the environment in which he or she is situated determines to a great extent the degree of stress and anxiety he or she will experience. It will influence how he or she reacts to it emotionally and physiologically. Life situations present a person with information and provide the necessary feedback for forming an understanding of the world. A person with HIV relies heavily on these sources of data. Behavioral responses are understood in relation to these situational conditions. Behavior does not exist in isolation from real life situations. Some persons with HIV are more vulnerable than others to the physical and psychological stressors associated with this diagnosis.

Stress and anxiety are not synonymous. Anxiety always involves stress, but the reverse is not necessarily true. An HIV diagnosis, for example, may lead to stress, but not necessarily to anxiety. Which stressors lead to stress depend upon the person's assessment of them as threatening. Although many clinicians like to separate the physical and psychological dimensions of stress, they are related.

Pastoral counseling may be one vehicle for assisting a person with HIV to manage some sources of stress. To do so, a pastoral worker must have a clear understanding of what these issues are, and how much and how disposed an individual is to explore these concerns. Knowing these things, the pastor can determine which issues might be addressed and on what timetable.

Pastors can do some practical things to help a person manage stress. The first is the simple recognition, acknowledgment, and acceptance that the person's situation is stressful. Recognition and rehearsal of these *facts* may assist a person to plan ways of dealing with subsequent crises. The second thing a pastor can do is to begin to work with feelings of helplessness, hopelessness, and demoralization by emphasizing the individual's personal and social coping resources. A person can be assisted to feel reasonably confident that he or she has the resources to face the current situation and manage well.

Persons with HIV can manage to live in spite of the serious physical, psychological, and spiritual threats they may perceive. A pastor can also assist an individual to work out plans for protecting himself or herself from sources of personal stress. A pastoral worker can help a person with HIV disease to maintain or regain independence so that he or she does not rely exclusively on others for protection from the sufferings and losses associated with HIV. In helping a person with HIV to manage stress, a pastoral counselor needs to strike a balance between the arousal of anticipatory grief and fear on the one hand, and realistic hope and genuine reassurance on the other. Some people can deal well with the facing reality, others cannot. A pastor needs to be able to recognize the difference.

Stigma

A person with HIV can feel stigmatized. When we speak about stigma, we refer to the ways in which society deals with undesirable differentness. In America today a person who is stigmatized is perceived as abnormal, deviant, and in some instances, is dehumanized. A person in our society who is stigmatized is set apart from others.

People treat the individual as dangerous, untrustworthy, objectionable. The person is not considered a fit member of society. The impact of stigma extends beyond the people so marked to affect the person's family, friends, and business associates, as well as those professionals who are involved with the stigmatized individual.

Many persons whose behaviors place them at high-risk for becoming infected with HIV bear stigma labels apart from their HIV status. Pejorative terms such as *junkies, druggies, whores, niggers, faggots*, and *queers* translate society's stigmatization of members of these groups. Although AIDS is a syndrome of diseases, the acronym has become a new stigma label.[5] Persons with HIV are legitimately afraid that others will learn of their diagnosis, realizing that they will be stigmatized if such knowledge is communicated further.

For the pastoral worker initiating ministry to a person with HIV, these issues have immediate relevance. A pastor will recognize the emotional effects of stigma. A person with HIV may feel unclean, despicable, unworthy. Although HIV is not easily transmitted, certainly not in ordinary non-sexual contact, some persons with HIV feel that others think they are contagious and thus to be avoided. Some are surprised when they are touched or embraced. A person with HIV may be embarrassed to face the pastor, fearing that he or she will be judged as deserving of this fate.

Stigmatization is emotionally scarring; it victimizes the person so branded. It is very important that a pastor recognize, acknowledge, and respond to the personal apprehension, frustrations, and tensions associated with the stigma of an HIV diagnosis. Pastoral care must encompass the family and friends, whose lives are also affected by the stigma of AIDS. As health care workers have experienced stigma because of their work with persons with HIV, so pastors must be prepared for the negative affect associated with our AIDS-related ministries.

Stigma can be reduced by effective education and modeling. As pastors we can do much to confront the attitudes, misinformation, and prejudices associated with this disease and the individuals who have become infected. The quality of our interpersonal relationships with persons with HIV will help to neutralize the negative effects of the stigma associated with this disease. As trusted leaders within our local communities, parishes, and congregations, pastors can do much to confront the injustices associated with the growing stigmatization of persons with HIV and the alienation of their families.

Communication

Whenever human beings interact, communication operates on a variety of levels. The most obvious level is when plain, direct words are exchanged. Another level involves non-verbal language or cues, posture, gestures, and facial movements. And finally, there is symbolic, verbal language. The images we select, the poetry we cite, and the jokes we tell all carry important messages. Too many of us limit what we receive in communication from another to the first level: plain language. Even then, we may not listen effectively to that message. There are many non-verbal cues that provide useful information about an individual's psychological and spiritual adjustment. An individual may not be able to express emotions or feelings in words, but they are being communicated nonetheless, even though the person may be unaware that they are being transmitted. How to interpret accurately the meaning of non-verbal cues—physical behaviors, facial expressions, gestures, postures—is an important and demanding task of the pastor in ministering to a person with HIV.

The sensitive pastor must be aware of all the ways in which the person with HIV is attempting to communicate. Non-verbalized feelings are an important component of human communication. They are the only reasonable alternative to spoken communication. Many people in life-threatening situations rely heavily on this latter form of communication. A comprehensive understanding of a person's needs and behavior is often contingent upon a correct assessment of the non-verbal cues and feelings. Correctly interpreting these various strata of communication will assist greatly in deciding how best to respond to the messages being sent and received.

Our discussion has identified areas of deficit that are related to HIV illness. This underscores the importance of accurate assessment of these issues prior to providing specific pastoral care to a person with HIV. It is equally important to assess the person's strengths. These are important resources upon which to build. In the face of the many disabling aspects of HIV, we may sometimes overlook the fact that a person has resources which are not necessarily weakened by the disease.

A Ministry of Hope to Persons with HIV

There are many ways to describe the role of a pastor in the care of persons with HIV. The enabling role, a ministry of hope, is certainly among the most important. Among HIV+ persons living in places where there is a high prevalence of HIV-related disease, there can be the perception that the whole world is dying of AIDS (Weiss 1989; Helquist 1989). This perception can contribute in great measure to feelings of hopelessness, depression, and despair. At a time when people most need encouragement and support, family, friends, health care professionals, and pastoral care professionals may directly or indirectly withdraw from them. Physical and emotional distancing is experienced by persons with HIV as abandonment and rejection. It is understandable why some individuals speak of feeling miserable, not only as a result of the effects of their illness, but because they feel they have no one on whom they can depend.

Effective and consistent support helps maintain hope. We know that persons with HIV adamantly resist being labeled as victims. In ancient religious usage the term *victim* referred to a living creature that was sacrificed. By definition, a victim has little hope. Victim implies passivity. Persons with HIV, by rejecting the label victim, assert their prerogative to be treated as persons. They retain full possession of their human rights and dignity, and maintain control over their lives as long as they are alive.

The human psyche is complex. How a person thinks significantly affects how he or she feels. If a person believes that life is controllable, then he or she will work to exercise control. From research with both animal and human subjects, psychologists have concluded that there is a demonstrable relationship between psychological surrender and physical death. If the judgment is made that there is no basis for hope of living a dignified life, then a person surrenders the will to live. That decision may act as a trigger that accelerates the process of dying.

Two issues of general significance to helping persons with HIV to maintain hope are worthy of mention. The first is the issue of support. It is difficult to sustain hope in the face of uncertainty unless there is real and perceived support. Although sources of support are available, some people may be unable to use them. A second issue has to do with control and pastoral intervention. Pastors must diligently avoid exercising control by projecting their own values onto a person with HIV. Bernie S. Siegal continually confronts the value questions related to life-threatening illnesses—"It's not for us to evaluate the worth of continued life for another person; as long as my patients are living in a way that has value for them, I'm there to help them continue" (Siegal 1986). A pastoral counselor might benefit from reflecting on this principle of care.[6]

For some individuals AIDS means death, and they may find little meaning in attempting to live with HIV. However, for the majority of persons with living with HIV and its related diseases, AIDS presents a formidable challenge to live, one many are ready to embrace. There are many variables that contribute to the determination of a person with HIV to live. It will be helpful to identify and comment upon some of these resources.

Principal Relationships

Whether it is a parent, sibling, lover, friend, or counselor, a person with HIV needs a deeper relationship with someone. The needs in terms of physical care are evident and should not be minimized in any discussion. However, the emotional and spiritual dimensions of a deeper interpersonal relationship deserve further discussion. A decision to attempt to live with HIV disease exposes some profound human feelings. They run the spectrum from moments of exhilaration to moments of despair; from great optimism about a new treatment or drug to profound disappointment when it does not prove to be the hoped for remedy. There are moments of almost symbiotic closeness and times of frightening distance; of tenderness and warmth, of hardness and stoic disregard.

These are but some of the multiple and changing faces of relationship with a person with HIV. Constancy weaves together the threads of these transformations. The sense that "we'll see this through together" forms the *cantus firmus* of all successful relationships with persons with HIV. The importance of a deep human relationship for maintaining a commitment to live is evident. In some cases the relationship involves primary responsibilities for providing physical care. In other cases those responsibilities may be discharged by a number of persons, while the principal emotional needs of the person with HIV are addressed by one individual.

Pastors frequently find themselves in the latter category. A pastor may find himself or herself moving out of traditional ministerial roles and assuming other nontraditional roles in caring for a person with HIV. For example, the pastor may be the one with whom the individual wishes to share an evening at the theater or a picnic on a warm summer day. Regardless of the way in which the pastoral role is exercised, all pastoral care tries to enkindle and sustain hope in the face of the serious challenges which HIV presents. The ability of the pastor to forge a deeper relationship with the individual with HIV and his or her family can influence significantly not only the effectiveness of spiritual ministrations, but the person's very will to live.

Changing One's Mental Outlook

For centuries people have debated the intrinsic relationship between mind and body. Persons involved in the practice of dynamic psychotherapy know experientially that if one is successful in helping persons alter the ways in which they think about themselves or about a particularly distressing issue, that change in thinking will affect both bodily functions and behavior. Pastoral care implicitly engages in helping people change the ways in which they think about many aspects of their lives. In Judeo-Christian traditions the scriptures have been read and explained to help people modify the ways in which they understand their relationship to God and to each other. The work of conversion is essentially the work of changing one's thinking in order to change one's behavior. The work of reconciliation helps people see what is disordered in their approach to life and relationships, and to commit themselves to act upon what they see.

The traditional religious notion of inspiration appeals to a divine influence directly and immediately exerted on the mind or soul of a person. The theological significance of such inspiration is apparent: a person is animated, influenced, affected to such a degree that the body actively responds and behavior is changed. The consoling ministries of the church strive to help people rid themselves of unhealthy thoughts and to discover inner peacefulness. Peacefulness is more than a static state of harmony, serenity, or tranquility. Achieving peace of mind involves active engagement in the tasks of confronting and challenging the mental outlooks that threaten the very foundations of bodily health.

If the work of pastoral counseling is successful, a person will be involved in changing the mental outlooks that compromise bodily health and integrity. From a holistic perspective, the relationship between effective pastoral care and physical health is assumed.

Some Practical Ways to Support a Person's Hopes

Let us look at some of the ways in which pastoral care to persons with HIV can influence bodily health. Few persons with HIV want to think about the disease as a terminal illness. As we stated in the introduction, language colors how a person thinks about a disease. In order to maintain hope and engagement with life, a person needs to believe there is some possibility of survival. As pastors, we need to be sensitive to the ways in which we talk about HIV. Just as health care providers can use words like *lethal* and *terminal* in conversation with persons with HIV, a pastor can inadvertently use the same language.

Unconsciously, language can destroy a person's hope, take away the will to survive, and force an individual to surrender the remaining controls he or she has over life. In the words of Peter Vom Lehn, an AIDS patient:

> I think that terminal is insulting, offensive to the patient, because it takes away all his hope and can discourage him immediately. And hope is a very important part of the patient's mental and physical health, and essential if he's going to get any better and not give in. It's not fair to take away someone's chances for survival by taking away his hope, and if he's told that he has a terminal disease, that's just what you do, right at the start (Peabody 1986, p. 192).

In the practice of pastoral counseling with persons with HIV there are some specific ways to assist a person to maintain a positive and engaged approach to life. It is imperative that the pastoral worker understand what the person with HIV holds as life values. It may take some time to create the appropriate emotional climate in which a person is willing to share these important values. Beyond understanding, the pastor needs to communicate acceptance of these values. Acceptance does not imply agreement or approval. Some pastors find it difficult to make this distinction. In working with persons with HIV it is to be anticipated that some of their expressed values will not be held by some religious faiths. Pastoral counselors must learn to be non-judgmental in dealing with clients' values that differ from their own or those of the religious tradition they represent.

A person with HIV needs to feel that a prospective helper understands his or her inner struggles. The person with HIV is helped when the pastor is effective in communicating that he or she also understands and shares the individual's feelings.

Because of the nature and course of the disease, there is a problem in finding anything positive to say. In working with persons with HIV there is a danger that the orientation in conversation often may be negatively skewed. In order to maintain a person's realistic hopes in the face of this disease, efforts must be focused on reinforcing small, positive gains. This might involve helping a person to communicate directly with parents or friends. It could involve the person's resumption of work on a limited schedule. Gaining two pounds might be an important milestone. Having a day without a debilitating reaction to a therapeutic drug can be a small victory. Pastors should be alert to identify and respond to these cues. Those with HIV need to find encouragement in efforts they may be making to survive. They need others to recognize and celebrate with them the small gains they may be achieving.

It is easy to think and treat persons with HIV disease as handicapped persons. At some stages of the illness, and when HIV infection expresses itself in certain ways, a person may need special forms of physical and emotional support. However, it is imperative that we not generally think of the person with HIV as handicapped. Rather, it is important to help the person with HIV to maintain autonomy and to retain control over his or her decisions and behaviors.

It is not uncommon to note among the behaviors of sick persons a certain amount of regression. This is evident in their passivity, their abrogation of decision-making, their expectations that others should take care of all their basic needs. These are normal reactions to illness, and such behaviors are sanctioned by our social mores. However, if these regressive tendencies are not challenged appropriately, a person can lose the motivation to recover.

Some people adopt the "sick role" as a habitual mode of being and resist getting better. Some of these psychological dynamics, common to many individuals with acute illnesses, are observable in some people with HIV. Care providers must be able to strike a balance between providing necessary services and creating a situation of over-dependency.

Pastoral care of persons with HIV always should be enabling, encouraging, and supportive. It should foster independence of thinking and choosing. It should create a feeling of partnership rather than of paternalism. In pastoral care the pastor needs to be aware of the potentially counterproductive effects of an overly paternalistic approach. Paternalism is expressed not only in behaviors but also in language. While words and gestures might appear to be accepted by the sick individual and ostensibly be comforting, at the same time they can contribute to passivity and dependence.

Pastoral care should strive to create an environment where the individual feels encouraged to do more for himself or herself, knowing that he or she has support. Interventions should aim to help the person seek personal solutions to problems rather than to solve problems for the person. Depression results when others take control and solve problems. A person needs to determine goals and decide ways to achieve those goals. An effective model of this strategy of pastoral care is found in the ministry to the paralyzed person who is cured by Jesus (Lk 5:18–25). In this passage some people carried a paralyzed man on a pallet and placed him before Jesus, hoping that he would cure him. In this situation the paralyzed person needed physical assistance. This was an appropriate use of other people's assistance. There were enormous crowds around the house in which Jesus was staying, so they had to climb up and lower the man through the roof. Recognizing their determination and faith, Jesus expressed forgiveness and healed the man. His dismissal to the formerly paralyzed man was: "Arise, take up your bed and go home." Luke notes that the man immediately arose, took up the stretcher upon which he had been lying, and went away to his house, glorifying God. Jesus placed direct responsibility for the future on the formerly paralyzed individual. He didn't say to the others, "Take his bed home for him." Healing is linked with belief and personal action. Faith and personal, responsible action are underscored in Jesus' statement to this individual. Pastoral care should attempt to facilitate both faith and the exercise of personal responsibility.

In his classic book, *On Dying and Denying*, Avery Weisman talks about hope as it relates to perceived self-worth and self-acceptance:

> Hope is not dependent upon survival alone. Hope means that we have confidence in the desirability of survival. It arises from a desirable self-image, healthy self-esteem, and belief in our ability to exert a degree of influence on the world surrounding us. . . . Hope is decided more by self-acceptance than by objects sought and by impractical aspirations. . . . Foreshortened life does not in itself create hopelessness. . . . More important is our belief that we do something worth doing, and that others think so, too. Thus, people lose hope when they are unable to act on their own behalf and must also relinquish their claims upon others (Weisman 1972, pp. 20–21).

Or, as Bernie Siegal puts it: "Hoping means seeing that the outcome you want is possible, and then working for it" (Siegal 1986, p. 178). The purpose of any form of assistance to persons with HIV should be to help the individual to achieve personal goals. Integrity, self-acceptance, and love are necessary, common, and realizable goals (see Kirkpatrick 1990). They presuppose emotional honesty. For some individuals infection with HIV may exposes areas of personal life that have been hidden or inadequately addressed. The nineteenth-century German philosopher Friedrich Nietzsche emphasized the importance of the will to power as the chief motivating force of both the individual and society. He asserted that the person who has the *why* to live can endure almost any *how*. Pastoral counsel can be effective in maintaining a spark of hope in the darkness of the world of a person with HIV. As many persons living with HIV acknowledge, they depend upon these caring partnerships to keep their hopes alive.

Epilogue

By way of conclusion, the following case may bring together many of the issues discussed in this chapter on ministry to persons with HIV. Matthew was twenty-nine years old when he was referred by his physician for pastoral counseling.

Matthew was the youngest in a family of twelve children. Both of his parents were alcoholics with erratic histories of sobriety. Matt had left home when he was fourteen; he survived through prostitution, selling drugs, and other criminal activities. In his late adolescence he met an older man with whom he lived for almost six years in return for sexual favors. After almost fifteen years living away from his family of origin, Matt found his way back to his place of birth. Soon after his return he developed symptoms related to an underlying immunodeficiency, was tested for HIV, and was found to be positive.

At the time of his referral for pastoral counseling to address his anxiety and related concerns, he had been drug-free for eleven months, and was asymptomatic. He had been seen previously in individual and group counseling settings by a hospital social worker experienced in working with HIV clients. These interventions did not appear to help alleviate his anxieties, fears, and night tremors. As part of his recovery he experienced a religious reawakening. His medical team thought that pastoral counseling might be able to do what more traditional psychotherapeutic interventions could not achieve.

Matthew came willingly for weekly conversations. Four months into his pastoral counseling he developed Kaposi lesions on his leg, a definitive diagnosis of AIDS. He maintained regular counseling contact throughout the final fifteen months of his battle with several HIV-related illnesses, four of which required hospitalizations. During his treatment he reviewed his family history, his adolescent and young adult experiences, and his struggles with HIV disease. He set some definite and realizable goals, and he solicited help in achieving these objectives. The most significant goal was to establish an independent residence for himself. With the help of a local AIDS Action Committee, he was able to rent and furnish a small apartment in a low-income housing complex.

Matt also needed to address his religious needs. As a child he had been baptized in the Roman Catholic faith, but he never benefitted from religious education and never received the sacraments of penance or eucharist. One of the ways in which pastoral counseling helped him in his "living with HIV" was by supplying basic religious education and preparing and celebrating sacraments with him.

A year before his death Matt received the sacraments of penance and the anointing of the sick, and shared holy communion at a eucharistic celebration attended by many members of his family, including both of his parents. The family organized itself sufficiently well for this milestone occasion to prepare and host a party following the small, private celebration of Matthew's first communion.

His several serious illnesses disposed Matt to direct and comfortable discussions about death. These conversations were thoughtful and uncovered a primitive but strong faith. He drew enormous comfort in the notion of "communion of saints." When he thought about his own death, he viewed it in terms of reunion with Jesus and Mary and many of the saints whom he was discovering through reading brief accounts of their lives.

Although Matt did not have the ordinary benefits of formal secondary education, he was naturally intelligent and articulate. He actively investigated how he might earn a high school equivalency diploma, although he never realized this goal. His life experiences had taught him many things, and he was instinctively a reflective person. He wanted to learn how to pray and responded well to traditional devotional practices. He used a small book of prayers that he received on the occasion of his first communion, and these brought him much consolation.

During his final years of life he met another person with HIV who was fifteen years his senior. They became close friends, and Matthew assumed the role of primary care provider for this other person, who, at the time they met, was considerably more advanced with AIDS. Matthew used pastoral counseling as a way to monitor this relationship, develop strategies to resolve conflicts that arose, and as a primary support to his need for independence and autonomy.

Before Matthew died in June of 1990, he received anointing and communion one final time. In his last conversation with his pastoral counselor before his death, he summarized what this relationship had meant to him. He noted that in his whole life he had never known a relationship with another man where there was not a sexual, exploitive, or manipulative agenda. He confessed that for a long time he wondered why anyone would do so much for him without expecting something in return. He said it occurred to him after about five months into the counseling relationship that there are some people in the world who do care and really don't look for anything in return.

In his mind this was the pivotal turning point, the time when he began to trust confidently, to hope enthusiastically, to accept being loved without the fear of abandonment. His final words to his counselor were these:

> Looking back on my life, I many times asked myself why God would send someone like you into my life at this time. Now I know the answer. God does love me, and sent me an angel to bring me home. You've been that angel, and I want you to know how much this has meant to me. When the days were the darkest, you were always there. You helped me through some rough times, You said you would stay with me, and you have. Thank you, my friend. I love you.

Notes

1. For an expanded treatment of many of the topics discussed in this chapter, with case studies that interpret key issues in pastoral care, see Smith (1988). The reader might also wish to consult Shelp, et al. (1986); Dilley, et al. (1989); and Kirkpatrick (1990).

2. The Centers for Disease Control (CDC) have classified persons with HIV disease in four groups: (1) Group I have acute HIV syndrome; (2) Group II are without symptoms (asymptotic); (3) Group III have persistent swelling of the lymph nodes (generalized lymphadenopathy); and (4) Group IV have specific manifestations of HIV disease, further delineated as constitutional symptoms (IVa), neurologic disease (IVb), infections (IVc), cancers (IVd), and others (IVe).

3. It may be helpful to read Barbara Peabody's account of her care of her son, Peter, who died from complications of AIDS (Peabody 1986). Reading Barbara Peabody's sensitive account of her relationship with her son during his final year of struggle with AIDS, one is aware that she tolerated a good deal of his anger, yet there were limits to how effective she was in the management of anger.

4. There have been several interesting chronicles of the government's response during the first decade of the pandemic, for example, see *And the Band Played On* (Shilts 1987).

5. For an insightful reflection on this issue, see *AIDS and Its Metaphors* (Sontag 1989). The reader may also wish to read her earlier work, *Illness as Metaphor* (Sontag 1979).

6. Readers may also wish to consult *Head First: The Biology of Hope* (Cousins 1989). An adjunct professor in the School of Medicine at UCLA, Cousins presents a lay person's perspective on scientific evidence that supports the place of faith, love, will to live, purpose, and humor in managing serious disease.

References

AIDS Education Project of the American Psychiatric Association. 1989. *A Psychiatrist's Guide to AIDS and HIV Diseases: A Primer.* Washington, D.C.

AMA (American Medical Association). 1986. Statement on AIDS reported by the Council of Ethical and Judicial Affairs of the American Medical Association (December).

Callen, Michael. 1990. *Surviving AIDS.* New York: HarperCollins.

Cousins, N. 1989. *Head First: The Biology of Hope.* New York: Dutton.

Dilley, J. W., Pies, C., and Helquist, M., eds. 1989. *Face to Face: A Guide to AIDS Counseling.* San Francisco: AIDS Health Project UCSF.

Helquist, M. 1989. "Too Many Casualites: HIV Disease in Gay Men." In Dilley, et al., *Face to Face.*

Kirkpatrick, B. 1990. *AIDS: Sharing the Pain: A Guide for Caregivers.* New York: Pilgrim Press.

Peabody, Barbara. 1986. *A Screaming Room.* San Diego: Oak Tree.

Shelp, E. E., Sunderland, R. H., and Mansell, P. W. A. 1986. *AIDS: Personal Stories in Pastoral Perspective.* New York: Pilgrim Press.

Shilts, Randy. 1987. *And the Band Played On: Politics, People, and the AIDS Epidemic.* New York: St. Martin's Press.

Siegal, Bernie S. 1986. *Love, Medicine, and Miracles.* New York: Harper & Row.

Smith, Walter J. 1988. *AIDS: Living and Dying With Hope.* New Jersey: Paulist Press.

Sontag, Susan. 1979. *Illness as Metaphor.* New York: Vintage Books.

Sontag, Susan. 1989. *AIDS and Its Metaphors.* New York: Farrar, Straus, Giroux.

Weisman, A. 1972. *On Dying and Denying: A Psychiatric Study of Terminality.* New York: New York Behavioral Publications.

Weiss, A. 1989. "The Aids Bereaved: Counseling Strategies." In Dilley, et al., *Face to Face.*

Notes on the Contributors

DAVID W. AUGSBURGER is Professor of Pastoral Care and Counseling at Fuller Theological Seminary, Pasadena, CA. A Mennonite minister, author, educator, musician, sculptor, traveler, gourmet cook, chocolate lover, academician, conflict mediator, consultant, friend, father, pacifist, cyclist, therapist, and lover of life, he is a graduate of Eastern Mennonite College and Seminary and holds the Ph.D. in Personality and Religion from the School of Theology at Claremont, CA.

DAVID BLACKWELDER possesses a M.Div., Th.M., and Ph.D. in Pastoral Counseling and has been an ordained Lutheran Pastor since 1961. He has served Pastorates in Maryland and Delaware for twenty years and is currently Director of Pastoral Counseling and Consultation of Tressler Centers of Delaware, adjunct professor at Neumann College in Pennsylvania, and a Fellow in A.A.P.C. Dr. Blackwelder is married to the former Theda D. Jones and has four children and two grandchildren. He resides in Middletown, DE.

RICHARD BYRNE, O.C.S.O., is a monk of the New Melleray Abbey, Dubuque, IA. Currently he is director of the Institute of Formative Spirituality at Duquesne University, Pittsburgh, PA. His teaching and research focus upon the following areas: the new discipline of formative spirituality and its relation to Christian mystical tradition, the contribution of formation science to pastoral counseling and spiritual direction, and contemporary personality theories in relation to transcendence development. He has conducted numerous workshops nationally and internationally on these topics.

RACHEL CALLAHAN, C.S.C., is a clinical psychologist. She has coauthored three books (all published by Paulist Press) for those who grew up in dysfunctional families and works at the Consultation Center, 1001 Spring Street, Silver Spring, MD 20910.

SHARON E. CHESTON is Assistant Professor and Associate Chair of the Pastoral Counseling Department at Loyola College in Maryland. As a counselor, educator, and supervisor, she has specialized in counseling adult victims of sexual abuse. Dr. Cheston has also written the book *Making Effective Referrals* and a journal article on clinical case presentation paradigms. She has a private practice at Bay Ridge Counseling Center near Baltimore and offers workshops to religious organizations.

JOSEPH CIARROCCHI teaches in the Graduate Program in Pastoral Counseling at Loyola College in Maryland and is a Director of Addictions Services, Taylor Manor Hospital, Ellicott City, MD. He holds the Ph.D. in Clinical Psychology from Catholic University and completed a graduate degree in theology.

MARIE M. FORTUNE grew up in North Carolina where she received her undergraduate degree from Duke University. She received her seminary training at Yale Divinity School and was ordained a minister in the United Church of Christ in 1976. After serving in a local parish, she founded the Center for the Prevention of Sexual and Domestic Violence where she serves as Executive Director. The Center, located in Seattle, is an educational ministry serving as a training resource to religious communities in the United States and Canada. Among her recent works are *Violence in the Family: A Workshop Curriculum for Clergy and Other Helpers* (Pilgrim Press, 1991) and *Is Nothing Sacred? When Sex Invades the Pastoral Relationship* (Harper and Row, 1989–1990 Book of the Year Award from the Academy of Parish Clergy).

DAVID W. FOY currently holds professorships in psychology at the Neuropsychiatric Institute, UCLA Medical School, and the Graduate School of Psychology, Fuller Theological Seminary. He also serves as Director of PTSD Research and Training at West Los Angeles VA Medical Center, Brentwood Division. His primary interests involve study and treatment of survivors of traumas.

EILEEN A. GAVIN serves as Professor of Psychology at the College of St. Catherine in Minnesota. She served as President of Psychologists Interested in Religious Issues, a division of the American Psychological Association, from 1978 to 1979 and has held other elected posts in that association. Her publications have been largely related to the history of psychology, teaching of psychology, and the psychology of women.

PAUL R. GIBLIN received the Ph.D. from Purdue University and M.Div. from Weston School of Theology. He is Assistant Professor of Pastoral Studies and coordinates the MA Program in Pastoral Counseling at Loyola University's Institute of Pastoral Studies in Chicago.

MARGARET GORMAN, R.S.C.J., received the Ph.D. from Catholic University of America and an MA from Fordham University. She is Adjunct Professor of Psychology and Theology, Boston College, and editor of *Psychology and Religion*. She has written several articles on faith and moral development and is psychological consultant to the United States Army and Air Force on adult and moral development.

ROY LEWIS is the Director of the Northeast Career Center, Princeton, NJ, Diplomate in AAPC, and member of AACD and AAMFT. He is the author of the book *Choosing Your Career: Finding Your Vocation,* published by Paulist Press, 1989.

PAUL D. LININGER is a Roman Catholic priest and a member of the Franciscan Community. He is a graduate of St. Anthony-on-Hudson, Albany, NY, where he received his graduate degree in theology. Later, after several years in parish and hospital ministry, he pursued continuing education and training as a graduate student in Pastoral Counseling at Loyola College, Baltimore, and went on to complete his doctoral degree in Pastoral Counseling. Currently, he is a member of the faculty at Johns Hopkins University, School of Medicine, Department of Psychiatry. He is also the Assistant Director/Clinical Director of two substance abuse treatment programs for the University.

ROBERT J. McALLISTER is Director of the Isaac Taylor Institute of Psychiatry and Religion and Adjunct Professor, Pastoral Counseling, Loyola College, Baltimore. Dr. McAllister is on the Board of Directors of the National Guild of Catholic Psychiatrists. He received the Ph.D. in Psychology from Catholic University, Washington, D.C. and his M.D. from Georgetown University.

REA McDONNELL, S.S.N.D. whose Ph.D. is in Biblical Studies, is a teacher, pastoral counselor, and spiritual director. She has co-authored three books (all published by Paulist Press) for those who grew up in dysfunctional families. She works at the Consultation Center, 1001 Spring Street, Silver Spring, MD 20910.

PAUL A. MICKEY is Associate Professor of Theology at Duke University Divinity School. He is a graduate of Harvard University and earned his M.Div. and Ph.D. from Princeton Theological Seminary. Dr. Mickey has pastored churches in Ohio and New Jersey. He is the author of several books, the most recent of which are *Of Sacred Worth: Biblical and Pastoral Perspectives on Homosexuality* and *Clergy Families: Is Normal Life Possible?* co-authored with Ginny Ashmore.

CHRISTIE COZAD NEUGER is an Assistant Professor of Pastoral Theology at Princeton Theological Seminary. An ordained United Methodist minister, she worked as a parish pastor, a hospital chaplain, and a pastoral counselor before coming to Princeton Seminary. She received a B.A. from the University of Minnesota, M.Div. from United Theological Seminary of the Twin Cities, and the Ph.D. in Personality and Theology from the School of Theology at Claremont. She lives in Princeton with her husband, Win, and her two teen-age children.

RICHARD D. PARSONS is Associate Professor of Counselor Education, West Chester University, and has a private practice in West Chester, PA. Dr. Parsons holds the Ph.D. in Psychology from Temple University. He has published nine books and over fifty articles in the area of mental health prevention and intervention. His most recent books include *Valuing Sexuality* (W. C. Brown), *Adolescence: What's a Parent to Do?* (Paulist Press) and *Counseling Strategies* (CHA).

JAMES POLING is Associate Professor of Pastoral Theology and Counseling at Colgate Rochester/Bexley/Croyer Divinity School. He is also author of *The Abuse of Power: A Theological Problem* (published by Abingdon Press).

CARROLL SAUSSY received clinical training at the Menninger Foundation in Topeka, Kansas, and the Ph.D. in Religion and the Personality Sciences from the Graduate Theological Union in Berkeley, CA. She is the Howard Chandler Robbins Professor of Pastoral Care and Counseling at Wesley Theological Seminary in

Washington, D.C. Her recent book is *God Images and Self Esteem: Empowering Woman in a Patriarchal Society.*

CHRIS R. SCHLAUCH (M.Div., Yale Divinity School, Ph.D., the Divinity School, University of Chicago) is Assistant Professor of Pastoral Psychology and Psychology of Religion at Boston University. He was formerly Assistant Director for Professional Services at the Danielsen Institute at Boston University. His writings in pastoral psychology have focused on the theory, practice, and supervision of pastoral counseling and psychotherapy.

EDWARD P. SHAFRANSKE, Ph.D., is Associate Professor of Psychology, the Graduate School of Education and Psychology, Pepperdine University. His interests include the application of psychoanalytic theory to psychotherapy, to the psychology of religion, and to the study of the arts. In addition to his academic and research commitments, Dr. Shafranske is in private practice in San Diego and in Irvine, CA.

WALTER J. SMITH, S.J., Dean and Clinical Professor of Psychology and Pastoral Care at Weston School of Theology, Cambridge, MA, has worked for almost two decades with individuals facing life-threatening illnesses. His book *Dying in the Human Life Cycle: Psychological, Biomedical and Social Perspectives* (Holt, Rinehart and Winston, 1985) summarizes many of the issues he has treated in his clinical practice. His book on AIDS pastoral care, *AIDS: Living and Dying With Hope* (Paulist Press, 1988) was named "Best Pastoral Book in 1989" by the Catholic Press Association.

WILLIAM J. SNECK, S.J., earned the doctorate in psychology at the University of Michigan. After teaching at Georgetown University and at the Jesuit Novitiate, Wernersville, PA, he now serves as Assistant Professor of Pastoral Counseling at Loyola College, Baltimore. He also conducts workshops in the "Hard Emotions" (hurt, anger, guilt).

SIANG-YANG TAN (Ph.D., McGill University) is Director of the Psy.D. Program in Clinical Psychology and Associate Professor of Psychology in the Graduate School of Psychology at Fuller Theological Seminary. His scholarly interests include lay counseling and lay counselor training, intrapersonal integration and spirituality, cognitive-behavior therapy, epilepsy, pain, and cross-cultural counseling, especially with Asian-Americans.

HOWARD W. STONE is Professor of Pastoral Psychology and Pastoral Care, Brite Divinity School, Texas Christian University, Fort Worth, TX. He is a Lutheran minister, psychologist, and diplomate in AAPC. Dr. Stone has written seven books, numerous articles, and is co-editor of the new Creative Pastoral Care and Counseling Series from Fortress. He is married and has one daughter and two granddaughters.

ANN BELFORD ULANOV, Ph.D., is the Christiane Brooks Johnson Professor of Psychiatry and Religion at Union Theological Seminary, a psychoanalyst in private practice, and supervising faculty member of the C. G. Jung Institute of New York. She is the author of *The Feminine in Jungian Psychology and Christian Theology, Receiving Woman, Picturing God,* and *The Wisdom of the Psyche.*

BARRY ULANOV, Ph.D., is McIntosh Professor of English Emeritus at Barnard College. Among his many books are *A History of Jazz in America, The Two Worlds of American Art, The Making of a Modern Saint, The Prayers of Saint Augustine,* and *Jung and the Outside World.*

Together, the Ulanovs have written *Religion and the Unconscious; Primary Speech: A Psychology of Prayer; Cinderella and Her Sisters: The Envied and the Envying; The Witch and the Clown: Two Archetypes of Human Sexuality;* and *The Healing Imagination: The Meeting of the Psyche and Soul.*

GAIL LYNN UNTERBERGER is Assistant Professor of Pastoral Care and Counseling at Wesley Theological Seminary in Washington, D.C. A United Methodist minister, she received the Ph.D. in Personality and Theology from the School of Theology at Claremont, CA. She is finishing a book on feminist pastoral counseling.

RICHARD W. VOSS received the D.P.C. from Loyola College, an M.S.W. from Fordham University, and an M.T.S. from the Washington Theological Union. He is Assistant Professor of Pastoral Counseling and the Coordinator of the Graduate Program in Pastoral Counseling at Neumann College. Dr. Voss also maintains a private practice in pastoral counseling and psychotherapy in West Chester, PA.

ROBERT J. WICKS is Professor and Director of Program Development of the Graduate Programs in Pastoral Counseling at Loyola College in Maryland. He has been a Visiting Lecturer at both Princeton Theological Seminary and Washington Theological Union. In addition, he is on the Editorial Board of *Human Development* and the Editorial Committee of *The Journal of Pastoral Care* (1991). His recent books include *Self-Ministry Through Self-Understanding, Living Simply in an Anxious World, Availability: The Problem and the Gift*, and *Seeking Perspective.*

Name Index

Abbott, S., 250
Abbott, W.M., 144
Abramczyk, L.W., 148
Adams, E.B., 34
Adams, J., 27
Adams, P., 150
Agudo, P., 394
Ahrons, S.J., 608
Ainsworth, M., 512
Alexander, C.N., 297
Alexander, F., 103
Alexander, P.C., 454
Allender, D., 28, 34
Alley, S., 27
Allport, G., 245
Ammerman, R.T., 623
Amundson, N.E., 669, 670
Andersen, A.E., 526
Anthony, B., 245–46
Anzaldua, G., 248, 252
Anzieu, D., 18
Apollinaire, G., 11
Aponte, H.J., 147, 150, 151, 152, 159, 160, 161, 167
Armstrong, J., 528, 529
Arnold, J.D., 148
Asquith, G.H., Jr., 51
Assagioli, R., 430
Astin, M., 625
Auden, W.H., 268
Auerswald, E.H., 145
Augsburger, D.W., 28, 131, 136–37, 239
Augustine, St., 9, 18
Auslander, G., 145
Axelrod, S.J., 150
Ayres, B., 150, 151

Backus, W., 28, 34
Bailey, L., 630
Baldwin, C.L., 28, 34
Baldwin, J., 268
Balint, M., 103–04
Balka, C., 257
Ballou, M., 191
Bandura, A., 604
Barber, S., 268
Barlow, S., 40
Barnard, G., 500
Barnett, 305
Barth, K., 271
Baruch, G., 297, 305
Basch, M.F., 84, 85, 86
Bass, E., 447, 452, 456, 458, 462, 463, 472, 475, 479, 480, 482, 483, 489, 499
Bassett, R.L., 32
Bathrick, D., 496, 497, 500
Bear, G., 28, 34
Beattie, M., 370, 580
Beck, A.T., 316, 317, 415, 419, 423, 425, 429
Beck, J.R., 42
Becker, E., 315, 319, 583
Becker, W.W., 27, 41–42
Bednar, R., 383, 384
Been, H., 118
Beirnaert, L., 210–11
Bellah, R.N., 307, 314
Bender, M.E., 623
Bennett, S.M., 536–37
Benokraitis, N., 188–89, 191, 192–93
Bentley, S., 146
Berger, B., 135
Berger, P., 135
Bergers, G., 525
Bergin, A.E., 102
Berman, J.S., 39, 40
Berzon, B., 250

Biller, H.B., 27
Billingsley, A., 150
Bilotta, V.M., 410, 411
Binder, J., 102
Birt, C.J., 150
Black, C., 577, 578
Blakeslee, S., 314
Blanchette, M.C., 36
Blanton, J., 27
Blau, M., 330, 338
Bloch, M.H., 150
Bloomfield, M., 417
Blume, S.B., 600
Boan, D.M., 37
Bobgan, D., 28
Bobgan, M., 28
Boff, L., 144, 153
Boisen, A., 51
Boland, F.J., 524
Boodhoo, J.A., 536
Booth, C., 150
Borgen, W.A., 669, 670
Boswell, J., 229, 268
Bourque, L.B., 191
Bowden, J., 577
Bowers, W.A., 529–30
Bowker, L.H., 146
Bowlby, J., 512, 528, 644
Boyer, E., 318, 325
Braceland, F., 211
Bradshaw, J., 394, 395, 581, 585
Brennan, A., 297, 299, 302, 303, 309
Breton, M., 145
Brewi, J., 297, 299, 302, 303, 309
Briere, J., 623
Britten, B., 268
Brock, R.N., 363, 374
Brock, R.T., 31
Brocollo, G., 314
Brooks-Gunn, J., 297
Brown, G., 151
Brown, L., 250
Brown, R.M., 130
Browning, D., 51, 52, 60, 62, 67, 95, 96
Bruch, H., 522
Brumberg, J., 522
Bryant, J., 192
Buchanan, D., 28
Buckler, R.E., 32
Budman, S.H., 120
Buell, B., 150, 151
Bufford, R.K., 32
Bugenthal, J., 354
Bullis, R.K., 146, 501
Burish, T.G., 40
Burlingame, G., 40
Burns, D., 581
Bush, B.J., 410, 411
Butcher, J.N., 107
Byrd, R., 226

Caddell, J.D., 623
Caesar, P.L., 489
Cain, A.C., 646, 647, 651, 652, 653–54
Calam, R.M., 536
Callahan, R., 583, 585, 587, 604, 607
Cameron, B., 243
Capps, D.E., 51, 52, 62, 67, 96, 273, 297, 303, 304
Carey, M.P., 40
Carkhuff, R.R., 238, 657
Carl, D., 250
Carlson, V., 497
Carnes, J., 59
Carroll, E.M., 623, 625
Carroll, J., 391–92
Cassisi, J.E., 623
Cather, W., 268
Cattanach, L., 532
Cavanagh, M., 212–13
Cerling, G.L., 33
Chandler, S.M., 628
Chapian, M., 28, 34
Chauncey, G., Jr., 268
Chavkin, W., 145

Chilstrom, C., 657
Chiriboga, D.A., 297, 303
Choisy, M., 210–11
Christiansen, E.M., 593
Ciarrocchi, J.W., 598, 600, 601, 606–07, 610
Cicchetti, D., 497, 508, 509–10, 511
Clausen, J., 145
Clinebell, H., 27, 342, 610
Cloninger, C.R., 53
Collins, G.R., 27, 28, 32, 33–34, 35
Collmer, C., 510
Colon, F., 151
Colt, G.H.C., 641, 642
Compton, J.R., 36
Congar, Y.M.J., 155
Conn, J.W., 307
Connors, M.E., 537
Cooper, J.L., 530
Corley, R., 234, 253, 255
Cousins, N., 710
Crabb, L., 27–28, 33, 34
Crews, D.W., 148
Cripe, J.A., 395
Crompton, L., 269
Crowther, J.H., 530
Cruikshank, M., 249
Curran, D., 315
Custer, L.F., 607
Custer, R.L., 597, 607

Damluji, N.F., 526
Dante, 17
Davanloo, H., 102, 104, 105, 107, 110, 111, 112, 113, 116, 117
Davis, D., 116
Davis, L., 447, 452, 456, 458, 462, 463, 472, 475, 479, 480, 482, 483, 489, 499
Delworth, U., 36
Denham, T.E., 146
Dick, K., 150
Dickinson, E., 20–21
Dilley, J.W., 709
Distad, L.J., 623
Dodds, L., 28, 38
Dohrenwend, B.P., 53
Donnerstein, E., 192
Donovan, M.E., 188
Doress, P., 190
Dostoevsky, F., 18, 392
Drakeford, J., 28
Draper, E., 51, 52, 61, 62, 76, 95
Droege, S., 304
Drury, M., 9
Duberman, M., 268
Duecker, S.J., 536
Dumas, L.S., 665, 666, 669
Dunne, E.J., 655
Dunne-Maxim, K., 655
Durlak, J.A., 39, 40, 41
Dutton, M.A., 630

Edwards, A.W., 151
Egan, G., 238, 239, 657
Egeland, B., 508, 511, 512–14, 516–17
Elbow, P., 73–74
Ellens, J.H., 52, 62, 96
Ellis, A., 581
Ellis, E.M., 628
Ellison, C.W., 32
Emmet, D.M., 10–11
Epstein, N., 316, 317
Erickson, M.F., 508, 511, 513–14, 516–17
Erikson, E., 300, 302, 307, 366, 394–95, 588
Estadt, B.K., 36, 52
Evagrian Ponticus, 415–16, 420–21
Ewing, 57

Fairbank, J.A., 623
Fairbanks, R.J., 51
Fairchild, R.W., 426, 443
Fast, I., 646, 647, 651, 652, 653–54
Faulkner, K.K., 536
Faulkner, W., 392
Feagin, J., 188–89, 191, 193

Feighner, J.P., 53
Fekken, G.C., 524
Feldman, L., 316
Feldman, R., 27
Ferenczi, S., 103
Ferguson, J.M., 525–26
Fields, R., 319, 320
Finklehor, D., 453
Fisher, B., 334, 339–40, 347, 349, 350, 352, 353, 354
Fisher, S.G., 39
Fiske, M., 297, 303
Fleischer, G., 151, 167
Foley, V., 151
Fortunato, J., 238, 257
Fortune, M., 489, 497, 499, 500, 501, 503
Foster, T., 28, 34
Foucault, M., 268
Fowler, J., 61, 62, 96
Fowler, J.W., 366
Foy, D.W., 623, 625
Franasiak, E.J., 412
Franco, K.S., 526
Frankl, V., 433
Freire, P., 278
Freud, S., 18–19, 104, 113, 210, 292, 392, 452
Friedman, E., 219
Fromm, E., 333
Furey, P., 257
Furniss, T., 161, 165

Gabalac, N., 191
Gadamer, H.G., 274, 284
Gallers, J., 623
Ganley, A.L., 492
Garanzini, M.J., 146
Garbarino, J., 508
Garfield, S.L., 102
Garfinkel, I., 329, 355, 356
Garfinkel, P.E., 522, 530
Garner, D.M., 522, 530
Gaskill, H.S., 52
Geismar, L., 150, 151
Gelles, R., 496
Gerkin, C., 52, 62, 67, 96, 135, 138
Gershon, M., 27
Gerson, R., 577–78
Giblin, P., 314
Gilbert, M.G., 31
Gilbert, S.D., 531, 532
Gill, M., 117
Gilligan, C., 306
Glaser, C., 257
Glaser, J.W., 397
Glen, A., 597
Gleser, G.C., 623
Goldman, R., 104, 111
Goldner, E., 53
Gordon, J.R., 547
Gorsuch, R.L., 38
Gottman, J., 318
Gould, R.L., 303
Grace, M.C., 623
Grahan, J., 231
Gramick, J., 229, 235, 270
Gravitz, H., 577
Greeley, A., 314, 323
Green, B.L., 623
Greenberg, L.S., 60
Greenfield, L., 550
Greenson, R., 78, 108
Greenspan, M., 201, 369, 382
Groth, A.N., 495–96, 499
Grove, D., 467, 469
Grove, W.M., 53
Groves, P., 246, 250, 251, 252, 253
Grunlan, S., 28, 34
Guerney, B.G., Jr., 27
Gutiérrez, G., 153, 154–55
Guze, S.B., 53

Habermas, T., 521–22
Hall, C.S., 282, 292
Hall, M., 239
Hallinan, H.W., 151
Hamberger, L.K., 489
Hanson, N.R., 59
Hardy-Fanta, C., 151

Harlow, H., 512
Harrar, W.R., 42
Harrell, F., 153
Harris, J., 39
Hart, G.M., 36
Hart, K., 319
Hart, T., 313, 319
Hartman, A., 145
Hattie, J.A., 39
Haugk, K.C., 28, 34
Hauser, M.J., 644, 646, 647
Hawkins, E., Jr., 253
Hawthorne, N., 21, 392
Hawton, K., 120
Heidegger, M., 440
Heitler, S., 318, 322
Helgesen, S., 314
Helquist, M., 701
Hendrix, H., 316, 320, 321, 322
Hennessey, M., 628
Henning, K.H., 146
Heraclitus, 544
Herbert, C.A., 460
Herbstein, J., 53
Herman, J., 453
Hersen, M., 623
Herzog, A., 657
Herzog, D.B., 527, 533
Hess, A.K., 36
Hesselgrave, D., 28
Heyward, C., 237, 246–47, 257
Hiltner, S., 52, 61, 62, 96
Hippocrates, 418
Hobbs, M., 537
Hoblitzelle, H., 320
Hoblitzelle, O., 320
Hobson, D.P., 52
Hochstein, L., 236
Hoffman, L.W., 36
Holbrook, T.L., 145
Holifield, E.B., 137–38
Holland, N., 56
Holmer, P., 51
Horney, K., 283
Horowitz, M., 102, 104, 105
Houskamp, B., 623
Hsu, L.K.G., 536
Huber, M., 536
Hudson, J.I., 537
Hudson, R.V., 148
Hudson, W., 236
Hughes, S., 28
Hunt, M., 232–33, 257
Hunter, S., 297
Hurding, R.F., 34
Husserl, E., 440

Ignatius Loyola, St., 404–05, 407–08, 583, 589
Imber-Black, E., 315
Innes, C., 191
Isely, Paul, 500
Isely, Peter, 500
Ivy, S.S., 61, 62, 96

Jacob, M., 11–13, 52
Jacobvitz, D., 516
Jaffe, A.C., 536
James, W., 141, 368, 603
Janoff-Bulman, R., 625
Jaques, E., 302
Javits, J., 156
Jernigan, R., 38
Johnson, C., 534, 537
Johnson, E.D., 146
Johnson, L.B., 156
Johnson, M., 60
Johnson, S., 581
Jones, J., 115
Jordan, M.R., 52, 386, 584
Jung, C.G., 11, 17, 24, 297, 298–99, 300, 302, 303, 308, 309, 545

Kaffman, M., 533, 534
Kafka, F., 392
Kahn, M., 23
Kaiser, H., 57
Kant, I., 440
Karen, R., 512

Karp, S., 533
Kaslow, F.W., 36
Katz, J.L., 527, 529
Kaufman, G., 588
Keane, T.M., 623
Kegan, R., 307
Kelley, K.E., 409
Kellner, 135, 143
Kempe, C.H., 507
Kierkegaard, S., 95
Kimper, F., 132, 143
Kinard, E.M., 507
King, C., 28
Kirk, J., 121
Kinsey, 231
Kirkpatrick, B., 706, 709
Klein, D., 146
Klein, R., 600
Kleinman, A., 67
Knapp, S., 42
Kohlberg, L., 308, 309
Kohn, M., 145
Kohut, H., 54, 57, 58, 68, 69, 75, 91, 93, 238
Kolb, L.C., 622
Koltow, E., 665, 666, 669
Koss, M.P., 107
Krantzler, M., 338
Krisberg, 151
Kroll, J., 216–17
Kübler-Ross, E., 669

La Sorte, M.A., 151
Lakoff, G., 60
Lambrides, D., 28, 34
Langan, P., 191
Langer, E.J., 297
Larocca, F.F.E., 537
Larson, D., 226
Laubach, F., 320, 321
Lawrence, K., 625
Lazare, A., 56
Lazarus, A., 316, 323, 440
Leavey, S.D., 593
Leckey, D., 319, 323, 325
Ledray, L., 489, 499
Leibermann, M.A., 338–39
Leonardo da Vinci, 268
Lepkowsky, C., 533
Lesieur, H., 593, 596–97, 600
Levin, J.D., 546, 559
Levinson, D., 297, 298, 300–03, 304, 307, 310, 369, 371
Lew, M., 449, 450, 451, 453, 455, 479, 482, 483, 485
Lewinsohn, P.M., 433, 434
Lewis, H.B., 392–93
Lewis, S., 246
Lieberman, R.P., 429
Lim, I., 28
Lim, S., 28
Lindberg, F.H., 623
Lindquist, S., 28
Lindy, J.D., 632
Lindzey, G., 282, 292
Lingswiler, V.M., 530
Lininger, P., 548
Linz, D., 192
Lipsker, L.E., 36–37
Litwin, H., 145
Lonergan, B., 292
Loulan, J., 241, 255
Love, B., 250
Luborsky, L., 102, 114, 116
Lukens, H.C., Jr., 28, 30, 31, 34
Lupfer, S.L., 454
Lystad, M., 496

Maas, H.S., 308, 310
McAdoo, H., 151
McCaffrey, R.J., 623
McCann, I.L., 632, 633
McDonald, N., 150
McDonnell, R., 583, 584, 585, 587
Mace, D., 316
McFague, S., 55, 60
McGoldrick, M., 577–78
McKenzie, J.L., 147
MacKinnon, C., 192
McLaughlin, E., 533

MacMahon-Herrera, E., 151
McNeill, J.J., 269, 272
Madge, N., 151
Maier, J., 405
Mailloux, N., 210
Major, B., 195
Malan, D.H., 102, 103–04, 107, 112, 113, 116
Mallarmé, S., 13
Malony, H.N., 32
Mandel, H., 102
Mandelstam, N., 391
Mann, D., 102, 104, 107, 111, 113
Marcel, G., 73
Maritain, J., 211
Marlatt, A., 547, 604
Maslow, A., 299–300, 309, 354
Mathews, R.K., 42
May, G., 315
May, R., 322, 354
Mayman, M., 56
Mead, D.E., 36
Mehrabian, A., 60
Meichenbaum, D., 322
Melville, H., 392
Menard, G., 233
Menninger, K., 56, 391
Meyers, J., 640
Michelangelo, 268
Mickalide, A.E., 526
Miller, A., 365, 367, 368, 581, 586, 588
Miller, G., 144, 145
Miller, J.B., 248
Miller, P.M., 28, 34
Miller, S., 318, 322
Millon, T., 56–57
Milt, H., 597
Minuchin, S., 145, 151
Mitchell, J.E., 522, 524, 536
Mitchell, K., 51
Moffic, S.H., 145
Mollat, M., 149
Mollencott, V., 257
Mondale, W., 156
Montalvo, B., 151
Moore, T.V., 210
Moraga, C., 248, 252
Moraga, L.C., 243
Morawetz, A., 332, 340–41, 343–44, 350
Morris, P., 28
Morrow, J.S., 593
Morton, N., 202
Moses, A., 253
Mott, P.E., 156
Muehl, W., 51
Murphy, B., 250
Muslin, H., 61
Myer, G., 51, 61, 62

Napier, N., 588
Nathan, P., 54
Nelson, J.B., 269, 271, 272
Nelson, M.B., 255
Neugarten, B.L., 302, 303
Neuger, C., 200
Neumann, D., 299, 623
Newton, P.M., 297, 303, 304, 305
Nichols, M., 250
Nicholas, W., 316, 331–32, 338, 340, 343
Nicoloff, L., 250
Nietzel, N.T., 39
Nietzsche, F., 392, 706–07
Nixon, R.M., 156
Norring, C., 532–33
Norton, N.C., 39, 40
Nouwen, H.J.M., 52, 62
Nugent, R., 229, 235, 270

O'Connor, F., 22
O'Neil, J.A., 549
Oden, T., 95
Olasov Rothbaum, B., 623
Oliver, J.E., 153
Olson, M., 256
Oraker, J., 28
Osato, S.S., 623, 625
Osborn, E.B., 34

Osterweis, M., 338
Othmer, E., 61
Othmer, S.C., 61
Overton, A., 151
Owens, T., 37
Oyebode, F., 536

Padesky, C., 250
Page, H.O., 150
Pande, S., 137
Pantano, M., 536
Parke, R., 510
Parkes, C.M., 644
Parks, 341
Parsons, 639, 640
Parsons, R., 145
Parsons, R.D., 273, 639, 640, 656, 658
Parzen, Z., 51, 61, 62, 95
Patton, J., 52, 62, 67, 75, 96
Paul, St., 63–64, 335, 547, 640
Peabody, B., 704, 709
Pearlman, L.A., 632, 633
Pellauer, M., 489, 499
Penrod, S., 192
Peterson, E., 28, 34
Peterson, S., 383, 384
Pianta, R., 511, 512–13, 516
Picasso, P., 11
Piercy, F.P., 340
Pierson, A., 150
Pincus, G., 625
Pittenger, N., 272
Ple, A., 210–11
Plummer, C., 198
Poling, J., 493
Politzer, R.M., 593
Pomeroy, C., 536
Pope, H.G., 537
Powell, J., 334, 336
Power, F.C., 106
Powers, S.K., 536–37
Prater, J.S., 35
Prather, R.C., 529
Pruyser, P.W., 52, 54, 55, 56, 60, 61, 62, 96
Rakoff, V., 527–28
Rank, O., 103
Raphael, S.J., 341, 673
Rappaport, J., 146
Rashke, R., 229
Redlich, F.C., 145
Regensburg, J., 151
Reid, C.H., 672
Reiter, L., 233, 235
Rencken, R., 448, 450, 451, 452, 453, 455
Resnick, H.S., 625
Resnik, H.L.P., 639, 657
Rice, L.N., 60
Rich, A., 242
Rich, M.D., 145
Richardson, R., 598, 601, 606–07
Richmond, M.E., 145
Ricketts, 236
Ricoeur, P., 74
Rilke, R.M., 325
Rivers, C., 305
Rix, S., 190
Rizley, R., 508, 509–10, 511
Rizzuto, A.M., 14, 376–77
Robbins, A., 36
Roberts, P., 297, 303, 304, 305
Robin, S.S., 27
Robins, E., 53, 231
Robinson, H.A., 145, 150
Rockwell, W.J.K., 537
Rodin, J., 532
Rogers, C., 515
Rogers, H.J., 39
Rose, A., 257
Rosenthal, R.J., 593
Rossi, A., 319, 320
Roth, D.M., 528, 529
Roth, S., 61, 84, 87, 240, 250
Royce, J., 610
Rubel, J.B., 538
Rubenstein, H., 150
Ruch, L.O., 628
Rueger, D.B., 623, 625
Russell, D.E., 494, 495

Russell, G.F.M., 530
Rutter, M., 151
Rutter, P., 497–98
Ryan, R.M., 532
Rybicki, D., 533
Ryncarz, R., 308–09

Sadeh, T., 533, 534
Sager, C., 316, 317
Saghir, M., 231
Salkovskis, P.M., 121
Sala, H., 28
Salk, J., 314
Sampson, H., 102
Samuelson, G., 52, 61, 62
Sanchez, G., 28
Sanders, C., 338, 339, 341, 349
Sandford, P., 483
Sanford, L., 188
Sarason, S., 145
Sarff, P., 37, 38
Satir, V., 339, 579, 587
Saussy, C., 364, 375
Scanzoni, L., 231
Schaef, A., 315, 370, 580
Schaefer, C.A., 38
Schaefer, G., 28
Schafer, R., 57, 58, 67
Schapira, K., 536
Schick, C., 148
Schillebeeckx, E., 153
Schlauch, C.R., 52, 57, 69
Schmidt, P.F., 32
Schmitt, A., 28
Schmitt, D., 28
Schneider, C.D., 52, 62, 96
Schneiders, S., 314
Schneidman, E., 639
Schuckit, M.A., 548, 552
Schwartz, L.S., 629
Seamands, D., 34
Seiden, R.H., 648
Seligman, L., 61
Sgroi, S., 489, 499, 500
Shafranske, E.P., 115
Shakespeare, W., 391
Shapiro, D., 57, 58
Sharpley, C.F., 39
Shaw, D., 38
Shearer, S.L., 460
Sheehan, W., 216–17
Sheen, F.J., 210
Shilts, R., 709
Siegal, B.S., 701, 706
Siegal, D., 190
Sieleni, G., 529–30
Sifneos, P.E., 102, 104, 107, 108, 110, 116
Simenauer, J., 331, 353
Singer, L.T., 536
Sipprelle, 623, 625
Sklar, I., 118
Slade, P.D., 536
Smith, M.T., 665
Smith, W.J., 709
Sobey, F., 27
Sobrino, J., 154–55
Solomon, C.R., 28, 34
Sontag, S., 709
Sophocles, 544
Souvaine, E., 307
Sparks, L., 28
Spence, D., 67
Spencer, J.C., 152
Spencer, S., 340, 354
Spitzer, R.L., 561
Spiz, R., 512
Sprenkle, D.H., 340
Sroufe, L.A., 516
Steadman, B., 52, 61, 62, 76, 96
Steadman, H.J., 593, 600, 601
Steinbron, M., 28
Steketee, G., 623
Steoin, G., 268
Stephens, M.A.P., 530
Stern, D., 85, 86
Stern, K., 210
Stiglitz, E., 250
Stock, M., 211
Stoltenberg, C.D., 36

Stone, H.W., 424, 426, 440, 443
Straus, M., 496
Strauss, J., 532
Strnad, L.J., 150
Strober, M., 529
Strupp, H., 102, 104, 118
Struzzo, J., 245, 249
Stuart, R., 316, 321, 322
Studzinki, R., 297, 303, 309
Sturkie, J., 28, 34
Sundel, M., 297
Sunderland, R., 27
Susskind, E., 146
Sweeten, G.R., 28, 33, 34
Swenson, N., 190

Tan, S.Y., 27, 28, 29, 30, 31, 33, 34, 37, 38
Taylor, A., 153
Tchaikovsky, P.I., 268
Tellenbach, H., 418
Teresa of Avila, 589
Thompson, C., 146, 629
Tillich, P., 62
Topper, C., 249
Torem, M.S., 530–31
Toufexis, A., 507
Toulmin, S., 106
Townsend, J.S., 32
Toynbee, A., 638
Tracy, D., 284
Trimble, J., 623
Tritch, T., 665

Ulanov, A.B., 10, 14, 15, 17
Ulanov, B., 9, 10, 15, 17
Underwood, R.L., 52

Val, E., 61
Van Buren, D.J., 536
Van Kaam, A., 274, 276, 278, 279, 288
Van Strien, T., 525, 527
Van-Hasselt, V.B., 623
Vance, C., 246
VandeCreek, L., 42
Vanderheyden, D.A., 524
Vann, G., 211
Varenhorst, B., 28
Vicinus, M., 230, 246, 268
Voiland, A.L., 150–51
Volberg, R.A., 593, 600, 601
Vom Lehn, P., 704

Wachtel, P., 315
Wagenfeld, M.O., 27
Wagner, C.P., 32
Wahking, H., 52, 62, 96
Wall, J., 230
Wallerstein, J., 314
Walters, R., 28, 30, 34, 39
Ward, W.O., 28, 34
Warren, R.L., 151
Wegscheider-Cruse, S., 578
Weick, A., 307–08, 309, 310
Weil, S., 22
Weisman, A., 706
Weiss, A., 701
Weiss, J., 102
Weiss, R., 332
Wells, G., 383, 384
Welter, P.R., 28, 34, 37–38
Wenzel, S., 416
Westberg, G., 349
Whitehead, E.E., 272, 287
Whitehead, J.D., 272, 287
Wichern, F.B., 32
Wicks, R.J., 273, 340, 656, 658
Wiedemann, F., 380
Wiley, M.O., 36
Williamson, D.A., 529, 536–37
Wilson, B., 545–46
Winnicott, D.W., 366, 374, 581, 588
Winston, A., 102
Wish, E.D., 549
Wittgenstein, L., 7
Wolberg, L.R., 102

Wolfet, A.D., 651, 652
Wolman, B., 61
Wood, K., 151
Worthington, E., 321
Worthington, E.L., Jr., 28, 34, 35, 36
Wright, H.N., 28, 34
Wright, W., 319, 322

Yalom, I., 354
Yates, W.R., 529–30
Yeomans, M., 52, 62, 96
Young-Eisendrath, P., 380

Zakin, D., 525
Zanotti, B., 257
Zikmud, B., 142
Zilboorg, G., 210
Zillman, D., 192
Zimering, R.T., 623
Zimmer, B., 536
Zoppa, R.M., 600
Zucker, P., 531

Subject Index

Accidie, 415–16, 429
ACoA. *See* Adult children of alcoholics
Acquired Human Immunodeficiency Virus (HIV). *See* AIDS
Addiction, 543–45; *see also* Substance abuse; Gambling, pathological
Adult children of alcoholics, 577–92; addictions studies, 579–80; affective issues, 582; "as if" personality, 581; autonomy, 588; catastrophizing, 581; co-dependency, 580, 583–84; cognitive therapy, 587; dysfunctional family systems, 577–79; false self, 581; family hero, 578; family mascot, 578–79; God images, 584; individual psychological issues, 580; lost child, 578; "oppositional bonding," 581; pastoral counseling, ministry to, 585–89; pastoral focus, 582–85; personalization, 581–82; scapegoat, 578; shame, 588; splitting, 581, 584
Adult development, 298–312; women, 303–07
Adult survivors of child sexual abuse. *See* Child sexual abuse survivors
Affect: adult children of alcoholics, 582; depression, 419–20, 428–32; marital conflict, 316–17, 319–20; pastoral diagnosis, 84–87
Affirmation, 279–80, 288–89, 290
Affirmation for United Methodists, 256, 270
AIDS, 679–710; acquiring infection, 680–81; anger, 692–94; case studies, 707–09; change of mental outlook, 703; communication, 700; cryptosporidiosis, 686; cytomegalovirus (CMV), 685; defense mechanisms, 691–94; denial, 691–92; immunodeficiency, 681–83; Kaposi's sarcoma (KS), 684–85; mycobacterium avium-intracellulare (MAI), 686; pastoral care, 687–707; pneumocystis carinii pneumonia (PCP), 684; regression, 705; relationships, 702; self-esteem, 695; stigma, 698–99; stress, 697–98; support, 701, 703–07; syndrome of diseases, 683–84; toxoplasmosis, 685–86
AIDS Education Project, 680
Al-Anon, 580, 608, 611
Alcoholics Anonymous, 545–46, 602; Twelve Steps, 545, 583, 590, 602, 611
Alcoholism, 607; illness versus moral lapse, 610; *see also* Adult children of alcoholics; Substance abuse
American Association for Marriage and Family Therapy, 42
American Association of Counseling and Development, 41–42
American Association of Pastoral Counselors, 236, 237

American Medical Association, 690
American Psychiatric Association, 51, 211–12, 226, 234, 268, 451, 522, 559, 622; AIDS Education Project, 680; *see also Diagnostic and Statistical Manual*
American Psychological Association, 42, 188, 234
Anger: adult survivors of childhood sexual abuse, 475–76; AIDS, 692–94; depression, 429; post-traumatic stress syndrome, 626; suicide survivors, 649, 657; traumatic experiences, 626
Anorexia, 522; borderline personality disorder, 530; secondary anorexia, 522; sexual orientation, 525; *see also* Eating disorders
Antisocial personality disorder, 403, 598–99
Anxiety: AIDS, 697–98; *see also* Stress
Application, 189–90, 280–81
Appraisal, 278–79, 283–84, 290
Apprehension, 277–78, 281–83, 290
"As of" personality, 367, 581
Association of Pastoral Counselors, 273
At-risk families. *See* Multi-risk families

BASH, 537
Battered Child Syndrome, 507
Batterers, 496–98
Beck Depression Inventory, 425
Behavioral therapy, 432–36
Behavior modification, 338–39
Behaviorism, 383
Bereavement, 644–60
Bible: and marriage counseling, 325; on traumatic experiences, 626–27
Biblical counseling, 27–28
Biblical Counseling Seminars, 33
Biblical feminism, 305–06
Biblical models and programs, 27–32
Bibliotherapy, 326
Bisexuality, 231, 292, 382
Blowup technique, 442
Borderline personality, 198, 540
Brecksville (Ohio) Veterans Administration Hospital, 597
Brigham Young University, 40
Bulimia, 522; depression and, 530, 532; *see also* Eating disorders
Burnout, 632–34

Catastrophizing, 581
Center for Church Renewal, Plano, Texas, 30
Center for Studies of Suicide Prevention (CSSP), 639
Centers for Disease Control, 709
Character Assessment Scale, 32
Child abuse, 145; *see also* Child sexual abuse survivors; Psychological/emotional child abuse
Child molesters, 494–95
Child sexual abuse survivors, 447–88; acknowledging reality of abuse, 464–67; anger, 475–76; confrontation, 479–80; coping with sexual abuse, 456–58; covert sexual abuse, 450–51, 452; decision to heal, 462–64; defense mechanisms, 456–59; definitions, 449–51; denial, 458, 465–66; developing a facade, 458; dissociation, 456–57; facing the pain, 467–70; family, 453–54; forgiveness, 481–83; grace, 484; group work, 479; guilt, 485–86; healing stages, 462–77; image of church, temptation to

protect, 490; low reporting rates, 448–49; misconceptions, altering of, 470–75; minimization, 457; negative feelings, dealing with, 475–76; professional boundaries, 478–79; regression, 448, 458–59; repression, 457–58; resolution and reconciliation, 476–77; 484–85; secrecy, 453; shame, 485; signs and symptoms of abuse, 455–56; society and, 451–52; spouse abuse, 492–93; termination of counseling, 477; therapeutic process, 462; therapeutic techniques, 477–79; treatment plans, 459–62; victim, 454–55; victim versus survivor, 450
Children of alcoholics. *See* Adult children of alcoholics
Christian Association for Psychological Studies, 30
Christian Family Movement (CFM), 325
Christian Lesbians Out Together (CLOUT), 256
Church Career Development Centers, 676
Church of the Savior, Wayne, Pennsylvania, 355
Clinical pastoral education (CPE), 235
Clinical Supervisor, The, 36
CLOUT, 256
Co-dependency, 370; alcoholic families, 580, 583–84; women, 198
Cognition: adult children of alcoholics, 587; depression and, 421–22, 439–44; marital conflict, 317, 320
Cognitive Error Questionnaire (CEQ), 532
Cognitive rehearsal, 441
Cognitive restructuring, 440
Collaborative translating, metaphor of, 67–68
Collegial model of therapy, 165
Community intervention: lay counselors, 28; marital conflict, 325; multi-risk families, 173–75; single parents, 342–43
Compassion, 279, 286
Compatibility, 278–79, 286
Competence, 279, 286–87; self-esteem and, 370–71
Confidentiality: lay counseling, 42; multi-risk families, 172–73; sexual abusers, 501
Congeniality, 278, 284–85
Congregation for the Doctrine of the Faith, 269–70
Conscience, 397–98
Counseling. *See* specific headings, e.g.: Gay males; Lay counseling
Counseling Resource Center of First Presbyterian Church, Boulder, Colorado, 30
Counseling with Power Seminars, 33
Counselor Education and Supervision, 36
Counselor Training for Young Life, 28
Counselor Training Program Questionnaire, 37
Countertransference, 14, 357; pastoral diagnosis, 89–93, 116–17; religion professionals, 212–13, 219, 221; short-term psychotherapy, 117; substance abuse, 547, 572
Creative Counseling Center, Hollywood Presbyterian Church, 30
Crisis intervention: pathological gambling, 603–10; single parents, 345–46, 347–48
Cross-cultural counseling, 129–43; characteristics of counselor, 136–37; intercultural counseling, 130, 131, 132;

interpathy, 131; intracultural counseling, 130–31; lay counseling, 35, 38; lesbians, counseling of, 239; narcissism, 135; pathos, 132; pluralism of values, 133; privatism, 133; relativism, 133; theological grounds for, 141–42; training of counselor, 138–39; tribalism, 133; transcultural counseling, 130, 131, 132
Cryptosporidiosis, 686
Cytomegalovirus (CMV), 685

Death, 336–37
Defense mechanisms: AIDS, 691–94; child sexual abuse, 456–59; religion professionals, 220; *see also* specific headings, e.g.: Dissociation
Denial: adult survivors of childhood sexual abuse, 458, 465–66; AIDS, 691–92; suicide survivors, 648
Dependence, 218–19
Depressants, 552–53; *see also* Substance abuse
Depression, 415–46; affect, 419–20; affective intervention, 428–32; alternative technique, 442; anger, expression of, 429; arbitrary inference, 439; assessment, 422–26; background and assessment, 422–26; behavior, 420, 432–36; blowup technique, 442; bulimia, 530, 542; causes, 418–19; cognition, 421–22, 439–44; cognitive rehearsal, 441; cognitive restructuring, 440; discussion of problem, 429; dis-identification, 430–31; diversion, 431; drug intervention, 436–37; emotion, expression of, 429; exercise, 437, 439; faith and, 422; grief and, 424; magnification and minimization, 439; overgeneralization, 439; pastoral counseling methods, 428–44; personalization, 439; physiology, 420–21, 436–39; "primary triad," 421; reattribution, 442–43; resignation, 430; selective abstraction, 439; self-identification, 430–31; sleep disturbances, 421, 438; spiritual direction, 443–44; suicide survivors, 658; suicide, risk of, 426–28; thought stopping, 441; traits, 419–22; women, 188–89, 195, 198, 201–03; worry time, 441–42
Diagnosis. *See* Pastoral diagnosis
Diagnostic and Statistical Manual, 51, 55, 61, 451, 453, 522, 523, 559–61, 595, 600
Diagnostic Survey for Eating Disorders (DESES), 530
Dignity for Roman Catholics, 256, 270
Dis-identification, 43–310
Dissociation, 456–57
Diversion, 431
Divorce mediation, 339–40, 345
Domestic violence, 146, 191–92; *see also* Sexual abuse
Drug abuse. *See* Substance abuse
Drug therapy, 436–37
Drunk driving, 550
DSM. *See Diagnostic and Statistical Manual*
Dysmorphobia, 535–36

Eating Disorder Inventory (EDI), 530
Eating disorders, 521–42; borderline personality disorder, 530; diagnostic

factors, 524–35; family dynamics, 527–29; ideational perfectionism, 533–35; monoideistic fixation, 533; negative self-image, 524–27, 529; psychiatric history, 521–24; psychopathology, 529–31; social dysfunction, 531–33; treatment, 535–37
Ecosystemic pastoral counseling, 157–64, 165, 170–71
"Emmaus walk" exercises, 406–07
Emotional child abuse. *See* Psychological/emotional child abuse
Entitlement, sense of, 220
Evangelical Women's Caucus, 305

Faith, 365–66; adult development and, 305–06; depression and, 422; human faith, 365; religious faith, 365
Faithful companioning, metaphor of, 65–67, 68
False self, 365–66, 367, 368, 377, 382, 385, 386, 387; adult children of alcoholics, 581
Families-at-risk. *See* Multi-risk families
Family abuse and violence, 143, 191–92; *see also* Sexual abuse
Family Service Association (FSA), 39
Family Service Plan (FSP), 174
Family systems: adult children of alcoholics, 577–79; lesbians, counseling with, 239–40, 253–54; marital distress, 203; single parents, 340–41, 344
Feminist counseling, 185–207; case studies, 185, 203–05; depression, 188–89, 201–03; group component, 195–96; marital distress, 203–05; patriarchal context, 197; patriarchy, awareness of, 188; psychology, 197–99; theology, 199–201; therapeutic relationship, 193–95; woman-centered approach, 196–97; woman's world, 189–90; *see also* Lesbians
First Presbyterian Church, Counseling Resource Center, Boulder, Colorado, 30
Focal psychotherapy. *See* Brief psychotherapy
Forgiveness: sexual abuse victims, 481–83; sexual abusers, 491; single parents, 334–35
"Fresh Start," 355
Friends, 230

Gamanon. *See* Gambler's Anonymous
Gamblers' Anonymous (GA), 598, 600–01, 604, 605, 607, 608, 613, 614–15
Gambling, pathological, 593–617; assessment of immediate risk, 607; abstinence control, 604–05; changing meaning of money, 611–13; crisis intervention, 603–10; developmental phases, 597–98; illness versus moral lapse, 610–11; indications of, 595–600; legal crisis, 606–07; long-term recovery, 609–10; manic depression, 609; marital/family crisis, 607–09; narcissism, 610; outpatient treatment, 603, 613; pastoral focus, 610–13; resolving financial crises, 605–06; self-help groups, 602–03; stimulus control, 604; suicide, 607; symptoms of disorder, 595–600; treatment, 601–03
Gay liberation, 267–68

Gay males, 267–94; affirmation, 279–80, 287–91; application, 280–81, 287–91; appraisal, 278–79, 281–84, 288, 290; apprehension, 277–78, 281–84, 288, 290; compassion, 279, 286; compatibility, 286; competence, 286–87; congeniality, 284–85; lesbian therapists, 239; pastoral counseling, 275–91
Gender/sexual abuse, 381, 388
Genogram, 579
God images, 14; children of alcoholics, 584; ideology and, 375–77; patriarchical societies, 377–80; self-esteem and, 375–80, 382–83; women, 200, 365, 379–80
Grace: sexual abuse victims, 484; sexual abusers, 491
Grief: depression and, 424; resignation, 430; single parents, 331, 337–38, 348–49; unemployment, 669–73
Group work: feminist counseling, 195–96; sex abuse victims, 479
Guided imagery, 467
Guilt, 390–413; "Emmaus walk" exercises, 406–07; examples, 393–95; healthy versus toxic guilt, 395–401; identity as "loved sinner," 401–03; interpreting guilt, 391–95; pastoral counseling, 403–12; sexual abuse victims, 485–86; shame distinguished, 392–93; single parents, 332; suicide survivors, 650, 656

Hallucinogens, 553; *see also* Substance abuse
Hamartia, 402
Hamilton Rating Scale, 425
Hate, 19, 20
Heterosexism, 236–37, 240, 242, 248, 257
HIV. *See* AIDS
Hollywood Presbyterian Church, Creative Counseling Center, 30
Homophobia, 241–42, 248, 268, 292
Homosexuality, 229–30, 233–34; church and, 268–75; culture and, 267–68; full acceptance, 244, 260, 272; qualified acceptance, 271–272; rejecting-non-punitive motif, 271, 272; rejecting-punitive motif, 271, 272; sin and, 235–37; *see also* Gay males; Lesbians
Human Immunodeficiency Virus (HIV). *See* AIDS
Hypnosis, 467
Hypnotic medications, 553; *see also* Substance abuse
Hysteria, 135

Incest, 449, 452, 454
Index of Attitudes Toward Homosexuals (IAH), 236
Individuation, 301–02
Infancy, ideology and, 372–74
Inhalants, 553; *see also* Substance abuse
Insanity: suicide as, 643–44
Insight therapy, 383
Integrity for Episcopalians, 256, 270
Intercultural counseling, 130, 131, 132; *see also* Cross-cultural counseling
Internal/external metaphor, 69, 70–72
Interpathy, 131
Intracultural counseling, 130–31; *see also* Cross-cultural counseling

JIM MOTSIGA, 76
Johns Hopkins Hospital, Department of Psychiatry, 555

Journal of Supervision and Training in Ministry, 36
Judaism, 230

Kaposi's sarcoma (KS), 684–85

Lay counseling, 27–50; biblical models and programs, 27–32; confidentiality, 42; effectiveness of, 37, 39–41; formal, organized model, 31; informal, organized model, 31–32; informal, spontaneous model, 31; legal and ethical issues, 41–43; malpractice insurance, 42; peer counseling, 28–29, 38; selection of counselors, 32–33; supervision, 35–37; training counselors, 33–35
Lesbians, 228–66; abuse, 381–82; bisexuals and, 231; case studies, 228–29, 244, 251–52; coming out, 231, 250–54; cross-cultural counseling skills, 239; cultural analysis, use of 240–42; definition, 230–33; desire to conform, 248; etiology, 233–34; family systems, use of, 239–40; "full acceptance," 244, 260; genuineness of counselor, 238–392; history, 246; illness or variation, 234–35; oppression, 242–43, 248, 381–82; as parents, 254–55; pastoral counseling, 238–59; secular psychotherapy and pastoral counseling distinguished, 244–45; psychological problems, 245–49; religious lesbians, 255–56; self-esteem, 248–49; social justice issues, 258–59; theologies and spiritualities, 257–58
Liberation theology, 153, 154–55, 236; *see also* Lesbians

Malpractice insurance, 42
Manic depression, 609
Marijuana, 553; *see also* Substance abuse
Marital conflict, 313–28; affective elements, 316–17, 319–20; behavioral/interpersonal elements, 317–18, 321–23; bibliotherapy, 326; cognitive elements, 317, 320–21; community and, 325; cultural context of marriage, 314; gambling, 607–09; imaging marital spirituality, 323–24; marital spirituality, 313–14; prayer and meditation, 325; resolution, 318–26; scripture study, 325; single parents, 345; silence and solitude, 325; spiritual direction, 325
Mediating a gift, metaphor of, 63–65
Melancholy, 417–18; *see also* Depression
Men Stopping Violence, 496
Metropolitan Community Churches, 230
Midlife transition, 297–312
Minimization: adult survivors of childhood sexual abuse, 457, 458; depression, 439; suicide survivors, 652
Minnesota Mother-Child Interaction Research Project, 513
Minnesota Multiphasic Personality Inventory, (MMPI), 32
Mirroring, 374
Misbelief therapy, 28
Monoideistic fixation, 533–34
Monotheism, 379
Moravian Church, 230

"More Light Churches," 256
Multi-risk families, 144–84; case studies, 168–72; clinical intervention, 172–75; collegial model of therapy, 165; community intervention, 173–75; ecosystemic pastoral counseling, 157–64, 165, 170–71; non-therapy activities, 165, 166; personal conversions of counselor, 164–66, 175; privatized model of therapy, 165; professional boundaries, 166–67; shared confidentiality, 172–73; single mothers, 355–56; studies, 161–64, 168–72; systemic convergence, 160; systemic fission, 160–61, 163–64; theological methodology, 153–55
Multiple personality, 456
Mycobacterium avium-intracellulare (MAI), 686
Myers-Briggs Temperament Type Indicator, 32

Narcissism, 135, 303, 610
Narcotics, 553; *see also* Substance abuse
National Coalition Against Domestic Violence, 381
National Committee for the Prevention of Child Abuse, 497
National Convention of the Christian Association for Psychological Studies, 30
National Council on Compulsive Gambling, 613
National Crime Survey, 191
National Highway Traffic Safety Administration, 550
National Institute of Drug Abuse, 594
National Institute of Mental Health, 342, 415
National Peer Helpers Association, 28–29
Navigators, 28
Networking, 341–42, 354–55
"New Life," 355
Nouthetic counseling, 27
Numbing, 456

Object relations school, 374
Obsessive compulsive disorders, 135
Ontario Bible College, 37
Open Hands, 240
"Oppositional bonding," 581
Out of body experiences, 456, 481
Outlook, 252
Overeaters Anonymous (OA), 537
Oxford Movement, 545–46

Pain. *See* Suffering
Parents: lesbians as, 254–55; self-esteem and parental acceptance, 368–69; *see also* Single parents
Parents and Friends of Lesbians and Gays (PFLAG), 253
Passivity, 19–20, 113
Pastoral counseling. *See* specific headings, e.g.: Gay males; Lay counseling
Pastoral diagnosis, 51–101; action, 87–89; affect, 77–78, 84–87; as theological diagnosis, 51–52; clinical attitude, 57–59, 68–93; collaborative translating, metaphor of, 67–68; content, 77, 78–84; countertransferase, 92–93, 117; diagnostic variables, 56–57, 75–93; doubting-believing, 69–70, 73–75; engagement of psychologist-theologian-ethicist, 68–69; faithful companioning, metaphor of, 65–67, 68; internal-external, 69, 70–72; introspective-

empathic attitude, 69–74; language, 85–86; mediating a gift, metaphor of, 63–65; process of engagement, 88–89; relationship, 89–93; root-metaphors, 59–62; self and suffering, 75–77, 78, 88; self-experience, 69–70; surface-depth, 69–70, 72–73; transference, 89–93, 117–18
Pathological gambling. *See* Gambling, pathological
Pathos, 132
Patriarchy, 188, 197, 242, 250, 369, 385; gender acceptance, 378; God images, 377–80
Pedophiles, 217, 494–95
Peer counseling, 28–29, 38
People-helping, 28
Personal Orientation Inventory (POI), 32, 38
Personalization, 581–82
Phipps Psychosocial Assessment, 555
Physicians' Desk Reference (PDR), 553
Pneumocystis carinii pneumonia (PCP), 684
Poor. *See* Multi-risk families
Posttraumatic stress disorder (PTSD), 621–37; anger, 626; burnout, 632–34; church and, 628–32; definition, 622–24; non-judgmentality, 630; non-traumatic factors, 625; role of pastoral counselor, 627–28; spiritual challenges of traumatic experiences, 625–27; validation, 630
Pre-marriage counseling, 346
Professional Psychology: Research and Practice, 36
Psychoanalysis, 17–18, 104
Psychological abuse, 492; *see also* Psychological/emotional child abuse
Psychological/emotional child abuse, 506–18; attachment theory, 512; child-based model, 510; definition, 507–09; pastoral approach, 514–17; psychiatric model, 510; social situational model, 510; sociological model, 510
Psychology: feminism and, 197–99; religion and, 7–26, 210–13, 238–45

Quakers, 234

Rape, 191
Rapists, 495–96
Reattribution, 442–43
Regression: AIDS, 705; adult survivors of childhood sexual abuse, 458–59; short-term psychotherapy, 117, 118–19
Relaxation training, 40–41
Religion professionals, 208–27; case studies, 216, 218–19; confidentiality, 223; countertransference, 212–13, 219, 221; defense mechanisms, 215–21; dependency, 218–19; entitlement, sense of, 220–21; low morale, 222–23; origin of treatment philosophies, 210–13; pastoral counselor, role of, 225–26; religious administration, responsibility to, 223–25; therapist, role of, 213–14; "uniqueness" of religion professionals, 214–21
Religion, psychology and, 7–26, 210–13, 238–45
Religious Status Interview, 32
Repression, 448, 457–58
Resurrection, 336–37
Resignation, 430
Resistance, 111, 112, 113, 116–17

Sadism, 496
San Francisco General Medical Center, 226
SCL-90, 530
Sedatives, 552; *see also* Substance abuse
Self, 91–93, 135, 138, 366–67; "as if" personality, 367, 581; faith in self, 364, 365, 387; false self, 365–66, 367, 368, 377, 382, 385, 386, 387, 581; sociohistorical dimension, 274; true self, 366, 377, 382, 385, 387
Self-acceptance, 371–72
Self-actualization, 137–38, 354
Self-esteem, 363–89; AIDS and, 695; avoidance, 384–85; competence, 370–71; confronting, 384; coping, 383–85; dimensions of, 367–72; faith, 365–66; foundational self-esteem, 367, 368, 382; God images and, 364, 375–80, 382–83; good enough self-esteem, 377, 382–86; ideology and, 368, 372–80; lesbians, 248–49; parental acceptance and, 367, 368–69; passion for life, 371–72; relationships, 369–70; secondary self-esteem, 367, 371; self, 366–67; self-acceptance, 372; substance abuse and, 571–72; women, 188, 200, 380–82
Self-experience, 69–70
Self-help groups, 602–03
Self-identification, 430–31
"Selfobject," 91
Self-pity, 658
Self-realization, 137–38, 402
Sex discrimination, 188–89
Sexism, 188–89, 240, 241, 243, 381
Sexual abuse, 191–92, 381, 449–50; categories of abuse, 492–93; covert sexual abuse, 450–51; disbelief, temptation of, 490; gender/sexual abuse, 381, 388; *see also* Child sexual abuse survivors; Sexual abusers
Sexual abuse survivors. *See* Child sexual abuse survivors
Sexual abusers, 450, 452–53; batterers, 496–98; blaming, 490; child molesters, 494–95; church and, 489–505; confidentiality, 501; consequences of behavior, temptation to protect from, 491; forgiveness, 491; grace, 491; intervention, 498–503; pedophiles, 217, 494–95; professions, abusers in the, 497–98; rapists, 495–96; sadism, 496; secrecy and deception, 501; sympathy with, 490–91; types of abusers, 493–98; women as, 493–94, 497; *see also* Child sexual abuse survivors
Sexual harassment, 497–98
Sexual orientation: anorexia and, 525; sexual identity and, 233
Shame, 395; adult children of alcoholics, 588; examples, 393; guilt distinguished, 392–93; sexual abuse victims, 485; suicide survivors, 641–44
Shepherd Scale, 32
Short-term psychotherapy, 102–23; appropriateness of client, 107–12; confrontational-interpretative process, 111–12, 117; countertransference, 117; interpretations, 111–12, 118; maintaining focus, 114–16; motivation for change, 109–10; object relatedness, 111; process of, 112–19; psychological mindedness,

109; reciprocal relationship, history of, 110–11; regression, 117, 118–19; resistance, 111, 112, 113, 116–17; termination, 113–14, 118–19; therapeutic alliance, 110–11; therapeutic focus, 104–07, 108; time, function of, 113–14; transference, 113, 117–18; working through process, 118
Sin, 217, 363, 402–03; homosexuality and, 235–37; suicide as, 642–43; women and, 199–200
Single parents, 329–59; behavior modification, 338–39; collaboration with other caregivers, 349–50; community, 342–43, 355–56; countertransference, 357; crisis intervention, 345–46, 347–48; custodial arrangements, 330–31; death and resurrection, 336–37; divorce mediation, 345; family systems approach, 340–41, 344; forgiveness, 334–35; freedom, 354; friendships, 351–52; grief and mourning, 331, 348–49; grief work, 337–38; growth and developmental approaches, 339–40; guilt, 332; individual counseling approaches, 341; legal concerns, 356; letting go, 350–51; love, 333–34, 352; marriage counseling, 345; networking, 341–42, 354–55; parents, 353; pastoral counseling opportunities, 342–43; post-crisis intervention, 346–47; poverty and welfare, 355–56; pre-crisis intervention, 345; pre-marriage counseling, 344, 346; process, 343–44; rebuilding stage, 350; referral, 349–50, 355; remarriage, 356–57; responsibility, 353; self-image and concept, 351; singleness, 353–54; stewardship, 336; subjectivity, 357; suffering, 335–36; support groups, 341–42, 354–55; theological implications, 333–37; trust, 352–53; victim self-concept, 351, 353
Sleep disturbances, 421, 438
Social Security Act, 156
Somatizing, 652
"South Oaks Gambling Screen" (SOGS), 600
Spiritual Leadership Qualities Inventory, 32
Spiritual Well-Being Scale, 32
Spirituotherapy, 28
Splitting, 581, 584
Spouse abuse, 191, 492–93
Stephen Series Leader's Training Course, 28, 33
Stewardship, 136
Steroids, 553; *see also* Substance abuse
Stimulants, 553; *see also* Substance abuse
Stonewall riots, 1969, 267
Stress: AIDS, 697–98; *see also* Post-traumatic stress disorder (PTSD)
Substance abuse, 543–76; definitions, 551–52; assessment and treatment, 553–58; case studies, 563–74; classification of drugs, 552–53; client's history, 555–58; countertransference, 547, 572; personality disorders and, 559; psychoactive substance use disorder, 558–63; relationships, importance of,

570–71; self-esteem and, 571–72; statistics, 548–51; transference, 546–47; treatment, 569–74
Suffering, 7–8, 11–12; self and, 75–77; single parents, 335–36
Suicide: age and sex factors, 436; as crime, 641–42; depression and risk of, 426–28; as insanity, 643–44; as sin, 642–43; gamblers, 607; levels of prevention, 640; plan, 426; stress and, 426; *see also* Suicide survivors
Suicide survivors, 638–63; anger, 649, 657; avoidance, 651–52; bereavement, 644–60; counselor as preventional, 639–40; denial, 648; depression, 658; disorganization, 645–46, 650–51; displacing, 651; grieving process, 646–57; guilt, 650, 656; intervention model, 654–66; minimizing, 652; pathogenic grief response, 651–54; postponing, 651; primary prevention, 640, 659–60; reorganization, 646; replacing, 651–52; secondary prevention, 640, 656–59; self-pity, 658; shame, 641–44, 657; shock, 644–45, 647–48, 656–57; somatizing, 652; tertiary level prevention, 640, 655–56; yearning and protest, 645, 649–50
Superego, 397, 398
Supervision, 35–37
Support groups, 341–42, 354–55
Surrealism, 11, 12
Systemic convergence, 160, 161
Systemic fission, 160–61, 163–64
Taylor Manor Hospital, 598, 601
Taylor-Johnson Temperament Analysis, 32
Theology: cross-cultural counseling, 141–42; feminism and, 199–200; lesbian theologies, 257–58; multi-risk families, 153–55; pastoral diagnosis as theological diagnosis, 51–52; single parents, 333–37
Therapeutic alliance, 110–11
Thought stopping, 441
Time, function of, 113–14
Time-limited psychotherapy, 102–04, 119; function of time, 113–14; regression, 118–19; *see also* Short-term psychotherapy
Toxoplasmosis, 685–86
Training: intercultural pastoral counselor, 138–39; lay counselors, 33–35, 37–39
Transcultural counseling, 130, 131, 132; *see also* Cross-cultural counseling
Transference: pastoral diagnosis, 89–93, 117–18; short-term psychotherapy, 113, 117–18; substance abuse, 546–47
Transitional objects, 376
Transitional space, 376
Trauma survivors. *See* Posttraumatic stress disorder (PTSD)
Tressler Lutheran Services, 356
Trial therapy, 111
Tribalism, 133
Twelve Steps of Alcoholics Anonymous, 545, 583, 590, 602, 611
Unemployed, 664–78; grief process, 669–73
Unitarian Universalists Association, 230
U.S. Conference of Mayors, 145

Wagner-Modified Houts Questionnaire, 32
Wellesley College Center for Research on Women, 305
Women: adult development, 303–07; borderline personality disorder, 198; co-dependency, 198; depression, 188–89, 195, 201–03; economic factors, 190–91; God images, 200, 364, 365, 379–80; media and, 192–93; rape, 191; self-esteem, 188, 200, 380–82; sex discrimination, 188–89; as sexual abusers, 493–94, 497; sin and, 199–200; violence against, 191–92, 196; *see also* Feminist counseling; Lesbians
World Health Organization Report, 191
Worry time, 441–42

Zung Self-Rating Depression Scale, 425